Dedicated to you:

The intrepid and skill-seeking librarian of the twenty-first century

Contents

Part II   Introduction to Major Reference Sources

4   Answering Questions about Books, Magazines, Newspapers, Libraries and Publishing, and Bibliographic Networks— Bibliographic Resources   **57**

5   Answering Questions about Anything and Everything— Encyclopedias   **75**

6   Answering Questions That Require Handy Facts— Ready Reference Sources   **103**

7   Answering Questions about Words—Dictionaries   **125**

Part III Special Topics in Reference and Information Work

Preface

Skill Sets

Well, of course it would be convenient if there were a genetic predisposition to being a librarian of worth and integrity. It is so much easier being born as something. Then again, it would not be as much fun. The process of maturing into a worthy reference librarian, skill set by skill set, is challenging, unending, hugely rewarding, and, yes, fun. *Reference and Information Services in the 21st Century*, Second Edition, is all about those skill sets. We identify them, analyze them, break them into their component parts and present it to you, the eternally maturing reference librarian, in ways that are reproducible.

The first edition of this book was dedicated to the intrepid librarian of the twenty-first century. The second edition continues to celebrate intrepidity because the reference librarian of the twenty-first century must, above all else, be fearless. Ambiguity, never a stranger to the field of librarianship in general and information studies in particular, seems particularly acute in the face of dramatic new technologies fostering equally dramatic new ways of doing reference. Google committed itself to the prodigious digitization of over 12 million manuscripts available for open reference, even as Twitter began peeping out reedy 140-character reference posts. The solid old desk across which the static transaction of reference questions and answers was conducted is competing or being replaced entirely by "Learning Commons" with roving librarians and mobile technology. Real-life librarians have spawned virtual reference librarians in social networks like Facebook and Quora, while funky reference avatars move surreally through Second Life's three-dimensional libraries, dispensing information and, coincidentally, reminding us that we are not in Kansas anymore.

The ferocious pace of change in three years compelled us to write a new edition in 2009 and to update over 300 sources in 2011. Search skills required to locate newly digitized government documents, for example, bear little resemblance to searches through the voluminous GPO publications of a few years ago. An augural job listing by the New York Public Library listed as one of its performance expectations, a knowledge of the library as a "location where new and emerging information technologies and resources are combined with traditional sources of knowledge in a user-focused, service-rich environment that supports today's social and educational patterns of learning, teaching, and research." No pressure intended.

The professional reference librarian must commit to an ongoing under-standing of the fundamental concepts, essential resources, search techniques, and managerial tasks inherent to reference, which are underwritten in large part by the wider social and educational patterns of information and research. The chapters contained in this edition support that commitment, even as they ease the pressure of trying to know too much without organized skill sets. The larger universe, where the primacy of information has never been felt more acutely, is kept in strict perspective throughout the text. The chapter on Refer-ence 2.0 tools introduced in the second edition has been updated to capture some of the restless flux inherent to emerging technologies and alerts the ref-erence professional to experimental trends and practices that are utilizing new technology in innovative ways. More important, it acknowledges the growing relevance of virtual reference and rising expectations on the part of the user, to access information freely, instantaneously, and in ways that are individually relevant and open to social feedback. While a mix of print and electronic resources was provided in the first edition, this revised second edition also spotlights free Web resources of depth and value, in deference to budget-con-scious institutions faced with continuing global recession. Valued suggestions by practitioners have been incorporated. The suggestion by an LIS faculty member to provide the uninitiated student with a comprehensive idea of the immense diversity in reference resources through an accessible list of RUSA Outstanding Reference Resources was adopted, so that a list of selected titles now appears as an appendix in the second revised edition.

What worked effectively for the first edition has been retained and enhanced with necessary updates. Care has been taken to both cull and expand the hundreds of resources listed in the text, with amendments and supplements on a companion Web site at www.neal-schuman.com/reference21st2nd/. Each of the chapters on resources provides an important section on selection and keeping current in the field. We have continued to treat reference transactions as an organic process that involves understanding both the text and subtext of a question, identifying the best resources, and providing an optimal answer. *Reference and Information Services in the 21st Century: An Introduction* differed from traditional reference texts in consciously linking questions to sources, rather than classifying resources and providing a general description of their use. Our approach, firmly grounded in real-world practices, was a direct result of the oft-heard remark from library school graduates who believed their experiences in real transactions felt remote from what they had studied at school. The progres-sion of question → reference interview → search process → resource options → answer was deemed to be a truer representation of what students would face in the real world and this second revised edition continues to uphold that structure.

Organization

While *Reference and Information Services in the 21st Century: An Introduction* is aimed at all reference librarians striving to acquire or affirm the necessary skill sets, it is organized to complement the syllabus of a prototypical library and information studies course. The four sections that make up the text provide a well-rounded grounding in the fundamental concepts of reference, the arsenal of major resources with which every reference librarian must become familiar to answer basic questions, special topics such as "readers advisory work" and user instruction (that fall within the purview of reference work), and tools to field the ongoing responsibility of developing and skillfully managing reference departments in the face of constant change and innovation.

Part I: Fundamental Concepts

Chapter 1, "Introducing Reference and Information Services," provides readers with both a brief history of reference service in libraries and an overview of the breadth of services housed under the reference rubric.

Chapter 2, "Determining the Question," outlines the first and perhaps most critical step in the reference process. Given that reference is, and always will be, predicated on contact and communication, even in times of change, this chapter takes into account in-person, telephone, and virtual reference interviews.

Chapter 3, "Finding the Answer," is in many ways a conclusion to Part I and a prelude to Part II. Having identified the question, the next step is to construct an answer. This hands-on chapter trains you to organize your thoughts, develop a strategy for the particular request, and find the optimal solution.

Part II: Introduction to Major Reference Sources

The nine chapters in this section focus on how, what, where, who, and when questions as they correlate to authoritative resources, rather than describe types of resources. Included in this section are:

Chapter 4, "Answering Questions about Books, Magazines, Newspapers, Libraries, Publishers, and Bibliographic Networks—Bibliographic Resources"

Chapter 5, "Answering Questions about Anything and Everything—Encyclopedias"

Chapter 6, "Answering Questions that Require Handy Facts—Ready Reference Sources"

Chapter 7, "Answering Questions about Words—Dictionaries"

Chapter 8, "Answering Questions about Events and Issues, Past and Present —Indexes and Full-Text Databases"

Chapter 9, "Answering Questions about Health, Law, and Business—Special Guidelines and Sources"

Chapter 10, "Answering Questions about Geography, Countries, and Travel Atlases, Gazetteers, Maps, Geographic Information Systems, and Travel Guides"

Chapter 11, "Answering Questions about the Lives of People—Biographical Information Sources"

Chapter 12, "Answering Questions about Governments—Government Information Sources"

Each of these chapters begins with an overview of materials and how they are used to answer the particular type of question. We provide sample questions (and answers) for which those sources are best used and describe the major print, electronic, and Web-based materials available. Resources are explored holistically since most major reference works exist in both print and electronic formats. There is also guidance for collection development and maintenance practices; further considerations and special information particular to the topic; a final list of the "Top Ten" reference sources in the subject area and a list of recommended free Web sites. As each chapter is uniformly structured, you will find it conducive to both advanced reading in preparation for service and as an effective reference source at the desk.

Part III: Special Topics in Reference and Information Work

Chapter 13, "When and How to Use the Internet as a Reference Tool," addresses one of the most challenging and ubiquitous reference resources to have emerged in our times. Outlining the strengths and weaknesses of the Internet as a reference source, this chapter also contains a five-step approach to using the Internet in reference transactions.

Chapter 14, "Reader's Advisory Work," brings together reference work and the other hallmark of librarianship—literacy. While readers' advisory (RA) is sometimes housed in departments other than reference (Adult, Children's, or Young Adult Services), the librarian sitting at the reference desk should and often must be prepared to field all questions, including an RA question. This chapter, authored by Mary K. Chelton, describes the most common types of RA queries, offers advice for handling RA requests, and provides a list of resources for consultation.

Chapter 15, "Reference Work with Children and Young Adults," also authored by Mary K. Chelton, expands the reference conversation to a new and sometimes tricky user group. With unique perceptions and needs, children and young adults present opportunities and challenges to librarians—instruction, homework help, and concerned parents or guardians. Reference work is more than simply answering questions—it can also be a learning experience for both the patron and the professional.

Chapter 16, "Information Literacy in the Reference Department," discusses the importance of information literacy in all types of libraries and offers suggestions for one-to-one classroom instruction and distance learning. In the right transaction, instruction can be a very appropriate and valued response to a query.

Part IV: Developing and Managing Reference Collections and Services

The selection of fast-disappearing or format-changing reference material has never required as much dexterity and flexibility as in the current climate. Management skills are essential for the library professional, as are the development of assessment tools that continually measure the library's success in cresting and controlling the ebb and flow of changing reference collections and services.

Chapter 17, "Selecting and Evaluating Reference Materials," provides sources for review and evaluation criteria. You will also find guidance for managing the materials budget, assessing collections, weeding titles, writing policy, and marketing the collection.

Chapter 18, "Managing Reference Departments," looks at staff, service, and department organization. This chapter provides options for managers and considerations for decision making. While aimed at the manager, it is also a helpful glimpse for any professional into the form and function of today's reference departments.

Chapter 19, "Assessing and Improving Reference Services," moves from the day-to-day practice of reference work to the vision and development of future service. In times of budget stringency especially, the emphasis on assessment and accountability is heightened. From why we should assess, what and how to assess, and what we should do with our findings, this chapter encourages a hands-on and proactive approach to improvement.

Chapter 20, "Reference 2.0," provides a comprehensive snapshot of the many tools and sites mined from Web 2.0 technology and used to enhance reference services by innovative libraries across the United States, Great Britain, and Canada.

Finally, Chapter 21, "The Future of Information Service," looks ahead to the models, materials, and service, which will continue to evolve and define reference services in the foreseeable future.

Round 2

In asking the user to absorb the skill sets provided in this book as a means to fearlessly navigate through the shifting sands of reference, we have been rather fearless ourselves. We have invited stringent critiques from theoreticians and practitioners, students and faculty, colleagues and friends on the ideas, organization, choices, and usability of the text. Our personal egos have been temporarily suspended in the search for an objectively good product. The four members of the Advisory Board (listed on the verso of the title page) have been invaluable in helping us toward this goal, with one exemplary role model providing a methodical thirty-page report covering every detail. We have been in safe hands and we hope to pass that security on to you.

David Lankes, a mover and shaker at Syracuse University, talks of libraries and reference as conversation and participatory networking. Round 1 of this book was birthed through intense conversation. We could see our fetal ideas gain bone, muscle, and tissue as we held focus groups at ALA conferences, deconstructed scores of reference syllabi, poured through publishers' catalogs and Web sites, and immersed ourselves in "participatory networking" with both aspiring students and grizzled practitioners. It was a heady experience. Round 2 has been a process of fine-tuning, of quieter contemplation, of more in-depth questioning and expanded experience. Comprehensiveness, currency, and readability have been the ternion values undergirding all additions, sub-tractions, and edits to the text. Tethering multiformat reference tools and services to the larger movements in society has provided context to the choices we have made. The product you hold contains both the energetic fire of its birth and the controlling waters of intensive calibration and expansion that marked Round 2. We hope this combination will find its resonance in your individual development as reference librarians of the twenty-first century.

Acknowledgments

We thank:

Charles Harmon, who has been a continuing source of positive energy and ideas through both the first and second edition of this project.

The members of our Advisory Board, Anita Ondrusek, Marie Radford, Cheryl Knott Malone, and Stephanie Matta. Their incisive observations were responsible for some of the most worthy revisions in the text.

The members of various listservs who generously responded to our requests with comments and real-life examples.

Jane Fisher and the many reference librarians who were willing to share their views and expertise.

Our friends for their understanding and support.

Kay thanks:

Marina I. Mercado for her support, patience, and love.

Uma for being the perfect co-author.

The library schools students I have taught for helping me to shape my ideas about reference service.

Uma thanks:

Kay for her trust.

Bala for "being there" as always.

Ayesha and Vani, the loves of my life.

Rajendra and Mohini for keeping the faith.

Part I
Fundamental Concepts

1

Introduction to Reference and Information Services

In this first decade of the twenty-first century reference and information services are a vital yet changing part of the function and mission of the library institution. While the continually expanding availability of electronic resources and digitized materials has changed the nature of reference, the essential service remains central. Indeed, far from minimizing the need for reference services, the rise of the Internet, and with it the availability of a tremendous number of subscription and free online resources, makes this aspect of library service all the more crucial. Librarians and their users are constantly bombarded with a wide range of information choices that must be evaluated for authenticity and accuracy. Whether at home on their computers or wandering through the stacks, many people feel as though they are drowning in a sea of information. New media and technologies are like tributaries leading to this great new body of knowledge, and each stream makes the waters deeper and more perilous. Reference services are at once a life raft, map, and compass to those who feel adrift. In providing them with a combination of personalized service in a timely manner, libraries reaffirm their centrality as twenty-first century public institutions par excellence.

> For all its contemporary relevance, the concept of reference service is more than a century old. In 1876, Samuel Green, librarian of the Worcester Free Public Library in Massachusetts, developed the idea of having librarians assist the user in the selection of books to suit their needs. This served a dual function, increasing the use of his library's collection and thereby demonstrating the need for the library. Green saw the role of the public library as one of welcoming users by having a pleasant and cultivated female staff (Genz, 1998). Some forty years later, in 1915 at the thirty-seventh meeting of the American Library Association, a paper on reference work was delivered by W.W. Bishop, the superintendent of the Reading Room of the Library of Congress. Bishop defined reference work as "the service rendered by a librarian in aid of some sort of study" holding that it was "an organized effort on the part of libraries in aid of the most expeditious and fruitful use of their books." (Genz, 1998: 511)

The idea of reference service was further developed by Charles Williamson in his 1923 report, "Training for Library Service: A Report Prepared for the Carnegie Corporation of New York," which included a course description for reference work:

> A study of the standard works of reference, general and special encyclo-
> pedias, dictionaries, annuals, indexes to periodicals, ready reference
> manuals of every kind, special bibliographies, and the more important
> newspapers and periodicals. Works of similar scope are compared, and
> the limitations of each pointed out. Lists of questions made up from
> practical experience are given, and the method of finding the answers
> discussed in the class. (Genz, 1998: 513)

Several authors, including James I. Wyer, Margaret Hutchins, William A. Katz, Richard E. Bopp, and Linda C. Smith wrote reference texts in which they continued to refine the role of the reference librarian over the subsequent decades.

Perhaps the most important point to remember is that reference service seeks to fulfill the greater mission of the library by helping individual users. Despite the many transformations that have been wrought on reference work by both developments of our information society and paradigm shifts in the self-understandings of the library, much has remained the same. First and foremost, it is still a service in which the librarian interacts with a patron on a one-to-one basis. This level of personal service has become even more important in the twenty-first century in light of the alienating and depersonalizing effects of many information technologies. On the other hand, the way such service is provided has changed considerably—it now extends beyond face-to-face assistance thanks to the availability of the telephone, e-mail, and the technology for chat and IM reference.

Ethical Awareness and Engagement

Ethical awareness and engagement is a crucial aspect of all library services, and the ideals that have been established for the profession generally apply fully to those working in reference services. Just as therapists would do their patients little good if they did not keep their information confidential, reference librarians must follow certain standards of behavior if the service they provide is to be effective. The American Library Association's current Code of Ethics, adopted in 1995, provides a useful guide. This code, composed of eight broad statements, upholds a variety of the principles essential to the modern library.

The first statement of the Code insists that librarians should provide the "highest level of service to all library users" and service that is equitable for all with information provided that is "accurate, unbiased and courteous." This statement is at the heart of good reference service, which strives to provide good quality information and information that can be documented. Reference staff must understand what constitutes a good reference interaction and must strive to meet that standard with each user query (Bunge, 1999).

The second statement of the Code calls for the protection of the "principles of intellectual freedom" and resistance to "all efforts to censor library resources." Library selection is reflected in this statement, as librarians attempt to provide information on a subject from many points of view. The third statement protects the user's right to privacy and confidentiality in requesting and using library resources. Reference librarians must be particularly cognizant of this professional obligation. They must respect the privacy of a user by keeping their reference interview and the resources used confidential.

According to the fourth statement, intellectual property rights should be recognized and respected. It is important that librarians keep current with changes in intellectual property laws, especially copyright, and keep their users aware of these laws. Librarians must know when copying is covered under the "fair use" provision of the law and when copying violates the copyright law. This is more than a good in itself; it also helps protect the institution, its employees, and its users from claims of copyright infringement and intellectual dishonesty.

The fifth through the eighth statements of the Code all treat the relationship between personal interests and professional responsibilities. The fifth encourages the respectful treatment of coworkers and colleagues and the safeguarding of the rights of all employees. This is a statement that encompasses the whole library and its staff. Every staff member should ensure that others are treated fairly.

In the sixth statement, library employees are cautioned not to put private interests ahead of library interests. This means that employees should be circumspect in their dealings with library vendors and others outside the library so their decisions are made on professional merit and are not influenced by personal interest.

The seventh statement cautions library employees not to put personal convictions or beliefs ahead of library interests. This is also of special significance to reference librarians. Sometimes a librarian must help a user research an area that is personally against the librarian's beliefs or philosophy. But by putting professional duties first, the librarian can successfully assist the user and provide the information needed.

The eighth statement encourages all library staff to continue to grow in their knowledge and skills and to assist those entering the profession. We live in a time when change is constant, so all library staff must continue to learn and change.

Other professional library organizations have their own codes of ethics. These include the American Society for Information Science (ASIS), the Society of American Archivists, the Medical Library Association, and the American Association of Law Libraries.

Kinds of Information Service

Information service, in the most general sense, is the process of assisting library users to identify sources of information in response to a particular question, interest, assignment, or problem. Sometimes referred to as reference service, the Reference and User Services Association (RUSA) of the American Library

Association defines reference transactions as "information consultations in which library staff recommend, interpret, evaluate, and/or use information resources to help others to meet particular information needs" (www.ala.org/ala/mgrps/divs/rusa/resources/guidelines/definitionsreference.cfm). These reference transactions can take place in person or via the telephone, e-mail, or virtual reference technologies. Librarians are also creating Web sites, answer archives, and links to answers to "frequently asked questions" all designed to anticipate user questions and help people find information independently. Traditional reference desk service continues to be highly valued by library users in many settings, but the newer forms continue to grow in popularity. Consequently, it is all the more important that librarians understand the range of inquiries that can be expected, allowing them to provide a full and ready answer, regardless of the form in which the query arises.

Answering Reference Questions

In light of the immense diversity and range of possible questions, being approached by a patron with a reference need can seem like a daunting prospect. Indeed, much of the difficulty of information services arises from uncertainty about the kind of service or breadth of information called for by a given question. Categorizing reference questions by type is a useful way to make sense of such concerns. Three common types of information service are ready reference questions, research questions, and bibliographic verification.

Ready reference questions such as "Where was Abraham Lincoln born?" "Who won the 1992 World Series?" "What is the capital of Nicaragua?" or "Where can I find a copy of the United States' Declaration of Independence?" can be readily answered using one or two general reference sources. The librarian may be tempted to tell the user the answer to simple ready reference questions. Yet here the old saying that "giving a man a fish feeds him for a day while teaching him to fish feeds him for a lifetime" is proven true. No matter how simple they seem initially, ready reference questions provide the possibility of teachable moments. Whenever possible, librarians should lead users through the process of looking up the information rather than simply providing the solution.

Librarians who assist users with ready reference inquiries on a regular basis sometimes choose to create a "ready reference" section of the most commonly used resources either in print or on the library's Web site to answer quick questions. Typically, such sections include a general all-purpose encyclopedia, dictionaries, almanacs, and handbooks. Care must be taken to keep the sources up-to-date and to avoid depending so heavily on this subset of the collection that other sources are overlooked by library users and librarians. Librarians may find that ready reference questions have diminished due to the ease of answering basic questions through online information portals such as Google. Nevertheless, ready reference remains a cornerstone of information services, and librarians should be primed to provide it at any time.

Research questions are more complex, may take much longer to answer, and typically require multiple sources of information. These questions often require the user to consider a variety of sources and viewpoints and to subsequently draw conclusions. Sometimes questions that initially seem like ready reference questions are far more complex as previously hidden facets of the user's inquiry are revealed. Here, the variety of possible sources increases with the complexity of users' questions. Librarians should, for example, guide the user in the use of bibliographic sources, citations, and the back-of-the-book bibliographies. Likewise, users with complex questions may need to be taught how to find or request the full text of articles for which only citations are given in a search of electronic databases, allowing them to move beyond cursory surveys of the literature.

Research questions, especially if the user is unable to fully articulate the nature of his or her query, require librarians to ask questions of their own, trying to get at the nature of the request before setting out to help the patron answer it. The librarian may, for example, have to determine how much information is needed, what level of information is needed, and what other sources have already been consulted. As will be discussed in Chapter 3, information services call for mutual engagement, especially with more complex questions. Reference librarians should never be passive participants, pointing the way to an answer. Instead, they should play the part of dynamic guides, joining users on their journeys to knowledge.

Naturally, the extent of such engagement may vary from one circumstance to another. Different types of libraries tend to have their own standards for how long librarians should spend with users on research questions. Many public libraries recommend that users be given five or ten minutes of personal assistance and then asked to return if more help is needed. A university library may have a similar standard, or depending on the institution, may be able to invite the user to make an appointment for more in-depth research assistance. Some libraries may suggest that users call or e-mail ahead of their visit so the librarian can be prepared to offer the best possible assistance. Other libraries, including special libraries, may only be able to provide a basic level of help during the first visit. Libraries may refer users to other libraries with more specialized materials in the area of the user's research or may offer to call back if additional information is found.

Finally a library user may seek *bibliographic verification* when he or she has already obtained the information needed but must verify the sources. Sometimes this service is a matter of fact checking, whereas on other occasions users may have completed their research but lack full citation information. As users increasingly depend on electronic databases for information, compiling and formatting bibliographic citations becomes easier. Verifying and citing material found on Web pages is more difficult since the information needed for the citation is not always easy to find.

Reader's Advisory Service

Reader's advisory service, sometimes considered a type of information service, is the quest to put the right book in the hands of the right reader. Librarians are increasingly expected to provide an answer to the dreaded question, "Can you help me find a good book?" Fortunately, as demand has increased, so too has the ease of providing this service. Although there is no substitute for one's own knowledge or experience, many new technologies serve to make the reader's advisory far easier than it was in the past. Many online databases, for example, have functions that automatically recommend other books for those who like a given title. Others have searchable lists of works by genre, helping readers match their favorite books to others like them. As always, however, remember that reader's advisory, like other reference work, is predicated on the interaction between librarian and library user. Asking directed questions, listening carefully to the users' responses, and tailoring assistance accordingly is the basis of excellent, truly helpful service.

The reader's advisory service is generally associated with public libraries and tends to be employed primarily by those looking for fiction. In academic libraries, it is far less common as users rarely come in searching for a mystery to read. Even so, reader's advisory may be needed to help lay researchers looking to deepen their knowledge of a particular field. A patron who has read and enjoyed Stephen Ambrose's *Undaunted Courage*, but is troubled by allegations about Ambrose's questionable accuracy and academic honesty, may want to know the titles of books about the Lewis and Clark expedition that are both reputable and engaging. Successful reader's advisory librarians are skilled at asking users questions that enable them to assess users' reading level, language, or educational background. They must know a great deal about various genres of fiction and nonfiction and be intimately familiar with their library's collection. Significantly, it is important that they be able to convey their expertise in a friendly and conversational manner. Truly mastering reader's advisory service requires a great deal of skill and practice, but the basics will be explored in more detail in Chapter 14.

Information Literacy

User instruction, which is now usually referred to as *information literacy*, may range from showing an individual how to use the library's online catalog and basic print reference sources to formal classroom sessions about conducting research in the library. The basic component of information literacy includes demonstrating how, when, and why to use various reference sources in an integrated way that will capture the user's attention at the teachable moment.

In today's educational settings, the ease of using electronic resources often results in a failure to teach more traditional research strategies. While finding superficial information has grown easier, in-depth information has become increasingly obscure for many students. In the library too, approaches to instruction may vary and librarians often question whether to simply answer questions posed by users or to teach users how to employ the available resources. This may be contingent on the mission or purpose of the library. Academic institutions may call on their librarians to help students understand how to engage effectively and independently in the research and information evaluation process. Public librarians, by contrast, may try to teach users about reference sources in a more informal manner as they lead users to the answers they seek. Thus, while instruction is always an important part of reference work, the degree to which they go about providing it is highly contingent on the circumstances.

In any case, all reference librarians must be skilled at helping users find information and answers quickly and be ready to teach users how to use the reference sources that are available. The best reference librarians develop an intuition for when to be information providers and when to be bibliographic instructors. In some libraries, only specific, designated librarians are charged with conducting library instruction courses. Nevertheless, an increasing number of librarians are required to participate in their libraries' bibliographic instruction program, and library school graduates are expected to be capable of teaching basic classes on the use of library resources. As should be clear, even those librarians not charged with providing formal instruction have the opportunity to teach those they serve. The various aspects of user instruction are covered in greater depth in Chapter 16.

Selecting and Evaluating Print and Electronic Information

Selecting and evaluating print and electronic information for the library's collection can be as professionally rewarding as providing expert information service. Reference librarians' involvement in evaluating and selecting titles for the collection helps them develop rich knowledge of the sources at their disposal, increasing their effectiveness.

The responsibility for selecting reference materials depends largely on the size and scope of the library. In large academic libraries, selecting reference materials may be assigned to subject bibliographers whose work may be limited to collection development responsibilities. On the other side of the continuum, the evaluation and purchase of resources in very small libraries may be the work of a single reference librarian or coordinator of reference. A range of shared evaluation and selection possibilities between these points include reference materials selection committees or group assignments.

The question, "What makes a book a reference book?" has long been debated in our profession. For the purpose of this discussion, reference books are those texts set aside to be consulted for specific information rather than to be read as a whole. In other words, reference books contain content meant to be "looked up." Typically, one turns to a reference source in search of something in particular rather than to the text as a whole. Another common characteristic of reference books is that they do not leave the library premises. This ensures that all works in the reference collection are always on hand, making for a consistently available body of knowledge. Note that labeling narrative or non-reference books as "reference" to deter theft or ensure that a popular volume is always available may lead to bloated reference collections, and it is not generally recommended. Finally, with the addition of electronic reference sources, which are increasingly available to remote library users from their homes, dorm rooms, offices, and elsewhere, reference collections encompass much more than print books and serials and may be available twenty-four hours a day.

As the present trend toward shrinking budgets for reference collections, lean reference collections, and the elimination of duplication among print and electronic collections continues, the careful evaluation and selection of reference materials is essential. Libraries should determine the criteria that will be used in selecting sources for its reference collection. The following criteria may help determine whether an item is a worthy addition to a library's collection: scope, quality of content, appropriateness for audience, format, arrangement, authority, currency, accuracy, ease of use, unique coverage and cost. Criteria for selecting electronic resources may vary, though all of the criteria used to evaluate print resources should be considered, especially in libraries that aim to avoid redundancy in their print and electronic reference collections.

Some libraries select reference materials by reading reviews in the library professional literature such as *Library Journal* and *Choice* and *Booklist*'s "Reference Books Bulletin." Other institutions insist on physically reviewing reference sources at trade shows or through special arrangements with publishers of reference materials. Most libraries employ a combination of these two. A more extensive discussion of selection and evaluation is found in Chapter 17.

Creating Finding Tools and Web Sites

Another strategy employed by many reference departments is the creation of finding tools and pathfinders for library users. Here, librarians act as cartographers, mapping out the best routes through familiar territory and pointing out interesting sites along the way. Pathfinders are often prepared for commonly requested subjects such as high school and college assignments about capital punishment, drug abuse, and the history of Native American tribes. Similarly, public libraries may prepare pathfinders that address frequently asked questions of a quotidian nature such as: finding job information, checking the credentials of a health care provider, or researching a family tree. Depending on the topic, audience, and needs, the pathfinder may guide the user to a selection of appropriate reference books, relevant databases and search terms, a selection of current and authoritative Web sites, and tips for searching the library's Online Public Access Catalog (OPAC) for additional materials.

Librarians also create Web sites of carefully evaluated links organized by topic, sometimes known as "webliographies" that serve as finding tools. Who better than librarians to organize the World Wide Web of information, pointing the users to "the best" sources and helping them steer clear of the dubious? Web-based finding tools offer several advantages to print pathfinders. They are available to users 24/7, they can be updated as often as needed, and they can include direct links to Web sites and electronic reference tools.

Depending on the circumstance and the nature of a library's Web presence such webliographies can be either general, providing direction to broadly targeted reference resources, or subject specific. General all-purpose lists of librarian-selected Web resources include the *ipl2* (www.ipl.org) and Infomine (http://infomine.ucr.edu). Examples of library subject-specific webliographies include The New York Public Library's *Best of the Web* (www.nypl.org/links/) and the University of Washington's *Information Gateway* (www.lib.washington.edu/subject/). Larger libraries, whether academic or public, often produce indexes of both types. Smaller libraries may be better served by developing webliographies for specific areas in which they have subject specialists and linking to a general reference site like the *Internet Public Library*.

Promoting and Marketing Libraries and Reference Service

Paying attention to promotion and marketing of libraries and reference service is becoming more important than ever. Without support from the community, the library will not stay viable. Promoting reference services among individual library users can go a long way toward achieving this goal, especially insofar as it demonstrates how the library can serve them. In large communities—urban public libraries, for example—promoting the library through individual users is not enough to attract new users and major marketing or publicity campaigns become important. In academic libraries, school libraries, and special libraries, promotion and marketing are equally essential. Use of print and online newsletters, Web sites, and opportunities to meet with faculty and staff can provide opportunities to promote the library's resources.

Evaluating Staff and Services

Libraries may seek to routinely evaluate their reference collections or reference service. In her book *Evaluating Reference Services: A Practical Guide* (Whitlatch, 2000: 1), Jo Bell Whitlatch wisely emphasizes the importance of defining the purpose of the evaluation before setting a strategy. "The most important questions you must ask," according to Whitlatch, are these: "Why am I evaluating reference services" and "What do I plan to do with the study results?"

The quality of the reference interaction, from either the user's or the librarian's perspective, may be assessed to help determine how effective the reference service is. Evaluating reference staff is one way to help determine how effective the reference service is, and is one way to help assure quality reference service. The American Library Association's Reference and User Services Association has developed "Guidelines for Behavioral Performance of Reference and Information Service Professionals," which are intended to be used in the training, development, or evaluation of library professionals and staff. The performance of reference librarians is typically evaluated on both the information conveyed to users and the satisfaction of the interaction on the library user.

The following factors are covered by the ALA Guidelines:

- Approachability: Are users able to identify that a reference librarian is available to help?
- Interest: Does the librarian demonstrate a high degree of interest in the reference transaction?
- Listening/Inquiring: Does the librarian identify the user's information need in a manner that puts the user at ease? Are good communication skills used throughout the transaction?
- Searching: Is the librarian skilled at creating search strategies that yield accurate and relevant results?
- Follow-up: Does the librarian determine if the user is satisfied with the results of the search/interaction?

These performance guidelines may form the backbone of a library's staff evaluation instruments, whether the instrument is a simple self-evaluation checklist, a peer-evaluation tool, or a formal evaluation system influencing earning potential.

In addition to evaluating staff, the library may measure its productivity or efficiency with quantitative measures that include the number of questions answered and the frequency with which print and/or electronic sources are consulted. Smaller libraries may continuously count the number and type of in-person questions answered by the reference staff. In larger libraries, quarterly one-week periods are frequently used to estimate the number of questions answered over the course of a year. Depending on the available resources, data may be recorded using hand-held computers, by making hash marks on a form, or by any means in between.

A variety of other evaluation strategies are also available to libraries: Assessing the quality of the resources available may, for example, be another useful measurement. Issues of resource allocation may also be incorporated into departmental evaluations, if one includes how the library's budget allocates for library staff, print and electronic resources, computers and networks, and buildings. Evaluation methods frequently used to gauge users' satisfaction with reference services and sources include questionnaires, surveys, focus groups, observation and interviews.

It is crucial that library administrators determine what is to be measured and against what standards before choosing the preferred method of evaluation. Many sources are available for detailed information on designing evaluation instruments for libraries. Selecting the best method, developing and field testing the instrument, administering the survey, questionnaire, or interview, planning the observation, avoiding interviewer bias and scores of ethical issues should be carefully considered. Analyzing data and developing conclusions and recommendations may require advanced training and in some cases evaluation experts are hired. These and other questions are considered in greater depth in Chapter 19.

The Changing Nature of Reference

As the form of the library has evolved in the years since Samuel Green's seminal pronouncements in 1876, so too has the nature of reference services. Today it stretches far beyond the walls of the library and strives to far loftier ends than welcoming users to the library with a "cultivated female staff." Academic libraries in particular have already seen a slowing of traffic to the physical library and the increasing use of the library's online resources. Users can ask questions 24/7 through virtual reference and expect an immediate response. Likewise, they can access electronic resources that the library provides through its Web site. Virtual reference is growing quickly; the appeal of instant messaging and like services point to a generational paradigm shift ahead. These online reference services have the advantage of being convenient and necessary in our fast-paced world.

In numerous forms and fashions, technology continues to change reference services. Libraries must be ready to learn new technology and adapt to the needs of users unable to imagine a world without technology. Like few other professionals, librarians must be willing to ride the waves of such change, adapting to meet the needs of their users. Whether it is the cell phone, the Palm Pilot, the MP3 player, or the iPod, users will want to receive and read their information on this new technology.

New models of reference are also developing to meet different user needs. Libraries are adding more points of service. For example, an information desk near the front of the library, a reference service point combined with other library services or an in-depth reference center where a user can sit down with a librarian and work out a plan for researching a paper have all been instituted to positive effect at libraries around the world. In other situations, librarians rove the reference area to help users who do not approach the reference desk.

These and other new strategies are changing the way information services are offered. As we look ahead, we must be aware that reference work will no doubt be based increasingly on electronic means of communication. It will at the same time continue to be a personal service although not necessarily face to face. There will be more emphasis on electronic materials while some older materials will still need to be consulted in print format. Even so, the way we find information and convey it is as fundamental today as it ever was. In the chapters ahead, we explore the cutting edge of contemporary reference, demonstrating how to keep this crucial service central to the modern library.

Recommendations for Further Reading

Austin, Brice. 2004. "Should There Be 'Privilege' in the Relationship between Reference Librarian and Patron?" *The Reference Librarian* 87/88: 301–311. An exploration of whether privilege should be extended to the librarian-patron relationship.

Fritch, John W., and Scott B. Mandernack. 2001. "The Emerging Reference Paradigm: A Vision of Reference Services in a Complex Information Environment."

Library Trends 50, no. 2 (Fall): 286–306. A proposal of ways to respond to changes in reference service.

Jacoby, Jo Ann, and Nancy P. O'Brien. 2005. "Assessing the Impact of Reference Service Provided to Undergraduate Students." *College and Research Libraries* 66, no. 4 (July): 324–340. Reports on how reference service can help students to learn to do research and to use the library.

Landesman, Margaret. 2005. "Getting It Right—The Evolution of Reference Collections." *The Reference Librarian* 91/92: 5–22. A history of the development of reference collections.

Lenker, M. 2008. "Dangerous Questions at the Reference Desk: A Virtue Ethics Approach." *Journal of Information Ethics* 17, no. 1: 43–53. A good article on ethics.

Puacz, Jeanne Holba. 2005. "Electronic vs. Print Reference Sources in Public Library Collections." *The Reference Librarian* 91/92: 39–51. A discussion of the impact of electronic resources on public library collections.

Samson, Sue, and Erling Oetz. 2005. "The Academic Library as a Full-Service Information Center." *Journal of Academic Librarianship* 31, no. 4 (July): 347–351. The development of an Information Center at the University of Montana-Missoula supports the changing nature of library service and combines one-stop service for library users.

Bibliography of Works Cited in This Chapter

Bopp, Richard E., and Linda C. Smith. 2001. *Reference and Information Services: An Introduction.* Englewood, CO: Libraries Unlimited.

Bunge, Charles. 1999. "Ethics and the Reference Librarian." *The Reference Librarian* no. 66: 25–43.

Genz, Marcella D. 1998. "Working the Reference Desk." *Library Trends* 46, no. 3 (Winter): 505–525.

Gorman, Michael. 2003. *The Enduring Library: Technology, Tradition, and the Quest for Balance.* Chicago: American Library Association.

Katz, William A. 2001. *Introduction to Reference Work.* 2 vols. New York: McGraw-Hill.

Nolan, Christopher W. 1999. *Managing the Reference Collection.* Chicago: American Library Association.

Tyckoson, David A. 2001. "What Is the Best Model of Reference Service?" *Library Trends* 50, no. 2 (Fall): 183–196.

Whitlatch, Jo Bell. 2000. *Evaluating Reference Services: A Practical Guide.* Chicago: American Library Association.

2

Determining the Question: In-person, Telephone, and Virtual Reference Interviews

The reference interview is more an art than a science, an ever-changing practice that requires responsiveness to context rather than just the application of a predetermined set of skills. While librarians should learn the elements of a good reference interview, they must also recognize that these steps must be adapted to match each situation. Each reference interview will be different since each user and each question is different. The overall structure has three phases: "establishing contact with the user, finding out the user's need, and confirming that the answer provided is actually what was needed" (Ross, Nilsen, and Dewdney, 2002: 5). Within this framework, librarians must learn to improvise like expert jazz musicians.

For librarians, answering the user's question correctly is the most important part of the reference interaction, yet studies and experience show that users react to the manner in which the reference interview is conducted, paying special attention to both verbal and nonverbal cues. They are more likely to return to a librarian who has handled their request respectfully whether or not their information need has been completely fulfilled. Librarians must learn the elements of a good reference interview. Each reference interview will be different since each user and each question is different. So they will have to adapt the elements of the interview to the specific situation. Conduct is as important as content.

Why Conduct the Reference Interview?

Sometimes it seems like the questions asked by users are very straightforward, prompting librarians to wonder why the reference interview is necessary at all. Upon looking into the matter, however, the librarian often discovers that the real question was not the first one asked. Users tend to believe they can ask a short question and get enough information to proceed on their own. In such circumstances, the ambiguity of their initial inquiry often leads to confusion. A user might, for example, ask for books about stars when, in fact, he wanted to know the constellations one can see south of the equator or maybe he is seeking information about the home addresses of movie stars. On another occasion a user might ask for books on baking when he wanted to find out about the chemistry involved in the rising of yeast rather than recipes for bread. In philosophy, errors prompted by the multiple meanings of words are known as "category mistakes," the grouping of dissimilar concepts under a single shared label. Errors of this kind may not have profound consequences in the library world, but they do waste the time of users and staff alike. By asking additional clarifying questions the librarian can avoid such problems, focusing on the meaningful content of the user's request.

What We Know about the Reference Interview

Many studies have been done about the reference interaction. Robert S. Taylor in his article "Question Negotiation and Information Seeking in Libraries" explored the reference interaction from the point of view of question negotiation. Taylor discussed "five filters through which a question passes and from which the librarian selects significant data to aid him in his research" (Taylor, 1968: 183). Elaine Z. Jennerich and Edward V. Jennerich approached the reference interview as a "creative art" and a "performing art" (Jennerich and Jennerich, 1987). Mary Jo Lynch studied the reference interview in public libraries and asked how reference librarians know when to interview a user, through what channels a librarian gathers information without asking questions, and what the characteristics are of an effective question sequence (Lynch, 1978).

Brenda Dervin and Patricia Dewdney's article, "Neutral Questioning: A New Approach to the Reference Interview," proposed the neutral questioning model—a user-oriented approach to answering reference questions (Dervin and Dewdney, 1986). Patricia Dewdney and Catherine Sheldrick Ross continued the research in this area by looking at the reference interview from the user's point of view (Dewdney and Ross, 1994). They asked Masters of Library and Information Science students to visit libraries and ask questions of interest to them and to report on the results. Only 59.7 percent said that they would return to the same librarian (Dewdney and Ross, 1994: 222).

Marie Radford in her 1998 article in *Library Trends* turned her attention to nonverbal communications. She identified five factors indicated by users that were critical in their decision as to whom to approach. They were initiation, availability, proximity, familiarity, and gender. Mary Jane Swope and Jeffrey Katzer studied the question of why people don't ask for assistance and found that dissatisfaction with their previous assistance, the belief that their query was too simple and the disinclination to bother the librarian affected their decision not to ask for assistance (Swope and Katzer, 1972).

Intercultural communication has been studied by Terry Ann Mood (1982) and R. Errol Lam (1988). Mood stated that foreign students learn best by hands-on experience. Lam emphasized more effective intercultural communication through the reference interview. Most recently, research has turned to the area of virtual reference and what are the differences and similarities with face-to-face reference with the work of Straw (2000), Kern (2003), Radford (2008), and Nilsen (2005).

Conducting the Reference Interview

The reference interview is composed of several parts, each of which is discussed in turn over the following pages:

- Establishing rapport with the user
- Negotiating the question
- Developing a strategy for a successful search and communicating it to the user
- Locating the information and evaluating it
- Ensuring that the question is fully answered—the follow-up
- Closing the interview

Establishing Rapport with the User

When users arrive at the library or contact a librarian remotely (whether by phone, e-mail, chat, or instant messaging), they expect to find someone willing to assist them. To make the initial approach easier, librarians must find ways to signal, verbally and/or nonverbally, that they are approachable. In Edward Kazlauskas's "An Exploratory Study: A Kinesic Analysis of Academic Library Public Service Points," he found that raising the eyebrow and lowering it when someone approaches, maintaining eye contact, nodding and smiling all help make the initial encounter more positive and comfortable (Kazlauskas, 1976). He also identified behaviors that make the librarian less approachable: lack of immediate acknowledgment of user, failing to change body stance as user comes closer, covering the eyes with the hand, reading, tapping one's finger, and twitching of the mouth (Kazlaukas, 1976).

Marie A. Radford "observed reference interactions for thirty-seven hours, interviewing 155 users who approached thirty-four librarian volunteers." Her purpose was to discover behaviors that influenced which librarian the user approached. She identified five factors indicated by users that positively shaped user decisions:

1. *Initiation.* The librarian begins the interaction by using one of the following nonverbal signals: eye contact, body orientation, movement toward the user, or verbal enforcement.
2. *Availability.* The librarian indicates availability by turning around, moving toward the patron, using eye contact, or otherwise signaling attention to the user nonverbally.
3. *Proximity.* Users decide who to approach based on their physical distance from the librarian.
4. *Familiarity.* The user had previously met or been helped by a particular librarian.
5. *Gender.* Users found it more comfortable to approach a female librarian. (Radford, 1998: 708–710)

The Jacoby and O'Brien study of undergraduate students documented the importance of reference staff being friendly and approachable. This makes it more comfortable for the users to request the help they need. It also impacts on the students' confidence to search for information on their own (Jacoby and O'Brien, 2005).

The librarian can also look approachable by roving through the reference area and helping users who may need assistance. Many users may not be comfortable initiating a conversation with a librarian when they need help, so roving gives users a less formal opportunity to get assistance. As they roam, librarians can simply ask users if they are finding what they need. They can approach users whom they have already assisted or perhaps users who have not approached the reference desk.

When serving users who telephone, send their requests by e-mail, or ask a question through a chat service, the librarian can make the process easier by greeting the user in a friendly, upbeat manner (i.e., "Hello. How can I help you?") and by responding to the information provided by the user. For example, the user may reveal that the reason he or she is using virtual reference is due to an illness or the inability to leave home. The librarian should respond to this comment by remarking on the situation in a friendly but neutral way—for example, by saying, "Hope you feel better soon."

Whatever the circumstances, the user must feel that the librarian is interested in his or her question. The librarian can accomplish this by facing the user and maintaining eye contact with him or her. The librarian signals his or her understanding of the user's question by responding verbally or by nodding. In a remote situation the librarian must stay in contact with the user by text messaging and conveying interest in the question in words. For example, the librarian could say, "What an interesting question."

Negotiating the Question

Once the possibility of dialogue has been established, the next step is to establish the patron's query. Many approaches to negotiating the question have been suggested by researchers and practitioners. Brenda Dervin has suggested "sense-making" as a way of finding out exactly what the user wants (Dervin and Dewdney, 1986). Sense-making is user oriented and approaches the reference interview in an organized way designed to ensure that the librarian understands what the user really needs. This method calls for an understanding of the user's situation, the gap that led to the question, and how the user plans to use the information. Dervin argues that it is important to understand that the "gaps individuals face (i.e., the questions they have) depend upon the way in which they see the situation and how they are stopped. The kind of answers they want is dependent on how they expect to use or be helped by the answers" (Dervin and Dewdney, 1986: 507). Two questions, alike in form, may not, in the end, be at all similar if the users who ask them differ in their views of the situation. Dervin and Dewdney went on to develop a further approach to questioning called "neutral questioning" which grows out of "sense-making"

(Dervin and Dewdney, 1986). Neutral questioning involves asking open questions that will help the librarian discover the true nature of the question. Dervin and Dewdney state that the librarian through questions must assess the situation, assess the gaps and assess the uses of the information (Dervin and Dewdney, 1986: 509). They suggest that the most useful neutral questions are the following:

> What kind of help would you like?
> What have you done about this so far?
> What would you like this book (information) to do for you? (Dervin and Dewdney, 1986: 512)

An example of this questioning in action is the following:

> Do you want annual reports? What sort of details do you want? If you could tell me the kind of problem you're working on, I'll have a better idea of what would help you. (Dervin and Dewdney, 1986: 510).

This form of questioning can be tailored to the needs of each individual by focusing on how the information will be used. Once learned, neutral questioning is not a long process since it is adapted to the needs of the individual. Neutral questioning can help librarians avoid the kind of category mistakes described above. It also helps facilitate other forms of disambiguation, by ensuring that all possible information about the information desired by the user is made known. Users may ask where books on a certain subject are, thinking that they can browse when they get to the section and find what they are looking for. Another patron may need some specific information and think the library does not have it just because a particular book is not on the shelf—unaware that a librarian may be able to answer the question with another source.

In order for a positive reference interview to take place, the librarian must listen carefully to the user and ask clarifying questions as necessary. The librarian must begin with open-ended questions, giving the user a chance to express reference needs. Often the first question asked by the user does not really describe what the user is seeking. The librarian must ask probing, open-ended questions such as "Please tell me more about your topic or what you want to know about (the topic)? What additional information can you give me?" The librarian should continue with clarifying questions that may be a combination of open-ended or closed questions until it is clear what the user wants. These clarifying questions might include the following:

Open-ended questions	Closed-ended questions
How much information do you need?	Do you need current or historical information?
What have you already found?	Do you need factual or analytical information?
What format for the information do you need?	Can you read languages other than English?

The librarian should rephrase the question to be sure that he or she really understands what is needed by the user. Of course, it goes without saying that the librarian should remain objective and does not make judgments about the subject of the question. The same is true of a virtual reference question. The librarian must ask the same open-ended questions to give the user a chance to type out his or her information.

Although the librarian should begin with open-ended questions that allow users to express their question more fully, there is also a place for closed-ended questions. Once the librarian understands the question he or she may want to narrow the search with some clarifying, closed-ended questions. The important thing to remember about closed-ended questions is that the response from the user will be brief. For example, if the librarian asks the user "Do you want books or just articles?" the user may respond with a one-word answer, such as "books" or "articles." Sometimes a mix of open- and closed-ended questions works best. As the librarian listens to the user's question, he or she must not make assumptions about the user or the question. Assumptions may lead the librarian in the wrong direction, bringing the search up short. By working to avoid the always mistaken belief that the horizon of the user is the same as one's own, the librarian can extend the limits of his or her vision.

For this interchange to be truly effective, the librarian should include the user in the search. For example, the librarian may turn the monitor toward the user to show the user the information being located in the database. This will enable the librarian to continue to test whether he or she is proceeding in the right direction, and it will be less isolating for the user. As the exchange proceeds, including the user will give the librarian the opportunity to other information about how to use the library that may be helpful to the user in the future.

In the course of assisting the user the librarian may need to help the user reframe his or her question. The question may be too general or too specific, and the librarian must then work with the user to better formulate the question. For example, the user may ask for information on the Civil War but actually want information on the Battle of Gettysburg. The librarian should try to find out in carefully crafted phrases how the information will be used and what level of material is needed.

Finally the librarian should paraphrase the question back to the user to be sure that the understanding is mutual. For example, "If I understand you correctly, you want information on the coral reefs in Key West, especially their geology, location, and water temperature?" It is easy to misunderstand the user's question so every effort should be made to make sure the user's needs are being communicated.

Developing a Strategy and Communicating It to the User

Once the subject is clear the librarian should construct a search, selecting search terms and identifying the most appropriate sources for the particular user. If the librarian has little knowledge of the subject, he or she should partner with the user in selecting the subject terms. No one, even a subject specialist, can ever expect to be an expert on that which might be of interest to library users, and the reference encounter is often as much a chance to learn as it is to teach. As long as one knows where to begin looking, the reference process can be exciting for both librarian and user. As the search is developed, the librarian should explain as much about the search as he or she thinks is of interest to the user. The librarian should also respect the user's time frame and work to assist the user to the fullest extent possible within that time frame.

Of the many kinds of information available on most subjects, the librarian must determine what information will fit the user's needs. Does the user want more general information or more technical information? This can only be judged by continuing to communicate with the user. The user may also have a preference as to the format of the information, the amount of information, and the level of the information. Ideally, much of this information should have been discovered in the earlier phase of determining the question. It is important that the librarian constantly keep in mind all he or she knows about the user's needs and work to plan the search accordingly.

Locating the Information and Evaluating It

Whatever the extent of a reference query, the librarian should continually check in with the user to determine whether the material being discovered complies with the user's needs. This process should continue until the user has the information needed or the user has resources to examine.

Instruction in the use of the resources should be provided to the user if the user is unfamiliar with the source(s). Attention should also be paid to the quality of the information by evaluating that information to be certain that the sources selected are of high quality. This can be done by using the guidelines for the selection of reference materials.

Ensuring That the Question Is Fully Answered—The Follow-up

The follow-up question is of great importance to the reference interview. It is necessary to check with users to see whether they have had their question answered. The librarian may want to ask if users found the information they sought or say, "Please come back if you don't find what you are looking for and we can look somewhere else." Or the librarian may be roving and check in with the user. Gers and Seward stated that the follow-up question "may be the single most important behavior because it has the potential for allowing one to remedy lapses in other desirable behaviors" (Gers and Seward, 1985: 34). Dewdney and Ross (1994) found that librarians often fail to ask follow-up questions. This can result in a situation in which the user lacks needed information but is unable to express the discrepancy.

Closing the Interview

Like the closing moves of a chess game, the conclusion of a reference interview is a highly specialized art. Once it has been confirmed that the user has all the information he or she desires, the consulting librarian should find a way to bring the conversation to a close without making the patron feel summarily dismissed. Christopher Nolan suggests that a reference department should develop goals for the interview, making it easier to know when the conversation should be brought to a close. He further states that "three factors are involved in the end of most interviews: knowledge or content of the interview, dynamics of the interpersonal interaction, and institutional or policy components" (Nolan, 1992: 515). Keep in mind that, as is suggested elsewhere in this book, reference services are one of the primary means to spotlight the value of the library itself, so the interview should close on an open note. In particular, the librarian can make a follow-up comment that will encourage the user to return.

Problematic Strategies in the Reference Interview

The Imposed Query

Most librarians and researchers have based their evaluations of the reference interview on the assumption that the questions are self-generated. This is not always true. Melissa Gross defines and discusses the imposed query, as "a process in which the imposer or end user passes the question to another who will act as the agent in the transaction of the query and then return to the imposer with the answer or resolution" (Gross, 1998: 291). Although we do not know all the implications of the imposed query, it is logical to suppose that the assumptions and stereotypes of both the person who asked the question and the person who transmits the query will affect the outcome. Gross points to the need for more research in this area. A good example of the imposed query is when a parent arrives in the library asking for information for a child's homework assignment. In this case the person who needs the information is not present and the parent may or may not be clear as to the actual information need. It is helpful to the librarian to identify this situation as the imposed query since the librarian will realize that the person asking the question may not be able to clarify the question for the librarian, making it more complicated to provide help.

The Communications Trap

Sometimes the problem between the user and the librarian is one of communication. The article, "Oranges and Peaches: Understanding Communication Accidents in the Reference Interview," points out this problem. This article begins by describing a scenario in which a student arrives at the library, claiming that he has been assigned a book to read titled *Oranges and Peaches*. The librarian is unable to find a book by this title and asks the student for the author. The librarian does not ask the student any open-ended questions or sense-making questions in order to get information on the context of the request. Finally the student does provide additional information, and the librarian realizes that the student is looking for Darwin's *On the Origin of Species* (Dewdney and Michell, 1996: 520–521).

Sometimes the librarian misunderstands the question because the pronunciation of the key words is slightly different or the librarian hears the word and relates it to something familiar to him or her. In another example, Dewdney and Michell describe a user who arrives at the library asking for material on Socrates. But the librarian has just been weeding in the sports section and hears it as "soccer tees." There are, of course, many words that sound the same but have completely different meanings such as China/china, Turkey/turkey and Wales/whales (Dewdney and Michell, 1996: 527–528). Other communication accidents happen when the user asks a question that he or she has heard from someone else. The solution to these miscommunications is first to restate the question, allowing the user the opportunity to restate it, and second, to ask follow-up questions, helping to introduce context into the discussion.

Behaviors to Avoid

Librarians should take care not to fall into the many traps that can easily occur during the reference transaction.

Keep in contact with the user. It is tempting to just start typing on the computer once the user has asked a question. This is extremely confusing to the user who neither knows what the librarian is doing nor if the librarian really understood the question. Before beginning a search, be sure that the question is clear by restating it and explaining to the user what is being searched. If possible, let the user see the screen so he or she can follow the search. If the librarian goes elsewhere to get the information for the user, he or she should try not to be out of sight of the user for any length of time so that the user knows the librarian is still working on the question.

Avoid the negative closure, i.e., a dismissive behavior that falls short of providing full service. In a negative closure the librarian is more interested in getting rid of the user than in answering the question and sends the user away without the information needed. Here are some examples of this:

- The librarian provides an unmonitored referral. This is when the librarian sends the user somewhere else without any clear direction. For example, the librarian gives the user a call number and suggests looking in that area or points to a particular area and suggests browsing there. Similarly problematic would be a situation in which the librarian refers the user elsewhere in the library or to an agency without confirming that the user will actually find information there.
- The librarian suggests that the user should have done some independent work before asking for help.
- The librarian tries to get the user to accept information more easily available than what the user needs.
- The librarian suggests that the information will not be found for one of a number of reasons, such as too hard, obscure, or elusive or simply not available in the library and perhaps not in any library.
- The librarian tries to convince the user not to pursue the question.
- The librarian leaves the desk and does not return.

- The librarian through a nonverbal action such as turning away from the user indicates that the interview is over (Ross and Dewdney, 1999: 151–163).

Ross and Dewdney offer recommendations for more positive behavior. They recommend that when the librarian refers the user to another part of the library or to another library or information source, the librarian should verify that useful information will be found by the user. The librarian should also encourage the user to return if the user does not find the information needed. Roving reference can help identify users who need more help or who need help but have not talked to a librarian. If the reference interaction is remote, the librarian might suggest a visit to the library for further information or encourage the user to contact the library again for more assistance.

Another behavior to avoid is simply not listening to the user. It is hard to listen intently to each user's question. But the librarian must do this in order to understand as completely as possible the user's question. To not listen closely and ask pertinent questions can lead to assumptions that will lead the librarian in the wrong direction. For example, the librarian might be asked about abortions and immediately go to the health section only to find out the person wants to know about aborting space flights.

Finally, avoid making the user feel stupid. Sometimes the user does not know the library jargon. They may use "bibliography" instead of "biography" or they may use "reference book" when they mean a circulating nonfiction book. The librarian should correct the user in a nonjudgmental manner. It is the librarian who must learn to understand the users (Cramer, 1998).

The Telephone Interview

The telephone interview is one step removed from the face-to-face interview. It does have the advantage of getting immediate feedback from the user. Although the librarian cannot see the user, the librarian can hear the tone and inflexions in the user's voice and can ascertain how he or she is communicating.

The librarian should develop a pleasant speaking voice to aid in phone communication, aiming to sound approachable and attentive. As always, it is important to rephrase the user's questions to clarify meaning and ask open-ended questions. In this more ethereal context, it is doubly important that the user be kept informed as to how the search process is proceeding and that silent time be kept to a minimum. Once the answer has been found, follow-up questions should be asked in order to confirm that the question has been properly answered. The librarian should also cite the source where the answer can be found (Ross, Nilsen, and Dewdney, 2002: 127–131). A recent study by Agosto and Anderton revealed that eighty-six out of 125 telephone reference transactions analyzed gave no sources for their answer. The authors defined the standard citation elements for print resources as "title, author, publisher and year and for Web sites, the author (if there is one) and URL"(Agosto and Anderton, 2007: 52–53).

Librarians can provide value-added information that will enhance the user's understanding of the answer while doing telephone reference. For example, when a user asks, "Who is the current governor?" it would be useful to explain that the state has an official Web site and a page for the governor in addition to giving the URL (Agosto and Anderton, 2007: 49–50). Finally, as in all good reference interviews, the user should be encouraged to call again or visit the library.

Virtual Reference—E-mail, Chat, IM, and SMS

Using electronic means to provide reference assistance has become part of the lives of most reference librarians. Answering questions by e-mail, chat, instant messaging (IM), and text messaging (SMS) is not so different from answering questions face to face. The problem is that virtual reference lacks the advantage of the face-to-face reference interview where the user's tone of voice, facial expressions and body language help the librarian to judge whether he or she is communicating well with the user. A handicap for some is, however, an *advantage* for others who cannot leave home or do not communicate well verbally, making it a powerful means to support the mission of many libraries to make their resources available to all. Librarians should approach the virtual reference question in the same way as a face-to-face one.

E-mail reference has been offered by libraries since the mid-1990s. The structure of the e-mail reference interview is a well-designed form that captures essential information. This is the best way for the librarian to get information from the user. Collecting enough information is essential since it is hard to go back, ask follow-up questions, and get a response from the user. Sample e-mail reference forms can be found on many library Web sites, but the Internet Public Library's (www.ipl.org) e-mail reference form is a good place to start. A study by Diamond and Pease identified eleven question categories for e-mail queries including factual ready reference, information for term papers and assignments, and library policies and procedures (Diamond and Pease, 2001). Powell and Bradigan's study of e-mail reference also attempted to categorize the kinds of questions being asked by users and stated that most of the questions fell into the following categories: assignments, holdings information, library services and policies, and consumer health (Powell and Bradigan, 2001). Although e-mail reference is slower, it has the advantage of giving the librarian time to do some research and provide a more thorough response. The e-mail response should also invite the user to return for more information or to use the service again.

Chat, IM (Instant Messaging) reference, and now SMS (text messaging) have considerable potential for the reference interview because they are done in real time. Chat reference was adopted by libraries wanting to be able to provide immediate answers to questions. The advantage of chat reference is that the reference interview can be used successfully in this format. There is an opportunity to communicate back and forth with the user, and an opportunity for providing guidance the user can use in future queries. When providing chat reference, the librarian should not assume that the user does not have time for the reference interview. The fact that the user has not chosen to come to the library does not indicate that the user is impatient or in a hurry (Kern, 2003). Librarians should greet users by name and acknowledge the receipt of the question. They should then proceed to do a reference interview, asking the user for the context of the query, followed by open-ended questions. He or she should explain that the questions are aimed at ensuring that the librarian understands the question, and should rephrase the question to that purpose. It is also important to tell the user what steps are being taken since the user cannot see what the librarian is doing. The librarian should read carefully the users' replies for clues as to whether they are communicating well since the chat is text-based with no opportunity to observe nonverbal clues. When information is identified, the librarian can provide a URL or can co-browse with the user. Attention should be paid that the information given to the user really answers the user's question. As in the face-to-face interview, the librarian should encourage the user to return for more information or with another question. A final advantage to chat reference is that the user can receive a transcript with all the information from the search.

IM and SMS are faster than chat because of the nature of the software, but they often lack context. The kinds of questions answered in this mode are usually ready reference questions, directions, policy information, or URLs. Since both the questions and answers are quite short, the librarian may not have contact information to follow up, and it is difficult to know when the question is finished. Librarians must be succinct when responding to IM or SMS (text messaging) queries. They should also try to get an e-mail address if they want to do some follow-up or encourage the user to come to the library. Because the quick back-and-forth nature of IM and SMS (text messaging) may become tiresome to the user, it is recommended that the librarian should "respond with a small amount of information plus a request for clarification" (Ross, Nilsen, and Dewdney, 2002: 199). If the information needed is not available electronically, the librarian should arrange to get the print information to the user by fax and other convenient means (Ronan, 2003: 158). Steiner and Long studied the attitudes of academic librarians toward IM and found that 80 percent of the librarians had used IM (Steiner and Long, 2007). User perceptions of IM software were examined by Ruppel and Fagan, who found that users valued IM reference for its convenience, anonymity, and quick help (Ruppel and Fagan, 2002). SMS (text messaging), the newest communication mode, is communication by text messaging through cell phones. A variety of software including Altarama, AIM, and "Text a Librarian" is being used.

Virtual reference librarians should aim to be approachable in the way they word their responses to the user. Just as in the face-to-face interview, the librarian will want to strive to make the user comfortable with the process so that the user will return to the library. Follow-up should encourage the user to use the library virtually or in person. Recent research shows that the same mistakes happen in virtual reference as in face-to-face interviews, that is, the lack of the reference interview, unmonitored referrals and failure to ask follow-up questions (Nilsen, 2005). Straw comments that "a well-written response not only answers a question eloquently, but it also tells the user about the importance that the library places on the question" (Straw, 2000: 379). Mon and Janes' study confirms this. They found that librarians who used more words in their answers tended to be thanked more often whereas librarians who resorted to the "canned" responses or the FAQs received fewer thank-yous (Mon and Janes, 2007).

As librarians reach out to where their users are, many are providing information about the library and answering questions on Facebook (www .facebook.com) and MySpace (www.myspace.com). Hennepin County Library in Minnesota and the University of Massachusetts Boston Healey Library can be found on Facebook, whereas Brooklyn College and the Denver Public Library are examples of libraries that can be found on MySpace.

Virtual reference is often underused simply because users don't know about its existence. It is important that libraries clearly mark the service and make it visible on all pages on their Web site. Virtual reference policies such as who can use the service should also be visible to the users. Marketing a virtual reference service is essential.

Assessment and Accountability

Many researchers have spent time examining virtual reference. Two studies have examined the accuracy of the questions answered and the satisfaction of the user. Arnold and Kaske analyzed chat transcripts and found that the accuracy rate was 92 percent (Arnold and Kaske, 2005). White, Abels, and Kaske (2003) also found a high level of accuracy in chat reference in both university and public library service.

Assessments have included examining librarian and user judgments of service values, examining how libraries are setting policies, assessing virtual reference quality, developing quality standards for virtual reference, and using survey instruments such as LibQual+ and WOREP (Wisconsin-Ohio Reference Evaluation Program) (Radford and Mon, 2008).

Librarians doing virtual reference can develop a peer-reviewing system to help one another to improve the quality of their work. Transcripts should be reviewed on a regular basis to ascertain that the best possible service is being provided.

RUSA Guidelines—A New, More Integrated Approach

The most recent guidelines for the reference interview, "Guidelines for Behavioral Performance of Reference and Information Service Providers," were approved by the Reference and User Services Association Board of Directors in June 2004 (www.ala.org/ala/mgrps/divs/rusa/resources/guidelines/guidelinesbehavioral .cfm). These guidelines cover approachability, interest, listening/inquiring, searching and follow-up. Each of these five areas includes general guidelines, in-person guidelines, and guidelines for remote reference, that is, telephone, e-mail, and chat. For the first time, the guidelines have been tied to remote reference as well as in-person reference. This provides the librarian with a way to begin to blend the various ways of answering a reference question rather than treating remote reference separately as it had been when first emerging. These guidelines stress the need for good communication skills, whether the question is asked in person or remotely stating: "In all forms of reference services, the success of the transaction is measured not only by the information conveyed, but also by the positive or negative impact of the patron/staff interaction. The positive or negative behavior of the reference staff (as observed by the patron) becomes a significant factor in perceived success or failure."

In discussing approachability: "Approachability behaviors, such as the initial verbal and nonverbal responses of the librarian, will set the tone for the entire communication process and will influence the depth and level of interaction between the staff and the users."

On the subject of interest: "A successful librarian must demonstrate a high degree of interest in the reference transaction. While not every query will contain stimulating intellectual challenges, the librarian should be interested in each patron's information need and should be committed to providing the most effective assistance."

About listening: "The reference interview is the heart of the reference transaction and is crucial to the success of the process. The librarian must be effective in identifying the patron's information needs and must do so in a manner that keeps users at ease."

On searching: "The search process is the portion of the transaction in which behavior and accuracy intersect. Without an effective search, not only is the desired information unlikely to be found but users may become discouraged as well."

About follow-up: "The reference transaction does not end when the librarian leaves the users. The librarian is responsible for determining if the users are satisfied with the results of the search and is also responsible for referring the users to other sources, even when those sources are not available in the local library."

Kwon and Gregory surveyed whether users would be more satisfied if RUSA Guidelines were used. Five behaviors were the strongest predictors of user satisfaction: "receptive and cordial listening, searching information sources with or for the patrons, providing information sources, asking patrons whether the question was answered completely and asking patrons to return when they need further assistance" (Kwon and Gregory, 2007: 137).

Understanding and Respecting Cultural Differences

The librarian should try to understand and respect the cultural differences of the users. Some users may have trouble asking their question. If they are difficult to understand, the librarian could ask them to write out their question. Librarians should avoid jargon and speak slowly and distinctly. When possible, give users struggling with English handouts that they can read. Other issues to be aware of involve differences in body language and personal space issues. In some cultures it is acceptable to stand very close to the librarian when talking to him or her. For others this can be uncomfortable. Etiquette also differs among cultures. In some countries it is important to greet someone formally before beginning the conversation and in others it is important to shake hands first. No matter what the cultural differences it is important to treat all people with respect.

A recent study by Shachaf and Snyder found that once African-American students asked a question, they asked more questions on follow-up in second and third e-mail messages to librarians than the Caucasian students did (Shachaf and Snyder, 2007).

Improving Our Skills

Doing a good reference interview takes skills that come only with practice. The new librarian should continually evaluate his or her abilities and try to improve them.

- Practice looking approachable. This means being relaxed and open and not looking so busy that the person will hesitate to ask a question.
- Practice active listening skills. Listening to the nuances as well as the words of the user will help the librarian to be sure that he or she understands the question.
- Develop knowledge of reference sources. Continuing to build knowledge of reference resources is essential in assisting the user.
- Practice posing questions. Think about how to craft and ask questions that will elicit more information from the user and help the librarian to better understand the question.
- Practice the follow-up questions and the closing of the interview. Both are essential in making sure the question is answered and making it comfortable for the user to return again.

A Look Ahead: Striving for Excellent Service

As we look to a future which is a mix of face-to-face, telephone, or virtual reference, the importance of the reference interview remains. It has been proven in all situations to be an important key to successfully answering the user's questions. It is also important in ensuring that the user feels that the librarian has tried his or her best to answer the question. It is interesting that the user values the behavior of the librarian often more than the answer. Consequently, the development of good people skills is of great importance no matter the form of the reference interview. Kathleen Kern summed up the reference interview as follows: "we need to remember that the type and quality of the service we offer must depend on our philosophy of reference service and not on the mode of communication with the user (Kern, 2003: 49). As the ways in which we work to help library users continue to change, we would do well to keep these words in mind, remembering that it is an orientation toward excellent service that leads to satisfied users.

Recommendations for Further Reading

Bobrowsky, Tammy, Lynne Beck, and Malaika Grant. 2005. "The Chat Reference Interview: Practicalities and Advice." *The Reference Librarian* 89/90: 179–191. This article offers practical information on how to conduct a chat reference interview.

Durrance, Joan. 1995. "Factors That Influence Reference Success." *The Reference Librarian* 49/50: 243–265. Based on the author's "Willingness to Return" study that identifies factors that are associated with successful reference interviews.

Dyson, Lillie Seward. 1992. "Improving Reference Services: A Maryland Training Program Brings Positive Results." *Public Libraries* 31, no. 5 (September/October): 284–289. Presents the Maryland Division of Library Development and Services survey and subsequent training program that identified verification and follow-up questions as the most important elements in the reference interview.

Fagan, Judy Condit, and Christina M. Desai. 2002/2003. "Communication Strategies for Instant Messaging and Chat Reference Services." *The Reference Librarian* 79/80: 121–155. The author discusses effective ways to communicate using instant messaging and chat reference.

"Guidelines for Behavioral Performance of Reference and Information Service Providers." 2004. *Reference & User Services Quarterly* 44, no. 1 (Fall): 9–14. A discussion of these guidelines for providing digital reference service.

Hill, J.B., Cherie Madarash Hill, and Dayne Sherman. 2007. "Text Messaging in an Academic Library: Integrating SMS into Digital Reference." *Reference Librarian* 47, no. 1: 17–29. Describes integrating SMS into the library's "Ask a Librarian" service.

Kern, M. Kathleen 2009. *Virtual Reference Best Practices, Tailoring Services to Your Library*. Chicago: American Library Association. This new title provides a wealth of up-to-date information on how to set up a virtual reference service.

McCain, Cheryl. 2007. "Telephone Calls Received at an Academic Library's Reference Desk: A New Analysis." *The Reference Librarian* 47, no. 2: 5–16. A study that documents that most telephone calls do not require a librarian.

Naylor, Sharon, Bruce Stoffel, and Sharon Van Der Laan. 2008. "Why Isn't Our Chat Reference Used More? Finding of Focus Group Discussions with Undergraduate Students." *Reference & User Services Quarterly* 47, no. 4 (Summer): 342–354. This study documents the reasons the Milner Library at Illinois State University's chat service was not better used.

Owen, Tim Buckley. 2006. *Success at the Enquiry Desk: Successful Enquiry Answering—Every Time*. 5th ed. London: Facet. A helpful and up-to-date manual on the particulars of providing reference service.

Portree, Martha et al. "Overcoming Transactional Distance; Instructional Intent in an E-mail Reference Service." *Reference & User Services Quarterly* 48, no. 2 (Winter): 142–151. Customization of the e-mail response is an important part of the transaction. This study documents how librarians provide instruction and as a result interact more directly with the user.

Ronan, Jana. 2003. "The Reference Interview Online." *Reference & User Services Quarterly* 43, no. 1 (Fall): 43–47. The author discusses how chat communication norms for online communities can be applied to real-time chat reference service following the RUSA Behavioral Performance of Reference and Information Services Professionals guidelines.

Ross, Catherine Sheldrick, and Patricia Dewdney. 1994. "Best Practices: An Analysis of the Best (and Worst) in Fifty-two Public Library Reference Transactions." *Public Libraries* 33, no. 5 (September/October): 261–266. This survey confirmed that 55 percent of the users would return to the same librarian again. Unhelpful practices in the reference interview are listed.

Stover, Mark. 2004. "The Reference Librarian as Non-Expert: A Postmodern Approach to Expertise." *The Reference Librarian* 87/88: 273–300. An exploration of the reference interview using the "postmodern psychotherapeutic view of the therapist as a non-expert."

Ward, David. 2004. "Measuring the Completeness of Reference Transactions in Online Chat." *Reference & User Services Quarterly* 44, no. 1 (Fall): 46–57. A study of the effectiveness of online chat reference and to see if the questions were answered completely.

Ward, David. 2005. "How Much Is Enough? Managing Chat Length." *Internet Reference Services Quarterly* 10, no. 2: 89–93. A discussion of how to handle long chat sessions—both policies and suggested practices.

Ward, David. 2005. "Why Users Choose Chat: A Survey of Behavior and Motivations." *Internet Reference Services Quarterly* 10, no. 1: 29–46. A study of why people choose chat and their overall satisfaction.

White, Marilyn Domas. 1981. "The Dimensions of the Reference Interview." *RQ* 20, no. 4 (Summer): 373–381. Discusses the importance of explaining to the user what is happening during the reference interview.

White, Marilyn Domas. 1998. "Questions in Reference Interviews." *Journal of Documentation* 54, no. 4 (September): 443–465. A discussion of the types of questions asked in a presearch interview.

Wikoff, Nora. 2008. "Reference Transaction Handoffs; Factors Affecting the Transition from Chat to E-mail." *Reference & User Services Quarterly* 47, no. 3 (Spring): 230–241.

Bibliography of Works Cited in This Chapter

Agosto, Denise E., and Holly Anderton. 2007. "Whatever Happened to 'Always Cite the Source?' A Study of Source Citing and Other Issues Related to Telephone Reference." *Reference & User Services Quarterly* 47(Fall): 44–53.

Arnold, Julie, and Neal Kaske. 2005. "Evaluating the Quality of a Chat Service." *portal: Libraries and the Academy* 5, no. 2: 177–193.

Cramer, Dina C. 1998. "How to Speak Patron." *Public Libraries* 37, no. 6 (November December): 349.

Dervin, Brenda, and Patricia Dewdney. 1986. "Neutral Questioning: A New Approach to the Reference Interview." *RQ* 25(Summer): 506–513.

Dewdney, Patricia, and Gillian Michell. 1996. "Oranges and Peaches: Understanding Communication Accidents in the Reference Interview." *RQ* 35, no. 4 (Summer): 520–536.

Dewdney, Patricia, and Catherine Sheldrick Ross. 1994. "Flying a Light Aircraft: Reference Service Evaluation from a User 's Viewpoint." *RQ* 34, no. 2 (Winter): 217–230.

Diamond, Wendy and Barbara Pease. 2001. "Digital Reference: A Case Study of Question Types in an Academic Library." *Reference Services Review* 29, no. 3: 210–218.

Gers, Ralph, and Lillie J. Seward. 1985. "Improving Reference Performance: Results of a Statewide Study." *Library Journal* 110 (November 1): 32–36.

Gross, Melissa. 1998. "The Imposed Query: Implications for Library Service Evaluations." *Reference and User Services Quarterly* 37, no. 3 (Spring): 290–299.

"Guidelines for Behavioral Performance of Reference and Information Service Providers." Available: www.ala.org/ala/mgrps/divs/rusa/resources/guidelines/guidelinesbehavioral.cfm.

Jacoby, JoAnn, and Nancy P. O'Brien. 2005. "Assessing the Impact of Reference Services Provided to Undergraduate Students." *College and Research Libraries* 66, no. 4: 324–340.

Jennerich, Elaine Z., and Edward J. Jennerich. 1987. *The Reference Interview as a Creative Art*. Englewood, CO: Libraries Unlimited.

Kazlauskas, Edward. 1976. "An Exploratory Study: A Kinesic Analysis of Academic Library Public Service Points." *Journal of Academic Librarianship* 2, no. 3: 130–134.

Kern, Kathleen. 2003. "Communication, Patron Satisfaction, and the Reference Interview." *Reference and User Services Quarterly* (Fall): 47–49.

Kwon, Nahyun, and Vicki L. Gregory. 2007. "The Effects of Librarians' Behavioral Performance on User Satisfaction in Chat Reference Services." *Reference & User Services Quarterly* 47, no. 2 (Winter): 137–148.

Lam, R. Errol. 1988. "The Reference Interview: Some Intercultural Considerations." *RQ* 27, no. 3 (Spring): 390–395.

Lynch, Mary Jo. 1978. "Reference Interviews in Public Libraries." *Library Quarterly* 48, no. 2 (April): 119–142.

Mon, Lorri, and Joseph W. Janes. 2007. "The Thank You Study" *Reference & User Services Quarterly* 46, no. 4 (Summer): 53–59.

Mood, Terry Ann. 1982. "Foreign Students and the Academic Library." *RQ* 21(Winter): 175–180.

Nilsen, Kirsti. 2005. "Virtual versus Face-to-Face Reference: Comparing Users' Perceptions on Visits to Physical and Virtual Reference Desks in Public and Academic Libraries." Reference and Information Services Section, World Library and Information Congress, Oslo.

Nolan, Christopher W. 1992. "Closing the Reference Interview: Implications for Policy and Practice." *RQ* 31, no. 4 (Summer): 513–523.

Powell, Carol A. and Pamela S. Bradigan. 2001. "E-Mail Reference Services: Characteristics and Effects on Overall Reference Services at an Academic

Health Services Library." *Reference and User Services Quarterly* 41, no. 2: 170–178.

Radford, Marie L. 1998. "Approach or Avoidance? The Role of Nonverbal Communication in the Academic Library User's Decision to Initiate a Reference Encounter." *Library Trends* 46, no. 4 (Spring): 699–717.

———. 1999. *The Reference Encounter.* Chicago: Association of College and Research Libraries.

———. 2008. "Encountering Virtual Users: A Qualitative Investigation of Interpersonal Communication in Chat Reference." *Journal of the American Society for Information Science and Technology* 57, no. 8: 1046–1059.

Radford, Marie L., and Lorri Mon. 2008. "Reference Service in Face-to-Face and Virtual Environments." In *Academic Library Research: Perspectives and Current Trends,* edited by Marie L. Radford and Pamela Snelson. (ALA/ACRL. Publications in Librarianship #59). Chicago: ACRL.

Ronan, Jana Smith. 2003. *Chat Reference: A Guide to Live Virtual Reference Service.* Westport, CT: Libraries Unlimited.

Ross, Catherine Sheldrick, and Patricia Dewdney. 1999. "Negative Closure: Strategies and Counter-strategies in the Reference Transaction." *Reference and User Services Quarterly* 38, no. 2 (Winter): 151–163.

Ross, Catherine Sheldrick, Kirsti Nilsen, and Patricia Dewdney. 2002. *Conducting the Reference Interview.* New York: Neal-Schuman.

Ruppel, Margie and Jody Condit Fagan. 2002. "Instant Messaging Reference: Users' Evaluation of Library Chat." *Reference Services Review* 30, no. 3: 183–197.

Shachaf, Pnina, and Mary Snyder. 2007. "The Relationship between Cultural Diversity and User Needs in Virtual Reference Services." *Journal of Academic Librarianship* 33, no. 3: 361–367.

Steiner, Sarah K., and Casey M. Long. 2007. "What Are We Afraid Of? A Survey of Librarian Opinions and Misconceptions Regarding Instant Messenger." *Reference Librarian* 47, no. 97, no. 1: 31–50.

Straw, Joseph E. 2000. "A Virtual Understanding: The Reference Interview and Question Negotiation in the Digital Age." *Reference and User Services Quarterly* 39, no. 1 (Summer): 376–379.

Swope, Mary Jane, and Jeffrey Katzer. 1972. "Why Don't They Ask Questions?" *RQ* 12, no. 2 (Winter): 161–166.

Taylor, Robert S. 1968. "Question Negotiation and Information Seeking in Libraries." *College & Research Libraries* 29 (May): 178–194.

White, Marilyn Domas, Eileen G. Abels, and Neal Kaske. 2003. "Evaluation of Chat Reference Service Quality." *D-Lib Magazine* 9, no. 2: 1–13.

3

Finding the Answer:
Basic Search Techniques

All the right questions have been asked in the reference interview. What next? In a perfect reference world as epitomized in a children's poem, the questions are asked, understood, and answered to the complete satisfaction of the user.

> *The Firefly*
> "How DO you make your bottom glow?
> How DO you make your sitter light?"
> The firefly cleared his throat and said,
> "Bioluminescence is the oxidation of an enzyme
> or protoplast called lucifern or luciferase."
> I thanked him and went home to bed.
>
> *—Jack Kent*

At a reference desk, however, the absence of that vocal, erudite firefly makes for a more challenging interaction. As described in the previous chapter, the reference interview is not merely conversation. It is skilled conversation with a definite purpose. It requires the use of pre-established procedures and practiced skills to be effective. The conscious use of tools such as keeping eye contact to be approachable, repeating the user's question to verify, and asking open-ended questions that can elicit further details are not a function of individual personality but requirements for which every reference librarian should be trained.

A less-studied aspect of the reference interview is the reference answer. It is assumed that once the user's question is understood to its fullest extent, reference librarians will, like the firefly, clear their throats and spill out a fully formed answer. As even the most experienced librarian can vouch, the clearing of one's throat is the closest one approaches to the above perfect scenario. The reference answer, much like the interview, benefits greatly from preconditioning, practice, and a conscious adoption of answering tools. With these tools, the reference answer is less vulnerable to the randomness of the librarian's knowledge coinciding with the user's idiosyncratic questions. A professional interaction is ensured regardless of the personalities involved.

Tools of the Answering Trade

Questions, queries, quests, and quizzes, the range of user needs is vast. It is both the most exhilarating and the most terrifying aspect of the reference librarian's job. Below is a list of requests received during a day at an academic library:

- I need examples of funerary sculpture from the eighteenth century.
- Do you have articles about deforestation in the Dominican Republic in Spanish?
- I have to write about how the Internet has negatively affected American society.
- Do you have an outline map of Georgia?
- What is the date for the first Seder in 2012?
- I need to do a paper on the relation between monasteries and printing.
- Are there cookbooks in this library?
- Which New Jersey governor signed the Declaration of Independence?
- For my senior thesis, I have to research the life of Emily Brontë.
- How can I tell if a journal has been peer reviewed?

The act of leaping reflexively from one type of answering level to another can be done by everyone, much as hitting back at an approaching tennis ball is done. To effectively leap, however, requires much the same dedicated training as a professional tennis player who learns to hit balls with skill combined with instinct. Answering skills can be developed, just as questioning skills can be developed in a successful reference interview. As the reference interview proceeds, the librarian should simultaneously consider the following three steps to avoid a scattershot search:

1. Categorize the answer
2. Visualize how the final answer will appear
3. Test the waters to check if the answer is proceeding in the right direction

Step 1: Categorize an Answer

Time-consuming or Quick?

Slotting an answer into ready reference versus time-consuming is of immense help:

- It helps in avoiding panic and frustration on the part of both the librarian and the user by setting up a level of expectation.
- It also helps in organizing the flow of a reference desk. Alerting the user that finding the answer could take five minutes or fifteen minutes or one hour or more allows the user to vacate the desk and plan his or her time more effectively.
- It assigns a more professional stamp on the interaction. For telephone reference, if the answer does not fall in the realm of ready reference, the librarian

can say "I will call you back with an answer within fifteen minutes." This way, the user is not left dangling in a seemingly endless abyss of waiting for the phone to ring.

- It alerts the librarian to possible complications. Approximating a time value to each answer can sometimes be miscalculated, but most questions in a school, public, and academic library are answerable within fifteen minutes of research. If not, the question may be based on incorrect assumptions, or must be upgraded to an in-depth research question rather than a quick reference question, or a referral may be in order. The question on the New Jersey governor who signed the Declaration of Independence, for example, was printed on a school assignment sheet and occupied two reference librarians. Almost one hour was squandered before it was finally deduced that such a governor simply did not exist. It was suggested that perhaps the assignment was alluding to the New Jersey governor who signed the Constitution rather than the Declaration.

Simple or Complex?

Simplicity allows the librarian to think "within the box" and allot relatively little time to finding the answer:

- A question can be simple because it is pedestrian. An outline map of Georgia, for example, has no hidden complexities. It is a graphic. Moreover, it is an ordinary graphic that can be found in well-established sources such as the Outline Maps folder published by Facts on File, Inc., or printed via a simple Google images search.
- A question can be simple because it falls within the purview of the librarian's own interests and therefore the resources are highly familiar. Locating, explaining, and presenting the best resources does not require fresh initiative or the rapid acquisition of "knowledge on the fly."
- A question can be deceptively simple such as the above request for cookbooks, which proceeded to develop into a search for obscure recipes for cocktails that could use cardamom as an ingredient. In such cases, when original searches balloon into quite another direction, time and simplicity estimates must be recalculated.

Current or Retrospective?

It can be useful to delineate questions that require current information from those that do not. Literary critiques, biographies, histories, word etymologies, and etiquette books are subject areas that require currency but do not put a premium on it. Stock reports, directories, almanacs, and statistical yearbooks do. Deciding on whether the question is retrospective helps to veer the search process to appropriate formats. A question on the life of Emily Brontë would most definitely benefit from an exhaustive print biography. Searches on a database for current articles on Brontë would be more likely to provide a single, scholarly perspective on some aspect of her work. The question on the first

Seder of 2012, on the other hand, would be most efficiently answered by an Internet search.

Specific or Cross-disciplinary?

Being alert to differences in questions aimed at facts versus analyses helps in structuring the search process. Factual information is usually to be found in one classification area, though not necessarily one source. Analyses requiring cross-disciplinary perspectives will have to be broken down into their component parts in order to select multiple classification areas. See, for example, the difference between the following two inquiries:

- What are the different kinds of illegal drugs?
- I need to do a five-page report on the impact and incidence of illegal drug abuse in the teenage population of the United States.

In the first question, the Dewey area of the 360s or the Library of Congress call numbers in the RC566–RC568 area would amply cover a listing of all the different kinds of illegal drugs. In the second assignment, however, additional research would have to cover the 306 or HV5825 area on drug culture; 613 or RA564.5 for impact of drugs on teen health; the 310 or KDZ32 area for criminal statistics; 909 or H35 for overviews such as those found in CQ Researcher; and databases for articles.

Single Source or Multisource?

Questions requiring no more than a single source are usually closed-ended questions. "I was born on 10 January, 1976; what day of the week was that?" The question requires one perpetual calendar. There is no need for further confirmation or evaluation. The World Almanac would suffice. A question on the "impact of ancient Roman architecture on the perceived power of Rome" on the other hand, would draw from multiple sources dealing, at minimum, with the history of Rome and the dynamics of architecture and architectural forms.

User Appropriate?

Academic librarians are faced with students attempting to pick up resources for absentee friends, just as public librarians are invariably approached by parents wanting resources for the "Civil War," "The Holocaust," or "a famous African American." A printed sheet in their hands, a slight disconnect in their enthusiasm for the subject, and a successful reference interview should establish their role as middlemen, rather than as end users of the information. For such "imposed queries" (Gross, 2001), ascertaining the age, grade level, or purpose of the end user's needs is critical in choosing the appropriate answer source. Recognition of the reading level of the user is also required. A question on the workings of democracy in America could be answered with Tocqueville's dense treatise or with *Cliffs Notes'* simple explanations in American Government.

Step 2: Visualize an Answer

This book describes hundreds of important resources. While envisioning the exact resource to consult for each question is an unlikely scenario, it is both possible and advisable to triangulate onto the category of sources. Indexes, guides, directories, catalogs, dictionaries, journals, statistical yearbooks, government publications, almanacs, Web sites and databases: the strengths of each are established so that a move toward any one appropriate category or format is a logical first step.

Most reference librarians follow the visualizing search strategy without consciously practicing it. The librarian who spends time looking for the "oversize commercial atlas that was right here in the business section" has admittedly used a visualization tool, but has been stumped by the change in shape as the publication has morphed into two smaller-sized publications, as was the case with the 135th edition of the *Rand McNally Commercial Atlas and Marketing Guide*. Conscious practice improves the visualizing process. As Tim Owen (2003: 27) suggests, "You can't see the fine detail, and you don't know yet whether there is a source... [but]... conjure up a picture in your mind's eyes of what the final answer will look like."

The focal points for successful visualization of answer resources are not color and size, but a rapid mental slide show of whether the answer would be in:

- Print/Internet/Database;
- Textual/Graphical/Statistical; or
- Reference/Circulating/Children.

While the first step of categorizing the answer is essential in visualizing the answer source, shuffling through rapid images of format, category, source type, and reading-level appropriateness not only helps triangulating onto the right resources, but aids the process of continuing to ask the right follow-up questions. Here are three questions on Africa:

1. What were some of the causes and effects of imperialism in Africa?
2. What are current crime statistics for countries in the African continent?
3. Is the African setting necessary for character and plot development in the novels of J. M. Coetzee?

Given the breadth of information and the analytical requirements inherent to Question 1, a circulating print textual manuscript may be the first choice in resource visualization. For Question 2, current crime statistics for all countries might be most accessible through the Internet with globally vested sites such as the United Nations at www.uncjin.org/Statistics/WCTS/wcts.html. Unless a specific critical study exists of all aspects of Coetzee's works, a database of literary criticism might be the best bet for answering Question 3.

Step 3: Test the Waters

In basketball, players are urged to use soft-focus techniques and peripheral vision to be aware of the entire playing area. While providing answers, it is useful to use a similar technique to continually gauge whether the answer is proceeding in the right direction.

Creative Browsing

Float a trial balloon with introductory information and check user response. Calibrate accordingly. As studies have shown, individual research can be highly nonlinear. Users are far more likely to recognize the information they need when they see it than know all the details of what they need before they start.

For example, a somewhat taciturn user asked this question: "Where is your section on airplanes?" A reference interview of some length established that the user needed "pictures of planes flying together." Faced with an illustrated encyclopedia of aircraft, the user was interested but continued to want more material. At this point the ongoing verbal interview was not producing new insight, so a trial balloon was floated. The user was asked which type of illustration was closest to what he wanted. He pointed to a V-formation of military aircraft, but remembered that the V was disrupted at one point during the flight. This was the clue that it was the classic "missing man formation" aerial maneuver enacted at parades and funerals to honor the MIA. That further piece of information led the user to remember that he had seen it in a broadcast of President Reagan's funeral. That was the exact image he wanted and the librarian was able to get it for him.

In short, the more inchoate the question and the more limited the ability to draw clues from a reference interview, the greater is the value of trial balloons in locating the right answer.

Subcategorizing

Draw the user into various subcategories of the question to see if any strike the right chord. As the user shows interest in one category over another, focus on the chosen material and add to it.

For example, a user was interested in sexually transmitted diseases (STDs). The topic, being of a somewhat sensitive nature, was treated to a less than exhaustive interview. Presented with monographs, statistical data material, a dictionary of diseases, an illustrated encyclopedia of diseases, and a quick sample of online sites, the user was most interested in graphic images of people afflicted with STDs. In this case the online option worked best as the user was a concerned mom who wanted gory pictures to scare her adolescent son into following the straight and narrow.

Overviews

Provide a range of synopses of material and ask, "Do any of these appear to answer your question?" While ready reference questions require a single source, broader queries can be answered through different perspectives requiring different resources. However, as Joseph Janes has correctly pointed out, "users often want a response that is good enough—not perfect but optimal" (Janes, 2003: 38). The user rather than the librarian, though, must necessarily decide the optimal response. A way to navigate between the lines separating the overzealous librarian flooding the user with material and the Spartan librarian assuming the optimal choice is to provide "bites." A quick look at the "About" icon in an online resource, or a scan of the preface, table of contents, or back-page blurb in print resources is enough to provide a sweeping overview of the kinds of perspectives available to answer the question.

Whether the user is gently pushed into creatively browsing through the material to clarify the research and enable the librarian to select the right answer source; or the librarian organizes the range into subcategories from which the user can choose; or the user is provided with a quick and sweeping overview of the resources available, the end result is still the same. The librarian tests the waters to see if the initial response to a question is heading into the right answer field.

Types of Answers

Like all of human language and communication, the phrase "reference answer" conceals as much as it conveys. An "answer," far from being a uniform entity, can be of many different types, and more pertinently, provide various levels of utility for the user. Both during and after a reference interaction, it helps to be clear about what kind of answer was given to a user and whether another level of utility could have been possible.

Levels of Utility
Value-added answer ← Skilled answer ← Elementary answer

While all of the three broad answer gradations given above are helpful to the user, the highest level of utility can be assumed to derive from the value-added answer.

Value-added

The value-added answer goes a step beyond merely providing the right resources. It organizes the material, prioritizes the resources, keeps an eye open for potential research needs being generated by the material, and presents the answer with élan.

- On paper, providing a cover letter annotating the various sources so that their relevance is made clear goes a long way to adding value to an answer. Corporate and law librarians are perhaps the best practitioners of value-added answers. Not only are the right resources to the question selected, but the relevance of each resource is made clear so that answers are presented as professional time-saving reports. Such reports, of course, are far from the fifteen-minute answers averaged by desk reference and can take up to weeks or months to prepare (Williams, 2002).

- In-person answers can benefit greatly from professional tips and the librarian's perception as to why one source is more relevant or reliable than another. If six print resources have been presented to the user, for example, the librarian can point out that the top two resources are the ones to begin with as they contain the most relevant information and are from highly reputable publishers. Alternatively, if different resource formats have been presented, the librarian can explain why a certain Web site would provide the most current updates, or how a database has a better chance of leading the user to a richer range of sources through hyperlinks.
- Answers provided via e-mail can employ simple cut-and-paste methods to consolidate the relevant facts from a variety of Web sites or database articles. With citations provided for each extract, the user has the option to do further research if necessary. If not, the user is provided with a high-utility answer that has saved both time and energy.
- In live or chat reference, thinking ahead and out of the box makes for a value-added answer. For example, a user had a question on the control of pests without the use of pesticides. The librarian was able to locate a perfect environmental Web site and a transcript of a radio interview on the subject. Most librarians would stop at this point, having provided a complete answer. This librarian picked up on the minor clue that the information was for a college paper and did a follow-up question on whether the user had access to a style guide to cite Web sites and transcripts. The user was most appreciative.
- Concerns, suggestions, and possible referrals can also be included in all formats, so that the user has the best possible overview of a topic before starting the research process.

Skilled

Value-added answers, however desirable, can be quixotic in the working life of many librarians. Often, there is just not enough time or staff to provide the icing on the answer cake. At this point, the skilled answer adequately serves the purpose. To provide such an answer, the right resources are located, sifted, and judged so that only the best sources are selected for research consumption. As Kathleen Kluegel (2001: 109) states, "Most of the decisions a searcher makes in the search strategy are made to achieve the appropriate balance between the two aims of information retrieval: precision and recall. 'Precision' refers to getting only relevant material. 'Recall' refers to getting all the relevant material."

Sifting through all the material available on a subject, especially in a large library with vast resources, is almost as daunting as having no information at all. While there is some truth and much humor in Roy Tennant's (2001) aphorism that librarians like to search and users like to find, a complete and calibrated answer includes both the challenge of a search and the satisfaction of a find. Fast and effective ways to vet multiple sources and create a hierarchy of utility for the user include the following:

- Check the table of contents to get a quick overview of subjects included and pertinent keywords included.
- Locate keywords in the index to see if there is a long list of entries or pages on the subject.
- Skim through the preface to gauge the focus of the author.
- When available, review excerpts on book jackets; these may also provide a clue to the strengths of the resource.
- Past experience with certain publishers or series can be used to expound on resource choices. For example, a Gale encyclopedia can be expected to have glossaries, boxes highlighting interesting important facts, enlivening illustrations, and extensive cross-references. A DK publication is guaranteed to have spectacular graphics. CQ Researcher can be relied upon to provide an unequivocal overview, chronology, statistics, and evaluative account of hard-to-find sociocultural issues.

In chat reference too, the skilled answer would require professional weighing of resources. For example, a question was asked about Turner syndrome. The librarian was able to locate two authoritative Web sites. One was the acclaimed *Merck Manual* and the other was a special-interest national organization, the Turner Syndrome Society. The user wrote back to say that he or she was confused because the occurrence rates listed in the two sites were variant. Here was the librarian's assured answer: "That's a tough call; they are both reputable sites. While the Merck is a reference book, the site for the Turner Syndrome Society may be more in touch with the actual statistics, because they deal exclusively with the condition" (Gurzenda, 2005).

Elementary

There are occasions when you simply do not have the right resources or you do not have the time to provide a value-added or skilled answer.

Collaboration

If the resources are not available, a strong system and ethic of referrals is both valid and highly useful for the user. As mentioned in Chapter 9, keeping a list of the nearest medical, legal, and business libraries is essential to all library reference services. The areas are specialized and invariably require more in-depth research. Keeping a list of databases available in other open-access libraries is also helpful. At the Harvard University Library Web site, links to catalogs far beyond the university are offered so that it is possible to check the British Library Catalog and Germany's Karlsruhe Virtual Catalog.

Encouraging the increasingly sophisticated system of electronic bookmarking and "blinklisting" can help when sufficient resources do not appear to be available. Traditionally, librarians have a list of "Favorites" bookmarked on reference desk computers. This tradition has carried over to roving librarians with laptop computers. However, with each computer needing to be bookmarked individually, there is a pattern of irregularity in what gets bookmarked in one and forgotten in another. With innovations such as "Blinklist" at www.blinklist.com, links can be stored online so that they can be accessed from any computer. A "tagging" system allows for a categorizing of the links. Yet another iteration currently gaining relevancy is "social bookmarking." Digg, Delicious, LibMarks and Frassle, to name a few, allow a "finding, keeping, and sharing" of online information (Fichter, 2004).

Strategizing

When time is scarce, some methods can stave off the inclination to simply not answer users' questions or to keep them waiting indefinitely.

- Ascertain whether the question can be "tabled" and answered at your convenience or whether it requires an immediate response.
- Hand over a handy introductory resource such as an encyclopedia to get the research started.
- Escort users to the right area to browse and inform them you will be rejoining them in a certain number of minutes.

Common Pitfalls in Reference Answering

Wrong Information

The pressure to "just answer" can sometimes be overwhelming. Take for example the following scenarios: An irate user on the telephone who wants the location and number for a gas station "right now" because she's running out of gas on some highway; the trusting teenager who asks a trivial question for which your mind draws a blank; the new coworker who is at the desk with you and looking to you for reference know-how—the world of human reference can be fraught with the pressure to "just answer." The point to remember is "do not do it."

Anticipating the pressure and recognizing that it is part of every reference librarian's experience helps in developing a resistance to "just answering." Wrong information can range from being irksome to dangerous. Rather than just answering, compromises can always be negotiated. The highway driver can be asked to pull over to the shoulder so you can conduct a more reliable search. The teenager can be drawn into a minute of conversation as you Google the trivia. The new coworker can learn along with you as you consult with a colleague.

Inappropriate Information

A poor cousin to wrong information is inappropriate information. Heaping a researcher with resources on African-American culture because of an inability to find a specific resource on Kwanzaa is counterproductive. It not only may not answer the question, it wastes the time of the researcher. In addition to librarian lassitude, a poor reference interview is usually at the root of inappropriate information. The school librarian who pulled out multiple biographies of Karl Marx even though the student had continued to expand on his need for a

Marx biography as part of a book report for Black History Month could easily have established the confusion between Marx and Malcolm X. The futile medical information plied on the user who needed to research "Wounded Knee" is a painful product of poor reference interviews leading to inappropriate information.

Avoidance

Avoidance of difficult questions is highly unprofessional and unethical. It is usually an outcome of momentary panic in the face of a seemingly impenetrable question. A guard against falling prey to avoidance techniques is to remember a few helpful tips when faced with a panic attack.

- Develop handy referral systems both within and outside the reference area. Knowing staff special interests or aptitudes can help refer users to the right person in the event of a difficult reference question in that area.
- Keeping pathfinders, how-tos, "knowledgebases," and referral lists on intractable subjects are other tools to prevent avoidance tactics. An interesting online incarnation of this can be found in the blog created by Q&A NJ, the virtual reference answering service established in New Jersey. The blog, inaugurated in October 2005, aims to keep a set of handy FAQs (Frequently Asked Questions) with successful search strings for the use of librarians conducting live answering sessions.
- Establish a context for the question. Technical jargon, for example, can be intimidating on its own, but is considerably tamed when located within a subject context for which material is handy. The user looking for "Mott insulator transitions in Bose condensates" is really looking for a basic textbook on condensed matter physics.
- Attack questions from different angles. If all the books on the Reformation in sixteenth-century Europe are out, you can still help a user by providing biographies of Martin Luther.
- If a resource simply cannot be located for a query, play Sherlock Holmes for a moment and reasonably deduce what institution might have a vested interest in creating, organizing, or advertising such information. An overview of soybean production in Argentina, for example, would most likely be located in online sites for organizations such as the Ministry of Economy and Production for the government of Argentina or the Economic Research Service of the U.S. Department of Agriculture.
- Finally, do not succumb to feeling that you must know everything. If the topic is unfamiliar, get familiar with it. Ask the user for clarifying information, or else consult a ready reference resource. Even wildly unfamiliar concepts and words can be decoded with a handy dictionary, encyclopedic entry, or a quick browse on the Internet. Having understood the word, the question no longer appears as unapproachable.

"Disappearing into the stacks," as one study found (Ross and Dewdney, 1998), is quite simply unthinkable.

Poor Knowledge of Resources

No librarian can escape from the inevitable errors committed by not knowing the reference collection. Most librarians have, at some point in their career, forgotten a perfect resource available in their collection; however, the experience must be avoided at all costs. The best way to minimize the margin of error is to consciously refresh familiarity with resources on an ongoing and unremitting basis. Studying a new acquisition as it is received provides bedrock knowledge that is both incremental and absorbed at an unhurried pace. Shelf reading, weeding, swapping stories of successful answering resources with colleagues, and testing alternate sources with hypothetical questions are all ways of getting intimate with the collection.

Lack of Follow-up

A less obvious but equally egregious error in answering reference questions is not following up after providing the resources. As mentioned in the chapter on the reference interview, user questions tend to grow roots as more research is done. It is good practice to return to the user to see if anything else is required. Even live reference usually has a preset message requiring the user to write back if "further information is required."

Competent Search Skills

The most powerful deterrent to the answering of complex questions, however, is an underlying sense of inadequacy in searching skills. This is easily remedied. All reference librarians can become proficient search strategists if they consciously practice the art of "searching," rather than fall into the habit of "browsing." Search skills can be practiced with three major tools of reference:

1. The local library catalog
2. Electronic databases
3. The Internet

Given that Internet searching has sounded a dominant note in the past few decades, Chapter 13 is devoted to the study of finding answers on the Internet. In the following sections, the other two search strategy tools are outlined.

The Library Catalog

As one reference veteran correctly remarked, the catalog is the "first-resort tool for identifying and locating reference works in the library and if the catalog records includes links, on the Web" (personal communication, 12/29/2005).

Catalogs in the majority of libraries use the Library of Congress Subject Headings (LCSH). A conscious recognition of the structure of authority headings goes a long way in honing the art of catalog searches. The LCSH, for example, can offer "magic searches" (Kornegay, Buchanan, and Morgan, 2005) if one acknowledges the efficacy of its form subdivisions. Form subdivisions, of little value in pre-online cataloging times when author and title searches predominated, allow "librarians to combine the precision of the cataloger with the freewheeling style of a Googler" (Kornegay, Buchanan, and Morgan, 2005: 46). They do this by establishing what the material "is," rather than what it is "about." So, for example, if a user is searching for primary documents on the Revolutionary War, a search strategy that recognizes form subdivisions would look like this:

<Revolutionary War—Diaries>

OR

<Revolutionary War—Correspondence>

OR

<Revolutionary War—Sources>

By directing the search to what the material "is," namely primary documents such as diaries, correspondence, and sources, the search avoids the necessary irrelevancies associated with random topical keyword searches. It also obviates the necessity for having any prior knowledge of a controlled vocabulary, as would be required for a strict subject search where the search string would have to look like this to get the same results:

<United States—History—Revolutionary War, 1775–1783—Diaries>

While the list of form subheadings runs into the thousands, a study of actual usage found a highly skewed pattern with barely 100 subdivisions being used 90 percent of the time (O'Neill et al., 2001). It is therefore both a productive and feasible exercise for reference librarians to keep a handy list of some of the most-used form subdivisions. The following is a selected list of twenty common LCSH form subdivisions:

Common LCSH Form Subdivisions	
Periodicals	Case studies
Biography	Dictionaries
Bibliography	Pictorial works
Directories	Guidebooks
Statistics	Indexes
Maps	Databases
Handbooks	Study guides
Poetry	Interviews
Fiction	Popular works
Scores	Tables

Similarly, in an effort to train new reference librarians, a list of "25 high-performance subdivisions" was created by the reference staff of the Hunter Library of Western Carolina University and reported in a study (Kornegay, Buchanan, and Morgan, 2005). A lengthier list of selected subdivisions can be seen at Princeton University's reference cataloging at http://library.princeton .edu/departments/tsd/katmandu/reference/formsubdiv.html. Having a handy kit of subdivisions that anchor topical keywords to subject areas allows a speedy and effective search of the online library catalog.

Database Searching

A bewildering array of interfaces prompts one to believe that databases are very different creatures. Although the differences in databases must be acknowledged, some basic search patterns and strategies prove effective, regardless of whether one is looking for images in *AccuNet/AP Multimedia Archive* or global equity pricing in *Mergent Online*.

Step 1 involves identifying the research topic.
Writing out the topic either as a full sentence or as a list of concepts central to the topic is critical in establishing the framework for starting the search. Database searches can quickly derail with misleading or unnecessary keywords. Search strategy worksheets and search tips such as that created by the Humboldt State University at http://library.humboldt.edu/infoservices/sstrawrksht.htm help researchers to organize their search strings in a methodical and productive way. Worksheets such as the one designed by the J. Paul Leonard Library at San Francisco State University and reproduced as Figure 3-1 can be used to clarify the initial topic for both the researcher and the reference librarian.

Step 2 requires identifying the appropriate database.
Database collections typically resemble a suburban mall. There are a few "big name" databases highlighted by the library, accompanied by a host of smaller or more subject-specific acquisitions. Each of these has an "About" or "Help" icon that lists the scope and focus of the collation. Combining a comprehensive "big name" database with a more specialized subject database can result in a well-balanced search. Randomly wandering through a mall of databases in search of specific information can conversely be an enervating, even fruitless, experience.

Step 3 encourages becoming familiar with the search screen and search functions.
A number of major databases are subscribing to a somewhat similar form interface where the entry box for search terms is typically followed by a set of limiters. The limiters are of tremendous value and should be exploited to the fullest extent possible. Searches can be variously limited by date ranges, full-text availability, peer-reviewed entries, within-text searches, subject descriptors, and formats. Boolean operators such as AND/ OR/NOT are also available to narrow, broaden, or eliminate unnecessary terms in a search string. Other standard search tools such as proximity operators, truncations, wildcards, and plurals are also part of the database search-polishing arsenal. A key describing what

Figure 3-1. Database Search Strategy Worksheet

Database Search Strategy Worksheet

Name_____ Date_____

Reference Librarian_____

Please fill out this form to help the Reference Librarians assist you in determining the best databases and search strategy for your topic.

I. **State your research topic (in complete sentence).**

Example: How has the relationship between blacks and Jews historically been portrayed in the popular media?

II. **List any limitations such as language, period of time, periodical title, etc.**

III. **Concept terms you think might be useful in searching your topic.**

Use another sheet of paper if your search has more than three concepts. Note: Terms within the same columns are connected by the Boolean operator "OR" and are called a "set." Sets are connected by the operator "AND."

Sources for relevant terms:

- natural language; that is, familiar words you know
- database thesaurus (see if one is available for the specific database you are using)
- subject headings and descriptors in relevant citations records you find
- terms from encyclopedias, textbooks, coursework, etc.

Concept 1	Concept 2	Concept 3	
Example: Blacks African Americans Afro-Americans Negroes	Jews Jewish	Mass Media Radio Film Newspapers	Broadcasting Television Movies

                    AND   AND

Search statement example: (black* or African American*) and Jew* and (mass media or broadcast* or televis* or film*)

The asterisk (*) symbol in this statement is used to truncate. Truncation symbols vary among databases. Look in the database help sections to find which symbol is used.

Source: San Francisco State University, J. Paul Leonard Library, www.library.sfsu.edu.

polishing tools can be found in any given database is always included. Sometimes the tools are nested within an "Advanced Search" button, and will perform more effectively than the "Basic Search." Figure 3-2 is an example of an archetypal form interface where the search terms are fine-tuned with a set of Boolean operators and followed up by a set of date, title, subject, images, and target audience limiters.

Step 4 urges a search that uses subject headings or/and refines keywords.
If keyword searches using the advanced limiters do not produce the desired results, be prepared to step up to a higher level of search strategizing. Refer to the controlled vocabulary inherent to each database. This can be done by consulting the thesaurus attached to most databases, or by retrieving the subject descriptors listed in every individual record. Most thesauri list terms with broader, narrower, and related terms as well. These can be methodically used to dredge up more accurate material. Alternately, retrieving subject headings listed in an initial search entry can achieve the same results. A great many databases are set up with subject headings. Many of these headings are linked and allow for a one-click entry to new descriptors. Institutions such as the Alvin Sherman Library of Nova Southeastern University in Florida provide detailed individualized instructions to aid users in creating the most effective database search. A small sample of the instructional pages is given in Figure 3-3.

Step 5 evaluates the results.
The results can be speedily evaluated both by the number of documents returned and by the occurrence of search keywords in the title, subject keywords, or

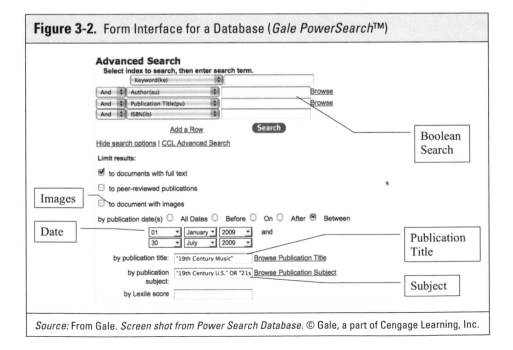

Figure 3-2. Form Interface for a Database (*Gale PowerSearch*™)

Source: From Gale. *Screen shot from Power Search Database.* © Gale, a part of Cengage Learning, Inc.

Figure 3-3. Refining a Database Search

◻ **Additional Features**

The Thesaurus is a controlled vocabulary list of subjects and related terms used to standardize the indexing in the database. You can select and search for synonyms, related, and preferred terms.

To use the Thesaurus

- click the **Thesaurus button**–left side of screen
- select **one or more databases**
- enter a **term** or **phrase**
- click **Start**

The results screen displays your term, or a related term, in a hierarchy. The report includes the database(s), and how many related records are available.

To clear the terms entered

- click **Clear** in the bottom taskbar

Search Thesaurus For:

| computers | **Start** |

Select one or more databases.
Enter a subject.
Click **Start**.

The Thesaurus is a list of suggested subject headings and related terms in the database's controlled vocabulary. You can look up and get information about subjects covered.

Thesaurus in Education Full Text.

http://www.nova.edu/library/dils/lessons/wilsonwebeducation/
Alvin Sherman Library, Research, and Information Technology Center, Nova Southeastern University

Source: Created by the Distance and Instructional Library Services department of the Alvin Sherman Library, Research, and Information Technology Center at Nova Southeastern University in Ft. Lauderdale, Florida.

---

abstract prefacing the document. Much like Goldilocks entering the bears' house and trying out things until she found them to be "just right," the number of documents returned in a search indicates whether the terms used were "just right." For the most part, searches that result in less than ten documents may suggest a search string that has been overly cautious and can be broadened by truncating the term or using the <OR> operator. More than 200 documents can be frequently defeating and may benefit from <AND> or <NOT> operators or any of the given limiters offered by the database. Any number in between is a good indication that the search string was "just right."

Search words are frequently highlighted by databases so that a quick eye-balling of the title, descriptors, and abstract is sufficient to suggest whether the result is worthwhile. Most results are also arranged in reverse chronological order, so that the timeliness of the articles can be gauged immediately. Some databases tab the results into scholarly and general categories; others list the citation and the number of words so that they need to be checked for evaluating levels of appropriateness.

Step 6 pulls together the search results into an organized whole.
Having conducted a successful search, it is important to remember that database results, unlike print material, disappear unless immediately organized. The results can be printed so that a hard copy is available. They can be saved on diskette, CD-ROM, or flash drives or exported directly into software such as EndNote or RefWorks. Students and staff at Yale University, for example, have open access to import citations into RefWorks. The globally renowned scientific database, SpringerLink, adopted CiteULike, a bookmarking Web site so citations can be instantly stored, shared, tagged with personal ratings and exported. Alternately, the results can be e-mailed, a welcome management addition for users who do not have the immediate means to print hard copies, and for research collaborators alerting members to pertinent research. The results can also be tagged as the search is being conducted. This is particularly useful when an introductory or overview of a research field is conducted and a large number of entries are being scanned for possible relevance.

However careful the original search strategy, it is vital to keep in mind that the strategy has to be constantly revisited and redefined as the research process continues. New subject descriptors suggest different tacks to the same topic. Indexed terms are certainly not graven in stone, and "related" terms can vary quite noticeably between databases. Searches may also have to be repeated over time since there can be significant time lags. As the University of Glasgow library Web site has noted, "MEDLINE gives priority to American titles and is notoriously slow to index non-U.S. specialty journals such as the *British Journal of General Practice*" (www.lib.gla.ac.uk/Docs/Guides/searching.html, accessed on 1/3/2006).

With the ongoing development of federated searching and open URL link resolvers, which allow a single query interface to trawl across multiple databases (Linoski, 2008), the future trend of database searching appears to be striving for increased search friendliness. Kids Search, Power Search, Metafind, Serials Solutions Article Linker, Muse Global Muse Search, and Innovative Interfaces Web Bridge are just some of the innovations that "offer a bridge between the reluctant searcher and the wealth of information in library databases" (Curtis and Dorner, 2005: 37).

Raison d'être: Finding the Answers

Finding answers is what we do as reference librarians. All of our skills in collection development, format management, and reference interviewing find their full flowering in the effective answering of user questions. It is quite simply our *raison d'être*.

Clarity in establishing the processes that go into the making of an answering strategy is a good thing. Deconstructing the process can appear as a slow-motion take that confirms and validates what the experienced reference librarian is doing almost instinctively. Or it can provide an instructive framework to condition and hone the librarian's techniques in answering queries of wildly different provenance. Either way, it aims to emphasize the pedagogical aspects of search strategies and the answering process.

Recommendations for Further Reading

Duckett, Bob, Peter Walker, and Christinea Donnelley. 2008. *Know It All, Find It Fast: An A-Z Source Guide for the Enquiry Desk*. 3rd ed. London: Facet. Cross-referenced and comprehensive, this book is a helpful guide for reference librarians confronted with unfamiliar enquiries.

Eurodesk. Available: www.eurodesk.org/edesk/Supportcentre.do?go=17 (accessed 11/27/2008). This Web site is an example of an answering process set up on "How to answer European questions." Designed for Eurodesk, an online support site for professionals working with young people in the European region, the site establishes an "enquiry answering checklist" and gives examples of successfully answered questions that followed the process.

"The Exchange." A one-time regular column in *RQ/Reference and User Services Quarterly*, "The Exchange" is an interesting way to study the asking and answering of tricky reference questions, some of which were never answered. The compilation of questions and answers is available to RUSA (Reference and User Services Association) members at www.ala.org.

National Health Service (NHS). Sponsored by the NHS, a national British pharmacy service available online at www.ukmi.nhs.uk, aims to provide collaborative and evidence-based information on medicines and supplies an interactive template for "standard search patterns" such as one for drug interactions. Templates such as these can be useful for searches that are repeated often. In academic libraries, subject-specific templates can be developed based on curricula. In public libraries, genealogy searches, relative car prices, personal finance resources, doctor information, and researching a house, are some general areas that one can find ready answers with prepared pathfinders.

Oder, Norman. "The End of LC Subject Headings?" 2006. *Library Journal* (May 15): 14. In a report both commissioned and publicized by the Library of Congress, it was suggested that the Library of Congress Subject Headings or LCSH, are becoming less necessary in an emerging research world where "we think of Google as the catalog." The debate between the use of free-text searching as epitomized by information searches online, and the use of controlled vocabulary as traditionally espoused in both print and online research, appears to have sharpened following the LC report.

Project Wombat. Since 1992, Stumpers-L was a popular reference listserv where librarians could post challenging questions that had "stumped" them. As of January 2006, Project Gutenberg hosted the new version of the listserv, known as Project Wombat, named after the mascot of the earlier listserv. Available at http://project-wombat.org, the list has various levels of subscription so that the user can choose between unmoderated and filtered lists.

Bibliography of Works Cited in This Chapter

Bell, Suzanne S. 2009. *Librarian's Guide to Online Searching*. 2nd ed. Englewood, CO: Libraries Unlimited.

Case, Donald O. 2007. *Looking for Information: A Survey of Research on Information Seeking, Needs, and Behavior*. 2nd ed. London: Academic Press.

Curtis, AnneMarie, and Daniel G. Dorner. 2005. "Why Federated Search?" *Knowledge Quest* 33, no. 3 (January/February): 35–37.

Fichter, Darlene. 2004. "Tools for Finding Things Again." *Online* 28, no. 5 (September/October): 52–56.

Fisher, Karen, Sanda Erdelez, and Lynne McKechnie, eds. 2005. *Theories of Information Behavior*. Medford, NJ: Information Today, Inc.

Gross, Melissa. 2001. "Imposed Information Seeking in Public Libraries and School Library Media Centers: A Common Behaviour?" *Information Research* 6, no. 2 (January).

Gurzenda, Mary-Jean. 2005. Q&A NJ live reference of April 26.

Hacker, Diana. 2006. *Research and Documentation in the Electronic Age*. Boston, MA: Bedford/St. Martins.

Janes, Joseph. 2003. *Introduction to Reference Work in the Digital Age*. New York: Neal-Schuman.

Kent, Jack. 2005. "The Firefly." *Cricket* 32, no. 11 (July): 4. (c)2005 by Jack Kent.

Kluegel, Kathleen M. 2001. "Electronic Resources for Reference." In Richard E. Bopp and Linda C. Smith, *Reference and Information Services*, 3rd ed. (pp. 97–124). Englewood, CO: Libraries Unlimited.

Kornegay, Becky, Heidi Buchanan, and Hiddy Morgan. 2005. "Amazing, Magic Searches." Library Journal 130, no. 18 (November): 44–46.

Linoski, Alexis and Tine Walczyk. 2008. "Federated Search 101." *Library Journal Net Connect* 133 (Summer): 2–5.

O'Neill, Edward T. O., Lois Mai Chan, Eric Childress, Rebecca Dean, Lynn M. El-Hoshy, and Diane Vizine-Goetz. 2001. "Form Subdivisions: Their Identification and Use in LCSH." *Library Resources & Technical Services* 45, 4: 187–197.

Owen, Tim Buckley. 2006. *Success at the Enquiry Desk: Successful Enquiry Answering— Every Time*. 5th ed. London: Facet Publishing.

Rethlefsen, Melissa L. 2007. "Tags Help Make Libraries del.icio.us: Social Bookmarking and Tagging Boost Participation." *Library Journal* 132, no. 15 (September 15): 26–29.

Ross, Catherine Sheldrick, and Patricia Dewdney. 1998. "Negative Closure: Strategies and Counter-Strategies in the Reference Transaction." *Reference and User Services Quarterly* 38, no. 42 (Winter): 151–163.

Sauers, Michael P. 2009. *Searching 2.0*. New York: Neal-Schuman.

Saxton, Matthew L., and John Richardson. 2002. *Understanding Reference Transactions*. Boston, MA: Academic Press.

"SpringerLink." 2008. *Online* 32, no. 6 (November–December): 14.

Tennant, Roy. 2001. "Avoiding Unintended Consequences." *Library Journal* 126, no. 1 (January 1): 38.

Williams, Sinead. 2002. "Teaming for Research Excellence." *Online* (November/December): 31–35.

Part II
Introduction to Major Reference Sources

4

Answering Questions about Books, Magazines, Newspapers, Libraries and Publishing, and Bibliographic Networks—Bibliographic Resources

Overview

Bibliographic resources remain vital in the age of electronic resources. They represent an organized and consistent way to present information about books, magazines, newspapers, media, libraries and publishing. Though this same information can be found piece by piece on the Internet, a bibliographic resource provides a way to compare and contrast information collected from many sources. With these resources in hand, the librarian can answer questions about everything from recently published novels and electronic journals to films and media distributors. Many requests of this kind arise from users' need to verify citation information for texts that they have previously consulted or verify the existence of new sources. Bibliographic resources can also assist in such tasks as finding a copy of a book published at the end of the eighteenth century, copies of a nineteenth-century magazine or the address of a new publisher. Further, they can help users find libraries with special collections and publishers who publish books in a specific subject area. In this chapter, the reader is introduced to the questions that call for these resources and the means of answering them.

Bibliographies are essentially lists of books or other materials that can be organized by author, title or subject. They record pertinent information about each item listed, including its author, title, edition, place of publication, publisher, and date of publication. The particulars of a bibliography's organizational structure inform and delimit the ways it can be used. For example, the bibliographic information may differ depending on whether the information is meant to facilitate verification of the title, location of a specific copy, or purchase of an in-print book. Bibliographies may be comprehensive—attempting to include everything within the scope of the bibliography—or selective. Some bibliographies are current and are regularly updated. Others are no longer published and record the existence of materials at a particular time and place. These bibliographies are referred to as retrospective. In the future most bibliographies will be compiled in an electronic format, making them easier to produce, more flexible to search, and easier to keep current.

Bibliographies have a long and distinguished history. Even before the rise of print, records were kept of written materials. As early as the seventh century B.C., the Library at Sennacherib at Nineveh kept a list of clay tablets (Harmon, 1989: 16). In the fourteenth century we find a catalog compiled by Franciscan monks, *Registrum librorum Angliciae*, which listed manuscripts in more than 180 English monasteries (Harmon, 1989: 17). One of the first bibliographies to be printed was a bibliography of ecclesiastical writers in chronological order, compiled by Johann Triheim, abbot of Spanheim, and published in 1494 (Stokes, 2003). Trade bibliographies began to be published with the invention of the printing press in the fifteenth century, as the need to make the public aware of new publications arose. In 1545, Conrad Gesner published *Bibliotheca Universalis*, a universal bibliography that listed 12,000 books arranged by the author's name, followed by an *Appendix* in 1555 with 3,000 additional works (Macles, 1961). Libraries began to print catalogs of their collections in the eighteenth century, including Leyden (1710), Oxford (1738), and Bibliothèque Royale (1743) (Harmon, 1989: 21). Scholars have compiled bibliographies either to record all books published in a single location or a single country, or a complete or selective list of books published on a certain topic, or a list of the works written by one author. These bibliographies have enabled librarians and scholars to know what books have been published and often where they can be found.

How Bibliographies Are Used

Bibliographies are used to:

- Identify or verify information
- Locate materials
- Select materials for the collection

A bibliography can be used to identify or verify information about a book or other type of material. For example, there may be two books with the same title. The bibliographic record, which includes the author, title, publisher, date of publication, and other useful information, may help to distinguish one from the other; the date of publication or the place of publication may be a guide as to which book it is. A list of books by date or by country can be used to verify the existence of a book. The *National Union Catalog* is an example of a bibliography used to both verify and locate books and other materials. In this case it lists materials held by the Library of Congress and by the many participating libraries. Bibliographies can also provide information for collection development by identifying new or retrospective titles on a certain subject. A library trying to build a new collection in a certain subject area may find bibliographies useful.

Questions Answered by Bibliographies

Q: Where can I find the name of the author of the book, *How Doctors Think*?

A: If this book is in print, the answer can be found in *Books in Print*. Otherwise, it could be found in a library catalog or in *WorldCat.org*.

Q: Where is the periodical *Reference and User Services Quarterly* indexed?

A: This information can be found in a directory of periodicals such as *Ulrich's International Periodicals Directory*.

Q: What publishers might be interested in publishing my book on new ideas for eating vegetarian?

A: The directory *LMP* is one source of information on this topic since it provides information on publishers and what subject areas they publish.

Q: Are there any academic libraries in Youngstown, Ohio?

A: The *American Library Directory* is a good source for this information.

Q: What U.S. publishers have published recent winners of the Nobel Prize for Literature?

A: *BooksinPrint.com* can be searched for this information.

Major Bibliographic Resources Used in Reference Work

National Catalogs and Bibliographies

National bibliographies provide listings of materials that are published in a particular country and often include materials received through the legal deposit. Each book or other material listed has been examined and cataloged, thus providing a high degree of accuracy. A national bibliography can answer the following questions: What books has a specific author written? What books are there on a particular subject? Who owns the following title?

The United States

Although there is no single, central national library covering all publications in the United States, the Library of Congress serves many of the functions of a national library. There is no legal deposit requirement that all published materials must be deposited in a national institution (often the national library), and it is not needed for copyright protection. However, since 1978 copies of all copyrightable works published in the United States must be deposited at the Copyright Office at the Library of Congress, but "not all works deposited are selected for inclusion in the collections of the Library of Congress" (Balay, 1996: 48). Because of this, all items published in the United States are not available in one location.

The *National Union Catalog*

The *National Union Catalog* (*NUC*) began as the card catalog of the Library of Congress in 1901. The first printed author catalog was produced in 1942 and included catalog cards from 1898 to 1942 from the Library of Congress and from other research libraries. In 1956 the *NUC* added the collections of other libraries to the *NUC* book catalog. From 1968 to 1981 the pre-1956 card catalog was published as *The National Union Catalog: Pre-1956 Imprints*, which was an author or main entry only catalog. This was published in both print and microfilm, called REMARC records. Today the *NUC* is available free through the Library of Congress at catalog.loc.gov (only books cataloged by the Library of Congress are included) and for a fee on the bibliographic network, OCLC. It includes books, maps, music, serials, visual materials, and many other materials. The Library of Congress itself has a collection of 139 million items that includes 21 million books, 61 million manuscripts, 13 million photographs, 5 million maps, 5.5 million pieces of sheet music, and 1.2 million moving images.

The *NUC* is a good source of retrospective bibliographic information and can be used to verify information on earlier editions of the writings of an author and to verify the existence of a particular work. Although most information from the *NUC* can be found in WorldCat, some bibliographic information is only available in the *NUC*.

Access to library catalogs online has made it easier to both identify and locate books, magazines, newspapers, manuscripts, maps, audiovisual materials, and other materials. In addition to its own catalog, the Library of Congress has an extensive list of online library catalogs on its Web site. The New York Public Library's online catalog CATNYP is available at www.nypl.org. This is another extensive database of U.S. and international titles owned by the New York Public Library.

When a catalog lists the records of several libraries, it becomes a union catalog. Many library consortia have union catalogs to make it easier for their members to identify and locate library materials. For example, the Five Colleges consortium in Massachusetts (Amherst College, Hampshire College, Mount Holyoke College, Smith College, and the University of Massachusetts Amherst) has an online union catalog (http://fcaw.library.umass .edu:8991/F/). Another example is "Tri-Cat," a union catalog for three medical center libraries in New York City: Memorial Sloan-Kettering Cancer Center, The Rockefeller University and Weill Medical College at Cornell University (http://lib3.rockefeller .edu/). On an international level WorldCat lists the holdings of libraries from all over the world and provides users with access to materials needed often close to their own location. A public version of WorldCat called "WorldCat.org" (www.worldcat.org) is now available through Google. Users can put in their location and find a copy of the book in a library near them. WorldCat is also available through mobile phones.

The United Kingdom

In the United Kingdom the *British National Bibliography* provides selective coverage of printed and electronic publications published since 1950. "The BNB is the single most comprehensive listing of U.K. titles. U.K. and Irish publishers are obliged by law to send a copy of all new publications, including serial titles, to the Legal Deposit Office of the British Library. The BNB is available as a weekly MARC Exchange File, a weekly printed publication and as a monthly CD-ROM" (www.bl.uk/reshelp/atyourdesk/docsupply/productsservices/ bnb/index.html). The *General Catalogue of Printed Books to 1975* and supplements to 1998 are available in print and are based on the country's legal deposit. *Catalogue* is now part of the British Library Integrated Catalogue (http://catalogue.bl.uk), which provides access to this world-renowned library collection.

Canada

In Canada, the Library and Archives Canada (LAC) maintains AMICUS, an online catalog, listing records from 1,300 Canadian libraries and has provided free online access to *Canadiana*, Canada's National Bibliography, since 1998. It "lists and describes a wide variety of publications produced in Canada, or published elsewhere but of special interest or significance to Canada" (www.collectionscanada.gc.ca/canadiana/index-e.html). Among the publications included are books, periodicals, sound recordings, video recordings, government documents, and electronic documents. "*Canadiana* provides standard cataloguing information for each item listed." *New Book Service* is a free, monthly service providing prepublication information on books in English and French (www.collectionscanada.gc.ca/newbooks/index-e.html).

Trade Bibliographies

Trade bibliographies are bibliographies usually produced commercially by the publishers and booksellers in a country to provide information on what is in print, what is out of print and what will be published. The primary purpose of a trade bibliography is to provide information as to what materials are available for purchase. The materials listed are supplied by the publishers. For this reason, price, publisher, and ISBN are listed. The ISBN (International Standard Book Number) is a system that allows each book published to have a distinctive number. The number includes a country code, a publisher identifier, a title identifier and a checkdigit. The materials listed have not been examined by the publisher compiling the information.

A trade bibliography can also answer questions such as these: Is this book still in print? What books by a certain author are still in print? What books on a specific subject are still in print?

Books in Print is a comprehensive annual trade bibliography for books, audio books, and video titles published or distributed in North America. *Books in Print* is available online through Bowker as well as through other online vendors. The online version combines in-print, out-of-print, and forthcoming titles, plus Fiction Connection and Non-Fiction Connection, which are online reader's advisory sites. *GlobalBooksInPrint.com* lists 16 million English- and Spanish-language titles published in 44 different markets. This is a useful tool for a library that needs to buy and locate materials outside the United States.

U.S. Retrospective Bibliography

A series of bibliographies make up the U.S. retrospective bibliography. These bibliographies are useful for establishing the existence and sometimes the location of books published before the twentieth century. For many scholars doing research on the history of the United States and the work of early authors and scholars, these bibliographies are a necessary part of their work. Charles Evans, a librarian, compiled *American Bibliography: A Chronological Dictionary of All Books, Pamphlets and Periodical Publications Printed in the United States from the Genesis of Printing in 1639 Down to and Including the Year 1800.* States Robert Balay, "The most important general list of early American publications... [it] includes books, pamphlets and periodicals, arranged chronologically by dates of publication. [It] gives for each book author's full name with dates of birth and death, full title, place, date, publisher or printer, paging, size and, whenever possible, location of copies in American libraries" (Balay, 1996: 45). In each volume there are indexes by author, subject, and printers and publishers. An author-title index to the whole set was published in 1959. It is now available in a digitized format with full text of the materials listed as *Early American Imprints, Series I. Evans (1639–1800).*

Ralph R. Shaw and Richard H. Shoemaker continued the Evans bibliography with *American Bibliography: A Preliminary Checklist for 1801–1819.* This bibliography was intended to fill the gap between the end of Evans and the beginning of Roorbach in 1820. Shaw and Shoemaker also include library locations. It was followed by Richard H. Shoemaker's *A Checklist of American Imprints for 1820–1829* and *A Checklist of American Imprints for 1830–1846.* This is also available on microform and online.

Orville Roorbach, a bookseller, published *Bibliotheca Americana: 1820–1861.* This "trade catalog of American publications, including reprints," was intended for use by booksellers (Balay, 1996: 46). The four volumes are arranged alphabetically by author and title and provide the publisher and sometimes the date of publication. Though incomplete and sometimes inaccurate, it is all we have for this period. James Kelly compiled *The American Catalogue of Books... January 1861 to January 1871,* picking up where Roorbach ended. It is also a trade bibliography providing similar information to Roorbach (Balay, 1996: 6). It is arranged alphabetically by author and title.

Joseph Sabin's *A Dictionary of Books Relating to America from Its Discovery to the Present Time* lists books, pamphlets and periodicals published in the Western Hemisphere and elsewhere with locations. It was published in 1936 having been finished by others. Arranged by author, each entry includes title, place, publisher, date, format, paging, and often information about the contents (Balay, 1996: 45). John Edgar Molnar published an author-title index to Joseph Sabin's *Dictionary of Books Relating to America* in 1974. *Sabin Americana 1500–1926* is now available in a digitized format with full text of many of the documents listed in the *Dictionary.*

American Book Publishing Record Cumulative 1876–1949 and *1950–1977* are early Bowker publications arranged by Dewey number with author and title indexes, with separate volumes for fiction and juvenile fiction. They document books published during this period.

American Catalogue of Books 1876–1910 was both a national and trade bibliography. The first volume lists the books under author and title and the second volume by subject. It "aims to include, with certain exceptions, all books published in the U.S. which were for sale to the general public" (Balay, 1996: 46).

The *United States Catalog* is an in-print list published by H.W. Wilson from 1899–1927. This was followed by *Cumulative Book Index*, subtitled "A world list of books in the English language," which was published by H.W. Wilson from 1928–1999. Each volume is a listing of works published in English anywhere in the world during that time period. Authors, titles and subjects are arranged in one alphabet.

Periodicals and Newspapers

Libraries receive many questions about magazines and newspapers. For example, where is a magazine published? Where is this journal indexed? What is the subscription price of this magazine? When did the journal begin? How much does it cost to advertise in this magazine or newspaper?

One of the top sources for information about current domestic and international magazines, journals and newspapers is *Ulrich's International Periodicals Directory*, which lists over 201,000 domestic and foreign serial publications including magazines, journals, newspapers, irregular serials, and online serials. *Ulrich's* provides bibliographic information about each title including address, subscriber information, a brief description of the serial, where the serial is indexed, whether the serial is available online, and the history of the serial as well as the ISSN (International Standard Serials Number). The ISSN, like the ISBN, provides a way to distinguish similar titles from one another. A listing of online databases is also included. The print version is a four-volume work arranged by subject. The online version, *Ulrichsweb.com*, lists over 300,000 titles including active, suspended, ceased, and forthcoming titles.

Magazines for Libraries, 16th Edition, is a source of recommendations for periodicals. Arranged by subject, it describes each magazine, evaluates it and recommends what kind of libraries might want to purchase this magazine. There are more than 6,850 magazines and databases reviewed. Title and subject indexes are included. *Magazines for Libraries* reviews are also included in *Ulrichs web.com*.

Although *Ulrich's* is often the first choice of librarians for information on magazines and newspapers, other directories provide similar information or supplement it. *The Standard Periodical Directory* is a smaller directory of periodicals listing over 60,000 U. S. and Canadian magazines and newspapers. It is published annually and is known for listing many house organs and trade publications not listed elsewhere. The online version is titled *MediaFinder*. The *International Directory of Little Magazines & Small Presses* is a source of information about little magazines and presses that may or may not get listed in the standard directories. Each magazine or press is described in nonevaluative terms. Subscription information is also provided.

As the number of electronic journals increases, users and librarians need to know what journals are available electronically, their subscription price and whether they are available in full text as part of a database. The *Gale Directory of Databases*, a listing of databases, CD-ROMs, database producers, and online services, is available in print and online. This reference work pulls together current information on databases and database products. For example, the librarian can find out what databases are available from the H.W. Wilson Company or from EBSCO. The librarian can also find out how to contact the publisher of the database. A number of other publications help librarians and users sort out the information on journals that are available electronically. *NewJour* (http://library.georgetown.edu/newjour/) is a free listing of all journals and newspapers available electronically. Users of the list are encouraged to send in new titles to add to the list. *Fulltext Sources Online (FSO)*, edited by Mary B. Glose, Tina D. Currado and Tracy Elliott, is "a directory of publications accessible online in full text, from 29 major aggregator producers." *FSO* is also available in print published two times a year. As open access journals have begun to flourish, the *Directory of Open Access Journals* lists over 3,700 free, full-text scholarly journals on all subjects and in all languages with about 1,300 searchable at the article level (www.doaj.org). *Gale Directory of Publications and Broadcast Media* is both an online and print publication listing periodicals and newspapers as well as radio and television stations and cable companies. This directory provides subscription rates, circulation, key staff, and advertising rates for both publications and media. It is organized geographically with city subdivisions for magazines, newspapers, radio, and TV, and also includes a subject index. Earlier compilations of serials titles and their locations were recorded in two volumes, which serve as a way to verify and locate serials titles that have been in existence for a long period of time or were being published before 1999. They are *Union List of Serials in the U.S. and Canada before 1950*, which ends in 1949, and *New Serials Titles* that continued the *Union List of Serials* and ceased publication in 1999.

Nonprint Materials

The nonprint equivalent to *Books in Print* simply does not exist. Librarians trying to identify, verify and often order DVDs, CDs, videos and audiotapes must search a series of sources in order to locate the information they need. *Video Source Book* provides information on a wide range of videos from children's features to documentaries to straight-to-video movies. The videos are arranged alphabetically by title and the list includes a detailed description. Six indexes are also available including subject, awards, and distributors. The *Internet Movie Database* (IMDB.com), now owned by Amazon.com, is a large online movie (feature film) database begun about 1990. For each movie the database provides the name of the director, the writing credits, the characters in the movie, the running time and viewer comments. It also indicates the formats available

(VHS, DVD) in the United States, the United Kingdom, Canada, and Germany. For educational, documentary, instructional, and independent productions there is the *NICEM Film and Video Finder Online* that is available by subscription. A print version is also available. This database covers over 660,000 items in all formats of media, for all age levels and provides both ordering information and MARC records. *Bowker's Complete Video Directory* lists 250,000 videos in four volumes with basic information needed in order to locate the titles. In addition to VHS listings, it lists Beta, ¾", U-matic, 8mm, and laser disc formats. This reference work includes educational and special-interest videos as well as entertainment videos. *Books Out Loud: Bowker's Guide to Audiobooks* (formerly *Words on Cassette*) provides detailed bibliographic information on audiobooks, both cassettes and CDs, including a content summary and an author/reader/performer index.

Bibliographies of Bibliographies

Theodore Besterman's *A World Bibliography of Bibliographies* is a retrospective bibliography of bibliographies separately published and arranged by subject. It includes information through 1963. Over 115,000 bibliographies in forty languages are listed. Alice F. Toomy produced a supplementary volume that spanned 1964–1974. For more recent works, the *Bibliographic Index Plus* is an online subject index to current bibliographies separately published or published in books, pamphlets and periodicals. A total of 2,800 periodicals are indexed with full-text bibliographies from 1,700 journals. It is available both online and in print as the *Bibliographic Index*.

Publishing Resources Found in Libraries

Questions about publishing and libraries come from the public and from librarians themselves. The library users often want basic information about a publisher, its location, and what types of material it publishes. They are often looking for a publisher to publish a book they plan to write. *Publishers, Distributors and Wholesalers of the United States* is available online and in print. The list of publishers is extensive, including small press and audiovisual publishers. Updated annually, it provides full contact information on publishing companies, distributors, and wholesalers in one alphabet. With over 140,600 entries it can help the user find information on the fields of activity, trade imprints, and subsidiaries.

The *American Book Trade Directory* lists over 25,000 retail and antiquarian book dealers, wholesalers, and distributors in the United States in a geographical arrangement. Librarians can use this directory to locate subject specialists, distributors of hard-to-find books and other materials, retail stores for specialized materials including books in languages other than English, and library collection appraisers.

Publishers Directory lists over 30,000 U.S. and Canadian publications, distributors and wholesalers listing contact information, key personnel and the number of titles published. It is also available online as part of the *Gale Directory Library*.

The Library and Book Trade Almanac is available in print. It provides reports on national and international library and book trade trends, events and news. The latest statistics ranging from the number of books published by subject to the average prices are included.

Literary Market Place is a guide to the American book publishing industry. An annual publication, it provides information on every aspect of the publishing business including publishers, what kinds of material they publish, and key personnel and related areas such as literary agents, translators, book fairs, printers, and manufacturers. This is a very useful reference work for authors and others working in the publishing industry.

American Library Directory, an annual publication available online and in print, is arranged by state and then by city and provides information and statistics about each library in that city, including special collections and key personnel.

World Guide to Libraries lists more than 630 institutions in 130 countries. This work is arranged by continent and country and then by type of library. All essential information about each library is listed including address, telephone, fax, e-mail, collections, and statistics.

Directory of Special Libraries and Information Centers, both a print and online publication, covers thousands of special libraries and information centers. Volume 1 provides information on subject-specific resource collections maintained by business, education, nonprofit organizations, government, etc. There are international listings as well as North America. Volume 2 provides geographical and personnel indexes.

Bibliographic Control

> Bibliographic control includes the standardization of bibliographic description and subject access by means of uniform catalog code, classification systems, name authorities and preferred headings; the creation and maintenance of catalogs, union lists and finding aids; and the provision of physical access to the items in the collection. (ODLIS)

Bibliographies perform this function of bibliographic control by organizing material by author, title, and subject so that it can be identified and then identify the location so that the material can be accessed. The best example of bibliographic control is the library catalog—either in card format or online. Cataloging each item in a library collection provides the means to retrieve each item in a variety of ways. Cataloging also provides consistency so that the same form of an author's name or a title is used each time and a standard set of subject headings is used.

The three elements that have made possible bibliographic control on an international level are Machine Readable Cataloging (MARC) records, the International Standard Bibliographic Description (ISBD) and Anglo-American Cataloguing Rules (AACR2) (Gorman, 2001). MARC records were developed by the Library of Congress and have been used since 1968. "MARC is the way we encode the results of the cataloging process" (Gorman, 2001: 3). The structure of the MARC record has made it possible to standardize the format of the data for each item cataloged. The ISBD "was seen...as a means of standardizing the presentation of descriptive data so that it could be machine-translated into MARC" (Gorman, 2002: 2). Finally the AACR2 was an effort to "bring uniformity to cataloguing practice in the English-speaking world" (Gorman, 2001: 2). The standardization has resulted in all permutations of a name being linked and a standard list of subject headings controlled by a thesaurus for consistency.

Verification and access are the results of bibliographic control. The more comprehensively an item is indexed the more accessible it will be since it can be searched from more access points.

In addition to individual library catalogs, there are also union catalogs that combine the catalogs of several libraries and make it possible to search for information and locations across several catalogs at one time. Bibliographic utilities also help the librarian to identify and locate books and other materials. The most noteworthy of these bibliographic utilities is OCLC (Online Computer Library Center). OCLC is a nonprofit membership organization with over 71,000 member libraries from 112 countries. Libraries use OCLC to locate, acquire, catalog, and borrow library materials. *WorldCat*, its union catalog, provides access to "nearly 900 million pieces of information about who holds what and where" (www.oclc.org/membership). The presence of bibliographic utilities has increased the standardization of cataloging and has greatly improved access to books and other materials.

Collection Development and Maintenance

Selection and Keeping Current

Librarians can turn to several sources to identify bibliographies. The primary source is the new *Guide to Reference*, an online-only resource that replaces Balay's *Guide to Reference Books*. The *Guide to Reference* has expanded its coverage to include many online resources. On a yearly basis *American Reference Books Annual* provides a comprehensive annotated list of reference books published in a specific year in the United States and Canada. It is available in print and online.

The British equivalent to the *Guide to Reference* is the *New Walford Guide to Reference Resources*, a three-volume work that is constantly revised.

Evaluating Bibliographic Resources

The basic criteria for evaluating any type of materials also apply to bibliographies. They include: accuracy, authority, scope, arrangement, methodology, bibliographical content, and currency.

- *Accuracy* is the most important criterion for bibliographies. Since bibliographies are used to verify information about a book or other type of material and often to locate it, the accuracy of the information is of the utmost importance. Each unit of the bibliographic record must be correct.

- The *authority* of the compiler and publisher helps the librarian or user to evaluate the credibility of the work.
- The *scope* can make a big difference particularly in subject bibliographies. The librarian will want to know if a subject bibliography covers the same ground as another bibliography or covers different dates or different types of material. The preface or introduction to the bibliography often describes the scope of the bibliography.
- The *arrangement* can make the bibliography easier or more difficult to use. How is the main body of the bibliography arranged—by author, title, subject, date, geography, etc.? And what indexes are provided to have alternative ways to access the material?
- The introduction of a bibliography usually describes both the scope and the *methodology* of the work. For example, it is important to know if the compiler examined each work listed in the bibliography. If not, the bibliography may not be very useful since listing items not examined usually produces some errors.
- *Bibliographical content* should be examined to see if the bibliographical entries include enough information to help the user to verify the titles and to proceed to locate them.
- A bibliography should be *current* within the boundaries of the work. The dates and material it covers should be inclusive unless otherwise stated.

Further Considerations

As one searches for bibliographic information for books, periodicals or non-print materials, there are certain basic considerations. First, it is important to know if the title is current or older. Sometimes the user does not know, so the librarian must try all sources—those listing current materials and those listing older material. However, if the item is current, the librarian should start the search with bibliographic sources that list current material, such as trade bibliographies or library catalogs. If a price and publisher are needed to order the item, a current trade bibliography such as *Books in Print* is a good beginning source. Many libraries also use the databases developed by library vendors such as Baker and Taylor and YBP, which provide bibliographic information and reviews from standard review sources. If the user wants to find the book in the library, then either the library's own catalog or a union catalog such as OCLC's *WorldCat* can be a good starting place unless the item is too recent to be listed.

For periodicals, librarians can use *Ulrich's International Periodicals Directory* to find subscription information and to verify the title. Library catalogs usually list the periodicals the library owns and the holdings. For information about electronic serials, librarians can turn to *Fulltext Sources Online*.

If the librarian understands the user's needs, it will be easier to determine the appropriate bibliographic source. Often more than one appropriate source is available. Even in this electronic world, a need exists to verify, identify, and locate materials. Bibliographies provide needed access to all formats of materials.

THE TOP TEN BIBLIOGRAPHIC RESOURCES

Title	Print	Online
American Library Directory, 1923– Medford, NJ: Information Today	Annual	Subscription www.americanlibrarydirectory .com
Books in Print, 1905– New Providence, NJ: R.R. Bowker	Annual	Subscription www.bowker.com
Gale Directory of Publications and Broadcast Media, 1969– Farmington Hills, MI: Gale	Annual	Subscription Gale Directory Library www.gale.cengage.com
Gale Directory of Databases, 1993– Farmington Hills, MI: Gale	Annual	Subscription Gale Directory Library www.gale.cengage.com
Guide to Reference, 2008 Chicago: American Library Association		Subscription www.guidetoreference.org
LMP (*Literary Market Place*), 1940– New York: R.R. Bowker	Annual	Subscription www.literarymarketplace.com
New Walford Guide to Reference Resources, 2005– London: Facet Publishing	3 vols.	
Publishers, Distributors and Wholesalers of the U.S., 1978– New Providence, NJ: R.R. Bowker	Annual	Subscription www.bowker.com
Ulrich's International Periodicals Directory, 1932– New York: R.R. Bowker	Annual	Subscription www.ulrichsweb.com
WorldCat, 1971– Dublin, Ohio: OCLC		Subscription www.worldcat.org

RECOMMENDED FREE WEB SITES

British National Bibliography. Available: www.bl.uk/reshelp/atyourdesk/docsupply/products services/bnb/index.html. All materials published in the United Kingdom are listed here.

Canadiana. Available: www.collectionscanada.gc.ca/canadiana/index-e.html. This is the primary source to identify and verify Canadian materials.

IMDB. Available: www.imdb.com. The best source for information on all aspects of film—actors, directors, etc.

Library of Congress Catalog. Available: http://catalog.loc.gov The Library of Congress' large collection makes it an excellent source for identifying and verifying titles.

New York Public Library Catalog. Available: www.nypl.org. The New York Public Library has another large and sometimes unique collection that is useful in identifying and verifying titles.

NewJour. Available: http://library.georgetown.edu/newjour/. This source provides a listing of all new e-journals.

Reference Resources Discussed in This Chapter

American Book Publishing Record Cumulative 1876–1949. 1980. 15 vols. New York: Bowker.

American Book Publishing Record Cumulative 1950–1977. 1979. 15 vols. New York: Bowker.

American Book Trade Directory. 1915–. Medford, NJ: Information Today. Annual.

American Catalogue of Books 1876–1910. 1880–1911. 8 vol. in 13. New York: Publishers Weekly.

American Library Directory. 2006. 59th ed. Medford, NJ: Information Today. Also available online: www.american librarydirectory.com.

American Reference Books Annual. 1970–. Littleton, CO: Libraries Unlimited. Annual. Also available online: www.arbaonline.com.

Besterman, Theodore. 1965–1966. *A World Bibliography of Bibliographies*. 4th ed. 5 vols. Laussane: Societas Bibliographica.

Bibliographic Index Plus. 1982–. New York: H.W. Wilson. Available online: www .hwwilson.com/databases/biblio.cfm.

Books in Print. 1948–. New Providence, NJ: Bowker. Annual. Also available online: www.booksinprint.com/bip/.

Books Out Loud: Bowker's Guide to Audiobooks. 2005. 20th ed. 2 vols. New Providence, NJ: Bowker.

Bowker's Complete Video Directory. 2005. New Providence, NJ: Bowker.

British Library. *Catalogue*. Available: http:///catalogue.bl.uk.

British National Bibliography. Available: www.bl.uk/reshelp/atyourdesk/doc supply/productservices/bnb/.

Canadiana. Available: at www.collectionscanada.ca/canadiana/index-e.html.

Cumulative Book Index. 1898–1999. New York: H.W. Wilson.

Directory of Open Access Journals. Lund, Sweden: Lund University Libraries. Available: www.doaj.org.

Directory of Special Libraries and Information Centers. 2005. 31st ed. Farmington Hills, MI: Gale. Annual. www.gale.cengage.com.

Evans, Charles. 1903–1959. *American Bibliography: A Chronological Dictionary of All Books, Pamphlets, and Periodical Publications Printed in the United States from the Genesis of Printing in 1639 Down to and Including the Year 1800*. 14 vols. Chicago: Self-published. Available online as Early American Imprints. Series I. Evans (1629–1800), Readex.

Fulltext Sources Online. Edited by Mary B. Glose and Tina D. Currado. Medford, NJ: Information Today. Available: www.fso-online.com.

Gale Directory of Databases. 1993–. Farmington Hills, MI: Gale. Annual. Also available online in Gale's Directory Library: www.gale.cengage.com.

Gale Directory of Publications and Broadcast Media. 1990–. Farmington Hills, MI: Gale. Annual. Also available online in Gale's Directory Library: www.gale .cengage.com.

Guide to Reference. 2008. Chicago, IL: American Library Association. Subscription. Available: www.guidetoreference.org.

International Directory of Little Magazines & Small Presses. Paradise, CA: Dustbooks. Annual.

Internet Movie Database. Available: www.IMDB.com.

Kelly, James. 1866–1871. *American Catalogue of Books...January 1861 to January 1871*. 2 vols. New York: Wiley.

The Library and Book Trade Almanac. 1957–. Medford, NJ: Information Today. Annual.

Literary Market Place: The Directory of the American Book Publishing Industry. 1940–. Medford, NJ: Information Today. Annual. Also available online: www.literarymarketplace.com.

Magazines for Libraries. 13th ed. New Providence, NJ: Bowker. Available online as part of www.ulrichsweb.com.

National Union Catalog, Pre-1956 Imprints. A Cumulative Author List Representing Library of Congress Printed Cards and Titles Reported by Other American Libraries. 1968–1981. 754 vols. London: Mansell.

New Books Service. Ottawa: Library & Archives Canada. Available: www.collections .canada.gc.ca/newbooks/g4-1000-e.html.

NewJour. Available at http:/gort.ucsd.edu/newjour.

New Serial Titles. 1953–1999. Washington, DC: Library of Congress.

New Walford Guide to Reference Resources, edited by Ray Lester. 2005–. 3 vols. London: Facet Publishing. Distributed in the United States by Neal-Schuman.

New York Public Library. CATNYP. Available: www.nypl.org.

NICEM Film and Video Finder Online. Albuquerque, NM: Access Innovations. Available: www.nicem.com.

Publishers Directory. Farmington Hills, MI: Gale. Annual. Available online as part of the Gale Directory Library: www.gale.cengage.com.

Publishers, Distributors and Wholesalers of the United States. 1978–. New Providence, NJ: Bowker. Annual.

Roorbach, Orville. 1852–1861. *Bibliotheca Americana: 1820–1861*. 4 vols. New York: Roorbach.

Sabin, Joseph. 1868–1936. *A Dictionary of Books Relating to America from Its Discovery to the Present Time*. 29 vols. New York: Sabin. Also available as *Sabin Americana 1500-1926*. Available: www.gale.com/digitalcollection/.

Shaw, Ralph R., and Richard H. Shoemaker. 1958–1966. *American Bibliography: A Preliminary Checklist for 1801–1819*. 22 vols. New York: Scarecrow.

Shoemaker, Richard H. 1964-1971. *A Checklist of American Imprints for 1820–1829*. 10 vols. New York: Scarecrow.

———. 1972–1993. *A Checklist of American Imprints for 1830–1846*. Metuchen, NJ: Scarecrow.

The Standard Periodical Directory. 1989–. New York: Oxbridge. Annual. Also available Online as *MediaFinder*: www.mediafinder.com.

Ulrich's International Periodicals Directory. 1932–. New Providence, NJ: Bowker. Annual. Also available online: www.ulrichsweb.com.

Union List of Serials in the U.S. and Canada before 1950. 1965. New York: Wilson.

World Guide to Libraries. Munich: K. F. Sauer; distributed by Gale.

Recommendations for Further Reading

Beaudiquez, Marcelle. 2004. "The Perpetuation of National Bibliographies in the New Virtual Information Environment." *IFLA Journal* 30, no. 1: 24–30. Examines whether national bibliographies should be maintained and makes recommendations for what is needed to provide access in an Internet environment.

DeZelar-Tiedman, Christine. 2008. "The Proportion of NUC Pre-56 Titles Represented in the RLIN and OCLC Databases Compared: A Follow-up to the Beall/Kafadar Study." *College & Research Libraries* 69, no. 5: 401–406. A study of the number of NUC pre-56 titles not in RLIN and OCLC databases.

Kieft, Robert H. 2002. "When Reference Works Are Not Books: The New Edition of the *Guide to Reference Books.*" *Reference & User Services Quarterly* 41, no. 4 (Summer): 330–334. A discussion of the development of the new edition of *Guide to Reference Books* that is being edited by Robert H. Kieft.

Kieft, Robert H. 2008. "The Return of the *Guide to Reference* (Books)." *Reference & User Services Quarterly* 48, no. 4: 4–10. A discussion of this new reference work by the editor.

Lenhardt, Thomas. 2007. "Constant Change." *Technicalities* 27, no. 4: 5–7. A discussion of change in bibliographic control.

Liptak, Deborah A. 2007. "Beyond WorldCat: Finding That Elusive Item." *Searcher* 15, no. 8: 24–31. This article lists a wealth of Web sites that can be searched for specific titles including national archives, union catalogs, portals and open access sources.

Morris, Susan, and Jane Mandelbaum. 2001. "Bibliographic Symposium: Control for the New Millennium." *Library of Congress Information Bulletin* 60, no. 1 (January): 16–18. A report on an LC symposium on bibliographic control. Lists recommendations from this conference.

Morrisey, Locke J. 2002. "Bibliometric and Bibliographic Analysis in an Era of Electronic Scholarly Communication." *Science & Technology Libraries* 22, no. 3/4: 149–160. Discusses some current issues in relation to the linkage of citations to publications.

White, Howard D. 2008. "Better Than Brief Tests: Coverage Power Tests of Collection Strengths." *College & Research Libraries* 69, no. 2: 155–174. Discussion of the coverage power tests for evaluating collections in all types of libraries by means of ranked holdings counts from OCLC's WorldCat.

Bibliography of Works Cited in This Chapter

Balay, Robert. 1996. *Guide to Reference Books*. Chicago: American Library Association.

Bell, Barbara L. 1998. *An Annotated Guide to Current National Bibliographies*. 2nd ed. Munich: K. G. Saur.

Gorman, Michael. 2001. "Bibliographic Control or Chaos: An Agenda for National Bibliographic Services in the 21st Century." *IFLA Journal* 27: 307–313.

Harmon, Robert B. 1989. *Elements of Bibliography: A Simplified Approach*. Rev. ed. Metuchen, NJ: Scarecrow Press.

Macles, Louise Noelle. 1961. *Bibliography*. Translated by T. C. Hines. New York: Scarecrow Press.

ODLIS. Online Dictionary for Library and Information Science. Available: http://lu.com/odlis/index.cfm.

Stokes, Roy B. 2003. "Bibliography." In *Encyclopedia of Library and Information Science*, edited by Miriam A. Drake. New York: Marcel Dekker.

5

Answering Questions about Anything and Everything—Encyclopedias

Overview

The basic informational core of any library is the encyclopedia. The thinking mind's dream, the needy mind's crutch, and every librarian's staple, the encyclopedia is quite simply the closest approximation to a bookish God, omniscient and omnipresent. A librarian at the desk, in fact, is often confused for an encyclopedia. "Excuse me, just one quick question: In what years was the French and Indian War fought?" Professional dignity can be maintained only with a quick dive into the nearest encyclopedia.

Given the ubiquity of today's World Wide Web and the easy availability of an encyclopedia for the past 200 years, what is obscured is the original encyclopedia's breathtaking vision and magnitude of purpose. To provide succinct, user-friendly information on *all* areas of cumulative human activity would be considered impossible in a pre-Internet age, if it did not already exist in the form of the encyclopedia.

Structure and Use of Encyclopedias

The etymology of the word "encyclopedia" is supposedly from *enkyklios paideia*, Greek for a "well-rounded education." While the inspiration of an encyclopedia to foment a well-rounded education has not changed since the days of Aristotle, changes in the audience and choices in the format have resulted in a bewildering variety of encyclopedias.

The earliest scholars who compiled information primarily for their own use did not have user-friendliness in mind. The information collated was idiosyncratic in both content and arrangement. Yet the act of collating diverse information into a cohesive unit must have fed into a basic human need since variations of encyclopedic undertakings can be found in all parts of the world over many centuries.

By the eighteenth century, the first prototype of the modern encyclopedia was presented in the form of John Harris's *Lexicon Technicum*, a compilation of alphabetically arranged articles written by multiple experts with a copious bibliography.

The three major structural elements of the modern encyclopedia slotted into place and have continued. Since then, the basic structure has been relatively unvarying, but encyclopedia choices have matured in response to different needs and innovations. Broadly, they are as follows.

Age Appropriateness

There is a welcome recognition that knowledge is not the preserve of the adult scholar alone. Age-focused encyclopedias have overtaken the field so that today it is impossible to equate the encyclopedia with exclusive and sophisticated research needs, as was the case in past centuries. Encyclopedias for elementary school readers, middle-school students and young adults in high school are primary audience foci as are all levels of adult readers.

Focus

Given the vast demographics that are now the target audience, encyclopedias are either general or specialized. Their breadth of coverage and ease of reading distinguish them from general titles. Specialized encyclopedias are known for intensity of focus on a single subject and in-depth accounting of all aspects related to that subject.

Scope

Encyclopedias come in all sizes to suit all needs and all pocketbooks. There are the single-volume encyclopedias with brief entries or highly specialized topics. The impressive multivolume series can be breathtaking in their scope to cover anything and everything.

Format

In the past decade, the formats available to encyclopedias have grown from simple print to a dizzying array of choices. Cheap little diskettes, courtesy of CD-ROM technology, and DVDs have been surpassed by online availability that is easily accessible, frequently updated, and either free or available through subscriptions. The future of encyclopedias is most definitely anchored to its online avatar. More interestingly, with the increasing popularity of open source, user-generated models, the avatar itself is morphing and maturing in ways that would have been unthinkable to creators of the traditional encyclo-pedic format.

Since the purpose of the encyclopedia is to be all encompassing, the potential to fall short is acute. It is imperative then that every reference librarian is completely clear about both acquiring and using the right encyclopedia for the right reasons. At a minimum cost of hundreds of dollars for a general, multi-volume set, the financial premium for carefully evaluating and making the most productive choice is also relatively steep.

Questions Answered by Encyclopedias

Adult or child, layperson or professional, the act of reaching out to an encyclopedic source, be it multivolume or a single volume, print or electronic, is conditioned by certain basic expectations.

Ready Reference

Q: Is Agricola a drink?

A: According to *Grolier Online*, "Agricola" was a Roman general who lived A.D. 40–93.

Encyclopedias provide quick and direct information on any topic. There are any numbers of sources that give statistical comparison charts of popular encyclopedias. Whether it be *Britannica*'s 64,926 articles or the *Americana*'s 40,000 entries, it is clear that a large number of questions can find an informational response within these pages. From straightforward biographies and country studies to more abstract conceptual ideas such as "values," the general encyclopedia is presumed to have it all.

Accessibility

Q: What are the workings of an electric motor?

A: *The World Book* has a clear 3-paged description with color graphics that is not technically abstruse and shows exactly how a motor works.

Entries in any encyclopedia are also geared toward high accessibility. From the simplicity of alphabetized entries, to the text of the writing that eschews specialized jargon, encyclopedias are primed to be easily digested. Anyone who has turned to the *World Book* to define "ethics" will feel the immense sense of gratitude that a good encyclopedic account is able to engender. Complex intellectual constructs such as deontology and teleology are worded in simple explanations and couched within a clear context that makes the dense study of ethics seem approachable.

Scope

Q: I need to compare the economic, social, and political features of Japan with Germany.

A: *Lands and Peoples* has specific sections on the land, people, economy, history and government of both nations. The *Grolier Online* version can create a customized side-by-side comparison chart as well.

Accessibility is traditionally married to scope as well, so that users expect to get a fully outlined sketch of any topic. If it is a country that is researched, an encyclopedia is expected to briefly cover a description of the people, topography, government, economy and history. If it is a biography, the important dates and achievements that merited an entry on the person are expected. The dimensions and definition of any topic are covered, however briefly, in an encyclopedia.

One-Stop Source

Q: My sixth-grader needs to do a report on arch construction and give descriptive examples of such architecture; where can she start?

A: *The New Book of Knowledge* defines and describes arch structures. You can also check for examples in the related articles mentioned about the Arc de Triomphe, Romanesque architecture, and bridges.

The "mall mentality" so pervasive in the modern era also applies to searches in an encyclopedia. It is frequently used as a one-stop source for multifaceted subjects so that if research on Picasso as a founder of the Cubist movement is required, entries for both the artist and Cubism are handily available.

Referrals

Q: Help! I know nothing about it and need to do a twenty-page report on the history and heritage of Korean Americans in my community.

A: The *Gale Encyclopedia of Multicultural America* will help and the *World Book*'s entry on Asian Americans provides additional resources that you can check out for more in-depth research.

While breadth of topics covered is the prime expectation of any encyclopedia, depth of coverage is not. Instead, users have come to rely on bibliographies and cross-references to extend their research in any subject. The system of cross-references in an encyclopedia was introduced as early as 1410 so that it is, by now, firmly embedded in user expectations. Encyclopedias are frequently used as shortcuts to find out where specialized information is available by consulting the bibliographic "further resources" and "recommended reading" lists included in all encyclopedias.

Synopses

Q: I am writing a novel set in the late nineteenth century and need a brief overview of how much training and what kind of training was required to be a physician.

A: It took barely two years of "deplorable" education to complete medical college in the United States. An interesting synopsis of "Medical Education" provided in Great Britain, Germany, and America can be read in the 1911 *Encyclopaedia Britannica*.

The encyclopedia is also useful in defining the years in which it was produced. As a definitive account of human experience, the encyclopedia reports and testifies to the various differing stages of human thinking. The standard encyclopedic description of marriage in 2005 was "the legal agreement between a man and a woman." With same-sex marriages continuing to acquire social currency and legal legitimacy, more recent descriptions have been attempting to capture the increased shades of meaning, so that the current *Encyclopaedia Britannica* describes it as "a legally and socially sanctioned union, usually between a man and a woman." Much as changing definitions in dictionaries offer tantalizing glimpses into human sociology, encyclopedic entries expand on those glimpses to provide a fuller, synoptic picture of the era in which they are written.

Value Add-ons

Q: Where can I research Middle Eastern national anthems and get to hear them as well?

A: The *Encyclopaedia of the Orient* at www.i-cias.com/e.o has a description of anthems as well as music clips you can hear.

Depending on the encyclopedia, users have also come to expect "extras." Maps, photographs, illustrations, diagrams, statistical tables, primary text or excerpts from historic documents, multimedia attachments on electronic encyclopedias that run the gamut of audio and video configurations are all increasingly feeding into user expectations. In all probability, the writers and compilers of thirteenth-century encyclopedias were the first to comprehend the human need for visual accompaniments as they delicately etched miniature illustrations and curlicue letterings into their laborious copying of encyclopedias. Those tiny, idiosyncratic additions to the script have certainly extended a long way to the multimedia encyclopedias that are continuing to develop since their recent inception in the 1990s.

The kinds of questions print encyclopedias are less suited to answer are as follows.

Analytical Phrases

Analytically connected nouns such as *the impact of Turkish immigrants in Germany* are better suited to monographs than to an encyclopedia. Structured to explain "Turkey" and "immigration" and "Germany" as separate entities, print encyclopedias would not be the source to consult for a merged analysis of divergent topics. Electronic encyclopedias with the capacity for Boolean searching and hyperlinks may prove more productive, but the search could be random and require multiple links.

Current Issues

Print encyclopedias are also intrinsically unsuited to dynamic, quick-developing areas of information such as statistics. Demographic figures, economic transactions, or sports tallies are best accessed from other sources. Online encyclopedias, however, are constantly updated and can be accessed for this kind of information.

New Technology

Rapidly growing fields such as computer technology are prone to entry lags in both print and online encyclopedias. The 2004 print editions of the major encyclopedias do not mention *MP3* technology or *blogs* or *zines*. The 2008 print editions do not include *RSS feeds* or *Ning*. Perhaps the traditional encyclopedia's age-old need to provide a well-rounded perspective on any topic provides a built-in brake against rushing into describing ongoing technological advancements.

The first editor of the venerable *Britannica* declined to edit the revised edition because the publishers wanted to include biographies of living persons. "How can we know if their lives merit an entry?" (Kogan, 1958) was his impassioned argument, elements of which account for a more restrained entry of dynamic developments. A.J. Jacobs, the editor of *Esquire*, who purportedly read all 33,000 pages of the *Britannica*, wryly wrote that Madonna was one of the few popular icons entered, though "you could tell the editors wrote the entry while wearing one of those sterile full-body suits people use when containing an Ebola outbreak" (Jacobs, 2004: 191). This restraint is less evident in the online versions of the major encyclopedias that must compete with the ever-bountiful and easily accessible *Wikipedia*, where the only restraint to including topics is a "notability" guideline that states subjects must have "received significant coverage in reliable sources that are independent of the subject" (http://en.wikipedia.org/wiki/Wikipedia:N, accessed 10/6/2008).

Major Encyclopedic Resources Used in Reference Work

While there is an inchoate expectation that encyclopedias are expected to answer anything and everything, there are in reality two major types of encyclopedias:

- *General:* Those that do answer everything
- *Specialized:* Those that answer anything to do with a specific subject

Type	Description	Examples
General	Covers all areas of information	• *Encyclopaedia Britannica* • *Encyclopedia Americana* • *World Book Encyclopedia*
Specialized	In-depth coverage of one area	• *Encyclopedia of Race and Racism* • *Encyclopedia of Global Warming and Climate Change* • *Encyclopedia of the Historical Jesus*

Both general and specialized encyclopedias can typically be acquired in multiple formats so that reference libraries have a choice between print, CD/DVD, and online versions. They can be single or multivolume print editions. Electronic versions provide multimedia options with audio and video in addition to text.

General Encyclopedias

William Smellie, the colorful, individualistic editor of the premier edition of the *Encyclopaedia Britannica* of 1768, was determined to expand the traditional audience for an encyclopedia from a limited, learned group, to an unlimited democratic one. "Utility," he wrote, "ought to be the principal intention." He then went on to expand on his utilitarian strategy "to diffuse the knowledge of Science" so that "any man of ordinary parts, may, if he chuses, learn the principles of Agriculture, of Astronomy, of Botany, of Chemistry, etc." (Kogan, 1958: 10–11).

"Utility" and "the greater good of the greatest number" continue to underwrite the relative popularity of encyclopedias. The descriptions of current works have been crafted to establish both their structural framework and present analytical reviews on their "utility" to the public. The structural components will focus on the LURES of each encyclopedia.

We have created LURES as a handy mnemonic to remind the busy reference librarian to check the following:

- Level of user
- Updating policies
- Research aids
- Electronic availability
- Special features

The analysis, deriving from the structure, will point out each encyclopedia's distinctive strengths, weaknesses, and overall utility.

The *World Book Encyclopedia*

Edition: 2011. Volumes: 22. Articles: 17,000. Illustrations: 27,500. Index entries: 170,000.

L The *World Book Encyclopedia* is a general encyclopedia that is aimed primarily at the reference needs of school-age students and secondarily as a general reference tool for families, educators, and the public.

U The print version is published annually with additions of new articles and selected revisions of existing articles and graphics. The additions derive from an ongoing "Classroom Research Project" that continually tests the actual use of the encyclopedia in selected North American classrooms.

R The *World Book* has an extensive system of cross-referencing that is additionally backed by a highly comprehensive index. "Related articles" point the user to other aspects of a topic. "Additional resources" provide a bibliography for further reading on more than 1,500 articles.

E It is available as a DVD that contains more articles than the print version, far fewer illustrations, and various electronic "perks" such as over two hours of videos, animation, and sounds and a handy embedded search engine. *World Book Online* is a veritable cornucopia of multilevel, multipronged encyclopedias available at *www.worldbookonline.com* through a paid subscription that is offered to individuals on an annual, one-month and even a three-day basis. *World Book Kids, Student, Discover, Advanced, Spanish and French* are all part of the online offering. In addition, the online versions have more articles than the print version as well as hyperlinks, videos, primary source documents, citation builders, state-of-the-art multimedia, and daily updates.

S The encyclopedia has certain unique features. It provides an instructional section in the final volume that aims to introduce the user to the basics of research and communication skills. It also adds on an annual *Year Book* supplement to cover major world events. A special graphics feature utilizes transparency in color overlays to display dual aspects of a single subject, so that the picture comes alive.

Analysis

The *World Book*, while ostensibly designed for the school-age student, is unarguably one of the most popular general encyclopedic sources used by all ages today. It marks high on readability, with articles that are clear and frequently illustrated. Technical words are italicized and defined. Larger articles employ a graduated, simple-to-complex method that mirrors the process of human learning. Difficult entries are appended with an outline, so that the user can opt to get a bird's-eye view of the subject as well as develop a sense of the interrelationships within the subject. Questions are provided at the end of major articles to help focus the user on the most important aspects of a difficult field. In terms of Smellie's mission of "utility," the encyclopedia scores very high.

Overall Utility

Think salt. This is a source of basic information that is a staple for very different genres of libraries. It is both attractive and accessible. Currently, it is the only major general encyclopedia, aimed at all ages, that has continued to steadily print an annual revised and updated edition in addition to its online edition and software choices. The only constituency for which it is inadequate is the one requiring in-depth information.

Encyclopedia Americana

Edition: 2006. Volumes: 30. Articles: Over 45,000. Illustrations: Over 23,000. Index entries: Approximately 353,000.

L   Like the *World Book*, it is advertised as a resource for "Grades 8–up." The inclusion of articles on subjects like "ceratopsia," "seaborgium," and "marginocephalia," however, attest to its aim to be something more than a resource for school students.

U   The print version, traditionally published on an annual basis, broke with tradition by not issuing a new edition since 2006 when over 9,500 pages had been either revised or added. However, the *Americana Annual* yearbook, which compiles the year's major developments, continues to be printed.

R   It has a very detailed and singular index so that the ratio of articles to index entries averages four entries for each article. Information that has not been covered by a full-length article, but is contained within a larger subject, is also indexed. Major subjects have complete outlines included in the index. Cross-references are provided both within and at the end of each article. Bibliographies aimed at representing "divergent points of view" are provided.

E   The *Americana* is available as part of a packaged bundle of eight databases, collectively called *Grolier Online*, and offered via subscription. The online version continues to offer *Americana Journal,* a global news source that adds 200 stories each week along with a Teacher's Guide.

S   The editors pride themselves on several features such as the unusual coverage of era surveys. Articles on each of the centuries are provided as separate entries. "Almost book length" articles have been written on issues such as the World Wars. A glossary of unwieldy or technical terms is provided with the index, listing all the words in the glossaries.

Analysis

Touted as being "prominent among Abraham Lincoln's scanty store of books" (preface) the *Encyclopedia Americana* has been part of the reference landscape since 1829. Does the fact that it is the first encyclopedia to be published in the United States give it added cache? Perhaps. The *Encyclopedia Americana* has been a familiar sight to generations of users and is therefore a trusted resource. Ostensibly a source for Americana, it is in reality not so limited and can be consulted for extensive general research. In fact, it has more than double the number of entries of the *World Book*, though far fewer illustrations. However, its greatest strength does lie in its fierce coverage of both the big and the small events of American history. Primary documents such as the Bill of Rights, the Declaration of Independence, and the Gettysburg Address can be found in the *Encyclopedia Americana*. A great many of the articles are signed, including short 100-word articles such as the one on "twill" and the 200-word article on "algorithm." The encyclopedia has been periodically criticized for being slow to include important current events in its print format. Given that the parent company is still "determining a print plan" for the future and has categorically stated that "the likelihood is there will not be the 2009 multivolume print version" (Cohen, 2008: 3), and that the online version is just one part of the larger *Grolier* bundle, suggests the *Americana* landscape is dimming.

Overall Utility

In terms of acquisition, the greatest selling point of the *Americana* is contained in its title. Medium-sized libraries acquiring the *Britannica* and the *World Book* may have no pressing need for the *Americana*, but might feel vulnerable when faced with questions regarding such topics as *Lochner v. New York*, the U.S. Coast Guard, Alan Greenspan, the Carnegie Institution of Washington, or the House Un-American Activities Committee. While being a solid general-purpose encyclopedia, the *Americana* has, in the past, been most trustworthy in its provision of domestic information. However, its flagging commitment to updates and revisions greatly compromises the overall utility of the resource.

Encyclopaedia Britannica

Edition: 2007. Volumes: 32. Articles: 64,900. Illustrations: 24,000. Index entries: 215,000.

L   The *Encyclopaedia Britannica* is globally renowned as a general informational resource. Yet the style, presentation, structure, and content of the entries are unabashedly directed to a higher level of readership.

U   The print version has been revised multiple times with a revision of articles on topics such as Pluto, stem cells, and nutrition. *Book of the Year* is an annual supplement that covers major events throughout the world and is included at no additional charge to all subscribers.

R   "The Great EB," as it is popularly known, has developed an elaborate system of research aids that can be overwhelming. Two full volumes are devoted to the indexing of entries. Over 500,000 cross-references are also allied to the index entries. The one-volume *Propaedia*, aimed at aiding the user to clarify topics through intellectual structure rather than alphabetical convenience, tends instead toward mind-numbing erudition.

E   The *Britannica* is available in an increasing variety of nonprint formats: CD-ROM, DVD, and online. The software, which is available for less than fifty dollars, can be tailored to suit three age levels. The *Britannica Ultimate Reference Suite* has over 100,000 articles and 19,000 graphics, as well as entries from the encyclopedia's famous past authors such as Sigmund Freud, Marie Curie, and Orville Wright. A "research organizer" offers software glitz that allows for note taking, saving bookmarks, and formatting reports. The online reference site is also available for younger (School Edition), experienced (Academic Edition) and all-purpose (Library Edition) readers. Over 3,000 audio-video animations plus links to 166,000 Web sites and full-text articles from EBSCO, combine to provide a formidable online presence. The most intriguing development of the online site, however, has been the 2008 adoption of modified open source entries at www .britannica.com. The modification consists of three categories of content: that created by the existing community of experts, by users, and by the encyclopedia itself, which integrates any part of the first two to create an "EBchecked" topic. In addition to the wiki facet, Britannica has added a cluster of Web 2.0 connectivity content such as widgets, blogs, and Twitter feeds.

S   To present what is "special" about the Great EB is to imply that there is something quotidian about it. There really isn't. Defined by a complex tripartite structure; an index that is analytical; nonstandardized vocabulary; an authorship that reads like a Who's Who of global and historical personalities; and a hoary history, the encyclopedia is unique at all levels.

Analysis

The *Britannica* claims almost 240 years of experience in delivering the "world standard in reference." Marketing hyperbole aside, the *Britannica* can rightly claim preeminence in name recognition. With past contributors like Einstein and Trotsky, its credentials are stellar. The twelve-volume *Micropaedia* is the core resource for general reference, providing breadth of coverage in short, authoritative articles. The *Macropaedia* offers depth of coverage on selected topics. International coverage has always been of a high order so that even nonbiographical or nongeographical subjects such as AIDS receive a global perspective. The *Britannica* is harder to navigate than most current encyclopedias.

The print is small and the *Micropaedia* is designed with three columns, separated by narrow margins that leave very little white space. Ease of readability is not a prime consideration as evident in the variant style of articles and the non-standardized vocabulary. There is no controlled vocabulary and a great many of the *Macropaedia* articles read more like academic treatises than as general reference resources.

Overall Utility

It is hard to imagine any library without the venerable and indomitable *Britannica*. It is the source that is reached for when something cannot be found in a more accessible, general reference encyclopedia. Ultimately, it remains the encyclopedia with the most gravitas.

Multimedia Encyclopedias

All the major print editions have been complemented or even eclipsed by digital or software versions. The formidable *Collier's Encyclopedia*, in publication since 1950, could only be found in parts of the *Encarta* digital encyclopedia, until that too was discontinued by 2010. The continuation of annual updates of the print version of *Encyclopedia Americana* remains a matter of serious conjecture. Globally, the honorable *Brockhaus* of Germany, printed since 1808, announced its intention of providing free online access to all of its 300,000 articles as of early 2008. While general encyclopedias were one of the earliest entrants into providing online editions, subject encyclopedias can now be found in multiple formats. *SAGE e-reference*, for example, was launched in January 2007 to provide electronic versions of its products at www.sagepublications.com/ereference.

Wikipedia

"Beware lest your dreams come true." While all of the general encyclopedias in the preceding section are available in nonprint formats, the dream of early encyclopedists to cater to the masses and generate a utilitarian source of encyclopedic information has led, in the twenty-first century, to a surreal point where the masses are feeding information to the masses. *Wikipedia*, born on January 15, 2001, is an online encyclopedia that offers "free-content," so that anybody is free to take the information, free to provide the information, and free to edit existing information. In the brave new world of burgeoning open-source software that feeds off voluntary authorship, *Wikipedia* hopes to be the ultimate people's encyclopedia. As of 2010, there were 17 million multilingual articles percolating in *Wikipedia*, of which more than 3 million were in the English language. This was reportedly being used by more than a third of adult American Internet users (2007 Pew Internet study), making it the seventh most visited Web site on the Internet (www.alexa.com). *Wikipedia* is also continually striving to "smooth the edges" as seen in its attempts at establishing "trust ratings" for its contributors (Giles, 2007).

Other Open-Source Encyclopedias

Citizendium, born in March 2007, was also fathered by Larry Sanger of *Wikipedia*. It was created with the sole aim of shoring up the single greatest criticism leveled at collaborative, open-source ventures, namely, their lack of accountability. Touting itself as the "world's most trusted encyclopedia and knowledge base," *Citizendium* continues to be a beta project with a little more than 15,000 carefully vetted articles.

The latest entry to open-source online encyclopedias was launched as a beta project by Google on July 23, 2008. *Knol*, as it has been named, differs from *Wikipedia* in that the contributors must sign their names and may even include a photograph and biography of themselves. Authors can also control the level of collaboration that they want from the community at large, choose between three different creative commons licenses, and exercise their option to include advertisements. Multiple articles by different authors on the same topic are allowed.

Most dramatically, "the Great EB," that has long touted itself as "the world's most famous and authoritative source of information" based on the authority of its contributors, is now guardedly opening the field to user-community input at its online site. A host of other beta sites such as *Scholarpedia* for "scholarly" peer-reviewed articles on a limited number of subjects testifies to the attraction of wiki encyclopedias.

Subject-specific open-source, collaborative encyclopedias are also making an appearance. *Proteopedia*, for example, which is aimed at biochemists and biologists, introduced the linking of text with spectacular three-dimensional information on biomacromolecule structures. Some 72,449 articles created by "page contributors, content donators and editors," since its inception in 2007, are updated weekly.

Bundled Encyclopedias

The "bundling" of encyclopedic resources is an additional characteristic of non-print resources. "Our greatest challenge is treading the fine line between too big and too niche," states Kevin Ohe of the Greenwood Publishing Group when speaking of electronic resource bundling (Roncevic, 2006: 10). The "fine line" is apparent in the newer bundles of online encyclopedias being offered by various publishers. While online editions were typically provided as a clutch of general and specific encyclopedias, the specific needs of specific user groups are also being introduced. So, for example, *Britannica* targets its online general encyclopedias for different types of libraries such as the academic, public and school libraries. *Grolier* and *EBSCO* cater to different age groups such as the elementary, middle and adult student. Oxford University Press is collating its subject encyclopedias into portal sites such as the breathtaking *Oxford Music Online* that provides "the most extensive and easily searchable online music resource available" (www.oxfordmusiconline.com/public/). Greenwood Publishing has fed more than 600 of its print editions on terrorism and security issues to create the online *PSIO: Praeger Security International Online*.

Although bundled encyclopedic offerings can appear to be prohibitively expensive, they serve multiple purposes and may be viewed in the budget as an accretion of many different line items. Conversely, the lengthy shopping list of resources bundled together may be dazzling in terms of what is included, but for the most part may not be relevant to institutional needs.

Use of Multimedia Encyclopedias

Multimedia encyclopedias have plenty to offer. The early CD-ROM versions that were simple transpositions of print to electronic format have gained both confidence and the necessary technology to burgeon into spectacular multimedia extravaganzas. A quick search for "Antarctica," for example, can explode into a mesmerizing display of interactive pictures, sounds, streaming video, multiple hyperlinks, animation, atlases, and timelines. Of course, the option to consult merely the text always exists, but invariably, the lure of a click into multimedia proves irresistible and fascinating. The factor of visual seduction segues neatly into some of the major considerations to keep in mind when reviewing the acquisition and use of an electronic encyclopedia. Reviews and ratings for the top ten encyclopedia software packages can be accessed at http://encyclopedia-review.toptenreviews.com/.

Options in Learning Styles
Electronic encyclopedias provide information in a variety of mediums—textual, auditory, and visual. If the education pundits are correct in believing that each person has the propensity to absorb information effectively through individualistic applications of all five senses, then the variety of choices inherent in an electronic format is certainly very appealing. The small print account of the Roman Empire as presented in the *Britannica* can blur before the eyes of a teenager who may respond more enthusiastically to the same subject when presented with voice-over narration and changing images as presented in *Grolier Online*.

Information Searching
Electronic encyclopedias can simplify and accelerate the process of information searching. Hyperlinks that leap from one aspect of an entry to a related one assist the careful user in covering vast ground in a short time. Keyword search capabilities can take researchers directly into multiple sources useful to their search.

Updates
Updating facts, figures, and statistical, biographical, and technological data is far easier to accomplish in an online resource. The researcher can thereby be relatively sure of the accuracy of current information. Quick editing also allows a majority of electronic encyclopedias to include popular culture, an area that most print encyclopedias are wary of covering.

Scope
Electronic articles are typically longer than print versions, since ultimate shelf space and production cost per page is not the issue it is with print

encyclopedias. In addition to longer articles, a greater number of articles are also the norm. There is, of course, a flip side to the obvious charms of nonprint encyclopedias.

- The usage mechanisms need a more complex infrastructure in order to provide multiple services at the same time. Print encyclopedias need shelving space. Many users can consult different volumes at the same time. Electronic encyclopedias need hardware, software, computer know-how on the part of the user, computer accessibility, and possible investments in multimedia apparatus such as headphones—in short, a far greater investment in infrastructure.

- The traditional allure of browsing through encyclopedias so that information on the Hebrides islands could just as well lead to a nonpertinent, yet exhilarating romp through the alphabetically proximate city of Hebron and the goddess Hecate is tamed in the electronic format. Browsing through hyperlinks is more suited to relevant related topics. The element of serendipitous knowledge, for which print encyclopedias are universally beloved, is dramatically muted in the more linearly conceived search technology of electronic encyclopedias.

- Librarians are a breed of professionals well suited to constant technological change. Yet the vulnerability never lessens. Electronic encyclopedias, in the past decade alone, have sprouted hydra-headed formats. CD-ROM technology led to a flurry of death announcements on the print encyclopedia in the 1980s. Paid subscriptions to online encyclopedias, with online access to patrons, led to another flurry of epitaphs on CD-ROM technology. The advent of free online encyclopedias has left the publishing world, the librarians, and the users poised for future changes. Open-source encyclopedias further complicate the current scenario. While the ongoing sense of vulnerability to change is certainly a function of time, it is vulnerability that has never been engendered by the stolid rows of print encyclopedias present in every library.

- Current user acceptance or use of online encyclopedias can also create a unique set of problems for the reference librarian. An alphabetical print resource requires little instruction and so the user has instant control. Electronic encyclopedias invariably require a set of instructions and, especially in public libraries, a process to sign up for the use of a computer. Troubleshooting can come in many forms. *Wikipedia*, for example, can be a "frame buster" that is hard to send directly; in order to send articles electronically one must instead employ a "copy and paste" method. Each unaware user needs to be informed individually. A sense of immediate control over the information resource is relatively lacking in the electronic format.

Specialized Subject Encyclopedias

Language has a peculiar impact on the way an object is perceived. Subject encyclopedias, unconsciously allied with the more popularly known general encyclopedias, are, in practice, acquisitions that cater to a very different constituency. The subject encyclopedia is "encyclopedic" only in that it is a comprehensive source of information arranged for easy access. The user of a specialized encyclopedia, however, is wholly different. Users are, for the most part, seeking relatively in-depth information on a highly specific topic—a topic that would merit perhaps a few pages in a general encyclopedia. Acquiring a subject encyclopedia, then, is really the equivalent of acquiring multiple books on a single topic, directed at a particular group of users. Acquiring a subject encyclopedia does not fulfill the traditional encyclopedia's "utilitarian" dictum of providing the "greatest good for the greatest number."

Being alert to this critical distinction can help the reference librarian choose among the thousands of subject encyclopedias that continue to flood the market at an ever-increasing pace. For the general encyclopedia, for which there is always a perceived need, the primary consideration is one of reliability. For the subject encyclopedia, the primary consideration would have to be demand or need. If there is an established constituency for the subject, only then can other considerations such as relative accuracy, reliability, and scope come into focus.

The word *subject* is also host to two important variations. Some subjects are really single topics such as the prize-winning three-volume *Encyclopedia of the World's Zoos*. Others are multiple topics within a field of knowledge, such as the well-established fifteen-volume *Encyclopedia of Religion* or the nine-volume *International Encyclopedia of the Social Sciences*, 2nd Edition. Single-topic encyclopedias require a crystal-clear demand for the topic, whereas some subjects encompassing a field of topics can be essential purchases for even the smallest libraries. For example, the valuable *Routledge Encyclopedia of Philosophy*, winner of an ALA Honorable Mention in 1999, or the more recent *The Encyclopedia of Philosophy* are handy compilations of philosophers, most of whom cannot be located in single-volume works. Similarly, the 2003 Dartmouth winner, the *Garland Encyclopedia of World Music*, is a comprehensive single purchase that covers vast areas of minor entries, not locatable in either the general encyclopedia or a topical manuscript. The absolute relief felt by a librarian in locating an account of "Tumbuka healing" in which African music is the equivalent of a prescription drug, is a feeling regularly engendered in reference librarians using subject encyclopedias. Multitopic research fields such as Canada or broadcasting or Judaism are well served by indispensable subject encyclopedias such as *The Canadian Encyclopedia*, the *Encyclopedia of Television* and *Encyclopaedia Judaica*. Equally noteworthy subject encyclopedias like the *Encyclopedia Sherlockiana* or *The Continuum Encyclopedia of Animal Symbolism in Art* or the *Encyclopedia of Body Adornment* are undeniably worthy acquisitions in and of themselves, but can be perceived as idiosyncratic luxury items unless the reference librarian has perceived a strong need in the constituency.

A handful of multidisciplinary titles are of use to any and every library. The *McGraw-Hill Encyclopedia of Science and Technology* covers a wide range of scientific topics written in an authoritative yet understandable style, with *McGraw-Hill AccessScience 2.0* (*MGHAS2*) as the online version. The thirty-four-volume

Dictionary of Art, despite its deceptive title, is an encyclopedic compendium of Western and non-Western art, art themes and cultural influences, artists and their biographies, art critics and art collectors, all supplemented with both color and black-and-white images. *Grzimek's Animal Life Encyclopedia* is the definitive compilation of information on insects, fishes, amphibians, reptiles, birds, mammals and other orders. Each order is discussed and brought alive with representative examples of species within the order. Photographs, illustrations, and maps provide graphic enhancements. Anything that runs, flies, leaps, crawls, slithers, and swims can be located in this seventeen-volume work. Finally, the *Gale Encyclopedia of Multicultural America*, although not as generically relevant as science, art, and animals, is a useful addition to all libraries within the United States, land of immigrants. There are 152 original essays written on the individual minority, ethnic, and ethno-religious groups that make up the American mosaic. Historical background information, patterns of settlement, and cultural mores associated with each group are described along with useful contact information on organizations and research centers that are relevant for further research.

Some of the most copious publishers of subject encyclopedias are the following:

- *ABC-CLIO:* Publisher of the "Companion" series that focuses on popular American issues.
- *Berkshire Publishing Group:* Entered the world of independent publishing as recently as 2005, and yet has forged a strong profile with "Outstanding Reference" recognition from *Library Journal* and ALA, among others.
- *Facts on File:* Publishes encyclopedias specifically for school and library consumption, with curriculum-based subject areas as the guiding framework.
- *Garland Science* and *Routledge Reference* of the Taylor & Francis Group: Specialize in scholarly niche publications.
- *Greenwood Publishing Group:* Includes Greenwood Press, Praeger Publishers, Heinemann USA, GEM, and Libraries Unlimited, thereby constituting one of the more copious publishers of reference encyclopedias.
- *Oxford University Press:* The behemoth of American university presses and a global publisher of reference encyclopedias.
- *Scribners:* Despite its relatively smaller output, Scribners looms large in the world of subject encyclopedias, as it has been awarded at least six of ALA's prestigious Dartmouth medals and Honorable Mentions in the past ten years. In 1999, Charles Scribner's Sons joined Thomson Gale.
- *Gale Cengage Learning:* Publisher of some of the most user-friendly subject encyclopedias and distinguished by its composite style, Gale products are also expanded by imprint publications from the likes of U.X.L. and Macmillan Reference USA.

Contact publishers directly if interested in updates of existing editions, or put out feelers about forthcoming plans, or even suggestions on what you may want to see published.

Reference librarians looking to fill a subject demand can check on a somewhat dated, yet wonderful resource: the two-volume *Subject Encyclopedias* by

Allan W. Mirwis (1999). The best picks from recent publishers can be culled from RUSA's annual *Outstanding Reference Sources* as well as the annual Dartmouth medal winners. Both lists are available at www.ala.org.

Encyclopedias for Children and Young Adults

Children's encyclopedias also cover vast swathes of information, but are usually short, heavily illustrated, and graphically simple with larger fonts and user aids.

- Aimed at grades 3–8, *The New Book of Knowledge* is available only as a database. The 9,200 articles are supplemented with more than 25,000 illustrations and over 1,300 maps, making it a child-friendly reference resource. The topics included range from the simple (George Bush) to the complex (Oriental Exclusion Acts). A clear indication of the target audience is evident in the value add-ons such as project and experiment manuals, homework help columns, and "wonder questions" such as what makes a stomach growl or the stars twinkle.

- The print version of Grolier's six-volume *Lands and Peoples* has not seen an update since 2005, but is available as one of the *Grolier Online* databases. It is aimed at grades 6–12, but can be used by upper-elementary students as well. The countries of the world are not arranged alphabetically, but by geographic continent, with each volume covering a separate continent. For young users who are not clear in which continent the country of Nauru is placed, there is an alphabetical index repeated in each volume. Geography, history, economy, lifestyles, and beliefs are described for each entry with the idea of re-creating a full social, cultural and physical milieu of the various peoples. It is a useful encyclopedia for the annual reports required by school curricula.

- *Compton's by Britannica* (2010), the incarnation of the earlier *Compton's Encyclopedia*, has been an effective teaching tool since 1922 when it was first published. Designed specifically for middle and high school students, *Compton's* 37,000 articles are deliberately allied to National Curriculum Standards. Larger articles are introduced with a boxed preview that explains the internal structure of the article. More than 23,000 images, including charts, lists, and graphs both enhance the text and summarize key data. Each of the twenty-six volumes includes a "Here and There" guide that provides an overview of subjects covered in the volume as well as a list of introductory questions that are aimed at stimulating reader interest. The most recent edition includes a reproducible worksheet to assist students in organizing their research steps. *Compton's* also prides itself on unique research aids such as the Fact Index, the final volume of almost 30,000 brief articles with an index.

- For upper-elementary students, *My First Britannica* (2008) is a pleasing thirteen-volume resource, hosted by the venerable Britannica publishing house. The distinction immediately apparent in this resource is the boldness in design, which comprises two-page articles with text on one page and illustrations on the facing page. Value add-ons include fun quizzes, factoids, and cross-references embedded into each entry. The font size is large and unfamiliar words are highlighted and defined in a comprehensive glossary. Like the previous resource, the entries are not alphabetical, but placed under subject headings for which consulting the separate index volume is a necessity.

- An alphabetic general encyclopedia aimed at the elementary student can be found in the thirteen-volume *The World Book Discovery Encyclopedia*. With 2,100 age-appropriate articles, and over 3,300 color illustrations, the encyclopedia contains succinct, easy-to-read text as well as prepares the child for more mature research techniques such as cross- and related references, pronunciation checks, and the relevance of guide words. The language is simple so that an earthquake, for example, is pithily defined as "the shaking of the ground."

Collection Development and Maintenance

Selection and Keeping Current

A number of established professional publications are also available to assist in finding the right encyclopedia. Among the most well-known sources are:

- *Kister's Best Encyclopedias*
- *Booklist* provides an annual update of existing encyclopedias in the September issue.
- *Word-of-mouth* opinions expressed by veteran reference librarians should always be welcomed. Preferred usage recommendations are one of the best indications of a good encyclopedia.
- *Bowker's Best Reference Books*
- *American Reference Books Annual*
- *Kirkus Reviews*—special editions
- Collated reviews of nonprint encyclopedias can be found in *Encyclopedia Software Review* available at http://encyclopedia-review.toptenreviews.com/.
- *Reference Reviews* available at www.gale.cengage.com/reference/ has guest columnists who provide handy, comprehensive, and current reviews of encyclopedias, both online and in print. While hosted by Gale, which is a part of Cengage Learning, the reviews are not restricted to Gale products.

Evaluating Encyclopedic Resources

Around the year 1230, Bartholomew de Granville published one of the most popular early encyclopedias, the *De proprietatibus rerum* or *The Properties of Things*. A typical entry described:

> Of A Maid: . . . a woman is more meeker than a man, she weepeth sooner. And is more envious, and more laughing, and loving; and the soul is more in a woman than in a man . . . (Steele, 2006: 22)

Despite intense competition among encyclopedias in the thirteenth century, Bartholomew's descriptions of the properties of things such as the meek, weeping, envious, laughing, loving woman with more soul, evidently struck the right chords. It was translated into multiple languages from its original Latin, and was a bestseller for over three centuries. Fifty to sixty fatted calves had to be slaughtered to provide enough vellum for a single copy, and multiple scribes and illuminators had to be employed, so that the process of acquiring the right encyclopedia was a far bloodier and exorbitant acquisition than it is today. The owning of an encyclopedia was certainly a luxury reserved for the aristocracy.

With the technological breakthrough of the printing press and the sociopolitical establishment of democratic ideals, the notion of encyclopedias as everyman's resource became more entrenched. Today we are inundated with scores of encyclopedias: general, age-specific, subject-specific, illustrated and multiformatted. Our energies are best spent in whittling down the choices to emerge with what best suits individual and institutional needs. In theory, this could prove to be a daunting task. In practice, the worth of an encyclopedia is relatively easy to gauge. Given the thousands of articles that continue to describe Bartholomew's ageless "properties of things," it is instructive to pick a few topics with which the reviewer is knowledgeable. A checklist composed of the following questions, *in order of preference*, can gird the reviewer with a sure sense of what is a work of quality and what deserves to be purchased.

Question 1: Is this encyclopedia reliable?

Above all else, reliability is essential. Given the thousands of articles penned by thousands of contributors, it is possible to gauge the reliability factor only through well-established indicators of authority. The list of contributors should be professionally qualified or known authorities on a subject. The publisher should be reputable. Both factors must be mirrored in articles that are accurate and current to the best of your knowledge. It is best to do the following:

- Choose a topic with which you are highly familiar or have a specific question that needs to be answered.
- Establish a list of expectations, preferably in writing, prior to gauging the article. If, for example, your field of expertise is the U.S. Civil War, set up an a priori checklist:
  - When was the Civil War waged?
  - Where were the major battles fought?
  - Who were the primary personalities involved in the war?
  - What were some of the probable causes of the war?
  - How did the war come to an end?
  - Why is the war so important in the context of American history?
  - Are there other reliable sources listed for continued research?
- Large subject topics such as the Civil War would merit the entire gamut of the reference librarian's reviewing arsenal of who, what, where, why, when, and how probes. Others, like a biography, might merit a more specific list such as this:

- ○ Who the person was
- ○ Why the person was famous
- ○ When the person was born and other significant dates
- ○ Availability of additional resources

Authoritative answers to an "a priori" set of questions that you are able to confirm is a simple and satisfying way of developing an educated preference for a much-used resource. In addition, you gain "added vision" while reading through professional critiques of encyclopedias, so that the ongoing evaluations offered by reference pundits has added resonance rather than the niggling uncertainty of a received truth.

Question 2: The source is reliable, but is it suitable for our constituency and the mission of our institution?

A clear perspective on the target audience can be mapped in terms of the following:

- Age/reading level: child, young adult, adult or all age groups
- Purpose: general knowledge, in-depth research
- Institutional size: small, medium, large
- Institutional type: public, academic, special

A child looking for general information on a subject in a small public library will both want and expect a very different encyclopedic source from an adult historian expecting to conduct research in a large special library.

Question 3: The source is both suitable and reliable, but can we afford to purchase it?

In increasingly financially strapped libraries, the relevance of cost cannot be underestimated. Given the variety of formats that encyclopedias can now be found, the variation in cost adds to the flexibility of choice.

- If the *Britannica* is available online for free, and the online version is a fraction of the price of print, what are the factors that would urge the buying of one format over another, or in addition to another?
- Are yearly updates necessary, or can the constituency live with a general encyclopedia set for five years, so that the average cost per year is less?

Question 4: Once the reference librarian has established that the encyclopedia is reliable, suitable, and affordable, it is time to ask this question: Will it hold the user's interest?

Perfectly comprehensive sources of information are undervalued or underused because of poor readability factors. The layout, graphics, font size, paper and binding quality all contribute toward a print source that is accessible. For online versions, quick loading, clean graphics, and updated Web links are of the essence in holding user interest.

Additional Criteria

If the major questions have been answered, additional criteria can help finetune the acquisition process.

- What is the scope of the encyclopedia? The length, breadth and intensity of coverage for all entries can be assessed.
- How are subjects treated? Are the entries intended for scholarly research or as popular information sources? Distinguishing between the two types is critical to both evaluation and user recommendation. Signed works and lengthy bibliographies supporting each entry are typically aimed at the serious researcher.
- Is there any bias, either unconsciously evident or explicitly professed in any of the entries? Controversial topics such as abortion and stem-cell research are potentially fertile areas to check for bias.
- Is the encyclopedia necessary because it is unique and would constitute a niche publication? Niche publications appear infrequently and may need to be acquired when available rather than when actively needed.
- Is the encyclopedia a rich resource for pre-research queries? Does it have a high potential for providing a guide to further research through suggested readings and the availability of cross-references?

A unique, unbiased publication with great sources for further research is, however, of little value if the first four criteria have not been met. The bottom line in evaluation then is as follows:

1. The encyclopedia must be reliable.
2. The encyclopedia must be suited to the needs of the institution.
3. The encyclopedia must be affordable.
4. The encyclopedia must be designed to hold user interest.

Further Considerations

Encyclopedias represent a significant and popular purchase. Even after careful evaluation of the product, an assessment of constituency needs and the reference department's mission plan are critical to making a choice. Visualizing some real-life scenarios can help prime the reference librarian in choosing the best possible options.

- You are head of reference in a medium-sized public library, serving a mixed-age constituency of 40,000 people. Your annual budget for reference acquisitions is $24,000 and you have ten public computers.
  Would you...
  ○ Budget for the thirty-two-volume *Encyclopaedia Britannica* 2007 with a prepublication offer of $1,095?
  ○ Consider the 56,000,000-word *Encyclopaedia Britannica Online* with its added access to the encyclopedia as well as the *Student, Elementary,* and *Concise* versions?
  ○ Purchase the inexpensive thirty-dollar DVD version of the *Encyclopaedia Britannica*?
  On what factors would you base your decision?
  ○ Computer-literate constituency and the demand for online information?
  ○ Option of remote access for online and a community that owns PCs?
  ○ Computer availability—can library afford a dedicated computer?

- ○ Shelf space for print?
- ○ Combination purchase possibilities?
- You are the chair of a small academic library with a total student population of 7,295. Your annual budget for reference acquisitions is $38,000. Would you…
  - ○ Purchase the well-received twenty-volume *Encyclopedia of Applied Physics* for $5,950?
    On what factors would you base your decision?
  - ○ Large physics department?
  - ○ Competing needs of other departments?
  - ○ At $295 per volume, option to buy some volumes rather than the entire set?
  - ○ Existing collection of older *Encyclopedia of Modern Physics* adequate?

TOP TEN ENCYCLOPEDIAS

Title	Print	Online
Compton's by Britannica, 2010 Chicago, IL: Encyclopaedia Britannica	26 vols.	Subscription http://corporate.britannica.com
Dictionary of Art, 1996 New York: Oxford University Press	34 vols.	Subscription www.groveart.com
Encyclopedia Americana, 2006 Danbury, CT: Grolier	30 vols.	Subscription http://auth.grolier.com/cgi- bin/authV2?bffs=N
Encyclopaedia Britannica, 2010 Chicago, IL: Encyclopaedia Britannica	32 vols.	Free and subscription www.britannica.com
Encyclopedia of Religion, 2004 Farmington Hills, MI: Thomson Gale	15 vols.	eBook subscription www.gale.com
Gale Encyclopedia of Multicultural America, 1999 Farmington Hills, MI: Thomson Gale	3 vols.	eBook subscription www.gale.com
Grzimek's Animal Life Encyclopedia, 2003–2004 Farmington Hills, MI: Thomson Gale	17 vols.	eBook subscription www.galegroup.com
The McGraw-Hill Encyclopedia of Science and Technology, 2007 New York: McGraw-Hill Professional	20 vols.	Subscription www.mhest.com/index.php
The New Book of Knowledge, 2008 Danbury, CT: Grolier	21 vols.	Subscription http://go.grolier.com
The World Book Encyclopedia, 2011 Chicago, IL: World Book	22 vols.	Subscription www.worldbookonline.com

---

RECOMMENDED FREE ENCYCLOPEDIA WEB SITES

Britannica. More than 25,000 short entries with a tab for additional content that provides basic bibliographic information is offered by the free version of the Great EB. Attempts to read more than the short entry lead to a frustrating blackout of the item page. Available: www.britannica.com.

Encyclopedia.com. More than 80 million Web articles from 6,500 publications, including *Oxford's World Encyclopedia*, the sixth edition of *The Columbia Encyclopedia*, and subject specific medical, computer, and science encyclopedias power this resource. Available: www.encyclopedia.com/.

Infoplease.com. The Columbia Electronic Encyclopedia of 2007 with its 80,000 cross-references and 57,000 articles make up this free encyclopedia. Updates, however, are slow and a search for Justin Bieber in 2011 was sterile, unlike the Britannica source. Available: www.infoplease.com/encyclopedia/.

Wikipedia. As the seventh most visited site, the charms of this open-source, collaborative encyclopedia are hard to ignore, even as each entry needs to be approached with due caution. Available: www.wikipedia.org.

Recommended Resources Discussed in This Chapter

Alexa. Available: www.alexa.com/.

Brockhaus. Available: www.brockhaus.de/.

Bunson, Matthew E. 1997. *Encyclopedia Sherlockiana*. New York: Hungry Minds, Inc. (now Wiley).

Citizendium. Available: http://en.citizendium.org/wiki/Welcome_to_Citizendium.

Compton's by Britannica. 2010. Chicago, IL: Encyclopaedia Britannica, Inc.

DeMello, Margo. 2007. *Encyclopedia of Body Adornment*. Westport, CT: Greenwood Press.

De Trevisa, John. 1988. *On the Properties of Things: De proprietatibus rerum*. Gloucestershire: Clarendon Press.

Dictionary of Art. 1996. Jane Turner, ed. New York: Oxford University Press.

Encyclopedia Americana. 2006. Danbury, CT: Grolier.

Encyclopedia of Applied Physics. 2004. George L.Trigg, ed. Hoboken, NJ: John Wiley and Sons, Inc. Available: http://mrw.interscience.wiley.com/emrw/9783527600434/home/.

Encyclopaedia Britannica. 2010. Chicago: Encyclopaedia Britannica, Inc.

Encyclopedia of Global Warming and Climate Change. 2008. George Philander, ed. Thousand Oaks, CA: Sage Reference.

Encyclopedia of the Historical Jesus. 2008. Craig A. Evans, ed. New York: Routledge.

Encyclopedia of Homelessness. 2004. David Levinson, ed. London: SAGE Publications.

Encyclopaedia Judaica. 2006. 2nd ed. Michael Berenbaum, ex. ed. Farmington Hills, MI: Macmillan Reference.

Encyclopedia of Modern Physics. 1990. Robert A. Meyers, ed. San Diego, CA: Academic Press, Inc.

The Encyclopaedia of the Orient. Available: www.i-cias.com/e.o (accessed October 7, 2008). Changed to the *LookLex Encyclopaedia* when checked January 2, 2011.

The Encyclopedia of Philosophy. 2005. 2nd ed. Donald Borchert, ed. Farmington Hills, MI: Macmillan Reference.

Encyclopedia of Protestantism. 2003. Hans Hillerbrand, ed. Oxford: Routledge.

Encyclopedia of Race and Racism. 2008. John Hartwell Moore, ed. Farmington Hills, MI: Macmillan Reference.

Encyclopedia of Religion. 2004. 2nd ed. Farmington Hills, MI: Thomson Gale.

Encyclopedia Software Review. Available: http://encyclopedia-review.topten reviews.com/ (accessed January 2, 2011).

Encyclopedia of Television. 2004. Horace Newcomb, ed. New York: Taylor & Francis.

Encyclopedia of the World's Zoos. 2001. Catherine E. Bell. Chicago, IL: Fitzroy Dearborn.

Gale Encyclopedia of Multicultural America. 1999. Farmington Hills, MI: Thomson Gale.

Garland Encyclopedia of World Music. 1999. Ruth M. Stone, James Porter, and Timothy Rice. New York: Garland Publishing.

Grolier Online. Available: http://teacher.scholastic.com/products/grolier/index.htm.

Grzimek's Animal Life Encyclopedia. 2003–2004. 2nd ed. Farmington Hills, MI: Thomson Gale.

Historica Foundation. *The Canadian Encyclopedia.* Available: www.thecanadian encyclopedia.com/index.cfm?PgNm=TCESubjects&Params=A1.

International Encyclopedia of the Social Sciences. 2007. 2nd ed. William A. Darity, Jr., ed. Farmington Hills, MI: Macmillan Reference.

Knol. Available: http://knol.google.com/k.

Lands and Peoples. 2005. Danbury, CT: Grolier.

The McGraw-Hill Encyclopedia of Science and Technology. 2007. 10th ed. New York: McGraw-Hill Professional. Also available online: www.mhest.com/index.php.

Mirwis, Allan N. 1999. *Subject Encyclopedias.* Phoenix, AZ: Oryx Press.

My First Britannica. 2008. Chicago, IL: Encyclopaedia Britannica, Inc.

The New Book of Knowledge. Available: http://teacher.scholastic.com/products/grolier/program_TNBON.htm.

Oxford Music Online. Available: www.oxfordmusiconline.com/public/.

PSIO: Praeger Security International Online. Available: www.greenwood.com/psi/online_info.aspx.

Proteopedia. Available: www.proteopedia.org/wiki/index.php/Main_Page (accessed October 7, 2008).

Routledge Encyclopedia of Philosophy. 1998. Edward Craig, ed. New York: Taylor & Francis.

Scholarpedia. Available: www.scholarpedia.org/.

Werness, Hope B. 2003. *The Continuum Encyclopedia of Animal Symbolism in Art.* London, New York: Continuum International Publishing Group.

Wikipedia. Available: www.wikipedia.org.

World Book Encyclopedia. 2011. Chicago, IL: World Book.

The World Book Discovery Encyclopedia. 2009. Chicago, IL: World Book.

Recommendations for Further Reading

American Reference Books Annual. 2011. Westport, CT: Libraries Unlimited. Also available at www.arbaonline.com. *ARBAonline* provides access to more than 20,000 reviews submitted within the decade. In addition, up to 200 new or updated reviews are entered at the start of each month. The print edition, organized by subject, has a section on "Dictionaries and Encyclopedias."

ARBA Guide to Subject Encyclopedias and Dictionaries. 1997. 2nd ed. Englewood, CO: Libraries Unlimited. Though dated, this selection of subject dictionaries and encyclopedias culled from ten years of *ARBA* reviews provides a broad overview of the breadth of material available. New reviews can be found in *ARBAonline.*

"Battle of Britannica." 2006. *The Economist* (April): 66. The attempt by *Nature* magazine to compare the accuracy of articles from the *Britannica* with those from *Wikipedia,* and the ensuing "battle" is covered in this thought-provoking article.

"Encyclopedia Update, 2010." 2010. *Booklist* 105, no. 2 (September 15): 68–70, 72, 74–75. Authored by B. Bibel and S. Yusko, the ever-reliable annual update covers three major print encyclopedias and some online encyclopedias in some detail. The accounts are descriptive rather than analytical. The January 1 and 15, 2008, issues of *Booklist* also describe encyclopedias in global languages.

Hane, Paula J. 2008. "Encyclopedias, Social Networks, and Health Resources Lead the News." *Information Today* 25, no. 1 (January): 7. The article gives a brief but telling overview of the new crop of beta products swarming in the world of collaborative online encyclopedias.

Howard, Jennifer. 2006. "State University Presses Create Regional Encyclopedias." *The Chronicle of Higher Education* (February 3). An interesting survey of the popularity of both print and online versions of local and regional encyclopedias such as the 2007 *Encyclopedia of Alabama* and the 2006 *Encyclopedia of North Carolina* that took fifteen years to create as well as the 2004 *Encyclopedia of Chicago* that required more than a decade. Regional encyclopedias require both print and online versions because they are regarded as a source of information, yet also serve as prized gifts and must-haves for local buffs.

Jacobs, A.J. 2004. *The Know-It-All: One Man's Humble Quest to Become the Smartest Person in the World.* New York: Simon & Schuster. A compelling and entertaining memoir that testifies to the age-old allure of encyclopedias, this book tells of Jacobs' attempt to read through all thirty-two volumes of the *Encyclopaedia Britannica.*

Janes, Joseph. 2005. "Pedias, Familiar and Otherwise." *American Libraries* 36, no. 9 (October): 76. A provocative, though brief, rumination on the world of wikis as opposed to traditionally developed encyclopedias.

Kister, Kenneth F. 1994. *Kister's Best Encyclopedias: A Comparative Guide to General and Specialized Encyclopedias.* 2nd. ed. Phoenix, AZ: Oryx Press. This is a must-read resource for understanding the immensity and internal organization of encyclopedic resources. Though well over a decade old, chapters on choosing, evaluating, and assigning relative values to available resources continue to provide welcome structure to collection development policies on encyclopedias.

Kogan, Herman. 1958. *The Great EB: The Story of the Encyclopaedia Britannica.* Chicago: University of Chicago Press. This is an engrossing account of the making of the *Encylopaedia Britannica*, and the towering ambitions that were passed from one visionary to the next so that the *Britannica* became a reality. It reads like a novel.

Pack, Thomas. 2004. "Specialized Encyclopedias for In-Depth Information." *Information Today* 21, no. 5: 29–30. This article argues the need for the dramatic upsurge in the production of specialized encyclopedias. Such encyclopedias, he claims, have far greater value and in-depth utility than general encyclopedias.

Pink, Daniel. H. 2005. "The Book Stops Here." *Wired Magazine* 13, no. 3 (March). Pink provides a quick tour of encyclopedia production principles from the One Smart Guy model (Aristotle), to the One Best Way model (Britannica) to the One For All model (Wikipedia).

Seymour, Ursula. 2007. "Encyclopedias Still Going Strong." *Australian PC World* (January): 38. A novel viewpoint provided in the reviews of DVD versions of *Encyclopedia Britannica 2007 Ultimate Reference Suite* and *Encarta Reference Library 2007*. Both are seen as useful format acquisitions for the computer wary, with *Encarta* getting higher points for providing information less biased toward an exclusively American market.

Shawn, Donna. 2008. "Wikipedia in the Newsroom." *American Journalism Review* 30, no. 1 (February/March): 40–46. Shawn provides a probing investigation of the citability of *Wikipedia*, which is treated more as "a road map to information than as a source to cite." The article ends with a list of "according to Wikipedia" attributions in the media by editors who have boldly gone where no media is usually willing to go, along with the editor's annotations.

"The 2008 Reference Review." 2008. *Kirkus Reviews* (November). An annual selection of significant reference publications, with a large percentage devoted to specialized encyclopedias.

Bibliography of Works Cited in This Chapter

Bailey, Annette. 1998. "The Good, the Bad, and the Dead! Using Encyclopedias." *School Library Media Activities Monthly* 15, no. 1 (September): 42–44.

Beede, Benjamin, R. 2001. "Editing a Specialized Encyclopedia." *Journal of Scholarly Publishing* 33, no. 1 (October): 1–10.

Bibel, Barbara, and Shauna Yusko. 2010. "Encyclopedia Update 2010." *Booklist* 105, no. 2 (September 15): 68–75.

Cohen, Noam. 2008. "Start Writing the Eulogies for Print Encyclopedias." *The New York Times* (March 16): 3.

Cohen, Steven, M. 2005. "Wiki While Your Work." *Public Libraries* 44, no. 4 (July/August): 208–209.

Foster, Andrea. 2008. "What Google's New Encyclopedia Means for Students and Professors." *Chronicle of Higher Education* 55, no. 2 (September 5): A17.

Giles, Jim. 2007. "Wikipedia 2.0 – Now with Added Trust." *NewScientist* no. 2622 (September 20): 28–29. Also available: http://technology.newscientist .com/.

Hamilton, B. 2003. "Comparison of the Different Electronic Versions of the *Encyclopaedia Britannica*: A Usability Study." *The Electronic Library* 21, no. 6: 546–554.

Jacso, P. 2000. "How the Reference Market Is Being Won." *Information Today* 17, no. 10 (November): 54–55.

Janes, Joseph. 2005. "What Does Google Know That We Don't?" *American Libraries* 36, no. 8 (September): 76.

"Life Isn't 2-D, So Why Should Our Encyclopedias Be?" 2008. *Pharma Business Week* (September 8): 106.

McArthur, Tom. 1986. *Words of Reference: Lexicography, Learning, and Language from the Clay Tablet to the Computer*. Cambridge, NY: Cambridge University Press.

Peek, Robin. 2008. "The New Encyclopedia Brigade." *Information Today* 25, no. 25 (October): 17–18.

Pew Internet and American Life Project. 2007. "Date Memo." (April). Available: www.pewinternet.org/pdfs/PIP_Wikipedia07.pdf (accessed October 5, 2008).

Roncevic, Mirela. 2006. "E-Reference on a Mission." *Library Journal* (September 15): 10.

Steele, Robert. 2006. *Mediaeval Lore from Bartholomew Anglicus*. Middlesex, UK: Echo Library.

Thompson, A.H. 2003. "The Ideal Electronic Multimedia Encyclopedia—Are We There Yet?" *Multimedia Information and Technology* 29, no. 4 (November): 111–113.

6

Answering Questions
That Require Handy Facts—
Ready Reference Sources

Overview

Moments of flamboyance in reference transactions are rare. When exhibited, they are invariably through the dramatic simplicity of a ready reference resource. Librarians seemingly pull out of a hat a string of dates, events, statistics, rankings, names, chronologies, and facts to ease the itch of patron queries that are short, factual, and nonanalytical.

Ready reference work includes all the joys and tribulations of instant gratification. It is quick. It is immediate. It is fun. It contributes to the stereotype of the all-knowing reference librarian. It also requires the reference librarian to assemble a stable of ready reference sources that are handy and entirely familiar.

A significant number of library Web sites, in fact, have an icon directing the user to ready reference sources. It is variously termed as "quick reference" as at the Purdue University Library (www.lib.purdue.edu/eresources/readyref); "virtual reference desk" as at the University of Delaware Library (www2 .lib.udel.edu/ref/virtual/index.htm); or just plain "reference desk" as at the Library of Michigan (http://web.mel.org). While online resources and the ability to "bookmark" and create "knowledgebases" has expanded the scope and range of ready reference resources, there continues to be a traditional substratum of established reference works to provide a footing for answering this genre of questions. This chapter delineates some of those handy reference resources specifically collated to cover the major who, what, which, where, when, and how questions faced by a reference librarian.

How Ready Reference Is Used

The need for ready reference sources is felt when:

- Quick, rather than multistep, answers are required.
- Factual, rather than analytical, information is required.
- Relative facts need to be located in a single source.
- The information required is wide ranging but not deep.
- Citations for primary research are required.
- The data found in a random Internet search are of dubious accuracy.

Ready reference is not necessarily "simple" reference. As Marydee Ojala writes, "it's the easy-sounding, fact-based questions that may be more difficult to answer" (Ojala, 2001: 59). There is usually only one right answer. Selecting the right resource to find these right answers is the first step in ready reference work.

Questions Answered by Ready Reference

Q: What is the Earth's distance from the sun?
A: 91.4–94.5 million miles according to the *World Almanac.*

Q: Where are the Amtrak and Greyhound stations located in Mobile, Alabama?
A: The address, telephone, and toll-free numbers are listed in *City Profiles USA.*

Q: How much would it cost to register copyright on a new computer software application?
A: $35—the Web site at www.copyright.gov can provide more detailed information.

Q: Who publishes historical romances in Virginia?
A: *The Literary Market Place* has a comprehensive list.

Q: Which character in the play version of *The Diary of Anne Frank* steals food?
A: Mr. Van Daan, according to the *MagillOnLiterature Plus* database.

Q: How do I address a letter to the Pope?
A: *Emily Post's Etiquette* suggests "Your Holiness" or "Most Holy Father."

Q: In the United States, what is the difference in earnings between men and women with professional degrees?
A: The *Statistical Abstract of the United States,* 2011 (Table 704) reports the mean income for males to be $43,131 and for females to be $25,076.

Major Ready Reference Resources Used in Reference Work

It is traditional to discuss differences between almanacs and yearbooks; annuals and compendiums; directories and indexes; and the many ready reference sources available to a librarian. Ready reference resources that will be emphasized in this chapter include almanacs, fact sheets, directories, consumer reports, synopses, handbooks, chronologies, and yearbooks. Selecting from this range of ready reference resources becomes easier if standard questions are visualized as falling into these question categories: who, what, where, which, when, and how. The subjects falling under the question categories can be interchangeable, and certainly not obedient to the examples given in this chapter. The generalized query is best served with an encyclopedia, an almanac, or Web portals such as *ipl2* at www.ipl.org, www.bartleby.com, www.libraryspot.com, and CredoReference at corp.credoreference.com.

Type	General Sources	Specific Source	Example
Who	Telephone books; government directories, almanacs	www.anywho.com	I need a telephone number for 5 Main Street, Anytown, USA.
What	Consumer and citizen guides; college guides, grant books; occupation handbooks.	www.cem.va.gov	What are the eligibility requirements to be buried in a National U.S. Cemetery?
Which	Literary synopses; yearbooks	*Masterplots*	Which Russian character murdered a greedy, old pawnbroker?
Where	Relocation directories, almanacs	*City Profiles USA*	Can I get the crime statistics, weather averages and school rankings for Boise, Idaho?
When	Timelines and events, chronologies, almanacs	*Chase's Calendar of Events*	What celebrities were born in the month of July?
How	Etiquette, statistics, manuals, almanacs	*Robert's Rules of Order*	What is the minimum number of people required to form a quorum?

General Facts

Almanacs are the epitome of a ready reference resource. They are crammed with general information that is concise, factual, and structured to broadly answer who, what, where, which, when and how questions. The earliest almanacs, dating back to the 1300s, were usually focused on the calendar and on weather. They gradually expanded to include a little bit of everything. Benjamin Franklin's beloved 1733 publication *Poor Richard's Almanac* even included lists of road names and a bit of poetry.

Poetry and road names have fallen by the wayside, yet the tradition of providing the widest common denominator of popularly requested facts continues to mark the successful almanac. In fact, the success of the almanac to provide wide-ranging and comprehensive data has, in tense times, been charged with assisting terrorists with "target selection and pre-operational planning" information, as was the case following 9/11 when heavily marked almanacs detailing American railways, dams, and reservoirs were found in the apartment of an al-Qaida sleeper agent. Librarians, among others, were quick to respond to the FBI bulletin warning against almanac-toting individuals with the retort that "Almanacs don't kill. People do" ("FBI Almanac Alert," 2004).

The most respected and used almanac in America is the annual *World Almanac and Book of Facts*. Published since 1868, and an annual since 1886, the *World Almanac* is crammed with facts, features, rankings, directories, and information. The index is comprehensive and a critical key to opening up the riches of the Almanac. The print edition is 1,008 pages and available in both paperback and hardcover editions. It is available in e-book format and is part of the Infobase Publishing eBook Master Collection for schools and libraries. A Kindle edition of the 2011 *Almanac* is available through Amazon.com. The *World Almanac for Kids* is available as an online database.

Marketed as a dual-format resource, the annual *Time Almanac* is prominently linked to the free Web site www.infoplease.com. Rather than the traditional table of contents and index bracketing the almanac, a detailed index prefaces the book. Graphical tabs listing the major sections replaces the table of contents, with "health and nutrition" given special focus and highlighted in red. Like the *World Almanac*, the *Time Almanac* has incorporated index marks on the edge of the book to facilitate quick delineation of different sections in the book. Free access to the Web site provides a distinct advantage to the almanac. There is a children's version of the almanac as well, the *TIME for Kids Almanac*, with a free Web site at www.factmonster.com.

Canada and the United Kingdom

While a great many reference works are globally useful, regardless of the place of publication, the almanac gains in value when directed to a specific audience. Users looking up the *World Almanac* or the *Time Almanac* will find universal facts on statistics, measures, calendars, science, biographies, and news, but will also find a great deal of information on the U.S. government, political structure, and personalities. So also, a copy of the *Canadian Global Almanac* and the hoary *Whitaker's Almanack* would be a worthwhile investment to ensure ready access to Canadian and British facts.

The 137th edition of *Whitaker's Almanack* continues a tradition that began in 1868, with the pledge to register "the people, institutions and processes [that] keep the modern world's cogs turning." In addition to global cogs involving statistics and general information, *Whitaker's* is an invaluable fount of facts on the United Kingdom. Summaries of the year's newsworthy events are supplemented with distinctly local information such as the winner of the Irish Derby, the year's productions at the Royal Opera House in Covent Garden, and local government listings that allow the user to verify, for example, whether Exeter is a parliamentary constituency. The table of contents divides the information into major categories and the all-important index is comprehensive. The almanac is not available online, though sample entries and Web links to useful sites can be found at www.whitakersalmanack.com.

The *Canadian Almanac & Directory*, published since 1847, prides itself on being Canada's preeminent sourcebook. It combines the essence of an almanac with that of multiple directories. In addition to providing scores of statistics, maps, weights and measures, national awards, Canadian symbols, and local forms of address, it also lists information on businesses, agencies, associations, health care facilities, publishers, and provincial utility companies amongst others. A bilingual article on the history of the country marks this "snapshot of Canada" as uniquely Canadian.

Local Facts

An essential component of ready reference is accessible local information. The resources for this can be diverse and less than formal. The onus of collating a useful collection is squarely on the reference librarian, based on the demands of the users. Some resources that can answer the who, what, when, where, which, and how questions of a municipality are the following:

- Town directory
- Town map
- List of elected officials and representatives
- Local government, institutions, agencies, and associations
- Visitor information
- List of services such as nearest fax, notary public, passport services, post office
- Transportation and directions to the library
- Local datasheet

The Parsippany-Troy Hills Public Library System in New Jersey had taken the initiative in producing a pathfinder titled "New to Parsippany" that listed all services needed by a new resident. Given the high number of immigrants in the region, information about ESL (English as a Second Language), adult education, and the certification of foreign transcripts was provided along with the more traditional facts of local day care, employment, newspapers, and service agencies. The pathfinder has since been supplanted by online links to "Selected Websites" in the region. Such online links can be found on most library sites, such as the Monona Public Library in Wisconsin (www.scls.info); the Jacobs Library of the Illinois Valley Community College (www.ivcc.edu); and the Tisch Library at Tufts University, Boston (www.library.tufts.edu).

The "Who" Facts

The "who" questions are typically answered by telephone directories or by biographical directories.

Letting your fingers do the walking with the ubiquitous telephone directory is good practice for the reference librarian. Given its commonality and public familiarity with usage, the SuperPages tend to be forgotten. They do, however, provide a slew of value add-ons in addition to business and name listings that can prove very handy to the busy librarian. Contact information for community agencies such as those for domestic violence, senior citizens, blood banks, and substance abuse can be found. Frequently needed numbers for local, county, state, and federal government offices are also listed in the Blue Pages. Verizon adds a Community Magazine to its directory, with area maps, graphics of airport and stadium layouts, local attractions, a recreation guide, and a calendar of events. Online telephone directories are highly effective resources as well; www.anywho.com, www.superpages.com, www.switchboard.com are all worthy sites to locate persons or businesses. Reverse lookups are also possible in all three. The switchboard site also offers search capabilities for Web addresses, area codes, and zip codes. An online source available at http://inter800.com locates 800/888 numbers by listing the product, service, or company name.

Specialty directories can be a positive addition to the basic telephone directory. Publishers like Gale Group and Omnigraphics have produced a series of specialty directories, some of more value to ready reference than others. Omnigraphics specializes in rearranging or expanding upon telephone directories so that a more exact search is facilitated. *The Toll-Free Phone Book USA*, *Headquarters USA*, and *Web Site Source Book* are annual directories with alphabetical listings of organizations. Entries can also be accessed through yellow-page-style subject classifications. In addition to their titular focus, the directories list complete mailing addresses and telephone numbers.

There are directories that act like yellow pages with a particular focus. The *National Directory of Corporate Giving* and the *National Directory of Nonprofit Organizations* are two examples. The former profiles over 1,000 funding sources in the United States. In addition to contact information, giving priorities and preferences are also analyzed. The latter lists names, addresses, telephone numbers, and annual revenues for over 180,000 nonprofit organizations. Popularly known as a "crisscross directory," the *Cole Cross Reference Directories* and the *Hill-Donnelly Cross Reference Directory* provide succinct answers to questions posed by users who have an address but are in search of a name or telephone number. Small business owners planning a marketing strategy as well as new homeowners scouting a particular area also use it extensively. Listings are most easily located either by the telephone number or by the address. Special sections include color-coded pages that provide locations via census tracts, zip codes, and street names. A "relative affluence rating" or income level estimate based on census data as well as medians of home value and income level accompanies each listing.

With 36,400 post offices serving more than 141 million homes, farms, and businesses through "snow, rain, heat and the gloom of night," the Postal Service publishes the detailed two-volume *National Five-Digit Zip Code and Post Office Directory*. The resource lists all the post offices in the country as well as the zip code for each named street. Arranged by state, each section is preceded by a map of the state, with three-digit zip code divisions outlined. A useful feature in Volume 2 is the listing of both new and discontinued zip codes as well as details of classes of mail and special services. The online version is freely available at www.usps.com. The "com" designation is based on the status of the Postal Service as an independent establishment of the Executive Branch, but users will be redirected even if they were to type in "gov." An online site for Canadian postal information is available at www.canadapost.ca/segment-e.asp. It provides information on postal (zip) codes and reverse searches, as well as a list of Canadian municipalities with defunct "old names" listed alongside.

Who's Who in America has been a familiar resource in America for over a century. First published in 1898, the current edition of *Who's Who* is a two-volume set that lists over 100,000 "high achievers." The value of this resource is that it covers living Americans about whom not much may be found otherwise. The mini-biographies are built around at least twenty set characteristics. Facts may be located not only for the glitterati, the literati, and the accomplished but relatively anonymous leaders of business, science, education, and the arts. There are two indexes to help the user find a name. One is by geographical location and the second is through an occupational category. *Who's Who in the World* is a valuable companion volume with the same format and coverage of over 50,000 global personalities. The publications are available online via subscription at www.marquiswhoswho.net. The online version is updated daily, and it is possible to search by name, gender, religion, and other access points. The online version also incorporates a total of twenty other *Who's Who* publications that focus on subject specialists. The subject coverage is useful for academic and special libraries but not necessary for the average public or school library.

A subject-special version of who is who can be found in the annual *Literary Market Place*, popularly known as the *LMP*. Given that the percentage of books published in the United States has risen at an exponential rate, the value of the LMP has risen in tandem. With many years of publishing history, the two-volume LMP has established itself as a reliable and exhaustive resource for the North American book-publishing world. The resource includes contact information for publishers, literary agents, and editorial services in America and Canada. The entries are alphabetical, as well as by subject, geographic location, and type of publication. The confusing world of imprints, subsidiaries, and distributors is also listed. A calendar of book trade and promotional events is provided along with relevant awards and prizes. The information is updated throughout the year and revised annually in print. The online version, available at www.literarymarketplace.com, has both the *LMP* and the *International Literary Market Place* and is updated continuously. Users have the option of free access to limited information such as a list of small presses or of becoming paid subscribers with access to all the information contained in both publications.

The "What" Facts

The "what" questions typically cluster around consumerist concerns. In an age of dizzying choice, what to choose based on what criterion is a recurring responsibility. From the more trivial questions of what is the best restaurant, vacuum cleaner, MP3 player, or car to the more weighty ones of what occupation, college, or government aid is available, consumer guides have increasingly become a staple of reference libraries. Monthly issues of *Consumer Reports* and the annual *Consumer Reports Buying Guide* are marketed as the consumer's most authoritative guides for "doing homework" on potential purchases. With ratings on home products that range from canned soups to minivans, the format is designed to aid the consumer in scoping the market, gauging trends, evaluating specific features, and scanning relative prices and advantages. The synoptic *Guide* is linked to the monthly *Reports*, which studies products in great detail. The *Guide* is handy in providing short overviews of popular items, but is more valuable as a comprehensive and cumulative index to the *Reports*. As a non-profit organization, *Consumer Reports* has staked much of its authority on the fact that it is independent of manufacturers' bias. It buys all the products it tests and accepts neither advertising nor free samples from commercial companies. The online version has a four-year searchable archive and can locate items by keyword or through an alphabetical index, or by category. It is available for a fee at www.consumerreports.org. It also includes a special section on "Canada Extra" for Canadian ratings on local goods.

A comprehensive source for pricing information on both new and used cars can be found in the Edmunds Guides. No longer in print version, the Guides are available online at www.edmunds.com and are popular, as the first free auto Web site for car ratings. They continue to provide free access to ratings as well as value add-ons such as a monthly payment calculator and used vehicle listings by geographic location. The small, yellow *N.A.D.A. Appraisal Guides*, also available at www.nadaguides.com, are another staple of ready reference and provide quick, continually updated prices on used and new vehicles of all types. *Kelley Blue Book*, available in print since 1926 and online at www.kbb .com, is yet another respected source for pricing on new and used cars.

A clear, well-organized synopsis of major occupational groups in the United States, the handy biennial *Occupational Outlook Handbook* is the resource to consult when the user needs to know what qualifications are required to be a recreational therapist; or what is the exact nature of an account collector's job; or if there is any future in a job as a machine setter. A great many of the 822 occupations detailed by the federal government are presented in organized sections describing the nature of the job, working conditions, current employment statistics, future job outlook through the year 2016, required training, median earnings, related jobs, and sources for further information that include the union or association covering the job type. The structure of the descriptions for each occupation is unvarying, providing ideal material for quick reference. The information is also freely available online at www.bls.gov/oco. Given that the *OOH* is updated only once in two years, it is supported by the *Occupational Outlook Quarterly* that is released both in print and online.

Information sources on financial assistance also abound. There are homes that are sold for a single dollar to local governing bodies. There are special education grants for infants with handicaps. There are guaranteed loans for veterans in need of housing. The *Government Assistance Almanac* is a user-friendly and commercial version of the government behemoth, the *Catalog of Federal Domestic Assistance*, published annually. With a comprehensive listing of domestic financial aid available through government agencies, the almanac lists the purpose of the grant, eligibility, range, and scope of aid and assistance provided, as well as a referral to the grant agency's headquarters, telephone number, and Internet address. The Omnigraphics edition, with its detailed index, is far easier to use than the *Catalog* that contains more detailed information such as grant deadlines, renewal policy, and application procedures, but is far too unwieldy to be used effectively for ready reference. The freely available Web site is available at www.cfda.gov and updated on a biweekly schedule. An advantage provided by the Web site is the easy access to all formal grant applications, including the generic Form 424 used for most assistance grants. A plug-in of the Adobe Acrobat Reader is required to download the forms.

Over $27 billion in grants were awarded in 2004 by independent, company-sponsored, community, and grant-making foundations. Some 10,000 of the largest of such foundations can be researched in some detail in the substantial *Foundation Directory*. First published in 1960, the *Directory* is updated and revised annually based primarily on the tax returns of relevant foundations. It aims at both describing and providing contact information to all major grant-giving institutions. Entries are arranged by geographic state, though seven supplementary indexes, including a subject index, are provided to aid in searching. The *Directory* does not cover grants to individuals. At www.fdncenter.org, the *Foundation Directory Online* is available at five levels of coverage, the *Basic, Plus, Premium, Platinum,* and *Professional.* It is updated weekly.

There was a time in the not-too-distant past when ready reference would include a messy collection of print catalogs and curricula from colleges and universities across the nation. While this collection is supplanted by the comprehensive online presence of individual educational institutions, wide-ranging information that can aid the college consumer still depends on collated guides. Peterson's six-volume *Annual Guide to Graduate Programs* is a definitive source for graduate and professional programs in accredited institutions, both in the nation and abroad. Profiles that cover the field of study, enrollment statistics, typical costs, computer and library facilities, housing, and contact information are provided for more than 1,800 institutions. Peterson's annual compilation of undergraduate institutions, *Two-Year Colleges* and *Four-Year Colleges* also deliver rounded profiles of junior and community colleges. In addition to the information provided for graduate colleges, these volumes state whether the institution is state supported, has an urban, suburban, or small-town campus, and the levels of difficulty in getting admission—from noncompetitive to most difficult. Barron's *Profiles of American Colleges*, College Board's *College Handbook*, and the *U.S. News & World Report Ultimate College Guide* are all worthy publications to aid the college consumer.

In addition to mainstream colleges, selections of specialized directories based on community interest are also of value to a collection. The *Handbook of Private Schools* lists selected, nonpublic educational institutions. *American Trade*

Schools Directory is a loose-leaf publication that has an amendment service to continually update the listings of schools for classified occupations that run the gamut from acupuncturist and accountant to welder and X-ray technician. The *Guide to Cooking Schools* provides a hard-to-find listing of culinary schools and recreational cooking schools both in the nation and abroad. The Law School Admission Council, in cooperation with the American Bar Association, publishes the annual *Official Guide to ABA-Approved Law Schools*. Peterson's also has a whole series of subject-specific school directories such as the ones for *Visual and Performing Arts*, *Nursing Programs*, and *MBA Programs*.

The "Which" Facts

"Which" questions are interchangeable with "what" questions, but tend to hone in on fewer or single options. Literary questions invariably fall under this category. Which chemical substance? Which song? Which film? Which drug? Which association? Which nonprofit company? Which poem, short story, drama? Ready reference in the "which" question field is scopic in range and more intimate in detail. Following are a few representative examples that should help you extrapolate rules for the "which" typology.

Masterplots is an ever-growing multivolume series that parses major bodies of literature such as fiction, drama, poetry, and short stories. Aimed at facilitating an understanding of all major literary works, this classical reference source has been around since 1949. In addition to a synopsis, some works are appended with critical evaluations, story segments, and review essays that have annotated bibliographies. The twelve-volume *Masterplots*, 4th Edition (2010) is a collection of all literary genres, whereas other series such as the eight-volume *Masterplots II, Short Story Series* and the four-volume *Masterplots II, Drama Series*, Revised Edition focus on one genre. The six-volume *Magill's Survey of American Literature* and six-volume companion *Survey of World Literature* offers biographies, bibliographies, abstracts, and analyses of 339 U.S. and Canadian authors and 380 globally renowned authors, respectively. A handy category list groups authors by genre, country, gender, and ethnic identity so that those questions on "which female Chinese-American poet..." or "which 18th century African dramatist..." are handily located.

The CRC Handbook of Chemistry and Physics, currently in its 91st edition, has long been the definitive text to find reliable and exhaustive data on the properties of organic/inorganic compounds and chemical/physical data. A CD-ROM version allows quick searches by keyword, physical properties, chemical name, or molecular formula. Ready reference is also facilitated with a cross-table searching tool that allows single searches to collate all material on a topic described in different sections of the printed text.

The "When" Facts

Published as a thirty-two-page booklet in 1957 by the Chase brothers, Chase's annual *Calendar of Events* is currently considered the most accessible and authoritative compilation of both famous and trivial events and holidays. The publication is arranged by each day of the calendar, so that all special events, celebrations, and birthdays of famous people on a particular day are clumped together. Presidential proclamations, religious observances, anniversaries of famous events, astronomical phenomena, and sponsored events provide the bulk of entries listed. A detailed index at the end of the book lists all events alphabetically so that a search is possible both by the name of the event or by the date on which it is celebrated. Obscure events also flood the pages of Chase's, as it is open to everyone to submit entries that will be added at the discretion of the editor. So, for example, Independence Day on July 4 is listed along with the World's Greatest Lizard Race in Lovington, New Mexico. National and state days of other countries around the world are also included.

For quick facts on what happened on a certain day in history, the "Any Day" site at www.scopesys.com/anyday provides an ambitious, global list of births, deaths, holidays, religious observances, and trivial and nontrivial happenings around the world from ancient times. A perpetual calendar for the years from 1901 to 2100 can be found at www.vpcalendar.net. The site also provides handy information on the exact years that define centuries and millennia as well as the dates of seasons in both hemispheres and Australia.

The *American Decades* and *American Eras* series are comprehensive sources for chronologies, headlines, and facts required for a specific time period in U.S. history. The eras of pre-twentieth-century America and the decades of twentieth-century America are presented in composite capsules that cover the major events, laws, entertainment, business, government, and personalities of the age. The source is a unique addition to "when" references because it covers dates of more abstract entities than the more easily located births, deaths, anniversaries, and calendar events. Cultural, social, and economic trends are covered; so, for example, the date for Levittowns, the first prototypes of mass-produced suburban complexes, can be located through an exhaustive index. The *UXL American Decades* series is a children's version of this resource and is available in both print and as an e-book.

The "Where" Facts

The *Statesman's Yearbook* is an annual one-stop source for the social, political, geographic, and economic profiles of all the countries of the world. More general information such as time zones and ISO country codes can also be found in the first part of the book. Published since 1863, the information is concise, authoritative, annually updated, and supplemented with a foldout color world map with flags from all 192 countries. An interactive online version available free with the purchase of the print edition can be accessed at www.statesmans yearbook.com/public/. It is updated on a regular basis and has links to over 2,000 other related sites. Similar information, updated frequently, can be found in *The World Factbook* at the Central Intelligence Web site available at www.cia .gov/library/publications/the-world-factbook/index.html. This site also contains one of the most current resources for checking on chiefs of state and cabinet ministers of nations and territories, as the information is updated on a biweekly basis.

Omnigraphics publishes a host of descriptive directories aimed at users looking for pertinent information on U.S. cities. The *Moving and Relocation Directory* and *City Profiles USA* are two examples. The *Directory* provides a list of over 100 major cities that are deemed to be "popular relocation locations." Much of the information provided is from primary sources, collected by contacting individual offices and firms. Statistics such as the "quality of life indicator" are taken from government sources. Whereas some of the features that have been included—such as time zone maps and area code tables—can be found in general almanacs, the directory is unique in its compiling of a comprehensive factual profile of the selected cities. Chambers of commerce, local moving companies, banks, television and radio stations, mass transit and telecommunications, employment agencies, and property appreciation rates are some of the included features listed for each of the 121 cities.

The "How " Facts

"How" questions are of two types: the "how many" variety that require statistical resources and the "how to" sort that require manuals.

How Many

Published since 1878, the preeminent print resource for statistical queries is the annual *Statistical Abstract of the United States*. It is an exhaustive compilation of the social, economic, and political profile of the United States, parsed into thirty sections and 1,363 tables. Each table is documented with a source that includes Web site information when applicable. An alphabetical index of all tables is provided at the end of the *Abstract*, along with a detailed guide to sources used. Given the torrent of statistical information contained in the book, the index is an invaluable lifeline to navigate through the numbers. Statistics as varied as the number of abortions in teens under fifteen years of age to the total production of wheat in the world can be found in the pages of the indomitable *Abstract*. It is available also on CD-ROM; this version has spreadsheets attached to each table so that more detail is available. The *Abstract* also acts as a handy guide to the far more extensive and dense statistical information to be found in the online version at www.census.gov/statab/www. Links to both macro and micro data on counties, cities, states, and metropolitan areas are available at the site.

Use of the census Web site at www.census.gov can quickly transform a ready reference question into a lengthy reference session. The site is rich. Despite clear icons, detailed instructions, and fast-loading screens, it is well worth the time of any reference librarian to get familiar with the vast information and search strategies available for the site. Keep in mind that the three factors of subject, time period, and location determine the data category and developing a search string for popularly asked questions goes a long way in making the best use of this seemingly infinite statistical resource. A suggested string for a demographic search, such as that created by reference librarian Lana Peker (2005), was sketched as follows:

- Click on: American Fact Finder
- Go to: Decennial Census and Get Data
- Choose: SF1 and click on: Detailed Table
- Choose: Place for Geographic Type
- Choose: State
- Select geographic area: Your Town
- Click on: Add and Next
- Choose a: Table (e.g., Show all tables)
- Select Race and: Add
- Click on: Show Results

Using the above string in the legacy American FactFinder, it would take the librarian or end user a few scant minutes to answer a question like: *"In Kalamazoo, Michigan, are there a larger number of inhabitants claiming Irish or German ancestry?"* While the search strings evolve along with a changing Web and must be updated periodically, the habit of setting up a few search strings for dense but rewarding Web sites makes for effective ready reference.

A similarly well-endowed statistical site is www.fedstats.gov. It acts as a portal to over 100 major federal agencies that expend more than $500,000 on any statistical activity. The information can be accessed either through the agency, by subject, alphabetically, or by keyword searches. The information is monitored and revised by each individual agency, so that the sites are not standardized and the librarian must be prepared to conduct different search strings for each search.

How To

A classic resource that has been around since 1922, *Emily Post's Etiquette* has been revised and rewritten by a great-granddaughter-in-law, Peggy Post (2011). The new edition includes netiquette, online dating, and cell-phone etiquette in addition to the traditional issues of manners, table settings, ceremonies, and how to address correspondence. Changing social realities are also covered in the book so that, e.g., a divorcee announcing her daughter's engagement is provided with clear guidelines as to how to phrase the invitation. A section on addressing Canadian government officials is also included. The index is comprehensive and the structure of the book is readily evident in the nine area sections laid out in the contents page. More recently, the *Etipedia* was created as an online etiquette reference resource.

The reigning authority on parliamentary procedures, *Robert's Rules of Order Newly Revised* was first published in 1876. It is an invaluable resource for checking on the correct procedure for conducting an institutional meeting. The composition of a meeting, the call to order, the bringing and passing of a motion, the types of motions, rules of quorum and debates, voting procedures, disciplinary action, and the taking of minutes are laid out in formal detail. The index is both clear and comprehensive so that the locating of abstruse issues is convenient. A Web site at www.robertsrules.com offers twenty frequently asked questions and provides an open forum to ask and answer questions. However, the fourth edition published in 1915 is public domain and can be freely accessed at a number of sites such as www.rulesonline.com and www.bartleby.com/176.

A host of e-government and legal questions also fall into this category and must be fielded by most reference librarians of public and academic libraries. How to research a deed, register to vote, file income tax, and file for a divorce are timeless questions that have gained in volume since the upsurge of online-only restrictions. Web resources listed in Chapters 11 and 12 provide lists of sites useful to address this category of "how to" questions.

Collection Development and Maintenance

Evaluation of Ready Reference Resources

Ready reference covers a wide range of materials. While authority, scope, cost, format availability, usability, reliability, and comprehensiveness are important in evaluating these materials, the prime directives are accuracy and currency. Ready reference must provide up-to-date facts that are definitive. Whereas keeping up on professional literature and reviews is the bedrock of validating resources, it is the reference librarian who is responsible for the following:

- Establishing which source serves which category of question
- Gauging whether the source is consistently accurate and current

Whether in print or online, the information provided needs to be constantly vetted for reliability. Most print sources have years of publishing experience and authority to back their use. Yet ready reference, with its compulsion for quick factual answers, draws heavily from online sources. Ninety percent of academic library Web sites have a ready reference section of selected sources that have presumably been selected by professionals. Public, school, and special libraries either provide an open-access ready reference section or collate their own "favorites" bookmarked for quick personal access. Social bookmarking services like *Delicious* at http://delicious.com have refined online ready reference by allowing all the staff computers in a library to share a single set of "favorites." These sites can be monitored by doing the following:

- Checking for dead links
- Checking the citation sources
- Being alert to sites with commercial endorsements
- Cross-checking answers to establish whether answers are consistently accurate
- Checking the updating timetables for each site

Selection and Keeping Current

Having an accessible selection of multiple resources for each question category is a reasonable strategy as billions of facts are accommodated at different levels of coverage and currency by each resource. An efficient way to keep current with new Web sites is to subscribe to a monthly newsletter provided by the hard-working team at the *ipl2*. The free newsletter at http://theipl.wordpress.com keeps abreast of reliable information sites.

"Current awareness services" such as search alerts, table of contents and citation alerts are possible through RSS (Really Simple Syndication). Web-based RSS Readers like Google Reader or Bloglines are free and regularly supply fresh content and real-time updates to relevant sites without having to actively look for it beyond the initial act of subscribing to the feed.

To keep a stable of ready reference online resources fresh and up-to-date, it is advisable to check in with some of the more reliable sources of recommendation. The Reference and User Services Association (RUSA), for example, has a committee that produces the Best Free Reference Web Sites each year. The list is published in the fall issue of the *Reference & User Services Quarterly* with an online version on the RUSA site.

Further Considerations

With so much of ready reference currently answerable through online or electronic resources, keeping lists of reliable sites, setting up RSS feeds for pertinent updates, and becoming wholly familiar with the content and structure of resources in each of the question categories allows this genre of reference to be handled deftly. Verifying the answer in more than one resource, print or online, is also key to accuracy.

The world of ready reference is as infinite as the minds of humans. Attempting to prefigure the range of queries is a paralyzing exercise. Almanacs, encyclopedias, dictionaries, and a selection of even five trusted resources for each category of the who, what, which, when, where, and how questions will arm the reference librarian with the tools to successfully answer 99 percent of ready reference questions. The stouthearted librarians of the New York Public Library proved this time and again as they boldly ventured into schools to play the game "Stump the Librarian." Students questioned the librarians, who then found an answer within three minutes from a small traveling collection of ten to fifteen ready reference tools. The good news? The librarians always won.

The following list is a sampling of some of the questions they fielded:

- This is my name in hieroglyphics: 𓈖 𓊪 𓆓. What is it?
- What years constitute 10 B.C.?
- What does it mean to die a "natural death"?
- How long can a person lie on a bed of nails?
- What percent of the globe's land is arable?

TOP TEN READY REFERENCE SOURCES

Title	Print	Online
World Almanac and Book of Facts, 2010 New York: World Almanac Books	Annual	
The Statesman's Yearbook, 2010 New York: Palgrave Macmillan	Annual	Subscription www.statesmansyearbook.com
Time Almanac, 2010 Upper Saddle River, NJ: Pearson Education	Annual	www.infoplease.com
The local telephone directory	Annual	www.superpages.com www.switchboard.com www.anywho.com
Statistical Abstract of the United States, 2011 Washington, DC: Government Printing Office	Annual	www.census.gov/compendia/ statab/
Occupational Outlook Handbook, 2010–2011 Washington, DC: US Department of Labor	Biennial	www.bls.gov/oco
Consumer Reports New York: Consumers Union of United States	Monthly	Subscription www.consumerreports.org
Chase's Calendar of Events, 2010 New York: McGraw-Hill	Annual	
CredoReference (Formerly Xrefer)	Ongoing	Subscription http://corpcredoreference.com
ipl.2	Weekly updates	www.ipl.org

RECOMMENDED FREE READY REFERENCE WEB SITES

Bartleby. Encyclopedias, dictionaries, thesauri, style books, quotation books, gazetteers, fact books, anthologies in the public domain, this site is akin to the attic of a historic home, packed with unique treasures and a rich, if idiosyncratic, source of ready reference answers. Available: www.bartleby.com.

Census.gov. A labyrinthine resource worth studying as it provides a rich vein of statistical information on the demographics of the United States. Available: www.census.gov.

Geohive. The site is a handy almanac of global statistics, with reliable links to international statistical organizations. Available: www.geohive.com.

Infoplease. "All the knowledge you need" reads the byline of *Infoplease*. It is one of the few free online versions of a popular general almanac and contains the necessary vastness of resources required for effective ready reference. Available: www.infoplease.com.

ipl2. The site selects, evaluates, and organizes online Web resources in a variety of subjects that make it a thoughtful resource for ready reference answers. This site also offers a 24/7 "Ask An ipl2 Librarian" service. Available: www.ipl.org.

Recommended Resources Discussed in This Chapter

American Decades. 1996–2011. Farmington Hills, MI: Gale Cengage Learning.

American Eras. 1997–1998. Farmington Hills, MI: Gale Cengage Learning.

American Trade Schools Directory. 1953–. San Diego, CA: Croner Publications, Inc.

Annual Guide to Graduate Programs. 2010. Lawrenceville, NJ: Thomson Peterson's Guides.

Canadian Almanac & Directory, 2011. 2010. Toronto, Ontario: Grey House Publishing Canada.

Catalog of Federal Domestic Assistance. 2006. Baton Rouge, LA: Claitor's Law Books and Publishing Division. Updates available at www.cfda.gov.

Chase's Calendar of Events, 2011. 2010. New York: McGraw-Hill.

City Profiles USA. 2010. Detroit: Omnigraphics.

Cole Cross Reference Directories. 2011. Lincoln, NE: Cole Information Services.

College Handbook. 2011. New York: College Board.

Congressional Directory. 1995–. Washington, DC: Government Printing Office. Updates available: www.gpoaccess.gov/cdirectory/index.html.

Consumer Reports. 1936–. New York: Consumer's Union of United States.

Consumer Reports Buying Guide 2011. 2010. New York: Consumers Union of United States.

Copyright. Available at: www.copyright.gov.

CRC Handbook of Chemistry and Physics. 2010. W.M. Haynes, editor-in-chief. Boca Raton, FL: CRC Press.

CredoReference. Available: http://corpcredoreference.com.

Etipedia. Available: www.emilypost.com/etipedia.

Foundation Directory. 2010. New York: Foundation Center.

Government Assistance Almanac. 2011. Detroit: Omnigraphics.

The Handbook of Private Schools. 2010. Boston: Porter Sargent Publishers.

Headquarters USA 2011. 2010. Detroit, MI: Omnigraphics, Inc.

Hill-Donnelly Cross Reference Directory. 2011. Tampa, FL: Hill-Donnelly Corporation.

ipl2. Available: www.ipl.org.

Kelley Blue Book. 2009. Irvine, CA: Kelley Blue Book Company.

Literary Market Place 2010. 2009. New Providence, NJ: Information Today.

MagillOnLiterature Plus. 2006. Pasadena, CA: Salem Press.

Magill's Survey of American Literature. 2006. Steven G. Kellman, ed. Pasadena, CA: Salem Press, Inc.

Magill's Survey of World Literature. 2009. Steven G. Kellman, ed. Pasadena, CA: Salem Press, Inc.

Masterplots. 2010. 4th ed. Lawrence W. Mazzeno, ed. Pasadena, CA: Salem Press.

Masterplots II, Drama Series. 2003. Rev. ed. Christian H. Moe, ed. Pasadena, CA: Salem Press.

Masterplots II, Short Story Series. 2004. Charles E. May, ed. Pasadena, CA: Salem Press.

The Moving and Relocation Directory, 2009–2010. 2009. Detroit: Omnigraphics.

N.A.D.A. Appraisal Guides. 2011. Costa Mesa, CA: National Appraisal Guides.
National Cemetery. Available: www.cem.va.gov.
National Directory of Corporate Giving. 2010. New York: Foundation Center.
National Directory of Nonprofit Organizations. 2011. Farmington Hills, MI: Gale
   Cengage.
National Five-Digit Zip Code and Post Office Directory. 2010. Baton Rouge, LA:
   Claitor's Publishing Division.
The New York Times Almanac 2011. 2010. New York: Penguin Group.
*New York Times Guide to Essential Knowledge: A Desk Reference for the Curious
   Mind.* 2008. New York: St. Martin's Press.
Occupational Outlook Handbook. 2010–2011. Washington, DC: U.S. Government
   Printing Office. Available: www.bls.gov/oco.
Official Guide to ABA-Approved Law Schools 2011. 2010. Newtown, PA: Law
   School Admission Council and the American Bar Association.
Post, Peggy. 2011. *Emily Post's Etiquette.* 18th ed. New York: HarperCollins.
   Available: www.emilypost.com.
Profiles of American Colleges. 2011. New York: Barron's Educational Series.
Robert, Henry M. 2000. *Robert's Rules of Order Newly Revised.* 10th ed. New
   York: Perseus Book Group.
The Statesman's Yearbook 2011. 2010. New York: Palgrave Macmillan.
Statistical Abstract of the United States. 2011. Available as CD-ROM and down-
   load: www.census.gov.
Time Almanac 2011. 2010. Borgna Brunner, ed. Upper Saddle River, NJ: Pearson
   Education.
TIME for Kids Almanac, 2011. 2010. New York: Time for Kids.
Toll-Free Phone Book USA 2011. 2010. Detroit, MI: Omnigraphics, Inc.
U.S. Census Bureau. 2011. *Statistical Abstract of the United States.* Washington,
   DC. Available: www.census.gov/statab/www/.
U.S. News & World Report Ultimate College Guide 2010. 2009. Naperville, IL:
   Sourcebooks.
UXL American Decades. 2003. Farmington Hills, MI: UXL (Gale).
Web Site Source Book 2008. 2008. Detroit, MI: Omnigraphics, Inc.
Whitaker's Almanack 2011. 2010. London: A & C Black. Available: www.whitakers
   almanack.com.
Who's Who in America 2011. 2010. New Providence, NJ: Marquis Who's Who, LLC.
Who's Who in the World 2011. 2010. New Providence, NJ: Marquis Who's Who,
   LLC.
The World Almanac and Book of Facts 2011. 2010. New York: Infobase Publishing.
The World Almanac for Kids 2011. 2010. New York: Infobase Learning.
The World Factbook. Available: www.cia.gov/library/publications/the-world-
   factbook/index.html.

Recommendations for Further Reading

Agosto, Denise A., and Holly Anderton. 2007. "Whatever Happened to
   'Always Cite the Source?'" *Reference & User Services Quarterly* 47, no. 1:

44–54. Citations are an established "best practice" for all reference transactions. An unobtrusive test conducted on twenty-five libraries in the United States and Canada found that ready reference questions like the population of Montana and the location of the Southern Poverty Law Center were answered without citing the source. The study brings out one of the pitfalls of ready reference, namely, the disregard for citing sources in the process of providing "quick" reference.

Bell, Suzanne S. 2009. *Librarian's Guide to Online Searching*. 2nd ed. Santa Barbara, CA: Libraries Unlimited. Given that ready reference requires both speed and accuracy, this book is invaluable in training reference librarians to navigate database searches with ease and confidence. Bell uncovers the inherent structure of databases, describes the tools of efficient searching, and provides helpful exercises and visual screenshots to enhance the text. The material effectively teaches ways for reference librarians to get adept at online retrieval.

Fast Answers to Common Questions: A Gale Ready Reference Handbook. 1999. Carolyn A. Fischer, ed. Farmington Hills, MI: Gale Cengage. As part of the *Ready Reference Handbook* series comprising four volume-specific guides and six industry-specific sourcebooks, this particular title presents common reference transactions in a question-and-answer format with citations.

Ford, Charlotte. 2008. "Finding Facts Fast: Ready Reference." In *Crash Course in Reference*. Santa Barbara, CA: Libraries Unlimited. A review and listing of ready reference resources that can be added to a basic reference collection is provided in this chapter of a book that provides a broad overview of reference services.

Frické, Martin, and Don Fallis. 2004. "Indicators of Accuracy for Answers to Ready Reference Questions on the Internet." *Journal of the American Society for Information Science and Technology* 55, no. 3 (February): 238–245. Just when you think a Web site without advertisements is a sign of site maturity, the authors claim that such commonly held indicators may be fallible signposts of accuracy. They go on to present Internet "link structures" as the more infallible way to gauge accuracy on a ready reference site.

Miller, William, and Rita Pellen. 2007. *Evolving Internet Reference Resources*. Binghamton, NY: The Haworth Press. This book provides a market list of both free and subscription-based Web sites and services for twenty-six subjects ranging from health to ESL (English as a Second Language). The hazards associated with ready reference sites are also discussed along with the new approaches adopted by reference librarians to create reliable online information.

Mudrock, Theresa. 2002. "Revising Ready Reference Sites: Listening to Users Through Server Statistics and Query Logs." *Reference & User Services Quarterly* 42, no. 3 (Winter). This article is a strong reminder to reference librarians that ready reference sites must constantly evolve according to the needs of users. Usability heuristics, feedback, and usage statistics can be employed to structure the evolution. Mudrock provides a practical example as applied to the University of Washington Libraries at Seattle.

Sowards, Steven W. 2005. "Structure and Choices for Ready Reference Web Sites." *Reference Librarian* 44, no. 91/92: 117–138. After studying both academic and public ready reference Web sites, the author finds commonality in the use of subject categories and the selection and use of free Internet content, but a lack of sophisticated search tools aimed at the end user.

Sowards, Steven, W. 2005. "Visibility as a Factor in Library Selection of Ready Reference Web Resources." *Reference Services Review* 33, no. 2: 161–172. By studying the ready reference Web sites of one hundred libraries, Sowards deduces that reference librarians typically select sites that receive recognition soon after the site is launched. It is also educative to check the sites that are included in different kinds of libraries.

Wilson, Paula, A. 2004. *100 Ready-To-Use Pathfinders for the Web: A Guidebook and CD-ROM*. New York: Neal-Schuman. This title features 100 convenient and logically constructed pathfinders on topics applicable to different kinds of libraries. The CD-ROM contains a blank template for creating pathfinders, as well as a copy of all the pathfinders in XHTML so they can be tailored to individual demands.

Bibliography of Works Cited in This Chapter

"Best Free Reference Web Sites: Twelfth Annual List." 2010. *Reference & User Services Quarterly* 50, no. 1 (Fall): 19–24.

Bulson, Christine. 2003. "Just the Facts: A Look at Almanacs." *Booklist* 99, no. 18 (May 15): 1684.

Byerly, Greg, and Carolyn S. Brodie. 2002. "Get Ready for Reference: Featuring the Internet Public Library and Websites to Use for Fact Finding." *School Library Media Activities Monthly* 19, no. 4: 31–34.

"Credo Reference Receives Highest Scores in Library Journal's E-Reference Ratings." 2009. *CREDOreference*. Available: http://corp.credoreference.com/index.php?option=com_content&task=view&id=2021&Itemid=77 (accessed March 21, 2009).

DiBianco, Phyllis, and Linda Chapman. 2003. "Ready Reference 24/7." *Information Searcher* 14, no. 2: 5–14.

Eggleston, Tim. 2008. "Managing Online Reference Enquiries." *inCite* 29 (December).

"FBI Almanac Alert Prompts Unintended Reactions." 2004. *American Libraries* (January 4). Available: www.ala.org/ala/alonline/currentnews/newsarchive/alnews2004/alnewsjan2004/fbialmanacalert.cfm (accessed January 22, 2008).

Fernandes, Maria Isabel. 2008. "Ready Reference: Thoughts on Trends." *Community & Junior College Libraries* 14, no. 3: 201–210.

Goldsborough, Reid. 2002. "Double-checking Your Facts." *Information Today* 19, no. 10 (November): 51–52.

Guz, Savannah Schroll. 2007. "The Promise of Xrefer." *Library Journal* 132, no. 1 (January): 152.

Kelsey, Sigrid. 2008. "What's New in Library Products and Services." *Louisiana Libraries* 71, no. 2 (Fall): 7–9.

Ojala, Marydee. 2001. "Don't Sweat the Small Stuff: Business Ready Reference Decoded." *Online* 25, no. 1 (January): 59.

O'Leary, Mick. 2002. "xreferplus Heats Up Ready Reference Race." *Information Today* 19, no. 10 (November): 12–14.

Peker, Lana. 2005. West Orange Public Library, New Jersey. With the launch of the 2011 new American FactFinder, the search string has been greatly simplified with a "Quick Search" option (factfinder2.census.gov).

Sims, Lee. 2004. "Academic Law Library Web Sites: A Source of Service to the Pro Se User." *Legal Reference Services Quarterly* 23, no. 4: 1–28.

7

Answering Questions about Words—Dictionaries

Overview

Humans may have started with a primordial grunt, but they sure have extended it. Fungible and pusillanimous; zephyr and logodaedalian; mook and zax; every nuance and twitch in human existence morphs into a word that aspires toward universal and timeless communication.

Dictionaries make a valiant attempt to list all the words in a language along with meanings, usage, pronunciation, grammatical provenance, and syllabication. Although there are many different types of dictionaries, they share one major characteristic: they provide definitions. Alexander Theroux, in fact, chose to refer to a dictionary as a "definitionary" (Saussy, 1989: xv).

In the past few years, the convenience and authority of definitions available through online dictionaries and those embedded in word processing software has led to a rapid increase in the proliferation of online sources and a noticeable sluggishness in the updating and publishing of traditional print dictionaries. New formats suggested by the emerging tools of Reference 2.0 are also coming into play so that collaborative, free-content dictionaries such as *Wiktionary* and *Wordia* are an available option.

How Dictionaries Are Used

- A question requiring a definition should automatically prompt a reference librarian to consult a dictionary. The need for definitions ranges across many types of words—simple, archaic, slang, idiomatic, foreign, literary, and technical.
- In addition to simple meanings, the etymology and usage of a word can also be clarified by a quick dictionary search. Confusion over the spelling of words, even everyday ones that might "embarrass/embarass," is referred to a dictionary.

- Dictionaries act as invaluable pronunciation and syllabication guides as well. These are accomplished through phonetic symbols, supplemented with keys to the symbols used. Online and electronic versions provide audio pronunciations.
- The root history of words can be found in dictionaries so that users get to know etymologies such as "algebra" being the sum of the Arabic fractions "al" (the) and "jabara" (to reunite).
- Dictionaries list classes of words, so simpler grammatical quandaries can be directed to a dictionary. The principal forms of the word are also included.
- Even a general dictionary provides synonyms for many words. More in-depth needs can be met with a dictionary of synonyms.
- A visual or illustrated dictionary provides text as well as graphical representations to provide further clarity to a word.
- A dictionary of regionalisms provides specialized definitions of less universal usage. It can, for example, help the reference librarian direct a Maine user to the genealogy rather than the gardening section when asked about "seed folk."

Questions Answered by Dictionaries

- **Definitions:**
  Q: I have been directed to "shelve my alb" in the second half of the play; is that integral to the Stanislavski school of method acting?
  A: Er, no. An alb is merely a full-length white linen ecclesiastical vestment with long sleeves, according to the eleventh edition of *Merriam-Webster's Collegiate Dictionary*.
- **Orthography:**
  Q: Is the wit of Wilde "mordint" or "mordent"?
  A: Neither. To paraphrase Wilde, "to foul one spelling may be regarded as a misfortune; to foul two smacks of carelessness." Wilde's "mordant" wit can be checked in the *American Heritage Dictionary*.
- **Pronunciation:**
  Q: When people say "nuclear" with a "nu-cu" sound, do I get a "me-graine" or a "my-graine"?
  A: You may want to indulge in a "my-graine," according to the *New Oxford American Dictionary*.
- **Etymology:**
  Q: Is "juggernaut" a bona fide English word?
  A: According to *The Oxford English Dictionary*, "juggernaut" is the English incarnation of Jagannath, a bona fide Hindu god.
- **Grammar:**
  Q: What is the transitive verb of "sequence"?
  A: If you sequence transitive verbs after the root noun, as directed by *NTC's American English Learner's Dictionary*, you would transit to "sequenced."
- **Synonyms:**
  Q: Is there a better word for "nice"?

A: There are eighty nicer synonyms for "nice" in *Roget's New Millennium Thesaurus*, available at http://thesaurus.reference.com.

- **Visual:**
  Q: What are the differences between a thumb knot, a reef knot, and a butterfly knot?
  A: Textual explanations are bound to tie one up in knots. Refer instead to the *Ultimate Visual Dictionary's* "Ropes and Knots" page for photographic representations.

- **Regionalisms:**
  Q: I just moved to northern Illinois and my neighbors asked me to "scramble." Should I be insulted?
  A: Accept your potluck invitation graciously, after checking the *Dictionary of American Regional English*.

Major Dictionaries Used in Reference Work

The use of dictionaries then, is ubiquitous, interesting, and widespread. Given such usage, the types of dictionaries that exist are many: general purpose, specialized, abridged, unabridged, rhyming, slang, polyglot, historical, illustrated, and etymological to name a few. Given such richness, the librarian has an important mandate to be aware of the choices, so that the reference collection has the right mix of dictionary selections to suit constituency needs.

General Dictionaries

"A definition is a snapshot of a word at rest" (McQuade, 2003: 1688). General dictionaries strive to provide that perfect snapshot. Depending on the number of "words at rest" that are captured in a publication, a general dictionary can be unabridged with over 265,000 entries; abridged with over 139,000 entries; or pocket-sized with anywhere from 30,000 to 55,000 entries (Reitz, 2004).

Unabridged Dictionaries

In unabridged dictionaries, depth and breadth of information is the prime directive rather than currency of words.

The twenty-volume *Oxford English Dictionary* (*OED*) took forty-four years to complete. With more than 590,000 entries that have multiple corollary word forms, extensive etymology, date of first recorded use of a word, and a "sense perspective" that includes the usage and status of the word, the *OED* with its "21,370 large pages of very small print" (Hoyle, 2008: 4) is the accepted authority of international English. While a second printing was published in 1989, a completely revised and updated version is continually in the works. The revisions and additions are being added to an accessible database rather than kept in storage for a printed third edition. Available both online and on CD-ROM, the *OED* online is updated quarterly. The online version, available at www.oed.com, is the most comprehensive version currently as it contains the second edition of the dictionary, a three-volume Additions Series, quarterly updates, and all the drafts for the third edition.

Webster's Third New International Dictionary, Unabridged is the direct descendant of Noah Webster's 1828 opus, *An American Dictionary of the English Language.* The cumulative weight of historical expectation is evident in the 470,000 descriptive entries that fill out the book. While the current edition dates to 1961, an addenda section has kept the dictionary somewhat updated to 2002. A CD-ROM version is available as well with 476,000 entries, color illustrations, and thirteen search options. An online version is also available at https://member.m-w.com/subscribe.php for a monthly or annual fee.

The *Random House Webster's Unabridged Dictionary*, 2nd Edition, is available on CD-ROM as well as a 2,300-page hardcover book. Both versions have 315,000 entries of which 1,000 are new words updated to 2001. In the print version, the updates are not integrated into the main text, but provide relative currency to the dictionary. A 2006 release of the same edition combines the book and CD-ROM. It is the smallest of the three unabridged behemoths, and the most affordable. The entries are short and focus clearly on American English. There is no online version of this dictionary.

Abridged Dictionaries

The United States

With 90,000 words, more than 4,000 color graphics, and a longstanding commitment to providing detailed usage information, the *American Heritage Dictionary*, 4th Edition is a respected standard in abridged dictionaries. The most recent edition is freely available online on sites such as www.bartleby.com. It is also a popular choice for "embedded lookups" in e-books so that a double-click, e.g., on any word in a Stephen King title available through Glassbook's open software provides a definition from the *American Heritage Dictionary.* Contemporary words such as "wiki" and "blogosphere" and "Amber Alert" are included in the 2006 print version. The CD-ROM version has certain value-added features such as the ability to enlarge all thumbnail illustrations; supply audio pronunciation to words; and provide optional search limiters including the ability to block "vulgar" words.

Clarity, simplicity, and speed of access seem to be the motivation behind the relatively recent *New Oxford American Dictionary*, 3rd Edition (*NOAD*). With 350,000 words, over 100,000 example sentences, and the publishing weight of the Oxford University Press to back it, the *NOAD* is establishing itself as a dictionary that goes to the heart of a definition. Rather than listing all the senses of a word in sequence, the "core" or most literal definition of a word is provided, along with related or less literal submeanings, all of which are derived from the 2-billion-word *Oxford English Corpus.* The pronunciation guide is harder to navigate, since a guide is provided at the start of the book, rather than applied to each word.

Merriam-Webster's Collegiate Dictionary, 11th Edition has more than 100 years of authority undergirding the current edition. With 165,000 entries in the eleventh edition, supported by 42,000 usage examples, it continues to be "runner-up to the Bible" as the "second best-selling English hardcover book in history" (McQuade, 2003: 1688). The new edition openly touts a belief in the "convergence" of formats to provide multiaccessibility, so that print, online, and CD-ROM versions are all provided as a single package. The online version is independently available at www.m-w.com and on AOL, with a huge clutch of value-added features such as a thesaurus, word stories, word of the day, kids' dictionary, and a message board to exchange word trivia. Some sections, such as "Signs and Symbols" available in print, are not included. In its latest avatar, an enhanced version of the dictionary with 225,000 entries can now be added on to iPhones.

The United Kingdom

Winston Churchill's droll observation that "England and America are two countries divided by a common language" is most evident in the distinctive collection of abridged dictionaries published in the United Kingdom. Unlike the venerable *OED*, which maintains a commanding global profile despite its British roots, the abridged dictionaries published in the United Kingdom are uniquely and unabashedly British.

"It's nice, rich, handy, modern. Obtain it!" is a charming anagram of the inimitable *Chambers Dictionary*, 9th Edition (www.anagramgenius.com/ archive/chambe.html), which continues to be floated even though the dictionary published its eleventh edition. Over 100 years old, the *Chambers* continues to pepper the collection with fey definitions such as "channel surf—switching rapidly between different television channels in a forlorn attempt to find anything of interest." These, of course, are not the norm and the 270,000 definitions making up the 2008 edition have clear definitions and include terms from dialects and historical forms. It is available as an online subscription at www.chambersreference.com.

The *Bloomsbury English Dictionary*, by contrast, is the British edition of *Encarta Webster's Dictionary of the English Language*. It eschews the British tradition of using the IPA (International Phonetic Alphabet) and has its own phonetic system. It is also distinguished by user-friendly additions such as cross-references to almost 1,000 of the most common misspelled words and labeling of words considered obscene.

The *Oxford Dictionary of English* 2010 has a total of 355,000 terms that have been updated based on the massive "Oxford English Corpus" database. Since its first edition in 1998, popular usage words such as "muggle," "data smog," and "vuvuzella [the sound of the 2010 World Cup]" have been included. In the Oxford tradition words have also been supplemented with brief etymologies.

The *Collins English Dictionary* is the most populist British dictionary in that its latest edition has, for better or worse, included highly "young" words— slang, dialect, and chat-group abbreviations that complement the collation of words derived from the 2.5-billion-word "Bank of English" database. Uniquely British terms like "stealth tax" (indirect tax); abbreviations like SOHF (sense of human failure); and dialect such as "thraiping" (thrashing) distinguish the *Collins*, just as much as the pointed beheading of monarchical terms distinguishes it within British circles. As an outraged citizen pointed out, "Tudor" has simply been defined as a style of architecture in the *Collins*. It also provides usage hints, so that the definition of a common word such as "actual" is followed by the hint that excessive use of the word in a sentence should and can be avoided, as it is "actually" unnecessary. Logodaedalians (wordsmiths) in the United Kingdom are up in arms as the current editors propose to shave away archaic words to make place for 2,000 new entries (Adams, 2008). The dictionary is available online at www.collinslanguage.com.

Canada

Recognizing the subtle and not-so-subtle differences in English pronunciation, usage, and spelling fostered by different cultures in different countries, the Oxford University Press has created a uniquely *Canadian Oxford Dictionary*. Compiled by Canadians, examining Canadian sources and perspectives, the 2004 edition has 130,000 terms and various appendices. Words such as "scraper," for example, include the Canadian usage of removing not only ice, but mud and paint as well. Canadian acronyms like "BQ" for Bloc Québécois, expressions like "jam buster" and spellings like "traveller" and "humour" make this a strong Canadian dictionary resource. Given "changing market conditions," the Canadian dictionary division of the publishers, Oxford University Press, was disbanded in 2008 so that the work of updating the dictionary has been outsourced to freelance lexicographers. The *Nelson Canadian Dictionary of the English Language* (until recently known as the *ITP Nelson*) has over 150,000 terms. It includes extensive Canadian biographies, history, government and folklore and uses Canadian spelling. However, the source has not been updated since 1997. In a country where a governmental ruling stated a preference for the "-our" spelling to the "-or," Gage Publications, while slow in adopting the usage, has currently updated the familiar *Gage Canadian Dictionary*. Distinctive Canadian words like "snowbird—a Canadian who goes south for the winter" also make the Gage a useful Canadian resource. It is marketed as a dictionary "written by Canadians for Canadians." An informative online presence focusing on Canadian spelling can be found at www.luther.ca/~dave7cnv/cdnspelling/cdnspelling.html.

Specialized Word Sources

Learners' Dictionaries

English, as spoken in McDonald's rather than by the Queen, is becoming the dominant lingua franca of the world; as a result there appears to be a rising market for dictionaries for learners. How is this different from a regular or even an abridged dictionary? For one thing, "less is more" (Dahlin, 1999), and the prime directives are not comprehensiveness and depth of meaning, but simplicity, ease of use, and frequency of words in daily American communication. This is largely calculated from computational analyses of electronic word corpora that cover popular media reports. So, for example, a learner's dictionary is far more likely to include an MTV word like "dude" than an obscure one like "ophiophagus" (serpent eating). All the major publishers of dictionaries such as NTC, Cambridge, Merriam-Webster, Random House, and Macmillan have published recent editions of learner's dictionaries.

The *Macmillan English Dictionary*, for example, bases its dictionary on the enlightening fact that 90 percent of all text consists of only 7,500 words. These are the words that are highlighted along with 80,000 examples of usage. *NTC's American English Learner's Dictionary* selects 22,000 basic words that are defined and used in context, but eschew other traditional dictionary additions like etymology and synonyms of a word. The *American Heritage Dictionary for Learners of English* has over 40,000 words, with attention paid to the more confusing aspects of English such as homonyms, idioms, and synonyms. A reference section with basic grammar and American factoids is included. With nearly 100,000 words and phrases and more than 160,000 usage examples, the 2008 publication of *Merriam-Webster's Advanced Learner's English Dictionary* is aimed at an international market in which proficiency in the use of English, and American English in particular, is being attempted by an estimated 1 billion nonnative speakers around the world. It includes a free e-book version as well as a Web site available at www.learnersdictionary.com/.

Visual Dictionaries

In a visual dictionary, the words presented are not alphabetical, but grouped under subjects. The focus is on providing a pictorial of the word. Since terms are illustrated, selection is limited to the noun family. The *Firefly Visual Dictionary* (Corbeil and Archambault, 2002) has 35,000 terms organized into seventeen chapters. Insects, geology, sports, and architecture all find pictographic representation in full color. DK, known for its splendid graphics, publishes the *Ultimate Visual Dictionary* (2006) with fancier artwork, incorporating cutaways and exploded views that display internal structures. The *Firefly Five Language Visual Dictionary* (Corbeil and Archambault, 2009) covers 35,000 words in English, Spanish, French, German, and Italian, illustrated with over 6,000 color images. The role of the visual dictionary comes into sharp focus when, for example, a muskrat and a mole are both described as blunt-nosed and short-eared, but the homeowner needs to identify which one is destroying his summer garden. Visual dictionaries are also handy for those perennial school assignments that require labeling parts of the anatomy or the layers of the earth or the structure of an insect. A free visual dictionary can be found online at http://visual.merriam-webster.com/. Over 6,000 images organized with fewer than fifteen broad subject headings are included. The site may be easily searched with a keyword that conveniently generates readalike results.

"Gated" Word Dictionaries

The user in search of words "gated" to a particular community, class, age group, region, or profession is best directed to dictionaries of slang, jargon, argot, regionalisms, or idioms.

Dictionaries of slang usually collate colloquialisms recurring within groups. Slang, by definition, is particularly vulnerable to passing fads so that what was "groovy" earlier and "sweet" today will, in all probability, be entirely different a few years from now. Publications such as *Dewdroppers, Waldos, and Slackers* (Ostler, 2003) present slang over the decades from 1900 to 1999. *Stone the Crows: Oxford Dictionary of Modern Slang* (Ayto and Simpson, 2008) includes over 6,000 words and phrases in the second edition of this compilation of slang derived from the *OED* database. The multivolume *Random House Historical Dictionary of American Slang* (Lighter, 1997–) has more than 300,000 slang words that date back to Colonial America, more of which will be added once the final fourth volume is published. For current slang, online options are a wise choice. Everything from hip-hop, to London, to street drugs and sex slang is available. For slang being used in the United Kingdom, a handy directory can be accessed through www.peevish.co.uk/slang. Particularly useful for virtual reference that caters to a high percentage of young adult users is www.urbandictionary .com. With both "exact" and "inexact" search options, the site provides meanings for urban slang as well as chat argot like g2g (got to go) and emoticons like :) which is a happy face, but not as happy as :O.

The preeminent dictionary for American regionalisms is the multivolume, exhaustive, and ambitious *Dictionary of American Regional English (DARE)*. Launched in 1960, it has yet to be completed. It alphabetically documents regional words unlikely to be found in standard dictionaries. The meaning of a word, spelling, pronunciation, area of usage, and actual recorded use is provided along with some maps that display the geographical distribution of the word. With entries completed from A to Sk, with the last volume scheduled for publication in 2011, *DARE* is both a dictionary of unfamiliar terms like "Irish confetti" (bricks and stones used while fighting), as well as an engrossing historical record of American culture. *DARE* has an explanatory Web site available at http://dare.wisc.edu.

AAD

AAD? The need for *Acronyms and Abbreviations Dictionaries* in every reference library has never been felt more keenly. A string of letters that abbreviate a word (Mr.); initial a term (www); or synopsize a proper noun (UN) is a growing trend in human communication. Electronic communication, with its natural affinity for short forms, has added to the global legitimacy and relevance of truncations.

The most distinguished source for decoding these truncations is the Gale Group's multivolume *Acronyms, Initialisms, & Abbreviations Dictionary*. Arranged alphabetically in the contracted form as well as a reverse expanded version, users can consult the dictionary both to decode an acronym and to discover the accepted truncation for a given term. In the newest edition, terms have been added primarily from areas dealing with the Internet, education, medicine, and associations. Contractions for bus and railroad stations, navigation systems, and stock exchange symbols have also been included. The Gale Group publishes three more specialized dictionaries, the *Subject Guide Series* focusing on computers, telecommunications, and business, the *International* series for global contractions, and one for *Periodical Titles*.

Available since the 1950s, a single-volume source can be found in the 267,000 entries of the *Abbreviations Dictionary* (Stahl and Kerchelich, 2001). The entries not only include abbreviations, initialisms, and acronyms, but symbols such as emoticons, signs such as $ (listed under "D"), and eponyms or "designations derived from names" such as "Legionnaire's disease." The entries are in alphabetical order, with signs listed under the first letter of the term it signifies. A person who does not know what "µ" stands for will therefore find it hard to locate it under "m," but is aided by the different subject areas that are also listed. Abbreviations for U.S. states, Canadian provinces, territories, and capitals, and both British and Irish counties are included.

An extensive online dictionary with over 409,000 entries can be found at www.acronymfinder.com. Search strategies allow for both exact searches and inexact ones that can use wildcard truncations, "begins with," and reverse lookups. Parented by the well-regarded STANDS4 LLC, a free online reference provider, www.abbreviations.com is a large and comprehensive directory and search engine for acronyms, abbreviations and initialisms on the Internet. For the reference librarian who refers a user to any of these word sources, it is critical to establish the context usage of a contracted term. Acronyms invariably stand for multiple terms, so that "AA," for example, could stand for Alcoholics Anonymous as well as American Airlines or Aerolineas Argentinas. It may even represent a bond rating, a bra size, or the width of a shoe.

Rhyming Dictionaries

Rhyming dictionaries were created to help poets, song makers, and verse creators. They list phonetic endings in alphabetical form so that if users need words to rhyme with "blue," they would look up the phonetic suffix of "oo." *Words to Rhyme With* (Espy, 2006) has a separate section on "eccentric" words that are difficult to partner with a rhyme, such as "aardvark." *Random House Webster's Rhyming Dictionary* (2008) is an expanded version of the earlier pocket edition and includes 60,000 words with cross-references and a glossary of poetic terms. The *Oxford Rhyming Dictionary* (Upton and Upton, 2004) has over 85,000 words in forty sound groups, but uses British pronunciation. Derived from Carnegie Mellon University's "Pronouncing Dictionary," a machine-readable collection of over 125,000 words, the online rhyming source available at www.rhymezone.com, has been freely available for over ten years and organizes rhymes by syllable or letter sound.

Metadictionaries

The online medium seamlessly lends itself to consolidating diverse resources while scavenging for individual requests. Why restrict oneself to a single dictionary resource when a simple click can trawl through so many more? This is the motivation behind the metadictionary.

For example, www.onelook.com is host to 19,044,271 words (as of 12/12/2010) culled from 1,062 dictionaries that includes everything from the well-known *Compact OED* and *Merriam-Webster's Online Dictionary*, 11th Edition, to lesser-known sources such as *Luciferous Logolepsy* and *The Phrontistery*. The dictionary also provides for a reverse feature that allows users to describe a concept in order to find a word.

Another popular metadictionary, *Dictionary.com* (http://dictionary.reference .com), is free and user friendly. A simple search box at the top of the page in which the word or an approximation of the word can be typed is all that is presented. Over 900 online sources such as *The American Heritage Dictionary* and *The World Factbook* provide an answer with the source for each entry listed below the answer. Metadictionaries, then, act as hosts rather than producers of dictionaries. The spottiness of sources that contribute to an answer makes them a less than fully reliable reference resource, but certainly constitutes a handy site to add to the "Favorites" of a busy reference desk.

Special Constituency Dictionaries

Children's Dictionaries

The reference world of word sources for children focuses on all-purpose dictionaries. The market for children's dictionaries is geared toward three types of institutions: the school library, the public library, and the family library. For the family, hundreds of desk-sized print dictionaries are available with 12,000 to 15,000 words and a grab bag of bonus information aimed at the student. *A Student's Dictionary*, for example, adds on political factoids about the United States, weights and measures, and global trivia such as the seven continents and the eight planets. These publications are handy but not geared for purchase by reference collections. The definitions are spare, the binding fragile, and the entry is usually without synonyms or etymology or context usage. Reliable publishers of children's dictionaries for reference collections are Macmillan, American Heritage, World Book, and Merriam-Webster's.

It is a pleasure to use the *Macmillan Dictionary for Children*. The physical construction includes sturdy binding, large fonts, colorful guidewords, and over 3,000 captioned color illustrations and photographs. The 35,000 entries have clear definitions, parts of speech, abbreviations, synonyms, etymology, pronunciation, and context usage. Homonyms are also included for many words, as are geographical and biographical entries. A critical addition is the spelling hints provided at the start of each letter. Children looking for "pneumonia" or "knighthood" under the phonetic "n" are directed to "pn" and "kn" spellings. Obscure words (which nonetheless have relevance in student life), such as "multiplicand" (the number that is to be multiplied), are included.

The educational psychologist Edward Lee Thorndike and the lexicographer Charles Lewis Barnhart aimed at producing dictionaries that were not "dumbed-down" versions of an adult dictionary. Thorndike-Barnhart has expanded its publications to a cluster of children's dictionaries, the *Thorndike-Barnhart Children's Dictionary*, the *Junior Dictionary*, the *Advanced Dictionary*, and the *Student Dictionary*. Whereas the *Children's* and the *Junior* are for very young children, there does not appear to be a significant difference between the *Student* and the *Advanced*. The *Student Dictionary* intends to help students both define words "in simpler language than the main word being defined," as well as develop a sense for vocabulary by mastering word sources and word family clues. Forty-three word sources that trace back to a common language source and seventy word families that trace back to a common root are included. Synonyms, etymology, pronunciations, a style manual for writing, and illustrations in black and white as well as color complete the *Student Dictionary*. The currency of words is maintained by the "Scott Foresman citation files," which monitor changes in word usage of the 100,000 entries listed in the book. Although there have been no updates since 1998, the ThorndikeBarnhart files continue to be used by various publishers of children's dictionaries.

On the other hand, the *World Book Dictionary*, also derived from Thorndike-Barnhart files, has been published in print since 1963 and the online version is continually updated. The most recent print edition has more than 225,000 entries and 3,000 illustrations, while the online version has 248,000 entries, making it one of the largest dictionaries accessible to children. Clarity in definition is the key directive. Illustrations, grammar notes, and a 128-page "guide to communication" are included. Biographical and geographical entries are excluded and instead referred to the *World Book Encyclopedia*. Available in print, and as part of an online *Reference Center* package, the *World Book Dictionary* is also one of the first to be available in handheld editions of pocket PCs and smart phones. The 2003 edition of the dictionary is freely available as a preview through Google Books.

The *DK Merriam-Webster Children's Dictionary*, with 35,000 entries and 3,000 visually arresting photographs and illustrations, is a reliable and delightful resource for ages eight to the lower teens. In addition to the alphabetical dictionary, there is also a thematic section on countries and related topics. The definitions are marked by their clarity and the graphics are outstanding. Word context is provided by sentence examples.

Bilingual Dictionaries

With porous national boundaries and an increasingly intimate world, the relevance of bilingual dictionaries appears heightened. The large "foreign language" tomes that traditionally graced academic libraries have multiplied into a dizzying variety of unabridged, dual, pocket-sized, and desk dictionaries suitable for academic, public, corporate, and personal libraries.

Cassell, NTC, Oxford, HarperCollins, and Random House are familiar names of brands and publishers that offer a range of bilingual dictionaries. While classic and European languages dominated the industry a century ago, today's landscape offers an extravagant choice of languages. Bilingual dictionaries are conveniently arranged so that the word can be looked up both by its English translation and in the original language.

The Cassell series has had more than 120 years of experience in publishing. *Cassell's Latin Dictionary*, first published in 1854, continues to be a classic addition for the serious researcher. *Cassell's Italian Dictionary* is typical of the later publications that are geared for both the beginner and the advanced speaker. Given that the many dialects of Italian would require multiple synonyms, the dictionary has "translate[d] rather than define[d]" words. In the Italian-English section, pronunciation is eschewed given the phonetic nature of Italian spelling, but included in the English-Italian section.

The Oxford University Press publishes a variety of world language dictionary series. *The Oxford Starter* series, the *Oxford-Duden Pictorial* dictionaries, the *Oxford-Hachette* and *Oxford-Paravia* dictionaries, and the *Compact, Pocket, Concise, Basic* series are all geared at varying levels of readership. Over forty different languages are published with most current projects in the area of pocket and desk editions. A complete list of editions more suited for library reference collections can be accessed at www.askoxford.com.

McGraw-Hill's *Vox/NTC* series has also established itself as an aggressive publisher of world language sources, especially known for its Spanish language series. *Larousse* is the traditional choice for French dictionaries. In the area of world language dictionaries, sometimes even the smallest of publishers become urgent sources of reference acquisition. For example, after the conflict in Kosovo and the sudden influx of Albanians into the United States in the late 1990s, the frantic scramble for stocking libraries and other places with Albanian dictionaries heightened the role of Hippocrene, a small New York press that was able to offer the only *Albanian-English/English-Albanian Practical Dictionary* in print.

Given the nexus between politics and the demand for world language dictionaries, the reference librarian is well advised to acquire the major language dictionaries, as well as keep alert to changing local demographics or global events that can create a sudden demand for lesser-known language groups.

Subject Dictionaries

A burgeoning use of the word "dictionary" has been in the area of subject dictionaries. These dictionaries also define words, but triangulate over an isolated subject area and focus with laser-sharp intensity on any and every word connected with that area. Be it medical, legal, business, scientific, technical, computer, mathematical, electronic, religion, or gardening, every subject appears to be inspiring its own dictionary.

Although it is entirely probable that a word presented in a subject dictionary could also be found in an unabridged dictionary, subject dictionaries tend to do the following:

- Provide more depth in definition. Some definitions are quasi-encyclopedic in coverage. For example, in the *Harvard Dictionary of Music*, the definition of "electroacoustic music" runs over a page.
- Be informed by subject specialists and rate high on reliability. *Black's Law Dictionary* or *Dorland's Illustrated Medical Dictionary* are authoritative additions to most reference collections. An online version of *Dorland's* is also available for a fee at www.dorlands.com.
- Complete gaps in coverage for relatively smaller fields such as librarianship. *ODLIS* or the *Online Dictionary for Library and Information Science* is an exhaustive glossary of well-designed and thoughtfully crafted library terminology.

FOLDOC or the *Free On-Line Dictionary of Computing*, supported by the United Kingdom's Imperial College in London, effectively provides over 14,000 definitions in the computing field. *Webopedia* also serves that purpose with daily updates in the world of computer and Internet technology.

- Provide quicker access to updated words. The most dramatic example can be found in the aftermath of the digital revolution, when even pocket-sized computer dictionaries were acquired by reference libraries in an effort to keep up with the torrent of new vocabulary flooding everyday global communication. In 1998, no general dictionary listed terms like "hypertext markup language," and a "mouse" was still just a rodent. The need for a subject dictionary on computer terms was dramatically demonstrated.

In most cases, however, the need is undramatic and subject dictionaries like *The Dictionary of Aquarium Terms* are acquired only when appropriate to the aims of the institution and the needs of its constituency.

Visual and Hearing Impaired

Two major special constituencies for whom authoritative dictionaries are available are the visual and the hearing impaired. While usage of special constituency dictionaries is sporadic, an absence of these dictionaries when needed can be felt very acutely. The need can appear in academic, public, corporate, specialized, and school libraries. Large-print dictionaries typically tend to have shorter definitions, but wider margins and large, clear font sizes. The *Oxford Large Print Dictionary* was first published in 1989 and is derived from the same database as the *New Oxford American Dictionary*. Definitions are clear and supplemented with usage contexts, notes on confusing or variant spellings, and updated biographical and geographical entries. Abbreviations are used sparingly. The physical design of the book has received input from the Royal National Institute for the Blind so that page quality allows for clarity in type, a maximum of white space brought about by generous margins and line spacing, and accessible font size.

Webster's New Explorer Large Print Dictionary defines more than 40,000 words with pronunciation. A special section on abbreviations is also included. Approved by the National Association for Visually Handicapped, the guidewords are in eighteen-point font with the entries in fourteen-point. *Random House Webster's Large Print Dictionary*, published in both the United Kingdom and the United States, is another resource that has received a Seal of Approval from the National Association. The latest edition includes a "New Words" section as well.

Sign language dictionaries are often confused with sign language manuals. Although much overlap occurs between the two, the dictionaries typically provide pronunciation guides, cross-references, and usage context in addition to sign entries with illustrations. *The American Sign Language Dictionary Unabridged* (Sternberg, 1998) has more than 7,000 sign entries accompanied by 12,000 illustrations that are arranged alphabetically. It has been updated to include new signs since it was first published in 1981.

The American Sign Language Handshape Dictionary published by the Gallaudet University Press does not, on the other hand, follow alphabetical order but is organized by a unique system of forty basic "handshapes." The more than 1,600 signs defined in the dictionary derive from these basic handshapes. Illustrations complement the entries and context usage is also provided. An alphabetical Index of English Glossaries at the end of the dictionary provides an alternative way of looking up the right word and sign. More recently, *The Gallaudet Dictionary of American Sign Language* was released with more than 3,000 illustrations and an attached DVD that demonstrates each of the 3,077 signs.

Speaking dictionaries available for handheld devices with handy expansion cards that can be added are also available for this constituency. *The Merriam-Webster* (M-W) *Speaking Dictionary and Thesaurus* offers *Merriam-Webster's Collegiate Dictionary*, 11th Edition, while an M-W Web application for iPhones and iPods also provides the dictionary and thesaurus in audio format. Free online dictionaries such as the meta-dictionary site available at www.dictionary .reference.com have partial audio formatting since only some of the dictionaries included, such as *The American Heritage Dictionary*, provide audio pronunciation icons for listening to a word.

Thesauri

Thesauri play a different role from dictionaries. Whereas dictionaries are primarily responsible for defining a word, a thesaurus helps the wordsmith to find the right word. Each word is partnered with strings of synonyms and antonyms. This provides users with both variety and the tools to choose the right shading in meaning. Thesauri are arranged either alphabetically or by categories.

Introduced over 150 years ago by Dr. Peter Roget, the term thesaurus is usually synonymous with Roget and hence used by a number of publishers. *Roget's International Thesaurus* is a strong resource. The sixth edition has 330,000 words and phrases organized into more than 1,000 categories arranged according to meanings. *The Oxford American Writer's Thesaurus* is innovative in that it has introduced short articles attached to certain word usages, provides writing tips with a language guide, and features words along with their opposites. It has 25,000 words, supported by 300,000 synonyms and 10,000 antonyms. An online resource is www.thesaurus.com based on *Roget's New Millennium™ Thesaurus* and produced by the creators of www.dictionary.com.

Quotations

Dictionaries often provide quotations to establish the usage of a word. Quotation books exploit that need and provide thousands of memorable quotes that highlight words and concepts. The arrangement of quotation books is varied. The seventeenth edition of the venerable *Bartlett's Familiar Quotations*, for example, is laid chronologically, though supported by an in-depth index of keywords and authors. It contains 25,000 quotations, most of which continue from John

Bartlett's original picks of 1855, updated with new quotes from modern personalities like Bill Clinton, Mother Theresa, and Jerry Seinfeld. *Bartlett's* quotes as listed in the tenth edition can be freely accessed at www.bartleby.com/100. It is searchable by keyword as well as through a chronological or alphabetic index of authors and a concordance index.

The Random House Webster's Quotationary (Frank, 2001), on the other hand, has 20,000 quotations arranged by subject. Chronology plays no part in the arrangement, though cross-references by author are provided. The third editions of the *Oxford Dictionary of Modern Quotations* and the *Oxford Dictionary of Phrase Sayings and Quotations* are both published by the Oxford University Press, with the former arranged chronologically and the latter by subject. *The Yale Book of Quotations*, while considerably smaller with its 12,000 notable quotes, is meticulously researched for original source, emphasizes American material, and is consciously modern and eclectic in its choice of quotes that range from political slogans and television catchwords to children's authors such as Dr. Seuss.

The role of quotation books in providing dramatic or elegant expression to a certain word or concept is straightforward. A few comprehensive quotation books should suffice for that role. Most reference collections, however, tend to stock a variety of books because of the possibility that a user needs to know a specific quote, in which case the chances of finding it increase by varying the range to cover general, humorous, biblical, political, gender focus, and other specialized quote sources.

Concordances

A variation of the quotation book, concordances are an alphabetical enumeration of major words in a book or a collection of books by an author, along with the immediate context of the word. Essential additions to any reference collection are concordances on Shakespeare and the Bible.

Much as Roget's, Bartlett's, and Webster's are public domain and used by multiple publishers to sell thesauri, quotation books, and dictionaries, Strong's, derivative of nineteenth-century theologian James Strong, is connected with biblical concordances. *Strong's Exhaustive Concordance of the Bible* is a reliable concordance of the *King James Bible*. Concise dictionaries of words in the Hebrew Old Testament and the Greek New Testament are given in addition to the Authorized and Revised English Versions. The prefaced goals of "completeness, simplicity, and accuracy" are evident while using this concordance. The *Unbound Bible*, offered by the Biola University in California, is a free online concordance available at http://unbound.biola.edu.

The nine-volume compilation *A Complete and Systematic Concordance to the Works of Shakespeare* and its single-volume version, the *Harvard Concordance to Shakespeare*, are both respected choices. The *Harvard* edition focuses on Volumes 4–6 of the nine-volume edition, covering the plays and poems of Shakespeare. The specific play, act, scene, line number, and line row in which the word appears is provided using the modern spelling laid out in *The Riverside Shakespeare*. The

Complete version has elaborate concordances for characters and individual plays, as well as statistics, stage directions, etc. James Farrow at the University of Sydney Information Technologies Web site at www.it.usyd.edu.au/~matty/Shakespeare/test.html has developed a well-reviewed online Shakespearean concordance.

Style and Usage of Words

Much as the perfect frame enhances a picture, words can come alive with the right grammar and punctuation. The bullet-spraying panda that eats, shoots and leaves because of an extra comma struck a punctuation chord in both the United Kingdom and the United States (Truss, 2004). Usage styles have become more elaborate with the explosion of formats, both print and electronic, that need to be cited. The printed book, pamphlet, thesis or article is compounded by the nonprint CD-ROM, video, CD or cassette; the oral interview, quote, broadcast, discussion, personal communication; and flourishing Web sites, databases, listservs, chat groups, et al., all require citations. Reference librarians must be prepared for two types of questions in the field:

- Grammar and punctuation
- Style and citation guidance

The Chicago Manual of Style is the top choice for the user interested in publication. Originating in the 1890s as a single proofreader's sheet, the sixteenth edition continues to be a crucial tool for countless writers and editors. Preparing a manuscript by dotting the right *i*'s and crossing the right *t*'s, conforming with editorial styles, checking on grammar pitfalls, outlining copyright restrictions, guiding one through the maze of citation differences, providing mathematical copy templates, and designing, producing, and marketing a printed or electronic publication, are all covered in *The Chicago Manual*. It is the source to consult when publication is the goal of the user. There is both a CD-ROM version and an online version available at www.chicagomanualofstyle.org/home.html that includes sample forms and letter styles.

For the undergraduate and high school student, the *MLA* (Modern Language Association) *Handbook for Writers of Research Papers* (Gibaldi, 2003) is the primary source. Traditionally listed as the bibliographic guide for students, the *MLA* is strong on citation guidance. The *MLA Style Manual and Guide to Scholarly Publishing* (2008) is the standard guide for professional writing. Every reference collection needs to stock the MLA simply because users will specifically ask for it by title. The latest edition includes simplified citation formats for electronic sources and helpful guidelines for creating electronic files.

For the professional, specifically the social scientist, the APA's *Publication Manual of the American Psychological Association* (2001) is the most suitable resource. The print manual is aimed at the writing of reports, presentations, and papers. Guides on presenting statistical data, graphics, and metrication are provided in addition to grammar and citation styles. Notes on avoiding plagiarism are also included. Its "most popular" tips, such as how to cite

Facebook or Twitter, are freely available online at www.apastyle.org/previous tips.html.

Technological breakthroughs in style management software are resulting in a new generation of management software that can manipulate citations into more than 600 styles including the above *APA, MLA,* and *Chicago* style. Products such as "Reference Manager," "EndNote," "RefWorks," "2collab," "BibSonomy" and "ProCite" have the capability to "search Internet databases, organize references, and format bibliographies" (Poehlmann, 2005). Academic libraries have been the first to offer bibliographic management software to students and faculty, such as the free subscription to RefWorks provided to all affiliates of the Johns Hopkins University, End Note, which is provided to students of Cornell University, and RefWorks and EndNote, which are provided to the community affiliated with the University of Kansas at Lawrence.

Given the different departments in academic institutions, a collection of subject-specific style manuals must also be part of the reference collection. The field of political science, for example, requires the *Style Manual for Political Science;* chemistry would refer to *The ACS Style Guide;* government documents follow *The Complete Guide to Citing Government Information Resources* (Cheney, 2002); journalism favors the *Associated Press Stylebook;* the *American Medical Association Manual of Style* guides the medical field; and mathematics is supported by the *Handbook of Writing for Mathematical Sciences* (Higham, 1998). The list is long and style manual acquisition, as always, would have to draw from a clear consideration of local demand.

For those who are stuck wondering whether to use "that" or "which," split an infinitive, or dangle a participle, the inimitable *Fowler's Modern English Usage* (Burchfield, 2004) has been consulted for more than seven decades. The most recent edition published has departed in controversial ways from the original. It has updated the pronunciation guidelines to cohere with the IPA; provided samples of English usage that are global rather than purely British; and updated "vogue words" and modern usage contexts. For those who are not amused by Burchfield's revised edition, the 1908 version, titled as *The King's English,* has been reprinted in hard copy with new contextualizing notes.

An admittedly descriptive, rather than prescriptive, usage book has been published in the United Kingdom by Cambridge University Press. *The Cambridge Guide to English Usage* is aimed at the "global and local communicators" of the twenty-first century. Two electronic databases, the British National Corpus and the Cambridge International Corpus, as well as hundreds of questionnaires, have been used to establish patterns that are presented in more than 4,000 alphabetical points of English usage and style.

Collection Development and Maintenance

Selection and Keeping Current

Keeping abreast of developments and updates of dictionaries is accomplished in a number of ways.

- Reading professional reviews
  - *Reference Books Bulletin*, though sectioned into *Booklist*, has its own editorial board and reviews all dictionaries, not just those recommended for purchase.
  - An annual *Supplement* to the *Library Journal* published in November each year lists recent and forthcoming reference titles with a separate subject listing for dictionaries.
  - Updates of prominent dictionaries are reviewed in multiple professional publications such as *Publishers Weekly, Booklist, Library Journal, Choice,* and *School Library Journal.*
  - *College & Research Libraries* publishes a semiannual selection of recent reference books that includes reviews of general reference works such as dictionaries.
  - Reviews of online and CD-ROM dictionaries are frequently found in *Database.*
- Referring to regularly updated reference works is another way to keep informed. The ALA's *Guide to Reference Books* and *ARBA* are authoritative sources of information.
- A subject-specific monograph such as the 1998 *Guide to World Language Dictionaries* by British librarian Andrew Dalby covers dictionaries for 275 languages in alphabetical order. *Kister's Best Dictionaries for Adults and Young People* reviews 300 English-language dictionaries along with comparative assessments and charts. While dated, it is still a valid resource for insights into the structure of gauging dictionaries and getting a sense of the breadth of material available.
- For an in-depth look at dictionary sources, subscribing to the Dictionary Society of North America is a fertile possibility. Available at http://polyglot.lss.wisc.edu/dsna/, the society is probably the most well-known professional organization of lexicographers. The newsletters and annual journal provide steady insight into the inner dialogues preceding the updating or launching of a dictionary. For a European perspective, membership in EURALEX is possible at http://www.euralex.org/.
- Individual dictionary updates are also possible. The *Oxford English Dictionary*, for example, provides a quarterly newsletter, the *OED News*, which reports research projects and new development initiatives planned for the dictionary. Regular reports on *OED* revisions and new features are guaranteed by signing up for an e-mail listing at www.oed.com/news/email.html.

Evaluating Word Sources

Authority and understandability are the prime criteria for evaluating a word source. If the definition of a word is presented in abstract or misleading ways, all other criteria become moot. Since constant and widespread usage of words decides on whether a word enters or is dropped from a dictionary, authority is as important as accuracy. In fact, there are times when the accuracy of a definition is decided by the authority of the lexicographer or lexical institution. For example, is "nigger" a noun or a racial slur, or both? The authority of Merriam-Webster and the Oxford University Press as responsible lexical giants has upheld the secondary definition of a noun despite charges of inaccuracy from the NAACP (National Association for the Advancement of Colored People). Similarly, the second sense of the term "anti-Semitism" as "opposition to Zionism" as defined in *Merriam-Webster's Third New International Dictionary* was criticized by the American Arab Anti-Discrimination Committee but has yet to be revised.

Other criteria for evaluating word sources are currency, cost, format, scope, comprehensiveness, and, of rapidly increasing importance, value-added features. Given the ubiquity of spell-checking software, availability and added access to embedded and machine-readable dictionaries is forging ahead as a criterion for evaluation. Online dictionaries have the unique ability to provide clusters of value-added features such as audio availability so the pronunciation can be heard, variant spellings available through wildcard searches, and hyperlinks to related material such as thesauri, similes, usage examples, and word games. Most large dictionary publishers are adding online availability to the print editions so that it has become an increasingly important component of purchase evaluation.

That said, reference evaluators must keep in mind that dictionaries attempt to be definitive about words, and words by definition are both ephemeral and mutative. As Dr. Johnson laments in his preface to *Cassell's Italian Dictionary* (1977: v), "Every other author may aspire to praise, the lexicographer can only hope to escape reproach."

Further Considerations

Having sampled just a few of the hundreds of dictionaries available, the reference librarian will need to apply the knowledge to these twin tasks:

- Acquisition of word sources
- Information referral

Acquisition

To paraphrase Ranganathan (1963): to every library its own collection of word sources. While general dictionaries, both abridged and unabridged, are staples of every collection, specialized word sources can play out in various permutations depending on the type, size, and in-built expectations of a particular library. Following are a few caveats to keep in mind while acquiring word sources.

- Not all books titled "dictionaries" are really dictionaries. They are merely alluding to the alphabetical arrangement of a book. For example, *A New Dictionary of Irish History* from 1800 lends little to the world of words, but a great deal to the world of history instead. Conversely, titles without the word "dictionary" may be just that. Clues can sometimes be found in publications that have "ABC" in the title, such as the classic subject dictionary *ABC for Book Collectors*, wherein a specialized term like "japon vellum" finds definition.

- Word sources can be highly derivative, even incestuous, in their capture of existing words and defining mores. For example, no dictionary listed obscene or "gutter" words until the *American Heritage* decided it was a necessary component of existing communication. Today, it is primarily the children's dictionaries that do not include such words. It is therefore not necessary to compulsively acquire every new title that comes up for purchase.

Referral

To paraphrase Ranganathan (1963) yet again: to every question its own word source. While reference librarians develop a "muscle" to efficiently field a wide variety of questions based on their knowledge of existing word resources, it is helpful to broadly deconstruct just what that "muscle" is.

- *Visualizing:* As the question is asked, fast-forwarding to the final answer helps establish the area for possible resources. If the question is *"What is a chassis?"* the final answer would read *"A chassis is _____."* A simple dictionary would suffice. If the question is *"What's another word for assessment?"* the final answer would read *"Another word is _____."* A simple thesaurus would suffice.

- *Complexity:* Is the question multitiered? Does it require analysis or oblique thinking? *"Was Thomas Edison aware that the use of mercury at his labs could adversely affect the health of his employees?"* With no recorded evidence of whether he did or did not, tracing the definition of "mercury" as it appeared in dictionaries at the turn of the century allowed one researcher to hazard a guess. For the librarian, the area of complexity lies in making the link between the question and the resource to be used.

- *Depth:* How much information does the question suggest? Instead of *"What is angst?"* if the question posed was *"Is angst an English word and can I use it to describe my teen years?"* more depth is required of the answer than a simple definition. A check into the etymology of the word as well as usage would provide a complete answer.

- *Context:* Given the mutability and infiniteness of words, placing words within a larger framework can sometimes ease the reference process. If a word is wholly unfamiliar, the context must be probed. For example, a graduate student wanted to know the meaning of "bovate," a word that could not be found in a general dictionary. The probe helped: *"Do you have the sentence in which this word appears?"* *"Did you hear this in a particular class at college?"* In this instance, the user had heard the word in the context of Elizabethan history. The possibility that it was an archaic word led the reference librarian to the *OED* where it was defined as a unit of land measure.

- *Format:* In the goal for conducting the most efficient search for the most efficacious answer, print or online resources are very often the personal choice of the librarian, but not always. In the world of word sources, for example, some words are more ephemeral than others and better served by online searches. A virtual reference question that was phrased as *"Are there any statistics available on zeroheros?"* had the librarian frantically looking through *Merriam-Webster's Collegiate*, before tracking the definition online to slang for "designated drivers." Current slang and outrageously marginalized words such as those found in one letter or all-vowel dictionaries usually suffer premature deaths and are best served by the Internet.

Following is a list of real questions asked at a library that can help exercise the reference "muscle" for answers deriving from word sources:

- *I did a phone interview with the mayor for my term paper. How do I cite his comments in my bibliography?*
- *Is the word "parsimony" ever mentioned in the Bible?*
- *I was reading the novel* The Kite Runner, *and the word "Baba" was used. Is that generic for "father" in Afghanistan?*
- *How do you spell the word that was the title of the poem by British poet William Henley and Timothy McVeigh's last words before he was executed?*
- *What is the most relevant definition of the word "browser"?*

Recommended Resources Discussed in This Chapter

Abbreviations. Available: www.abbreviations.com.
Acronyms. Available: www.acronymfinder.com.
Acronyms, Initialisms & Abbreviations Dictionary. 2011. Farmington Hills, MI: Gale/Cengage Learning.
The ACS Style Guide: A Manual for Authors and Editors. 2006. 3rd ed. Annie M. Coghill and Lorrin R. Garson, eds. New York: Oxford University Press.
Albanian-English/English-Albanian Practical Dictionary. 2006. New York: Hippocrene Books.
AMA Manual of Style. 2009. 10th ed. New York: Oxford University Press. Also available online at www.amanualstyle.com with a subscription.
The American Heritage Dictionary for Learners of English. 2002. Boston: Houghton Mifflin.
The American Heritage® Dictionary of the English Language. 2006. 4th ed. Boston: Houghton Mifflin.
American Medical Association Manual of Style: A Guide for Authors and Editors. 2007. 10th ed. New York: Oxford University Press.
The American Sign Language Handshape Dictionary. 1998. Washington, DC: Gallaudet University Press.
APA. 2009. *Publication Manual of the American Psychological Association.* 6th ed. Washington, DC: American Psychological Association.
The Associated Press Stylebook. 2010. New York: The Associated Press.
Bartlett, John. 2002. *Bartlett's Familiar Quotations.* 17th ed. Boston: Little, Brown.

TOP TEN DICTIONARY AND WORD SOURCES		
Title	**Print**	**Online**
The American Heritage Dictionary, 2006 Boston, MA: Houghton Mifflin	4th ed.	www.bartleby.com/61/
Bartlett's Familiar Quotations, 2002 London: Little, Brown Book Group	17th ed.	www.bartleby.com/100/ 1919 edition www. Archive.org—1968 edition
Dictionary of American Regional English, 2002– Cambridge, MA: Harvard University Press	5 vols. + 1	100 entries available at: http://dare.wisc.edu
Macmillan Dictionary for Children, 2007 New York: Simon & Schuster Children's Publishing		
Merriam-Webster's Collegiate Dictionary, 2003 Springfield, MA: Merriam-Webster	11th ed.	www.m-w.com
MLA Style Manual and Guide to Scholarly Publishing, 2008 New York: Modern Language Association of America	3rd ed.	
New Oxford American Dictionary, 2010 New York: Oxford University Press	3rd ed.	Subscription to "Premium" www.oxfordreference.com
The Oxford English Dictionary, 1989 New York: Oxford University Press	20 vols.	Subscription www.oed.com
Roget's International Thesaurus, 2010 New York: HarperCollins Publishers	7th ed.	www.bartleby.com/110 1922 edition
Webster's Third New International Dictionary of the English Language, Unabridged, 2002 Springfield, MA: Merriam-Webster		Subscription http://corporate. britannica.com/ library/online/mwu.html

Black's Law Dictionary. 2004. 8th ed. Bryan A. Garner, ed. Eagan, MN: West Publishing Company.

Bloomsbury English Dictionary. 2004. London: A & C Black.

Burchfield, R. W. 2004. *Fowler's Modern English Usage*. Rev. 3rd ed. Oxford: Oxford University Press.

Cambridge Advanced Learner's Dictionary. 2008. Cambridge, UK: Cambridge University Press.

The Cambridge Guide to English Usage. 2004. Cambridge, UK: Cambridge University Press.

RECOMMENDED FREE WEB SITES

Dictionary.com. This site is quick, reliable, and effective. It is a multi-source dictionary service, with the pleasing simplicity of a clean interface featuring a simple blue search box. It also features a thesaurus and translation dictionary that can toggle between twenty different languages. Available: http://dictionary.reference.com/.

Acronym Finder. More than four million acronyms, abbreviations, and initialisms are searchable in this popular site. They can be located by either keyword or through listed categories such as "Information Technology." Available: www.acronymfinder.com/.

The fourth edition of the reputable *American Heritage Dictionary of the English Language* is freely available through this site. 90,000 entries with 70,000 audio pronunciations, 900 visual illustrations, language notes and word-roots build up to make this a powerful free online dictionary resource. Available: www.bartleby.com/61/.

Merriam-Webster's Collegiate Dictionary, 11th Edition, is freely available at this site along with a thesaurus, and medical and Spanish-English word search capability. Available: www.merriam-webster.com/.

Netlingo. Updated daily, the site is invaluable in navigating the ever-changing shores of "cyberterms", the terminology, acronyms, and emoticons that populate the online universe. Available: http://netlingo.com/.

Canadian Oxford Dictionary. 2004. 2nd ed. Katherine Barber, ed. Oxford: Oxford University Press.

Canadian spelling. Available: www.luther.ca/~dave7cnv/cdnspelling/cdn spelling.html.

Carter, John, and Nicolas Barker. 2004. *ABC for Book Collectors.* 4th ed. New Castle, DE: Oak Knoll Press.

Cassell's Italian Dictionary. 1977. New York: Macmillan.

Cassell's Latin Dictionary. 1977. London: Cassell.

Chambers Dictionary. 2008. 11th ed. Edinburgh: Chambers Harrap.

Cheney, Debora. 2002. *The Complete Guide to Citing Government Information Resources.* 3rd ed. Bethesda, MD: Congressional Information Service.

The Chicago Manual of Style. 2010. 16th ed. Chicago: University of Chicago Press.

Collins English Dictionary. 2010. 30th anniversary ed. New York: HarperCollins.

A Complete and Systematic Concordance to the Works of Shakespeare. 1968. Marvin Spevack, compiler. New York: G. Olms.

Concordance—Shakespeare. Available: www.it.usvd.edu.au/~matty/Shakespeare/test.html.

Corbeil, Jean-Claude, and Arianne Archambault. 2009. *The Firefly Five Language Visual Dictionary: English, Spanish, French, German, Italian.* New York: Firefly.

———. 2002. *The Firefly Visual Dictionary.* New York: Firefly.

Dictionary. Available: www.dictionary.com.

Dictionary of American Regional English, Volume IV. 2002. Joan Houston Hall, chief ed. Cambridge, MA: Harvard University Press.

DK Merriam-Webster Children's Dictionary. 2008. New York: DK Publishing.

Dorland's Illustrated Medical Dictionary. 2007. 31st ed. New York: Elsevier/Saunders. Also available: www.dorlands.com.

Encarta Webster's Dictionary of the English Language. 2004. 2nd ed. New York: Bloomsbury.

Espy, Willard R. 2006. *Words to Rhyme With.* 3rd ed. New York: Facts on File.

FOLDOC. Denis Howe, ed. Available: http://foldoc.org.

Fowler, H.W. 2009. *A Dictionary of Modern English Usage: The Classic First Edition.* David Crystal, ed. Oxford: Oxford University Press.

Frank, Leonard Roy. 2001. *The Random House Webster's Quotationary.* New York: Random House Reference.

Gage Canadian Dictionary. 2000. Scarborough, Ontario: Thomson Nelson.

The Gallaudet Dictionary of American Sign Language. 2006. Clayton Valli, editor-in-chief. Washington, DC: Gallaudet University Press.

Gibaldi, Joseph. 2003. *MLA Handbook for Writers of Research Papers.* 6th ed. New York: Modern Language Association of America.

Harvard Concordance to Shakespeare. 1973. Marvin Spevack, compiler. Cambridge, MA: Belknap Press.

The Harvard Dictionary of Music. 2003. 4th ed. Don Michael Randel, ed. Cambridge, MA: Belknap Press.

Hickey, D. J., and J. E. Doherty. 2003. *A New Dictionary of Irish History from 1800.* Dublin, Ireland: Gill & Macmillan.

Higham, Nicholas J. 1998. *Handbook of Writing for the Mathematical Sciences.* 2nd ed. Philadelphia, PA: SIAM.

Lighter, Jonathan E. 1997. *Random House Historical Dictionary of American Slang,* Volume II. New York: Random House Reference.

Macmillan Dictionary for Children. 2007. New York: Simon & Schuster.

The Macmillan English Dictionary. 2007. 2nd ed. New York: Macmillan.

McGraw-Hill's Dictionary of American Idioms and Phrasal Verbs. 2006. New York: McGraw-Hill.

Merriam-Webster's Advanced Learner's English Dictionary. 2008. Springfield, MA: Merriam-Webster.

Metadictionary. Available: www.onelook.com.

MLA Style Manual and Guide to Scholarly Publishing. 2008. 3rd ed. New York: Modern Language Association of America.

Nelson Canadian Dictionary of the English Language. 1997. Scarborough, Ontario: ITP Nelson.

New Oxford American Dictionary. 2010. 3rd ed. New York: Oxford University Press.

NTC's American English Learner's Dictionary. 1998. Richard A. Spears, ed. New York: McGraw-Hill.

OED Online. Available: www.oed.com.

Ostler, Rosemarie. 2003. *Dewdroppers, Waldos, and Slackers: A Decade-by-Decade Guide to the Vanishing Vocabulary of the 20th Century.* New York: Oxford University Press.

The Oxford American Writer's Thesaurus. 2008. Christine A. Lindbergh, ed. New York: Oxford University Press.

Oxford Dictionary of English. 2010. Oxford: Oxford University Press.

Oxford Dictionary of Modern Quotations. 2008. 3rd ed. Elizabeth Knowles, ed. New York: Oxford University Press.

Oxford Dictionary of Phrase Sayings and Quotation. 2006. 3rd ed. New York: Oxford University Press.

Oxford English Dictionary. 1989. 2nd ed. John Simpson and Edward Weiner, eds. New York: Oxford University Press.

Oxford Large Print Dictionary. 2002. New York: Oxford University Press. Reissued in 2006 as the *Oxford Large Print Dictionary, Thesaurus, and Wordpower Guide.*

The Oxford Rhyming Dictionary. 2004. Clive and Eben Upton, eds. New York: Oxford University Press.

The Oxford Starter Bilingual Dictionary Series. New York: Oxford University Press. Copyright varies.

Random House Webster's Large Print Dictionary. 2007. New York: Random House.

Random House Webster's Rhyming Dictionary. 2008. New York: Random House Reference.

Random House Webster's Unabridged American Sign Language Dictionary. 2008. New York: Random House Reference.

Random House Webster's Unabridged Dictionary. 1997. New York: Random House Reference.

Reitz, Joan M. 2007. *ODLIS.* Available: http://lu.com/odlis/index.cfm.

Rhyming dictionary. Available: www.rhymezone.com.

Roget's International Thesaurus. 2010. Barbara Ann Kipferer, ed. New York: HarperCollins Publishers.

Saussy III, George Stone. 1989. *The Logodaedalian's Dictionary of Interesting and Unusual Words.* Columbia, SC: University of South Carolina Press.

Shakespeare concordance. Available: www.it.usyd.edu.au/~matty/Shakespeare/test.html.

Slang dictionary. Available: www.urbandictionary.com.

Stahl, Dean, and Karen Kerchelich. 2001. *Abbreviations Dictionary.* 10th ed. Boca Raton, FL: CRC Press.

Stedman's Medical Dictionary. 2006. 28th ed. Philadelphia, PA: Lippincott Williams & Wilkins.

Sternberg, Martin L. A. 1998. *The American Sign Language Dictionary Unabridged.* New York: HarperCollins Publishers.

Stone the Crows: Oxford Dictionary of Modern Slang. 2008. 2nd ed. John Ayto and John Simpson, eds. New York: Oxford University Press.

Strong's Exhaustive Concordance of the Bible. 2007. Peabody, MA: Hendrickson Publishers.

A Student's Dictionary. 2004. Charleston, SC: The Dictionary Project.

The Style Manual for Political Science. 2001. Washington, DC: American Political Science Association.

Thesaurus. Available: www.thesaurus.com and http://thesaurus.reference.com.

Thorndike-Barnhart Children's Dictionary. 1998. Upper Saddle River, NJ: Pearson Education.

Tullock, John H. 2000. *The Dictionary of Aquarium Terms.* New York: Barron's.

Ultimate Visual Dictionary, Revised and Updated. 2006. New York: DK Publishing.

Webopedia. Available: www.webopedia.com.

Webster's New Explorer Large Print Dictionary. 2006. Darien, CT: Federal Street Press.
Webster's Third New International Dictionary, Unabridged. 2002. Springfield, MA: Merriam-Webster.
Wiktionary. Available: www.wiktionary.com.
Wordia. Available: www.wordia.com.
World Book Dictionary. 2005. Chicago: World Book.
The World Factbook. Available: www.cia.gov/library/publications/the-world-factbook/index.html.
The Yale Book of Quotations. 2006. Fred R. Shapiro, ed. New Haven, CT: Yale University Press.

Recommendations for Further Reading

Clark, Joe. 2008. *Organizing Our Marvellous Neighbours: How to Feel Good About Canadian English.* E-book: http://en-ca.org/buy/. A short, ferocious and readable e-book that discusses the distinctiveness of Canadian spellings that is inconveniently individualistic since they are neither wholly British nor American. Clark correctly points to the insidious undermining effects of spell checkers that downplay Canadian spellings in favor of British and American ones. The book also serves as an intriguing example of the perceived value of dictionaries as lexical symbols of national identity.

Coleman, Julie. 2008. *A History of Cant and Slang Dictionaries*, Volumes I–III. New York: Oxford University Press. Coleman provides us with an exhaustive and fascinating three-volume account of the colorful history of slang in the English-speaking world. The history is supported with the etymology of slang words and the context within which they were embedded. Also featured are the spiritualists, criminals, soldiers, journalists, aristocrats, schoolboys, and others who made up a motley crew of slang lexicographers through the ages.

Dalby, Andrew. 1998. *A Guide to World Language Dictionaries.* London: Library Association. This evaluative single-volume collation of dictionaries covering 275 languages from around the world provides the most updated information in the area of language dictionaries. The listings are both annotated and listed alphabetically, so it is not necessary to have additional knowledge of language groups.

Harris, Roy. 2008. "Defining the Undefinable." *Times Higher Education* 1827 (January 10): 20. Harris, an emeritus professor of general linguistics at the University of Oxford, prolific author, and co-editor of the journal *Language and Communication*, presents us with a brief but stimulating essay on the importance of dictionaries to the self-understanding of society and the need to address a society where definitional anarchy in dictionaries is the norm.

Kabdebo, Thomas, and Neil Armstrong. 1997. *Dictionary of Dictionaries and Eminent Encyclopedias.* New Providence, NJ: Bowker-Saur. This edition provides a comprehensive and evaluative bibliography of 24,000 subject, online, historical, and language dictionaries and encyclopedias. While an updated edition would be welcome, the resource continues to be useful in providing an overview of the breadth of dictionaries available.

Kister, Kenneth. 1992. *Kister's Best Dictionaries for Adults and Young People: A Comparative Guide*. Phoenix, AZ: Oryx Press. Kister has written the definitive study of dictionaries. While the facts describing each dictionary are obsolete, the essays on the history, typology, and comparative evaluation of dictionaries continue to be powerful.

Reitz, Joan M. 2004. "ODLIS: Online Dictionary for Library and Information Science." Available: http://lu.com/odlis/. Also available in print as the *Dictionary for Library and Information Science*, Westport, CT: Libraries Unlimited. First popularized as an online resource, the author has now published this wonderful resource in a print version as well. Definitions for all kinds of dictionaries are provided in a clear style with helpful "compare with" suggestions for relevant entries.

Romero, Joseph M. 2004. "Life Among the Lexicographers." *Humanities* 25, no. 2 (March/April): 20. This is both a well-researched and elegant article on the creation of a unique dictionary, the *Dictionary of American Regional English*.

Sweetland, James H. 2001. *Fundamental Reference Sources*. 3rd ed. Chicago: American Library Association. The author, who was president of the Reference and User Services Association in 1990–1991 and is currently professor at the School of Information Studies, University of Washington-Milwaukee, is highly qualified to write this "reference on reference" that configures a workable method to both determine and pick out the most useful print and nonprint reference resources.

Wallraff, Barbara. 2004. "Dictionaries." *The New York Times Magazine* (October 5): 18. Written by the author of *Your Own Words*, this article alerts users to the fallibility of dictionaries in terms of differing and idiosyncratic entries and styles.

World Wide Words. Available: www.worldwidewords.org/reviews/re-fou1 .htm. Michael Quinion, an established British lexicographer, author, and contributor to the *Oxford English Dictionary*, is the creator of this delightful online newsletter on the English language and reviews of new books dealing with language.

Bibliography of Works Cited in This Chapter

Adams, William Lee. 2008. "War of the Words." *Time International* (Europe Edition) 172, no. 16 (October 20): 42.

Alford, Henry. 2005. "Not a Word." *The New Yorker* (August 29): 62.

Andriani, Lynn. 2008. "Merriam-Webster Joins Learner's English Market." *Publishers Weekly* 255, no. 28 (July 14): 6.

Dahlin, Robert. 1999. "You're as Good as Your Word." *Publishers Weekly* 246, no. 46 (November 15): 33.

"Dictionary Resists Pressure to Clean Up Language." 1998. *Newsletter on Intellectual Freedom* 47, no. 4 (July).

Douglas, Matthews. 2005. "The Devil's Dictionary." *The Indexer* 24, no. 3 (April): 161–162.

Hoyle, Ben. 2008. "Mafflard Left with Onomatomania after Reading Oxford Dictionary from A to Z." *The Times (London, England)* (October 4): 4.

Levett, John. 2003. "The Death of the Dictionary?" *Australian Library Journal* 52, no. 4 (November): 309–310.

McKean, Erin. 2004. "Lexicographer." *The New York Times Magazine* (November 14): 46.

McQuade, Molly. 2003. "Defining a Dictionary." *Booklist* (May 15): 1688.

"Merriam-Webster's Collegiate Dictionary now available for iPhone and iPod Touch." 2008. *Science Letter* (September 30): 3714.

Nunberg, Geoffrey. 2004. "What Defined." *The New York Times*, Section 4 (April 11): 7.

"Oxford Closes Canadian Dictionary Division." 2008. *Canwest News Service* (October 1). Available: www.canada.com/components/print.aspx?id=c74519ed-c8d5-4312-869b-af7508dd65cc (November 7, 2008).

Poehlmann, Christian. 2005. "Software Reviews." *Technology and Libraries* 21, no. 1 (November 16). Available: www.lita.org/ala/lita/litapublications/ital/2101software.htm (January 5, 2006).

Quinn, Mary Ellen, and Christine Bulson. 2008. "Atlas and Dictionary Update, 2008." *Booklist* 104, no. 18 (May 15): 80, 82.

Ranganathan, S. R. 1963. *The Five Laws of Library Science*. Bombay, India: Asia Publishing House.

Truss, Lynne. 2004. *Eats, Shoots and Leaves: The Zero Tolerance Approach to Punctuation*. New York: Gotham Books.

8

Answering Questions about Events and Issues, Past and Present— Indexes and Full-Text Databases

Overview

Indexes first came into being in the nineteenth century. The first index ever published was *Poole's Index to Periodical Literature* 1802–1906. It indexed articles from 479 American and English periodicals by subject only. For many decades printed indexes provided access to periodicals and newspapers. Today we have few paper indexes, but even before the more recent shift to digital media, new ways of presenting indexes began to take shape in the 1960s. Dialog, beginning in 1966, and BRS (Bibliographic Retrieval Service), beginning in 1976, provided libraries an interface that allowed them to search a large number of indexes by computer. Mead Data Central released the online databases LexisNexis in 1973 and 1980, respectively. By 1982 Dialog and BRS introduced flat rate simplified versions for home use. In 1985 Infotrac, a videodisc product that enabled the user to search databases in one alphabet, was produced by IAC (Information Access Company). CD-ROMs provided an even better and more economical way to store large amounts of data in a small space. Libraries were able to network CD-ROMs to serve their public. Libraries began to lease database indexes, often loading the information on their own in-house servers so users could access the information through the OPACs (Online Public Access Catalogs) (Machovec, 1995). The advent of the World Wide Web made it possible for libraries to subscribe to databases that the user could view over the Web and to provide full text for many or all articles. This has revolutionized indexes and made it possible to give access to massive amounts of regularly updated information while guaranteeing flexible, open access.

How Indexes Are Used

"The primary objective of the database (index) is to help the reader find entire documents, typically journal articles, on specific topics within some large document collection" (Diakoff, 2004: 85). Indexes dissect what is inside a periodical or newspaper so that the user has access to the individual articles. This enables the user to more easily find material on a specific subject or a specific article.

Indexes are used to find articles in periodicals and newspapers. They are most often employed to research topics of current interest. In some cases they can also be used to help develop one's understanding of a contemporary debate, as a variety of material can be found on any controversial topic from many different points of view. It is also helpful to use periodical and newspaper indexes to research a subject not yet written about in books.

For example, new medical treatments are usually discussed in journals, newspapers and magazines long before receiving treatment in longer print media, thanks to the quick turnaround of periodical publishing. Many indexes are now full text databases that allow users to access the complete article along with the bibliographic citation. Also advantageous with today's indexes is their easy searchability, a feature that sometimes makes them an expedient supplement to printed reference resources. Along these lines, note that, in addition to material published in periodicals and newspapers, indexes sometimes allow quick access to the contents of books, further streamlining the searching process.

Indexes are also useful for doing retrospective research. Many indexes have been in business for many years and have digitized their complete run. This enables researchers to quickly search for older material. Also, the digitization of newspapers from the beginning of their publishing has also provided an excellent tool for researchers.

As always, it is important to understand the kind and quality of information desired by the user before starting an index search. If the user just wants general, non-scholarly articles on a subject, then multidisciplinary periodical and newspaper indexes are probably the proper place to begin. Should the user's interests be more specialized, however, it is important that a more appropriate subject-based index be chosen.

Libraries have spent a great deal of time designing their electronic resources pages to lead the user to specialized indexes. Simply pointing out resources is, of course, not enough, so bibliographic instruction is also important in this regard. Librarians can design tutorials or courses that introduce the user to specialized indexes in their field of study and demonstrate how to use them. Federated searching using products such as Webfeat, Ex Libris' MetaLib and Serial Solutions' Central Search can also help users search appropriate databases by allowing the user to search across several databases at the same time without having to know the names of specific databases and learning individual searching protocols for each database. The area of full-text databases is a rich one and useful to both the librarian and the user.

Questions Answered by Indexes

Q: Where can I find information on Hispanic immigrants to the United States?
A: The answer can be found in a general full-text periodical index such as *Academic Search Premier* or in a more specialized index such as *PAIS International*.

Q: Where can I find articles on companies that provide day care for working mothers?

A: A general full-text periodical index such as *ProQuest Research Library* will have articles on this subject. Newspaper indexes such as *InfoTrac Newstand* would be good sources as well.

Q: How can I locate information about the effect of the Internet on American society?

A: A general full-text periodical index such as *Academic OneFile* will have articles on this or a more specialized index such as *Social Sciences Full Text*.

Q: Where can I find five pieces of criticism for the Faulkner short story "A Rose for Emily"?

A: Use a subject index like *Humanities Full Text* that will have full text for many articles. If you need to find more in-depth material and/or older material, use the *MLA International Bibliography*.

Q: Where can I find articles on deforestation in Mexico?

A: *PAIS International*, from the political and economic perspective, or *Biosis Previews*, with scientific articles on the environment, might be good places to start.

Q: What is the best place to look for research about the psychological effects of adoption on children?

A: *PsycInfo* is the best place to start for psychological topics. Be sure to look at the thesaurus to pick the best terms for your search.

Q: Where can I find information about which digital cameras are the best?

A: General full-text periodical indexes such as *Reader's Guide Full Text* include consumer magazines and computer magazines are a good source of information.

Major Indexes Used in Reference Work

Indexes can be multidisciplinary periodical or newspaper indexes or specialized indexes covering a particular subject area. Multidisciplinary periodical indexes provide a way to do research on a wide range of topics. They index periodicals that are widely used, usually providing the full text. General newspaper indexes do the same for newspapers. Some index a single newspaper while others index several newspapers. The subject indexes can be as specific as *GeoRef* or can be broad-based such as *ERIC* (*Educational Resources Information Center*) or the *PAIS International*.

Multidisciplinary Periodical Indexes

Several companies, including EBSCO, ProQuest, Gale Cengage Learning and H.W. Wilson, dominate the index field. All of these companies to a greater or lesser extent act as conglomerates continually buying other companies or leasing content in order to offer more databases to libraries. Some databases produced by outside organizations are available by subscription from more than one company. Each of these companies has its strengths and weaknesses, but overall the librarian will find any of them quite satisfactory. The choice a library makes should be predicated on the criteria important to their specific situation.

Academic Search Complete, EBSCO's largest multidisciplinary database, indexes 12,800 journals of which 8,500 are full text. Covering a wide range of subjects from the sciences, social sciences, and humanities to law, music, and many interdisciplinary subjects such as women's studies and area studies, this database indexes many peer-reviewed and scholarly journals. EBSCO also offers several other multidisciplinary indexes to fit the needs of different types and sizes of libraries. *Academic Search Elite* is designed for smaller academic libraries but would also be useful in community college libraries and public libraries. Over 3,650 titles are indexed and abstracted, and 2,100 periodicals are available in full text. Coverage dates from 1985. For libraries wanting a richer collection of resources there is *Academic Search Premier*, which indexes almost 8,500 titles with 4,600 full-text and back files beginning in 1975. EBSCO also has three indexes especially designed for public libraries. *MasterFILE Complete* is the largest of the indexes with more than 2,000 full-text periodicals and 1,000 reference books. *MasterFILE Premier* and *MasterFILE Elite* index fewer titles. These databases available through EBSCO have good search facility. One can search by keyword in the article title, subject descriptors, author and abstract fields.

ProQuest's largest multidisciplinary index database is *ProQuest Central*, a database of more than 11,500 titles with over 8,700 titles in full text, indexes journals, magazines, and newspapers as well as dissertations and company reports and is useful to all types of libraries, providing information on a wide range of subjects including business, humanities, education, social sciences, and sciences. The titles indexed begin in 1995. Its search methods are the usual—Boolean operators, advanced search, and natural language—with complete subject indexing and a controlled vocabulary. *ProQuest Research Library* is a full-text database that covers the top 150 core academic subject areas. *CBCA Complete* is a database of Canadian periodicals that includes bibliographic citations and a great deal of full text. It indexes more than 1,600 titles with coverage back to the 1970s.

Gale Cengage Learning's multidisciplinary full-text database, *Academic One-File*, is geared to undergraduate, graduate students and faculty. It indexes over 13,000 periodical titles as well as newspapers (including the *New York Times*, *Financial Times*, and the *London Times*) and wire services. The majority of the titles are full text and peer reviewed, and back file full-text coverage begins in 1980. Another of Gale Cengage Learning's full-text databases is *Expanded Academic ASAP*, which includes material for the undergraduate but is also useful for high schools and public libraries. *Expanded Academic ASAP* indexes over 4,300 titles, of which 2,500 are full text. It also indexes the *New York Times*. *General OneFile* indexes 7,000 full-text titles, 3,000 of which are peer reviewed. This database indexes five newspapers with full text of the *New York Times* from 1985 to date. The Gale Cengage Learning indexes have good searching capability and the ability to limit searches by full text, refereed publications, by date and by journal title.

The H.W. Wilson Company has the longest record in the index business beginning at the end of the nineteenth century. It is known for the quality of its indexing and its name and subject authority files. Most of the Wilson indexes are now available electronically. The *Readers' Guide to Periodical Literature*, which began publication in 1890, is a general index that is useful in high schools, public libraries, and four-year colleges. Indexing more than 400 periodicals, the *Readers' Guide* now publishes *Readers' Guide Full Text Mega Edition* with the full text of 215 publications back to 1994 and with indexing and abstracts of 400 periodicals dating back to 1983. Wilson also publishes *Readers' Guide Abstracts*, which indexes and abstracts over 300 periodicals. In addition, Wilson now offers *Readers' Guide Retrospective 1890–1982* to provide the earlier years of the index in electronic format. *Wilson OmniFile Full Text Mega Edition* combines full text, abstracts and indexing from six Wilson indexes, *Education Full Text*, *General Science Full Text*, *Humanities Full Text*, *Readers' Guide Full Text*, *Social Sciences Full Text*, and *Wilson Business Full Text*, back to 1982. It also includes full text of titles indexed in five of Wilson's other subject indexes. This index includes the full text of articles from more than 2,200 publications and abstracts and indexing from over 3,600 publications. The broad coverage makes this index useful as a general multidisciplinary index. Wilson continues to make back files of their many indexes available electronically, although many of these electronic indexes do not have full text.

LexisNexis has several general reference indexes aimed at academic institutions, public libraries, and high schools, all providing a variety of full-text information on current events, legal issues, and issues in the news that can be searched by keyword as well as by subject headings. The extensive searching capability of the LexisNexis products makes this database extremely useful. The range of publications indexed in the LexisNexis database goes far beyond the usual magazines and newspapers and includes reports, official documents, television and radio broadcast scripts, wire services, conference proceedings, and organizational newsletters. *LexisNexis Academic* provides national and international current events information as well as legal information, business and financial news, information on companies, and medical and science information from more than 10,000 publications, documents, and access to 9,500 news sources. *LexisNexis Library Express* is a recent database designed for public libraries.

First Search from OCLC (Online Computer Library Center) provides access to more than eighty-five subject databases including *PAIS International*, *ABI/INFORM*, the *MLA International Bibliography*, *PsycInfo*, and FRANCIS. Libraries can subscribe to a selection of these databases that fit their situation. *Electronic Collections Online*, accessible through *First Search*, provides bibliographic access to over 6,000 electronic journals in practically every subject area with coverage since 1994. Libraries can subscribe to a selection of these journals including the full text. Users also have access to *WorldCat*, where they can identify locations of books and other information, and *Article First*, where they can identify the journal for each article and locations for the journal title. Basic, advanced and expert search is available.

Dialog (ProQuest), one of the earliest companies in the field, is still a player providing more than 900 databases from many different publishers covering such subjects as science and technology, business, energy and environment, food and agriculture, medicine, social sciences, and reference. *Dialog* has more than one database and more than one pricing model. *Dialog 1*, a basic easy-to-use database, and *DialogClassic*, for experienced searchers, are two of its most popular databases offering excellent search capabilities.

JSTOR is a nonprofit developed to provide long-term preservation of an archive of important scholarly journals. Complete journals on subjects in all fields from volume 1 are available. The most current years are now being made available. Libraries must become a participant in JSTOR to subscribe to this service. Participant fees are based on the type of library (www.jstor.org).

Google Scholar (scholar.google.com) is a free service that provides access to scholarly literature. Most of the access is to citations and abstracts. All subjects are covered; articles, books, theses, papers, etc., are indexed. Libraries can link to their full-text holdings.

Access: The Supplementary Index to Periodicals (1975–present) indexes about 85 popular periodicals including city and regional magazines not indexed elsewhere. It often provides the first indexing for a new periodical and is available in print and electronically.

Alternative Press Index, founded in 1969, is a biannual subject index to more than 300 alternative, radical, and left-wing periodicals, newspapers, and magazines often not found in other indexes. It is international and interdisciplinary in scope covering such topics as labor, indigenous peoples, feminism, ecology, gays and lesbians, and socialism.

Newspaper Indexes and Databases

Newspaper databases are exceedingly useful to libraries and library users. These databases provide access to current and retrospective articles in many newspapers—often many more than the library might subscribe to. Many provide the full text of newspapers from smaller towns and cities. *Newspaper Source Plus* (EBSCO) provides full text for over 170 U.S. newspapers and 20 international newspapers including the *New York Times, The Christian Science Monitor, USA Today*, and *The Washington Post*, selective full text from 410 regional U.S. newspapers, and TV and radio news transcripts.

InfoTrac Newstand (Gale Cengage Learning) is a full-text database that provides access to 1,000 U.S. national, regional, and local newspapers as well as international newspapers. Gale also offers *Gale Custom Newspapers* which provides full text for more than 300 national and international newspapers.

ProQuest Newsstand allows libraries to develop a customized database of full-text newspapers from the over 350 daily national and international newspapers offered with a core of the *New York Times, USA Today, Wall Street Journal, Washington Post, The Guardian, El Norte, Jerusalem Post*, and the *South China Morning Post*. Coverage begins for many titles in the 1980s and 1990s. In addition to current newspapers ProQuest also offers its *Historical Newspapers*. This collection is continuing to grow. Libraries can subscribe to the full text of major newspapers such as the *New York Times* from 1851–2005, *Wall Street Journal* from

1889–1991, *Washington Post* from 1877–1992, *Christian Science Monitor* from 1908–1995, and *Los Angeles Times* from 1881–1986. The full text of many more newspapers is available.

Newsbank provides access to the full text of many newspapers. *America's News* provides complete full-text electronic editions of more than 1,500 U.S. news sources. A second database, *Access World News*, includes not only full-text newspapers from the United States but also newspapers from many other countries, translated into English when written in other languages.

Subject-based Indexes

Although many users just want to use the general database indexes, they should be introduced to the subject-based indexes since many journals are not indexed in the general database indexes. Subject-based indexes index more specialized journals, newspapers, and documents. When researching a subject in depth, it is necessary to use subject-based indexes to find more detailed and usually more scholarly material. Indexes in major subject areas are described in the following paragraphs.

Science and Technology Indexes

Two indexes that have for many years been the only science indexes for the layperson are the *General Science Index* (Wilson) and the *Applied Science and Technology Index* (Wilson). *General Science Full Text* is designed for the student and nonspecialist. It includes the full text of more than 100 periodicals from 1995 to date, as well as abstracts and indexing for 300 periodicals from 1984 to date. The subjects covered include astronomy, chemistry, biology, food and nutrition, physics, mathematics, and the earth sciences. *Applied Science & Technology Full Text* provides full text of articles from more than 220 journals from 1997 to date as well as abstracts and indexing of 800 periodicals from 1984 to the present. The subjects covered include automotive engineering, transportation, petroleum and gas, plastics, robotics, textiles, the food industry, construction, etc. There is also *Applied Science and Technology Retrospective 1913–1983*. *Science Full Text Select* is a database that includes the full text from three index databases—*General Science Full Text*, *Applied Science & Technology Full Text*, and *Biological & Agricultural Index Plus*—packaged together and aimed at the high school and community colleges. This product covers 400 journals.

Science in Context (formerly *Science Resource Center*) includes articles from newspapers and journals and the text of science reference titles as well as links to Web sites and audio and video clips. Aimed at a wide user base from students to the general public, it focuses on earth science, life science, the history of science, physical science, space science, and science and society. *Biology Digest* (Plexus Publishing) covers all aspects of the life sciences from 1987 to the present. Intended for high school and undergraduate students, it provides abstracts of journal articles ranging from botany and ecology to biochemistry, physiology, and zoology and is updated nine times a year.

For academic audiences, many in-depth subject indexes meet specific needs. Among these, *SciFinder Scholar* is the online version of *Chemical Abstracts* and includes CAplus database, the CAS (Chemical Abstract Service) registry file and Medline as well as information on chemical substances and reactions. This database includes citations and abstracts from journals, conference proceedings, patents, and dissertations from 1907 to the present. *Biosis Previews* is a comprehensive index to life science and biomedical research covering biology, biochemistry, genetics, zoology, environmental sciences, and many more subjects. It provides citations and abstracts to more than 5,000 international journals from 1990 to the present. *Scopus* (Elsevier) is an indexing and abstracting service covering more than 18,000 science, technology, and medical (STM) sources (journals, conference proceedings, scientific Web sites and more) as well as the social science and historical material from 5,000 publishers back to 1996. This large, powerful database provides good searching capability.

Many more scientific databases exist for those specializing in specific fields. For the geosciences, the *GeoRef* database produced by the American Geological Institute and distributed by ProQuest/CSA, covers geology of North America from 1693 to the present and geology for the rest of the world from 1933 to the present. This database includes bibliographic information and index terms for geoscience journal articles, books, maps, conference papers, reports, and dissertations as well as the publications of the U.S. Geological Survey. *Oceanic Abstracts* (ProQuest/CSA) includes citations and abstracts for literature on marine biology and physical oceanography, fisheries, aquaculture, and much more from 1981 to the present. *Zoological Record Plus*, now produced by Thomson Scientific and formerly by BIOSIS and the Zoological Society of London, covers the literature of zoology and animal science. This database provides bibliographic references to serial publications, books, and other kinds of publications that are indexed by a well-developed online thesaurus. It is regarded as the unofficial register of taxonomic names and systematics.

MathSciNet is an international bibliographical resource for the literature of mathematics and statistics. Begun in 1940 and produced by the American Mathematical Society, *MathSciNet* provides libraries full-text access to the material for which they have journal or online subscriptions. *INSPEC*, produced by the Institution of Electrical Engineers, provides bibliographical access to science and technology literature in physics, electrical engineering, electronics, computers, computing, and information technology. More than 3,500 journals are indexed as well as conference proceedings. Produced cooperatively by the Institute of Electrical and Electronics Engineers in the United States and by the Institution of Engineering and Technology in the United Kingdom, *IEEE Xplore*, which is also called *IEEE/IEE Electronic Library*, covers the fields of electrical engineering, electronics, computer science, information science, materials science, physical science, and biomedical engineering. Full text is provided for 140 journals as well as conference proceedings and standards beginning in 1980. The *ACM Digital Library* is an important database for computer science produced by the Association for Computing Machinery. More than 200 sources including journals, maps, newsletters, and conferences are indexed with a great deal of full text.

Education Indexes

Education is represented by two excellent indexes. *Education Full Text* (Wilson) is the *Education Index* with the full text of articles from 350 journals from 1996 to the present and abstracts and indexing for 770 back to 1983. *Education Full Text* indexes journals not indexed by ERIC. Its subject coverage ranges from Comparative Education and Educational Technology to Parent-Teacher Relations and Teacher Evaluation. *Education Index Retrospective: 1929–1983* provides electronic access to the back files of this index.

ERIC (Education Resources Information Center) (www.eric.ed.gov) is a free database funded by the U.S. Department of Education since 1966. It has been online since 1996. ERIC provides broad subject coverage in the field of education and extends into some related fields such as library science. It includes citations and abstracts from over 1,000 educational and education-related journals, books, reports, and other relevant materials, many with full text. One of its strengths is that it provides full-text access to a great deal of gray literature in the subject areas covered. The *Current Index to Journals in Education*, once a separate publication, is now part of ERIC online.

Social Science Indexes

The social sciences are a rich area for indexes due to the changing nature of information in this field. *Social Sciences Full Text* (Wilson) includes the full text of more than 215 publications from 1995 to the present. Its content covers social science journals published in the United States and elsewhere and includes such diverse subjects as environmental studies, ethics, political science, and urban studies. The *Social Sciences Index* indexes over 625 publications from 1983 to the present. *Social Sciences Index Retrospective 1907–1982*, which provides electronic access to the retrospective indexing of social science journals, is also available.

Sociological Abstracts (ProQuest/CSA) is a resource for literature in the social and behavioral sciences that includes a wide variety of sociological research. With back files to 1952 it provides indexing and abstracting of articles in more than 2,000 journals as well as books, conference papers, and dissertations. The subjects covered include culture and social structure, family and social welfare, rural and urban sociology, and social development. *SocINDEX* (EBSCO), with full text that complements *Sociological Abstracts*, also covers many aspects of sociology including criminology, ethnic and racial studies, and gender studies. Full text is available for 860 journals as far back as 1908 as well as books and conference papers. Author profiles are available for the most prolific and cited authors. Produced by the National Association of Social Workers, *Social Work Abstracts* (EBSCO) indexes over 900 journals and dissertations providing citations and abstracts. This index covers a wide range of subjects in the social work field including homelessness, child and family welfare, aging, and substance abuse.

PAIS International, published since 1914, covers such subjects as government, legislation, public policy, economics, sociology and political science. The online version begins in 1972. Now owned by ProQuest/CSA, it indexes journals as well as books, government documents, gray literature, research reports, and conference reports. As its title suggests, it is international in scope and indexes material in English, French, German, Italian, Portuguese, and Spanish. Although this is an index only, not a full-text source, it is a very good one indexing material not found elsewhere. *PAIS Archive 1915–1976* is also now available, providing a historical perspective on many social and public policy issues.

Project MUSE is a collection of more than 400 not-for-profit scholarly journals that can be searched across the full text of all the journals or one journal at a time. It provides both citations and abstracts and full text. Although in many ways a multidisciplinary database covering the arts and humanities, the social sciences and even mathematics, its strength is in the social sciences. Johns Hopkins University Press manages this venture that includes journals from the United States and abroad including Duke University Press, Indiana University Press, Edinburgh University Press, and the Liverpool University Press.

SIRS Researcher (ProQuest) is a reprint service providing full-text material from more than 1,600 magazines, newspapers, journals, and government publications with a focus on social sciences, economics, political science, and current events worldwide. This database index is designed for high schools and community colleges. It does not index complete journals or newspapers, but instead selectively indexes articles.

Historical Abstracts (ABC-CLIO) is a historical bibliography of world history from 1450 to the present (excluding the United States and Canada). It includes English language abstracts from journals of history and the social sciences and articles from academic historical journals since 1955 in more than forty languages. For the most part it provides only citations and abstracts; it does provide links to articles through open URL compliance. It is multidisciplinary in approach and can be used for researching sociology, psychology, women's studies/gender studies, religion, anthropology, political science, multicultural studies, etc. Citations for books and dissertations are also included.

America: History and Life (ABC-CLIO) provides citations, abstracts, and the full text of articles on U.S. and Canadian history and related fields from prehistory to the present in more than 1,700 journals. As with *Historical Abstracts, America: History and Life* is interdisciplinary and can be used to research many different disciplines including cultural studies, gender studies and literary studies. There are links to more than 215,000 articles.

U.S. History in Context (formerly *History Resource Center: U.S.*) (Gale Cengage Learning) is a collection of primary source documents, reference documents, more than 2,000 photographs, maps, and illustrations, and full-text coverage of history-related scholarly journals. Person, time period, and subject can be searched. *World History in Context* (formerly *History Resource Center: World*) (Gale Cengage Learning) provides full-text primary and secondary sources for the study of world history for all countries and all parts of the world. If the library subscribes to both the U.S. and World databases, they can be cross searched.

Humanities Indexes

Humanities has been the last area to develop electronic resources, probably due to the nature of the scholarship that has relied more heavily on book material.

Humanities Full Text (Wilson) includes the full text of 250 journals from 1995 to date and indexes over 600 periodicals. The subjects covered include classical studies, history, literature and religion as well as original works of fiction, drama and poetry, book reviews and reviews of ballets, theatre, film, etc. The *Humanities and Social Science Index Retrospective: 1907–1983* electronic access is also available indexing the *International Index*, the *Humanities Index*, and the *Social Science Index*.

FRANCIS (ProQuest/CSA) is an international, multilingual database with citations and abstracts in English and French to more than 4,000 journals, books, and other documents. The coverage includes the humanities and social sciences with an emphasis on European publications. The *ATLA Religion Database*, published by the American Theological Library Association, indexes journals representing all major religions and denominations. Its wide coverage extends to archeology and social issues as well as art. More than 1,600 journals with back files to 1908 are indexed.

Language and Literature Indexes

The Modern Language Association (MLA) produces the *MLA International Bibliography*. It is a subject index for literature and linguistics with more than 4,400 periodicals indexed as well as books and dissertations. The *Bibliography* dates back to the 1920s, but the online version dates from 1963. It is international in scope and includes bibliographic records in French, Spanish, German, Russian, Portuguese, Norwegian, and Swedish. The *MLA International Bibliography* has its own thesaurus. It is an excellent index for researching literary criticism or any other aspect of literature even though it does not have full text. It is available through several database vendors.

Two literature resources, *Literature Resource Center* and *Literature Online*, are the result of integrating several literature databases into one easy-to-search database. *Literature Resource Center* (Gale Cengage) combines three major Gale databases, *Contemporary Authors*, *Dictionary of Literary Biography*, and *Contemporary Literary Criticism*, into one large searchable full-text database. Users can search for both literary criticism from periodicals and books and biographical information about authors. *Literature Online* (ProQuest/Chadwyck Healey) is also a collection of full-text literary criticism and reference materials as well as the full text of poetry, prose, and drama in English. It includes *ABELL* (*Annual Bibliography of English Language and Literature*) that provides full-text access to 312 current literary journals. *Linguistics and Language Behavior Abstracts* (ProQuest/CSA) covers all aspects of the international literature on linguistics and the language sciences providing citations and abstracts to journals, books and dissertations.

Music Indexes

The world of music scholarship is represented by two indexes. The *Music Index Online* covers 850 music periodicals from many countries with subject and author indexing. This index includes all aspects of music and musicians. The original print index began in 1949; the digitized content began in 1973. *RILM*

Abstracts of Music Literature provides citations and abstracts for more than 950 scholarly journals as well as books, bibliographies, conference proceedings, dissertations, films, videos, and much more beginning in 1967.

Art Indexes

Art has three strong indexes that complement one another. Used together they provide wide coverage in art. *Art Full Text* (Wilson) includes the full text of articles from more than 270 journals from 1997 to the present, as well as article abstracts and indexing of 500 publications from 1984 to the present. It is international in scope including material in languages other than English and a wide variety of subjects including antiques, architecture, art history, costume, and crafts. *Art Index Retrospective: 1929–1984* is also available, providing indexing to more than 600 publications.

ARTbibliographies Modern (ProQuest/CSA) provides indexing and abstracts for journal articles, books, exhibition catalogs, PhD dissertations, and exhibition reviews on all aspects of modern and contemporary art including crafts, photography, theatre arts and fashion, as well as painting and sculpture from the nineteenth century forward. The coverage dates from 1974. Material in both English and in sixteen other languages is included. This index has a well-developed thesaurus.

The *International Bibliography of Art* (ProQuest/CSA) is a bibliography of scholarly writing about the history of western art. It is the successor to the *Bibliography of the History of Art*. All aspects of art are covered from paintings and sculpture to crafts and folk art. Indexing more than 500 journals, the citations include detailed abstracts. This bibliography is the successor to *Repertoire d'Art et d'Archeologie* from 1973–1980 and the *International Repertory of the Literature of Art* from 1973–1989.

Library and Information Science Indexes

Library science indexes include *Library Literature & Information Science Full Text*, *Library and Information Science Abstracts*, and *Library, Information Science and Technology Abstracts* (LISTA) and *Library, Information Science and Technology Abstracts with Full Text*. *Library Literature & Information Science Full Text* (Wilson) includes periodical articles, conference proceedings, pamphlets, books, and theses on library science. *Library Literature* indexes 400 periodicals dating back to 1984 with full text of articles from 155 periodicals back to 1997. It is international in scope and can be searched by keywords, subject headings, personal names, title words, publication, year, and type of article. *Library Literature & Information Science Retrospective: 1905–1983* provides electronic access to the early years of this index.

Library and Information Science Abstracts (ProQuest/CSA) is an international index with abstracts of over 440 periodicals from more than sixty-eight countries in more than twenty languages beginning in 1969. It covers all aspects of library science and information science. LISA has its own online thesaurus.

LISTA (*Library, Information Science and Technology Abstracts*) (EBSCO) is an index with abstracts of journal articles, books, research reports, and conference proceedings. *LISTA* covers librarianship, classification, bibliometrics, information retrieval, and information management. *Library, Information Science and Technology Abstracts with Full Text* provides full text for more than 560 journals and some monographs.

Psychology Indexes

PsycINFO, published by the American Psychological Association since 1967, has long been a major index in the field of psychology. It is arranged into twenty-two major categories including psychological, social, and behavioral sciences and related fields such as psychiatry, neuroscience, medicine, and social work. The scholarly, peer-reviewed, online bibliographic index provides comprehensive coverage of more than 1,000 journal titles relevant to psychology and covers more than 1,800 titles including books, dissertations, and reports. The publications included come from more than fifty countries in twenty-eight languages. Each listing includes the bibliographic citation and abstract. A separate thesaurus guides users through the subject headings. A separate database, *PsycArticles*, was developed to provide full-text access to the articles from more than eighty journals. Most go back to volume 1. *PsycINFO* is available from several of the major database vendors.

Psychology journals can also be searched through EBSCO's *Psychology and Behavioral Science Collection*, a comprehensive database with about 400 full-text titles covering topics such as emotional and behavioral characteristics, psychiatry and psychology, mental processes, anthropology, and observational and experimental methods. EBSCO's *Academic Search Complete, ProQuest Central*, and Gale's *Health Reference Center* are also sources of information on psychology.

Ethnic Indexes

The *International Index to Black Periodicals Full Text* (ProQuest/Chadwyck Healey), an index to scholarly and popular material in Black Studies, began in 1902. There are citations for retrospective records from 1902–1997. From 1998 forward there are citations and abstracts for 150 journals, newspapers, and newsletters published in the United States, Africa, and the Caribbean as well as full-text coverage of forty-two core Black Studies titles. This index provides bibliographic and full-text resources for a wide range of related issues including economics, history, religion, sociology, and political science. It is both international and interdisciplinary in scope.

EthnicNewsWatch (ProQuest/CSA) is a full-text online database that covers 1990 to the present. It includes a wide variety of newspapers, magazines and journals from the ethnic, minority and native presses. A total of 315 titles are now indexed in subject areas ranging from history and politics to the humanities and social sciences. It is searchable in both English and Spanish with titles in both languages. This unique database provides the researcher with alternate points of view on subjects of current interest.

Hispanic American Periodicals Index Online (*HAPI*) indexes and abstracts books, articles, reviews, bibliographies, literary works, and material appearing in 500 scholarly journals published in Latin America, the Caribbean, and in the United States from 1970 to the present. It is available online and links to full-text articles. *HAPI* is produced by the UCLA Latin American Center.

Business and Medical Indexes

Among the excellent business indexes are *Business Source* (EBSCO), *ABI/ INFORM Complete* (ProQuest), *Business and Company ASAP* (Gale Cengage Learning), *Factiva* and *Business Full Text* (Wilson). These business indexes offer the librarian and user a good deal of choice. These indexes are discussed in more depth in Chapter 9 as are the following medical and consumer health indexes: *PubMed, Health Source* (EBSCO), *Health Reference Center* and *Health and Wellness Resource Center* (Gale Cengage Learning), and CINAHL.

Open Access Journals

The amount of full text in online databases has grown due to the open-access journals. These journals, produced with alternative business plans so that the user does not have to pay for access, are particularly important in the sciences. Many are to be found through Highwire Press (http://highwire.stanford.edu) and through the Directory of Open Access Journals (www.doaj.org); both of which can be searched by subject. Many government databases provide access to open-access journals and articles. They include arXive.org (http://xxx.lanl.gov/), which offers access to e-prints in the sciences; Department of Energy Information Bridge (http://www.osti.gov/bridge/), which provides full-text articles and bibliographic citations in all areas related to energy; E-Print Network (http://www.osti.gov/eprints) offering e-prints primarily in physics but also in related scientific areas; NIST Virtual Library (http://nvl.nist.gov), which includes databases and other information on chemistry research; and PubMed Central (http://www.pubmedcentral.nih .gov), which provides journal literature in the biomedical and life sciences.

Citation Indexes

Citation indexes are very useful to researchers since a researcher can follow an idea from the original writer to others who have cited the original writer in their work. A researcher can also determine which writers have influenced others or how a basic concept is now being used. Originally there were three citation indexes: the *Science Citation Index* (1900–present), the *Social Sciences Citation Index* (1956–present) and the *Arts and Humanities Citation Index* (1975–present). These three citation indexes plus *Index Chemicus* (1993–) and *Current Chemical Reactions* (1986–) are now part of *Web of Science* (Thomson Reuters), an international citation index with coverage of 10,000 authoritative journals with links to the full text of articles cited. Librarians should introduce their users to the *Web of Science* if they are writing substantial research papers.

Indexes to Special Types of Material

ProQuest Dissertations and Theses is a database in which U.S., Canadian, British, and European dissertations and master's theses from 1861 to the present are listed. Abstracts exist for dissertations since 1980 and theses abstracts began in 1988. Some full text is included. This is a valuable resource for researchers providing in-depth research on many subjects.

Essay and General Literature Index (Wilson) indexes books, about 300 single and multi-author collections and twenty selected annuals and serials annually. It is a unique source of essays found in book collections that include literary criticism and essays on a wide variety of subjects. The online coverage begins in 1985. Users can search by keyword, subject, title, author, and date of publication as well as by names of fictional characters and titles of literary works. This database has no full text but can be linked to the library's catalog.

Short Story Index (Wilson) indexes short stories by author, title, subject, genre and technique. The online version goes back to 1984. This work indexes both collections of short stories and stories from 150 periodicals indexed by the *Readers' Guide* and *Humanities Index*. Most of this index simply provides bibliographic information, but there is full text for 5,000 stories. This index helps the user to locate short stories that are in multi-author collections or in periodicals.

The Play Index (Wilson) is now available electronically from 1949 to date. This valuable resource indexes more than 31,000 plays published individually or in collections. Full-length plays, radio and television plays, and one-act plays are indexed. Users can search by author, title, subject, style, genre, and cast type. This resource provides the librarian with a way to find individual plays in collections.

LitFinder (Gale Cengage Learning) is a source for finding the full text of poems, short stories, essays, speeches, and plays. This easy-to-use database allows searching by title, subject, author nationality, gender, and date. International in scope, it covers all time periods. Users can locate the text of more than 135,000 works of literature as well as additional information sources.

Book Review Digest has been published by H.W. Wilson since 1905. In addition to the bibliographic citation, each entry includes a summary of the book and excerpts from reviews. In order to be listed, a book must have two reviews of nonfiction and three reviews of fiction. *Book Review Digest Plus* is the electronic version covering 1983 to date and expanding the number of periodicals covered by adding entries from other Wilson indexes. Some full-text reviews are included in this version. This index is useful for readers' advisory work and collection development as well as finding reviews of books. *Book Review Digest Retrospective 1905–1982* provides the earlier years of *Book Review Digest*.

Book Review Index Online Plus (Gale Cengage Learning) includes the entire back file of the print index from 1965 to the present. More than 5.6 million review citations on more than 2.5 million titles are listed. There are links to full text from other Gale databases, and it does cover more titles than *Book Review Digest*.

The *Columbia Granger's World of Poetry* provides online access to more than 250,000 poems in full text with biographical information and critical essays. The poems are indexed by subject, first line, author, and title.

Indexes for Children and Young Adults

Librarians can choose from several indexes for young people. *Searchasaurus* combines several EBSCO databases, including *Primary Search, Middle Search Plus*, and *Book Collection: Nonfiction*. *Primary Search*, designed for elementary schools and children's rooms, is aimed at grades four through six. It provides full text of more than eighty of the most popular elementary school magazines. It indexes such titles as *Highlights for Children, National Geographic Kids, National Geographic World, Ranger Rick, Cricket*, and *Science World*. *Middle Search Plus*, designed for middle and junior high school students, is aimed at grades seven through nine. It provides full text of more than 140 popular middle school magazines. It indexes both kids' magazines and easy-to-read adult magazines such as *Time, National Geographic, Sports Illustrated, Popular Science*, and *Popular Mechanics*, as well as some reference book information. *Book Collection: Nonfiction* provides abstracts and full text of more than 4,000 popular nonfiction books.

eLibrary Elementary (ProQuest) offers 130 full-text magazines, newspapers, reference books, and transcripts as well as maps, images and multimedia resources concentrating on general interest areas including social science, general science, humanities and business. This index is aimed at K–6 students. *InfoTrac Junior Edition* (Gale Cengage Learning) is aimed at junior high and middle school students. This full-text online database indexes more than 300 general interest magazines of which 230 are full text. Newspaper articles are also included as are several reference sources including the *Columbia Encyclopedia, Merriam-Webster's Biographical Dictionary*, and *Merriam-Webster's Collegiate Dictionary* (10th Edition). *InfoTrac Student Edition* (Gale Cengage Learning), designed for secondary school students, indexes 1,200 magazines of which 1,100 are full text. It also includes newspaper articles, reference books, and maps on a wide spectrum of topics, along with some of the same reference works as *InfoTrac Junior Edition*. *Readers' Guide to Periodical Literature* (Wilson), discussed elsewhere in this chapter, is suitable for high school students.

Collection Development and Maintenance

Selection and Keeping Current

Indexes are expensive, so libraries must take care in selecting them. In many cases there is now more than one index in a particular subject area so that libraries have a choice and can make decisions based on the selection of materials indexed, the price, and other criteria that are important to a particular library.

Indexes continue to change rapidly as publishers try to expand their coverage and better fit their products to the market. Most index publishers have several products, usually for different types of libraries and often different size packages so libraries can choose which package they need and can afford. The publishers continue to develop new products as well as acquire smaller companies or form partnerships with other companies. Major publishers are also developing linking agreements in order to offer more full-text services to their users. This fast-changing field makes it difficult to keep current. Many periodicals such as *Library Journal, Computers for Libraries, Online,* and *Searcher* report on new index and database products. These same periodicals also include full-length articles from time to time summarizing the state of the field or a particular part of the field. The publishers themselves are active in contacting libraries as they develop new products or upgrade existing ones.

Evaluating Indexes

Due to the number of indexes now available, the evaluation of indexes requires a careful examination of a number of factors:

- Authority of publisher
- Scope/subjects covered
- Number and quality of periodicals/newspapers indexed
- Number of titles with full-text coverage
- Currency and frequency of updating
- Accuracy of citations
- Subject headings/controlled vocabulary and access points
- Statistics and training for staff
- Cost

The publisher of the index is of prime importance since the track record of a publisher will usually tell a great deal about what the librarian can expect in terms of quality. Librarians also want to be assured that the publisher will stay in business. This is particularly important with indexes since they are a major purchase, and the library needs assurance that the index will continue.

The librarian should consider the scope of the index, that is, the subjects covered and the beginning date of coverage. Often more than one choice in a subject area is available, so the librarians should strive to get the best fit of the subject coverage and the dates included for their particular library. The number of periodicals or newspapers indexed and their quality should be examined. This is not just a numbers game. Any publisher can state that it has more periodicals and newspapers indexed than another. But this can be a hollow statistic if the periodicals and newspapers indexed are not of good quality. In fact, indexing articles of lesser quality only serves to make it more difficult to find the better quality material. To determine where particular periodicals are indexed, *Ulrich's* or *Magazines for Libraries* can be checked. Since many indexes offer a great deal of full text, it is important to find out if full text is offered for the periodicals most needed. The librarian can check a resource such as *Fulltext Sources Online*. Sometimes none of the indexes offer the full text of a particular periodical because the publisher of the periodical has not agreed to it. But sometimes only one index has the rights to a certain periodical that is in high demand. Another issue surrounding full text is whether the whole periodical has been included in the full text. Sometimes only the main articles in a periodical are provided while smaller articles, columns, letters to the editor, and even book reviews are omitted.

The currency of the index is of utmost importance, as is the frequency of the updating. Unfortunately one cannot assume that just because an index is available electronically that it is up-to-date. Pick a current subject in the news and check it out in several indexes to determine how fast they are updating their indexes. One should also note the accuracy of the indexing, especially the bibliographic citations. Frequent errors indicate that the quality control of the index is below acceptable standards.

Examine the consistency and the depth of the subject headings used. Many indexes use the Library of Congress Subject Headings or the Sears List of Subject Headings. Other subject-based indexes such as the *MLA International Bibliography* and *PsycINFO* develop a thesaurus to provide more specificity in the range of subject headings offered. The use of controlled vocabulary in order to have consistency is important to an index so using an authoritative list of subject headings is absolutely necessary.

Compare the searching power of various indexes. Are some of them more user friendly than others? Do they use Boolean searching? Note whether it is easy to find what you want.

Some services are not seen by the public but are important to the librarian. First, the library needs to have statistics on the use of each index. The company producing the index must be able to supply these statistics on a regular basis to enable the library to determine how much each index is being used. Second is the issue of training staff. Since each index is slightly different from the other, staff needs training on each new index. Many companies are prepared to send a trainer to introduce the index to the staff. This is an important benefit.

Finally there is the cost. Costs vary tremendously, and most publishers negotiate individually with a library or group of libraries. Publishers usually have more than one way of determining the cost, so it is wise to be familiar with the various possibilities. Many now offer flat fees for their databases. Often publishers' fees are based on the size of a user group. For example, in a university, it might be based on the number of students and faculty. Sometimes companies offer "pay per view" plans to attract infrequent users. Publishers may also be willing to charge based on simultaneous uses. In this case the library pays for a certain number of simultaneous uses depending on how much they judge the database will be used. In any case, costs can be steep and for this reason libraries often join consortia so that the price for the database can be spread over several libraries and thus lower the cost.

Further Considerations

What to Do When There Is No Full Text

Users have become accustomed to having full text in indexes. But not all indexes have full text. For example, the Wilson indexes have some full text but not for all citations. Also the *MLA International Bibliography*, an essential index for those researching literature, has no full text. So what is a librarian or a user to do? First, the software programs Serials Solutions or EBSCO A-Z can be used to find out if the full text of an article is available in another database owned by the library. New software, link resolvers, can be used to direct the user to full text of an article in another database owned by the library. If the library does not own the full text online, the librarian should turn to the library's print collection to see if the periodical is owned by the library and is available in bound volumes or in microform. If this is also unsuccessful, the library must either order the article through interlibrary loan or turn to a document delivery service such as Ingentaconnect (www.ingentaconnect.com), ISI Document Solution (http://ids.isinet.com), or the British Library Direct (http://blorderform.bl.uk) and purchase the needed article.

Searching

One of the most difficult parts of the rich array of general and subject databases is that the searching protocols differ from company to company and from database to database. Librarians must become familiar with the databases owned by their library. Librarians in an institution often work together to become knowledgeable about databases. Each studies different databases and then shares the information with the others. It is important to look at both the similarities and differences between databases. Librarians need to know the basics of doing a search in each database and understand some of the useful additional features. Many vendors will provide training on their databases, and libraries should take advantage of this.

Final Thoughts

Index databases are one of the most useful and most popular reference tools available in a library. The advent of so much full text has made it much easier for the user to find the full text of articles. Each new software innovation makes it even more seamless to the user, who is always in a hurry. As more index databases develop, librarians can make more careful choices. Just as with reference books, duplication in databases is not always necessary. Libraries need to develop plans and annually reevaluate their holdings including looking at use statistics for each index.

Recommended Resources Discussed in This Chapter

Academic OneFile. Farmington Hills, MI: Gale Cengage Learning. Subscription. Available: www.gale.com.
Academic Search Complete. Ipswich, MA: EBSCO. Subscription. Available: www.ebscohost.com.
Academic Search Elite. Ipswich, MA: EBSCO. Subscription. Available: www.ebscohost.com.

Academic Search Premier. Ipswich, MA: EBSCO. Subscription. Available: www
    .ebscohost.com.
Access: The Supplementary Index to Periodicals. 1975–. Evanston, IL: John Gordon
    Burke Publisher. Available: www.jgburkepub.com.
Access World News. Naples, FL: Newsbank. Subscription. Available: www.news
    bank.com.
ACM Digital Library. 1985–. Association for Computing Machinery. Subscrip-
    tion. Available: http://portal.acm.org/dl.cfm.
Alternative Press Index. 1969–. Baltimore, MD: Alternative Press Center. Sub-
    scription. Available in print or online: www.altpress.org.
America: History and Life. 1964–. Santa Barbara, CA: ABC-CLIO. Subscription.
    Available: www.abc-clio.com.
America's News. Naples, FL: Newsbank. Subscription. Available: www.newsbank
    .com.
Applied Science & Technology Full Text. 1997–. New York: H.W. Wilson. Sub-
    scription. Available: www.hwwilson.com.

THE TOP TEN INDEXES		
Title	**Print**	**Online**
Academic Search Premier		Subscription www.ebscohost.com
Alternative Press Index, 1969– Baltimore, MD: Alternative Press Center	Quarterly	Subscription www.altpress.org
Dialog 1 Cary, NC: Thomson Reuters		Subscription www.dialog.com
Expanded Academic ASAP Farmington, MI: Gale Cengage Learning		Subscription www.gale.com
First Search Dublin, OH: OCLC		Subscription www.oclc.org
JSTOR		www.jstor.org
LexisNexis Academic Bethesda, MD: LexisNexis Academic & Library Solutions		Subscription www.lexisnexis.com
ProQuest Newsstand Ann Arbor, MI: ProQuest		Subscription www.ProQuest.com
ProQuest Research Library Ann Arbor, MI: ProQuest		Subscription www.ProQuest.com
Wilson Omnifile Full Text, 1982– Bronx, NY: H.W. Wilson		Subscription www.hwwilson.com

---

RECOMMENDED FREE WEB SITES

Directory of Open Access Journals. Available: www.doaj.org. Through this database open-access articles can be searched.

ERIC. Available: www.eric.ed.gov. This excellent education database produced by the U.S. Department of Education is available at no charge.

Google Scholar. Available: http://scholar.google.com. This site indexes a wide variety of journal articles. Some full text is available free of charge.

Highwire Press. Available: http://highwire.stanford.edu. This site provides free access to many journal articles.

LISTA Abstracts. Available: www.libraryresearch.com. This is the LISTA database available at no charge.

Applied Science & Technology Retrospective 1913–1983. New York: H.W. Wilson. Subscription. Available: www.hwwilson.com.

Art Full Text. 1983–. New York: H.W. Wilson. Subscription. Available: www .hwwilson.com.

Art Index Retrospective. 1929–1984. New York: H.W. Wilson. Subscription. Available: www.hwwilson.com.

ARTbibliographies Modern. 1974–. Ann Arbor, MI: ProQuest/CSA. Subscription. Available: www.ProQuest.com.

Article First. Dublin, OH: OCLC. Subscription. Available: www.oclc.org.

ATLA Religion Database. 1949–. Ann Arbor, MI: ProQuest/CSA. Subscription. Available: www.ProQuest.com.

Biology Digest. 1989–. Medford, NJ: Plexus Publishing. Subscription. Available online through Newsbank: www.newsbank.com.

Biosis Previews. 1990–. Philadelphia, PA: Thomson Reuters. Subscription. Available: www.thomsonscientific.com.

Book Review Digest. 1905–. New York: H.W. Wilson. Subscription. Available: www.hwwilson.com.

Book Review Digest Plus. 1983–. New York: H.W. Wilson. Subscription. Available: www.hwwilson.com.

Book Review Digest Retrospective 1905–1982. New York: H.W. Wilson. Subscription. Available: www.hwwilson.com.

Book Review Index Online Plus. 1965–. Farmington Hills, MI: Gale Cengage Learning. Subscription. Available: www.gale.com.

CBCA Complete. Ann Arbor, MI: ProQuest. Subscription. Available: www.ProQuest .com.

Columbia Granger's World of Poetry. New York: Columbia University Press. Subscription. Available: http://cup.columbia.edu.

DialogClassic. Ann Arbor, MI: ProQuest. Subscription. Available: www.dialog.com.

Dialog 1. Ann Arbor, MI: ProQuest. Subscription. Available: www.dialog.com.

Education Full Text. 1983–. New York: H.W. Wilson. Subscription. Available: www.hwwilson.com.

Education Index Retrospective: 1929–1983. New York: H.W. Wilson. Subscription. Available in print and online: www.hwwilson.com.

Electronic Collections Online. Dublin, OH: OCLC. Subscription. Available: www
.oclc.org.

eLibrary. Ann Arbor, MI: ProQuest. Subscription. Available: www.ProQuest
.com.

ERIC. 1966–. Washington, DC: U.S. Department of Education. Free. Available:
www.eric.ed.gov.

Essay and General Literature Index. 1985–. New York: H.W. Wilson. Subscription.
Available: www.hwwilson.com.

Ethnic NewsWatch. 1991–. Ann Arbor, MI: ProQuest. Subscription. Available:
www.ProQuest.com.

Expanded Academic ASAP. Farmington Hills, MI: Gale Cengage Learning. Subscription. Available: www.gale.com.

First Search. Dublin, OH: OCLC. Subscription. Available: www.oclc.org.

FRANCIS. 1984–. Ann Arbor, MI: ProQuest/CSA. Subscription. Available:
www.ProQuest.com.

Gale Custom Newspapers. Farmington Hills, MI: Gale Cengage Learning. Subscription. Available: www.gale.com.

General OneFile. Farmington Hills, MI: Gale Cengage Learning. Subscription.
Available: www.gale.com.

General Science Full Text. 1984–. New York: H.W. Wilson. Subscription. Available: www.hwwilson.com.

GeoRef. 1966–. Ann Arbor, MI: ProQuest/CSA. Subscription. Available:
www.ProQuest.com.

Google Scholar. Free. Available: http://scholar.google.com.

Hispanic American Periodicals Index Online. 1970–. Los Angeles: UCLA Latin
American Center Publications. Subscription. Available: http://hapi.ucla
.edu.

Historical Abstracts. 1955–. Santa Barbara, CA: ABC-CLIO. Subscription. Available: www.abc-clio.com.

Humanities Full Text. 1984–. New York: H.W. Wilson. Subscription. Available:
www.hwwilson.com.

Humanities & Social Science Index Retrospective: 1907–1983. New York: H.W.
Wilson. Subscription. Available: www.hwwilson.com.

IEEE Xplore. 1988–. IEEE/IEE (Institute of Electrical and Electronics Engineers
and the Institution of Engineering and Technology). Subscription. Available: http://ieeexplore.ieee.org.

InfoTrac Junior Edition. Farmington Hills, MI: Gale Cengage Learning. Subscription. Available: www.gale.com.

InfoTrac Newstand. Farmington Hills, MI: Gale Cengage Learning. Subscription.
Available: www.gale.com.

InfoTrac Student Edition. Farmington Hills, MI: Gale Cengage Learning. Subscription. Available: www.gale.com.

INSPEC. 1969–. Institution of Electrical Engineers. Subscription. Available:
www.theiet.org/publishing/inspec/.

International Bibliography of Art. 2008–. Ann Arbor, MI: ProQuest/CSA. Subscription. Available: www.ProQuest.com.

International Index to Black Periodicals Full Text. Ann Arbor, MI: ProQuest. Subscription. Available: www.ProQuest.com.

JSTOR. Subscription. Available: www.jstor.org.

Language and Linguistics Behavioral Abstracts. Ann Arbor, MI: ProQuest/CSA. Subscription. Available: www.ProQuest.com.

LexisNexis Academic. Bethesda, MD: LexisNexis Academic & Library Solutions. Subscription: Available: www.lexisnexis.com.

LexisNexis Library Express. Bethesda, MD: LexisNexis Academic & Library Solutions. Subscription. Available: www.lexisnexis.com.

Library and Information Science Abstracts. 1969–. Ann Arbor, MI: ProQuest. Subscription. Available: www.ProQuest.com.

Library, Information Science & Technology Abstracts (LISTA). Ipswich, MA: EBSCO. Subscription. Available: www.ebscohost.com.

Library, Information Science & Technology Abstracts with Full Text. Ipswich, MA: EBSCO. Subscription: Available: www.ebscohost.com.

Library Literature & Information Science Full Text. 1984–. New York: H.W. Wilson. Subscription. Available: www.hwwilson.com.

Library Literature and Information Science Retrospective: 1905–1983. New York: H.W. Wilson. Subscription. Available: www.hwwilson.com.

Literature Online (LION). Ann Arbor, MI: ProQuest/Chadwyck Healey. Subscription. Available: www.ProQuest.com.

Literature Resource Center. Farmington Hill, MI: Gale Cengage Learning. Subscription. Available: www.gale.com.

LitFinder. Farmington Hill, MI: Gale Cengage Learning. Subscription. Available: www.gale.com.

MasterFILE Complete. Ipswich, MA: EBSCO. Subscription. Available: www.ebscohost.com.

MasterFILE Elite. Ipswich, MA: EBSCO. Subscription. Available: www.ebscohost.com.

MasterFILE Premier. Ipswich, MA: EBSCO. Subscription. Available: www.ebscohost.com.

MathSciNet. 1940–. American Mathematical Society. Subscription. Available: www.ams.org.

Middle Search Plus. Ipswich, MA: EBSCO. Subscription. Available: www.ebscohost.com.

MLA International Bibliography. 1922–. New York: Modern Language Association. Subscription. Available (multiple vendors): www.mla.org/bibliography/.

Music Index Online. 1973–. Harmonie Park Press. Subscription. Available (through EBSCO): www.harmonieparkpress.com.

Newspaper Source Plus. Ipswich, MA: EBSCO. Subscription. Available: www.ebscohost.com.

Oceanic Abstracts. 1981–. Ann Arbor, MI: ProQuest/CSA. Subscription. Available: www.ProQuest.com.

PAIS Archive 1915–1976. Ann Arbor, MI: ProQuest/CSA. Subscription. Available: www.ProQuest.com.

PAIS International. 1972–. Ann Arbor, MI: ProQuest/CSA. Subscription. Available: www.ProQuest.com.

The Play Index. 1949–. New York: H.W. Wilson. Subscription. Available: www.hwwilson.com.

Poole's Index to Periodical Literature. Boston: Houghton Mifflin, 1802–1906.

Primary Search. Ipswich, MA: EBSCO. Subscription. Available: www.ebscohost.com.

Project MUSE. Baltimore: Johns Hopkins University Press. Subscription. Available: http://muse.jhu.edu.

ProQuest Central. Ann Arbor, MI: ProQuest. Subscription. Available: www.ProQuest.com.

ProQuest Dissertations and Theses. Ann Arbor, MI: ProQuest. Subscription. Available: www.ProQuest.com.

ProQuest Historical Newspapers. Ann Arbor, MI: ProQuest. Subscription. Available: www.ProQuest.com.

ProQuest Newsstand. 1977–. Ann Arbor, MI: ProQuest. Subscription. Available: www.ProQuest.com.

ProQuest Research Library. 1989–. Ann Arbor, MI: ProQuest. Subscription. Available: www.ProQuest.com.

PsycArticles. 1988–. Washington, DC: American Psychological Association. Subscription. Available: www.apa.org.

Psychology and Behavioral Science Collection. Ipswich, MA: EBSCO. Subscription. Available: www.ebscohost.com.

PsycINFO. 1967–. Washington, DC: American Psychological Association. Subscription. Available (from multiple vendors): www.apa.org.

Reader's Guide Abstracts. New York: H.W. Wilson. Subscription. Available: www.hwwilson.com.

Reader's Guide Full Text. 1994–. New York: H.W. Wilson. Subscription. Available: www.hwwilson.com.

Reader's Guide Retrospective 1890–1982. New York: H.W. Wilson. Subscription. Available: www.hwwilson.com.

Reader's Guide to Periodical Literature. 1890–. New York: H.W. Wilson.

Répertoire International de Littérature Musicale (RILM). 1967–. Ipswich, MA: EBSCO. Subscription. Available: www.ebscohost.com.

Science Full Text Select. New York: H.W. Wilson. Subscription. Available: www.hwwilson.com.

Science in Context. Farmington Hills, MI: Gale Cengage Learning. Subscription. Available: www.gale.cengage.com.

SciFinder Scholar. 1907–. Columbus, OH: American Chemical Society. Subscription. Available: www.acs.org.

Scopus. New York: Reed Elsevier. Subscription. Available: www.scopus.com.

Searchasaurus. Ipswich, MA: EBSCO. Subscription. Available: www.ebscohost.com.

Short Story Index. 1984–. New York: H.W. Wilson. Subscription. Available: www.hwwilson.com.

SIRS Researcher. 1988–. Ann Arbor, MI: ProQuest. Subscription. Available: www.hwwilson.com.

Social Sciences Full Text. 1995–. New York: H.W. Wilson. Subscription. Available: www.hwwilson.com.

Social Sciences Index Retrospective 1907–1982. New York: H.W. Wilson. Subscription. Available: www.hwwilson.com.

Social Work Abstracts. Washington, DC: National Association of Social Workers Press. Subscription. Available:. www.naswpress.org.

SocIndex. Ipswich, MA: Subscription: Available: EBSCO.www.ebscohost .com.

Sociological Abstracts. 1952–. Ann Arbor, MI: ProQuest/CSA. Subscription. Available: www.ProQuest.com.

U.S. History in Context. Farmington, MI: Gale Cengage Learning. Subscription. Available: www.gale.cengage.com.

Web of Science. Philadelphia, PA: Thomson Reuters. (Combines Science Citation Index, Social Science Citation Index, and Arts and Humanities Citation Index.) Subscription. Available: www.thomasscientific.com.

Wilson Omnifile Full Text. 1982–. New York: H.W. Wilson. Subscription. Available: www.hwwilson.com.

World History in Context. Farmington, MI: Gale Cengage Learning. Subscription. Available: www.gale.cengage.com.

Zoological Record Plus. Ann Arbor, MI: ProQuest/CSA. Subscription. Available: www.ProQuest.com.

Recommendations for Further Reading

Bucknall, Tim. 2005. "Getting More from Your Electronic Collections Through Studies of User Behavior." *Against the Grain* 17, no. 5 (November): 1, 18–20. Discussion of ways libraries can increase use of electronic resources by using such technologies as link resolvers.

Chen, Xiaotian. 2005. "Figures and Tables Omitted from Online Periodical Articles: A Comparison of Vendors and Information Missing from Full-Text Databases." *Internet Reference Services Quarterly* 10, no. 2: 75–88. A comparison of vendors of full-text databases and how they deal with charts, diagrams, figures, and tables that were part of the original periodical articles. Focus of article is on databases from EBSCO, Factiva, First Search, Gale, LexisNexis, ProQuest, and Wilson.

Mi, Jia, and Frederick Nesta. "The Missing Link: Context Loss in Online Databases." *The Journal of Academic Librarianship* 31, no. 6 (November 2005): 578–585. A study of online databases and how the context of an article is sometimes lost with suggestions as ways publishers could index articles to maintain the context.

Persson, Dorothy, and Carlette Washington-Hoagland. 2004. "PsycINFO Tutorial: A Viable Instructional Alternative." *Reference & User Services Quarterly* 44, no. 1 (Fall): 46–56. An evaluation of the effectiveness of a tutorial developed to increase students' understanding of PsycINFO.

Tenopir, Carol, and Donald W. King. 2002. "Reading Behaviour and Electronic Journals." *Learned Publishing* (October): 259–265. A study of the use of scholarly journals by scientists. The authors found that scientists are reading traditional journals both in print and electronic format as well as other electronic sources of information.

Tyler, David C., Signe O. Boudreau, and Susan M. Leach. 2005. "The Communications Studies Researcher and the Communications Studies Indexes." *Behavioral & Social Sciences Literature* 23, no. 2: 19–46. A comparison of the online specialty indexes and the large, multisubject databases showing that the multisubject databases perform better.

Bibliography of Works Cited in This Chapter

Diakoff, Harry. 2004. "Database Indexing: Yesterday and Today." *The Indexer* 24, no. 1 (October): 85–88.

Golderman, Gail, and Bruce Connolly. 2003. "One-Stop Shopping." *NetConnect* (Summer): 30–35.

Machovec, George. 1995. "Identifying Emerging Technologies." In *The Impact of Emerging Technologies on Reference Services and Bibliographic Instruction*, edited by Gary M. Pitkin (pp. 1–24). Westport, CT: Greenwood Press.

9

Answering Questions about Health, Law, and Business— Special Guidelines and Sources

Overview

Medical, legal, and business questions constitute one of the most specialized, sensitive, and expensive areas of reference. The eternal realities of birth, death, and taxes that color all human existence feed inexorably into an urgent and steady stream of questions on health, legalities, personal finance, and business.

> *"I have taken only one abortion pill, but wish to stop. Will that affect my pregnancy?"*
> Hmm...
>
> *"If I donate my house to charity, will I fall below the poverty line so I could apply for Medicaid?"*
> Well...
>
> *"What was the value of $300 in 1829 America relative to the current dollar in terms of the Consumer Price Index and the GDP per capita?"*
> Er...

Like most medical, legal, and business questions, these three demonstrate the hallmarks that mark this as a "handle with care" area of reference work.

- The questions are invariably weighty.
- The answers are typically multilevel so that some degree of specialized knowledge becomes necessary.
- A strong code of ethics must govern the answers.
- The resources swallow a significant percent of reference budgets and require constant updates.
- Finally, and most important, reference librarians, who are trained in the art and science of answering questions, must be constantly aware that they are nonspecialists and should calibrate their responses accordingly.

A careful balance that requires pre-established parameters of appropriate service combined with in-depth knowledge of available reference resources and referrals is the responsibility of every reference librarian. The American Library Association (ALA) recognizes this responsibility; In 1992 a set of specific guidelines for medical, legal, and business responses was prepared and subsequently updated. It is a useful reminder that the stated role of the reference staff is a vital first step in organizing reference services in these areas. "Libraries should develop written disclaimers.... The level of assistance and interpretation provided to users should reflect differing degrees of subject expertise between specialists and non-specialists" (ALA—updated 2001). Why is the line between the specialist and the nonspecialist so important in these areas? After all, librarians have unflinchingly responded to questions about SQml, Kantian metaphysics, electrical codes, and pointillism without any specialized knowledge of computer science, philosophy, construction, or art. The answer lies in the nature of the beast.

How Medical, Legal, and Business Resources Are Used

The Nature of the Beast

Medical, legal, and business questions are of a different order based on seven characteristics distinctive of these three areas of research.

Criticality

The psychologist Abraham Maslow had argued that there was a hierarchy of needs so humans would fulfill their wish to be a ballerina, for example, only if they had first fulfilled their need for basic security. So also, there is a hierarchy of criticality in providing the right reference resource. In all probability, the obsolete cancer resource has far more of a negative impact than an obsolete book of linguistics. The right resource for the pro se litigant battling for child custody is potentially more critical than the right resource for dining etiquette. Medical, legal, and business issues, while not always of dramatically inflated consequence, have a powerful built-in predilection for criticality. The issues they cover can conceivably fall into Maslow's first level of need (health, financial, and civic security) and must be recognized as such.

Knowledge

A medical doctor takes approximately six years to complete a professional education, and a lawyer is ready to face the bar after three years of specialized study. The level of professionalism is marked by a distinctive and highly specialized vocabulary. Given the density, even consumerist keys to the information can require further decoding. The traditional crutches used by reference librarians while searching in unfamiliar territory, namely the index, table of contents, or "About" icons on a Web site, are sometimes not enough, so that "staff must have the knowledge and preparation appropriate to meet the routine legal, medical, and business information needs of their clientele" (ALA Guidelines 2001). It helps, for example, to know how a bill passes into public law, so that when a user wants to know more about a citation preceded by

"P.L." rather than "H.R.," the librarian is clear about looking into laws rather than resolutions. A crash course in basic legal structure is possible through publications like *Legal Research in a Nutshell* or *Legal Research for Beginners*. Business resources such as investment reports can be deciphered after a quick study of guides such as *Business Information: How to Find It, How to Use It*.

Restraint

However knowledgeable the librarians, they can only play "doctor on television." Even lawyers who have become librarians, of whom there appear to be an appreciable number, must show restraint in the dispensing of legal advice. Instead, the role of providing guidance to resources and instruction in the use of resources must be adopted both formally as a written directive and behaviorally. The latter can be very hard to do given the neediness and urgency of many users. A strong referral system and relevant pathfinders are both a necessary antidote and a mandatory addition to medical, legal, and business reference services.

Ethics

The "guess what" quotient of medical, legal and business questions can be high. "Guess what, that woman is going through a messy divorce... that teen wants a book on the treatment of syphilis... that man wants to invest in Saudi oil." Discussing patron issues with coworkers must be scrupulously avoided. Questions can be of a highly personal nature, and confidentiality must be consciously maintained. In addition, the best possible resource recommendation is dependent on a successful interview, so that tact in conducting the interview is a necessity. The user must feel comfortable about providing the fullest possible information relevant to the question.

Volume

It is no accident that there are specialized libraries devoted to medical, legal, and business collections. The demand for this information is high. As the hapless pages in even nonspecialized public libraries will attest, it is the 300 and the 600 section of the collection that is in never-ending need of shelving and shelf alignment. The 300s and 600s are the meat of public libraries primarily because the volume of questions is significant. Publishers, too, have realized this, as attested by the staggering 7,382 medical consumer books published in 2004. A survey conducted by Pew in 2008 also corroborated consumer interest in health with the statistic that between 75 and 80 percent of Internet users have looked online for medical information (Fox, 2008).

Updating

Given the premium on currency of resources in these areas, an inordinate number of print publications are loose-leaf, or require inserts and pocket parts, or are supplemented by regular updates. Reference librarians will need to set clear guidelines on discarding procedures and updating schedules, as well as monitor the correct placement of inserts and loose-leaf substitutions, pocket parts, or additions. The individual nature of these weekly, monthly, bimonthly, or quarterly additions, so unlike the simple edition updates of other reference material, further sets apart these three fields as a more specialized area of reference. Users who do not have to fumble through bloated *Value Line* binders that show no signs of the weekly inserts having been discarded; or miss out on an updated law because the annotated insert is not placed in the back pocket; or face rows of dusty *Mergent's Bond Records* because staff is not sure whether they are of "some use" are users who will appreciate the librarian's recognition that these resources require informed attention.

Expense

Once again, given the depth of information and overriding need for currency, a significant portion of reference budgets must be kept aside for medical, legal, and business resources. A single volume of *Weiss Ratings' Guides*, for example, may be between $250 and $300. However, the volume is redundant in four months, when a new quarterly appears.

Questions Answered by Medical, Legal, and Business Resources

The need to understand the nature of the beast is not so that the reference librarian shirks responsibility in tackling such questions, but approaches such questions with a full awareness of its necessary limiters.

Q: Can you find any recommendations for a Dr. Mount E. Bank, with whom I have a colonoscopy scheduled?

A: I could certainly find you a biographical sketch instead that lists his certifications and specialty background, in the *Official ABMS Directory of Board Certified Medical Specialists*.

Q: I am suing my contractor for bad faith. He claims it is a case of negligence. What is the difference and does it mean he can get away with shoddy construction?

A: *West's Encyclopedia of American Law* explains the difference between bad faith and negligence, but you do need professional legal representation to ensure your rights in the matter.

Q: Who are the five largest private employers in the United States and are they financially secure?

A: The U.S. Postal Service, Burger King, Express Personnel, Carlson, and Blue Cross are the five largest according to *Hoover's Handbook of Private Companies 2008*. You could analyze their financial viability by checking the revenue history, net incomes, background information, and structure as given in the Handbook.

Q: Are there any contraindications to the drug Coumadin?

A: Consult the latest copy of the *Physicians' Desk Reference* for information, and then I would suggest double-checking with your doctor or pharmacist.

Q: My lawyer left a message to say that inheriting my grandfather's mansion could be "damnosa hereditas." Is that good or bad?

A: Bad! "An injurious inheritance" is the definition given by *Black's Law Dictionary*, so you may want to check into the costs of inheriting it.

Clarity in defining the limits of what can and cannot be answered is critical to these areas of reference. A thorough knowledge of existing medical, legal, and business resources, such as the ones described below, goes a long way in encouraging clarity when faced with a user's real-life question.

Major Health Resources Used in Reference Work

The days of the family doctor who made house calls sounds like a long-forgotten myth in today's frenetic world of specialists and insurance-sensitive health systems. For better or for worse, consumer empowerment in health decisions is the order of the day and replaces the old unthinking reliance on the family doctor. Given this climate of empowerment, both the demand for and the supply of health information have reached epic proportions. The reference librarian therefore plays a vital role in slimming down the large amounts of information published and offering an improved selection of comprehensive and comprehensible medical information.

Medical Dictionaries

Inopexia and pallidotomy, cirrhonosus and amusia—the involved language created to describe the vast functions and malfunctions of the human body is almost mystical in its incomprehensibility. For a prosaic understanding of it, however, a stellar dictionary that can bridge the gap between professional terminology and amateur understanding is vital. Even comprehensible words must be checked in a medical dictionary if the context is one of health. For example, an innocuous word like "bay" that may mean an estuary or a barking sound or a leaf in the nonmedical world is, in anatomy, a recess containing fluid.

- A resource that has provided a bridge for many years is *Stedman's Medical Dictionary*, 28th Edition. With over 107,000 terms accompanied by graphics and photographs, the dictionary is used by both health professionals and laypersons. User-friendly features include, but are not limited to, a separate listing of "high profile terms"; synonyms distinguished by blue print; all subentries positioned on a new line to provide more visual simplicity; densely labeled illustrations; and a detailed index. A free online version is available at www.stedmans.com and can be searched by keyword with wildcard capabilities. A CD-ROM supplement has a medical spellchecker, as well as videos, animations, four-color images, and the ability to keep a record of search histories. The dictionary is also available for PDAs with searches through headwords and multiple hyperlinks.
- First published as a pocket medical dictionary in 1898, *Dorland's Illustrated Medical Dictionary*, 31st Edition, currently defines more than 120,000 terms supplemented with over 1,100 color plates. The dictionary is invaluable for its clean line drawings, photographs, and radiographic images. In the most recent edition, the dramatic inclusion of color graphics after more than 100

years of black-and-white images has further enhanced the usability of the reference, as has the addition of more than 800 complementary and alternative medical terms. Color boxes, tables for complex information, and medical terms printed in bright red to enhance readability all contribute to a resource that is both user friendly and comprehensive. The authority of the resource can be testified by the National Library of Medicine, which uses it to establish MeSH, its own controlled vocabulary of subject headings. The dictionary is available on CD-ROM, and can also be accessed freely at www.dorlands.com.

- Though dated, *Melloni's Illustrated Medical Dictionary*, with its 30,000 terms and 3,000 illustrations continues to be a popular choice for students of the health sciences. Close to one-third of each page is devoted to careful two-color line drawings that bring life to terms that are boldfaced. Whereas the previous two dictionaries are suitable for practicing physicians and others, this dictionary is primarily for beginning students, nurses, allied health workers, and the amateur user.

Medical Encyclopedias

Thompson Gale, Omnigraphics, and Facts on File publish health series that are comprehensive, authoritative, and user friendly.

General

- The *Gale Encyclopedia of Medicine* and the *Gale Encyclopedia of Alternative Medicine* are reliable general encyclopedias available in print and as e-books. The five-volume "one-stop" work on human diseases, disorders, syndromes, procedures, therapies, and drugs, the *Encyclopedia of Medicine* was first published to rave reviews in 1999. The third edition, published in 2006, continues the format of alphabetical entries covering a range of diseases with information on causes, symptoms, diagnosis, prognosis, treatment, and prevention included. The structure of information is standardized, so that looking up information on unfamiliar topics becomes relatively easy. Graphics supplement many of the entries in the third edition, and a detailed index with a cross-referencing system aids usage.
- With a national statistic that claims more than one-third of adults in the United States use complementary and alternative medicine, the four-volume *Encyclopedia of Alternative Medicine* is a useful addition to reference collections. It presents forty types of alternative medicine, from ancient Indian ayurveda to the modern Feldenkrais Method of healing. The information is careful to avoid any bias. Resource lists of printed information and relevant institutions are also given. Color photographs of medicinal plants provide an invaluable key to identifying obscure herbs. Side effects and general acceptance levels for each entry are also included.
- The thirty-two-volume *Encyclopedia of the Life Sciences*, with more than 4,300 specially commissioned and peer-reviewed articles, is the definitive text

for life scientists. "Introductory," "Advanced," and "Keynote" gradients of coverage, specificity, and complexity help in making this a user-friendly resource for students and specialists. Color illustrations, tables, taxonomies, acronyms and synonym listings all contribute toward the user-friendly aspects of these scholarly volumes. A subscription-based online version, with limited free content, is available at www.els.net.

Specialized

- The *Gale Encyclopedia of Children's Health* is a four-volume compilation of pediatric diseases and disorders aimed primarily for children under the age of four years. In addition to a catalog of diseases, the encyclopedia also covers developmental issues, immunizations, and drugs. The volumes are also available as an e-book through the Gale Virtual Reference Library. The *Gale Encyclopedia of Surgery and Medical Tests* covers 450 surgical procedures. The information is enhanced with much-needed descriptions of the diagnostic procedure for each type of surgery as well as the aftercare that will be required. Morbidity and mortality rates and alternate techniques are included. The encyclopedia is aimed directly at patients and caregivers, as evident in the defining of medical jargon, the use of second opinions, lists of questions to ask doctors, procedures for hospital admission and presurgery, and an extensive bibliography of support organizations, associations, and literature on the subject. It is also available as an e-book.

- A comprehensive and widely respected source of information for over 3,000 drugs, the *Physicians' Desk Reference—PDR* is a staple of all health collections. Drugs can be located by manufacturer, as well as by product or generic name and category. Usage information includes warnings, dosages, overdosages, contraindications, and use-in-pregnancy ratings. The print edition is published annually and updated monthly via eDrug Updates. Photographs of over 1,800 drugs are included, even though they are inserted as a group rather than as accompaniments to the written descriptions. The free online version, available at www.pdrhealth.com, on the other hand, includes photos with the description, which is written in lay terms. The Web site also provides information on herbal medicine such as echinacea; over-the-counter drugs such as Alka-Seltzer; and nutritional supplements such as vitamins. A collation of *PDR* and related sources is available on CD-ROM as well as mobile devices.

- A complete and reliable online drug index can be found in *RxList: The Internet Drug Index*, which is freely accessible at www.rxlist.com. Founded by pharmacists in 1995, the index covers both brand and generic drug names. Handy tools, such as a "pill identifier," which can put a name to a drug through color, shape, or the identifier code indented on every pill, make this a valuable free drug resource.

- The accessible two-volume *Gale Encyclopedia of Mental Health* covers all disorders listed in the *DMV-IV-TR*, a dense manual described in the next section. It also covers various therapies and medications. All entries are standardized to include, among other things, coverage of definitions, causes, diagnoses, prevention, and additional resources. The language is relatively clear of jargon and illustrations, photographs, and graphics complement entries. Key terms in any description are highlighted in a definition box to simplify understanding of complex issues.

Handbooks and Manuals

- With the cautionary principle that "memory is treacherous" guiding its publication, the *Merck Manual of Diagnosis and Therapy* has been an aid to physicians since 1899, when a slim version was first published. Albert Schweitzer is said to have carried a copy to Africa in 1913 and Admiral Byrd to the South Pole in 1929. The layman's version of the *Merck*, published as recently as 1997 and since updated, is titled *The Merck Manual Home Health Handbook*. Based on the original *Merck*, the home edition uses everyday language to give in-depth information on a complete range of disorders. The information is supplemented with original graphics. The table of contents lists all entries under various disorders, but the detailed index guides the user so that it is not necessary to know which disorder contains the word abetalipoproteinemia. Marketed as a "not-for-profit" service to the global community, the home manual is freely available at www.merck.com. The site can be searched by keyword, an alphabetical index, or through a subject section such as "blood disorders" or "infections." Once linked, the page displays a navigation area clearly stating the section, chapter, or topic that has been selected. Relevant hyperlinks and diagrams are also included.
- Published primarily as a diagnostic tool, the *DSM-IV-TR* (*Diagnostic and Statistical Manual of Mental Disorders*) is published by the American Psychiatric Association. It has become a fixture in libraries because of its unique coverage of psychiatric illnesses and its authority as a source for standard nomenclature of all mental disorders. Prevalence, genetic predisposition, age, gender, culture, and other features are included for each disorder. The presentation is dense and aimed at the professional rather than the lay user. The fourth edition is available for use on PDAs and Smartphones. The fifth edition is not due until May 2012. *DSM-II* is freely available online at www.psychiatryonline.com/DSMPDF/dsm-ii.pdf. The recent edition can be searched as a subscription database at www.psychiatryonline.com/DSMPDF/dsm-ii.pdf.

Medical Directories

Locating a particular doctor or hospital; scanning listings for relevant doctors and medical centers in a certain area of specialization; and vetting doctors and hospitals are frequent requests. Medical directories provide answers for this category of questions.

- The annual three-volume *Official ABMS Directory of Board Certified Medical Specialists* has comprehensive biographies of over 695,000 medical specialists in the United States and Canada, who have been certified by the twenty-four medical specialty boards of the American Board of Medical Specialties. Certification is voluntary, so it is not necessary that each qualified physician be in the directory. The directory can be used to locate a physician by specialty and by geographical area. It can also be used to verify a specialist's educational background, professional associations, and general credentials. The print edition includes access to a companion Web site. The CD-ROM version of the directory is updated twice a year and titled *ABMS Medical Specialists PLUS* (Elsevier). The database version, available at www.boardcertifieddocs.com is updated daily and has special features such as "alerts" tailored to specific notifications and downloadable records. A free certification search is accessible at www.abms.org/login.asp, but the user must log in and complete a registration form. Physicians can also be verified by calling the toll-free number, 1-866-ASK-ABMS.

- A popular consumer guide to physicians can be found in Castle Connolly's guide, *America's Top Doctors*. Over 230,000 physicians are surveyed and nominated by their peers so that a total of over 6,000 "top doctors" can be found. The procedure is highly subjective but provides a first cut to users looking for a starting point in their search for the right physician. Listings are by area of specialization so that twenty-five specialties and ninety subspecialties can be studied for both institutional and physician listings. The information is also available online for an annual fee at www.castleconnolly.com, though a portion of the database can be accessed free after completing a registration form.

- More than 814,000 fully licensed physicians can be found on the freely available DoctorFinder provided by the American Medical Association at http://webapps.ama-assn.org/doctorfinder/home.jsp. Physicians who are not fully licensed are best located in the printed *Directory of Physicians in the United States* published by the American Medical Association that covers residents, researchers, teachers, administrators, and retired physicians.

- A unique resource that has not been updated since 2000 is the consumer watch publication from Public Citizen, *20,125 Questionable Doctors: Disciplined by State and Federal Governments*, National Edition. The doctors pilloried in the four volumes are from across the nation and collectively account for more than 34,000 disciplinary actions ranging from fines to license suspensions. Detailed information on whether the physician has been disciplined for substance abuse, sex offenses, or incompetence is included. With a majority of the physicians listed continuing to practice, the volumes provide an authoritative resource for users looking for further information on specific doctors. A continuing focus on transparency and accountability in the health profession is offered by the group at www.citizen.org/hrg.

- *DIRLINE*, a comprehensive directory of health and biomedical organizations, can be found in the free government Web site at http://dirline.nlm.nih.gov. With over 8,000 records of agencies, referral centers, professional organizations, self-help and community groups, and research institutions, the directory can be searched by keyword or a subject search of the disease or condition. The results include an abstract of the organization's aims, history, and budget, as well as complete contact information.

Medical Databases and Indexes

- *PubMed* is both freely accessible and the most extensive bibliographic database for health issues. It covers the information contained in the National Library of Medicine's *MEDLINE*, which has 18 million citations dating back to 1948; OLDMEDLINE, with 2 million citations ranging between 1950 and 1965; and special out-of-scope citations primarily from the life sciences. The coverage is not limited to North American journals. While full text is not available on *PubMed*, a "Link Out" feature allows the user to access full-text articles from a specific citation. Many of these links, however, require subscriptions or fees to access the full text, which can be procured through vendors such as EBSCO or OVID. Available at www.pubmed.gov, the database has the authority of the National Institutes of Health and is invaluable as an index tool for researchers.

- *EMBASE* is a comprehensive biomedical and pharmacological bibliographic database that can be accessed at www.embase.com. It contains more than 19 million indexed records collated since 1947, with more than 600,000 additions made on an annual basis. With 1,800 additional biomedical journals in its repertoire, it is more extensive than *PubMed*, especially in its coverage of European drug trials and pharmaceuticals that are undergoing research and development.

- Gale Cengage Learning at www.gale.com is responsible for a set of well-known and respected medical databases and indexes to medical journals, newspaper articles, and pamphlets. The two major ones are *Health Reference Center Academic* and the *Health and Wellness Resource Center* available through the *Gale PowerSearch* platform. Similar in content, though different in interface, access, and search strategies, the Gale databases are user friendly, authoritative, and provide both full-text articles and indexing to additional titles. The index covers articles in books, overviews, pamphlets, and journals. The *Academic* database has a built-in translating tool for on-demand document translation as well as the ability to create alerts with RSS Export.

- EBSCO Information Services at www.ebsco.com parents a host of bibliographic and full-text medical databases of which *Health Source* and *CINAHL* are notable for their coverage and ease in searching. *Health Source*, available as both a *Consumer* and an *Academic* edition, is an extensive database with access to health periodicals, reference books, pamphlets, drug monograph entries, and patient education fact sheets. Full-text documents as well as abstracts and indexes are available, with convenient links that can guide the researcher to more in-depth study. *CINAHL* is less general, but provides the most exhaustive index for issues related to nursing and allied health. *CINAHL Full Text* is the expanded version that allows for full-text searches. Almost 3,000 journals in the nursing field are indexed by this database, as well as nursing dissertations, conference proceedings, and standards of practice. Together, there are more than 2 million records, some of which date back to the early 1980s. Aimed at a more specialized user, full-text articles from more than 600 journals, legal cases, and clinical trials are also available.

- For special reference collections, the subscription-based *Dialog* is a rich source of medical and pharmaceutical databases; it has 121 million records directly focused on biomedical and pharmaceutical literature. It also includes the 10,000 foundations listed in the *Foundation Directory* that is invaluable for the constant grant seeking required in the medical field.

Health Information Sites

Changes in medical wisdom have far-reaching effects. The miracle cure of today can become the pariah of tomorrow. Fast-changing knowledge of medical research can oftentimes only be available on the Internet, a medium that is capable of handling and disseminating news speedily and globally. Bookmarking at least five to ten valuable Web sites for medical news and updates is a necessity of good health reference service.

- The National Library of Medicine is the largest medical library in the world. *MedlinePlus*, a component of the aforementioned *PubMed*, was started in 1998 as the library's consumer health Web site at http://medline plus.gov. It now covers over 800 topics with over 700 available in Spanish and 18,000 links to authoritative health sites. It is also a strong resource for checking on drugs, clinical trials, hospitals, and physicians. The information is updated daily and fed by both government agencies and health organizations. A medical dictionary and encyclopedia are included. Some of the sources that cover drug information, such as the *USP-DI*, give Canadian brand names as well, so that, e.g., Sinutab in Canada can replace an antihistamine like Sinarest in the United States after a quick check of the Web site.
- While *MedlinePlus* is a valuable all-purpose site, specialized sites such as www.cancer.gov and www.cancer.org provide authoritative and timely information on specific diseases. Sponsored by the National Cancer Institute and the American Cancer Society respectively, both sites are written in lay terms and cover the various stages faced by cancer patients.
- A valuable site for drug information can be found at www.drugdigest.org, which provides the unique Drug Interactions database that allows the user to check for interactions between two drugs. Niggling questions on whether one can take an aspirin for headache while taking a particular prescription drug for diabetes are solved by use of this site. More than 6,000

images of pills also helps users who need to confirm that what they are about to swallow is indeed what they meant to swallow, especially when pill makers change the shape or color of the pills. Freely accessible to all, the Web site also includes data from the subscription database *Clinical Pharmacology*.

* An interesting source for up-to-date medical news articles, with a bias toward news from the United Kingdom, can be found at http://news .bbc.co.uk/1/hi/health/. The "Health" section of the BBC news can be checked for current medical stories, as well as searched for archival material by keyword or through an A-Z index. More extensive yet is the National Library for Health site at www.library.nhs.uk that provides medical updates, news, links to special libraries, and acts as a "digital hub" for services across the country.

* Medical updates in the United Kingdom can also be accessed from the *BMJ* (*British Medical Journal*), a popular and highly reputable online site at www.bmj.com that attracts over 1.5 million unique users each month and was awarded the Medical Publication of the Year in 2008. More dramatic medical updates can be found in the well-known and well-loved journal, *The Lancet*, available at www.thelancet.com. *The Lancet* is unabashedly activist in that it publishes both medical science such as its groundbreaking identification of the viral cause of SARS in 2003, and champions public health causes such as child survival and climate change.

Health Statistics

The National Center for Health Statistics accessible at www.cdc.gov/nchs is the primary source for health statistics. Data collected from birth, death, and medical records as well as through widespread surveys, testing, interviews, and examinations are collated to provide "surveillance information" that can be used to limn the nation's health problems. The site has a simple overview of datasheets so that it is possible to access a rich vein of statistical information with minimal burrowing. Each datasheet has links to a range of additional sources so that more in-depth research is also possible. Hard-to-find statistics on teens with live births (444,899 in 2007) or tuberculosis in the United States (11,545 in 2009) or persons without health coverage (43.0 million in 2007) can be accessed easily.

Major Legal Resources Used in Reference Work

On January 2, 2003, the Judicial Council of the California County Law Librarians decided to include an icon for 24/7 legal reference help in every page of its site. The effect was immediate. From an average of 100 questions per month, the number of legal queries shot up to an astonishing 2,045 questions. There has never been any doubt that we live in an increasingly litigious society. However, the exponential rise in amateur lawyers and pro se litigants has come as a surprise. The person on the street is now potentially able to draw up a living will; expand a home in accordance with local zoning laws; or fight a custody battle. Prohibitive lawyer fees, coupled with extensive access to legal precedent and rules via the Internet, have put the onus of legal responsibility on the common person, and by extension, the neighborhood librarian.

Given this trend, a collection that includes basic printed legal material and access to online resources is a necessary component of reference service in all libraries. While all libraries must have a dictionary to decode legalese and an encyclopedia to cover a breadth of legal topics, more specialized resources such as directories, indexes, and primary and secondary legal material can be acquired based on the needs of the community.

Legal Dictionaries

* Currently in its ninth edition, the invaluable *Black's Law Dictionary* was first published in 1891 under the stewardship of English legalist Henry Campbell Black. It is reportedly the most cited law dictionary in the country and covers more than 45,000 definitions. A large number of the entries are cross-referenced to cases in the *Corpus Juris Secundum* to aid further research. The last edition also provides a useful appendix of more than 4,000 legal abbreviations and another on legal maxims. Pronunciations of arcane legalese such as the feudal "feoffee" are provided, as well as equivalent terms and alternate spellings for more than 5,300 terms and senses. A pocket, an abridged, and a deluxe edition of the dictionary are also available. The dictionary is available as a digital dictionary that can be integrated with individual word processors and Web browsers and is searchable on *Westlaw*. It is also available as an app for iPhones, iPads, and iPods, and a version for Androids and BlackBerrys is planned.

* With more than 10,000 definitions of over 5,000 legal terms defined with phonetic pronunciations, *Ballentine's Law Dictionary* has been a popular alternative to *Black's*. An all-important case citation, from which a particular definition derives authority, is also supplied, thereby providing a starting point of research for many users. It is particularly useful in its coverage of old Saxon, French, and Latin phrases. The *Ballentine's Law Dictionary and Thesaurus* combines the dictionary with a thesaurus for legal research and writing so that synonyms, antonyms, and parts of speech are also attached to each definition, making for a more exact understanding of each legal term. The appendix includes *The Chicago Manual of Legal Citation* and a guide to doing research.

* Free online legal dictionaries can also be used for quick searches. *Merriam-Webster's Dictionary of Law* can be accessed through Findlaw at http://dictionary.lp.findlaw.com. A basic legal dictionary that can be searched by legal term, by letter of the alphabet, and by all definitions that include the word can be found at http://dictionary.law.com. A historical dictionary of legal terms can be accessed at www.constitution.org/bouv/bouvier.htm, where a copy of the indomitable 1856 *Bouvier's Law Dictionary* provides definitions for such legal entities as "female" (the sex which bears young).

Legal Encyclopedias and Yearbooks

- The word "weal" is defined as the common good or the welfare of the community at large. It is also the motivation and acronym of the preeminent legal encyclopedia, *West's Encyclopedia of American Law (WEAL)*. Formerly published as the *Guide to American Law*, the thirteen-volume set covers 5,000 legal issues. Terms, cases, statutes, documents, issues, forms, time lines, and over 600 biographies are presented without specialized jargon so that it is accessible to the layperson. With a determined focus to provide "legal ease" rather than "legalese," even complex and far-ranging issues such as *Roe vs. Wade* are condensed into understandable packets of knowledge with the inclusion of lawyer arguments, majority and dissenting opinions, and the reasoning of the judges. Graphics, cross-references, time lines, and focus boxes enhance the text. The encyclopedia is also available in an e-book format.

- The *American Law Yearbook* is a corollary to *WEAL*. It annually updates the encyclopedia and provides expanded versions of entries. Cross-references, time lines, and photographs that accompany the biographies make this a highly user-friendly resource. Each edition carries the U.S. Supreme Court docket as well as other cases not argued at the level of the Supreme Court. The recent inclusion of legal issues pertaining to YouTube, eminent domain law and steroid scandals amongst athletes, attests to the currency of each edition. It is available in e-book format through *Gale Virtual Reference Library*.

Legal Directories

- Published for 140 years, the *Martindale-Hubbell Law Directory* is an established authority for locating and checking on the credentials of law firms and lawyers. The twenty-six-volume print edition lists more than 1 million lawyers and firms in 160 countries. The entries are arranged by geographical location so that smaller libraries have the option of purchasing single volumes that cover their own home state. An extensive indexing system allows searches by name as well. The volumes are also available on a two-disc CD-ROM that allows for twenty-seven different search criteria. Search results can be exported to a spreadsheet or database program, with more than one application running at the same time. Free online access is available via the *Lawyer Locator* at www.martindale.com and through new mobile apps. Solicitors and law firms in the United Kingdom can also be freely accessed at www.lawyerlocator.co.uk. The biographical information provided is also supplemented with peer ratings and reviews, a unique practice begun since the 1896 edition of the directory. The directory is not only a global standard for information on the legal profession; it also acts as a marketing or fact-checking tool for lawyers as well. All lawyers and law firms can complete the Practice Profile listings, so that an unlisted firm or lawyer is invariably considered to be suspect.

- A single-volume directory with almost 2,000 pages packed with information can be found in the annual editions of the *Law and Legal Information*

Directory. Over 21,000 legal agencies, programs, institutions, facilities, and services are listed under different categories as diverse as "National and International Organizations" and "Awards and Prizes." Each listing provides a brief description and contact information.

Legal Databases and Indexes

Subscription databases such as *Lexis*, *Westlaw*, and *LAWCHEK* aim to provide a wide range of legal information relevant to the most heavily used areas of legal research.

- Started as early as 1973, *Lexis* was a pioneer in providing full-text legal information. As the *LexisNexis* database, it continues to be the most authoritative index of legal and government documents, as well as a resource for full-text legal material. Various permutations of the master database are available so that custom packages can be created for different levels of libraries, the primary three being corporate, government, and law libraries. Case law, codes, legal analysis, public records of property, news transcripts, and regulations are all part of the powerful array of legal resources provided by *LexisNexis*. Indexes such as H.W. Wilson's *Index to Legal Periodicals* are also part of the array. The database has continued to expand and in 2005 became the exclusive provider of legal content for a major repository of business intelligence, *Factiva*, at www.factiva.com. Given the richness of the database, the endless customization available, and the high costs of purchase, an involved study of each community's legal reference demands must be made before choosing the right package at www.lexisnexis.com.
- *Quicklaw* is the Canadian branch of *LexisNexis* and can be accessed at http://ql.quicklaw.com. Tailored to Canadian legal information needs, the same mix of case law, court and tribunal decisions, procedures, legal news, and commentary are provided for a fee. Legal information can also be found in French and the Web site itself is bilingual.
- *LexisNexis UK* is accessible for a subscription fee at www.lexisnexis .co.uk. With lawyer-locator services, studies and citations of English, Irish, Scottish, Commonwealth, and European cases, all fifty volumes of *Halsbury's Laws*, tax and pension information, and fully amended texts of statutes, etc., *LexisNexis UK* is a comprehensive legal resource for the United Kingdom. A new initiative to provide online legal service was inaugurated in June 2005.
- *Westlaw* is another powerful provider of legal documents such as case law, statutes with annotations and court corrections, directories, law reviews, and public records such as real property deeds. While aimed at the legal professional, *Westlaw* has introduced user-friendly search aids such as "Smart Tools" that attempts to flag any word or acronym that appears to be spelled incorrectly or appears out of context. So for example, even a "correct" spelling like "statue" is flagged if it mistakenly appears in the context of the term "statute of limitations." Related terms are also suggested to aid the nonprofessional. Directories can be scanned by single word search terms

and words are automatically searched along with their plurals, irregular plurals, and possessives. The density of information offered is tempered with these search enhancements, details of which can be found at the Web site, www.Westlaw.com.

- *LAWCHEK* was created as a direct result of the 1991 ALA study that found the most problematic area of reference research in any library was in the field of law. It is aimed at the layperson and the reference librarian. Fashioned as a tutorial for twelve selected legal disciplines found to be the most heavily trafficked areas of public research, *LAWCHEK* provides fee-based access to legal forms, glossaries, guides, letter templates, and legal directories associated with these areas. It is also linked to both state and federal codes and cases. The Web site can be accessed at www.lawchek.com/.

Legal Online Resources

- Winner of the 2005 Webby Awards for best legal Web site, *FindLaw* at www.find law.com is a popular free site for legal professionals, students, and the layperson. Packed with legal links, information, lawyer directories, forms, and news, the site is a rich source for both primary and secondary legal material.
- *Hieros Gamos* is a respected Web site for extensive directory listings of lawyers, law firms, expert witnesses, court reporters, investigators, and process servers both in North America and globally. Legal and bar associations, law libraries around the world, legal events, and news are all part of the site available at www.hg.org.
- In January 1995, *THOMAS* became the first and foremost source for free online information on federal legislation. The *Congressional Record Index* supplies an invaluable index. Also available are historical documents; summaries of congressional activity; the legislative process; committee reports and information; and bill text, summaries, and status. Accessible at http://thomas.loc.gov, the site is easy to use and provides a valuable resource for any information related to legislation in the United States. Edward Elsner, a listserv participant, provided the tip that summaries of laws and acts could also be accessed by a Google search with the name of the law in quotation marks followed by the word "summary" (Publib, August 5, 2005).
- Access to global laws is also becoming freely available. For British law a good portal to law sources can be found at http://legal-directory.net. It provides free access to specialized legal information such as family, property, medical negligence, and personal injury law in the United Kingdom. A comprehensive portal to information about Canadian legal resources, set up by the nonprofit Canadian Legal Information Institute, can be found at www.canlii.org.

Major Business Resources Used in Reference Work

It is a jungle out there. Business resources run the gamut from tissue-thin pamphlets on personal finance to multivolume works on global marketing. The whys and wherefores and how-to's of making, consolidating, and propagating wealth root into a dense thicket of publications on accounting, taxation, banking, human resources, industrial relations, labor, personal finance, international finance, insurance, advertising, company profiles, product development, biographical directories, commodity statistics, rating guides, statistical overviews, et al. Whereas a set of inclusive online or print business dictionaries, encyclopedias, handbooks, indexes, and directories is required of all reference collections, more in-depth acquisition is required primarily in two of the most heavily trafficked areas of business queries: that of personal finance and business entrepreneurship.

Business Dictionaries

- When users are stumped as to whether they should be putting an "accelerator clause" in their lending document; or whether a "variable markup policy" is advisable for their small business, it is time to consult the Oxford University Press's *A Dictionary of Business and Management*. First published in 1990 as *A Concise Dictionary of Business*, the 2009 edition has over 7,000 entries, with a focus on e-commerce terms. The definitions provide pithy background information and are strengthened by a systematic web of cross-references, illustrations, synonyms and abbreviations.
- The distinct red-covered Economist Series on the *Dictionary of Business* and the *International Dictionary of Finance* provide simple definitions on a wide range of business activity. Brief analyses of business concepts are also provided, along with cross-references, acronyms, and business jargon. More than 2,000 terms are listed in each dictionary. Given the global nature of business, many of the terms included are common to countries other than the United States. However, the dictionaries are relatively vulnerable in the area of e-commerce as they have not been updated since 2003.
- Strong in current terminology is the online business dictionary *BusinessDictionary*, which is freely available at www.businessdictionary.com. With over 20,000 definitions that can be approached as keywords or through forty-two subject categories, and 115,000 links between related terms, the site also offers a free daily e-newsletter.
- Libraries that require a more specialized breakdown of dictionary meanings in all the various aspects of business can look into the Barron's Educational Series. Separated into the *Dictionary of Business Terms* with 7,500 entries; the *Dictionary of International Business Terms* with 5,000 entries; the *Dictionary of Marketing Terms* with 4,000 entries; the *Dictionary of Insurance Terms* with 4,500 entries; the *Dictionary of Accounting Terms* with 2,500 entries; the *Dictionary of Finance and Investment Terms* with 5,000 entries, etc., the series is physically small and hard to shelve, but useful and inexpensive.

Directories and Handbooks

- The multivolume annual *Thomas Register of American Manufacturers* published since 1906 ceased publishing print editions in 2007 and is now freely available online at www.thomasnet.com. It is the standard authority for finding information such as contact numbers, addresses, subsidiaries, sales offices, and affiliations for 607,000 companies. There are 72,000 product and service categories listed alphabetically under city and state. Contact information, as well as product details, is accompanied by millions of detailed CAD drawings of component pieces and company catalogs. Searches can be made via keyword and product category or limited by geographic location. Manufacturing information for the United Kingdom, Canada and twenty-six other countries can be accessed freely at www.solusource.com.

- First published in 1928, the three-volume *Standard & Poor's Register of Corporations, Directors and Executives* is a panoptic directory of 75,000 corporations and 290,000 executives across the United States, Canada, and parts of the world. Volume 1 covers corporations with contact information that includes Web site addresses when applicable, as well as a brief listing of key personnel, number of employees, products, total sales, and North American Industry Classification System (NAICS) codes. Volume 2 alphabetically lists officers, directors, trustees, and patrons of business organizations, with both contact information and biographical details such as year and place of birth, college and year of graduation, and noncollege fraternal memberships. Volume 3 contains indexes. The entries are democratic in that Bill Gates is given the same space as an officer of a florist company in Kentucky. An extensive system of cross-references is also provided so that a user can locate companies under NAICS codes, geographical location, and subsidiary and parent company information. Tracking the ultimate parent company in a corporate family hierarchy, so that the relation between, say, ABC Inc. as a subsidiary of the Walt Disney Company becomes clear, elevates this resource to more than just a simple directory. The annual is further updated through cumulative supplements. An online paid subscription to *NetAdvantage* at www.netadvantage.standardandpoors.com provides access to the *Register* as well as a bundle of other *S&P* resources.
- "Who Owns Whom" is the succinct description supporting the title of the extensive eight-volume *LexisNexis Corporate Affiliations*. The directory lists almost 225,000 international and American companies with revenue in excess of $50 million and $10 million, respectively. A master index can be used to locate the ownership status, corporate hierarchy, nationality, geographic coverage, personnel, Standard Industrial Classification, and brand name correlations for each company. Users wanting to know if the Bridgestone Corporation is American, or if there are links between the Tokyo office of Bridgestone and the Cobra Tire Company Inc. in Phoenix are well served by the clear nexus provided by this resource. The directory is available as a fee-based online subscription at www.corporateaffiliations.com, where the family tree is traced all the way down to the "seventh level of reporting relationships" and covers nearly 700,000 companies.

- Published in 1991 as a single handbook profiling 500 corporations, Hoover's now publishes multiple handbooks that are updated annually. *Hoover's Handbook of American Business* focuses on 750 influential American companies with in-depth coverage of personalities and analyses of successful company strategies. *Hoover's Handbook of Private Companies* profiles 900 such companies including hospitals, charities, universities, and cooperatives. *Hoover's Handbook of World Business* covers 300 public, private, and state-owned businesses located outside the United States, but intimately webbed in today's global market so that the iconic American 7-Eleven stores are shown to be controlled by Ito-Yokado, a Japanese retail monolith. *Hoover's Handbook of Emerging Companies* aims to highlight 600 of the most vibrantly growing small businesses, with in-depth profiles on 200 of them. *Hoover's Handbook of Industry Profiles* is the latest addition and covers analysis and trends for 300 industries. All five handbooks emerge from a company database of 65 million companies that allows Hoover's Business Press to offer a dizzying variety of online business resources that can be accessed via subscription at www.hoovers.com.

- *Brands and Their Companies* is a useful directory of more than 426,000 brand names. For users wanting to know which company manufacturers the Frisbee toy (Wham-O Manufacturing Co.); or what the brand Diazinon is (a household pesticide); or whether Big Time candy is still in production (no), this is the directory to consult. The entries are listed alphabetically by brand name and briefly list the product description and the manufacturer or distributor. Brands no longer in production are marked as such, whereas brands that have morphed into generic words such as "Xerox" are also included. Brands not registered with the patent office are also entered, making this a unique resource for hard-to-find information. The directory is also available as part of the *Gale Directory Library*, a subscription database available at www.gale.com.

Investment Guides

- In the volatile world of financial investing, a steady guide has been provided by *Value Line Investment Survey*. Published since the 1930s, the survey is a weekly investment advisory that comes in three loose-leaf parts. The main part is the *Ratings and Reports* section that covers 1,700 stocks. Each stock is analyzed and graded for timeliness, safety, and volatility. Background information on the company is provided along with a graph charting a decade of price ranges. Given the careful mix of recommendation and information, *Value Line* has become a staple of reference collections. Subscription to an online version can be found at www.valueline.com.

- A Financial Ratings Series powered by Weiss Ratings and The Street Ratings publishes a series of quarterly investment guides for both the novice and seasoned investor. The beginning user can be directed to the *Ultimate Guided Tour of Stock Investing*, in which a pith-helmeted cartoon safari leader leads the investor through the wilds of stock figures, analyses, and analysts.

However, the bulk of publications are aimed at the practicing and amateur investor. There are *Ratings Guides on Bond and Money Market Mutual Funds, Exchange Traded Funds, Common Stocks, Stock Mutual Funds, Banks and Thrifts, Health Insurers, Life and Annuity Insurers, Property and Casualty Insurers.* A careful system of ratings is established so that each bond, mutual fund, bank, insurance company, and brokerage firm is analyzed and judged according to a stated set of criteria. Weiss, which has been publishing guides for over thirty years, stresses objectivity so that no compensation is accepted from any of the institutions rated. Libraries have the option of buying one annual issue, or subscribing to the quarterly editions that are published for each guide. Individual rating reports are commercially available at www.weissratings.com or the more recent www.financialratings series.com.

Business Entrepreneurship Aids

- The 2011 edition of the annual *Market Share Reporter* is a combination of both the North American market and the international market that was previously published as the *World Market Share Reporter*. With more than 2,000 entries arranged under SIC/NAICS codes, the *Reporter* acts as a unique resource for users interested in comparing and ranking the market share of companies and their products. Products ranging from top disposable diaper brands (Huggies Ultratrim) to the leading aircraft maker for the defense department (Boeing Co.) are listed along with the percentage share of the market and, in some cases, the dollar amounts as well. An alphabetical table of topics is provided along with a table of contents listed in numerical SIC ascending order. Pie and bar charts supplement some of the entries, and each entry cites the source.
- Previously published as the *Source Book of Franchise Opportunities, Bond's Franchise Guide* profiles nearly 900 franchises, divided into business categories such as "recreation and entertainment" and "automotive products and services." Each entry provides contact information. The entries are derived from a forty-point questionnaire and are therefore highly detailed, requiring an a priori reading on how to use the data. In addition to contact information, background history, and a description of the business franchiser, criteria for granting a franchise are also given along with legal and financial requirements. Franchise seekers are well served by this resource. It is also available online at www.worldfranchising.com.

Business Databases and Indexes

- A sweeping database with a powerful indexing component, Gale's *Business and Company ASAP* covers over 200,000 directory listings, full-text public relations newswires for up-to-the-minute information, and thousands of entries from business journals, trade periodicals, and management serials from 1980 to the present. The corollary *Business Index ASAP* is integrated so that indexes for the financial section of *The New York Times*, the *Asian Wall Street Journal*, and *The Wall Street Journal* are available. User aids include a controlled vocabulary, a subject guide, cross-references, and customizable search strategies. Subscription information is available at www.gale.cengage.com.

- *Mergent Online* is an incisive business database that provides global business and financial information that includes filings from *Electronic Data Gathering Analysis and Retrieval* as well as *D&B's Million Dollar Directory Plus*; the annual reports of both U.S. public and international companies; financial reports for more than 10,000 Canadian and U.S. companies; and insider trading data that records all transactions within a six-month period. The database provides the tools to compare and analyze up to 200 companies against a set of variables that can be mixed and matched. The ability to create a customized company report is also offered. The database at www.mergentonline.com is available with several varieties of configurations and can be adapted to suit the needs of basic business information such as looking up a company to more involved cross-border searches.

- Begun as a graduate project in 1971, *ABI/INFORM Complete* (ProQuest) is a pioneer in the online indexing and abstracting of business information. It currently contains about 2 million documents, of which approximately half are in full text. The meticulous 150-word abstracts for which it was renowned have also been pared down to a mix of long and short, indicative entries as a wider variety of business sources are being added to the database. More than 60,000 company profiles; full-text journals from academic publishers such as Kluwer, John Wiley, and Palgrave Macmillan; and entries from thousands of local, national, and international management and business publications are offered by *ABI/INFORM* at www.proquest.com/products/pt-product-ABI.shtml.

- EBSCO's *Business Source* databases come in different packages: *Elite, Premier, Corporate, Complete,* and *Alumni*. The *Premier* and *Complete* include monograph and reference books in addition to articles from serials. A special "business-specific interface" allows for relatively sophisticated fine-tuning of search results so that lists can be limited by preferred sources and search options can be conducted through more than just company name or subject entry. A breakdown of titles available through each database is available at www.ebsco.com. EBSCO's user-friendly and standardized search bars, title list management tools, and comprehensive coverage of business resources make it an attractive choice for all levels of libraries.

- Formerly known as *Dow Jones Interactive*, *Factiva* is an innovative provider of global business content. Indexes, abstracts, and full-text content from over 9,000 resources including *The Wall Street Journal*, the *Financial Times*, television and radio transcripts, individual company reports, the *Dow Jones* and *Reuters* newswires, and publications from 118 countries succeed in providing a content-rich and wide-ranging business database. The content is universally indexed and enables searches in multiple languages. Subscription information is available at http://factiva.com.

Collection Development and Maintenance

Selection and Keeping Current

One of the distinctive aspects of medical, legal, and business resources is that once selected, a large number of the publications tend to fall into the category of a "standing order." Whether it is *Mergent's* reports, reviews, and handbooks or individual states' annotated statutes, the overriding need for currency fuels a system of constant updating that can only be feasible as a standing order. The onus of decision making, then, is on the initial selection for which there are a few effective ways for identifying new resources.

Published Reviews

In addition to reviews found in mainstream publications such as *ARBA*, *Library Journal*, *Reference and User Services Quarterly*, *Booklist*, and *Choice*, reviews can also be located in professional journals.

- For health and medicine, the *Medical Reference Services Quarterly* (book reviews and from the literature), the *Journal of the American Medical Association* (books, journals, new media), and the *New England Journal of Medicine* (book reviews) are relevant resources. Doody Enterprises at www.doody.com offers subscriptions to review sets, *Doody's Core Titles: Basic* or *Premium*; *Doody's Review Service*, a larger service that integrates the titles in the Core List; and *Catalog Connect*, which provides access links to the Doody database from any library catalog. The J.A. Majors Company at www.majors.com offers complementary collection development resources such as *BestSellers*, *Forthcoming*, and *Just Released* for new and noteworthy medical titles.
- For legal resources, reviews are available in the *Law Library Journal* (Keeping Up with New Legal Titles). A free monthly online resource can be found in *The Law and Politics Book Review*, sponsored by the Law and Courts Section of the American Political Science Association at www.bsos.umd.edu/gvpt/lpbr.
- A uniquely consolidated update of business resources can be found at the Business Reference and Services Section of the American Library Association. Titled as the *Public Libraries Briefcase*, the quarterly column put out by the section provides an organized bibliographical account of both old and updated resources in all the disparate areas of business. The October 2008 issue, for example, covers *The Top Ten Best Business Reference Sources for the Non-Business Librarian*.

Publisher Sites

As mentioned earlier, the proclivity to publish series is strong among the publishers of medical, legal, and business resources. Librarians looking for new resources on health, for example, can browse through these Web sites:

- Omnigraphics Health Reference Series at www.omnigraphics.com
- Facts on File Library of Health and Living at www.factsonfile.com
- Thomson Gale encyclopedias at www.gale.cengage.com
- The *R2Library* launched by Rittenhouse Book Distributors, Inc. at www. rittenhouse.com offers collection building in digital content as well as a *Quarterly Report* of updates that is freely accessible.

Some legal publications aimed at the layperson are published by the following:

- West Nutshell series at www.thomson.com
- Journals and resource series from the American Association of Law Libraries at www.aallnet.org/products
- Legal products at www.reed-elsevier.com
- Nolo legal series at www.nolo.com

Some business and finance publications can be checked on the following sites:

- Mergent's products at www.mergent.com/productsServices.html
- Financial Services pages at www.mcgraw-hill.com
- Hoover's books at www.hoovers.com/free

Online Catalogs

Given the number of specialized libraries devoted to medicine, law, and business, nonspecialist reference librarians need not reinvent the wheel.

- A periodic check of new titles acquired by specialized libraries such as the National Library of Medicine, which lists a column titled *Bookshelf,* is freely accessible at www.ncbi.nlm.nih.gov and can provide timely clues.
- The Harvard Business School brings out a list of new business acquisitions by the fifteenth of each month that is arranged under subject headings. The *New Books at Baker* list can be perused at www.library.hbs.edu/baker books/recent/.
- The *New Acquisitions* listed monthly by the Lillian Goldman Law Library at Yale Law School provides an alphabetical list that can be accessed at www.law.yale.edu/library/acquisitions.asp.

Listservs and Alerts

In a research world that is increasingly comfortable with the ethos of social networking, joining a subject-specific listserv can be very rewarding. The larger group of medical, legal, or business librarians are able to contribute toward any and every question that you may have, including that of collection development. The generosity of listserv participants cannot be underestimated.

- Medical librarians can be tapped via the MEDLIB-L listserv. E-mail listserv @list.uvm.edu with the message "subscribe medlib-l <firstname lastname>".
- Legal librarians have a vibrant community in LAW-LIB. E-mail listproc @ucdavis.edu with the message "subscribe lawlib <name>".

- Business librarians are available at BUSLIB-L. E-mail listserv@lists.nau.edu with the message "set buslib-l mail."

Questions on the best new resources in a particular area, relative rankings of subject sources and feedback on specific titles bring on a range of responses in listserv discussions that can be original, sincere, and illuminating.

Signing up for Announce Lists, E-Alerts and RSS Feeds from institutions and professional associations can also instantly flag the reference librarian about new or upcoming publications of possible interest to the collection. All of the online catalogs listed in the previous section, for example, offer signups on their sites.

Evaluating Medical, Legal, and Business Resources

While scope, accuracy, authority, and cost are basic criteria for evaluating medical, legal, and business resources, of heightened importance are the factors of currency, usability, and utility.

Currency

The urgent need for current information has resulted in a number of publications that have a constant schedule of updates. The type and frequency of these updates must be registered so that older copies are discarded immediately and the processing of updates is done at a priority level. For resources that do not have an updating service, weeding must be punctilious. No information in these three areas is preferable to outdated information. The currency of a publication can be gauged by looking up issues about which new information has been released. What does a 2011 drug reference say about Halaven or Egrifta? Does a legal yearbook document the controversy over "waterboarding"? Is AOL's buyout of Huffington Post recorded in a profile of companies?

Usability

All three fields are thick with specialized terminology and jargon. Reference resources aimed at the layperson need to be vetted for linguistic and graphic simplicity. Resources that cannot avoid terminology must have boxed definitions, legends, keys, glossaries, highlights, or other aiding devices. The indexes must be infallible as the material is relatively unfamiliar and pattern recognition on the part of the user will play an important part in navigating through the material.

Utility

Given the thousands of titles available in each of these areas, the resources must be evaluated in direct correlation to their use for the given community. Publishers are prone to produce series or sets of health, legal, and finance publications. The series follow a standard format, share a distinctive look, and attempt to cover the most heavily trafficked areas of public demand. For example, the temptation to buy all of Omnigraphics's distinctive red-and-white hardcover publications on 140 health topics is understandable, but not entirely necessary. A community may need the most updated version of the *Alzheimer Disease Sourcebook* but not the *Ethnic Diseases Sourcebook* or vice versa. The attractive binders of *Entrepreneur's Business Start-Up Guides* provide a uniform layout to almost fifty different businesses and are a valuable addition to libraries, but again, the *Freight Brokerage Service* may be more useful to some communities and the *Gift Basket Service* to others. Keeping the subject demands of the community in focus is one way of not succumbing to the siren call of professional and well-made series.

Further Considerations

Sources Are Not Enough

In the world of medical, legal, and business resources, despite excellent acquisition skills, a worthy collection, and an acute knowledge of the resources available in multiple formats, there may always be the need to do more. Resources must be supplemented with referrals, research guides, disclaimers, alternate sources, and policies for all kinds of usage.

Alternate Sources

What is considered the ideal source for a general reference question must be approached as just one of the sources for a medical, legal, or business question. There is value in providing alternatives so that the user can make comparisons. This effectively supplants the role of advice and reinforces the role of the nonspecialist librarian as the provider, rather than the interpreter, of information. The *Directory of Special Libraries and Information Centers* is a handy resource to provide a definitive list of alternate sources in special libraries, resource centers, medical collections, and documentation centers that may be consulted.

The importance of a referral sheet cannot be underestimated. A list of the nearest law, medical, and business libraries must always be handy, so that the user can be referred to a greater variety and depth of resources if necessary. A directory of lawyers, doctors, and business professionals must also be available so that the user can access professionals for additional information if required. Care must be taken, however, to resist personal recommendations of any one specific professional.

Disclaimers

Constant reminders on the currency of the resource must be provided. For example, if the *Physicians' Desk Reference* was provided as the resource to consult for a certain drug, the user must be reminded to check for currency on a Web site such as www.drugdigest.org, as well as consulting with his or her doctor or pharmacist. An instructive case in point is that despite its widely reported recall in 2004, the drug Vioxx had no mention of any controversy in the 2005 edition of the *PDR*.

Research Aids

For popular subject areas, consulting written or online aids in identifying, demystifying, and evaluating medical, legal, and business reference sources is advisable. It is not only of enormous help as a visual crutch to the user who is faced with specialized information, but provides a guard against librarians forgetting to include vital pieces of information while explaining a complex document. Sources such as *Business Information: How to Find It, How to Use It* (Lavin, 1992), despite being an older publication, provide a clear X-ray of the skeletal structure of data-rich financial reports, surveys, and analyses. The data packed into a single page of the *Value Line Investment Survey*, for example, are clearly labeled and explained in the book, so that a condensed key can be prepared by librarians for first-time users. An online example of an effective aid to understanding Mergent publications can be found in the New York Public Library's *A Guide to the Mergent Manuals* at http://tinyurl.com/98vxc4.

Remote Access Usage

Finally, provisions must be made for remote access usage, especially telephone reference. To inform a user on the telephone that a certain disease reads as being fatal or to attempt reading aloud the annotations and updates of a certain law is not only awkward but also ripe for misunderstanding and liability. Text-based responses must also be handled with care. Emphasis on in-house resources that the user can consult, compare, and interpret is far preferable in most medical, legal, and business queries.

Reference versus the Radiendocrinator

In the early part of the twentieth century, the entrepreneur William Bailey sold the all-purpose "Radiendocrinator." It professed to cure everything from acne to memory loss by "ionizing the endocrine glands" (Ware, 2002: 3). The cost to the user was what would today amount to over $10,000. With scopic medical, legal, and business resources available to users through their libraries, and effective informational roles played by reference librarians, it is hoped there will be a decrease in the sale of modern-day radiendocrinators.

Recommended Resources Discussed in This Chapter

Medical

Alzheimer Disease Sourcebook. 2008. 4th ed. Detroit: Omnigraphics.
America's Top Doctors. 2010. New York: Castle Connolly Medical Ltd.
BMJ (British Medical Journal). Available: www.bmj.com.
Cancer. Available: www.cancer.gov and www.cancer.org.
CINAHL. Available: www.cinahl.com/cp.gsm.com.
Dialog. Available: www.dialog.com.

TOP TEN MEDICAL, LEGAL, AND BUSINESS SOURCES		
Title	**Print**	**Online**
Black's Law Dictionary, 2009 Eagan, MN: Thomson West	9th ed.	Subscription www.Westlaw.com
Hoover's Handbooks Austin, TX: Hoover's Business Press	4 vols. Annual	Subscription www.hoovers.com/free/
Martindale-Hubbell Law Directory, 1931– New York: Martindale-Hubbell Law Directory	Annual 26 vols.	www.martindale.com www.lawyers.com
The Merck Manual Home Health Handbook, 2011 Whitehouse Station, NJ: Merck & Company	1 vol.	www.merck.com
Official ABMS Directory of Board Certified Medical Specialists, 1993– Philadelphia, PA: W. B. Saunders	Annual 4 vols.	Subscription www.boardcertifieddocs.com
Physicians' Desk Reference, 1945– Montvale, NJ: Thomson PDR.	Annual 1 vol.	www.pdrhealth.com
Stedman's Medical Dictionary, 2005 Philadelphia, PA: Lippincott Williams & Wilkins	28th ed.	www.stedmans.com
Thomas Register of American Manufacturers, 1905– New York: Thomas Publishing		www.thomasnet.com
Value Line Investment Survey New York: Value Line Publications	Weekly	Subscription www.valueline.com
West's Encyclopedia of American Law, 2005 Farmington Hills, MI: GaleCengage Learning	2nd ed. 13 vols.	e-book subscription www.gale.com

Directory of Physicians in the United States. 2008. 41st ed. Chicago: American Medical Association.

DIRLINE. Available: http://dirline.nlm.nih.gov.

Doody's Review Service. Available: www.doody.com.

Dorland's Illustrated Medical Dictionary. 2007. 31st ed. Philadelphia, PA: W. B. Saunders Co. (Elsevier).

Drug information. Available: www.drugdigest.org/DD/Home.

DSM-IV-TR (*Diagnostic and Statistical Manual of Mental Disorders*). 2000. Arlington, VA: American Psychiatric Association.

EMBASE. Available: www.embase.com.

RECOMMENDED FREE HEALTH, LAW, AND BUSINESS WEB SITES

Health

British Medical Journal. This is both a print publication and a free online resource of depth and variety. It is peer-reviewed and the online site is updated daily. Available: www.bmj.com.

Healthfinder. Sponsored by the U.S. National Health Information Center, this site draws from over 1,600 government and nonprofit organizations to provide a wide range of popular health topics. Available: www.healthfinder.gov.

MedlinePlus. As the world's largest biomedical library, the U.S. National Library of Medicine provides this free Web site with access to the health database *MedlinePlus*. Available: www.nlm.nih.gov.

Mondofacto. A subject-specific dictionary of terms related to medicine and the sciences, this resource also includes acronyms, eponyms, conventions, and the history of terms. Available: www.mondofacto.com.

WebMD. Appropriately titled, this site provides timely and reliable health information for the general management of health. Available: www.webmd.com.

Law

American Law Sources Online (ALSO). This resource provides an extensive compilation of links to freely available sites on U.S., Canadian, and Mexican law sources (cases, statutes), commentary (law reviews), and practice aids (court information, official forms). Available: http://lawsource.com/also/.

FindLaw. A popular, easily navigable site that offers a mix of cases, statutes, news, and legal directories. Available: www.findlaw.com.

Glin. This site is an extensive searchable database that freely provides global documents in the legal categories of laws, judicial decisions, legislative records, and legal literature. Available: www.glin.gov.

Hieros Gamos. This is a dense, content-rich site of legal directories from around the world, as well as news, guides, and legal reference material. Available: http://hg.org.

THOMAS. This is the definitive site for U.S. federal legislative information, bills, resolutions, committee information, congressional records, treaties, and presidential nominations. Available: http://thomas.loc.gov.

Business

Big Charts. A personal investment research Web site that offers interactive charts, market commentary, and industry analysis. The 'Historical Quotes' tab allows a user to research stock quotes dating back to 1985. Available: http://bigcharts.marketwatch.com.

Department of Commerce. The site of the U.S. Department of Commerce has descriptions of all the various departments important for business owners, as well as portals to other pertinent sites that may be of interest to the business owner. Available: www.commerce.gov.

IRS. Particularly popular in the month of April, this is the main site for the U.S. Internal Revenue Service. Downloadable forms, publications, and tax-related information are packed into this site. Available: www.irs.ustreas.gov.

THOMASNET. More than 607,000 industrial companies (as of 2/5/2011) in North America are listed in this free online resource that no longer publishes its traditional multi-volume print edition, *The Thomas Register*. Available: www.thomasnet.com.

Yahoo! Finance. An all-purpose site for the personal investor, *Yahoo! Finance* updates its quotes automatically, unless there is over 25 minutes of inactivity in trading. Personal finance (such as retirement, taxes) and investing (such as bonds, currency) have their own tabs. Available: http://finance.yahoo.com.

Encyclopedia of the Life Sciences. 2006. Malden, MA: John Wiley & Sons, Inc. www.els.net.

Ethnic Diseases Sourcebook. 2001. Detroit: Omnigraphics.

Gale Encyclopedia of Alternative Medicine. 2008. 3rd ed. Jacqueline L. Longe, ed. Farmington Hills, MI: Gale Cengage Learning.

Gale Encyclopedia of Children's Health. 2005. Kristine Knapp and Jeffrey Wilson, eds. Farmington Hills, MI: Gale Cengage Learning.

Gale Encyclopedia of Medicine. 2006. Jacqueline L. Longe, ed. Farmington Hills, MI: Gale Cengage Learning.

Gale Encyclopedia of Mental Health. 2007. Laurie J. Fundulian, ed. Farmington Hills, MI: Gale Cengage Learning.

Gale Encyclopedia of Surgery and Medical Tests. 2008. 2nd ed. Anthony J. Senagore, ed. Farmington Hills, MI: Gale Cengage Learning.

Health Reference Center—Academic. Available on InfoTrac Web or CD-ROM: www.gale.com.

Health Source—Consumer and Nursing/Academic editions. Ipswich, MA: EBSCO Publishing. Available: www.epnet.com.

Health and Wellness Resource Center. Farmington Hills, MI: Gale Cengage Learning. Available: www.gale.com/HealthRC.

JAMA: The Journal of the American Medical Association. 1960–. Chicago: American Medical Association. Available: http://jama.ama-assn.org.

The Lancet. Available: http://www.thelancet.com.

Medical Reference Services Quarterly. 1982–. Philadelphia: Taylor & Francis. Available: www.taylorandfrancis.com.

MedlinePlus. Available: http://medlineplus.gov.

Melloni's Illustrated Medical Dictionary. 2001. Ida G. Dox, Biagio John Melloni, Gilbert M. Eisner, and June L. Melloni. Baltimore, MD: Williams and Wilkins.

Merck Manual of Diagnosis and Therapy. 2006. Mark H. Beers and Robert S. Porter, eds. Hoboken, NJ: John Wiley & Sons.

The Merck Manual Home Health Handbook. 2011. Mark H. Beers, ed. Whitehouse Station, NJ: Merck & Co.

National Center for Health Statistics. Available: www.cdc.gov/nchs.

National Library for Health. Available: www.library.nhs.uk.

New England Journal of Medicine. 1928–. Waltham, MA: Massachusetts Medical Society. Available: http://content.nejm.org.

Official ABMS (American Board of Medical Specialties) Directory of Board Certified Medical Specialists 2009. 2008. 41st ed. Philadelphia, PA: W. B. Saunders Company.

Physicians' Desk Reference—PDR. 1974–(annual). New York: Thomson Reuters.

PubMed. 1957–. Bethesda, MD: National Library of Medicine. National Institutes of Health. Available: www.pubmed.gov.

RxList: The Internet Drug Index. Available: www.rxlist.com.

Stedman's Medical Dictionary. 2005. Philadelphia, PA: Lippincott Williams & Wilkins.

20,125 Questionable Doctors: Disciplined by State and Federal Governments, National Edition. 2000. Washington, DC: Public Citizen Group.

Legal

American Law Yearbook. 2009. Farmington Hills, MI: Gale Cengage Learning.

Ballentine's Law Dictionary. 1994. New York: Cengage Delmar Learning.

Ballentine's Legal Dictionary and Thesaurus. 1995. New York: Cengage Delmar Learning.

Black's Law Dictionary. 2009. 9th ed. Bryan A. Garner, ed. Eagan, MN: Thomson West.

Bouvier, John. 1856. *Bouvier's Law Dictionary.* Jamaica Plain, MA: Boston Book Company.

Canadian Legal Information Institute. Available: www.canlii.org.

Corpus Juris Secundum. Eagan, MN: Thomson West. Copyright varies.

Hieros Gamos. Available: www.hg.org.

Law and Legal Information Directory. 2011. Farmington Hills, MI: Gale Cengage Learning.

Law Library Journal. 1908–. Washington, DC: American Association of Law Libraries.

LAWCHEK. Available: www.lawchek.com.

LexisNexis. Available: www.lexisnexis.com.

LexisNexis UK. Available: www.lexisnexis.co.uk.

Martindale-Hubbell Law Directory. 1931–. New York: Martindale-Hubbell Law Directory, Inc.

Merriam-Webster's Dictionary of Law. 1996. Linda Picard Wood, ed. Springfield, MA: Merriam-Webster, Inc.

Quicklaw. Available: http://ql.quicklaw.com.

Westlaw. Available: www.Westlaw.com.

West's Encyclopedia of American Law. 2004. Jeffrey Lehman and Shirelle Phelps, eds. Farmington Hills, MI: Gale Cengage Learning.

Business

ABI/INFORM Complete. Available at www.proquest.com.

Bannock, Graham, Evan Davis, Paul Trott, and Mark Uncles. 2003. *Dictionary of Business.* New York: Bloomberg Press.

Bannock, Graham, and William Manser. 2003. *International Dictionary of Finance.* London: Profile Books.

Bond's Franchise Guide. 2010. Oakland, CA: Source Book Publications. Also available: www.worldfranchising.com.

Brands and Their Companies. 2010. Farmington Hills, MI: Gale Cengage Learning.

Business and Company ASAP. Available: www.gale.cengage.com.

BusinessDictionary.com. Available: http://www.businessdictionary.com.

Capela, John J., and Stephen W. Hartman. 2004. *Dictionary of International Business Terms.* New York: Barron's Educational Series.

A Dictionary of Business and Management. 2009. 5th ed. London: Oxford University Press.

Downes, John, and Jordan Elliott Goodman. 2006. *Dictionary of Finance and Investment Terms.* New York: Barron's Educational Series.

EBSCO Business Source. Subscription available at www.ebscohost.com.

Factiva. Available: http://factiva.com.

Friedman, Jack P. 2007. *Dictionary of Business Terms.* New York: Barron's Educational Series.

Hoover's Handbook of American Business. 2009. Austin, TX: Hoover's Business Press.

Hoover's Handbook of Emerging Companies. 2010. Austin, TX: Hoover's Business Press.

Hoover's Handbook of Industry Profiles. 2010. Austin, TX: Hoover's Business Press.

Hoover's Handbook of Private Companies. 2010. Austin, TX: Hoover's Business Press.

Hoover's Handbook of World Business. 2010. Austin, TX: Hoover's Business Press.

Imber, Jane, and Betsy-Ann Toffler. 2008. *Dictionary of Marketing Terms.* New York: Barron's Educational Series.

LexisNexis Corporate Affiliations. 2010. New Providence, NJ: LexisNexis Group.

Market Share Reporter. 2010. Farmington Hills, MI: Gale Cengage Learning.

Mergent Online. Available: www.mergentonline.com.

Mergent's Bond Record. 1999–(monthly). New York: Mergent FIS.

Standard & Poor's Register of Corporations, Directors and Executives. 2008. New York: McGraw-Hill.

TheStreet.com Ratings Guides. 2010. Millerton, NY: Grey House Publishing.

Thomas Register of American Manufacturers. Available: www.thomaspublishing.com.

Value Line. Available: www.valueline.com.

Value Line Investment Survey. 1995–(weekly). New York: Value Line Publications.

Recommendations for Further Reading

American Library Association, Reference and User Services Association, Business Reference and Services Section. 2001. *Guidelines for Medical, Legal, and Business Responses.* Available: http://tinyurl.com/9ne6mm. A clear set of guidelines prepared for both specialist and non-specialist reference librarians in dealing with issues on the role of staff, the currency and accuracy of sources, and the special care required for off-site users in need of medical, legal, or business questions.

Ambrogi, Robert J. 2004. *The Essential Guide to the Best (and Worst) Legal Sites on the Web.* New York: ALM Publishing. The author, who introduced "legal.online," a syndicated column in 1995, has organized relevant legal Web sites into major practice areas. Each site is also rated along a five-star rating system that covers utility, design, content, accessibility and innovativeness. Although the book has yet to see a third edition, the author continues to cover new legal Web sites, blogs, commentary, and legal resources at www.legaline.com/lawsites.html.

Bookman, Jo Anne, and Fred W. Roper, eds. 2008. *Introduction to Reference Sources in the Health Sciences.* 5th ed. New York: Neal-Schuman Publishers. A comprehensive collection of health resources, the fifth edition of this book continues to pinpoint the major bibliographic and informational sources relevant to health reference collections. Print, electronic, and online formats are all included.

Carey, Benedict. 2008. "Psychiatry's Struggle to Revise the Book of Human Troubles." *The New York Times* (December 18): 1, A27. A fascinating article that highlights the sensitive nature of medical publications and information. The proposed publication of the DSM-V in or around 2012 has already fomented heated battles over what should and should not be included, since "the manual is both a medical guidebook and a cultural institution" that provides insurance companies with reimbursement codes.

The Directory of Business Information Resources, 2008. 2008. New York: Grey House Publishing. A useful overview of the most relevant business newsletters, trade shows, special associations, trade journals and magazines, industry-specific databases, directories, and Web sites for almost 100 broadly grouped industries.

Encyclopedia of Business Information Sources. 2008. Farmington Hills, MI: Gale Cengage Learning. The twenty-fourth edition of this book is a dense compilation of an unusually broad spectrum of print, electronic, and online business resources arranged by subject. Within each subject, types of resources such as indexes, directories, almanacs, and databases are listed with a brief description and complete contact information.

Jankowski, Terry Ann. 2008. *The MLA Essential Guide to Becoming an Expert Searcher: Proven Techniques, Strategies, and Tips for Finding Health Information.* New York: Neal-Schuman. The difference between "Googling" a health topic and diving deep into a database is highlighted in this thorough treatise on search strategies and database construction. Specific health databases are discussed and a list of thirty exercises for becoming a skilled health information specialist is provided.

Medical and Health Care Books and Serials in Print. 2008. New York: Bowker. An extensive listing of over 115,000 books and nearly 24,000 serials related to the health and biomedical field. The two-volume set can be searched by subject and title as well as by author and publisher. It is a useful resource to consult for updates in a field where currency is of paramount value.

Moss, Rita W. 2004. *Strauss's Handbook of Business Information.* Westport, CT: Libraries Unlimited. A clear and well-organized handbook describing business reference sources and formats. It also covers the tricky area of loose-leaf services.

Spatz, Michelle. 2008. *Answering Consumer Health Questions.* New York: Neal-Schuman. Recognizing the delicate nature of health reference, Spatz provides interesting scripts and strategies that can be employed for common health inquiries. Both in-person and virtual reference are taken into account when establishing guidelines for confidential inquiries.

Wood, Sandra, ed. 2008. *Introduction to Health Sciences Librarianship.* New York: Routledge. A wide, informative net is cast over the length and breadth of health resources, services, libraries, and information in original ways that include screen captures and "A Day in the Life of..." accounts of the health reference librarian.

Worley, Loyita. 2006. *BIALL Handbook of Legal Information Management*. Burlington, VT: Ashgate Publishing Company. Though applied to the laws of the United Kingdom, this is an authoritative handbook on critical aspects of law librarianship applicable to all information providers. Search techniques and organization of legal resources along with chapters on the practical management and training of staff in ongoing legal research and ethics, combine to provide a compelling focus on legal information services as a whole.

Bibliography of Works Cited in This Chapter

"Accessing Legal and Regulatory Information in Internet Resources and Documents." 2006. *Journal of Library Administration* 44, no. 1/2: 263–324.

American Library Association, Reference and User Services Association, Business Reference and Services Section. 2001. *Guidelines for Medical, Legal, and Business Responses*. Available: http://tinyurl.com/9ne6mm.

American Reference Books Annual. 2008. Westport, CT: Libraries Unlimited. Also available: www.arbaonline.com.

Cohen, Morris, and Kent C. Olson. *Legal Research in a Nutshell*. 2003. Eagan, MN: Thomson West.

Directory of Special Libraries and Information Centers. 2011. Vols. 1 and 2. 39th ed. Farmington Hills, MI: Gale Cengage Learning.

Ebbinghouse, Carol. 2008. "The New Surge of Open Legal Information on the Internet." *Searcher* 16, no. 6 (June 1): 8–16.

Fox, Susannah. 2008. "The Engaged E-Patient Population." *Pew Internet and American Life Project—Reports: Health* (August 26).

Goodman, Lisa A. 2008. "Legal Ethics Is Not a Laughing Matter." *AALL Spectrum* 13, no. 1 (September 1): 32–33.

Habermann, Julia. 2005. "Weblogs as a Source of Business News and Information." *Online* 29, no. 5 (September/October): 35–37.

"Health and Medical Resources: Information for the Consumer." 2006. *Journal of Library Administration* 44, no. 1/2: 395–428.

Ketchum, A. M. 2005. "Consumer Health Information Websites: A Survey of Design Elements Found in Sites Developed in Academic Environments." *Journal of the Medical Library Association* 93, no. 4 (October): 496–499.

Larson, Sonja, and John Bourdeau. 1997. *Legal Research for Beginners*. New York: Barron's Educational Series.

Lavin, Michael, R. 1992. *Business Information: How to Find It, How to Use It*. Phoenix, AZ: Oryx Press.

Moulton, Sara E. 2008. "Response to a Consumer Health Query." *Journal of Consumer Health on the Internet* 12, no. 3 (July 1): 237–249.

Ojala, Marydee. 2006. "The New Life Cycle of Business Information." *Online* 30, no. 1(January/February): 48–50.

"Outstanding Business Reference Sources: The 2007 Selection of Recent Titles." 2007. *Reference & User Services Quarterly* 47, no. 2 (Winter): 132–136.

Pettinato, Tammy R. 2008. "Dealing with Pro Se Patrons." *Public Services Quarterly* 4, no. 3 (October 1): 283–289.

Ross, Celia. 2008. "Keeping Up with Business Reference." *Journal of Business & Finance Librarianship* 13, no. 3 (January 1): 363–370.

Scarr, Carrie. 2008. "Business/Economics." *Library Journal (Reference Supplement)* 133 (November 15): 32–34.

Ware, Leslie, and editors of *Consumer Reports*. 2002. *Selling It*. New York: W. W. Norton & Co.

Welch, Jeanie M. 2005. "Silent Partners: Public Libraries and Their Services to Small Businesses and Entrepreneurs." *Public Libraries* 44, no. 5 (September/October): 282–286.

Whisner, Mary. 2006. *Practicing Reference: Thoughts for Librarians and Legal Researchers*. Buffalo, NY: William S. Hein and Co.

10

Answering Questions about Geography, Countries, and Travel— Atlases, Gazetteers, Maps, Geographic Information Systems, and Travel Guides

Overview

Geography is an interdisciplinary area of study spanning both earth science (physical geography) and social science (human geography). Today geography "explores the relationship between the earth and its peoples through the study of place, space and environment. Geographers ask the questions where and what; also how and why" (Unwin, 1992: 13). "Individuals with diverse interests are tied together through their interest in understanding how places or locations affect activities (human or otherwise), how places are connected, and how those connections facilitate movement between places or cause an event at one location to impact another location" (Johnson, 2003: 1).

As our perspectives shift to a more global outlook, the importance of geographic information increases, allowing more learning about the world in which we live. The information provided by geographic sources is remarkable and extensive and includes information in print and electronic formats. Geographic sources provide information in narrative form through gazetteers and other text resources and visually through maps. Although geographic information is available in other information sources, sources specific to the field provide the most precise and accurate information. For example, in an atlas the user can find not only the location of a country or city but also its latitude and longitude and its relationship to other geographic entities.

How Geographic Information Is Used

Geographic information sources are used to answer a variety of queries. First, they can be employed to find the location of towns, rivers, mountains, countries, continents, and so on. Geographic sources make it possible for users to more easily visualize the relationship between countries and continents. They do more than just show boundaries; they may show the makeup of a particular land area—its mountains, valleys, rivers, and plains. Other geographic tools show the environmental and climatic or ecological factors in an area so we can better understand how this affects the ability of the area, for example, to develop agriculturally. Geographic sources may deal with the past as well as the present. For example, historical maps and atlases trace changing country boundaries to provide the reader with a way to visualize what has happened in a particular country and how history has been affected by these changes. Because many atlases provide other related information, users can find information on demographics and population trends for a particular area.

Questions Answered by Geographic Information

Q: What countries surround Austria?

A: This answer can be found by looking at a current map of Austria in an atlas.

Q: What is the present name of the country called Burma?

A: A gazetteer such as the *Columbia Gazetteer of the World Online*, which will cross-reference Burma to its present name, Myanmar, can provide this information.

Q: Where is Rabat located?

A: Either an atlas with a good index or a gazetteer can be used to find this answer. It is a city in the country of Morocco.

Q: What were the boundaries of the countries in Europe in 1848?

A: This can be found in *Shepherd's Historical Atlas*.

Major Geographic Information Resources Used in Reference Work

Geographic information sources come in many formats, such as gazetteers. Gazetteers are text-based sources of information about geographic places and features. They are arranged alphabetically and describe as concisely and precisely as possible where, for example, a particular town or mountain range is located and other pertinent facts about it.

In contrast to gazetteers, maps are a way to visualize the world. They take an enormous amount of information and put it into a format that can be more easily understood (Liben, 2008). The most common types of maps are route and street maps that show the streets and highways so that someone can determine the best route to get from one place to another. Topographic maps show the natural land features through the use of color so that the user can see clearly the mountainous areas, the rivers, and the plains. Political maps show the boundaries of major cities, towns, and villages, and the boundaries of countries. Thematic maps usually deal with a narrow theme such as religion, ethnic diversity, or history, using the visual format of maps to convey information.

The digital revolution has brought new possibilities to mapmaking, but the end of the paper map is not in sight. Although digital mapmaking has made it possible to produce interactive maps, to provide for route finding, to search for place name and convert maps into electronic form, paper maps still have some distinct advantages. They allow subtleties of color and text that are not possible with digital maps. Maps that appear on a computer screen are limited by the screen resolution. Paper maps also allow the user to look at a wider expanse at one time than is possible on a screen (Ashworth, 2003: 56). Route and street maps are particularly useful in electronic format. Such vendors as Mapquest.com and Google Maps (http://maps.google.com) make it possible for the user to type in a starting location and destination. These programs then provide a map and written directions to the location. Alternately, these programs allow a user to type in a specific address and get a map of that location. In some major metropolitan areas, Web sites such as HopStop.com are being developed to help plan routes on foot and via public transportation.

An atlas is a collection of maps with some unifying theme. Atlases may include a series of maps for a particular country or continent, showing both the overview and more specific areas such as a state, province, city, or a world atlas that covers the entire globe. Atlases offer more than maps since they often include other geographic information such as population, the environment, and statistics on countries, with a detailed index. But there are also collections of historical maps that show the changes in political boundaries through time. Thematic or subject atlases have become popular to show visually a particular subject, for example, an atlas on some aspect of history. A third type of map is a globe. Globes provide a way to see the relationship between continents and land masses and provide a more accurate visualization of the earth. There is less geographic detail on a globe. Another source of geographic information is travel guides. Travel guides come in many forms. Some simply list places to see, restaurants, and hotels, whereas others provide more detailed information about a particular city or country with maps, detailed information on the history and culture of the city or country, and interesting descriptions of historical sites.

Gazetteers and Geographical Dictionaries

"A gazetteer is an alphabetical list of place names with information that can be used to locate the areas that the names are associated with" (Johnson, 2003: 49). Often users do not need a map but simply want information about the location of a particular city, town, river, or mountain. For this information, the librarian can turn to a gazetteer or geographical dictionary.

The *Columbia Gazetteer of the World* is a standard source for reference librarians. This three-volume set contains more than 170,000 detailed entries listing geographical sites such as countries, cities, lakes, and mountains worldwide and using the 2000 census figures. The online version of the *Gazetteer* (www.columbia gazetteer.org) is available by subscription.

Merriam-Webster's Geographical Dictionary, 3rd Edition Revised, is a one-volume gazetteer and a good choice for libraries not needing the more extensive

Columbia Gazetteer of the World. It contains more than 54,000 brief entries with economic, political, and physical data and 250 black-and-white maps. Countries, cities, natural features, and historical sites are listed.

The *Getty Thesaurus of Geographic Names Online* (www.getty.edu/research/tools/vocabulary/tgn) is a free online gazetteer developed by the Getty Research Institute. Listing nearly 1 million place names, it provides information about the preferred name for a place (a place could be a city, a village, or a land feature such as a mountain) and all variants by language and through history. The latitude and longitude is given for each place as well as its hierarchical position. For example, Milan's hierarchical position is World (facet), Europe (continent), Italy (nation), Lombardy (region), Milano (province), Milan (inhabited place). It also places Milan in its historical hierarchy and adds a note about its history. Sources of information for this thesaurus are listed and include the *Columbia Lippincott Gazetteer, Merriam-Webster's Geographical Dictionary*, and the *Encyclopaedia Britannica.*

Geographic Names Information System (GNIS) (http://geonames.usgs.gov/) provides a way to verify the correct version of place names. It lists more than 2 million physical and cultural geographic names in the United States, the U.S. territories, and Antarctica. It was developed in cooperation with the U.S. Board of Geographic Names. Users can search for names of towns, rivers, streams, valleys, airports, schools, and much more. For example, the search for a town will give the user the elevation, the population, history notes, and the latitude and longitude.

NGA GEOnet Names Server (http://earth-info.nga.mil/gns/html/index .html), a database of 5.5 million foreign place names, is hosted by the National Geospatial-Intelligence Agency. This is the official source for all names of foreign geographic features and places.

The U.S. Bureau of the Census's *U.S. Gazetteer* (www.census.gov/geo/www/gazetteer/gazette.html) provides detailed maps of all incorporated towns, counties, and county subdivisions in the United States. The user can search by place names or zip code. There is a link to a Topographically Integrated Geographic Encoding and Referencing System map. The 2000 and the 1990 census are used.

Geographical Names of Canada (http://geonames.nrcan.gc.ca/index_e.php) is a source to verify place names for Canada in the same way that GNIS does for the United States.

Worldmark Encyclopedia of the Nations, also available online, is a good source of information on over 200 countries and dependencies around the world. In addition to the detailed information on each country, there are biographical essays on national leaders.

Maps and Atlases

Mapmaking has a long history. Even in ancient times the Babylonians drew maps on clay tablets. The Greeks were among the early mapmakers. The maps of Ptolemy were still being used in the fifteenth century when his book *Geography* was published in 1482 in Latin. The European discovery of America and the explorations of Africa and Asia diminished the importance of Ptolemy's works. Geographers from all over Europe contributed new information and corrected the maps of Ptolemy during the sixteenth century. Among those mapmakers were two Dutchmen, Abraham Ortelius and Gerard Mercator. The invention of printing coincided with these explorations so that new maps could be more easily produced and distributed. "Governments began to use maps as tools not only for foreign conquests and economic exploitation but to establish control at home and for purposes of national defense" (info@maphistory.info).

Major World Atlases

Called by *Booklist* the "pinnacle of atlases," the *Times Comprehensive Atlas of the World* is the highest quality world atlas available. The maps are the work of John G. Barthlomew of Edinburgh, Scotland. It has digitally produced maps that have light but easy-to-distinguish colors and a readable typeface. This atlas has tried to provide a balanced coverage of all parts of the world and includes extensive mapping of all continents with at least ten maps per continent. Thematic world maps covering such topics as climate, population, energy, and minerals are included. The *Times Atlas* pays careful attention to detail and uses easy-to-read symbols. Its excellent index lists more than 200,000 place names at latitude/longitude coordinates and can serve as a gazetteer. The *Times Atlas* does, however, lack city maps.

The *National Geographic Atlas of the World*, though smaller than the *Times Atlas* with fewer pages, maps, and index entries, is nevertheless a very good atlas that particularly excels in U.S. maps. It provides city maps for each continent with the largest number from the United States. Completely revised, it contains the latest information on political and natural changes. A group of thematic world maps provide information on climate, biodiversity, the economy, and other issues. A companion Web site is available for owners of the print atlas that provides updated information and the ability to customize maps.

Oxford Comprehensive Atlas of the World reflects recent changes in country boundaries. This atlas includes 290 pages of maps and a fifty-six-page section on different aspects of world geography including climate change, biodiversity, and global warming.

The *DK Great World Atlas* includes 370 maps, 320 satellite images, and 750 full-color photographs as well as industry maps, communication maps, agricultural maps, and natural resource maps. It has a list of countries of the world with some basic statistical information on each of them. This atlas is very user friendly with good layout of each page.

Many of the publishers of atlases publish a series of atlases in various sizes and at different prices.

Medium-Sized Atlases

Although there is no comparison to the unique and oversized *Times Comprehensive Atlas of the World*, many atlases in the medium-sized category provide good coverage at a moderate price and are very useful in a library.

The *Times Concise Atlas of the World* is a smaller version of the *Times Atlas*. It includes the usual Bartholomew maps, the detailed index of 200,000 place names, and a list of countries with concise information on each country and a picture of the flag. City maps are inset on the page of the country.

The *Hammond World Atlas* is one of a series of Hammond atlases. The new edition of this medium-sized atlas has more than 200 digital maps, a sixty-four-page "Thematic Section" with information ranging from the solar system to global warming and a forty-five-page "Satellite Image Section." The physical maps are from digital elevation data. The index features 110,000 entries. Major metropolitan areas are dealt with as inserts on regional maps. Commentary relating to each continent precedes each section. The *Hammond World Atlas* uses a smaller scale for countries other than the United States, which makes comparisons difficult. Nevertheless, it is an excellent atlas for its size and price.

The *Oxford Atlas of the World*, which is revised annually, includes 179 pages of full-color, computer-generated maps with an index of 83,000 entries. The major part of this atlas is devoted to maps of the continents including physical maps, political maps, and maps of specific regions. There is a separate section with thirty-one pages of maps for sixty-nine urban areas. A thirty-two-page gazetteer that provides ready reference information is arranged alphabetically with country summaries and official flags. The index uses the latitude and longitude as well as a letter/figure grid reference.

The *HarperCollins New World Atlas* also features Bartholomew maps. It provides a new approach to an atlas with a variety of maps for each continent on such subjects as countries, issues, and environments, and a number of excellent physical/political maps covering all parts of the continent. The index of 80,000 place names is particularly useful.

The Dorling Kindersley *Traveler's Atlas* provides physical maps for every section of the world as well as a box with a list of cities and places to see in that country or group of countries and another box with possible activities. Introductions to each continent provide maps on climate, transportation, languages, and standard of living.

Desk and Student Atlases

Smaller atlases are also published by the same publishers. Though not as detailed as larger atlases, they are often useful to students. *Goode's World Atlas* is an excellent compact atlas with world thematic maps, physical/political regional maps, a section on tectonic plates and an index and geographic tables. It is highly recommended. In addition, it is worth considering the following: the *Oxford Essential World Atlas* and the *National Geographic Concise Atlas of the World*.

Some atlases are specifically designed for children. The *National Geographic World Atlas for Young Explorers* provides twenty-five thematic maps. The maps throughout the atlas are of good quality and easy to use. The flags and facts about each country, including population, the capital and language are provided. An interesting feature is the fifteen pages devoted to the oceans. *World Book Atlas* is another good choice.

Historical Atlases

Maps provide information about the past as well as the present. They can be arranged by theme or by date. *Shepherd's Historical Atlas* is a rich source of historical maps, especially European maps. *Shepherd's* shows the changes in boundaries throughout the ages, providing the user with an understanding of the impact of wars and treaties on the face of Europe.

Times History of the World, edited by Richard Overy, begins with a twelve-page "Chronology of World History." It presents a balanced view of world history, including information on social history and on the cultural achievements of the various civilizations.

The *Concise Atlas of World History* provides a series of maps combined with a narrative and photographs for each time period, beginning with the Ancient World and continuing to the year 2000. It also contains an alphabetical list of events, people, and places. This atlas provides an added dimension to our understanding of world history through its visual approach.

The *Historical Atlas of the U.S.* provides a visual approach to U.S. history. It alternates the thematic sections, e.g., land, people, boundaries, economy, networks, and communities, with the five chronological sections—1400–1606, 1607–1788, 1789–1860, 1861–1916, and 1917–1988. The atlas includes time lines of U.S. history along with text and photographs. A bibliography includes the sources of the maps and illustrations as well as additional sources of information and an index.

The *Historical Atlas of Canada* is a three-volume interdisciplinary effort to capture the history of Canada—both of the indigenous people and the Europeans. The three volumes are titled *From the Beginning to 1800*, *The Land Transformed, 1800–1891*, and *Addressing the Twentieth Century, 1891–1961*. The maps range over a wide variety of subjects from population, workforce, and transportation to trade, agriculture, and fishing. This atlas presents its material in clear, easy-to-read maps with accompanying text. There is no index, but there is a detailed table of contents.

The *Barrington Atlas of the Greek and Roman World* by William Rand Kenan, Jr., is a comprehensive atlas of the classical world that includes all the regions that the Greeks and Romans penetrated between 1000 BC and 640 AD. It is an attempt to re-create the landscape of that time.

David Rumsey and Edith M. Punt have produced *Cartographica Extraordinaire: The Historical Map Transformed*. This work reflects the way even historical maps are being transformed by geographic information systems (GIS). The maps in this work are also available on Rumsey's Web site (www.davidrumsey.com). The David Rumsey Map Collection also provides 17,400 free of copyright maps specializing in eighteenth- and nineteenth-century maps, focusing on the Western Hemisphere but including historic maps of other continents as well. These maps can be searched by country, state, publication author, or keyword and can be printed.

Other sources of historical maps online are the History of Cartography Gateway (www.maphistory.info), which links to map sources, and the Library of Congress American Memory Collection (http://memory.loc.gov/ammem/index.html), which features mostly U.S. maps from 1544 to 2004 in the public domain. Users can search the American Memory Collection by cities and towns or by subject, e.g., conservation and environment, discovery and exploration, cultural landscapes, military battles and campaigns, and transportation and communication. Yale University provides on its Web site a selection of maps from its historical map collection. This is a good source of antiquarian maps and historical city maps (www.library.yale.edu/MapColl/index.html).

Thematic Atlases

The atlas format is being used for thematic maps, which may or may not depend on geography. These atlases usually deal with a subject that could be history, ethnic diversity, religion, etc. Thematic atlases are characterized by photos, drawings, graphs, charts, and maps. Some examples of thematic atlases are the following: *Oxford New Historical Atlas of Religion in America*, edited by Edwin Gausted, is an excellent atlas using both text and maps to show by century and region the growth of each religion. In addition to the more traditional religions, the atlas includes coverage of Muslim, Hindu, Sikh, Buddhist and other religious groups. Bibliographical references are included at the end of each section. *Penguin Atlas of Women in the World* by Joni Seager provides analysis of current data on many issues facing women throughout the world including motherhood, changing households, domestic violence, and women in government. The *Penguin State of the World Atlas* (Smith, 2008), a very powerful representation of the world, provides a visual survey of current events and global trends. It includes statistics on international trade, energy resources and consumption, aging, health risks, and much more.

Thematic atlases also include subject matter on the ocean and astronomy. For example, *Hidden Depths: Atlas of the Oceans* was written by NOAA scientists and covers the current state of oceans and future trends with emphasis on natural systems along with new, full-color photos. *Atlas of the Universe* by Mark A. Garlick, written especially for children, provides colorful, dramatic space photographs as well as good star charts, portraits of the solar system, stars and galaxies, and aids for amateur explorers.

Rand McNally Commercial Atlas and Marketing Guide (annual) is available online as well as in book form. This atlas provides maps for 120,000 places in the United States with information on population, the economy and economic activity, and transportation and communications. State tables list principal cities and business data by county. It is an excellent business planning tool.

Road Atlases

Librarians will want to buy road and street maps for their community, county, and state. Many good local and regional map companies exist and can be located through the yellow pages of local telephone directories. Maps are also produced by city, county, and state governments.

The best-known road atlas is the *Rand McNally Road Atlas*. This atlas, updated annually, provides maps of every state in the United States, every Canadian province, and a map of Mexico. This atlas also includes maps of 300 cities and twenty U.S. national parks. A list of town names by state is available at the end of the atlas as well as a nationwide mileage chart and a map showing interstate mileage and drive time. This atlas is used by people needing to determine the best route to a destination. It is integrated with www.randmcnally .com via codes on the map pages.

The National Geographic Society provides some free maps, and many for purchase from its Web site. The Map Machine (www.nationalgeographic.com/maps/map-machine) can be used to obtain a free street map. The National Geographic Xpeditions (www.nationalgeographic.com/xpeditions) provides printer-friendly maps.

MSR Maps (http://msrmaps.com/Default.aspx) provides public access to maps and aerial photographs of the United States. Users can look at their own neighborhood or at some famous place such as a national park.

Mapquest (www.mapquest.com), a popular Web site, provides the user with directions to locations even beyond the U.S. borders, and locations of a particular address.

A more recent addition to online maps is Google's maps. At http://maps .google.com the user can find a map for a particular location, find a map to locate a business, or get directions from one location to another. In addition to these maps, Google Earth available at earth.google.com provides satellite maps. Google now has MyMaps where users can create personalized, annotated maps. Libraries are using this feature to create local maps showing library branches, local historical sites, etc. (Jacobsen, 2008).

Maps

Individual maps are often needed by users. The following are some of the sources of individual maps, both current and historic.

The Perry-Casteñada Library, University of Texas, Web site (www.lib.utexas.edu/maps/) provides 5,000 digitized maps country by country from the library's collection. It is strong in historical maps and is a good source for printing out a small-scale map.

National Atlas of the United States (www.nationalatlas.gov) is an interactive geological and topographical map produced by the U.S. Geological Survey that provides a wealth of information about the United States on a variety of topics from agriculture to government. Users can access more than 400 data layers. Many files require GIS software, but it is, on the whole, a user-friendly site.

The *Atlas of Canada* is a bilingual online product. There are many interesting thematic maps showing both current and historic information in visual form on such subjects as the environment, the economy, history, climate, and health (http://atlas.nrcan.gc.ca/site/english/index.html).

The *American Fact Finder*, located on the U.S. Census site (http://factfinder2 .census.gov), provides maps based on historical information. There are both reference and thematic maps that have been developed using census data.

Odden's Bookmarks: The Fascinating World of Maps and Mapping (http://oddens .geog.uu.nl) provides over 4,000 links to map collections and cartography resources from all over the world on the Web. Users can search under a variety of subjects including maps and atlases, sellers of cartographic materials, departments of cartography, and libraries.

Infomine (http://infomine.ucr.edu), a site developed by librarians, has a selective list of map links primarily of the United States.

For British maps a good place to start is the British Library Map Collection (www.bl.uk/onlinegallery/index.html), which includes old and new maps. Other important map collections in the United Kingdom include the Bodleian Library at Oxford University, the National Library of Scotland, the National Library of Wales, and the Royal Geographic Society.

The United Nations also has a growing collection of country maps that can be accessed at www.un.org/Depts/Cartogaphic/English/htmain.htm.

U.S. Government Publications and Maps

Maps are available from many departments of the U.S. government. The largest number of maps is produced by the U.S. Geological Survey (www.usgs.gov). They include geological maps, topographical maps, and GIS maps on a wide range of topics including agriculture and farming, atmosphere and climate, and health and disease. They make aerial photographs available for purchase through EROS (Earth Resources Observation Systems) (http://eros.usgs.gov).

The U.S. Bureau of the Census (www.census.gov/geo/www/maps) provides maps that enable the user to visualize the information in the census. The Bureau of the Census also provides online mapping resources of U.S. locations through the TIGER mapping service. The Environmental Protection Agency (EPA) has developed EnviroMapper (www.epa.gov/emefdata/em4ef.home), which provides maps by location showing eligibility for Superfund monies and information about such issues as hazardous wastes and toxic emissions. The Federal Emergency Management Agency (FEMA) (www.fema.gov/hazard/ map/index.shtm) provides multiple hazard maps showing locations vulnerable to floods, landslides, tornadoes, and hurricanes.

The Geography and Map Division of the Library of Congress (http:// memory.loc.gov/ammem/gmdhtml/gmdhome.html) provides both historic and more recent maps showing changes in the U.S. landscape, e.g., maps showing the growth and development of the U.S. National Parks.

Canadian maps including topographic, geological, forest, and mining maps as well as aerial photographs and satellite images are produced by the Earth Sciences Section of Natural Resources Canada (http://ess/nrcan.gc.ca/ mapcar/index_e.php).

GIS Sources

Geographic Information Systems (GIS) use "computer hardware, software, data and people combined to answer spatially based questions and to provide new ways of looking at geographic information to find solutions or make decisions" (Johnson, 2003: 177). GIS has added a whole new dimension to the study of geography, going far beyond the study and use of maps. Using GIS software requires advanced study or training. Some of the sites providing GIS products are U.S. Geological Survey's GIS Web site (http://egsc.usgs.gov/isb/pubs/gis _poster), the Census Bureau's American Fact Finder, and EPA's EnviroMapper.

A number of companies provide GIS software. These include ESRI (www .esri.com), which has a suite of GIS software (ArcGIS Explorer, ArcGIS Engine, ArcView, ArcInfo, ArcEditor), Microsoft (Map Point), and Calipher (Mapitude 4.7) (Cline, 1005: 27). Open-source software such as GRASS developed by the U.S. Army Corps of Engineers and Map Server developed by University of Minnesota are also available.

Travel Guides

An often overlooked geographic source is travel guides. Travel guides are available from a diverse array of authors and publishers. Although some may seem too subjective to be used as a reference source, others provide a great deal of factual, up-to-date information on cities and countries. Some of the most factual of the guidebooks are the *Michelin Green Guides*, *Fodor Travel Guides*, *Baedeker Guides*, the *Rough Guides*, *Lonely Planet*, and *Moon Handbooks*. All of these guidebooks provide detailed information about the history of a city or country and information about museums and other cultural sites. They often provide maps of the interiors of museums and noted buildings and detailed descriptions of important rooms within these buildings.

Useful specialized travel guides provide information on such subjects as accessibility, guides to special kinds of sites such as the national parks, Native American landmarks, and ecotourism sites. In addition to these there are guides to campgrounds, e.g., Woodall's *Campground Directory*.

Collection Development and Maintenance

Selection and Keeping Current

Information about geographical sources as well as reviews of new monographs and online information sources help the librarian to identify new and updated materials. Geographical sources are regularly reviewed in *Booklist*, *Choice*, *Library Journal*, and *American Reference Books Annual*.

The U.S. government remains a key source of information producing a wide variety of maps. The TIGER mapping service from the U.S. Bureau of the Census produces detailed maps of locations throughout the United States using census data. Other maps are produced by the National Oceanic and Atmospheric Administration (NOAA), the U.S. Geological Survey (USGS), the U.S. Department of Housing and Urban Development (HUD), the U.S. Department of Defense's National Imagery and Mapping Agency (NIMA), the Environmental Protection Agency (EPA), and others.

Information about new geographic sources is available through the following groups: American Library Association's Map and Geography Round Table (MAGERT) newsletter, *base line*, and its listserv, maps-l; the Information Bulletin of the Western Association of Map Librarians; and the Bulletin of the Association of Canadian Map Libraries and Archives.

Numerous monographs include Mary Lynette Larsgaard's *Map Librarianship: An Introduction*, Jenny Marie Johnson's *Geographic Information: How to Find It, How to Use It*, and Barbara Farrell and Aileen Desbarats's *Guide for a Small Map Collection* that provide information on map librarianship.

In addition to some of the geographic sources listed in this chapter, ALA's Map and Geography Round Table has suggested in its publication "Helpful Hints for Small Map Collections" that libraries acquire topographic maps of their county and state, city maps of nearby cities, and aerial photographs of their area. These can be acquired through commercial map dealers or through the U.S. Geological Survey (geography. usgs.gov). Libraries needing to acquire maps should look at the catalogs or Web sites of the major publishers of maps.

Evaluating Geographic Resources

The criteria for good-quality accessible maps includes currency and accuracy, authority, legibility, scale and projection, color, symbols, format, index, and price.

The currency of the maps must be a primary consideration. Boundaries continue to change and even place names change. Maps must be current in order to be useful. Before purchasing geographic sources, the currency of the source should be verified by checking to see if current boundaries of countries are shown and to see that it reflects changes in names of cities and countries.

Accuracy is essential for a good-quality map. Accuracy and currency are closely linked, since a large part of accuracy has to do with being up-to-date. Authority is particularly important to mapmaking. The major publishers of maps and atlases are Times Books, Rand McNally, C. S. Hammond, the National Geographic Society, DK, and Oxford University Press. Other publishers are known for the quality of their maps. Among them are John G. Bartholomew (Edinburgh) and George Philip & Sons, Ltd. in the United Kingdom, and Michelin in France.

Legibility and readability of the map is crucial. This may be influenced by the scale of the map, the color contrast of the map, and the way symbols are used to indicate certain features of the map. "Scale is the ratio of distance on the map to linear distance on the earth" (Monmonier and Schnell, 1988: 15). Scale can be represented as a ratio l:10,000 or 1/10,000 or it can be represented as a bar scale or a verbal scale of "one inch equals 64 miles."

Color is often a subtle but important part of mapmaking. A well-done map will be pleasant to look at and yet offer enough contrast to understand the different kinds of land areas. Symbols are used to distinguish between geographic features and make them easier to locate. Symbols must have a good legend and be adequately explained. The use of a good type style is needed to enable the user to easily find the desired information.

Atlases should display a balanced coverage of the world or a balanced approach to the continents or countries that they cover. Mary Lynette Larsgaard suggests determining the number of pages in an atlas and then counting the number of pages devoted to the United States and the number of pages devoted to Africa as a way to ascertain whether the atlas is providing balanced coverage (Larsgaard, 1998: 113). Larsgaard also suggests comparing the same area in two or more atlases to determine which atlases provide the best treatment (Larsgaard, 1998: 114).

As much as possible, the same scale should be used throughout an atlas. In this way it is possible to compare the size of countries or continents. "Map projection is the method employed to transfer a curved area—a section of earth—to the flat, two dimensional plane of the page" (Sader and Lewis, 1995: 164). All flat maps distort to some extent the shapes and areas. The larger the area covered by the map, the greater is the distortion; the smaller the area, the less distortion there will be. Various methods of projection are used to lessen the distortion. The kind of projection used depends on the use of the map. Within an atlas different map projections are often used to best capture a particular area.

Atlases need to be accessible. This involves both the arrangement of the atlas as it moves from area to area, the need for a clear and easy-to-understand legend, and finally a comprehensive index with both cross-references to other names or spellings and a good grid system. Many indexes use latitude and longitude to describe the location of a particular place while others use a grid system. If it is hard to find specific places after locating them in the index, then the indexing has failed.

Because maps are now produced both on paper and electronically, it is necessary to evaluate whether the format serves the source well. Is this, for example, an appropriate map for an electronic format or would it be better in paper? Sometimes the purpose of the source will dictate which format is more appropriate. If the format is paper, it is important to note the ease of handling the atlas, the convenience of use and the binding, and whether some of the maps fall into the book's gutter, making them hard to read.

Price is the final consideration for any atlas. It may pay to have fewer atlases and purchase those of high quality.

Further Considerations

For many reasons users need geographic information. They may want to see a map of a particular area of the world to better understand what is happening there. They may want to know where Saudi Arabia is in relation to Iraq or they may want to know where Bali is in relation to Penang. Maps often provide an understanding of how events affect other countries in a region.

People planning a trip want maps and guidebooks to chart their trip. For example, they might be planning a trip to Thailand and want to know which other countries they could easily visit. Maybe friends have given them names of towns to visit, and they need to see where they are.

A businessman has just been told that he is being sent to Kiev in the Ukraine. He is researching Kiev to find out about the area, the temperature for the time of year he is going, what he can expect in terms of access to e-mail, and whether he can expect to be able to use a wireless laptop. Maps and guidebooks will provide him with a great deal of information, as will Web sites.

Currency is important with maps. Librarians need to be aware of the publication of new editions of atlases and acquire the new edition. If the older edition is fairly recent, it could be put in the stacks. But keeping old editions in the stacks may lead users to inaccurate information.

For information on citing maps the University of North Texas Libraries has useful instructions at www.library.unt.edu/govinfo/browse-topics/citation-guides-and-style-manuals/citing-maps.

Recommended Resources Discussed in This Chapter

American Fact Finder. Available: http://factfinder2.census.gov.
American Library Association. 1981–. *Base line: A Newsletter of the Map and Geography Round Table.*

TOP TEN GEOGRAPHIC INFORMATION SOURCES		
Title	Print	Online
Commercial Atlas and Marketing Guide Chicago: Rand McNally	Annual	www.randmcnally.com
Times Comprehensive Atlas of the World New York: Times Books	11th ed.	
National Geographic Atlas of the World Washington, DC: National Geographic Society	8th ed.	
Oxford Atlas of the World New York: Oxford University Press	Annual	
Columbia Gazetteer of the World New York: Columbia University Press	2nd ed.	Subscription www.columbiagazetteer.org
Rand McNally Road Atlas Chicago: Rand McNally	Annual	
Perry-Casteñada Library		www.lib.utexas.edu/maps/
Google Maps		Maps.google.com
Mapquest		www.mapquest.com
Shepherd's Historical Atlas Totowa, NJ: Barnes & Noble	9th ed.	

RECOMMENDED FREE GEOGRAPHIC WEB SITES

Geographic Names Information System (GNIS). Available: http://geonames.usgs.gov. A source to provide the correct names of places in the United States and Antarctica.

Google Maps. Available: http://maps.google.com. A source of maps of most locations.

Library of Congress. Geography and Map Division. Available: http://memory.loc.gov/ammem/gmdhtml/gmdhome.html. Good source of historical maps.

Mapquest. Available: www.mapquest.com. Provides driving directions and maps of specific locations.

National Geographic Society Map Machine. Available: www.nationalgeographic.com/maps/map-machine. A source of free street maps.

Perry-Casteñada Library Map Collection. Available: www.lib.utexas.edu/ maps/. An excellent source of maps past and present.

U.S. Bureau of the Census. U.S. Gazetteer. Available: www.census.gov/geo/www/gazetteer/gazette.html.

Association of Canadian Map Libraries and Archives. 1968. Bulletin. Ottawa, ON. Triannual.

Atlas of Canada. Available: http://atlas.nrcan.gc.ca/site/english/index.html.

British Library Map Collection. Available: www.bl.uk/onlinegallery/index.html.

Columbia Gazetteer of the World. 2008. 3 vols. New York: Columbia University Press.

Columbia Gazetteer of the World Online. Available: www.columbiagazetteer.org.

Concise Atlas of World History. 2002. New York: Oxford University Press.

DK Great World Atlas. 2004. London: Dorling Kindersley.

DK Traveler's Atlas. 2005. New York: Dorling Kindersley.

Earth Sciences Sector. Natural Resources Canada. Available: http://ess.nrcan.gc.ca/mapcar/index_e.php.

Environmental Protection Agency. EnviroMapper. Available: www.epa.gov/emefdata/em4ef.home.

FEMA maps. Available: www.fema.gov/hazard/map/index.shtm.

Garlick, Mark A. 2008. *Atlas of the Universe.* New York: Simon and Schuster.

Geographic Names Information System (GNIS). Available: http://geonames.usgs.gov.

Geographical Names of Canada. Available: http://geonames.nrcan.gc.ca/index_e.php.

Getty Thesaurus of Geographic Names Online. Available: www.getty.edu/research/tools/vocabulary/tgn.

Goode's World Atlas. 2010. Chicago: Rand McNally.

Google Maps. Available: http://maps.google.com.

Hammond World Atlas. 2008. 5th ed. Spring House, PA: Hammond.

HarperCollins New World Atlas. 2003. New York: HarperCollins.

Hidden Depths: Atlas of the Oceans. 2007. New York: Harper Collins.

Historical Atlas of Canada. 1987–1993. 3 vols. Toronto: University of Toronto Press.

Historical Atlas of the U.S. 1988. Rev. ed. Washington, DC: National Geographic Society.

History of Cartography Gateway. Available: www.maphistory.info.

Infomine. Available: www.infomine.ucr.edu.

Johnson, Jenny Marie. 2003. *Geographic Information: How to Find It, How to Use It.* Westport, CT: Greenwood Press.

Kenan, William Rand, Jr. 2000. *Barrington Atlas of the Greek and Roman World.* Princeton, NJ: Princeton University Press.

Library of Congress. American Memory Collection. Available: http://memory .loc.gov/ammem/index.html.

Library of Congress. Geography and Map Division. Available: http://memory .loc.gov/ammem/gmdhtml/gmdhome.html.

Mapquest. Available: www.mapquest.com.

Merriam-Webster's Geographical Dictionary. 2001. 3rd ed. rev. Springfield, MA: Merriam-Webster.

MSR Maps. Available: http://msrmaps.com/Default.aspx.

National Atlas of the United States. Available: www.nationalatlas.gov.

National Geographic Atlas of the World. 2010. 9th ed. Washington, DC: National Geographic Society.

National Geographic Concise Atlas of the World. 2007. 2nd ed. Washington, DC: National Geographic Society.

National Geographic Society. Map Machine. Available: www.nationalgeo graphic.com/maps/map-machine.

National Geographic World Atlas for Young Explorers. 2007. 3rd ed. Washington, DC: National Geographic Society.

National Geographic Xpeditions. Available: www.nationalgeographic.com/ xpeditions.

NGA GEOnet Names Server. Available: http://earth-info.nga.mil/gns/html/ index.html.

Oddens's Bookmarks: The Fascinating World of Maps and Mapping. Available: http://oddens.geog.uu.nl.

Oxford Atlas of the World. 2010. 17th ed. New York: Oxford University Press.

Oxford Comprehensive Atlas of the World. 2008. New York: Oxford University Press.

Oxford Essential World Atlas. 2010. 6th ed. New York: Oxford University Press.

Oxford New Historical Atlas of Religion in America. 2001. Edwin Gausted, ed. New York: Oxford University Press.

Perry-Castañeda Library Map Collection. Available: www.lib.utexas.edu/ maps/.

Rand McNally Road Atlas. Chicago: Rand McNally. Annual.

Rumsey, David, and Edith M. Punt. 2004. *Cartographica Extraordinaire: The Historical Map Transformed.* Available: www.davidrumsey.com.

Seager, Joni. 2003. *Penguin Atlas of Women in the World.* New York: Penguin Books.

Shepherd's Historical Atlas. 1980. 9th ed. Totowa, NJ: Barnes & Noble.

Smith, Dan. 2008. *Penguin State of the World Atlas.* New York: Penguin Books.

Times Comprehensive Atlas of the World. 2008. 12th ed. New York: Times Books.

Times Concise Atlas of the World. 2006. 10th ed. London: Times Books.

Times History of the World. 1999. 5th ed. Richard Overy, ed. New York: Times Books.

2008 Commercial Atlas and Marketing Guide. Chicago: Rand McNally. Annual. United Nations Map Library. Available: www.un.org/depts/dhl/maplib/maplib.htm.

U.S. Bureau of the Census. Available: www.census.gov/geo/www/maps.

U.S. Bureau of the Census. American Fact Finder. Available: http://factfinder2.census.gov.

U.S. Bureau of the Census. U.S. Gazetteer. Available: www.census.gov/geo/www/gazetteer/gazette.html.

U.S. Geological Survey. Available: www.usgs.gov.

U.S. Geological Survey. EROS (Earth Resources Observation Systems) Data Center. Available: http://eros.usgs.gov.

U.S. Geological Survey. GIS Web site. Available: http://egsc.usgs.gov/isb/pubs/gis_poster.

Western Association of Map Librarians. 1970–. Information Bulletin. Triannual.

Woodall's North American Campground Directory. Guilford, CT: Globe Pequot. Annual.

World Book Atlas. 2005. Chicago: Rand McNally.

Worldmark Encyclopedia of the Nations. 2003. 11th ed. Farmington Hills, MI: Gale.

Yale University Map Collection. Available: www.library.yale.edu/mapColl/index.html.

Recommendations for Further Reading

Allen, David Y. 2003 "Helpful Hints for the Paperless Map Librarian." Chicago: ALA/MAGERT. Available: www.ala.org/ala/mgrps/rts/magert/index.cfm.

Behler, Ann, Beth Roberts, and Karen Dabney. 2006. "Circulating Maps Collection at Pennsylvania State University Preservation Challenges and Solutions." *DttP* 34, no. 4: 33–36. A good how-to-do-it article on balancing user access with preservation.

Berenstein, Paula. 2006. "Location, Location, Location: Online Maps for the Masses." *Searcher* 14, no. 1 (January): 16–25. A discussion of new online maps including Google maps, Google Earth, and Yahoo maps.

Buckland, Michael et al. 2007. "Geographic Search: Catalogs, Gazetteers and Maps." *College & Research Libraries* 68, no. 5: 376–387. An interesting article on the use of geographical information to enhance catalog records for place names.

Kemp, Jim. 2008. "Lost in Space: On Becoming Spatially Literate." *Knowledge Quest* 36, no. 4: 32–39. On using maps in the classroom.

Kollen, Christina. 2006. "Map Scanning Registry." *DttP* 34, no. 4: 25–27. Describes a Map Scanning Registry developed and maintained at the University of Arizona Library and sponsored by the ALA Map and Geography Round Table (MAGERT) to record map scanning projects to avoid duplication.

McDermott, I. 2002. "Where Was I? Maps on the Web." *Searcher* 10, no. 6: 75–78. A guide to map sources on the Web.

Mitchell, Susan. 2003. "Where in the World? An Online Guide to Gazetteers, Atlases and Other Map Resources." *Internet Reference Services Quarterly* 8, no. 1/2: 183–194. An annotated guide to map resources on the Web.

Northedge, Richard. 2008. "The Medium Is Not the Message: Topic Maps and the Separation of Presentation and Content in Indexes." *The Indexer* 26, no. 2: 60–64. Explores the idea of developing a model for topics maps that separates index content from presentation.

Ramos, Miguel, and Dawn Gauthier. 2007. "Mash It Up! Removing the Information Superhighway." *Searcher* 15, no. 6: 17–22. Describes the use of maps to enhance text such as combining Google Maps with housing sale prices.

Singh, Sawtantar, and Ashwani Krush. 2006. "Google Earth versus MSN Virtual Earth." *DESIDOC Bulletin of Information Technology* 26, no. 6: 23–27. Provides information on Google Earth and MSN Virtual Earth.

Smith, Agnes, and Claudene Sproles. 2004. "Don't Get Lost!: The Basics of Organizing a Library's Map Collection." *Kentucky Libraries* 68, no. 2: 22–27. A useful article that deals with handling print map collections.

Smith, Linda C., and Myke Gluck. 1996. *Geographic Information Systems and Libraries: Users, Maps and Spatial Information*. Urbana, IL: University of Illinois. Graduate School of Library and Information Science. Papers from the 32nd Annual Clinic on Library Applications of Data Processing addressing accessing spatial data use of GIS systems and related issues.

Tenner, Elka, and Katherine H. Weimer. 1998. "Reference Service for Maps: Access and the Catalog Record." *Reference & User Services Quarterly* 38, no. 2: 181–186. A discussion of the cataloging of maps. Tenner states that subject analysis is the most important access point. Digital format may necessitate changes in cataloging to emphasize intellectual content.

Weessies, Kathleen. 2001. "Electronic Maps: Sources and Techniques." *Reference Services Review* 31, no. 3: 248–256. This article focuses on how to work with electronic maps including saving them to a disk, pasting them into PowerPoint, and cropping them.

Bibliography of Works Cited in This Chapter

Ashworth, Mick. 2003. "Paper or Pixels: Where to Next for Maps?" *Geographical* (December): 56–60.

Cline, Michael E. 2005. "Mapping Solutions Under $500." *Online* 29, no. 3 (May/June): 27–30.

Cobb, David. 1990. *A Guide to U.S. Map Resources*. 2nd ed. Chicago: American Library Association. (A new edition is planned.)

Farrell, Barbara, and Aileen Desbarats. 1981. *Guide for a Small Map Collection*. Ottawa: Association of Canadian Map Libraries.

Jacobsen, Mikael. 2008. "You Are Here." *Library Journal* 133 (October 15): 26–28.

Johnson, Jenny Marie. 2003. *Geographic Information: How to Find It, How to Use It*. Westport, CT: Greenwood Press.

Kenny, Ann Jason. 2002. "More Than Just Maps." *School Library Journal. Net Connect* (Fall): 45–47.

Larsgaard, Mary Lynette. 1998. *Map Librarianship: An Introduction*. 3rd ed. Englewood, CO: Libraries Unlimited, Inc.

Larsgaard, Mary, and Katherine Rankin. 1997. "Helpful Hints for Small Map Collections." Revised by Stephen Rogers. Chicago: ALA/MAGERT. Available: www.ala.org/ala/mgrps/rts/magert/index.cfm.

Liben, Lynn S. 2008 "Understanding Maps: Is the Purple Country on the Map Really Purple?" *Knowledge Quest* 36, no. 4: 20–30.

Map History of Cartography: The Gateway to the Subject. Available: www.maphistory.info or info@maphistory.info.

Monmonier, Mark, and George A. Schnell. 1988. *Map Appreciation*. Englewood Cliffs, NJ: Prentice Hall.

Sader, Marion, and Amy Lewis, eds. *Encyclopedias, Atlases & Dictionaries*. 1995. New Providence, NJ: R. R. Bowker.

Unwin, Tim. 1992. *The Place of Geography*. Burnt Mill, England: Longman Scientific and Technical Press.

Wood, Denis, with John Fels. 1992. *The Power of Maps*. New York: Guilford Press.

11

Answering Questions about the Lives of People— Biographical Information Sources

Overview

Many reference questions are about well-known people. Where were they born? How old are they? How many times were they married? How many children do they have? Biographical sources answer these and many more questions. Although biographical information is widely available in many other reference sources, biographical resources provide more extensive and often more accurate information about people who are important historically and people who are presently in the news. To these ends, a wealth of biographical sources exists. Some are published by major publishers and others by small, sometimes vanity, presses.

How Biographical Resources Are Used

Biographical sources provide information about the lives of both living and deceased people; these print and electronic resources may concentrate on one country such as *Who's Who in America*, on people in a certain field such as *American Men and Women of Science*, or may be more general in nature such as Biography.com. The information may be brief—such as, correct name, dates of birth and death, the field of work of the person and the person's nationality— or may be more extensive, discussing in great detail the person's life and accomplishments and including a bibliography for further research.

Since biographical sources are a source of information about people, they are of use to the user who is simply seeking minimal information about a person, including what their field of work is or was, dates of birth and maybe death, and nationality. Sometimes biographical sources are used to determine that the user has the correct person if there is more than one person with the same or a similar name. On the other hand, the user may be looking for more extensive information on a person and should be directed to a source that provides a lengthy biography and perhaps a list of sources for more information. Sometimes biographical sources are used to find well-known people in a certain field such as engineers, jazz musicians, or philosophers. For this reason, some biographical sources have an index by profession.

Questions Answered by Biographical Resources

Q: When did Harriet Tubman die?
A: The answer can be found in the *American National Biography*.

Q: What are the birth and death dates for Virginia Woolf?
A: This can be found in *Oxford Dictionary of National Biography*.

Q: How can I find articles about Twyla Tharp?
A: *Biography Index* is a good source to check for articles on contemporary people.

Q: Where can I find a biography of the present king of Thailand?
A: *Biography in Context* can be searched by occupation and nationality to find this information.

Major Biographical Resources Used in Reference Work

Indexes

Indexes are a good place to begin when uncertain where the biography of a certain person will be found. Two indexes can be helpful, particularly if biographical information on a person is difficult to locate. One, the *Biography and Genealogy Master Index*, indexes over 1,600 biographical reference sources such as biographical dictionaries, Who's Who, indexes, and literary criticism with biographical information. About 5 million biographical sketches of persons, both living and deceased, from every field and from all areas of the world are included in this index. Each reference work is listed where the biographical information can be found for a certain person. This index is particularly useful when it is not obvious which biographical source would have information. It is available online and updated twice annually.

The second index, *Biography Index*, indexes biographical material in 3,000 periodicals indexed in other H.W. Wilson databases and in 2,000 books per year. The online coverage is from 1984 to the present. The value of this index is that it provides access to biographical material on contemporary people that would not be easily found elsewhere. *Biography Index* is also indexed in the *Biography and Genealogy Master Index*.

Biographies of Contemporary People

For concise information about contemporary people, the user can turn to the *Marquis Who's Who* series of publications. *Who's Who in America* is perhaps the best known of the series. The 2010 edition of this annual publication provides current biographical information on about 110,000 noteworthy Americans. Some of the entries are new listings; many are updated entries. Questionnaires are sent to those listed to update their information annually. A typical entry includes the person's name, occupation, date of birth, family information, education, career summary, publications, civic and political activities, memberships, and address. This valuable biographical source includes a geographic index, a professional index, a retiree list, and a necrology for those deceased since the last edition.

Marquis also publishes regional *Who's Who* for each part of the United States such as *Who's Who in the East, Who's Who in the Midwest,* and *Who's Who in the West* as well as others such as *Who's Who of American Women* and professional sources such as *Who's Who in American Education* and *Who's Who in American Politics.* The format for all the print *Who's Who* is similar. *Marquis Who's Who on the Web* provides access to more than 1.4 million biographies of people from twenty of the "Who's Who" print publications. It covers both people from the past and present from all walks of life. This online database allows the user to search by such criteria as name, gender, occupation, college/university, date of birth, or a combination of them. According to the publisher, the online sub-scription database is updated daily.

Who's Who is the British resource that lists contemporary people of note— mostly British but a few Americans as well. With more than 30,000 biographies, this resource follows the typical pattern of listing the name, present position, date of birth, family details, education, and career in order of date, publica-tions, recreations, and address. *Who's Who* is updated through a questionnaire to the people listed. An obituary section with the death date is also included. This database is now available online.

Although *Canadian Who's Who* began in 1910, it did not become an annual reference work until 1980. Questionnaires are sent out annually to update the 14,000 biographical sketches in this work. Date and place of birth, address, family details, education, career information, memberships, and awards or other achievements are listed for each person.

World Who's Who includes information on more than 60,000 noteworthy men and women from all professions and from all parts of the world. A typical entry includes the person's name, nationality, profession, date and place of birth, family information, education, career summary, awards, publications, leisure interests, and contact information. Obituaries are included in addition to a section that lists all the reigning royal families in the world. This online resource allows the user to search by name, nationality, place and date of birth, and profession. Routledge also produces a series of international "Who's Who" by profession such as *International Who's Who in International Affairs* and *Inter-national Who's Who in Classical Music.*

Current Biography provides biographical information on people in the news. Each of its eleven issues per year provides profiles of eighteen to twenty people from the arts, politics, literature, sports, film and television as well as obituaries of people previously profiled. This well-written biographical source is useful for students as well as adults. The articles are 2,000 to 3,500 words in length and include a photograph of the person and a bibliography of additional sources of information. An annual volume is published compiling the individual issues for the year. *Current Biography Illustrated* is the online version of *Current Biography*. In this format users can search the entire database from 1940 to the present by name, profession, place of origin, birth or death date, ethnicity, and gender.

A recent publication, *Current Biography International Yearbook*, began in 2002. This annual focuses on people outside the United States making international news and history. The yearbook includes profiles of about 200 people, covering a wide range of professions. Each article includes the subject's own opinions and the observations of journalists and colleagues. Photographs and a bibliography are included.

Newsmakers: The People Behind Today's Headlines is similar to *Current Biography*. Each biography of 1,500 to 3,000 words includes the person's address, date of birth, family details, education, career summary, awards, writings, and a biographical essay. A photo of each person and a bibliography of additional sources of information are included. People listed in each issue come from all walks of life including business, television and film, entertainment, literature, politics and government, and science. This publication contains indexes by nationality, occupation, and subject as well as an obituary section. In addition to the four issues published annually, there is an annual cumulative volume. An e-book of the annual volume is also available.

Biography in Context (formerly *Biography Resource Center*) is an extensive online database providing biographical information about persons currently in the news and those deceased. Each profile includes personal information, career information, the person's writings, "sidelights," and a bibliography for further readings about the person. This Gale Cengage Learning resource includes full text from *The Marquis Who's Who*, 250 periodicals, and other Gale Cengage Learning biographical resources including *Encyclopedia of World Biography*, *Dictionary of American Biography*, and *Scribner's Encyclopedia of American Lives*. Over 600,000 biographies of more than 525,000 people from more than 170 Gale Cengage Learning resources are included as well as full-text articles from more than 265 magazines. Searches can be done by name, occupation, year of birth, nationality, ethnicity, or place of birth.

Biography Reference Bank combines several H.W. Wilson databases into one biography subscription database. This database includes *H.W. Wilson Biographies Plus Illustrated*, *Biography Index*, and links to other full text from H.W. Wilson publications including *Current Biography*. More than 550,000 people are listed in this database, which can be searched by name, profession, place of origin, gender, ethnicity, birth and death dates, titles of works, and keyword. More than 36,000 images are also included.

Biography.com is a free database that includes 25,000 biographies of well-known people from ancient times to the present. Each entry includes birth and death dates, career information and often a photograph, list of works and related Web links. Information for this Web site comes from *Cambridge Dictionary of American Biography* and *Cambridge Encyclopedia Database* as well as information from the cable station, A&E (Arts and Entertainment).

Biographical Dictionary (www.s9.com) is another online source of biographical information covering more than 33,000 people both past and present. Brief information is given for each person including birth and death dates, profession, position held, and literary and artistic works produced. Anyone can add content to this site.

Who2? (www.who2.com) provides basic information of more than 32,000 people with links to other related Web sites.

Retrospective Biography

American National Biography is a recent work published in print and available online that is a companion to the *Dictionary of American Biography* (*DAB*). It is a completely new work "that resulted in the more expansive understanding of who is a notable American" (Bryant, 1999: 82). There are 17,500 lengthy biographies that include more women, minorities, and people from other countries who have lived in the United States and made contributions to it than the original *DAB*. Not all people in the *Dictionary of American Biography* are included in the new *American National Biography*. As in the *Dictionary of American Biography* all persons listed are deceased. This new work is updated quarterly online and can be searched by name, occupation, gender, birth and death dates, birthplace, and ethnic heritage. Entries include a photograph of the person and a bibliography. A useful feature is the hyperlinks to related biographies.

The *Dictionary of American Biography* was commissioned by the American Council of Learned Societies. It has been for many decades the premier source of American biography. The last supplement was published in 1985 and includes people who died before 1980. A total of 19,000 biographies are included in the volumes of this work.

Oxford Dictionary of National Biography, published in 2004, is a major revision of the *Dictionary of National Biography* (*DNB*), which was completed in 1900. Available both in print and online, this new version includes both 55,000 new biographies and rewritten or revised biographies of the lives of people included in the thirty-three volumes of the original *DNB* and its supplements. The coverage includes Britons from all walks of life who have made their mark in Great Britain or elsewhere, as well as people from other countries who have played a role in British history and life. As in the original *DNB*, people listed in this work are all deceased. Searching online can be done by person, place, dates, and fields of interest. Three updates online are made each year.

The original *Dictionary of National Biography* covered 29,333 people. It was reissued in 1908–09 in twenty-two volumes. Additional supplements were published between 1912 and 1996. As is the case with the *DAB*, the *DNB* has been the primary source of biographical information about people of British origin.

The *Dictionary of Canadian Biography* states in the introduction that those omitted are those "who have not set forth in what is now Canada, or at least approached its shores" (*DCB*, 1966: xvi). The volumes are arranged in chronological order as determined by the person's death date. Volume 1 covers 1000 to 1700. Each biographical sketch is 400 to 1,200 words. A general bibliography and an index is included at the end of each volume. Fourteen volumes have been published to date. The *Dictionary* is also available in French. The *Dictionary of Canadian Biography Online* is the online version of the *Dictionary of Canadian Biography*, which also includes some of the biographical sketches for the upcoming volume.

World Biographical Information System (WBIS Online) compiles biographical articles from microfiche archives including information from the sixteenth to the twentieth century and provides facsimiles of the original documents online. This online tool will include 5 million digitized biographical articles when it is completed and is available in German, Spanish, English, French, and Italian. Searches can be done by name, gender, year of birth and death, occupation, and country.

Who Was Who and *Who Was Who in America* are the retrospective versions of *Who's Who* and *Who's Who in America*. Once a person is deceased he or she becomes part of the retrospective version. *Who Was Who* is grouped in four-year segments. Volume 11, for example, contains the entries of people who died between 2001 and 2005. The entries are as they appeared in *Who's Who* with the death date added as well as posthumous publications. There is also a *Who Was Who, A Cumulated Index 1897–2000* that provides easy access to *Who Was Who* listing the person's name, birth and death years and the volume number. *Who Was Who in America* now has fourteen volumes beginning in 1897 and continuing through 2008. In addition, a historical volume covers the years 1607–1896. This is a specially compiled volume since *Who's Who in America* did not begin until 1899. Parts of *Who Was Who in America* are available online as part of the *Marquis Who's Who on the Web*. The complete *Who Was Who* is available online with links to the *Oxford Dictionary of National Biography*.

The National Cyclopedia of American Biography is subtitled "Being the History of the United States as illustrated in the lives of the founders, builders and defenders of the Republic and of the men and women who are doing the work and moulding the thought of the present time." The volumes are groupings of individuals and not in alphabetical order. Each person has a fairly lengthy biography and a photo or line drawing as well. Many of these people were alive when the volume was published. Because the listings are not in alphabetical order, each volume has an index. The uniqueness of this biographical source is that it lists many people who are not in other biographical sources such as prominent business people, clergy, etc.

The Scribner Encyclopedia of American Lives presents very readable signed biographies of deceased people with a photo of each person and a bibliography. Each volume is arranged in alphabetical order with an occupations index. The latest volume includes people who died between 2003 and 2005. These volumes are supplements to the *Dictionary of American Biography*.

Encyclopedia of World Biography, 2nd Edition, is a multivolume work that includes in-depth portraits of more than 7,000 persons, both living and deceased, from all time periods and all walks of life both living and deceased. The biographies are very readable and include a bibliography and often a photograph or drawing of the person. Because of the emphasis on the international, it is a good place to find information on persons from other countries such as government officials. This is also available as an e-book that includes the supplements to the *Encyclopedia*.

One-Volume Biographical Dictionaries

Chambers Biographical Dictionary is a large one-volume biographical dictionary (1,669 pages) that includes 17,500 biographies of "people who have shaped, and continue to shape, the world in which we live" (preface). In a user-friendly format, the dictionary provides short biographical sketches of people both living and deceased. The entries are written in prose describing the achievements of the person. For a few select people the biographical sketch is highlighted in a box with an appropriate quote by or about the person. *Chambers* is also available online (www.chambersharrap.co.uk). It is also published under the title *The Cambridge Biographical Dictionary*.

Merriam-Webster's Biographical Dictionary is a compact one-volume biographical dictionary listing concise biographical information about 30,000 persons from ancient times to the present day who are deceased. It is useful as a ready reference source.

Obituaries

Obituaries are often requested by library users searching for details of someone's life. Because of such easy access to the retrospective issues of *The New York Times*, it is not as necessary to have separate volumes with obituaries; however, these two print volumes can be quite useful and easy to check. The *New York Times Obituaries Index, 1885–1968* and *New York Times Obituaries Index, 1969–1978* are an accumulation of obituaries for these periods of time. It is rather interesting to note the different policies throughout the decades about murders and suicides. But Volume 2 does cover these deaths. *Newsbank* has also developed an online obituaries database, *America's Obituaries and Death Notices*, which includes information from newspapers throughout the United States. Another source to try is Obituaries.com, which provides access to obituaries from 700 newspapers in the United States and Canada.

Subject-Based Biographical Tools

Contemporary Authors is an excellent source of information on current authors, especially nonfiction writers whose biographical information can be hard to find. Available in print and electronic formats, it includes a wide range of authors publishing fiction, nonfiction, poetry, etc. The information provided includes personal information, career information, awards, "sidelights," which is an essay about the author's work, writings by the author and writings about the author. Periodically, these biographies are updated. Over 120,000 authors are included. *Contemporary Authors* is also included in Gale Cengage Learning's

Literature Resource Center, which also includes *Contemporary Literary Criticism Select* and the *Dictionary of Literary Biography Online*. The *Dictionary of Literary Biography Online* contains more than 10,000 biocritical essays on authors and their works. This information has been compiled from other Gale Cengage Learning publications and from 260 literary journals. The user can search by name, ethnicity, nationality, genre, literary theme, and literary movement. Web sites on the author's life and work are included. The print version of the *Dictionary of Literary Biography* has more content than the online version so librarians might want to compare the two to decide which version is the best for their users.

Voices from the Gaps: Women Artists and Writers of Color (http://voices.cla.umn .edu) is maintained and updated by the English Department of the University of Minnesota. This site provides biographical information on North American women artists and writers of color. Users can search by name, birthplace, or geographical location, racial/ethnic background or significant dates.

The American Historical Association's *Guide to Historical Literature* includes references to biographies throughout each of its three editions (1931, 1961, and 1995). This is an excellent source of biographies from a particular time period.

Directory of American Scholars provides short biographical sketches similar to those found in *Who's Who in America*. Each of the five volumes covers specific disciplines: History; English, Speech, and Drama; Foreign Languages, Linguistics and Philology; Philosophy, Religion, and Law; and Social Sciences. There is a separate index volume that includes an alphabetical index, discipline index, institutional index and geographical index. This resource provides information about many in the academic world not easily found in other biographical sources.

American Men and Women of Science; A Biographical Directory of Today's Leaders in Physical, Biological and Related Sciences is an invaluable source of information about contemporary scientists in both the United States and Canada who have made significant contributions in their field. The information is provided in a concise format and includes birth date, birth place, citizenship, family details, field of specialty, education, honorary degrees, professional experience, honors and awards, memberships, research information, address, e-mail. There are seven volumes of biographical information with an eighth volume devoted to a discipline index organized by field of activity and within each subject the names are arranged by state. Volume 1 also lists the winners of various scientific prizes. This reference work is available online through Gale Virtual Reference Library. The *New Dictionary of Scientific Biography*, a biographical dictionary for mathematicians and natural scientists, which is often called a DAB for scientists, has been updated; it is now a twenty-six-volume set. The additional volumes can be ordered separately or the whole set can be purchased as an e-book that is part of the Gale Virtual Library. A free Web site on mathematicians (www-history.mcs.st-and.ac.uk/BiogIndex.html) has been produced and kept up-to-date by the School of Mathematics and Statistics of the University of St. Andrews, Scotland. The biographies are quite extensive and are signed.

Notable American Women, 1607–1950: A Biographical Dictionary and its companion volume, *Notable American Women, the Modern Period: A Biographical Dictionary*, provide excellent background on the role of American women in history. *The Palgrave Macmillan Dictionary of Women's Biography* provides biographical information on over 2,100 women both current and from the past. It provides information on many contemporary women from all parts of the world who have received little recognition. The National Women's History Museum (www.nwhm.org/education-resources/biography/biographies/) lists women by area of contribution such as environmentalists, activists, entertainers, and journalists. There is a short biographical sketch for each woman with a photograph and a short bibliography.

Eric Weisstein's World of Biography (scienceworld.wolfram.com/biography/) provides brief biographical sketches of over 1,000 people in the sciences with a short bibliography for each person.

Biographies of philosophers can be found in the *Stanford Encyclopedia of Philosophy*, a free Web site (http://plato.stanford.edu). It provides extensive signed biographies of philosophers.

The *Biographical Directory of the United States Congress, 1774 to Present* is now available online (http://bioguide.congress.gov/biosearch/biosearch.asp). Users can search by name, position in Congress (senator, representative, Speaker of the House, etc.) state, party, etc. Photos of recent members of Congress are included.

Modern and Contemporary Artists and Art (www.the-artists.org) can be searched by the name of the artist or by art movement, style or medium in this free Web site. The listings provide information about the artists and their work. The *Union List of Artist Names* (*ULAN*) is produced at the Getty Museum in California (www.getty.edu/research/tools/vocabularies/ulan/index.html). It lists over 220,000 names of artists. Its scope is global, and it covers antiquity to the present. Each record includes variations of the artist's name, dates of birth and death, geographic locations, relationships such as student-teacher relationships, biographical notes and the source of the information.

Biographical information on people in the movies can be found on the *Internet Movie Database* site (www.imdb.com). Another Internet site, www.whata character.com, lists biographical information on character actors with photos and lists of their film and TV roles.

An alphabetical list of biographical information on jazz musicians can be found at www.pbs.org/jazz/biography/.

Biographical Resources Featuring Ethnic/Cultural Heritage

Who's Who Among African Americans provides biographical sketches of prominent African Americans. The main part of this reference work lists each person's personal data, occupation, educational background, career information, organizational affiliations, honors or awards, special achievements and military service. This resource includes geographical and occupational indexes as well as an obituaries section for people that are recently deceased. This resource is also available as an e-book through the Gale Virtual Reference Library. The *African American National Biography* provides substantial, scholarly biographical information on more than 4,100 African Americans. Some of the information comes from the *American National Biography*. The online version is available in *Oxford African American Studies Center*.

Although very few biographical reference sources exist for individual ethnic groups, many of the electronic reference sources in this chapter can be searched by ethnic groups, allowing the user to find information on contemporary African Americans, Hispanic Americans, Asian Americans, and others.

Collection Development and Maintenance

Selection and Keeping Current

Biographical sources are reviewed by the journals that review reference materials. The librarian can find new biographical resources reviewed in *Library Journal, Booklist, Choice*, and *American Reference Book Annual*. Standard titles are discussed in ALA's *Guide to Reference* and in *New Walford Guide to Reference Resources*. Biographical resources are listed in the *ARBA Guide to Biographical Resources 1986–1997*, which includes international sources arranged by country and sources of biographies in professional fields organized by profession.

Evaluating Biographical Resources

Criteria for evaluating biographical resources include the following:

- Scope
- Accuracy
- Length of entry
- Criteria for inclusion
- Audience
- Authority
- Frequency of updates
- Photo
- References for further reading

Scope is particularly important in biographical sources since it applies to the coverage of the resource. Does the resource cover both living and deceased people? Does it only cover certain professions or certain countries? What are the parameters of its coverage? In a library's collection the librarian will want to have biographical sources that describe the lives of well-known people of the past, called retrospective biography, as well as sources that describe the lives of people who are alive today, called current biography. The collection should also have resources with information on people from other countries as well as the United States. Sometimes biographical sources include people from many different parts of the world whereas others provide information on people from a region or a country.

Attention to accuracy is needed in biographical resources. Fact checking biographical entries is recommended. In addition to checking the birth and death dates against another credible source, read some entries in the reference source to see if they are objective and comprehensive within the parameters of the entries. If the work is not available, reviews will often point out inaccuracies in a reference work.

The length of the entry is important because sometimes users need a short biographical sketch and sometimes they need lengthy, more detailed information. Libraries will want resources with short and longer biographies.

Criteria for inclusion are of great interest. Perhaps those included filled out a questionnaire or perhaps authors made an effort to find everyone who fit their criteria for inclusion. This is often explained in the preface or introduction to the biographical resource. If, however, it appears that everyone in the book was required to pay to be included, this may not be a very objective source.

The audience for the resource should be noted. Determine the reading level of the biographical source and the intended audience. Some sources provide scholarly biographies, whereas others are more popular in content and tone and are aimed at a general audience.

The authority of the work must be examined, which may be either the publisher or the author. Signed biographies and biographies with a bibliography are good signs of a quality resource. Not all biographical sources are published by major publishers. This does not mean they are not useful additions to a library collection. But it does mean that the librarian should review these resources more carefully.

Determine how often the publisher plans to update the book, especially if most of the people listed are currently alive. Many biographical sources are updated annually. Be aware that many biographical reference sources build on previous volumes and may issue or include an index to assist users to find the needed material. The *Dictionary of Literary Biography* is a good example of this. Multiple volumes are issued in one year with an index providing cumulative indexing. If online, the biographical source can be expected to be updated more regularly. Note if the biographical source includes a photograph of the person. Many sources do not, but it is extremely useful to have biographical sources with photographs since many users are interested in knowing what the person looks or looked like.

Finally, it can be useful for the biographical source to include a bibliography of other sources of information about the person to assist in doing more extensive research.

Further Considerations

Biographical information is both easy and difficult to find. Well-known people are listed in many different biographical resources. However, some people can be very hard to locate in biographical resources. It can be useful to narrow the kinds of biographical resources that would possibly be relevant by attempting to categorize the person, assuming the user has some information. First, the user should try to determine if the person is living or dead. If the person is living, for example, the user can eliminate biographical resources that include only deceased persons. The next step is to determine the nationality of the person. This can definitely narrow the number of possible sources as not all biographical sources are international. If the user knows the profession of the person, this can also be useful. Subject encyclopedias can often be useful for finding information on a person known in a particular field. For example, the user could find an extensive biography on Mozart in *The New Grove Dictionary of Music and Musicians* or a biography of Picasso in the *Grove Dictionary of Art* (also available as *Oxford Music Online* and *Oxford Art Online*). It can also be helpful to try large comprehensive resources that cover many resources and provide a single way to identify biographies in multivolume works such as *Biography and Genealogy Master Index*. Sometimes it is necessary to go beyond these biographical sources and try some of the periodical and newspaper databases for information on people currently in the news.

THE TOP TEN BIOGRAPHICAL SOURCES		
Title	**Print**	**Online**
American National Biography, 1999 New York: Oxford University Press	24 vols.	Subscription www.anb.org
Biography and Genealogy Master Index Farmington Hills, MI: Gale Cengage Learning	Biannual	Subscription www.gale.com
Biography Index, 1946– Bronx, NY: H.W. Wilson	Quarterly	Subscription www.hwwilson.com
Biography in Context Farmington, MI: Gale Cengage Learning		Subscription www.gale.com
Current Biography, 1940– New York: H.W. Wilson Online, *Current Biography Illustrated*	Monthly	Subscription www.hwwilson.com
World Who's Who Independence, KY: Routledge Distributed by Taylor & Francis	Annual	Subscription www.worldwhoswho.com
Literature Resource Center Farmington Hills, MI: Gale Cengage Learning		Subscription www.gale.com
Oxford Dictionary of National Biography, 2004 New York: Oxford University Press	60 vols.	Subscription www.oxfordlonline.com/ online/odnb
Who's Who, 1897– New York: St. Martin's Press	Annual	
Marquis Who's Who on the Web New Providence, NJ: Marquis Who's Who		Subscription www.marquiswhoswho.com

RECOMMENDED FREE WEB SITES

Biographical Dictionary. Available: www.s9.com. A source of biographical information that anyone can edit.
Biographical Directory of the United States Congress, 1774 to Present. Available: http://bioguide.congress.gov/biosearch/biosearch.asp. A guide to Congress from the beginning of the Republic.
Biography.com. Available: www.biography.com. A good general biographical source.
Eric Weisstein's World of Biography. Available: http://scienceworld.wolfram.com/biography/. A biographical source for people in science.
Internet Movie Database. Available: www.imdb.com. An excellent source for information on people in the motion picture industry.
National Women's History Museum Web site. Available: www.nwhm.org/education-resources/biography/biographies/. Information on outstanding women in history.
Obituaries.com. Available: www.obituaries.com. A good source of obituary information.
Stanford Encyclopedia of Philosophy. Available: http://plato.stanford.edu. Biographies of philosophers.
Union List of Artist Names (ULAN). Available: www.getty.edu/research/tools/vocabularies/ulan/index.html. A good source of information on artists.

Recommended Resources Discussed in This Chapter

African American National Biography. 2008. Edited by Henry Louis Gates, Jr. and Evelyn Brooks Higginbotham. New York: Oxford University Press.
American Historical Association. 1931. *Guide to Historical Literature.* New York: Macmillan.
American Historical Association. 1961. *Guide to Historical Literature.* New York: Macmillan.
American Historical Association. 1995. *Guide to Historical Literature.* New York: Oxford University Press.
American Men and Women of Science: A Biographical Directory of Today's Leaders in Physical, Biological and Related Sciences. 2005. 22nd ed. Farmington Hills, MI: Gale Cengage Learning.
American National Biography. 1999. 24 vols. New York: Oxford University Press. Available: ww.anb.org.
ARBA Guide to Biographical Resources, 1986–1997. Edited by Robert L. Wick and Terry Ann Mood. Englewood, CO: Libraries Unlimited.
Biographical Dictionary. Available: www.s9.com.
Biographical Dictionary of Hispanic Americans. 2001. 2nd ed. Edited by Nicholas E. Meyers. New York: Facts on File.
Biographical Directory of the United States Congress, 1774 to Present. Available: http://bioguide.congress.gov/biosearch/biosearch.asp.
Biography and Genealogy Master Index. Farmington Hills, MI: Gale Cengage Learning. Annual. Also available online: www.gale.cengage.com.
Biography in Context. Farmington Hills, MI: Gale Cengage Learning. Available online: www.gale.cengage.com.

Biography Index. 1946–. Bronx, NY: H.W. Wilson. Quarterly with annual cumulations. Also available online: www.hwwilson.com/database/bioind.htm.

Biography Reference Bank. New York: H.W. Wilson. Available online: www.hwwilson.com/databases/BioBank.htm.

Biography.com. Available: www.biography.com.

Canadian Who's Who. 1980–. Toronto: University of Toronto Press.

Chambers Biographical Dictionary. 2008. 8th ed. Edinburgh: Chambers. Available online: www.chamberssharrap.co.uk.

Contemporary Authors. 1962–. Farmington Hills, MI: Gale Cengage Learning. Available online as part of the *Literature Resource Center*.

Current Biography. 1940–. New York: H.W. Wilson. Monthly with an annual cumulative volume. Online version, *Current Biography Illustrated*.

Dictionary of American Biography, 1927–1936. 20 vols. and index. New York: Scribner. Supplements, 1944–1980 with index, 1996.

Dictionary of Canadian Biography. 1966. 14 vols. and index. Toronto: University of Toronto Press. Also published in French. Available: www.biographi.ca/.

Dictionary of Literary Biography. Available: www.gale.cengage.com/Dictionary LiteracyBio/.

Dictionary of National Biography. 1885–1900. London: Smith, Elder. Supplements 1912–1996.

Dictionary of Scientific Biography. 2007. New York: Simon and Schuster. Available as part of the Gale Cengage Learning Virtual Library.

Directory of American Scholars. 2001. 5 vols. Farmington Hills, MI: Gale Cengage Learning.

Encyclopedia of World Biography. 1998. 2nd ed. Farmington Hills, MI: Gale Cengage Learning.

Eric Weisstein's World of Biography. Available: scienceworld.wolfram.com/biography/.

Internet Movie Database. Available: www.imdb.com.

Jazz Musicians. Available: www.pbs.org/jazz/biography.

Literature Resource Center. Farmington Hills, MI: Gale Cengage Learning. Available by subscription online.

Marquis Who's Who on the Web. Available by subscription: http://marquis whoswho.com.

Merriam-Webster's Biographical Dictionary. 1995. Springfield, MA: Merriam-Webster.

Modern and Contemporary Artists and Art. Available: www.the-artists.org.

National Cyclopedia of American Biography. 1898–1984. New York: White.

National Women's History Museum Web site. Available: www.nwhm.org/education-resources/biography/biographies/.

New York Times Obituaries Index, 1885–1968. 1970. New York: New York Times.

Newsmakers: The People Behind Today's Headlines. Quarterly. Farmington Hills, MI: Gale Cengage Learning.

Notable American Women, 1607–1950: A Biographical Dictionary. Cambridge, MA: Belnap Press of Harvard University Press.

Notable American Women, the Modern Period: A Biographical Dictionary. Cambridge, MA: Belnap Press of Harvard University Press.

Obituaries.com. Available: www.obituaries.com.

Oxford Dictionary of National Biography. 2004. 60 vols. New York: Oxford University Press. Available: www.oxfordonline.com/online/odnb.

Palgrave Macmillan Dictionary of Women's Biography. 2005. 4th ed. Edited by Jennifer S. Uglow, Frances Hinton and Maggy Hendry. New York: Palgrave Macmillan.

School of Mathematics and Statistics, University of St. Andrews, Scotland. Available: www-history.mcs.st-and.ac.uk/BiogIndex.html.

Scribner Encyclopedia of American Lives. 1998–. New York: Scribner. Biennial.

Stanford Encylopedia of Philosophy. Available: http://plato.stanford.edu.

Union List of Artist Names (ULAN). Available: www.getty.edu/research/tools/vocabularies/ulan/index.html.

Voices from the Gaps: Women Artists and Writers of Color. Available: http://voices.cla.umn.edu.

What a Character Database. Available: www.whatacharacter.com.

Who2? Available: www.who2.com.

Who Was Who. 1897. London: A&C Black, with a cumulated index 1897–2000.

Who's Who. 1897–. London: A&C Black. Annual.

Who's Who Among African Americans. 2006. 19th ed. Farmington Hills, MI: Gale Cengage Learning.

Who Was Who in America. 1897–. Chicago: Marquis Who's Who. Historical volume, 1607–1896.

Who's Who in America. 2010. New Providence, NJ: Marquis Who's Who. Annual.

World Biographical Information System (*WBIS Online*). Farmington Hills, MI: K.G. Saur. Available by subscription online.

World Who's Who. Independence, KY: Europa Publications, distributed by Taylor & Francis. Available by subscription online.

Recommendations for Further Reading

Aycock, Anthony. 2006. "Where's Waldo: A Primer on People-Searching Online." *Online* 30, no. 1 (January/February): 28–33. A guide to using the Internet to locate information on people.

Bridge, Noeline. 2003. "Verifying Personal Names on the Web." *The Indexer* 23, no. 3 (April): 149–156. A guide to indexes on verifying personal names serves as a good guide to biographical resources.

Ojala, Marydee. 1994. "The Never-ending Search for People." *Online* 18 (September/October): 105–109. Resources for finding biographical information on business executives.

Schreiner, Susan A., and Michael A. Somers. 2002. "Biography Resources: Finding Information on the Famous, Infamous, and Obscure." *College and Research Libraries News* 63, no. 1 (January): 32–36, 39. An interesting review of biographical Web resources from specific fields of study.

Thomsen, Elizabeth. 2000. "When You Need to Know Who's Who: Biographical Resources on the Web." *Collection Building* 19, 2: 76–77. A listing of biographical resources on the Web.

Bibliography of Works Cited in This Chapter

Bryant, Eric. 1999. "Assessing American National Biography." *Library Journal* 122 (July): 82.

Fialkoff, Francine. 1998. "Dueling Dictionaries." *Library Journal* 123 (November 15): 54.

LaGuardia, Cheryl. 2005. "Oxford Sets the Bar High." *Library Journal* 129 (October 15): 24–25.

McDermott, Irene E. 2003. "What's What With Who's Who on the Web." *Searcher* 11 (July/August): 49–51.

Quinn, Mary Ellen. 1998. "Brief Lives." *Booklist* 95 (September 1): 164.

Rollyson, Carl E. 1997. "Biography as a Genre." *Choice* 35 (October): 249–258.

Schreiner, Susan A., and Michael A. Somers. 2002. "Biography Resources: Finding Information on the Famous, Infamous and Obscure." *College and Research Libraries News* 63 (January): 32–35, 39.

Thomsen, Elizabeth. 2000. "When You Need to Know Who's Who: Biographical Resources on the Web." *Collection Building* 19, 2: 76–77.

Whiteley, Sandy. 2005. "An Undertaking of Exceptional Magnitude." *Booklist* 101 (January 1–15): 901.

12

Answering Questions about Governments—Government Information Sources

Overview

Every level of government, from federal agencies to the local municipal authorities, publishes. Perhaps unsurprisingly these works are often referred to, in reference services and beyond, as "government documents." In the U.S. government publications are defined as "informational matter which is published as an individual document at government expense, or as required by law" (44 U.S. Code 1901). This definition encompasses records of government administrations, research publications including statistics and other data, and popular sources of information on such subjects as nutrition, health, jobs and travel. They are as varied as "Botanic Garden for the Nation: The United States Botanic Garden" from the U.S. Botanic Gardens, "Empowering Youth with Nutrition and Physical Activity" from the U.S. Department of Agriculture, "Eyes on the Bay," from the Maryland Department of Natural Resources and "Malaria & Children: Progress in Intervention Coverage" from UNICEF. These publications come in many formats: books, CD-ROMs, periodicals, pamphlets, films, maps, and online publications. Every country produces its own government publications, and international organizations such as the United Nations and the World Bank also produce many publications.

How Government Publications Are Used

Government publications are an excellent source of information about many important issues. In fact, information on some subjects is only available from government publications. If one looks at the array of subjects covered by government departments and agencies, it becomes apparent that the government deals with nearly every part of a citizen's life. For this reason it is important to know about government publications and how to organize, access, and then add them to a library's collection.

Questions Answered by Government Publications

Q: How can I find National Parks where I can hike?

A: Go to the "Find a Park" section of the National Parks System site (www .nps.gov/findapark/index.htm), and you will find a list of National Parks where you can hike.

Q: Do I need immunizations to visit in South Africa?

A: Go to the Center for Disease Control site (www.cdc.gov/travel/) and you will be able to find the recommended immunizations for South Africa.

Q: How can I find out about eligibility requirements for Medicaid?

A: Go to the Centers for Medicare and Medicaid Services section of the Department of Health and Human Services Web site (www.cms.hhs.gov/ home/medicaid.asp) and you can find information on Medicaid eligibility and how to apply.

Q: How can I find information on small business loans?

A: Go to the Small Business Administration site (www.sba.gov) where you can find out about the services and loan programs that are available and how to apply.

The U.S. Government Printing Office and Its Future

The U.S. Government Printing Office (GPO) is "the largest information processing, printing and distribution facility in the world" (www.gpo.gov/pdfs/gpo_faq.pdf). It produces an enormous number of publications annually on every conceivable subject, e.g., census information, reports on education, information on immigration procedures and advice on health issues. The Government Printing Office is making a sea change in the way it publishes and distributes publications. First of all, in an effort to cut costs, the U.S. Government Printing Office will in the future be basically an online publisher. A selected number of publications will remain in print, but most publications will only be available online. This is a huge adjustment for libraries that have housed vast print collections of government publications. For users it means they can access free of charge most government publications as long as they have a computer and preferably a printer. Second, the government has put more responsibility on government agencies. The E-Government Act of 2002 has mandated agencies to improve public access to their information resources. "Agencies will have to follow standards in organizing information and making it easily searchable, and to provide basic information on agency mission, structure, and strategic plans" (Hernon, Dugan, and Shuler, 2003: 9). Finally, in May 2002 the Office of Management and Budget (OMB) "indicated that when the private sector can provide the better combination of cost, quality and timely delivery, agencies should contract with the private sector" (Drake, 2005: 46). This has produced many questions from librarians since if government information can be printed by private publishers, will these publications be part of the government's publications, or only available through the private publisher, thus increasing the cost?

All in all, the face of government publishing is drastically changing. With this new online world the public and libraries alike must become adept at searching and accessing the information they need. All librarians will want to learn more about government information and how it can benefit their users.

Depository Libraries

Depository libraries were established in their present form by the Printing Act of 1895 in order to keep the citizenry informed and to provide a way to distribute the publications to all parts of the country. These depository libraries receive government information from the Government Printing Office without charge with the agreement that they will provide free access to the public. There are two kinds of depository libraries: regional depository libraries and selective depository libraries. The regional libraries receive all items distributed to the depository system, while the selective depository libraries can receive the materials that meet their needs. Each state can have two regional depository libraries and each congressional district can have two selective depository libraries. There are about 1,250 federal depository libraries including public libraries, academic libraries, and special libraries. The list of depository libraries is available at http://catalog.gpo.gov/fdlpdir/FDLPdir.jsp.

Most depository libraries arrange their publications according to the Superintendent of Publications (SuDoc) classification numbers. These numbers are based on a classification system that identifies the name of the agency, the sub-agency, the publication type, and a cutter number that represents the title. For example, if a publication had the classification C3.134/2:C83/2/994, the C would indicate that it was a Department of Commerce publication, the 3 would indicate that it is a Census Bureau publication, the numbers after the decimal point would indicate the type of publication, and the numbers after the colon would be the individual cutter number of the publication.

Because the majority of government publications are now available online, the role of the depository libraries is being reevaluated. It is possible that they may take on an enhanced role and that there may not be as many depository libraries. The future of the depository library program is currently being discussed by the Depository Library Council and librarians administering depository library collections. Charles A. Seavey wrote recently that "we are moving into an era when every library in the country has the potential to become a depository in the sense that each one could potentially provide users with access to government information at a level previously unavailable (Seavey, 2005: 44).

Major Government Publication Resources Used in Reference Work

Guides to the U.S. Government

Fewer books have been published about government publications in recent years, perhaps due to fast pace of change. Judith Schiek Robinson's *Tapping the*

Government Grapevine: The User-friendly Guide to U.S Government Information Sources (Oryx Press, 1998) remains a useful text. More indicative of the new direction of government publications is Peter Hernon et al.'s *U.S. Government on the Web: Getting the Information You Need* (Libraries Unlimited, 2003), which deals with government publications as they appear on the Web. A more recent one is *Managing Electronic Government Information in Libraries*, edited by Andrea M. Morrison for GODORT (ALA, 2008).

In addition to books, many good Web sites link librarians to a wealth of information on government publications. Core Documents of U.S. Democracy can be found at http://thomas.loc.gov. This site leads the user to the Declaration of Independence, the U.S. Constitution, and the Emancipation Proclamation, as well as the U.S. Code, the Congressional Record, and many other key documents. The government documents Web site at the Vanderbilt University Library (www.library.vanderbilt.edu/romans/fdtf) is an excellent site with a good subject guide to help the librarian or user to find pertinent publications on a wide variety of subjects. Another Web site is housed at the University of Michigan and can be found at www.lib.umich.edu/government-documents-center/explore/. Both are very complete and a good starting place for researching not only U.S. government publications but also state and international publications. Google Uncle Sam (www.google.com/unclesam) is still another source of government information where the user can conduct a subject search and find both federal and state legislation on the same subject.

CQ Press Encyclopedia of American Government is a new fee-based online resource providing concise information on all aspects of U.S. government, the presidency, the Supreme Court, Congress and elections. It includes information about the organization and powers of each branch of government as well as current and past presidents, justices, and members of Congress.

Directories

The *U.S. Government Manual* is the best single source of information about the various branches and agencies in the federal government. It provides basic information about each government department and agency and quasi-government agencies including chief officials, addresses, phone numbers, and a summary of the areas of responsibility. It is available in print and online at www.gpo.gov/fdsys/browse/collection.action?collectionCode=GOVMAN. The commercial version of this manual is the *Washington Information Directory* (Congressional Quarterly), an annual publication available in print and online that provides contact information and a brief description for each government agency or congressional committee. It also includes information on nongovernmental agencies such as associations, lobbying organizations, and foundations.

Each branch of government has its own directory. For Congress there is the *Congressional Directory* (www.gpo.gov/fdsys/browse/collection.action?collectionCode=CDIR), published by the GPO. The *Congressional Staff Directory*, the *Federal Staff Directory* for the Executive Branch, and the *Judicial Staff Directory* for the Judicial Branch are published by Congressional Quarterly Press three times a year with an annual volume. They are all available in paper and online.

Periodicals and Their Indexes

The U.S. government is a prolific publisher of periodicals. These periodicals are indexed in the *ProQuest Government Periodicals Index*, to provide access to articles in over 160 federal government publications. This quarterly index is published online and can be searched by keyword. The U.S. government periodicals indexed include *FDA Consumer, International Economic Review, Environmental Health Perspective, Science and Technology Review, Monthly Labor Review, Survey of Current Business*, and *Occupational Outlook Quarterly*.

Other fee-based indexes provide access to government publications. *PAIS International* indexes governmental as well as many nongovernmental publications in the areas of its coverage. *LexisNexis Academic, ProQuest Congressional*, and *ProQuest Statistical Insight* also index government material and provide the full text of many government publications online. (See Chapter 8 for more information.)

U.S. Government Branch Publications

To understand the organization of government publications, it is necessary to understand the organization of the U.S. government. The U.S. government has three branches: Legislative Branch, Executive Branch, and Judicial Branch. Each branch has many agencies within it. The branches of the U.S. government and their publications are described in the sections that follow. The most direct access to the key publications of each branch is the Federal Digital System (FDsys) (www.gpo.gov/fdsys/).

Legislative Branch Publications

The Legislative Branch consists of Congress—the Senate and House of Representatives—and its supporting agencies that include the Library of Congress, the Government Printing Office, the General Accountability Office, and Congressional Budget Office. The legislative branch of government produces a huge number of publications as it moves from congressional bills to committee hearings and reports to discussions and votes on the floor of the House and Senate and then to the public laws that are eventually written into the United States Code. At each step of the way there is a document that is being discussed and often revised. All the information about the actions of the U.S. Congress can be found on FDsys (www.gpo.gov/fdsys/). It provides the history of bills, the text of all congressional bills, the Committee reports, and the text of the laws. The most important document is the *Congressional Record* (www.gpo.gov/fdsys/browse/collection.action?collectionCode=CREC), which is the official record of what takes place on the floor of the House and the Senate. A *Congressional Record Index* is available on FDsys from 1983 to date as an online publication.

This legislative process is documented by THOMAS (http://thomas.loc.gov), a Web site of the Library of Congress named for Thomas Jefferson. With THOMAS the user can easily follow the progress of a bill. THOMAS provides the text of the bill, its status, committee schedules and reports, the debate in either house of Congress as documented by the *Congressional Record*, the roll call vote, and the text of the public law when passed. Users can search by keyword or bill number. Within the *Congressional Record* users can search by subject or by member of Congress. THOMAS also provides information about the legislative process and the text of historical publications such as the Constitution of the United States and the Declaration of Independence.

A number of commercially produced publications document the progress of bills through Congress. The *CIS Index* is the most comprehensive index to bills and resolutions, committee prints, and congressional hearings. It indexes the publications of House, Senate, and joint committees and subcommittees. Each monthly issue has an index volume and an abstract volume. The index volume indexes publications by subject, name, title, bill number, and publication number. The abstract volume provides bibliographic information, SuDoc numbers, and summaries of the contents, including such detail as the names of witnesses and their affiliations. This index is published in an annual volume at the end of the year. It is also available through ProQuest. Since 1984 Congressional Information Service (CIS) has also published an annual legislative history volume with material indexed by subjects and names. CQ Press publishes numerous guides to Congress. *CQ Weekly*, an online resource, reports on a weekly basis on the activities of Congress. Flexible searching allows the user to search by keyword, date, etc. This database has expanded to include coverage of the executive branch and government regulations. *CQ Congress Collection*, another online resource, integrates a large amount of information into one database including information on legislation, members of Congress, key floor votes as far back as 1945, and other information about the legislative branch of government. The U.S. Serial Set and the American State Papers, available through *ProQuest Congressional*, provide researchers with access to the congressional legislative history documents from 1789 to 1969. *CQ Researcher*, available in print and online, provides reports on individual topics such as social, political, environmental, and health issues. Each report is about 13,000 words. Forty-four issues are produced each year.

Executive Branch Publications

The Executive Branch includes the Office of the President and many agencies that report directly to the president, such as the Council of Economic Advisors, the Office of Management and Budget, the National Security Council, and the Domestic Policy Council. The cabinet-level departments, i.e., Department of Commerce, Department of Defense, Department of Education, Department of Health and Human Services, Department of State, and others, are also part of the Executive Branch, as well as a number of independent government agencies such as Environmental Protection Agency, Federal Reserve, the Peace Corps, and the National Science Foundation.

Many excellent publications on the presidency have been published including the *Encyclopedia of the American Presidency* by Michael Genovese (Facts on File, 2010), which provides information on many aspects of the American presidency from George Washington to the current president. Information is included on the relationship between the presidency and other branches of government and on court cases, elections, and scandals in the *Guide to the Presidency Online Edition*. Other sources are the Presidential Library System Web site, which can be found at www.archives.gov/presidential_libraries/ and the American Presidency Project at www.presidency.ucsb.edu.

The *Federal Register* (www.gpo.gov/fdsys/browse/collection.action?collection Code=FR), produced by the National Archives and Records Administration, is this branch's most important publication. It provides information on a daily basis about presidential publications such as executive orders and proclamations, rules, proposed rules, and notices from agencies. This is a good place to look for the guidelines for government-funded programs. The database can be searched by subject or by agency. A *Federal Register Index* is also available. The *Code of Federal Regulations* (www.gpo.gov/fdsys/browse/collectionCfr.action?collectionCode =CFR) codifies the rules into public laws. Many rules and regulations are now published on the agencies' Web sites as a result of the E-Government Act of 2002.

The cabinet-level departments of the U.S. federal government are located in the Executive Branch. Each has its own Web site. These Web sites are gold mines of information. Sometimes it takes some hunting to find certain resources. The following is a description of a selection of government departments to provide the reader with a sense of the vast amount of information on these departmental Web sites.

Department of Education

Through the Department of Education Web site (www.ed.gov) one can find information on the latest education policies, financial aid information, education publications, grants, and, of course, ERIC, the Educational Resources Information Center, which is found at www.eric.ed.gov (see Chapter 8). A couple of interesting features are the teaching resources for teachers and parents and the National Center for Education Statistics (www.nces.ed.gov), which provides nationwide statistics on education such as enrollment trends in public and private elementary and secondary schools.

Department of Labor

The Department of Labor Web site (www.dol.gov) provides information on safety and health standards (OSHA), wage, hour, and other workplace standards, labor statistics, information about job seeking and careers (*Occupational Outlook Handbook*), and information for working women from the Women's Bureau. The Bureau of Labor Statistics (www.bls.gov) is a source of local data and includes the Consumer Price Index and unemployment rate.

Department of Interior

Through the Department of Interior Web site (www.doi.gov) one can find information on fish and wildlife, including endangered species and wildlife refuges (United States Fish and Wildlife Service), maps from the U.S. Geological Survey, and information from the National Park Service about each National Park.

Department of Health and Human Services

The Web site of the Department of Health and Human Services (www.dhhs .gov) provides a wealth of information on diseases and conditions, safety and wellness, drugs and food, as well as information on aging issues, family issues, and issues for specific populations. This well-organized Web site provides easy access to many important resources. The Department of Health and Human Services includes the Centers for Disease Control and Prevention, Centers for Medicare and Medicaid Services, Food and Drug Administration, and the National Institutes of Health, which publishes *MedlinePlus*, an important source of consumer health information.

The Department of Commerce

The Department of Commerce (www.commerce.gov) includes the Bureau of Economic Analysis, which publishes the journal, *Survey of Current Business*, as well as the International Trade Administration, which provides reports on U.S. trade and the U.S. industry and trade outlook and the Bureau of the Census. The Minority Business Development Agency resides here as does NOAA (National Oceanic and Atmospheric Administration). On the NOAA site one can find all kinds of weather and climate information including hurricane information and other kinds of weather advisories. The National Technical Information Service is also housed in this department. This clearinghouse for government-funded engineering, scientific, technical, and business-related information has an online library and bookstore.

The Department of State

The State Department (www.state.gov) provides information on U.S. embassies and consulates, travel information, and information on international issues. *Background Notes* is published and updated by the U.S. State Department. These publications provide concise information about countries including the land, people, history, government, political conditions, economy, foreign relations, and travel and business. They are updated frequently.

Central Intelligence Agency

The CIA publishes *The World Factbook*, which provides maps and some general information about 267 countries (www.cia.gov/library/publications/the-world-factbook/index.html). This excellent free source, which includes information on geography, people, government, economy, communications, transportation, military, and transnational issues, is current and quite extensive.

Library of Congress

The Library of Congress (www.loc.gov) is often treated as a national library, but it is actually the research arm of Congress. Its Web site states as its mission "to make its resources available and useful to Congress and the American people and to sustain and preserve a universal collection of knowledge and creativity for future generations." It houses the THOMAS Web site and the

Congressional Research Service, which works for Congress. On the Library of Congress Web site there are resources especially for librarians, researchers, publishers, kids and families, and teachers. The Copyright Office is of interest to many. Here one can find out how to register a copyright or how to search copyright records. The American Memory project provides a wealth of digitized text and images on many aspects of American history, e.g., women's history, African-American history, immigration, and culture and folk life.

Judicial Branch Publications

The Judicial Branch consists of the Federal Courts, including the Supreme Court and special courts such as the Court of International Trade. The Judicial Branch contains administrative units such as the Federal Judicial Center. The Web site for the U.S Supreme Court is www.supremecourt.gov. Here one can find the history of the court, biographies of past and present members of the Supreme Court, and even speeches by members of the Supreme Court.Opinions of the Supreme Court can be found at www.supremecourt.gov/opinions/opinions.aspx.

Other sources of court decisions can be found in the fee-based databases of Westlaw and LexisNexis. An online source is *CQ Supreme Court Collection*, which includes information on the history of the Supreme Court, important cases, and the impact of these decisions on American life.

Statistical Resources

All libraries receive many questions about statistics on population, jobs, education, health, crime, income, and much more. Since so many statistics are collected by government entities, this is often a good place to start.

The *Statistical Abstract of the United States* (www.census.gov/compendia/statab/), published by the Bureau of the Census annually in paper and online, is a compilation of tables and graphs of statistics from every government agency about the United States. Sources for each table and graph are noted. When U.S. government statistics are not available, statistics from other reliable national organizations are used. This source covers such areas as population, health and nutrition, vital statistics, education, labor, agriculture, law enforcement, manufacturing, trade, and housing. *FEDSTATS* (www.fedstats.gov/), maintained by the Federal Interagency Council on Statistical Policy, provides links to federal statistics by topics and agencies. Links are provided to agency databases such as the Bureau of Labor Statistics and the Center for Education Statistics. One can also search by state or by subject and then by state or city. It also is possible to search across agency Web sites. *American Fact Finder* is a user-friendly Web site from the Bureau of the Census (http://factfinder.census.gov/home/saff/main.html?_lang=en). This Web site provides statistics on population, housing, economic, and geographic data. In addition to the data from the last census, it provides information from the American Community Survey, which surveys about 3,000 households annually from every county in the United States for population and housing information and will substitute for the Census' long form. The Economic Census is taken every five years.

Three indexes are produced that cover statistics at the federal, state, and international levels. They are all published by ProQuest. *American Statistics Index (ASI)* provides statistics from publications in all parts of the federal government. Published monthly, it includes an index and abstracts with an annual cumulation. It is available in paper and on *ProQuest Statistical Insight*. *Statistical Reference Index (SRI)* includes sources of statistics from private-sector organizations and state governments. Over 1,000 sources are included. This publication is produced monthly in an annual cumulation with an index and abstracts. It is available in paper and on *ProQuest Statistical Insight*. *Index to International Statistics (IIS)* includes all kinds of statistical publications from more than 100 international intergovernmental organizations including all major Intergovernmental Organizations (such as the United Nations, European Union, Organization of Economic Co-operation and Development, and Organization of American States). It is published monthly with an index and abstracts and with an annual cumulation and is also available on *ProQuest Statistical Insight*.

Business and economic statistics are available from several sources. The Bureau of Economic Analysis (www.bea.gov) provides statistics such as the gross domestic product, the balance of payments, international trade, and personal income. *USA Trade Online* (www.usatradeonline.gov), a publication of the Foreign Trade Division of the U.S. Census Bureau, provides export and import data by commodity. Individuals can subscribe to it for a fee. The Bureau of Labor Statistics (www.bls.gov) provides a wealth of labor statistics. Here one can find the consumer price index, import/export indexes, wage statistics, demographics about the workforce, and career information. There is also statistical information on a state-by-state basis. The National Center for Health Statistics (www.cdc.gov/nchs) provides health statistics on all kinds of health issues nationwide such as injuries, infant mortality, and food allergies.

Government Publications by Subject

The government has also made it possible to access information by subject. The overall Web site, USA.gov, was designed to provide access to government publications for the general public. This portal provides gateways for citizens, businesses, and government employees. Users can search for information by topic such as health, jobs, education, money, or recreation or by department or agency; users can also download forms for jobs, benefits, passports, social security, etc., and can even receive an e-mail newsletter. Many subject-specific Web sites can also be accessed by the public or the librarian. They include www.science.gov, www.disability.gov, and www.seniors.gov. Each site is tailored to the needs of the target group or subject area.

Maps

The U.S. government produces many maps. Among the agencies producing maps are the U.S. Geological Survey, the Bureau of the Census, the National

Park Service, and the National Oceanic and Atmospheric Administration. These are described in more detail in Chapter 10.

Information on Elections

Elections have become an important part of our national life, as they are in other countries. Many places contain information on current and historical elections. USA.gov, which provides a great deal of user-friendly information, is a good place to start. Another source is the Federal Election Commission Media Guide, available at www.fec.gov. The Open Secrets site (www.opensecrets.org) from the Center for Responsive Secrets repackages the FEC information into a more accessible form. Other sites of interest include America Votes (www.americavotes.org), Project Vote Smart (www.votesmart.org), the League of Women Voters (www.vote411.org), and the U.S. Election Atlas (www.us electionatlas.org).

Historical Data

Historical Statistics of the United States has recently been updated by Cambridge University Press and is now available in print and online. It includes historical statistics on every aspect of American society from colonial times to the present including population, labor and employment, agriculture, manufacturing, and transportation. Another historical series of great interest is the *U.S. Congressional Serials Set*, which includes the House and Senate documents and House and Senate reports, bound by session of Congress, beginning with the first session of the 15th Congress in 1817. The earlier records are found in the *American State Papers*.

The States

State governments also produce a wide array of interesting and essential publications. They usually have a Web site that can be checked to find their publications either in print or online. Two useful Web sites are State and Local Government on the Net (www.statelocalgov.net), which is arranged by state and by topic, e.g., arts, aging, health, education, and libraries; and USA.gov, which has a link to local government information. A state-by-state list of links to state agency databases can be found at wikis.ala.org/godort/index.php/State_Agency_Databases. Information on state depository library systems is available at wikis.ala.org/godort/index.php/State_Depository_Library_Systems.

The Book of the States, published by the Council of State Governments, provides data about state government including articles on trends and issues in state constitutions, the three branches of state governments and major policies and programs, information about legislatures, governors, and other state officials, information on agricultural policy, women in government, environmental spending, education, mental health, etc. *City and County Data Book*, a supplement to *Statistical Abstract*, includes statistics for 1,078 cities, all U.S. counties, and places with 2,500 or more inhabitants and provides a way to make comparisons among cities and counties. It is available online.

State Rankings 2010, edited by Kathleen O'Leary Morgan and Scott Morgan, is a commercially published book on the states. It includes tables comparing the states in such areas as education, health, crime/law enforcement, welfare, and taxes.

For Kids

Kids.gov, divided into grades K–5 and 6–8, provides basic information about the federal government. In addition, many government agencies such as the EPA, CIA, FBI, Federal Trade Commission, and the Forest Service have developed clever, well-designed Kids' Pages. Access to them is available through www.kids.gov.

E-Government

E-government is online government services, that is, any interaction one might have with a government agency using the Internet. The access to government information on the Internet has made it possible to provide more government information no matter the library. Although depository libraries are still important, many questions about the federal government as well as state and local government can be answered by any reference librarian. Once librarians ascertain that a question is related to the government they should proceed to www.usa.gov or to www.gpo.gov where numerous ways are available to search for government information including Browse Topics developed by librarians, the A-Z list, and even e-mail and chat reference if assistance is needed. Most forms needed by users are available online and can easily be printed.

United Nations Publications

Although the United Nations is the first organization that comes to mind when we say international, many international organizations are included, as well as the numerous agencies that are part of the United Nations and the many other international organizations worldwide.

The United Nations has made its official documents available for free at www.un.org/en/documents/index/shtml. The majority of the documents in this database are from 1993 onward, but older publications are added all the time. The Official Publications of the United Nations (ODS) "provides access to the resolutions of the General Assembly, Security Council, Economic and Social Council and the Trusteeship Council from 1946 onwards" (http://unp.un.org). It does not include the UN Treaty Series or the UN Sales Publications.

The U.N. publications that are for sale, both print and online, are listed at http://unp.un.org. The Yearbook of the United Nations provides data on the world economy, its structure and major trends, population and social statistics, economic activity, and international economic relations. It is published in English and French. The *Demographic Yearbook*, published by the United Nations, is an international source of statistics that provides basic statistical data on more than 200 countries. The information, presented in tables, includes basic demographic statistics such as population trends and size, fertility, mortality, marriage and divorce, and migration. This yearbook is published in English and French and is available online. The *Population and Vital Statistics Report* is available in print. Libraries can set up standing orders with the United Nations and can set up alerts for new publications.

U.N. publications have a similar organization system to the Superintendent of Documents. They are arranged by the issuing body and any subordinate body, and the form and a number for a specific publication. There are U.N. depository libraries throughout the world. UNIBISNET provides free bibliographic access to U.N. documents and publications from 1979 forward. Check the U.N. Library site for a wealth of information on the United Nations at www.un.org/Depts/dhl/. *AccessUN* is a subscription database providing access to U.N. documents and publications.

Selected International Resources

Canadian Publications

The Canadian government's Web site for publications can be found at http://publications.gc.ca/site/eng/home.html. This site provides information about Canadian government publications. Users can search by topic, by title, or by keyword in a database that lists all kinds of government publications. Users can also access a list of recent releases, and information guides. A Weekly Checklist of new publications is available online. The only full-text publication is the *Canada Gazette*, the official paper of the government of Canada. This publication, begun in 1841, publishes weekly information on new statutes and regulations, decisions of administrative boards, government notices, and public notices from the private sector. Similar to the United States, Canada has a library Depository Service Program. Established in 1927 to provide access to federal government information, there are presently 680 depository libraries in public and academic libraries. Of these depository libraries only fifty-two are full depositories and the rest are selective depository libraries. A list of the depository libraries can be found at http://publications.gc.ca/site/eng/locatingOur Publications/depositoryLibraries/index.html. The selective depositories select their publications from the Weekly Checklist.

Government Publications in the United Kingdom

The Office of the Public Sector Information (www.opsi.gov.uk) manages and provides access to U.K. government information. The UKOP (www.ukop.co.uk) houses the catalog of official U.K. publications since 1980. The House of Commons publications and the Command Papers, those presented by a government minister to Parliament "by Command of Her Majesty," can be found at www.official-documents.gov.uk. Copies of all government publications can be

purchased from the TSO Parliamentary and Legal Bookshop (www.tsoshop.co
.uk/parliament). Further information on the U.K. government is available
through *Directgov* (www.direct.gov.uk/en/index.htm).

Collection Development and Maintenance

Selection and Keeping Current

The primary access point for U.S. government publications is FDsys (www.gpo
.gov/fdsys/). This portal provides free access to federal publications produced
by the various government departments and agencies. Users can search by
branch of government, i.e., legislative, executive, or judicial, or can search by
title or topic.

The FDsys (Federal Digital System), an online index and database, includes
bibliographic records from 1994 to the present as well as full text when available. The print version of the catalog, begun in 1895, was called the *Monthly
Catalog of U.S. Government Publications* and is the major access point for pre-
1976 documents. Government publications can also be accessed through
WorldCat, which includes all items from the *Monthly Catalog* and its successors
since July 1976.

In order to purchase government publications, one can turn to the U.S.
Government Online Bookstore (bookstore.gpo.gov), which allows searching
by subject. A weekly list of new publications is also available. Libraries can
purchase publications from the GPO by setting up a deposit account or paying
by credit card or check. Federal publications can also be purchased from the
Federal Citizen Information Center (www.pueblo.gsa.gov). These are mostly
low-cost or free publications on such subjects as education, small business,
health, and employment.

The Government Documents Round Table (GODORT) on the American
Library Asssociation's Web site is available at www.ala.org/ala/mgrps/rts/
godort/index.cfm. It provides links for the librarian to a great deal of useful
information on government publications. It is the best place to start for the
beginner and the experienced librarian. GODORT produces guides to government publications and up-to-date information on the status of the Government
Printing Office and the Government Depository Library Program.

Evaluating Government Documents

Because government documents are published by a governmental body, they
are assumed to provide accurate, reliable, and up-to-date information. For this
reason there is no need to apply the usual evaluation criteria. However, since
some government information is also published by trade publishers, librarians
will want to compare the products to see which will be the most useful to their
clientele. For example, material published by a trade publisher might be easier
to use, easier to search, or have a more acceptable layout. Cost will enter into the
librarian's decision since government publications tend to be less expensive

than those published by a trade publisher. Format will continue to be an issue. Librarians should pay attention to which documents remain in print, since at least for U.S. documents, it has been stated that only a small number will continue in print format. The access issue will remain. If important information is not available for a reasonable cost online, librarians must make a case for access. Or if information is made available and is then withdrawn, librarians must call that to the attention of appropriate officials. Even with government information some evaluation criteria will apply, and librarians must be alert to these issues.

Further Considerations

Having so much information accessible on the Internet has made searching for government publications much easier. Efforts are being made to digitize older material. The FDsys (Federal Digital System) is the way to begin since one can search from a number of access points. However, having some rudimentary knowledge of the organization of the U.S. government will still come in very handy in finding the document needed. Getting familiar with the Web sites of departments and agencies will also be useful. They are not equally user friendly, and many times the user needs some knowledge to make use of them. The *U.S. Government Manual* is helpful in finding out where a particular agency is housed. This is a time of change in the area of government publications.

TOP TEN U.S. GOVERNMENT PUBLICATIONS		
Title	**Print**	**Online**
Bureau of the Census publications		www.census.gov
Congressional Record	Daily	www.gpo.gov/fdsys/browse/collection.action?collectionCode=CREC
FDsys		www.gpo.gov/fdsys/
Federal Register	Daily	www.gpo.gov/fdsys/browse/collection.action?collectionCode=FR
Library of Congress		www.loc.gov
Statistical Abstract of the United States	Annual	www.census.gov/compendia/statab/
THOMAS		http://thomas.loc.gov
USA.gov		www.usa.gov
U.S. Government Manual	Annual	www.gpo.gov/fdsys/browse/collection.action?collectionCode=GOVMAN
The World Factbook		www.cia.gov/library/publications/the-world-factbook/index.html

---

RECOMMENDED FREE WEB SITES

FDsys. Available: www.gpo.gov/fdsys/. This site provides access to major documents from all three branches of government.

Statistical Abstract of the United States. Available: www.census.gov/compendia/statab/. This is an excellent online source providing government statistics on a multitude of subjects.

THOMAS. Available: http://thomas.loc.gov. Housed at the Library of Congress, THOMAS provides access to congressional bills past and present, the Congressional Record and other information on Congress.

United Nations. Available: www.un.org/en/documents/index/shtml. This provides access to many UN *documents.*

USA.gov. Available: www.usa.gov. This user-friendly site provides access to government information for all.

Recommended Resources Discussed in This Chapter

America Votes. Available: www.americavotes.org.

American Statistical Index. New York: LexisNexis. Published monthly with an annual cumulation. Available online through *ProQuest Statistical Insight.*

The Book of the States. 1965–. Lexington, KY: Council of State Governments. Annual.

Canada. Depository libraries. Available: http://publications.gc.ca/site/eng/locatingOurPublications/depositoryLibraries/index.html.

Canada Publications. Available: http://publications.gc.ca/site/eng/home.html.

Central Intelligence Agency. *The World Factbook.* Available: www.cia.gov/library/publications/the-world-factbook/index.html.

CIS Index. 1970–. New York: Congressional Information Service/LexisNexis. Annual volume. Also available online through LexisNexis.

City and County Data Book. 2007. Washington, DC: Government Printing Office. Available: www.census.gov/prod/www/abs/ccdb07.html.

Code of Federal Regulations. Available: www.gpo.gov/fdsys/browse/collection Cfr.action?collectionCode=CFR.

Congressional Directory. Available: www.gpo.gov/fdsys/browse/collection .action?collectionCode=CDIR.

Congressional Record. Available: www.gpo.gov/fdsys/browse/collection.action? collectionCode=CREC.

Congressional Record Index. Available: www.gpo.gov/fdsys/browse/collection .action?collectionCode=CRI.

Congressional Staff Directory. Washington, DC: CQ Press. Published three times a year with an annual volume. Also available online: http://library .cqpress.com/csd.

Core Documents of U.S. Democracy. Available: http://thomas.loc.gov.

CQ Congress Collection. Washington, DC: CQ Press. Available: www.cqpress.com.

CQ Press Encyclopedia of American Government. Washington, DC: CQ Press. Available: www.cqpress.com.

CQ Researcher. Washington, DC: CQ Press. Forty-four issues a year and an annual volume. Also available online: www .cqpress.com/researcher.

CQ Supreme Court Collection. Washington, DC: CQ Press. Available: www.cqpress.com.

CQ Weekly. 1983–. Washington, DC: CQ Press. Available online: www.cqpress.com.

ERIC (Educational Resources Information Center). Available: www.eric.ed.gov.

FDsys (Federal Digital System). Available: www.gpo.gov/fdsys/.

Federal Citizen Information Center. Available: www.pueblo.gsa.gov.

Federal Register. Available: www.gpo.gov/fdsys/browse/collection.action?collectionCode=FR.

Federal Staff Directory. Washington, DC: CQ Press. Published three times a year with an annual volume. Also available online: http://library.cqpress.com/fsd.

FEDSTATS. Available: www.fedstats.gov.

Genovese, Michael. 2010. *Encyclopedia of the American Presidency.* New York: Facts on File.

Google Uncle Sam. Available: www.google.com/unclesam.

Government Documents Round Table (GODORT). Available: www.ala.org/ala/mgrps/rts/godort/index.cfm.

Guide to the Presidency. Washington, DC: CQ Press. Available online.

Historical Statistics of the United States. 2006. New York: Cambridge University Press. Also available online: http://hsus.cambridge.org.

Index to International Statistics. New York: ProQuest. Published monthly with an annual cumulations. Also available online through *ProQuest Statistical Insight.*

Judicial Staff Directory. Washington, DC: CQ Press. Published three times a year with an annual volume. Also available online: http://library.cqpress.com/jsd.

Kids.gov. Available: www.kids.gov.

League of Women Voters. Available: www.vote411.org.

Library of Congress. Available: www.loc.gov.

National Center for Education Statistics. Available: http://nces.ed.gov.

National Center for Health Statistics. Available: www.cdc.gov/nchs.

Presidential Library System. Available: www.archives.gov/presidential_libraries/.

Project Vote Smart. Available: http://votesmart.org.

ProQuest Government Periodicals Index. 1988–. New York: ProQuest. Quarterly. Available online.

State Agency Databases. Available: wikis.ala.org/godort/index.php/state-agency_databases.

State and Local Government on the Net. Available: www.statelocalgov.net.

State Depository Library Systems. Available: wikis.ala.org/godort/index.php/state_depository_library_systems.

State Rankings 2010. Edited by Kathleen O'Leary Morgan and Scott Morgan. Washington, DC: CQ Press.

Statistical Abstract of the United States. Available: www.census.gov/compendia/statab/.

Statistical Reference Index. New York: ProQuest. Published monthly with an annual cumulation. Also available online through *ProQuest Statistical Insight.*

THOMAS. Available: http://thomas.loc.gov.

TSO Parliamentary and Legal Bookshop. Available: www.tsoshop.co.uk/parliament/.

United Kingdom. *Command Papers and House of Commons Papers.* Available: www.official-documents.gov.uk.

United Kingdom. Directgov. Available: www.direct.gov.uk/en/index.htm.

United Kingdom. Office of the Public Sector Information. Available at www.opsi.gov.uk.

United Kingdom. Official Documents. Available: www.official-documents.gov.uk.

United Nations. *Demographic Yearbook.* Available: http://unstats.un.org/unsd/demographic/products/dyb/dyb2008.htm.

United Nations Documents. Available: www.un.org/en/documents/index/shtml.

United Nations Publications. Available: http://unp.un.org.

United States Depository Libraries. Available: http://catalog.gpo.gov/fdlpdir/FDLPdir.jsp.

University of Michigan Government Documents Web site. Available: www.lib.umich.edu/government-documents-center/explore.

U.S. Bureau of the Census. *American Factfinder.* Available: http://factfinder.cenus.gov/home/saff/main.html?_lang=en.

U.S. Bureau of Economic Analysis. Available: www.bea.gov.

U.S. Bureau of Labor Statistics. Available: www.bls.gov.

U.S. Department of Commerce. Available: www.commerce.gov.

U.S. Department of Health and Human Services. Available: www.dhhs.gov.

U.S. Department of the Interior. Available: www.doi.gov.

U.S. Department of Labor. Available: www.dol.gov.

U.S. Department of State. Background Notes. Available: www.state.gov.

U.S. Election Atlas. Available: www.uselectionatlas.org.

U.S. Government Manual. Washington, DC: Government Printing Office. Annual. Also available: www.gpo.gov/fdsys/browse/collection.action?collectionCode=GOVMAN.

U.S. Government Online Bookstore. Available: http://bookstore.gpo.gov.

U.S. Serial Set Digital Collection. New York: ProQuest.

U.S. Supreme Court. Available: www.supremecourt.gov.

U.S. Supreme Court. Opinions. Available: http://supremecourt.gov/opinions/opinions.aspx.

USA Trade Online. Available: www.usatradeonline.gov.

Vanderbilt University Government Documents Web site. Available: www.library.vanderbilt.edu/romans/fdtf.

Washington Information Directory. Washington, DC: CQ Press. Annual.

Recommendations for Further Reading

Bahr, William L. 2008. "Quick Guide to Finding U.S. Supreme Court Cases." *Reference Services Review* 36, no. 3: 232–244. Useful for those not very familiar with searching this area.

Burroughs, Jennie M. 2009. "What Users Want: Assessing Government Information Preferences to Drive Information Services." *Government Information Quarterly* 26, no. 1: 203–218. Results of a University of Montana Library study on use of government information.

Evans, Donna, and David C. Yen. 2005. "E-Government: An Analysis for Implementation; Framework for Understanding Cultural and Social Impact." *Government Information Quarterly* 22, 3: 354–373. This article explores the implications of e-government for U.S. citizens and the international community.

Fagan, Jody Condit, and Bryan Fagan. 2004. "An Accessibility Study of State Legislative Web Sites." *Government Information Quarterly* 21, 1: 65–85. A study of the barriers to state legislative Web sites for users of assistive technology.

Herman, Edward. 2008. "The American Community Survey: An Introduction to the Basics." *Government Information Quarterly* 25: 504–519. An important subject by an experienced government information person.

Jacobs, James A., James R. Jacobs, and Shinjoung Yeo. 2005. "Government Information in the Digital Age: The Once and Future Federal Depository Library Program." *The Journal of Academic Librarianship* 31, 3: 198–208. The authors argue that even with the technological changes in the delivery of government documents, the Federal Depository Library Program is still needed.

Liptak, Deborah A. 2005. "Congressional Research Service Reports Revealed." *Online* 29, no. 6 (November/December): 23–26. Information on where to find the Congressional Research Service Reports that are written for Congress on such subjects as copyright, global climate change, AIDS, and stem cell research.

Mann, Wendy, and Theresa R. McDevitt, eds. 2003. *Government Publications Unmasked: Teaching Government Information Resources in the 21st Century.* Pittsburgh: Library Instruction Publications. An excellent guide to teaching government publications.

Martin, Mary, ed. 2005. *Local and Regional Government Information: How to Find It, How to Use It.* Westport, CT: Greenwood Press. A recent guide to local and regional government information online and in print.

Morrison, Andrea. 2007. "Resources for Art in Online Government Information." *Indiana Libraries* 26, no. 2: 47–53. Discusses government information as a source of fine art, graphic art and images.

Nour, Mohammed A., Abel Rahman, A. Abel Rahman, and Adam Fadlalla. 2008. "A Context-based Integrative Framework for E-government Initiatives." *Government Information Quarterly* 25, no. 3: 448–461. The development of a model for e-government efforts and initiatives.

Prophet, Mary, Megan Fitch, and Joy He. 2004. "Ohio5 Government Documents." *Against the Grain* 16, no. 3 (June): 38–39. Describes a cooperative arrangement among five college libraries in Ohio who are all Federal Depository libraries.

Reddick, Christopher G. 2005. "Citizen Interaction with E-government: From the Streets to the Servers." *Government Information Quarterly* 22, 1: 38–57. A study of the demand of citizens for e-government.

Rogers, Michael. 2005. "Illinois Libraries/OCLC Tackle Government Information Online." *Library Journal* 130, no. 10 (June 1): 35–36. Discussion of the development of an Illinois State Library, the University of Illinois at Chicago and OCLC sponsored virtual reference desk for government information using thirty librarians from federal depository libraries.

Shuler, John A. 2004. "New Economic Models for the Federal Depository System—Why Is It So Hard to Get the Question Answered?" *The Journal of Academic Librarianship* 30, no. 3 (May): 243–249. A discussion of the need for a new economic model that will enable the Government Printing Office to survive and the future role of depository libraries.

Singer, Carol A. 2003. "The Transition of U.S. Government Publications from Paper to the Internet: A Chronology." *Internet Reference Services Quarterly* 8(3): 29–35. A year-by-year chronology of the transition of U.S. government publications to the Internet.

Staley, Robert A. 2007. "Electronic Government Information Dissemination: Changes for Programs, Users, Libraries and Government Documents Librarians. *Collection Management* 32 (3/4): 305–326. A helpful update on e-government.

Wilson, Yvonne, and Deborah Richey. 2005. "State and Local Documents Roundup. A Basic Primer on Collecting Government Publications." *Documents to the People* 33, no. 4 (Winter): 9–11. Includes information on collecting financial reports, annual reports, statistical surveys, municipal codes, and planning documents, etc.

Bibliography of Works Cited in This Chapter

Drake, Miriam A. 2005. "The Federal Depository Library Program: Safety Net for Access." *Searcher* 13, no. 1 (January): 46.

Herman, Edward. 1997. *Locating United States Government Information: A Guide to Sources*. 2nd ed. Buffalo, NY: William S. Hein.

Hernon, Peter, Robert E. Dugan, and John A. Shuler. 2003. *U.S. Government on the Web: Getting the Information You Need*. 3rd ed. Westport, CT: Libraries Unlimited.

Johnson, Linda B. 2004. "Electronic Moves Center Stage." *Library Journal* (May 15): 52–57.

Morrison. Andrea M., ed. 2008. *Managing Electronic Government Information in Libraries*. Edited by Andrea M. Morrison for GODORT. Chicago, IL: ALA.

Robinson, Judith Schiek. 1998. *Tapping the Government Grapevine: The User-friendly Guide to U.S. Government Information Sources*. 3rd ed. Phoenix, AZ: Oryx Press.

Seavey, Charles A. 2005. "Publications to the People." *American Libraries* 36, no. 7 (August): 42–44.

Smith, Diane H., ed. 1993. *Management of Government Information Resources in Libraries*. Englewood, CO: Libraries Unlimited.

Smith, Lori L., Daniel C. Barkley, Daniel D. Cornwall, Eric W. Johnson, and J. Louise Malcomb. 2003. *Tapping State Government Information Sources*. Westport, CT: Greenwood Press.

Wilson, Paula. 2003. "Electronic Publications to the People." *Public Libraries* 42, no. 6 (November–December): 362–363.

Part III
Special Topics in Reference and Information Work

13

When and How to Use the Internet as a Reference Tool

The Facts

The most seductive and ubiquitous reference resource to emerge in the twentieth century was the Internet. Virtually unknown to the general population until the advent of the World Wide Web in 1990, the explosion of Internet use in less than two decades has been nothing short of spectacular. It took many centuries for an encyclopedia to be viewed as an all-purpose resource accessible to the common person. In contrast, it has taken less than a decade for 95 percent of libraries in postsecondary degree-granting institutions to establish open access to the Internet. As of today, almost 99 percent of public libraries and a little over 90 percent of school media centers have Internet access (ALA Fact Sheet 26). This access can feed off a stratospheric 4.3 billion IP addresses (ISC Internet Domain Survey). With so much material and access freely available, usage statistics are also high. Some 80 percent of eighteen- to twenty-four-year-olds use the Internet on a regular basis, and according to a Generational Media Study, the Internet has predominated as "the medium of choice" (Greenspan, 2004). It seems clear then that the Internet is here to stay, perchance to flourish.

The Puzzle

Yet reference librarians have been curiously sluggish in wholly claiming, organizing, and charting the course of Internet research.

At the start of the twenty-first century, a fascinating and important study by Ross and Nilsen found that reference librarians "seem to regard the Internet as an external resource that users can search independently...but not as a full-fledged reference tool for which reference librarians have a responsibility to help users search and evaluate" (Ross and Nilsen, 2000: 147). By 2005, the *Chronicle of Higher Education* published a special segment on libraries in which Elizabeth Breakstone, author of the concluding article, wrote, "librarians not only participate in the information revolution but help direct its course"

(Breakstone, 2005: B6). However, there were no great moves toward actively "directing the course" of Internet searches. It was only at the close of 2008 that a serious proposal was launched by OCLC and the information schools of Syracuse University and the University of Washington to recast Internet sources as "full-fledged reference tools." The creation of a comprehensive search engine based on librarian recommendations and the automatic gathering of reliable URLs from digital references selected by libraries for their own institutional sites is the underpinning of this new venture aptly titled *Reference Extract* (Oder, 2008). A $100,000 grant from the MacArthur Foundation is financing the project and it remains to be seen whether a search engine trawling for the collective, though restricted, information contained in selected Web sites is a feasible and effective way to harness the power of Web resources without inheriting a large part of its unreliability as well.

Curiously enough, Google too appears to be aiming for control over the seeming chaos of Web research in its continuing bid to develop the "perfect search engine . . . that understands exactly what you mean and gives you back exactly what you want" (Carr, 2008: 58). Rather than relying on individually selected Web resources, as *Reference Extract* aims to do, Google is refining its internal search algorithms. A systematic analysis of behavioral data is collated as users conduct Google searches, with an aim to create a vast collective artificial intelligence that is larger than the sum of its parts. For example, the Google tool *Flu Trends* appears to supply early detection warnings for regional flu outbreaks at a sustained average of seven to ten days before the venerable Centers for Disease Control makes the announcement. The unintentional behavioral data resulting from individual searches on flu and flu-related words is intentionally collated by *Flu Trends* to produce this nontraditional yet effective way of maximizing Internet research.

Much like the canonical "Hausfrau," the Internet is also being used in any number of ways by reference librarians, without being given the necessary recognition or attention due to a "full-fledged reference tool." Various applications of Internet protocol such as electronic mail, chat, remote login, and file transfer are being appropriated by reference librarians to conduct e-mail reference, chat reference, wikis, blogs, and instant messaging reference, as well as remote access to reference databases. So in addition to the ubiquitous use of Web sites and search engines, the larger technological domain covered by the Internet is also being used in dynamic and ever-increasing ways, as highlighted in Chapter 20. Some reference librarians are more immersed in Internet reference than others, but no librarian can claim complete immunity.

The Solution

It seems clear that rather than holding on to the tail of the Internet tiger and bumping along wherever it goes, Internet reference must be recognized as a "full-fledged reference tool" so that reference librarians can "help direct its course" in creative ways. This can be achieved through an understanding of the nature of the beast and a considered blueprint for actual use.

Nature of Internet Reference

The portable book was invented in the Middle Ages; in all these centuries we have developed a visceral acceptance of the strengths and weaknesses of the format. With the Internet, this has yet to happen. Both paeans and dirges are sung with equal passion and sincerity as we grapple with the possibilities and ramifications of the format. A spotlight on the major strengths and weaknesses of the Internet is a step toward understanding the best ways to use the medium to its most effective advantage.

Strengths

Ease

Intuitively, the act of plugging into a universe of information, 24/7, at the click of a finger is enticing. Despite all the wrong or unfiltered information for which the Internet is known, the number of right answers for information that would otherwise have taken extended time, energy, and resources is impressive. The process of getting these right answers is not only trivial, but also instantaneous and handy.

For example, a question like *"Who is the person listed at 708-555-1212?"* could potentially have been time-consuming for a user. The knowledge that a criss-cross directory existed, followed by the search for a library that subscribed to a printed criss-cross directory for the 708 area, followed by a study of the arrangement of the directory, would be the minimum requirement. A reverse lookup in any of the online directories is accomplished in a matter of a minute.

In a 1999 study it was found that fully one-third of the traditional reference questions used as class assignments for library students had to be discarded because finding an answer required neither logic nor knowledge of sources. Instead, the answers were available with a minute's worth of Googling (Ross and Nilsen, 2000: 148). Ease of use and the potential instant gratification of needs contribute greatly to the perceived strengths of Internet research.

Currency

Internet resources are stereotypically valued for their currency. Print resources, by definition, have built-in time delays to accommodate the vetting and printing process. Even a newspaper takes twenty-four hours to print the day's news. The Internet, on the other hand, can potentially update news as it is made. The print directory listing new Congress members, for example, was published as the *Congressional Directory* in April 2011, four months after the inaugural session of the 112th Congress. In the interim, users wanting to contact a congressional representative or browse the roster had little choice but to consult Web sites such as www.senate.gov. In a dramatic bid for currency, in 2009, the 100-year-old *Christian Science Monitor* became the first nationally circulated newspaper to shift from a daily print format to a constantly updated online publication in the interests of "improving the *Monitor*'s timeliness and relevance" (Cook, 2008).

Audiovisual

Useful or even critical to some research is the need for audiovisual information. The Internet has the capability to provide it in composite forms that can include text, visual, and audio packages. A reference question on the unique positions of Sirius, Mirzam, Wezen, and Adhara, the major stars of the Canis Major constellation, could be partially answered with a print resource. However, their positions at changing times, dates, and latitudes could only be answered with the interactive simulations of a sky chart provided online by www.outerbody.com/stargazer. In children's reference, recurring school projects on country or ethnic studies, for example, gain immeasurably when textual descriptions are enhanced by a rendering of the national anthem of the country, or by videos of the celebration of local festivals and cultural programs. A student presenting a project on Pueblo tribes in southwestern America was able to dress and present a truncated kachina dance of the Hopi tribe based on a streaming video found online.

Exclusivity

Given the ease in both entering and accessing information, there is an increasing number of publications, proceedings, transcripts, and data that are available only on the Internet. Conference proceedings, government documents, state job listings and application forms, news blogs, subject wikis, and even professional communications can be found exclusively on the Internet.

The most dramatic example of exclusivity appeared in 1991 when Paul Ginsparg, a physicist at the Los Alamos National Laboratory, launched an online archive of preprint research communications that would, in effect, circumvent print publications. The initiative, currently owned, operated and funded by Cornell University, has proven to be wildly successful. Acknowledged as a leader in "e-print" service, arXiv, as it is known currently, attracts monthly submissions numbering over 5,000, a big jump from the less than 500 submissions received in 1991–1992. Reference questions dealing with the cutting edge of physics must frequently be referred to the Web site at http://arxiv.org.

Interactive

Print information informs, but rarely "listens." Internet information has the capability to be interactive. Discussion groups, listservs, e-mail newsletters, wikis, live interviews, and ongoing comment pages are possible so that an information dialogue can be created. Interactivity in research is quite possibly one of the most dynamic areas of future development in reference librarianship. Even as major initiatives such as *Q&A NJ* in New Jersey, and *ASKaLibrarian* in Florida are maturing at a hectic pace, instant messaging (IM) reference is taking shape as a less costly and more personalized alternative.

According to a 2004 survey, 80 million Americans are using instant messaging on a regular basis; it is likely that IM, chat, and SMS will not remain unfamiliar technologies for long (Houghton and Schmidt, 2005: 26–30). Teens are particularly involved in IM techniques and are the "targeted group" for new

IM ventures such as the one begun in 2005 at the Marin County Free Library (Houghton, 2005: 192–193). The extent of IM reference can be seen in the 436 practicing libraries within the United States listed with hyperlinks in *Library Success: A Best Practices Wiki* accessible at www.libsuccess.org. The libraries of the University of Alberta, University of Calgary, University of Toronto, Carleton University and the Ottawa Public Library are among at least fifteen other libraries in Canada that offer IM reference as does the Heriot-Watt University Library and the University of Teesside Library in the United Kingdom.

Given the unmistakable allure of *Wikipedia*, wiki resources are maturing at an even faster rate. There are now credible moves toward establishing "reference wikis" that are less open than *Wikipedia*, and are therefore less vulnerable to the charge of being unreliable or inaccurate. The *Psychology Wiki* with over 28,000 articles, the *Thomas Jefferson Encyclopedia*, and the *Encyclopedia of Earth* created on wiki platforms, and the successful *Peer-to-Patent* wiki that is speeding the patent review process are examples of authoritative wikis (Bell, 2009: 20–24). In October 2010, the third *Peer-to-Patent* pilot was launched, based on the evident success of the first two pilots.

Another area where interactivity is playing a major role is in statistical information (Foudy, 2000: 49–53). Web sites are beginning to offer data in formats that permit users to transpose data directly onto spreadsheets or Excel and Access programs, to create graphs, or extract selective line data. The National Economics Accounts at the U.S. Department of Commerce, for example, provides "Interactive Access" for all of its tables. A reference question on changes in the market value of goods and services in the American economy before and after the 9/11 terrorist attacks could require multiple printed resources, which are relatively difficult to locate. With the "Interactive Access" tables, however, changes in current-dollar Gross Domestic Product can be tailored to fit any selected range of years with the frequency of data tweaked to present annual, quarterly, or monthly figures.

Mass Convenience

Unlike single-book sources, Internet information is accessible to multiple users at the same time. A user spending hours over the *Occupational Outlook* need not be disturbed if Internet access is available for the twenty high school students with "career assignments" who can do research and access the same resource online at www.bls.gov/oco.

Scope

Reportedly, three new pages are added to the Internet every second of the day. That is a lot of material. Then again, many print resources are published every day as well; so why is "scope" treated so holistically for the Internet? The reason lies in the different forms of print versus Internet resources. The clicking of the same mouse to switch almost instantaneously from one resource to another gives the admittedly misleading impression that the scope of the Internet is one vast composite whole. In reality, the criterion for scope should be applied to each individual site, much as is done for each individual book.

However, in terms of the appeal of Internet research, the perception of scope, voiced as "you can find everything," is powerful.

Weaknesses

Given the scope, accessibility, ease, currency, convenience, and value-added features of Internet use, it is curious that the Internet is taking so long to be treated as a full-fledged reference tool. The explanation for this time lag can reasonably be located in the following vulnerabilities peculiar to Internet research.

Lack of Regulated Quality Control

Both the attraction and the detraction of Internet research is that for any and every reason, anyone can write anything, from anywhere in the world, and leave it for any amount of time for anyone to read. With the insouciant littering of information and wisdom, knowledge and factoids, learning and vitriol flung haphazardly into Everyman's existence, it is no wonder that librarians, with their trained beliefs and classical training in classification and subclassification, have indulged in nervous speculation that the end of the information world was imminent (Crawford and Gorman, 1995; Anhang, 2002). Without any checks on authorship, reliability, accuracy, currency or validity, information can quite literally run amok. The fast developing Internet religion of the "pastafarians," followers of the Flying Spaghetti Monster, a parodist creation originally designed to mock the inclusion of intelligent design in Kansas school curricula, is a case in point. This illuminating parody can be accessed at www.venganza.org.

Evaluation Falls to the User

Given the absolute lack of quality control, the onus of evaluating sites falls squarely on the shoulders of the user. Evaluation, as librarians are aware, is a complex undertaking, requiring both the awareness and the skills to navigate between trustworthy and untrustworthy sites. Since users are conditioned to accept all printed material as valid information, the pitfalls of Internet-generated research become more acute. Public librarians faced with the directive to "print something from that Internet," and undergraduates laboring under the IKIA (I Know It Already) syndrome (Wilder, 2005) are daily examples of users unaware about the fallible nature of Internet information.

Lack of Overview

Thomas Mann, the venerable reference librarian at the Library of Congress, describes how scholarship can be affected in the way information is presented. Direct and physical access to subject-classified shelves can result in information that may not be possible through digital access dependent on the use of keywords because of the following:

1. Researchers invariably do not have all the exact keywords prior to starting the research, but do recognize the information when it is "immediately in front of them within a manageably segregated group of likely sources" (Mann, 2005: 45).

2. Even with the right keywords specified in advance, results cannot "build bridges *among* multiple sets" so that an overview of the research topic becomes difficult (Mann, 2005: 46).

Mann has a valid point and has voiced a widespread nostalgia for the serendipity of shelf browsing that is so intrinsic to print reference. However, in the place of visual browsing a new set of skills can establish keywords, link words, and search terms to circumvent the apparent lack of an overview. This is further outlined in the chapter.

Overwhelming Results

Oftentimes, the Internet is just not the right resource. Given the powerful belief that all information is available on the Internet, much time can be wasted in looking for information that can be found far more efficiently through other formats. In addition to the waste of time engendered by choosing the wrong resource, time can be wasted in sifting reliable from unreliable material, or getting caught in the hop-skip-and-jump allure of hyperlinks. "Relevance ranking" or the ability of search engines to sift through the frequency, uniqueness, and positioning of search keywords and pull those to the top of the returns list, is not always the searcher's best friend. For example, an overly creative title that does not use words directly relevant to the subject matter may receive a lower "weight" and get buried further down the results list. If the file size is small, such as in a brief book review, but uses the search keyword the same number of times as a larger document (such as a literary analysis of the book), it is the smaller book review file that accrues a higher "density" rating. As a result it is the brief review that gets pushed to the top of the returns list relative to the analysis, for which the user may have been searching.

No Guarantee of Free Full Text

Full-text articles from journals are also not always free to the Internet user. Research-quality articles have traditionally clustered under expensive subscription databases. This would not ordinarily be considered a "weakness." After all, full-text articles in print journals are also available only through purchase. However, Internet research has accrued the impression of being free. As Joe Thompson of the Baltimore County Public Library laments, "Good information still costs money, and people forget that" (Selingo, 2004: G5). The cost of information, accepted as normal for print, is paid unwillingly for Internet sources, fueled no doubt by the lurking suspicion that the information might indeed be free "somewhere" on the Internet. Increasingly, however, with projects such as Google Scholar and its Print Library Project, the HathiTrust digital repository, which already has the "digital equivalent of 25 miles of books on library shelves"(Hadro, 2008: 21), as well as the Open Content Alliance scheduled to run Yahoo's library digitization venture, the extent of open-access journals will probably increase.

Spotty Coverage of Historical Material

The presence of historical material on the Internet is relatively limited. Even databases usually do not go far back into archival material so that journal articles prior to the 1980s are hard to find via the Internet. If included, historical coverage tends to be spotty, almost as if it is included only if and when time and personal interest permit such inclusions. With digital initiatives like *American Memory*, Yale University's *Avalon Project*, *Gallica* from the National Library of France, and the University of Michigan's *Making of America*, the information drought on historical material may be lessening.

Volatility

With content being added, modified, deleted, or forgotten, there is a constant level of volatility built into the medium. What was vetted yesterday as being a "good" site will have to be vetted again today before it is used, because it might have changed. The *Internet Yellow Pages*, which become partially obsolete within the first year of publication, are prime exhibits of this volatility. Documenting the Web site to the last letter or number of the URL (Uniform Resource Locator) address is one way of coping with the mercurial quality of Internet-generated answers. While it does not retrieve a lost site, it both testifies and provides clues to the earlier structure of a site. The Internet Archive at www.archive.org can also be consulted with its storehouse of 150 billion pages of dead Web sites and extinct pages.

Five Steps to Successful Internet Reference

The Internet is *surfed*. It should be *searched*. Rather than crest every passing "information wave," the following five steps should be followed.

Step 1: Ask Yourself, Is the Internet the Right Medium?

"Type first and think later" has been the instinctive reaction to using the Internet. The considered reaction should be this:

- Is it the best resource to use?
- Is it the only resource to use?

Clarity in the advantages and disadvantages of Internet use is a necessary first step. Being open to a combination of formats can also pay dividends. For example, on the morning of August 29, 2005, when Hurricane Katrina struck the Gulf Coast region of the United States, the Web site for the American Red Cross was jammed. Loading the page took an average of twenty-five to fifty-five minutes, if it opened at all. By contrast, referring users to the information for Disaster Relief at the American Red Cross headquarters, found in print resources such as the *Washington Information Directory*, took a minute. Picking up the telephone or consulting a colleague can also prove to be more efficient in certain situations. A focus group study by Milner Library at Illinois State University found that their chat reference service was proving to be a disappointment primarily because the time it took for a student to complete a chat query was far greater than a one-on-one interaction with a reference librarian in person or over the telephone (Naylor et al., 2008: 342). The first step, then, involves a clear choice of using the Internet in tandem, or in preference, to print or other information mediums.

Step 2: Select the Right Internet Tool

The second step is using the most efficient Internet search tool—a search engine, a metasearch engine, or a subject directory.

Search Engines

If the question requires a broad overview, single keywords or phrases typed into a search box can provide a flood of hits. This option requires eyeballing a list of random resources that may or may not be productive, but at minimum, helps formulate the research query. General search engine technology, yet in its relative toddlerhood, is growing in leaps and bounds so that various tools are now available to fine-tune the keyword search. Some of the more popular search engines are Yahoo! Search, Google, MSN Search, Ask (formerly known as Ask Jeeves), Gigablast, AOL, EarthLink, Exalead, and MyWay. A brief overview of some of the major general engines available to users can be seen in Table 13-1.

For seven-to-twelve-year-old users, child-friendly search engines are available. They typically provide a mix of information and ready entertainment. The pages are bright and loaded with contrasting colors and graphics. The sites are usually geared to providing both directories and search engine capabilities. The highly popular Ask Kids, available at www.askkids.com, uses natural language technology so the importance of keywords is lessened. It only accepts links that are "G-rated" and written specifically for children. There is no option for chat. Yahooligans!, on the other hand, available at http://kids.yahoo.com, provides safe surfing guidelines and places the onus of responsibility on parents and the child.

New ways to display results are also appearing so that the "Grokker" system, available at www.grokker.com, can organize more than 150 results into a single pictorial that can be previewed by the user to gauge what might be the most relevant groups of results. The domain, however, has been on sale since the start of 2011. Factbites at www.factbites.com, sells itself as a perfectly matched cross between a search engine and an encyclopedia. It provides natural language sentences for every site listed in the search results so that there is more information on the search page.

Metasearch Engines

Metasearch engines produce far more results, given that they collate sites from multiple search engines. Searches can be overwhelming and search statements can be read differently so that metasearches are best used when a very broad overview of a subject is required. Some of the best-known metasearch engines are Ixquick, ez2find, QueryServer, and Dogpile. A brief overview of Dogpile and Ixquick is provided in Table 13-2.

Subject Directories

Because directories employ subject headings based on standardized vocabulary, organized by human rather than robotic logic, specific questions can

Table 13-1. Sample General Search Engines

	GOOGLE	YAHOO!	ASK.COM
Debut Year	1998	1994	1996
Site	www.google.com	www.yahoo.com	www.ask.com
Name Etymology	From "googol," a number represented by 100 zeros following the numeral 1	Acronym for: "Yet Another Hierarchical Officious Oracle"	Originally "Ask Jeeves"; rebranded to self-explanatory "Ask.com"
Indexed Pages	Over 8 billion	Over 4 billion	Over 2 billion
Traffic	72.07% of U.S. searches in December 2008	17.79% of U.S. searches in December 2008	3.15% of U.S. searches in December 2008
Boolean	Capitalized OR; Default AND	Capitalized AND, OR, AND NOT, NOT	Capitalized OR; Default AND
Unique Features	1. At least forty-four special features such as local business listings in the US, UK and Canada. 2. Special tools such as blogging and services such as a system for organizing medical records online. 3. Sites "cached" so that if page is unavailable, original page can be displayed.	1. Both a general search engine and a directory that can be used in tandem. 2. Signature exclamation mark directs user to specific service so that "travel!", for example, goes to Yahoo! Travel. 3. Communication services such as chat and commerce services such as investing and personal finance.	1. Can refine search results through word filters and stated suggestions. 2. Results show context of search terms. 3. Editorial comments on Web links are often provided.
Ranking Algorithm	Page Rank™—general popularity usage calculated from over 100 factors.	Relevancy—through keyword density.	Subject Specific Popularity—number of same subject pages that reference a site. Since Teoma's rebrand to Ask.com, the algorithm is called ExpertRank.

Table 13-2. Sample Metasearch Engines

	DOGPILE	IXQUICK/STARTPAGE
Debut Year	1996	1998
Site	www.dogpile.com	www.ixquick.com
Name Etymology	Term used to describe Rugby players piling on top of one another to celebrate	The "i" for intelligence, the "x" for "times," and the "quick" for speed. In 2009, "Startpage" deemed to be easier to remember than "ixquick."
Metasearches	Google, Yahoo!, Bing, Ask, and content from Kosmix and Fandango	Ask, Blekko, EntireWeb, Gigablast, Open Directory, Statesman, Wikipedia, Yahoo!, Yebol, Yoozila
Unique Features	1. Default search settings can be customized to include filtering. 2. Searches can be conducted over ten languages. 3. The fifteen-most recent searches can be displayed at right of page. 4. New search widget featuring Arfie, the Dogpile mascot, who also functions as a Search Spy displaying "what the rest of the world is searching." 5. Radio buttons for audio, video, images, news and directories	1. Awarded the hard-to-get European Privacy Seal for its privacy-driven searches of the Internet. No recording of IP addresses or tracking cookies and supports HTTPS and proxy service. 2. Searches can be conducted in 18 languages. 3. Stars awarded for each result based on top search-engine ratings. 4. Provides total of 50–70 results, "more than enough to answer most questions." 5. Option to set family-friendly setting and filter adult-content sites.

benefit from a directory. Conversely, if users are unclear about search terms within a subject area, the directory supplies terms, much as a thesaurus supplies synonyms. These Web sites are relatively vetted and therefore produce a more limited, yet pertinent set of results. The directory is also useful in mining the "invisible Web," those sites such as specialized searchable databases that are typically not locatable in a general search engine (Sherman and Price, 2001). An overview of three subject directories is given in Table 13-3.

If the past is a true predictor of the future, the above search engines, metasearch engines, and directories will morph into sleeker technology and different ranking and selecting systems. Search engine names such as Lycos, Hotbot, and Excite are no longer what they were a few short years ago. Sudden death or transpositions of engine technology and ownership is the order of the day, so that the tables provide a brief, time-bound snapshot of ways to synopsize a tool as and when it appears on the search horizon.

Table 13-3. Sample Subject Directories

	INFOMINE	**ipl2 (2008)**	**INTUTE (2006)**
Debut Year	1994	1993	1998
Site	http://infomine.ucr.edu/	www.ipl.org	www.intute.ac.uk
Links	Over 100,000 links, of which 26,000 are by librarians and the rest by robots/crawlers	Over 20,000 Web sites	Over 100,000 linked resources, confirmed only until July 2011
Traffic	Current figures not known—over 20,000 accesses in 3/1996	An average of 10 million hits a month in 2006	3,547,630 searches performed between 8/02–7/03
Boolean	NEAR, NOT, AND, OR are executed in that order.	Default AND. NOT and OR can be used.	Default AND. OR and minus sign for NOT is used.
Unique Features	1. University-level research with sites vetted by librarians from the University of California, Wake Forest University, California State University, and others. 2. Rich resource for the "invisible Web" of databases, electronic journals and books, and bulletin boards. 3. Nine major subject headings. 4. Concise descriptions for each record.	1. Free of commercials. 2. Sites vetted by permanent staff and 100 contributors from libraries in California and Washington. 3. Free weekly newspaper for resource updates. 4. Fourteen primary subject headings and many sub-headings.	1. A collaboration of seven universities and multiple education and research organizations in the UK aimed at higher-level research. 2. Four "hubs" that focus on a subject specialty. Within a hub are sub-specialties. 3. Highly useful inter-active Web tutorials. 4. A set of online case studies provided for each hub. 5. Live RSS feed for "Behind the Headlines" news service.

Step 3: Construct the Right Search Terms

The third step, possibly the most critical in establishing the difference between a wild surfing session and a professional search strategy, is in constructing the most effective search terms. To succumb to the siren call of typing in terms as they pop like flashbulbs in one's head is to be vulnerable to a lengthy and possibly frustrating search.

Make a List

Instead, the trained response should be to pick up a pencil and draw up a list. Starting with a blanket strategy, all words and phrases associated with the question should be jotted down in two categories that differentiate between key representative terms and related terms. Once the brainstorming of words is over, a hierarchy needs to be imposed, however tentative the ranking. Stratification would help to both structure preresearch thinking and save an immense amount of time and energy as the research proceeds. Dubious leads can be tweaked and search terms revised based on this list. Repetition can be avoided and time saved. The Zen insight of finding equal importance in absence as in presence is also instructive in that dead-end terms can throw critical light on the relative relevance of different aspects of a research topic. For example:

Query: *I need to research separatist movements in Sri Lanka.*

Representative search terms: *Sri Lanka, Sri Lanka and politics, Sri Lanka and separatists, Sri Lanka and ethnic conflict*

Related terms: *Ceylon Tamils, Tamils and Sinhalese, LTTE, Tamil Tigers, TULF, PLOTE, EPRLF, Thimpu Talks, Prabhakaran/Pirabhakaran, Sri Lanka and India, eelam, Jayewardene, Kumaratunga*

Hierarchy:
1. *Sri Lanka politics*
2. *Sri Lanka and ethnic conflict*
3. *Liberation Tigers of Tamil Eelam*

Free online tutorials on developing list skills can be found at www.vts.intute.ac .uk/, a national initiative in the United Kingdom that presents wonderfully detailed tutorials designed for subject areas ranging widely from engineering to gardening.

Alternate Spellings

In addition to setting up a hierarchy of search terms, an awareness of the syntax, spelling, and alternate spelling of terms can both ease and enhance a search. For example, an Internet search on the history of Myanmar, the Democratic Republic of Congo, or Surinam may be incomplete without using the recently discarded names of Burma, Zaire, and Dutch Guiana. While existing awareness of alternatives is not necessary, it is necessary to be aware of the possibility of alternatives so that clues offered in one search string can be hoarded for another search.

Context

Vague or generic keywords and search terms can result in a frustrating, never-ending, or dead-end search. If a word is generic, the trick to relieve it of its anonymity is to use combination terms that establish the context of the word. For example, a user wanting biographical information on the-singer-formerly-known-as-Prince cannot type a search term as generic as "prince." The results would no doubt cover the singer, but the information would be embedded within millions of sites on the scions of Great Britain, Monaco, the Netherlands, and various African countries, the history of Russia and the Indian subcontinent, bestsellers from today's Rowling and yesterday's Machiavelli, counties in Maryland and Virginia, and fond owners' descriptions of dogs answering to that name. Combining the term "prince" with "singer," or even searching the notorious phrase "formerly known as prince" provides the necessary limiters to bracket the search.

Step 4: Use the Right Search Operators

Having established the best possible hierarchy of productive search terms, consideration of the most effective search operators is the logical corollary. In theory, Boolean operators, truncations, wild cards, quotation marks or parentheses, and proximity matrices are helpful tools that can streamline the search process or extend it in the right direction. The inclusion of the Boolean "and" between two terms narrows an overlarge search result. If the results are too limited, the use of the Boolean "or" can expand it. For example, a search for <conservatives and republicans> would produce a narrower result than <conservatives or republicans>. Parentheses or quotation marks allow the searcher to nest Boolean operators and refine the search considerably. For example, search strings like <(Clinton and (Hillary or Chelsea)) not Bill> would lighten the search considerably by removing all references to the past president.

In practice, however, search operators vary from site to site so that Gigablast, for example, accepts Boolean operators AND, OR, NOT, parentheses, and plus and minus signs, while at AltaVista the Boolean only works in the Advanced Search page. The best way to take control over idiosyncratic operators is to check the "Help," "About," or "Tip" icons included on each Web site, directory, or search engine. A comparative chart on the various operators allowed and disallowed by major search engines is provided in effective detail by Greg Notess at http://searchengineshowdown.com/features/; and by Joe Barker at http://infopeople.org/search/chart.html. With most searchers favoring one engine over another, it is expedient to be wholly familiar with the effective and timesaving tips provided by each engine. Even trivial shortcuts, such as hitting the "Return" key rather than clicking on the "Search" button as suggested by Google, can shave away search time.

Step 5: Evaluate the Search Results

The moment of truth is at hand. Carefully selected search terms are rewarded with a clutch of sites that can number anywhere from a few pages to thousands. How best to pick the best sites and evaluate them in more detail?

Given the complete absolution from traditional vetting agencies such as personal name accountability, publisher standards, editorial expertise, or professional evaluation, all Internet information must be treated as "guilty unless proven authoritative." This sounds harsher than it is. It merely reminds the Internet user to establish the validity of each informational site using some of the same criteria used for print evaluation, along with recognition of the working mechanics of the Internet medium. The need for this is greater when providing Internet reference for minors. A comprehensive checklist of Web site evaluation for kids can be found at www.ala.org/ala/alsc/greatwebsites/greatwebsites forkids/greatwebsites.htm.

Authority

Placing authorship is a traditional way of establishing the authority of any piece of information. It is no different in the Internet medium, though the ways of gauging the author's reputation may require keener detection.

- Who is the author? Is the work signed, and if so, is the name familiar or well regarded in the field?
- If the name is unfamiliar, is there more detailed contact information about the author? Open accountability can usually be regarded as a sign, though not a guarantee, of reliability.
- Is there any professional review or affiliation of the author provided on the site? Affiliations can provide clues to author validity.
- Is the link that led to this site one that can be trusted? Most trustworthy sites feel responsible about the hyperlinks they allow and thereby act as a vetting agent. Links from libraries are a classic example.
- What appears to be the motive of the author? Is there any indication that the author might be biased? If so, is the bias a necessary part of the research angle or liable to skew the research?
- Does the author exhibit a grasp of the subject, provide an overview of the field, or allude to existing theories in the field? While known authors are reviewed and slotted into comfortable perception fields, unknown Web authors must prove their expertise in the field and these exhibits provide some indicators of the level of expertise.

Reliability

Reputable print resources gain stature because of their credentials, authority, and transparent documentation of publishing pedigree. Given that the Web is a vast public forum for both individual and institutional output, Internet resources need to be held up to equally strict, and infinitely more creative, indices of reliability.

- Does a known organization or institution sponsor the site?
- If unknown, what does the "About Us" icon say about the organization? This may be termed with alternative phrases such as "Background" or "Our Philosophy." Truncate the URL until it reaches the domain name succeeded by a front slash, as this is the main home page of the site and may be the only page containing accountability information.
- Are clear contact details provided? Once again, accountability can vouch for some degree of reliability. If the only contact information is e-mail, it

should act as a red flag. As a last resort in such cases, e-mailing for more information is advisable.

- Is the URL indicative? For example, when researching for information on Winston Churchill, the reliability of a URL such as www.chu.cam.ac.uk/archives/collections/churchill_papers can be considered very high, even without actually delving into the site. Why is that? Because of URL clues such as "uk," which stands for the United Kingdom, home to Churchill; the "ac," which stands for academia much as "edu" does in the United States; and "cam," which stands for the prestigious University of Cambridge. A URL with a tilde (~) could be a highly useful source of information, but needs a more critical eye as it is the personal site of an individual rather than a known institution.
- The URL is also valuable in establishing the context of the resource. An account of the relevance of insurance ratings by various companies as presented on the Weiss Web site will quite naturally present a point of view that is favorable to the Weiss ratings system. This is perfectly valid information but must be recognized as information that has a vested interest.
- Another prominent aspect of reliability is accuracy. This is gauged much as it is in print. Is there a bibliography or hyperlinks to other resources with which the searcher is familiar? Does the link seem like a good choice? Is the literature overview or the factual information used correct in the areas with which the user is familiar? If the background research is solid, it is an indication that the rest of the information may be reliable.
- Are quotations, referrals, graphics, or statistical data well documented and fully cited? If statistical data are presented, are the data solid or does the data resort to dubious phrases such as "a majority of " or "a large percentage" or "a significant amount" without any real numbers?
- Are there typos, spelling mistakes, or egregious grammar errors evident throughout the document?

Finally, the wheel need not be endlessly reinvented. Reliable Web sites vetted by experts have already been listed in *INFOMINE*, which is a virtual library of Internet sources relevant for university-level researchers; the *ipl2* that deems "serving the public by finding, evaluating, selecting, organizing, describing, and creating high quality information resources" (as part of its 2008 Vision Statement); or the United Kingdom's *Intute* that has as its byline "best of the Web."

Currency

Relative to print resources, Internet reference is most valued for providing the kind of currency that print formats cannot possibly supply. Minute-by-minute game plays, hourly stock updates, daily foreign news updates, weekly conference proceedings, monthly cost-of-living estimates—the scope of instant communication of information as provided by the Internet is breathtaking. The relevance of checking for currency in areas where it is required can therefore pose a very important part of evaluation. Follow these steps to check for currency.

- Scroll down to the bottom of the page where a "last updated" message may be provided.
- If unavailable, check the site directory to see the "last modified" date.
- Check for copyright dates.
- Check for statements that verify that the data will be updated on a recurring basis according to a set schedule.
- If no obvious statements of currency are available, check for more subtle signs such as whether a current event or statistic you are sure about has been included.
- Check for giveaway statements that mention the date such as "According to a 2006 study..." or "Next week, the 111th Congress will open...."
- Check for multiple dead links, a sure sign that the site has been abandoned for some time.

In general, if information found on the Internet appears suspicious or dubious, it probably is. Erring on the side of caution is recommended. However, the power of Internet research is irresistible and need not be resisted. Librarians must learn to evaluate resources speedily and effectively so that snap judgments on the millions of available sites become second nature. With this skill, the nature of the medium is accepted, absorbed, and engaged. In addition, establishing a conscientious system of bookmarking favorite Web sites and creating a "Web-based reference desk" (Sauers, 2001) is an effective way of adding on source-specific searches that are more akin to print research.

Practicing with the excellent *Virtual Training Suite* of free, interactive tutorials provided by the United Kingdom's *Resource Discovery Network* is a good way to develop evaluation skills. Available at www.vts.intute.ac.uk, the site has sixty-six tutorials in various subject areas. Developing a content evaluation tool such as the one given in Figure 13-1 is another way to practice appraising a site with consistency. The chart is a representative example. Aspects of the criteria listed above are included in the chart. For example, much of the "Authority" factors are covered under "Information Providers" in the chart; whereas "Reliability" is approximated by the "Information Quality" category. However, developing your own ratings using all of the evaluation criteria could be immensely helpful.

Recommendations for Further Reading

Bell, David A. 2005. "The Bookless Future." *The New Republic* (May 2–9): 27–33. The ever-elegant Bell writes a supremely cogent treatise on the "democratizing effects" of Internet research, as well as its associated risks and ways of dealing with it. Ideas, arguments, and language come together seamlessly to provide a thought provoking and pleasurable read.

Bell, Suzanne. 2009. *Librarian's Guide to Online Searching*. 2nd ed. Santa Barbara, CA: Libraries Unlimited. Written as a textbook, the book is a thorough treatise on how to go about mastering the art of online retrieval. The inherent structure of databases is described as are the arsenal of search tools using Boolean logic, proximity, truncation, et al., in a clear and practical way.

Figure 13-1. WWW Cyberguide Ratings for Content Evaluation

Site Title: _____ Subject: _____

URL: _____ Audience: _____

Purpose for exploring this site:

_____

Notes on possible uses of this site and URLs for useful linked sites:

_____

_____

_____

To determine the worth of the Web site you are considering, evaluate its content according to the criteria described below.

Circle "Y" for "Yes", "N" for "No", "NA" for "Not Applicable"

1. First look

A. User is able to quickly determine the basic content of the site.	Y	N	NA
B. User is able to determine the intended audience of the site.	Y	N	NA

2. Information Providers

A. The author(s) of the material on the site is clearly identified.	Y	N	NA
B. Information about the author(s) is available.	Y	N	NA
C. According to the info given, author(s) appears qualified to present information on this topic.	Y	N	NA
D. The sponsor of the site is clearly identified	Y	N	NA
E. A contact person or address is available so the user can ask questions or verify information.	Y	N	NA

2. Information Providers

A. The author(s) of the material on the site is clearly identified.	Y	N	NA
B. Information about the author(s) is available.	Y	N	NA
C. According to the info given, author(s) appears qualified to present information on this topic.	Y	N	NA
D. The sponsor of the site is clearly identified	Y	N	NA
E. A contact person or address is available so the user can ask questions or verify information.	Y	N	NA

3. Information Currency

A. Latest revision date is provided. Date last revised _____	Y	N	NA
B. Latest revision date is appropriate to material.	Y	N	NA
C. Content is updated frequently.	Y	N	NA
D. Links to other sites are current and working properly.	Y	N	NA

(Cont'd.)

Figure 13-1. WWW Cyberguide Ratings for Content Evaluation *(Continued)*

4. Information Quality

	Y	N	NA
A. The purpose of this site is clear: business/commercial-entertainment-informational—news—personal page-persuasion.	Y	N	NA
B. The content achieves this intended purpose effectively	Y	N	NA
C. The content appears to be complete (no "under construction" signs, for example).	Y	N	NA
D. The content of this site is well organized.	Y	N	NA
E. The information in this site is easy to understand.	Y	N	NA
F. This site offers sufficient information related to my needs/purposes.	Y	N	NA
G. The content is free of bias, or the bias can be easily detected.	Y	N	NA
H. This site provides interactivity that increases its value.	Y	N	NA
I. The information appears to be accurate based on user's previous knowledge of subject.	Y	N	NA
J. The information is consistent with similar information in other sources	Y	N	NA
K. Grammar and spelling are correct.	Y	N	NA

5. Further Information

	Y	N	NA
A. There are links to other sites that are related to my needs/purposes.	Y	N	NA
B. The content of linked sites is worthwhile and appropriate to my needs/purposes.	Y	N	NA

Totals

Based on the total of "yes" and "no" answers and your overall observations, rate the content of this site as:

_____ Very useful for my information needs   _____ Worth bookmarking for future reference

_____ Not worth coming back to

Source: Karen McLachlan, 2002. Used by permission.

Boyd, Rhonda S. 2005. "Assessing the True Nature of Information Transactions at a Suburban Library." *Public Libraries* (July/August): 234–240. While the article deals with far broader issues than just the assessment of transactions as suggested by the title, it offers a strong quantitative argument on the impact of Internet research on reference services and the reference staffing model best suited to accommodate this impact.

Bradley, Phil. 2004. *The Advanced Internet Searcher's Handbook.* 3rd ed. London: Facet Publishing. The strength of this title, in a long list of titles that hope to enhance the process of Web research, is its inclusion of real-life examples for all the techniques provided. Different types of search engines are ana-lyzed by structure to help choose according to individual engine strengths. Tips for searching for multimedia information, the "hidden" Web, blogs, and information gateways are also provided along with fifty tips for better searching such as suggestions for truncating an unwieldy URL. The author also keeps up a Web site with extensive search engine information avail-able at www.philb.com/whichengine.htm.

Hacker, Diana. 2006. *Research and Documentation in the Electronic Age.* 4th ed. Boston, MA: Bedford/St. Martins. The author, recently deceased, was able to complete a final update to this classic guide to finding, understanding, and evaluating online resources. Distinguishing between "narrow," "chal-lenging," and "grounded" research questions, Hacker introduces the text with suggestions for mapping out an appropriate search strategy, and concludes with an extensive annotated bibliography of specialized library and Web resources.

Henninger, Maureen. 2007. *The Hidden Web: Finding Quality Information on the Net.* 2nd ed. Sydney: University of New South Wales Press. This is a more specialized guide to Internet research in that it aims to uncover "hidden" information tucked into the folds of an HTML document, or one deeply embedded into a Web site, or a full-text document that does not require subscription to a database.

Janes, Joseph. 2003. *Introduction to Reference Work in the Digital Age.* New York: Neal-Schuman. This book is a formal study of emerging reference strate-gies, couched in a deceptively informal tone. It focuses on the importance of identifying user needs and utilizing new, hybrid formats and technology to supply those reference needs.

Radford, Marie L., Susan B. Barnes, and Linda R. Barr. 2005. *Web Research: Selecting, Evaluating, and Citing.* 2nd ed. Boston, MA: Allyn and Bacon. The authors provide a comprehensive and valuable overview of initiating research on the Web, mining for the best resources, and concluding Web searches with the most appropriate citations. The sensitive issue of Web copyright is also addressed.

The Scout Report. Available: http://scout.wisc.edu. Published by the reputable Internet Scout Project, the weekly report provides an update of new and evolving Internet resources that can be accessed on the Web or via direct e-mail. Each resource is annotated. The *Report* is a handy way to keep abreast of new and noteworthy Web sites.

Sherman, Chris. 2005. *Google Power: Unleash the Full Potential of Google.* Emeryville, CA: McGraw-Hill/Osborne Media. Recognizing that "Googling" is fast evolving into a regular verb, the author provides a hands-on study of different search techniques that can enhance the results from this search engine. Some of the lesser-known charms of Google, such as retrieving information from dead links and setting up automated search tool mechanisms, are also outlined.

Tancer, Bill. 2008. *Click: What Millions of People Are Doing Online and Why It Mat-ters.* New York: Hyperion. "We are what we click" is the interesting basis of this general book on the nature of Internet searching. While ideas range from the peculiarities of the average searcher to pointers for online marketers, the parts that analyze how users navigate the Web and search for information can be useful for students of Internet reference.

Bibliography of Works Cited in This Chapter

American Library Association. *ALA Fact Sheet Number 26: Internet Use in Libraries*. Available: www.ala.org.

American Memory. Available: http://memory.loc.gov/.

Anhang, Abe. 2002. "Be It Resolved That Reference Librarians Are Toast." *American Libraries* 33, no. 3 (March): 50–51.

Avalon Project. Available: www.yale.edu/lawweb/avalon/avalon.htm.

Bell, Suzanne. 2009. "Wikis for Reference, Enthusiasts, and Government Information." *Online* 33, no. 1 (Jan–Feb): 20–24.

Breakstone, Elizabeth. 2005. "Libraries." *Chronicle of Higher Education*, Supplement, 52, no. 6 (September 30): B6.

Carr, Nicholas. 2008. "Is Google Making Us Stupid? What the Internet Is Doing to Our Brains." *The Atlantic* 302, no. 1 (July–August): 56–62.

Cook, David. 2008. "Monitor Shifts from Print to Web-based Strategy." *The Christian Science Monitor* (October 28). Available: www.csmonitor.com/2008/1029/p25s01-usgn.html.

Crawford, Walt, and Michael Gorman. 1995. *Future Libraries: Dreams, Madness, and Reality*. Chicago: American Library Association.

Encyclopedia of Earth. Available: www.eoearth.org.

Foudy, Geraldine. 2000. "Wide, Wide World of Statistics: International Statistics on the Internet." *EContent* 23, no. 3 (June–July): 49–53.

Frauenfelder, Mark. 2007. *Rule the Web: How to Do Anything and Everything on the Internet—Better, Faster, Easier*. New York: St. Martin's Griffin.

Gallica. Available: http://gallica.bnf.fr/.

Greenspan, Robyn. 2004. "OPA: Online Most Favored of All Media." (September 21). Available: www.clickz.com.

Hadro, Josh. 2008. "HathiTrust: 80 Terabytes and Growing." *Library Journal* (November 1): 21.

Helft, Miguel. 2008. "Google Uses Web Searches to Track Flu's Spread." *The New York Times* (November 12): A1.

Hock, Randolph. 2007. *The Extreme Searcher's Internet Handbook: A Guide for the Serious Searcher*. 2nd ed. Medford, NJ: CyberAge Books.

Houghton, Sarah. 2005. "Instant Messaging: Quick and Dirty Reference for Teens and Others." *Public Libraries* 44, no. 4 (July–August): 192–193.

Houghton, Sarah, and Aaron Schmidt. 2005. "Web-Based Chat vs. Instant Messaging: Who Wins?" *Online* 29, no. 4 (July–August): 26–30.

Infomine. Available: http://infomine.ucr.edu/about/index.shtml.

Internet Public Library. Now known as *ipl2*. Available: www.ipl.org.

Internet Systems Consortium. ISC Internet Domain Survey Background. Available: www.isc.org.

Intute. Available: www.intute.ac.uk/.

Making of America. Available: http://moa.umdl.umich.edu/.

Mann, Thomas. 2005. "Google Print vs. Onsite Collections." *American Libraries* (August): 45–46.

Miller, William, and Rita Pellen. 2006. *Evolving Internet Reference Resources.* Binghamton, NY: The Haworth Press, Inc.

Naylor, Sharon, Bruce Stoffel, and Sharon Van Der Laan. 2008. "Why Isn't Our Chat Reference Used More? Finding of Focus Group Discussions with Undergraduate Students." *Reference & User Services Quarterly* 47, no. 4 (Summer): 342–355.

Oder, Norman. 2008. "Too Late or Just Right?" and "Reference Extract Web Project Debuts." *Library Journal* no. 19 and 20 (November 15 and December 15).

Peer-to-Patent. Available: www.peertopatent.org.

The Psychology Wiki. Available: http://psychology.wikia.com/wiki/main_page.

Ross, Catherine Sheldrick, and Kirsti Nilsen. 2000. "Has the Internet Changed Anything in Reference? The Library Visit Study, Phase 2." *Reference & User Services Quarterly* (Winter): 147–155.

Sauers, Michael P. 2001. *Using the Internet as a Reference Tool.* New York: Neal-Schuman.

Search Engine Statistics. Available: www.hitwise.com.

Selingo, Jeffrey. 2004. "When a Search Engine Isn't Enough, Call a Librarian." *New York Times* (February 5): G5.

Sherman, Chris, and Gary Price, 2001. *The Invisible Web: Uncovering Information Sources Search Engines Can't See.* Medford, NJ: Cyber Age Books.

The Thomas Jefferson Encyclopedia. Available: http://wiki.monticello.org.

Veldof, Jerilyn. 2008. "From Desk to Web: Creating Safety Nets in the Online Library." In *The Desk and Beyond: Next Generation Reference Services,* edited by Sarah K. Steiner and M. Leslie Madden (pp. 120–134). Chicago, IL: ACRL.

Wilder, Larry. 2005. "Changes in Reference Service in Academic Libraries." *Illinois Library Association Reporter* 23(1): 9.

14

Reader's Advisory Work

Mary K. Chelton

Reader's Advisory and Reference: A Marriage of Convenience

Introduction

Reader's Advisory (RA) services encompass more in practice and concept than is usually included in the conventional scope of reference/information services. The latter is often defined as a method of information retrieval by a person needing utilitarian information from an information system of some kind, with or without the help of an intermediary.

Consequently, reference as such tends to focus on individual service, especially on determining the specification of the user's question, the user's ability to locate information independently, and the training necessary for the development of his or her information literacy skills. RA services, on the other hand, reach out to a broader audience, including casual browsers and groups, using displays, lists, formal presentations, and discussions. Further, RA is as much concerned with the potential for enjoyment as it is with the solving of problems based on a user's situation, information gap, or needs.

Organizationally, RA service can be situated in other library departments, such as adult, children's, or young adult services. School libraries, especially at the elementary level, often emphasize RA service to enhance literacy development through read-alouds and author studies. Regardless of this distinction, however, the fact remains that in most libraries RA is delivered face to face as a part of reference, making it a crucial element of this volume. The inclusion of RA within reference flies in the face of the false dichotomy that exists, both within the profession and the larger culture, between "information" and "entertainment." "Information" supposedly encompasses useful knowledge, whereas "entertainment" is purely frivolous. Fiction is generally relegated to the second category and skills in retrieving or suggesting fiction to readers as a result, have been marginalized to the point that they can literally be forgotten in discussions of core services (Wiegand, 2000). This attitude is bad enough when adults are the clientele, and drove many of them to bookstores prior to interactive reader Web sites on the Internet, but it is particularly problematic for youth services, where language and literacy development are emphasized and prized. Under such circumstances, the degradation of any form of engagement with users as readers is to be avoided at all costs.

In addition, many youth reference queries are at least partially RA. For example, students required by a teacher to read a historical novel set in a certain period in U.S. history, or a book about an animal, or in some instances, just to read a book in a particular genre, might need to take advantage of the reference department.

Information-Seeking Utility of RA

Catherine Ross (1999a) has explored specific information readers get from fiction in "Finding Without Seeking: The Information Encounter in the Context of Reading for Pleasure," in which she lists the non-goal-oriented information (i.e., problem-solving information) encountered by readers in their interactions with texts. She also directly challenges the prevalent cognitive model of information seeking in the profession and reiterates the importance of an affective dimension in finding information:

> Constructing the searcher/reader as a rational, goal-directed individual who is engaged primarily in problem-solving downplays the role played by feeling. The reported research with pleasure-readers suggests that the affective dimension is involved throughout the process, from choosing a book according to mood to valuing a book for its emotional support in providing confirmation, reassurance, courage or self-acceptance. What readers said about risk-taking—that the choice of familiar and unchallenging vs. novel and challenging materials depends on the level of stress in the rest of their life—may turn out to be generalizable to goal directed information seeking situations as well. (Ross, 1999a: 796)

Ross's research with readers, like Kuhlthau's on the information search process (Kuhlthau, 2004; Kuhlthau et al., 2008), makes the point that information seeking has both cognitive and affective dimensions, and that the affective dimension is particularly important for pleasure readers who do find information in their reading.

Jessica Moyer (2004), following Ross's lead, examines the educational outcomes of reading fiction, hypothesizing that reading a book can have both educational and recreational outcomes. Based on a factor analysis of her interview data, she finds such outcomes in four categories: (1) people and relationships; (2) other countries, cultures, and time periods; (3) enriching one's life; and (4) gaining access to different perspectives.

Although such research is sparser than might otherwise be desired, the fact that information science actually has a term for it—"incidental information"

(Williamson 1998)—suggests that pleasure readers are relegated too easily to the "entertainment" and opposite side of the false dichotomy between "information" and "entertainment." In RA services, librarians must understand that both information and entertainment are involved in reading when they help readers locate books. The arrival of the computer does not mean that all information and learning is now electronic, nor that readers avoid electronic resources that support their reading.

Common RA Questions

Nearly every practicing librarian has, at some point in his or her career, received any one of three variants on a common question. Some users are content to simply ask, "Can you recommend a good book to read?" Others, aiming for the personal, go further, querying, "What have you read lately that's good?" A few more tend toward the specific with requests such as "I just read Jodi Picoult's book, *My Sister's Keeper*, and loved it. Could you recommend another one like it?"

These three questions are all variations on the same theme, and the answer depends on what the user means by a "good book." In addition, the first two questions are deceptive because "good book" does not necessarily mean "of high literary quality." Nor do they mean the librarian's own definition of "good." The reference librarian needs to find out what "good book" means to the person asking. It is helpful at the outset to ask the person to tell about a book he or she has enjoyed or loathed; once that is understood, to find out whether the individual is in the mood for the same kind of "good" book or something different, and if the latter, *how* different. Depending on whether the user has given an author or title, one can use NoveList's "Find" field to search by author, title, series, or plot limited to the age of the person requesting. If the person cannot remember a specific title, the librarian can ask for a description of an ideal story and use NoveList's (www.ebscohost.com) "Find" > "Describe a Plot" feature to pull up likely titles. If the library does not have NoveList, try another tool, such as RA Online or Books and Authors. If no electronic tools are available, remember that RA has many print sources, but they are not as easily searchable as electronic sources.

For the third question, the reference librarian needs to find out what the person liked about the book, whether he or she might like to try another one by the same author who, in this case, tends to write compelling stories with similar appeal, or a different author. In other words, find out why the person thinks this title is a "good book," and depending on what the person says, proceed exactly as in the first question with NoveList.

Scenario: *I've been put in charge of our book club group for our next meeting and have no clue what to do. Can you help me?*

The reference librarian needs to find out more about the book group, whether the group has already picked a title for discussion, and what the person wants specifically. If the group has picked a title, check NoveList's left menu under "Book Discussion Guides" by age level if the person needs questions for discussion. If nothing appropriate is found there, a variety of online resources are available, such as www.readinggroupchoices.com and Reading GroupGuides.com. Many major book publishers also have book group guides available on their Web sites like Random House's Book Club Center (www.ran-domhouse.com/rgg/) or Harper Collins (www.harpercollins.com/Readers/readingGroups.aspx) as do the major online bookstores (Amazon and Barnes and Noble), and at least one library vendor, Ingram, through its electronic newsletter, *Ingram Insights*. If no guide already exists, or if the group has not yet selected a title, the person should be directed to one of the many books on organizing book discussion groups, such as the *New York Public Library Guide to Reading Groups*, or *What to Read: The Essential Guide for Reading Group Members and Other Book Lovers*.

Unfortunately, many reader's advisory questions go unasked. It is important to realize that many people looking for something "good" to read will never approach a reference librarian to ask anything for reasons not well understood, but rather, will browse displays and shelves. It is important to watch for and offer help to these people when they exhaust their own resources. Setting up appropriate displays is another means of helping them. Although such activities are usually not discussed in the reference context, books on reader's advisory services explain how to do this.

The Reader's Advisory Interview

Once the encounter with a patron seeking reader's advisory help has begun, it is crucial that the librarian determine as much information as possible about the user's needs and interests. Most people call this dialogue the "RA Interview," but the word "interview" usually implies a question-and-answer interrogation that would be controlled by the librarian from the outset. Such an approach is better suited for the retrieval of facts for information seekers than for discovering what someone likes to read. In RA interactions, where mapping moods and attitudes is more important than determining how much factual information is needed and how it is to be used, another strategy is called for.

Consider the example of two different kinds of reference requests about travel. If someone is planning a trip to Australia, the classic reference interview format is sufficient, insofar as it allows the librarian to determine what the user needs to know. If, on the other hand, their interest is in vicarious journeys, it is important to seek out clues that will reveal the tone of the texts they enjoy, as opposed to the amount of raw information they need. Getting the user to reveal, for example, that he or she loves funny travel books, regardless of where they take place, is less straightforward. That person may be an ideal reader of, e.g., Bill Bryson's books. The other aspect of the RA encounter that distinguishes it from the reference interview is that even within the limitations of this kind of assessment, there is no immediate way to assess the aptness of a recommendation until the user actually sits down and reads it. Accuracy, in fact, is irrelevant to many fiction readers who want to escape from mundane reality.

Saricks (2005), in *Readers' Advisory Services in the Public Library,* suggests that the librarian start the RA encounter like a conversation by asking the person to tell about a book that he or she has recently read and enjoyed. Most people cannot say specifically what kind of story they want or why they have enjoyed it, except for the vague "good book," which is meaningless in RA terms without knowing what they mean by it; but they can usually talk about a title they have liked or disliked and why. With knowledge of those aspects of books that readers like—the book's appeal factors—the librarian can then listen for descriptors that suggest whether a person may like plot- or character-driven books, contemporary or historical or fantastic settings, male or female narrators, or any other such distinguishing information. The librarian can also listen for rejection factors such as the common ones of "too much sex and violence," or "alternating viewpoints."

A failure to understand appeal factors can lead to a mistake where books suggested are based only on theme, topic, or some genre subcategory similarity such as "legal thriller," which are the most common ways librarians group or index titles; the authors themselves handle the themes or subcategories quite differently in terms of appeal. This is not to say that some readers are not varied in their tastes, nor omnivorous in terms of a subcategory, but the range of their interests cannot automatically be assumed. One such mistake of this kind would be to offer books on serial killers for those who enjoyed *The Lovely Bones,* a book that is really about a family's healing from the unimaginable loss of their daughter, simply because the protagonist in it is murdered by a serial killer.

Ross (1999b) and Ross and Chelton (2001) suggest that one of the most important factors for avid adult readers in selecting books is what reading experience they are in the mood for. They may be looking for something different from the title they have just described, regardless of whether they remember enjoying it or not, so the librarian should ask them about their current needs before starting to look for possible reading suggestions.

Ross (2001) describes mood preferences along six dimensions:

1. Familiarity versus novelty
2. Safety versus risk
3. Easy versus challenging
4. Upbeat and positive versus hard-hitting/ironical/ cynical
5. Reassuring versus stimulating/frightening/amazing
6. Confirming of beliefs and values versus challenging them

Mood, of course, varies. When readers are busy or under stress, they often want safety, reassurance and confirmation. They will reread old favorites or read new books by trusted authors. When life is less stressful, they can afford to take more risks and may want to be amazed by something unpredictable. After finding out what kinds of books appeal to readers, the next most important thing to ask them is whether they are in the mood for something similar or different.

Common Mistakes in the RA Encounter

Poor Interpersonal Communication

As with the other forms of reference service described throughout this text, poor communication can severely mar the process, making it an unsatisfactory experience for the user. The first interpersonal mistake librarians make is to lose eye contact with the reader. This avoidance behavior is often compounded by the pretense that everything the librarian is doing on the computer is some sort of silent secret ritual that the user should just accept without explanation. Continuing to pay attention to users and inviting them to look at the computer while the librarian searches and explains what he or she is doing is more appropriate. Failing to provide such information and attention can leave the user confused, uncertain whether a service is actually being provided. This sense of bafflement also occurs when librarians leave the desk to search for specific books or colleagues to help answer the query without providing some indication as to where they are going, when they will return, or inviting the user to come along.

Beyond increasing the user's comfort, observation of his or her nonverbal reactions and listening to the reader's unsolicited as well as solicited comments can be useful so the librarian knows if he or she is on the right track. The users have to be regarded as the primary source of information in a reader's advisory interaction, just as they are in a classic reference interview.

Before the interaction with patrons begins, librarians often do not appear "askable," nor do they always greet users. Users occasionally have to interrupt conversations between librarians at the desk, a move with which many may not be comfortable. Other patrons have to calm librarians visibly upset because they don't know how to answer RA questions, are unfamiliar with sources when they do use them, or are visibly irritated with users because it is too close to closing time. This is bad service regardless of whether it involves reader's advisory or classic reference inquiry. Needless to say, none of these scenarios are desirable nor result in positive user experiences.

Inappropriate OPAC Use

Foreclosing—the premature assumption that the librarian knows what the person wants before he or she has finished explaining it, or before the librarian has finished eliciting enough information to understand the question—is as common in RA work as in conventional reference. Many librarians turn immediately to Online Public Access Catalogs (OPACs) to identify other titles by the same author before asking the reader whether he or she has read other books by the author, or what the reader likes about the particular book. This problem is now rampant in public libraries, and the increased computer dependence of staff combined with their lack of background in popular reading seems to be making it worse. Worse still, these librarians never tell or show the user what they are doing on the computer, making it all look hermetic, magical, and obscure.

Looking up other books by the same author in an OPAC gives the librarian something to do, but it is rarely the correct initial action for an RA encounter. Instead, the librarian should continue the interpersonal interaction with the reader until certain of what the person wants. Since good subject headings for fiction are not specific enough in traditionally catalogued OPAC databases, and keyword searching may be just a sort of "scattershot" approach, first resorting to an OPAC before talking more to the reader and consulting RA reference tools is usually not helpful. Librarians who do not read popular fiction or know anything about the genre being described by the user should remember that many authors write books in different categories. Assuming that another title by the same author will have the same appeal is therefore often a mistake. Nora Roberts, for example, writes historical, paranormal, and contemporary romances, many of them in miniseries. Although they are all romances and many readers want anything she has written, others may have subcategory preferences not satisfied by just any book by the author.

Query Avoidance and Lack of Follow-up

It is generally not considered ethical for reference librarians to refuse to answer a question about which they have no personal knowledge. The same is true when they are in the reader's advisor role; refusal to answer is dismayingly common when librarians are asked RA questions about a genre they do not read personally. Excusing one's own ignorance is not the same as answering the user's question, nor is it professional behavior. A librarian asked about cancer would never dream of saying, "I have never had cancer, so I cannot answer that," but many feel no problem with saying, "I do not read that kind of book," and ending the interview there.

Documenting Sources

Reference librarians are obliged to document the sources for the information they provide and avoid off-the-cuff responses to ensure the accuracy of responses, and reader's advising practice demands no less. The numerous reference tools devoted to books in general as well as to specific genres should be consulted before checking availability in an OPAC. One of the biggest myths among librarians about RA services is that the librarian must have read the book personally to suggest it, without resorting to any reference sources. At an absolute minimum, librarians should be familiar with the "Top Ten RA Tools" (listed below). Tempting as they are, the automatic recommendation lists generated by, e.g., amazon.com and Barnes and Noble online (bn.com), should be avoided. While these suggestions do pick up "readalikes," they are generated through patterns of "associative buying," *not* designed by a careful analysis of the appeal factors of particular books. Depending on the query, this can be as misleading as helpful. Instead, librarians should look to the appropriate professional resources when met with the unknown.

When readers are referred to shelves to search for themselves, it is important to follow up and see if they find anything. Often librarians act as if their job is sending everyone off to help themselves, assuming that they will find what they want. At a minimum, the librarian should tell the user to come back if he or she does not find anything, a simple suggestion that is almost never implemented. If a library has few sources, like displays and lists available to readers, in addition to staff, referring users to shelves arranged in alphabetical order, spine out, makes follow-up even more important (since browsing is more difficult under those circumstances).

Reader's Advisory Reference Tools

The ideal RA tool should have multiple access points, be linked to a library or library system's holdings, and be indexed by those factors (or terms) that most appeal to readers, such as pacing (fast-paced) and characterization (complex characters), in addition to more traditional index terms such as genre, setting, historical period, award category (if any), and gender or occupation of the protagonist. Such a tool would have to be digital, featuring flexibility of access in searching, with a combination of both natural language and controlled vocabulary in its search options. Unfortunately, such a perfect tool does not yet exist, and formal cataloging for OPACs does little to rectify the situation, despite some overdue attention given to genre subject headings a few years ago in a project cosponsored by ALA's Association for Library Collections & Technical Services division and Online Computer Library Center. Annalise Pejtersen (1983, 1984) has done pioneering work of this kind in Denmark, but it has not been replicated in the North American context.

The usefulness of any RA tool will vary based on the kinds of questions asked, but RA tools generally fall into and should be evaluated against reference needs in five categories:

1. content (general or specific),
2. scope (time period covered, genre or mainstream, adult or juvenile, in print or out of print),
3. originator (librarian or librarian/fan or fan/nonlibrarian),
4. format (print or electronic), and
5. purpose (reader's guide or collection development tool).

All tools are only as good as their currency, the expertise of their creators, the way they are indexed, how they may be searched, whether they include annotations and/or cover art, and whether they are or can be linked to local library collections. Identifying something a reader wants, only to have to borrow it from another library on interlibrary loan, unless the reader is a diehard fan of whatever is requested, can be a frustrating experience. This problem can be solved, however, when reference librarians can suggest more than one item to fit the reader's mood and interests drawn from RA tools.

Many tools useful to RA reference queries are also or primarily concerned with collection development designed to keep librarians apprised of current publishing trends and provide selection advice. While *Publisher's Weekly* magazine has provided this service to the profession for years, there are now other book-related magazines, Web sites, and notification systems that are helpful to both collection development and reference librarians. Since good RA service depends on responsive collection development, some of them are included in the following list.

The Top Ten RA Tools

1. *NoveList/NoveList Plus* (www.ebscohost.com/novelist)

The nearest thing to the ideal tool, and the one that librarians should be most familiar with, NoveList is a licensed searchable fiction database of over 169,000 titles for readers of all ages from EBSCO Publishing. The newer NoveList Plus is an upgraded version of NoveList, which includes 240,000 titles (170,400) fiction and (68,500) readable nonfiction titles sortable by lexile reading levels with additional customized information on nonfiction as well as all the content from NoveList. A related product is NoveList K-8 Plus for children's and elementary school librarians. NoveList adds 20,000 new fiction and nonfiction titles annually to these databases.

Developed initially by Duncan Smith and Roger Rohweder, the tool allows searching by author, title, series, Dewey number or class, a variety of traditional index terms, natural language terms or phrases, and Boolean combinations. The latter are particularly important because the elusive appeal and mood factors are more often captured in a reviewer's or reader's own words and adjectives, than in more formally assigned subject headings. Saricks calls this "the vocabulary of appeal" (2005). Using the advanced (Boolean) search function, the librarian can also search for reviews that mention when a title is written much like "so and so's book" or in the same style as "so and so's book" and then use NOT to exclude the titles by that author. Links to readalike title lists appear frequently in the citation field of individual titles. For example, a link at Cody MacFadyen's *Shadow Man* leads to a list of other "serial killer" titles called "Hunting Humans." These lists can be saved to a personal computer, printed, or e-mailed directly to readers. The "Readers' Advisory" section of NoveList includes self-help sections to teach librarians how to get started in RA and also how to search NoveList and take advantage of all advanced search features.

A menu with links to customized content, organized by age (adults, teens, older kids, younger kids) includes readalikes, award winners, book discussion guides, feature articles and recommended reads. There is also now a section called "Working with Kids" that includes booktalks, curricular information, "Grab And Go" booklists, and "Picture Book Extenders." Individual title citations in NoveList can also include links to author Web sites and to this value-added content. One of the best value-added features of NoveList is the *RA News Newsletter* written by David Carr, who has taught RA to MLS students at Rutgers and UNC, Chapel Hill, besides being a voracious reader himself.

NextReads is another resource from NoveList that expands and enhances readers' advisory service. Hosted on the library site and branded with the library's logo and name, this service delivers reading selections in more than twenty fiction and nonfiction categories and genres to readers. NextReads also allows staff to create their own newsletters delivering the staff's expertise directly to their readers. NoveList also allows linking to all major ILS systems, which allows readers to check to see if titles they discover in NoveList are available in a local library's collection.

2. *Readers Advisor Online and the Genreflecting series* (http://rainfo.lu.com/)

The *Readers Advisor Online* is a subscription Web-based book-finding tool for RA librarians that brings the content of all nineteen genre-specific print titles in Libraries Unlimited's Genreflecting series together in one place. Other titles are added based on carefully selected RA and genre experts. Besides offering multiple choices for finding readalikes and "related reads," the database includes fiction and nonfiction, offers printable lists, links to library OPACs, and is informed by advice from top RA experts around the country, such as Diane Herald, the author of *Genreflecting*. The searchable database is augmented by a blog updated twice a week by Cynthia Orr, formerly head of collection development at the Cleveland Public Library, as well as *Readers' Advisor News*, an electronic newsletter with articles about RA for library educators and practitioners.

Despite the existence of this online tool, readers and librarians alike will enjoy using and browsing the individual genre-specific print *Genreflecting* titles, if currency is not an issue.

3. *Books and Authors and the What Do I Read Next? series* (www.gale.cengage .com/booksandauthors/)

A subscription-searchable database "powered by" Gale's What Do I Read Next? Series (all of which are also available in print format) that offers author, title, genre, readalike, and awards searches, as well as advanced Boolean searching options and a graphical search of Who, What, Where, and When. Users can save searches as well as rate and review books themselves and see what others have done. There are direct links to author information from the book pages and the ability for local libraries to customize and add content relating to library events and book clubs, for example.

4. *AllReaders.com*

This Web site duplicates the previous resources in some ways, although with far fewer titles (30,000). What makes it so useful is its Gordonator Precision Search Function for genre categories, which allows searchers to match many appeal characteristics such as "difficult/unusual lover" for romance, or "spying/terrorism" for thrillers, etc. Searchers can even specify the age and gender of the character. Reviewers are asked to specify certain things about the books they review. While it does not get at all reader appeal factors, it includes more than many others for the titles included in the database. AllReaders was created by Steve Gordon, a writer himself, who realized "that fiction, unlike non-fiction, was very difficult to classify" and "that people didn't just like books, they liked certain plots in books, certain kinds of characters in books, certain kinds and amounts of action and dialogue in books."

5.   *BookSpot.com*

Describing itself as "a free resource center that simplifies the search for the best book-related content on the Web," BookSpot provides a compendium of news about books, publishing, authors, and awards, covering all ages, with numerous reviews and a great deal of genre-specific information. Also included are links to the book review pages of major U.S. newspapers, book-related magazines such as *BookPage* and *Bookreporter*, and to book excerpts; this site is enormously useful, though reference librarians need to be familiar with it to use it well. The excerpts are particularly important because first paragraphs or selections of text allow readers to sense the "feel" or "frame" of a story to get an idea of whether they might like it or not. This site provides direct access to *Publishers Weekly*. After NoveList, BookSpot.com offers more one-stop looking. Links are also provided to related sites in the StartSpot network.

6.   *EarlyWord.com*

Calling itself the "publisher-librarian connection," this blog and Web site founded and owned by Nora Rawlinson, former editor of *Publishers Weekly* and *Library Journal* and Fred Ciporen, former publisher of *Library Journal* and *School Library Journal*, gives collection development and readers advisory librarians the earliest possible information on books so "they can stay ahead of demand" and give their readers what they want when they want it.

Besides providing news of the publishing industry, the site keeps librarians up-to-date on lists of bestsellers, annual "best" lists, award winners, movie tie-ins (worth it for this alone), book events, and programs. Online publishers' catalogs and publisher contact information are linked. The site contains occasional columns by editors such as Talia Ross Sherer at Macmillan, as well as reviews from newspapers, weekly magazines such as *The New Yorker* and *Business Week*, or television and radio shows.

7.   *FictionDB.com*

Started in 1999 with the intention of providing "accurate and reliable information for readers of genre fiction," this subscription site (although the first month is free) offers reviews, author pseudonyms, series, and upcoming releases information, author Web sites and a way to buy and sell books to keep track of one's own reading. Links are also provided to other related genre and publisher sites. Among the free offerings here are the complete booklists of 50,000 authors and 200,000 titles. A keyword search of books about serial killers turned up seven screens of annotated titles.

8.   *Fiction_L* (www.webrary.org/RS/FLmenu.html)

Started by Roberta Johnson while she was still a library school student and working at the Morton Grove Public Library (MGPL) in Illinois, the Fiction_L Listserv is a godsend for many librarians doing RA work because it functions as a communal mind of collegial professional helpers. Many posts begin with

"I have a patron who..." followed by further elaboration about desired reada-likes, queries about forgotten titles of favorite books, and so on. Although one often wishes that all the list subscribers did better RA interviews before going online, at least frantic reference librarians are guaranteed some level of help very quickly. The list is housed on the MGPL home Web site, along with all the member-generated readalike lists. Beside readalike and title identification assistance, the list members identify and comment on useful tools, discuss titles and discussion guides for library-based reading groups, and even discuss briefly books that they have read. A staple is the "Best Books of the Year" list.

9. *AudioFile Magazine* (www.audiofilemagazine.com/audiofileplus.html)

The popularity of audiobooks, especially in new downloadable formats, necessitates knowledge of and attention to what is going on in the industry, and there is no place better than the expanded version of *AudioFile Magazine* online. Besides discussions of industry trends, it also has the "golden-voiced" narrators who read the books, the award winners in various genre and age categories, as well as reviews of current and forthcoming audiobooks; the expanded electronic version offers access to 17,000 archived reviews, links to audiobook publishers, a reference guide to the industry, and search capability.

10. *Reader's Guide to Genre Fiction*

Based on the work that Joyce Saricks and her staff at the Downer 's Grove Public Library did in their "genre studies," this book lists key authors and titles in specific genres, explains the appeal of the genre and its subgenres, and provides lists for people coming into or willing to leave a favorite genre to try something new. The book should probably be at every reference desk to assist users and self-training during downtime. Since, at this writing, the tool is getting dated—an increasing problem with print tools—a new edition is planned for 2009.

Keeping Current

To keep current, one should read genre fan magazines and Web sites specific to one's interests, e.g., *Romantic Times Book Club* and the *Romance Readers of America* Web site (www.rwa.com) for romance and romance hybrids; *Locus* and www.sfsite.com/home.htm for science fiction, fantasy, and horror; *Deadly Pleasures* and cluelass.com for mysteries, especially for awards, features, and author profiles; the feature articles, author interviews and reviews in magazines such as *Publishers Weekly* (www.publishersweekly.com/) and *Book Reporter* (http://bookreporter.com/) are helpful, as are *Bookmarks* (www.bookmarksmagazine.com) and *BookPage* (http://bookpage.com/), to name just a few.

Since NoveList/EBSCO, ALA Editions, Thompson/Gale and Greenwood/Libraries Unlimited are the main publishers of RA tools, looking at their Web sites for new offerings regularly will help identify both new tools such as NoveList's readalike lists, and updates of old favorites, such as Libraries Unlimited's Genreflecting. EarlyWord.com offers information about publishing, awards, bestsellers, the book review sections of major papers, etc., in one place.

Both the Public Library Association (PLA) and the Reference and User Services Association (RUSA), divisions of ALA, have standing committees devoted to RA services. Their publications, *Public Libraries* from PLA and *RUSA Quarterly* from RUSA, usually include articles on RA services and reviews of tools. Both divisions offer programs at ALA's annual and divisional regional conferences on RA topics. The other way of staying current at the local level is to use part of every staff meeting to share new questions (and answers) and new tools with each other, and to know about and use colleagues' expertise for mini-workshops on particular questions about what they know best.

Bibliography of Works Cited in This Chapter

Kuhlthau, Carol Collier. 2004. *Seeking Meaning: A Process Approach to Library and Information Services*. 2nd ed. Westport, CT: Libraries Unlimited.

Kuhlthau, C.C., J. Heinström, and R.J. Todd. 2008. "The 'Information Search Process' Revisited: Is the Model Still Useful?" *Information Research* 13, no. 44: paper 355. Available: http://InformationR.net/ir/13-4/paper355.html.

Moyer, Jessica E. 2004. "Learning from Leisure Reading: Educational and Recreational Outcomes of Leisure Reading—A Study of Adult Public Library Patrons." (Certificate of Advanced Study Project Report). Urbana-Champaign: University of Illinois, September 21.

Pearlman, Mickey. 1999. *What to Read: The Essential Guide for Reading Group Members and Other Book Lovers*. Revised and updated. New York: HarperCollins.

Pejtersen, Annelise Mark, and Jutta Austin. 1983. "Fiction Retrieval: Experimental Design and Evaluation of a Search System Based on Users' Value Criteria. Part 1." *Journal of Documentation* 39, no. 4 (December): 230–246.

———. 1984. "Fiction Retrieval: Experimental Design and Evaluation of a Search System Based on Users' Value Criteria. Part 2." *Journal of Documentation* 40, no. 1 (March): 25–35.

Ross, Catherine Sheldrick. 1999a. "Finding without Seeking: The Information Encounter in the Context of Reading for Pleasure." *Information Processing and Management* 35, no. 6 (November): 783–799.

———. 1999b. *A Model for the Process of Choosing a Book for Pleasure*. Handout. Public Library Association Spring Symposium.

Ross, Catherine Sheldrick, and Mary K. Chelton. 2001. "Reader's Advisory: Matching Mood and Material." *Library Journal* 126, no. 2 (February 1): 52–56.

Sall, Rollene. 1995. *New York Public Library Guide to Reading Groups*. New York: Crown.

Saricks, Joyce G. 2005. *Readers' Advisory Service in the Public Library*. 3rd ed. Chicago: American Library Association.

Wiegand, Wayne. 2000. "Librarians Ignore the Value of Stories." *Chronicle of Higher Education* 47, no. 9 (October 27): B20.

Williamson, Kirsty. 1998. "Discovered by Chance: The Role of Incidental Information Acquisition in an Ecological Model of Information Use." *Library & Information Science Research* 20, no. 1: 23–40.

15

Reference Work with Children and Young Adults

Mary K. Chelton

Introduction: Challenges of Working with Young Audiences

Young people are a special reference audience for several reasons. First of all, they are a major clientele in public libraries, where librarians themselves reported in 1995 that 60 percent of their users were under eighteen (NCES, 1995), and in school libraries they are the primary clientele. Although children and young adults have personal information needs and interests like anyone else, young people usually use library reference services primarily for homework assignments that have been imposed on them by adults. These "imposed queries" (Gross, 1995) pose interesting problems for reference librarians because of the difficulty inherent in interviewing someone who may not know nor care enough about what he or she needs. Clarifying the question without forcing an answer is difficult, and, even in the best of circumstances, is hardly the ideal situation for a good reference interview. Most reference interviews assume genuine personal interest in the topic and depend upon the user's prior knowledge of, need for, or potential use for the requested information (Dervin and Dewdney, 1986). Many children and adolescents are given the same assignments at the same time, stretching resources beyond what they may have been intended for. Further, parents coming to "help" their children with homework queries often add to the confusion as they tend to know even less about what is needed than the young person does.

Public librarians sometimes mistakenly assume that every homework assignment is intended to teach students how to do research, or that school librarians have already taught them how to do it so they do not have to make the effort. Compounding this possible confusion, teachers are often clueless about how much research and how many resources are needed to do something they regard as a simple assignment, or they forbid Internet use for their assignments without understanding that Web-based databases are available to their students in libraries. Many young people bypass their school libraries for the public library closer to their home after school where they can see friends, even when the school library has more resources tailored to their assignments.

Because of an overwhelming preference for electronic resources and the instant gratification of the familiar point-and-click world of the Internet, many young people have little patience for using print reference sources and complicated indexes, especially without full-text access. All of this can make reference service to youth a very frustrating experience for everyone concerned unless these issues are understood at the outset and necessary strategies are put into place.

Special Topics in Reference and Information Work with Youth

Information Literacy Instruction and Youth Information-Seeking Behavior

Information literacy, which is discussed in greater detail in the next chapter, is not only the ability to access, evaluate, and use information responsibly (American Association of School Librarians and Association for Educational Communications and Technology, 1998), but also now includes multiple literacies, including digital, visual, textual, and technological as crucial skills for the twenty-first century (American Association of School Librarians, 2007). Whether or not an instructional role is mandated—as it is in school libraries through national professional standards—librarians doing reference work with young people in today's highly technological library environments need to make information literacy instruction a large part of their interactions with kids. Since most reference librarians feel that their job is either to locate information for people or help them locate it for themselves, they need to understand that many youngsters lack both the cognitive structure and the experience needed to evaluate and synthesize the information they find into something meaningful. Even clarifying the question for these users can position the reference librarian in the role of an instructor of information literacy. Locating information comes at the end of an often frustrating and anxiety-ridden reference search process that is not anticipated by many youths (Kuhlthau, Heinström, and Todd, 2008). Good reference librarians understand and often need to explain this to young people, as the following examples from a New York City school librarian demonstrate eloquently:

1. A middle-school student needed a picture of Mary Todd Lincoln, and typed "Mrs. Lincoln" into Google's search field. The student printed out the photo of a New Jersey woman in full wedding regalia from her wedding photos posted on the Web. Only upon subsequent questioning by the librarian did she decide that Abraham Lincoln's wife probably had neither looked nor dressed that way, nor had her picture taken in a school gym full of kids.

2.   An assignment required a student to "research" the foods eaten by the Iroquois. He asked to go online; I guided him to the subscription we have to *World Book* online, promising to return momentarily; I left him for a minute to go help another child with a book on the Iroquois.

Of course, the child had no interest in using the encyclopedia and instead went directly to Google. From the back of the library I heard the printer running and flew back to the front to look into the breaking of Library Cardinal Rule #1: "no printing without asking"—because I really do need to sit with them to teach them how to determine if the 6,000 pages they are about to print actually have anything to do with what they are looking for. Most do not read before printing; most do not even skim what they are about to print. The child had printed the entire Web site for the Iroquois Hotel in Manhattan, including pages with menus of food served in the hotel's restaurant; after all, the report was to be about food of the Iroquois. I like to believe it was edifying for this child to retrace his steps and actually read the page that came up at the top of Google's results list when he typed in "The Iroquois." It did not take him long at all to realize that the Iroquois Hotel and the Iroquois tribe were not one and the same. Nor did it take him long to realize that more than likely, the tribe did not generate printed menus (complete with prices) upon returning from a day hunting deer and harvesting beans, corn, and squash . . . and, also more than likely, appetizers (as a separate food entity) did not yet exist. The youth needed to READ and THINK/QUESTION simultaneously (Nesi, personal communication, 2008).

The ideas of broadening or narrowing a topic, using quotes to join words together in a search string, or using Boolean logic to join or exclude terms and concepts, to give just three examples, are largely unknown to most young people. Not only do they not know where to go beyond Google, they probably do not use Google as well as they might (Google "Improve Your Search Experience" and "Web Search Help Center," 2008). Likewise, few young students have been taught to evaluate the materials they find in their research efforts for quality, relevance and authority. If a word they find matches the word in an assignment, they print it out, going no further. They also do not know what to do when they get stuck during a search with no idea what to do next, are unaware of simple navigation commands to shortcut the search process, and are easily distracted by essentially meaningless visuals (Fidel, Davies, and Douglas, 1999; Shenton and Dixon, 2004). Knowledge is essential, not only of the common mistakes in information-seeking behavior by kids, but also of specialized research resources geared toward their needs, such as NoodleTools (2008).

Finally, the idea of intellectual property is alien to kids used to cutting and pasting their way around the Internet, or downloading audio and video, in the belief that all of it is free for the taking (Braun, 2006). All of these problematic behaviors (also shared by many adults), have a silver lining in that they present eminently teachable moments for information literacy instruction by good school and academic librarians, as eloquently discussed by Harris (2005). Unfortunately, they can also be an endless source of annoyance to overworked, time-strapped public and school librarians alike.

Developmental Barriers and Perceptions of Helpfulness

Developmentally, young people often lack the vocabulary to generate synonyms or the specialized vocabulary for a new subject they are still learning (Brown, 2004). Lacking hypothetical thinking strategies, they wait until the last minute to do dreaded assignments. They can also lack background knowledge on topics they are asked to research, and many do not understand that surfing the Web is not the same as searching for specific information using well-defined search strategies (Hirsch, 2004; Large, 2004). Worst of all, they do not perceive many adult reference librarians as helpful because they have long experience of being treated shabbily by librarians and many other adults who act as though they do not want them around. The following quote from a harried public library reference librarian is an example of a common attitude toward adolescents:

> I'll be happy to tell you why I find this age group "problematic." So many come to the reference desk with no idea of why they are there. They shove a sheet of paper in my face and say, "This is my homework. Where I can I find this?" When I ask them what the assignment is, they appear to be looking at it for the very first time. Or they simply mumble, "I don't know." It's the total lack of concern and the assumption that I'll figure it all out for them and go fetch the materials that irritates me.
>
> We have OPACS, and many of these patrons won't even go near them. When I ask them if they've checked the catalog, they reply they don't know how to use it. They will ask for staples, paper, directions, permission to use the phone, but they won't ask for help using the OPACS. They don't come to library for any other purpose than to socialize and bother patrons who have legitimate business in the library. We're across the street from a high school. At 2:45, it's like a parade that crosses the street and enters the library. We hired a monitor to do nothing else but to keep order in the library when the teenagers are here. In contrast to those who won't use the OPACS are the ones who love to bring a terminal down by screwing around in the DOS program. We have security features, but some have figured this out. One will bring it to my attention that a terminal is down, then two or three of his friends eagerly wait for me to log back on so they can watch. (I'm wise to this.)
>
> I know I sound "negative" but so many patrons in this age group don't need the services of the library or the librarians. They simply want a place to hang out until their parents pick them up. I love helping a kid find stuff for a tough research project. I enjoy taking vague questions and formulating reference questions. But having homework assignments and reading lists shoved in my face by healthy, intelligent, able-bodied young people who have no interest in their own homework just plain "bugs" me. (Chelton, 1997: 17)

This perception of unhelpfulness carries over beyond homework help to everyday personal information seeking. For example, Julien (1998, 1999) noted that libraries were rarely seen as a source of information by teenagers in career decision making. Meyers (1999) reiterated this in a summary of what young people involved in the DeWitt-Wallace Reader's Digest Fund Libraries as Partners in Youth Development Initiative said they wanted to change to make libraries be "cool" for them.

Research and Assignment Topics

Because so many youth research or report topics are determined by school curricula, a seasonal redundancy allows reference librarians to anticipate demands, so they are not caught off guard. A recent query to relevant professional listservs asking for the top five repeat assignments generated the following list, which varied only by grade level or local specifics (e.g., California missions): science fair projects; biographies of just about anybody past or present (the more obscure the better, especially if an ethnic minority); countries and states; ancient civilizations; careers; biomes; diseases and medical conditions; animals; author studies; genre fiction; battles of the American Revolution or Civil War; local people; insects; wildflowers, etc.; controversial contemporary issues; Constitutional amendments; famous court cases (AASL-Forum et al., 2008).

Many topics that are self-chosen by students within teacher-mandated parameters can be controversial. They hear about the topics on the news and want to know more. On other occasions, well-intentioned social studies teachers assign debate questions, or the students are told to write something rhetorical about a topic from a specific point of view. These choices make the *Opposing Viewpoints* series published by Greenhaven Press and Gale's accompanying Resource Center database particularly valuable for reference work with youth. Now encompassing more than 400 volumes, the *Opposing Viewpoints' At Issue and Current Controversies* series in the Resource Center:

> draws on the acclaimed social issues series published by Greenhaven Press, as well as core reference content from other Gale and Macmillan Reference USA sources, including selections from *Bioethics for Students*. The result is a dynamic online library of current event topics—the facts, as well as the arguments, of each topic's proponents and detractors. *Opposing Viewpoints Resource Center*'s unique features include Topic Overviews—frameworks that allow students to explore each topic's many facets—and exclusive electronic access to Gale's *Information Plus* reference series of statistics, government data, information on legislation and more. (Gale Cengage Learning, 2008)

Solutions to Common Problems in Reference Work with Youth

Mass Assignments

It would be nice if mass assignments disappeared, but they probably will not, because curricula determine that a certain number of children or adolescents must cover certain topics in a specific order during the year. Asking teachers to customize each report or research project for the convenience of librarians is as unrealistic as it is misguided for librarians to vilify teachers for not doing so. Being familiar with local school curricula topics and sequencing should help reference librarians plan better responses through strategies such as acquiring duplicate materials in advance of assignment deadlines, creating temporary reserve lists of relevant circulating materials, and creating reference pathfinders on repeated topics. In schools, collaboration with classroom teachers in the design of assignments also helps.

School and public librarians should keep in touch with one another about both upcoming assignments and those that become problematic. Student frustration can be averted if faculty are reminded at the beginning of each semester to state in writing on assignments that librarians are allowed to offer alternatives when all resources are out or in use. Librarians can also distribute teacher alert forms and business cards with contact information in order to improve the early warning system. Should things get especially bad, the use of some sort of standard notification form to teachers might be helpful if the tone is right. Examples of such forms from *Connecting Young Adults and Libraries* (Jones et al., 2004) appear in Figures 15-1, 15-2, and 15-3. Mass assignments will never go away entirely, but the frustration they cause librarians, parents, and students can be managed with good communication, anticipation, and preparation.

Figure 15-1. Assignment Alert Form

Dear Media Specialist,

As you know, often students will use the public library to find resources to complete assignments. Help us help them by alerting us as soon as possible to assignments which require library use. Together, we can help students use the wide variety of resources available in libraries, both school and public.

MEDIA SPECIALIST: _____ DATE: _____

SCHOOL: _____ TEACHER: _____

GRADE: _____ CLASS: _____ # STUDENTS: _____

ASSIGNMENT: _____

_____

DATE ASSIGNMENT IS DUE: _____

SPECIAL REQUIREMENTS (# OF SOURCES, LIMITS, ETC.): _____

_____

_____

Source: From Jones et al., 2004. Used by permission.

Figure 15-2. Letter to Teacher

Dear Teacher,

During the past week, I've been able to help several students from your _____
class work on their homework assignment/term paper. I'm delighted to see that you have
encouraged them to use our library. Thank you.

There is one thing that you could do to help us help your students learn even more. Some
students won't ask for assistance, and others simply won't come to the library. You could
help us help your students by:

- Arranging for them to visit the library as a group to receive library instruction
- Notifying us (and your school librarian) at least a week in advance of assignments
  so we may gather materials for them
- Allowing us to prepare pathfinders or other handouts which would help them help
  themselves

Again, I'm pleased to see so many of your students in our library. Please contact me so we
can arrange the activities mentioned above to benefit your students. In this "information
age," it is important that all students learn how to access the vast amount of information
available to them; that is why we're here and we'd like the opportunity to work with your
students at your convenience.

Sincerely,

<Librarian's name and contact information>

Source: From Jones et al., 2004. Used by permission.

Reference librarians should remember that if they were notified of every
assignment in advance, they would have time to do nothing else, making universal notification an ideal that ultimately leads to its own frustrations.

Parents Doing Homework

Public librarians can get very moralistic about parents who come in to get
materials for a child's report, and this secondhand interview with someone
who is even more distant from the query can lead to total confusion. That being
said, such professional judgments are self-defeating and do nothing to make
the "problem" go away. The solution is to do the best job possible under the
circumstances and leave the person with the impression that the librarian has
been helpful. Whatever family situation prompts the parent to act as proxy for
a child, it is neither of the librarian's making nor within his or her purview to
change. Since confusion usually occurs in such encounters, the librarian should
offer to take follow-up calls, e-mails, or visits to clarify the assignment further
if necessary, and also offer multiple options to address the query so the parent
does not leave with an incorrect resource.

Figure 15-3. Materials Unavailable Card

LIBRARY: _____ DATE: _____

Dear Teacher,

Your student _____ came to the library today to find materials

on _____.

We are sorry to report that we were unable to help your student because:

_____ All materials were checked out.
_____ A reasonable search failed to find materials.
_____ Materials are for "in library" use only.
_____ Clarification of request is needed.
_____ Other: _____

If you have any questions, please contact me. Often we can better help students and reduce their frustration in using libraries when we are notified in advance about school assignments like this one. Then, we can provide instruction and gather materials and other services to benefit all of your students.

LIBRARIAN: _____ PHONE: _____
E-MAIL: _____

Source: From Jones et al., 2004. Used by permission.

If the child or adolescent is with the parent, try to talk directly to the young person, although this can be difficult, because inevitably the parent answers. Usually, if they are there together, it is because the youth is clueless and the parent is frustrated already, so the best the librarian can do is "no harm."

Preference for Electronic Sources

Although wide disparities still occur in access and skill by socioeconomic status, most young people are much more comfortable with technology than previous generations, and this experience leads to increased expectations of library services. One study has documented that youth preference for using the Internet is a major reason for disuse of public libraries, especially if they dislike reading to begin with (Abbas et al., 2008). As early as 2001, researchers noticed that teenagers were using the Internet for information about health (Borzekowski and Rickert, 2001), a trend that has grown since that time. This led to the creation of specialized Web sites for delivering that information, such as KidsHealth (2008).

Smart reference librarians are learning to tailor services to the online formats that kids prefer such as texting, instant messaging, and chat (Braun, 2008; Connaway-Silipigni and Radford, 2007; Valenza, 2003; Thompson, 2003), or social networking sites like MySpace and Facebook (Young Adult Library Services Association, 2008).

Reader's Advisory Questions in Youth Reference Services

Many youth reference questions arrive as reader's advisory questions, such as being assigned to read a novel about a period in history or a novel that has won an award, or just a request for a book on the Accelerated Reader list (AR BookFinder, 2008). Reference librarians should stock and consult one of the many youth references sources designed to help with such queries and be ready to involve youth services colleagues in answering queries. Examples include titles such as *Middle Ages in Literature for Youth: A Guide and Resource Book* by Rebecca Barnhouse (2004); *World's Best Thin Books: Or What to Read When Your Book Report Is Due Tomorrow* by Joni Bodart (2000); *Guide to Collective Biographies for Children and Young Adults* by Sue Barancik (2004); ALA's *Newbery and Caldecott Awards: A Guide to the Medal and Honor Books* (2009), or *YALSA Annotated Book Lists for Every Teen Reader* by Pam Spencer Holley and Julie Bartel (2009).

Conclusion

It seems silly to remind reference librarians that children and adolescents are worthy of their professional assistance, but unfortunately, it is a point that needs repeating. Too many people who are attracted to reference service for the intellectual thrill of playing information detective fail to develop a strong service orientation grounded in the needs of real users. Fortunately, the needs of contemporary youth—informational as well as social—are well documented in library and information science research literature. The real question is whether librarians' attitudes can adjust to meet those kids who deserve—and need—more from reference librarians than impatience and neglect. Whether they remain an underserved group or are tapped as an ideal audience for formative instruction and assistance depends greatly on the attitudes of the librarians they encounter.

Bibliography of Works Cited in This Chapter

AASL-Forum, ALSC-L, and PUBLIB, multiple responses, December, 2008.

Abbas, June, Melanie Kimball, Kay Bishop, and George D'Elia. 2008. "Youth, Public Libraries, and the Internet, Part Four: Why Youth Do Not Use the Public Library." *Public Libraries* 47, no. 1: 80–85.

American Association of School Librarians. 2007. *Standards for the 21st-Century Learner*. Available: www.ala.org/aasl/standards.

American Association of School Librarians and Association for Educational Communications and Technology. 1998. *Information Power: Building Partnerships for Learning*. Chicago, IL: American Library Association.

AR BookFinder. 2008. Available: www.renlearn.com/arbookfinder/.

Association for Library Service for Children. 2009. *Newbery and Caldecott Awards: A Guide to the Medal and Honor Books*. 2009 ed. Chicago, IL: American Library Association.

Barancik, Sue. 2004. *Guide to Collective Biographies for Children and Young Adults.* Lanham, MD: Scarecrow Press.

Barnhouse, Rebecca. 2004. *Middle Ages in Literature for Youth: A Guide and Resource Book.* (Literature for Youth Series, #4). Lanham, MD: Scarecrow Press.

Bodart, Joni R. 2000. *World's Best Thin Books: Or What to Read When Your Book Report Is Due Tomorrow.* Rev. ed. Lanham, MD: Scarecrow Press.

Borzekowki, D., and Rickert, V. 2001. "Adolescent Cyber-Surfing for Health Information: A New Resource That Crosses Barriers." *Archives of Pediatric and Adolescent Medicine* 155: 813–817.

Braun, Linda W. 2006. "Torrent of Free Downloads, or Who Cares If It's Legal. Tag Team Tech: Wrestling with Teens and Technology" [column]. eVOYA. Available: http://pdfs.voya.com/VO/YA2/VOYA200602TagTeamTech.pdf.

Braun, Linda W. 2008. "Teen Texting in the News." YALSA Blog. Available: http://blogs.ala.org/yalsa.php?title=teen_texting_in_the_news&more=1&c=1&tb=1&pb=1.

Brown, Anita. 2004. "Reference Services for Children: Information Needs and Wants in the Public Library." *Australian Library Journal* 53, no. 3. Available: http://alia.org.au/publishing/alj/53.3/full.text/brown.html.

Chelton, Mary K. 1997. *Adult-Adolescent Service Encounters: The Library Context.* Brunswick, NJ: Rutgers University. Doctoral dissertation.

———. 2002. "The 'Problem Patron' Public Libraries Created." *Reference Librarian* no. 75–76 (June): 23–33.

Connaway, Lynn Silipigni, and Marie L. Radford. 2007. "Service Sea Change: Clicking with Screenagers Through Virtual Reference." Presented at the Association of College and Research Libraries 13th National Conference, "Sailing into the Future—Charting Our Destiny," March 29–April 1, 2007, Baltimore, Maryland (USA), and forthcoming in the conference proceedings. Preprint available online: www.oclc.org/research/publications/archive/2007/connaway-acrl.pdf.

Dervin, Brenda, and Pat Dewdney. 1986. "Neutral Questioning: A New Approach to the Reference Interview." *Research Quarterly* 25, no. 4: 506–513.

Fidel, Raya, Rachel K. Davies, and Mary H. Douglas. 1999. "Visit to the Information Mall: Web Searching Behavior of High School Students." *Journal of the American Society for Information Science* 50: 24–37.

Gale Cengage Learning Opposing Viewpoints Resource Center. Available: www.gale.cengage.com/servlet/ItemDetailServlet?region=9&imprint=000&titleCode=GAL74&cf=n&type=4&id=176168.

Google. "Improve Your Search Experience." Available: www.google.com/intl/en/help/features.html.

Google. "Web Search Help Center." Available: www.google.com/support/?ctx=web.

Gross, Melissa. 1995. "Imposed Query." *RQ* 35, no. 1: 236–243.

Harris, Frances Jacobsen. 2005. *I Found It on the Internet: Coming of Age Online.* Chicago: American Library Association.

Hirsch, Sandra. 2004. "Domain Knowledge and Search Behavior." In *Youth Information-Seeking Behavior: Theories, Models, and Issues*, edited by Mary K. Chelton and Colleen Cool, pp. 241–270. Lanham, MD: Scarecrow Press.

Holley, Pam Spencer, and Julie Bartel for YALSA. 2009. *YALSA Annotated Book Lists for Every Teen Reader: The Best from the Experts at YALSA-BK*. New York: Neal-Schuman.

Jones, Patrick, Michele Gorman, and Tricia Suellentrop. 2004. *Connecting Young Adults and Libraries*. 3rd ed. New York: Neal-Schuman.

Julien, Heidi. 1998. "Adolescent Career Decision Making and the Potential Role of the Public Library." *Public Libraries* 37, no. 6: 376–381.

Julien, Heidi. 1999. "Adolescents' Information Seeking for Career Decision Making." *Journal of the American Society for Information Science* 50, no. 1: 38–48.

KidsHealth.org. Available: http://kidshealth.org/parent/kh_misc/nemours_foundation.html.

Kuhlthau, Carol C., Jannica Heinström, and Ross J. Todd, 2008. "The 'Information Search Process' Revisited: Is the Model Still Useful?" *Information Research* 13, no. 4: paper 355. Available: http://InformationR.net/ir/13-4/paper355.html.

Large, Andrew. 2004. "Information Seeking on the Web by Elementary School Students." In *Youth Information-Seeking Behavior: Theories, Models, and Issues*, edited by Mary K. Chelton and Colleen Cool, pp. 293–320. Lanham, MD: Scarecrow Press.

Meyers, Elaine. 1999. "Coolness Factor: Ten Libraries Listen to Youth." *American Libraries* 30, no. 10: 42–45.

National Center for Education Statistics. 1995. *Services for Children and Young Adults in Public Libraries*. (NCES 95-731). Washington, DC: U.S. Government Printing Office. (Unfortunately, these data have never been updated in exactly the same form for a comparison with present-day trends.)

Nesi, Olga. School Library Media Specialist, I. S. 281, New York City. Personal communication, December 21, 2008.

NoodleTools. 2008. Available: www.noodletools.com/index.php.

Shenton, Andrew K., and Pat Dixon. 2004. "Issues Arising from Youngsters' Information-seeking Behavior." *Library & Information Science Research* 26, no. 2 (Spring): 177–200.

Thompson, Joseph. 2003. "After School and Online." *Library Journal NetConnect*: 35-37. Available: www.libraryjournal.com/article/CA266437.html.

Valenza, Joyce Kasman. 2003. "Wrestling with Teens & Technology: IMing Means Never Having to Say You're Not There." *Voice of Youth Advocates* 26, no. 4: 291.

Young Adult Library Services Association of the American Library Association. *Teens & Social Networking in School & Public Libraries: A Toolkit for Librarians & Library Workers*. 2008. Updated and expanded. Available: www.ala.org/ala/mgrps/divs/yalsa/profdev/SocialNetworkingToolkit_Jan08.pdf.

16

Information Literacy in the Reference Department

Contemporary libraries—whether public, academic, special, or otherwise—are far more than mere storehouses for books and magazines. The dusty monastic scriptoriums of the ancient past, in which volumes were literally chained to the shelves and kept from all but a select few, have disappeared. With few exceptions, today's libraries exist as spaces of dynamic learning in which we actively engage with the products and processes of our culture, exploring the associations and connections between the disparate elements of our changing world. To do so, however, we first need to understand how to use the resources available to us. Many users, daunted by the complexity of our information organizations, give up before reaching this point, content to find what they are looking for on a bookstore's bestseller tables or with a quick Google search. Faced with such despair, passionate librarians have an obligation to make the library a less forbidding space.

Reference services are one of the most ideal means to make the library a nonthreatening environment because it is here that we have the opportunity to teach our users how the library really works. This may seem a surprising proposition at first. After all, isn't the primary function of the reference librarian to point users to the information they seek? To some extent, this is, in fact, the case, but reference is also teaching users how to make sense of the library for themselves—encouraging them to become self-directed, critical thinkers. As has been suggested elsewhere in this book, the reference librarian should be the user's guide on the quest for knowledge, not his or her proxy. We can walk beside our users, but it is rarely a good idea to walk the road for them. In leading them on their path, we can help them find their own sense of direction, developing the skills known as information literacy.

Information literacy is defined as a set of abilities enabling individuals to "recognize when information is needed and have the capacity to locate, evaluate, and use effectively the needed information" (ALA, 1989). Instruction in these activities evolved from Bibliographic Instruction (BI), which sought to "meet basic needs and at the same time teach skills that users can transfer to new situations, new information tools, and new environments to help them learn how to learn" (Grassian, 2004: 52). Typical activities of BI included orientations to the library, classes, tours, pathfinders, credit courses, and development of new instructional materials and guides to using reference tools; it also included experiments in integrating bibliographic instruction into the curriculum. Two pioneers in this area were Evan Farber at Earlham College in Indiana and Patricia Knapp with the Monteith College Library Experiment (Knapp, 1966). Information literacy encompasses and expands the concepts of bibliographic instruction to include outreach, collaboration, and sequenced learning beyond the library (Grassian, 2004).

The American Library Association (ALA) turned its attention to information literacy in 1989, creating a Presidential Task Force on Information Literacy. This led to the creation of the definition cited above and further resulted in the creation of the National Forum on Information Literacy, an organization of more than seventy-five national organizations. Nine years later, ALA issued "A Progress Report: An Update on the ALA Presidential Committee on Information Literacy: A Final Report." This report discussed the activities of the National Forum on Information Literacy.

Education organizations and agencies have also been concerned with information literacy, particularly in relation to new technologies. The National Research Council produced a report on this topic titled "Being Fluent with Information Technology." The term FIT (fluent with information technology) was used to describe people who have achieved a sufficient degree of mastery to use information for problem solving and for critical thinking (Committee on Information Technology Literacy, 1999). The National Council for the Accreditation of Teacher Education has also included information literacy competencies in its standards, as have many other accrediting agencies including the Middle States Commission on Higher Education and the Commission on Colleges and Universities of the Northwest Association of Schools and Colleges.

In the past few decades, a consciousness of the need to foster universal information literacy has been central to libraries' approaches to user orientation. Instead of focusing only on content, libraries now focus on user outcomes and the need to connect users to knowledge. Whether this involves working one-on-one with users, developing online tutorials, presenting information in classroom situations, or working with teachers and faculty to integrate information literacy skills into their lesson plans, the library has a major role to play in information literacy. In the process, the face of information literacy has changed from simply teaching skills to placing an emphasis on encouraging curiosity and creativity. The ability to think and to evaluate information is at the core of this new information literacy. Randy Burke Hensley expresses this well, stating, "fostering an individual's sense of curiosity and creativity in tandem with developing his ability to find, locate, and evaluate information is the essence of information literacy" (Hensley, 2004: 35).

Standards for Information Literacy

In the past decade many organizations have developed standards for information literacy. The first were developed by the American Association of School Librarians (AASL) and the Association of Educational Communications and

Technology (AECT) in 1998. "Information Literacy Standards for Student Learning," in *Information Power*, provided standards by competency area for students in K–12 including standards for information literacy. These standards were replaced by *Empowering Learners: Guidelines for School Library Programs* (AASL, 2009) that emphasized the importance of technology and evidence-based learning and the library as a place that is influenced by its surroundings. AASL also developed *Standards for the 21st-Century Learner* as a guide to learning standards for students. In these standards, students use their skills, resources, and tools to:

Inquire, think critically, and gain knowledge

Draw conclusions, make informed decisions, apply knowledge to new situations, and create new knowledge

Share knowledge and participate ethically and productively as members of our democratic society

Pursue personal and aesthetic growth. (AASL, 2007)

The Association of College and Research Libraries (ACRL) in its 2000 publication *Information Literacy Competency Standards for Higher Education* defined information literacy as the basis for lifelong learning. These standards were instrumental in providing a framework for a discussion of information literacy within higher education (Arp and Woodward, 2002). The standards define an information-literate person as able to:

1. Determine the extent of information needed;
2. Access the needed information effectively and efficiently;
3. Evaluate information and its sources critically and incorporate selected information into one's knowledge base;
4. Use information effectively to accomplish a specific purpose; and
5. Understand the economic, legal, and social issues surrounding the use of information, and use information ethically and legally. (ACRL, 2000)

Approaches to Information Literacy

Many have outlined the components involved in teaching information literacy. One approach is "The Big 6," which was proposed by Eisenberg and Berkowitz (2000) and is now available on a Web site, www.big6.com. The authors outlined a practical six-step strategy for working with learners that could be applied equally well to the reference interaction:

- Defining the information problem;
- Determining the possible sources;
- Locating the sources;
- Using the information and extracting the information needed;
- Organizing the material and presenting it; and
- Evaluating the product and process. (Big 6 Skills Overview, www.big6.com)

Another strategy was proposed by Cunningham and Lanning (2002), who presented various approaches for librarians working with faculty to integrate information literacy into the curriculum including information literacy presentations in a class, working as a liaison with an academic department, and providing workshops for faculty. Conceptual frameworks for instruction were defined by Kobelski and Reichel (1987) and included methods such as teaching systematic literature searching, teaching about primary and secondary sources, understanding citation patterns, understanding how different forms of publications are designed, and understanding index structure and how it is designed to describe content.

Reporting on the ACRL Institute for Information Literacy, Susan Barnes Whyte states, "when we teach, we need to think less about the right way to do research, the right databases. We need to think more about who we're teaching. Ask them what they think they need to know. . . . I think that teaching is a succession of minor epiphanies. . . . It cannot be accomplished in one session or in one year of education. Build upon those epiphanies!" (Whyte, 2001: 2). This approach is further supported by Carol Collier Kuhlthau, who states that a user's needs are best fulfilled by a series of instructional sessions over a period of time rather than just one session. She describes the need for the librarian to intervene and help the user when and where the user's need arises and asserts that this is an individual need (Kuhlthau, 1999).

Information Literacy by Type of Library

Information Literacy in School Media Centers

School media centers try to provide a structured approach to teaching students how to do research in order to prepare them for lifelong learning and for academic research. School media specialists have found that collaborating with teachers is very important to success and that students are best taught using real examples from their school assignments. School media specialists and teachers work together to help students learn to evaluate information sources and to develop search strategies. School media specialists have also found it useful to take high school seniors to a university library and introduce them to the library and its resources. In addition to the AASL standards, school librarians continue to develop and share their strategies for integrating information literacy into new education programs.

Information Literacy in the Academic Library

The academic library is responsible for helping the student to make the transition to more structured research, e.g., researching an assigned topic. The academic librarian must begin wherever the school library left off, continuing to blend the skills of structured information seeking with independent information seeking (Hinchliffe, 2003). In order to do this successfully, the librarian must work with the faculty so that the students learn through subject-specific content rather than just through abstract presentations. As is the case with elementary and high school students, the teachable moment is important. The best time for a student to learn is when he or she has a topic to research. In order to make information literacy sustainable in the university setting, librarians must encourage the faculty to take ownership of information literacy (Bridgeland and Whitehead, 2005: 59).

Information Literacy in the Public Library

The public library is often the first library the child encounters. Here the child learns how to use a library and how to use the information technology independently or with the help of the librarian. The introduction may be one-to-one or may be a class visit to the library. The public library provides for children and adults a continuing experience in independent learning. Here they can explore and grow on their own (Hinchliffe, 2003). Public libraries have become more interested in developing their own approaches to information literacy in recent years. They often partner with the school library to help students learn to use library resources and work with adults returning to school. A library advocacy program developed in 2000 by the ALA continued the articulation of information literacy in the public library with the statement: "Librarians will partner with government, education, business, and other organizations to create models for information literate communities" (ALA, 2000: 5). Public libraries have developed structured programs to introduce users to computers and online databases. Literature in this area of public library information literacy is still sparse but will no doubt continue to increase.

Information Literacy in the Special Library

The special library provides information literacy on a one-on-one basis. Many users of special libraries have already gained some information literacy from public, school, or academic libraries. Because special libraries vary widely, the librarian must introduce the user to the library individually (Hinchliffe, 2003).

Carmel O'Sullivan points out the need for information literacy in a corporate setting. She states that many of the skills needed by workers are part of information literacy including advocacy and inquiry, the ability to learn, networking, resource investigation, IT skills, problem solving, and the ability to review risks, opportunities, and successes (O'Sullivan, 2002). She also points out that the librarian must move beyond the walls of the library and "apply corporate terminology to relevant information concepts" in order to work successfully with employees (O'Sullivan, 2002: 12). Just as in schools and universities, librarians in a special library setting must make their information literacy relevant to the employees.

Social and Ethical Uses of Information

Plagiarism has become one of the greatest problems in the use of information. Real information literacy is more than the simple ability to find what one is looking for; it is the ability to parse, recombine, and make use of such knowledge.

Those who simply appropriate materials without thinking critically about them do not understand how to use information. One of ACRL's standards states that students should be able to "understand the economic, legal, and social issues surrounding the use of information, and access and use information ethically and legally" (ACRL, 2000). The *Information Literacy Standards for Student Learning* also address the social responsibilities of students. Standard 8 states: "The student who contributes positively to the learning community and to society is information literate and practices ethical behavior in regard to information and information technology." This standard goes on to say that the student "respects the principles of intellectual freedom and the rights of producers of intellectual property... [and] applies these principles across the range of information formats—print, nonprint, and electronic."

Lynn D. Lampert has pointed out some of the issues surrounding plagiarism. Often there is no consistent approach by faculty, so the student does not have good guidelines. In other circumstances, it is not clear who is responsible for enforcing plagiarism guidelines, so no one puts them into practice. Finally, Lampert says it is not clear whether the faculty is teaching students to integrate and cite information sources they have used and incorporated into their writing (Lampert, 2004: 349). Arp and Woodward point out that "technology has blurred the once clearly delineated and separate processes of the use of information and its creation. Cutting, pasting, and cropping are simple keystrokes. The knowledge of when these actions are appropriate or inappropriate is not so easily imparted" (Arp and Woodward, 2002: 130). Librarians can improve this situation by teaching how to deal with exact quotations and with paraphrasing and by providing the faculty with resources for explaining what constitutes plagiarism. Many academic libraries provide information on quoting and paraphrasing on their Web sites. Some good examples of online tutorials on plagiarism are: Rutgers University Library at Camden http://library.camden.rutgers.edu/EducationalModule/plagiarism/ and the Library at Acadia University http://library.acadiau.ca/tutorials/plagiarism. The Web site, www.plagiarism.org, is also a good source of information.

One-on-One Instruction

Although we may think of information literacy as a group activity, librarians have traditionally done a great deal of information literacy instruction on a one-on-one basis. In many library situations, librarians use the opportunity of a reference question to provide some individualized library instruction. At times, the help they provide may be as simple as teaching the user how to search the catalog. Where circumstances permit, they may then move on to instruct the user in how to search a particular index or construct a Boolean search string. Alternately, they might be called on to provide a more in-depth research consultation, allowing them the space and time to educate the user about more detailed but important aspects of doing research in a specific subject area.

Those who recommend making instruction a part of the reference encounter advise that the librarian find out what the user already knows to avoid pedantically reteaching familiar skills. The librarian should query the user as to whether he or she would like to learn more about a database or catalog before proceeding, so as to allow the user to learn at his or her own pace. Beck and Turner (2001) recommend that librarians prepare mini lessons that they can teach at the reference desk, supplementing lessons with handouts. Confronted with those unwilling to listen to more formal lessons, librarians can verbalize the search process so that the user understands the steps the librarian is taking and the decisions the librarian is making.

Librarians should also be aware of "the teachable moment." They must decide if the user is receptive to learning and, if so, use this opportunity to impart appropriate information. Susan Avery suggests that librarians should be sure that the user is at the computer keyboard since the user will, no doubt, learn more by doing the search himself or herself (Avery, 2008: 115). This idea of the teachable moment can be extended to chat reference where many librarians mix library instruction with the reference transaction (Johnson, 2003).

Asking questions along the way also helps keep the user engaged in his or her research, thereby demonstrating that the process is as important as the answer. Lisa A. Ellis (2004) describes a topic development exercise that is used in her institution to help students think about their paper topic. This exercise can be done via chat or e-mail. In this exercise, questions are asked about the topic in an effort to further its development. The questions center on what the student already knows and what the student needs to know about the topic. This process helps the student to refine and narrow his or her topic. Jeanne Galvin (2005) suggests that the library should take advantage of out-of-class opportunities to promote and support information literacy. She discusses the use of library pathfinders, individual instruction at the reference desk, instruction in the virtual reference environment, and library Web pages. Galvin points out that the use of assignment-specific pathfinders that are readable and accessible and that can be used by students for completing assignments are more useful than more general pathfinders (Galvin, 2005).

For virtual reference, the librarian can develop short scripted messages to include in the interview or to attach to the information that is provided to the user in order to instruct as the question is answered (Beck and Turner, 2001). "Instruction via chat reference is a prime example of 'learning at the point of need' and librarians have found users very open to learning in the chat reference situation" (Alternative Strategies, 2005: 4).

The librarian can also use the library's Web site as a way to introduce the students to library resources. They can provide Web tutorials or other kinds of Web-based instruction, or list good free Web sites that have been evaluated by the library staff. "A well constructed and carefully maintained portal would be a good vehicle for breaking down the border between the free Internet resources favored by students and authoritative, scholarly databases not available via Google" (Galvin, 2005: 355).

Information Literacy in a Classroom Setting

School and college libraries and, to a lesser extent, public libraries, have tried to integrate information literacy into the classroom. They have worked with teachers and faculty to teach information literacy at the moment when the student most needs it in order to complete a project. By providing this instruction at such a turning point in the research process teachers can maximize the learning experience for the students and guide them to appropriate resources. The teacher or librarian must ask the "why" questions such as "Why would I use one source rather than another?" The openness of such questions forces students to settle on their own answers, ensuring that they will develop the information literacy strategies most suited to their own needs.

Molly R. Flaspohler (2003) studied the effectiveness of an instruction program at a four-year liberal arts college. In this study, librarians, working with faculty who taught an introductory course, taught three library sessions focused on active learning and aimed at improving the students' ability to use library resources including online indexes, and to evaluate and identify appropriate periodical literature. This study showed improvement in the ability of the students to use quality academic resources when information literacy skills are integrated into the curriculum.

Many promote the idea of an across-the-curriculum model in which information literacy is fully integrated into the curriculum. In this way, students learn about research and problem solving as part of whatever subject they are learning. The framework should include:

- Recognizing the need for information;
- Developing skills in using information technologies;
- Accessing information from appropriate sources;
- Critically analyzing and evaluating information;
- Processing and organizing information;
- Applying information for effective and creative decision making;
- Effectively communicating information and knowledge;
- Understanding and respecting the ethical, legal, and sociopolitical aspects of information and its technologies; and
- Developing an appreciation of lifelong learning. (Orr, Appleton, and Wallin, 2001: 459)

D'Angelo and Maid reported on an information literacy program at Arizona State University. In a collaboration between the Multimedia Writing and Technical Communications (MWTC) program and the Library at Arizona State University East, D'Angelo and Maid described a three-credit course "InfoGlut: Deal with It." The course emphasized how to incorporate new information; how to effectively select information; and how to understand issues related to information, including economic, legal, and ethical issues. They reported that students advocated for the inclusion of information literacy in their program; as a result, other courses were identified in which an information literacy component would be added (D'Angelo and Maid, 2004).

Impact of New Technology on the Teaching of Information Literacy

Through the rise of information technology we have taken great steps to expanding and universalizing our access to knowledge. To many, the way the World Wide Web and other innovations have leveled the playing field seems almost like a utopia, a better world in which all are potentially equal. We must remember, though, that the word *utopia* literally means "no place." The price we pay for living in such a world is the obligation to shape it ourselves, making meaning out of the inchoate mass of information with which we are met. As a result, it has become much more important to be able to critically evaluate information sources in order to select the best. The librarian is challenged daily to present to the user information about reliable sources and the differences between leased electronic resources and sources on the Internet.

Information literacy instruction's purpose is to change the way students approach the search for information and to teach them more complex research methods and strategies. This can be done through a variety of instructional approaches including online tutorials (Bloom and Deyrup, 2003: 238). Southeastern Oklahoma State University has developed an interactive tutorial (www.se.edu/lib/distanceedtutorials.htm) that helps students to write a paper. It covers areas such as:

- The types of sources available, such as magazines, books, newspapers, indexes, and the World Wide Web
- Selecting sources, including the difference between library sources and Internet information
- Topic selection and how to narrow the topic
- How to search the catalog
- How to search an index

The University of California at Berkeley Library has developed a tutorial for its students to use in evaluating Web pages. The site, located at www.lib.berkeley .edu/TeachingLib/Guides/Internet/Evaluate.html, encourages students to ask questions that will help them to evaluate a Web page and decide whether it is a reliable source of information. The site suggests:

- Examine the URL to see what it reveals about the site—for example, whether it ends in .edu, .org, or .com
- Examine who the author is, whether it is current, and the author's credentials
- Look for indicators of quality information such as footnotes, permissions to reproduce or copyright information, links to other resources, and what other sites link to this resource

This tutorial shows how complicated it is to examine a site and decide whether it is a good reference to use.

Librarians are also exploring how to integrate information literacy into the various learning management systems such as Blackboard, WebCT, and Sakai.

It is clear that a good way to reach students is to have information literacy tutorials embedded in the learning management systems. Pamela Alexandra Jackson (2007) surveyed California State University librarians about their use of learning management systems as a teaching tool. Based on her survey she made several recommendations as to strategies librarians could use. She suggested having a library learning management system liaison, creating a partnership with the learning management system administrator and the faculty involved in using the learning management system, training librarians to be comfortable using the system, developing information literacy packages that can be included in a learning management system, and participating in discussion boards. Jackson gives examples of information literacy packages developed and used at San Diego State University: Evaluating Information, Popular versus Scholarly, Primary versus Secondary Sources in the Sciences, Developing a Research Strategy, and Avoiding Plagiarism (Jackson, 2007: 458).

Assessment and Evaluation of Information Literacy

Teaching assessment and evaluation is equally as important as teaching the basic research skills found in information literacy programs. To judge the effectiveness of the program, learning outcomes must be determined. These outcomes are influenced by the environment, that is, the type of educational institution or library. The use of multiple assessment tools is recommended, including surveys, focus groups, and assessment built into the assignments.

ACRL's "Characteristics of Programs of Information Literacy That Illustrate Best Practices" states that the ideal information literacy program is one that "establishes a process for assessment at the outset" (ACRL, 2003). In the Assessment/Evaluation section it identifies both outcomes for program evaluation and student outcomes. For program evaluation, it recommends using multiple methods for assessment/evaluation, including formative and summative evaluation and short-term and longitudinal evaluation. For student outcomes, it recommends using a variety of appropriate outcome measures, such as portfolio assessment, oral defense, quizzes, essays, direct observation, anecdotal, peer and self-review, and experience to allow for differences in learning and teaching styles (ACRL, 2003).

Molly R. Flaspohler describes three assessment tools used in her study of the information literacy project conducted at Concordia College. She used an information literacy questionnaire developed by the UCLA libraries, a comparison of the bibliographies of the pilot groups and the control groups to see if the instruction had been successful, and a start/stop exercise that asked the students to write "what they will start doing in the library and what they will stop doing as a result of their session with a librarian" (Flaspohler, 2003: 133). This is a good example of using multiple assessment methods in order to have more than one perspective on the gains achieved.

The most recent information literacy assessment efforts are Project SAILS (Standard Assessment of Information Literacy Skills) and ETSs iSkills™ Assessment (Katz, 2007). Project SAILS began in 2001 as an initiative of Kent State

University. The goal of this project was to develop a standardized test for information literacy skills that would allow librarians to document the skills levels of groups of students. The three-year research and development project in partnership with the Association of Research Libraries in 2003 with funding from IMLS produced the SAILS test. It is a multiple-choice test based on ACRL's *Information Literacy Competency Standards for Higher Education* (www.projectsails .org/sails/aboutSAILS.php?page=aboutSAILS).

The work on the ETS iSkills™ Assessment tool began with an International ICT (Information and Communications Technology) Literacy Panel in 2001. In 2003 a National Higher Education ICT Literacy Initiative was developed that was a consortium of seven colleges and universities working with ETS to develop an assessment test. One of the driving forces behind this effort was the belief of many that the present generation of students are less information savvy and do not have well-developed critical thinking skills. This test is a scenario-based assessment tool that "focuses on the cognitive problem-solving and critical-thinking skills associated with using technology to handle information" (Katz, 2007: 4). The results allow educators and librarians to assess students' strengths and weaknesses in their use of information.

Information-Seeking Behavior

In order to assist users, it is important to understand the stages of the information-seeking process. Carol Kuhlthau's important research into the information-seeking process has been key to understanding these stages. She describes the users' process from the time they become aware of needing information, to their selection of a topic, their exploration of the topic and its various facets, their formulation of a more focused topic based on their exploration, their actual collection of information for their project, and finally their presentation of the results of their findings (Kuhlthau, 1993: 170–172). In order to successfully help a user, the librarian must try to understand where the users are in their information seeking. Kuhlthau further defines the various degrees of assistance librarians can offer as they interact with users from simply organizing the materials in order for the users to work on their own to actual counseling of users in need of more assistance as they progress in the search process (Kuhlthau, 1993: 175).

Further Considerations

Information literacy is an ongoing topic of interest; it is no more likely to go away than the books we store on our shelves. Staying at the cutting edge of this fundamental part of our professional activities, especially as it applies to reference services, is an obligation. Fortunately, many of the leading library publications have taken up the call to provide this information: The *Reference & User Services Quarterly*, *Reference Services Review*, *College and Research Libraries*, and the *Journal of Academic Librarianship* are among the journals that regularly publish articles on information literacy. Articles can also be found in *Knowledge Quest* and *School Library Journal*. The American Association of School Librarians and the Association of College and Research Libraries have started an information literacy listserv to allow librarians to share information.

Concepts regarding information literacy have changed. Concepts have progressed from a concentration on content to a concentration on how people learn. The idea of presenting information about the library and research in small amounts and integrating it into the curriculum are important new directions for this vital service. Finding quality information can be challenging for the user. Librarians can help the user identify high-quality information sources through well-thought-out information literacy programs.

Recommendations for Further Reading

Avery, Elizabeth F. 2003. *Assessing Student Learning Outcomes for Information Literacy Instruction in Academic Institutions*. Chicago: ACRL.

Badke, William. 2008. "Information Literacy Meets Adult Learners." *Online* 32, no. 4 (Summer): 386–391. An interesting article on techniques for working with adults who are going back to school and need to understand how to do research in the digital age.

Brier, David J., and Vickery Kaye Lebbin. 2004. "Teaching Information Literacy Using the Short Story." *Reference Services Review* 32, no. 4: 383–387. An approach to information literacy through the use of short stories. Provides course instructors with examples of how to use the short story to discuss information literacy standards.

Brown, Cecelia, Teri J. Murphy, and Mark Nanny. 2003. "Turning Techno-Savvy into Info-Savvy: Authentically Integrating Information Literacy into the College Curriculum." *The Journal of Academic Librarianship* 29, no. 6 (November): 386–398. Describes an approach to information literacy that combines the traditional instruction with novel approaches that appeal to college students' reliance on Internet search engines.

Bury, Sophie, and Joanne Oud. 2005. "Usability Testing of an Online Information Literacy Tutorial." *Reference Services Review* 33, no. 1: 54–65. Discusses the usability testing of an online information literacy tutorial designed for freshman undergraduates at the Wilfrid Laurier University Library. The findings were useful in making revisions and enhancements to the tutorial.

Buschman, John, and Dorothy A. Warner. 2005. "Researching and Shaping Information Literacy Initiative in Relation to the Web: Some Framework Problems and Needs." *Journal of Academic Librarianship* 31, no. 1 (January): 12–18. A discussion of the need to develop other frameworks of analysis to shape our knowledge of academic information seeking and the Web.

Collen, Lauren. 2008. "Teaching Information Literacy in the Public Library." *Knowledge Quest* 37, no. 1 (September/October): 12–16. An exploration of the role public libraries can play in helping students develop good research skills.

Davis-Kahl, Stephanie, and Lisa Payne. 2003. "Teaching, Learning and Research: Linking High School Teachers to Information Literacy." *Reference Services Review* 31, no. 4: 313–319. Teacher professional development, and university and library outreach activities and influences are described to provide an overview of the Compton Teacher Information Literacy Institute curriculum development. Curriculum remodeling after a mid-year assessment is also discussed.

Gilstrap, Donald L., and Jason Dupree. 2008. "Assessing Learning, Critical Reflection and Quality Educational Outcomes: The Critical Incident Questionnaire." *College and Research Libraries* 69, no. 5 (September): 407–426. The article documents a successful use of the critical incident questionnaire to evaluate information literacy.

Harding, Jane. 2008. "Information Literacy and the Public Library." *Australasian Public Libraries and Information Services* 21, no. 4 (December): 157–167. With an international focus, Harding discusses examples of public library information literacy programs in many different countries.

Harris, Benjamin R. 2008. "Communities as Necessity in Information Literacy Development: Challenging the Standards." *Journal of Academic Librarianship* 34, no. 3 (May): 248–255. Looks at the role that communities, defined in the broadest sense, can play in information literacy.

Hoffman, Paul S. 2002. "The Development and Evolution of a University-Based Online Library Instruction Course." *Reference Services Review* 30, no. 3: 198–211. Describes the development and evolution of an introduction to library research course into an online course that integrated information literacy into the curriculum through the general education program at the University of Nebraska.

Johnson, Anna Marie. 2003. "Library Instruction and Information Literacy." *Reference Services Review* 31, no. 4: 385–418. An annotated bibliography of literature on library instruction and information literacy for all types of libraries. Most articles are from 2002.

Johnson, Anna Marie, and Sarah Jent. 2004. "Library Instruction and Information Literacy—2003." *Reference Services Review* 32, no. 4: 413–442. An annotated bibliography of literature recently published on the topic of library instruction and information literacy in academic, school, public, and special libraries.

Kenney, Barbara F. 2008. "Revitalizing the One-Shot Instruction Session Using Problem-Based Learning." *Reference & User Services Association Quarterly* 47, no. 4 (Summer): 386–391. The author focuses on the need to develop a curriculum and be very focused in a one-shot instruction session.

Lenholt, Rob, Barbara Costello, and Judson Stryker. 2003. "Utilizing Blackboard to Provide Library Instruction: Uploading MS Word Handouts with Links to Course Specific Resources." *Reference Services Review* 31, no. 3: 212–218. Librarians at Stetson University describe how they integrated library instruction materials into the course management system.

Lindauer, Bonnie Gratch. 2004. "The Three Arenas of Information Literacy Assessment." *Reference & User Services Quarterly* 44, no. 2 (Winter): 122–129. A solid article on information literacy assessment that includes organizations and resources dealing with this area.

Malenfant, Chuck, and Nora Egan Demers. 2004. "Collaboration for Point-of-Need Library Instruction." *Reference Services Review* 32, no. 3: 264–273. Describes a project in which the librarian and member of the teaching faculty collaborated on an advanced information literacy experience. They found that offering advanced information literacy to upper-class students at their point of need increased their interest and participation in the program.

McMillen, Paula S., Bryan Miyagishima, and Laurel S. Maughan. 2002. "Lessons Learned about Developing and Coordinating an Instruction Program with Freshman Composition." *Reference Services Review* 30, no. 4: 288–299. Describes a collaboration between the Oregon State University Libraries and the university's freshman composition program. The article outlines the process followed by the coordinators of the instruction program and the important role they can play.

Neely, Theresa Y. 2007. *Information Literacy Assessment: Standards-Based Tools and Assignments*. Chicago: American Library Association. A useful guide that provides librarians with information about using assessment measures in their assignments.

Ondrusek, Anita 2008. "Information Literacy." In *Academic Library Research: Perspectives and Current Trends*, edited by Marie L. Radford and Pamela Snelson. Chicago: ALA. A good overview of the subject.

Owusu-Ansah, Edward K. 2004. "Information Literacy and High Education: Placing the Academic Library in the Center of a Comprehensive Solution." *The Journal of Academic Librarianship* 30, no. 1 (January): 3–16. The author suggests a comprehensive approach to help all students receive instruction in information literacy.

Phillips, Lori, and Jamie Kearley. 2003. "TIP: Tutorial for Information Power and Campus-Wide Information Literacy." *Reference Services Review* 31, no. 4: 351–358. A description of the Web tutorial developed by the University of Wyoming Libraries focused on the ACRL Information Literacy Competency Standards.

Radcliff, Carolyn, Mary Lee Jensen, Joseph E. Salem, Jr., Kenneth J. Berhann, and Julia A. Gedeon. 2007. *A Practical Guide to Information Literacy Assessment for Academic Librarians*. Santa Barbara, CA: Libraries Unlimited. This recent work discusses both formal and informal methods of assessment in detail.

Ragains, Patrick. 2006. *Information Literacy Instruction That Works: A Guide to Teaching by Discipline and Student Population*. New York: Neal-Schuman.

Seamans, Nancy H. 2002. "Student Perceptions of Information Literacy: Insights for Librarians." *Reference Services Review* 30, no. 2: 112–123. First-year students at Virginia Tech were questioned about their use of information using both e-mail questioning and face-to-face interviews. The data collected resulted in ways to improve library services for first-year students.

Sharkey, Jennifer K., and F. Bartow Culp. 2005. "Cyberplagiarism and the Library: Issues and Solutions." *The Reference Librarian* no. 91/92: 103–116. Deals with plagiarism in academic institutions influenced by the easy availability of online resources.

Somerville, Mary M., and Frank Virotto. 2005. "If You Build It with Them, They Will Come: Digital Research Portal Design and Development Strategies." *Internet Reference Services Review* 10, no. 1: 77–94. A pilot that builds information literacy into academic curricula of agribusiness through the portal Web-based design process.

Wood, Gail. 2004. "Academic Original Sin: Plagiarism, the Internet, and Libraries." *The Journal of Academic Librarianship* 30, no. 3 (May): 237–242. Describes an information literacy and integrity model to help students distinguish between their own ideas and those of others.

Bibliography of Works Cited in This Chapter

American Association of School Librarians. 2007. *Standards for the 21st-Century Learner*. Chicago, IL: AASL. Available: www.ala.org/aasl/standards.

American Association of School Librarians. 2009. *Empowering Learners: Guidelines for School Library Programs*. Chicago, IL: AASL.

American Association of School Libraries and the Association of Educational Communications and Technology. 1998. *Information Power: Building Partnerships for Learning*. Chicago: ALA. Available: www.ala.org/ala/aasl proftools/informationpower/informationliteracy.htm.

American Library Association. 1989. *Presidential Committee on Information Literacy*. Chicago, IL: ALA.

———. 2000. *Library Advocacy Now! Action Pack: A Library Advocate's Guide to Building Information Literate Communities*. 2000. Chicago, IL: ALA.

Arp, Lori, and Beth S. Woodward. 2002. "Recent Trends in Information Literacy and Instruction." *Reference & User Services Quarterly* 42, no. 2 (Winter): 124–132.

Association of College and Research Libraries. 2000. *Information Literacy Competency Standards for Higher Education*. Chicago, IL: ACRL. Available: www .ala .org/ala/acrl/acrlstandards/informationliteracycompetency.htm.

———. 2003. "Characteristics of Programs of Information Literacy That Illustrate Best Practices: A Guideline." Chicago, IL: ACRL.

Avery, Susan. 2008. "When Opportunity Knocks: Opening the Door Through Teachable Moments." *The Reference Librarian* 49, no. 2 (#102): 109–118.

Beck, Susan E., and Nancy B. Turner. 2001. "On the Fly BI: Reaching and Teaching from the Reference Desk." *The Reference Librarian* no. 72: 83–96.

Bloom, Beth, and Marta Deyrup. 2003. "Information Literacy Across the Wired University." *Reference Services Review* 31, no. 3: 237–247.

Bridgeland, Angela, and Martha Whitehead. 2005. "Information Literacy in the 'E' Environment: An Approach for Sustainability." *Journal of Academic Librarianship* 31, no. 1 (January): 54–59.

Committee on Information Technology Literacy. 1999. *Being Fluent with Information Technology*. Washington, DC: National Academies Press. Available: www.nap.edu/catalog/6482.html.

Cunningham, Thomas H., and Scott Lanning. 2002. "New Frontier Trail Guides: Faculty-Librarian Collaboration on Information Literacy." *Reference Services Review* 30, no. 4: 343–348.

D'Angelo, Barbara J., and Barry M. Maid. 2004. "Moving Beyond Definitions: Implementing Information Literacy Across the Curriculum." *Journal of Academic Librarianship* 30, no. 3 (May): 212–217.

Eisenberg, M. B., and R. E. Berkowitz. 2000. *Teaching Information and Technology Skills: The Big 6 in Secondary Schools*. Worthington, OH: Linworth Publishing.

Ellis, Lisa A. 2004. "Approaches to Teaching through Digital Reference." *Reference Services Review* 32, no. 2: 107.

Flaspohler, Molly R. 2003. "Information Literacy Program Assessment: One Small College Takes the Big Plunge." *Reference Services Review* 31, no. 2: 129–140.

Galvin, Jeanne. 2005. "Alternate Strategies for Promoting Information Literacy." *Journal of Academic Librarianship* 31, no. 4: 352–357.

Grassian, Esther. 2004. "Building on Bibliographic Instruction." *American Libraries* 35 (October): 51–53.

Hensley, Randy Burke. 2004. "Curiosity and Creativity as Attributes of Information Literacy." *Reference & User Services Quarterly* 44, no. 1 (Fall): 31–36.

Hinchliffe, Lisa Janicke. 2003. "Examining the Context, New Voices Reflect on Information Literacy." *Reference & User Services* Quarterly 42, no. 4 (Summer): 311–317.

Jackson, Pamela Alexondra. 2007. "Integrating Information Literacy into Blackboard: Building Campus Partnerships for Successful Student Learning." *Journal of Academic Librarianship* 33, no. 4 (July):454–461.

Johnson, Patricia E. 2003. "Digital Reference as an Instructional Tool: Just in Time and Just Enough." *Searcher* 11: 31–33.

Katz, Irvin R. 2007. "Testing Information Literacy in Digital Environments: ETS's iSkills Assessment." *Information Technology and Libraries* 26, no. 3: 3–12.

Knapp, Patricia. 1966. *The Monteith College Library Experiment*. Metuchen, NJ: Scarecrow Press.

Kobelski, Pamela, and Mary Reichel. 1987. "Conceptual Frameworks for Bibliographic Instruction." In *Conceptual Frameworks for Bibliographic Education: Theory into Practice*, edited by Mary Reichel and Mary Ann Ramey, pp. 3–10. Littleton, CO: Libraries Unlimited, Inc.

Kuhlthau, Carol Collier. 1993. *Seeking Meaning: A Process Approach to Library and Information Services*. Norwood, NJ: Ablex Publishing Corp.

———. 1999. "Accommodating the User's Information Search Process: Challenges for Information Retrieval System Designers." *Bulletin of the American Society for Information Science* 25, no. 3 (February-March): 12–17.

Lampert, Lynn D. 2004. "Integrating Discipline-Based Anti-plagiarism Instruction." *Reference Services Review* 32, no. 4: 347–355.

Orr, Debbie, Margaret Appleton, and Margie Wallin. 2001. "Information Literacy and Flexible Delivery: Creating a Conceptual Framework and Model." *Journal of Academic Librarianship* 27, no. 6 (November): 457–463.

O'Sullivan, Carmel. 2002. "Is Information Literacy Relevant in the Real World?" *Reference Services Review* 30, no. 1: 7–14.

Project SAILS. Available: www.projectsails.org/sails/aboutSAILS.php?page=aboutSAILS.

Whyte, Susan Barnes. 2001. "From BL to IL: The ACRL Institute for Information Literacy." *OLA Quarterly* 7, no. 2 (Summer): 14–15.

Woodward, Beth S. 2005. "One-on-One Instruction: From the Reference Desk to Online Chat." *Reference & User Services Quarterly* 44, no. 3 (Spring): 203–209.

Part IV
Developing and Managing Reference
Collections and Services

17
Selecting and Evaluating Reference Materials

Of all the sections of a library collection, the reference collection must be the most focused, specific and selective. Although far smaller than circulating collections, the works they contain are often more expensive than those found elsewhere. Consequently, developing a reference collection must be carefully orchestrated, each step requiring great thoughtfulness and care. To stay balanced and keep the collection from toppling over into the abyss of redundancy and irrelevance, the book selector must combine knowledge and experience to great effect. Each choice must be made with care, allowing the library to best leverage its resources and ensuring that neither money nor shelf space goes to waste. As has been suggested in the previous chapters, thoughtful evaluation of relevance and currency is crucial with each individual purchase, but those responsible for development must also possess the following:

- Knowledge of the library's community of users and their needs and interests
- Knowledge of how different types and formats of reference materials are used
- Knowledge of subject areas and how much updating they need
- Knowledge of how to evaluate reference materials

More often than not, these areas are interdependent. Note, for example, that an understanding of the library's users often goes hand in hand with the type of library and the educational level of the community it serves.

The takeaway-point here is that selectors must be willing to think out of the box and look beyond their immediate spheres of influence. Thus, academic librarians must take the various disciplines studied at their university or college into account when considering purchases. The needs and interests of this community are defined by the college or university's curriculum as well as the research needs of both students and faculty. As the curricula change, the academic library must respond by adding new reference materials that will meet these new needs. Likewise, public libraries must respond to the requests for information from members of their communities. The response should reflect users' wide-ranging information needs and interests from educational and career interests to hobbies and leisure reading. Public libraries have the most diverse user body. Their audience includes children, teens, and adults of all ages and all backgrounds. Consequently, reference collection development must take into account the widest possible range of users. School libraries serve a community of students and faculty. They tailor their collections to the subject areas being studied in the school as well as the interests of their user group. Special libraries serve the needs of their community of users, be they museum curators, hospital employees, businesspeople, or others. Their users have very specific information needs and interests that may change over time.

The ways in which knowledge is sought out and used by a library's patrons also plays a crucial part in the shaping of the reference collection. If the users tend toward factual information, the library may collect a large number of ready reference materials or build a ready reference section on its Web site. If queries tend more toward in-depth research, the library should concentrate on indexes and other reference sources that lead the user to full-text information. Sometimes libraries will need specialized materials such as maps or government documents. Alternatively, they may need collections of directories to meet certain kinds of requests.

By understanding characteristics of specific types of materials the libraries can tailor their collections to meet user needs. Formats of reference materials are much more important than ever before. In particular, libraries must decide how to balance print and electronic acquisitions. This may be based on the way the library's users request and utilize materials or the most suitable format for particular types of material. In general, there is now less demand for print resources since users tend to prefer electronic resources. Resources may also be purchased on CD-ROM or microform if they are necessary, but rarely used, guaranteeing patron access while freeing up shelf space. Alternate media may also be selected in some circumstances if they provide a more inexpensive way to provide access to the information.

A comprehensive knowledge of relevant subject areas will help the librarian decide how much material is needed to fully cover any given topic. Again, it is helpful here to think in terms of what users need and want. Sometimes, if demand is low, a single book or database is sufficient coverage for a given subject area, while in other subject areas multiple titles are needed to support the user requests. Further, titles about subjects in flux will have to be weeded and replaced with much greater rapidity, meaning that those responsible for reference collection development must stay abreast of changes in the field. Returning to the question of formats, note that frequent content changes in a subject area may call for the purchase of or subscription to online resources that are regularly updated.

Finally, as should by now be obvious, knowing how to evaluate reference materials is key to the success of a reference department. This requires both knowledge of how reference materials are used and knowledge of the subjects of the materials. Careful examination of the many important criteria is essential, as well as deciding for a particular work what the most important characteristics are. For many subject areas there may be more than one choice. Knowing the library's users ensures that the librarian can select the materials best suited to this particular audience.

Although reference collection development may appear to be one-dimensional, it actually includes a number of different tasks, such as:

- Identifying, selecting, and evaluating new reference material
- Management of the reference budget, including approval plans, standing orders, exchange agreements, and cooperative collection development
- Ongoing assessment of the reference collection
- Weeding the reference collection
- Writing and updating a reference collection development policy
- Promoting and marketing new reference materials to the library's users

Identifying, Selecting, and Evaluating New Reference Materials

Many reference materials are published both in print format and as an electronic database, whereas others are available in only one of these formats. Since most reference collections can acquire only a selection of the available titles, all decisions must be made thoughtfully. Reference materials should be selected either through personal examination, reference to literature produced by the publisher, reading of reviews, or some combination of the three.

Sources of Reviews

Reviews are one way of obtaining information about reference materials. *Booklist*'s *Reference Books Bulletin, Library Journal, School Library Journal, Choice,* and *Reference & User Services Quarterly* are the review sources most frequently consulted by librarians searching for reviews of new reference titles.

Booklist is published by the American Library Association twice monthly September through June and monthly in July and August. The purpose of *Booklist* is "to provide a guide to current library materials in many formats appropriate for use in public libraries and school library media centers. Materials are recommended for reasons relating to both quality and demand." "Reference Books Bulletin," a section of each issue of *Booklist,* states "reference sources are those designed by their arrangement and treatment to be consulted for specific items of information rather than to be read consecutively... that would be of interest primarily to public libraries and school media centers" (www.ala.org/ala/aboutala/office/publishing/booklist_publications/booklist/insidebooklist/booklistpolicy/booklistselection.cfm). The reviews in "Reference Books Bulletin" are prepared and critiqued by members of the editorial board and by contributing reviewers and represent the board's collective judgment. Each issue includes reviews of adult and youth reference titles. The reviews are well written and thorough. Occasional special sections on types of material or one subject area such as an annual review of encyclopedias or a page devoted to science databases are among the best to be found. This review source is available online.

Reference & User Services Quarterly is published by the Reference and User Services Association of the American Library Association. This journal is devoted to articles on all aspects of reference services. Each issue includes a "Reference Books" column that reviews twenty-five to thirty reference titles. The signed reviews both describe and critically evaluate each work.

Library Journal, a publication of Media Source, Inc., is published twice a month. A "Reference" section in each issue looks at about fifteen to twenty reference titles with a recommendation as to whether the title is recommended and for what type of library. Cheryl LaGuardia writes an "eReviews" column in each issue reviewing in depth one subscription database. *LJ* also publishes regularly on its Web site many reviews of e-reference materials (www.library journal.com).

School Library Journal, also published by Media Source, Inc., is a magazine for librarians who work with young people in schools or in public libraries; in it are two reference-related columns "Digital Resources" and "Reference Reviews." Suggestions as to which titles should be purchased are clearly made.

Choice is published monthly by the Association of College and Research Libraries. It is a book review service designed to support undergraduate library collections. *Choice*'s reference reviews are divided into General, Humanities, Science & Technology, and Social & Behavioral Sciences. More than sixty reference titles are reviewed in each issue. These reviews are written by academic scholars and librarians and, similar to the other titles discussed above, include a recommendation as to whether the text should be purchased and the types of libraries for which it is recommended. Electronic resource reviews are integrated with the print material reviews. Each issue includes a bibliographic essay pointing to resources in a particular subject area. *Choice* reviews are also available online at www.cro2.org.

ARBA (*American Reference Books Annual*), published by Libraries Unlimited, reviews all new reference works in print, online, or on CD-ROM published in the United States and Canada during the year. The reviews are arranged by four broad subject categories—general reference, social sciences, humanities, and science and technology. It is an important source of information about reference materials and includes some professional materials. This reference tool is also available online. The online version (www.arbaonline.com) covers 1997 to date and is updated monthly with 100 to 150 additional reviews.

In addition to the publications described previously, a number of annual lists of recommended reference titles are produced by committees and publications. These include *Outstanding Reference Sources*, a list compiled annually by a RUSA committee and published in May in *American Libraries*, and *Best Reference Sources*, an annual list compiled by *Library Journal* and published in the April issue. Reference reviews also appear on the Gale site (www.gale. cengage.com/reference/) under "Guest Columnists." The four columns include "Peter's Digital Reference Shelf," in which Peter Jacso reviews online and CD-ROM products; a review of public and academic reference resources by John R. M. Lawrence called "Lawrence Looks at Books"; "Reference Unbound" by Wendy Stephens that reviews print and online resources for

K–12; and "Doug's Student Reference Room" that reviews both print and online resources for K–12 as well as a "Reference Archive."

Other retrospective guides to reference materials include *Guide to Reference*; *The New Walford Guide to Reference Resources* (three volumes); *Recommended Reference Books for Small and Medium-Sized Libraries and Media Centers*; and *Reference Sources for Small and Medium-Sized Libraries*. For further information about these titles, please see the "Resources Discussed in This Chapter" section.

Evaluation Criteria

In order to determine which reference materials to purchase, the materials must meet certain evaluation criteria. In general, these criteria apply to both print and electronic materials:

- Scope
- Quality of content
- Accuracy of content
- Currency
- Authority of author and/or publisher
- Ease of use including usability, searching capabilities, and response time (for electronic resources)
- Arrangement of material
- Appropriateness to the audience/meeting of user needs
- Format
- Cost

When evaluating a reference work, it is important to understand its scope and purpose. In printed works the author usually discusses this in the preface or introduction. This should include a discussion of what the work covers, including topics such as how comprehensive it is, whether it covers allied fields, the dates covered, and whether the work includes only information from the United States or is international in scope. Reference to this information will give the librarian a way to compare this work with similar reference works on the same subject and to decide if this one is a necessary addition to the collection. Determining the scope of an electronic database is often more difficult, as there is rarely a direct equivalent to the preface and access to nonsubscribers may be limited. Often the printed material from the publisher describing the electronic database includes information on scope, and the Web site of the company may also be a source of information. In electronic versions of print resources, coverage is still an issue, as it is important to determine whether the digital version offers anything newer than the print version and, if so, what time period it covers. Questions of duplication are critical because most libraries cannot afford to have identical print and electronic resources.

The quality of the content has become particularly important in electronic resources because the librarian appears to have less control over what content the publisher chooses. Quantity is not as important as quality here. Quality content can be defined as accurate, up-to-date information of sufficient depth for the intended audience. Given the diversity of reference titles on almost every subject imaginable, librarians must try to distinguish between the good and the bad. A close examination of a title will reveal whether it has material that is not found in other similar titles or presents the material in a unique way. This would be a good reason for purchasing this title.

The authority of the reference work is indexed by the qualifications of the author or the publisher. The author may be someone known for authoring reference materials. Some publishers have a good track record in a certain area of reference material, meaning that the selector can begin the examination of the work with some confidence that the publisher will produce a credible work. Remember, though, that even the most seemingly authoritative work still needs to be examined for accuracy and currency. Accuracy can be tested by comparing it to other works on the same topic. Currency can be tested by checking to see if recent information on a specific topic is included in the work and checking the dates of resources cited. It is also important to note the cutoff date in relation to the publication date for this reference work. To test this, in the case of electronic databases, choose a current topic or a recent world event and see how current the information on that topic is.

Electronic resources should be examined for usability. Here, the most relevant factors are whether the program is easy to search and how quickly it responds to commands and queries. In addition, the resource should be examined to see if it can accept Boolean operators, whether it has both basic and advance search capabilities and whether it can easily be browsed. These issues of manipulating the database are one set of criteria that applies exclusively to electronic resources. The electronic resource should also provide a "Help" option and a "How to" guide.

Examining the arrangement of the reference work will determine whether its sections are organized and indexed in such a way as to facilitate easy access to the information it contains. Good organization separates a truly useful reference work from a text or simply a well-written work on a subject. The print reference work needs to have good page layout with many headings to make it easy to scan the pages. A sufficient amount of white space is needed, and a typeface that is clear and easy to read. The reference work must also have a good table of contents and index with cross-references where appropriate. An electronic work should use a thesaurus or accepted list of subject headings such as the Library of Congress Subject Headings as well as cross-references to enable the user to find the information easily. An intelligible interface and searchable help files are equally significant ways to enable the user to understand how to search the database easily. Because choices must often be made about which format materials should be purchased, it is important to consider the form that will best convey a title's content. Some information is still appropriately in print format whereas other material lends itself to electronic format. If the content changes often, it may be best in electronic format since the changes are easily made online. Indexes for periodicals and newspapers are far superior in electronic format since new material is being indexed constantly. Directories are another good candidate for the electronic format since addresses, phone numbers, e-mail addresses, etc., are constantly changing. Other reference works may be best or very acceptable in print. These include atlases, some ready reference materials, and handbooks.

The audience for the reference work must be considered in purchasing. A good reference work that is not for the audience of a particular library is not a good purchase. For example, a science handbook that is aimed at a university or professional audience will not be appropriate in a high school library. Reference works on the same subject are usually available on a variety of levels so that there is an appropriate title for the library's audience. On this account, it may be helpful to consider where in the professional literature a work has been reviewed. A text spotlighted in a school library publication will probably be inappropriate for the main research library of a large university. An astute selector should be able to determine this information on his or her own, however, as it should be clear on consideration of the text.

Format has been a tremendously complicated issue for librarians as reference sources have changed from print to electronic. The choices continue to be complex for a variety of reasons. First, not all reference sources are available in both print and electronic versions, so librarians who need a particular work must acquire it in whatever format is available. Second, if both print and electronic versions are available, the choice will depend on the library's user population and the library's budget. Academic libraries, for example, want most reference sources in electronic format since their user population wants off-site access. Public and school libraries have more choices since they have users who want print and users who want electronic. Also, public and school libraries do not always have a large enough budget to support a large number of electronic resources. Third, some reference resources are very acceptable in print such as atlases and maps and some ready reference sources.

Cost may be the final determination as to whether to purchase a specific reference work. For most subjects several reference works are available and the librarian can choose based on any or all of the criteria above. But in the end—all other factors being equal—price may be the determining concern. In the case of electronic resources the library may want to be part of a consortium in which it can share costs to afford the more expensive electronic resources.

Choosing Between Print and Electronic Resources

Many factors go into the decision as to which format to buy. Usually it is a decision based on the library's own needs. Some factors that may influence a library's decision are how often the resource is updated, whether everything in the print version is included in the electronic version, the years of coverage, the ease of use, and whether the resource is compatible with the library's technology infrastructure. For many academic libraries electronic resources are the best choice for many materials since students want to use the resources out-side of the library and at any hour. In public libraries the choice may not be so clear, because most public libraries have a wide range of users—many of whom are probably not accustomed to doing all their research electronically or simply prefer print resources. Sometimes the decision must be to duplicate the resource in print and electronically because it is so heavily used that it makes sense to have both. Encyclopedias are an example of a resource that is useful to have in both print and electronic format, as the print set will accom-modate more users at one time. Some reference materials are really still best in print, because not all digital conversions are as good as their original sources. Materials where visual browsing within the text is useful are still best in print. Although there is not a large place for CD-ROMs in the library today, there may still be occasions when it makes sense to buy a CD-ROM. Some examples of this might be a seldom updated bibliography or a dictionary.

Management of the Reference Budget

Librarians must learn to manage and maximize the library's reference budget. Reference departments typically have a specific annual budget. Depending on the size and administrative complexity of the institution this may be one budget or may be divided into a number of categories such as print, electronic, approval plans, standing orders, and specific subject areas. Either way, the staff must make a plan at the beginning of the year as to how the budget will be distributed. In academic and large public libraries approval plans and standing orders play a major role in the reference budget. Money must be allocated at the beginning of the year to pay for these plans. Reference works may come as part of a larger library approval plan or the library may set up approval plans with reference publishers. Electronic resources may include contracts paid for by the library and cooperative arrangements with library consortia. Most libraries have found it economical to join or form consortia for the purpose of purchasing electronic resources. This has made it possible to buy more titles for a more reasonable price. Another way to build collections without spending more money is to develop exchange agreements with other institutions and libraries. Some institutions publish quality journals as a way of being able to exchange with other institutions.

Ongoing Assessment of Reference Collections

Collections should be assessed on a regular basis to ascertain whether the materials meet the needs of the users and whether the selections are worth the cost. This is a two-pronged process that involves both determining gaps in the existing collection and evaluating the quality of available resources. On the former count, the library might want to look at the questions it received and could not answer and the interlibrary loans placed because the material was not available at the library. In addition to this, it is wise to browse the shelves to see if the collection appears balanced in relation to the current interests of the library's users. Is there too much material on subjects no longer of interest to the users? Is more material needed on subjects that have recently become more popular?

Collections may be assessed in a number of ways. For example, the staff could check the collection against standard lists such as the *Guide to Reference, Resources for College Libraries, Recommended Reference Books for Small and Medium-Sized Libraries and Media Centers,* or *Reference Sources for Small and Medium-Sized Libraries.* Alternatively, the staff could use the conspectus approach developed by the Research Libraries Group, which evaluates the level of materials in each subject area (i.e., 1 is the minimal level, 2 is the basic information level, 3 is the instructional support level, 4 is the research level, and 5 is the comprehensive level) and whether the level reflects the emphasis and interest in the subject area as reflected in the use of the materials. Third, the library could compare its holdings with comparable libraries using OCLC's WorldCat Collection Analysis or comparable programs.

User satisfaction can also be ascertained by questionnaires to the library's users—in person, by mail or e-mail, through interviews, and through feedback at the reference desk.

Weeding the Reference Collection

Weeding or deselection is an important part of reference collection development. Reference collections by their very nature must have the most current information to accurately answer users' questions. Anything less than the most current information possible is simply not acceptable. Accordingly, removing dated materials from the collection must take high priority. Current thinking dictates that print reference collections should be smaller since many materials are available electronically and are much more suitable in that form.

The criteria for weeding reference materials in any type of library are as follows:

- The content is no longer up to date or accurate.
- A new edition is available.
- The reference work is seldom used.
- The information is duplicated in another reference work.
- The book is worn out.

Libraries may want to use the same guidelines for weeding reference materials as for circulating nonfiction. Libraries will want to identify subjects that date quickly and weed those areas more often. History, art, literature, philosophy, and religion are seldom weeded, whereas science, medicine, and some of the social sciences require continual updating. Libraries do not necessarily replace all annuals each year. Because of the cost considerations some annuals are replaced every two or three years. Encyclopedias are often rotated out of the collection; five years is the longest an encyclopedia should be kept in a reference collection (Nolan, 1998: 162–163). Cumulative sets are usually maintained such as *Current Biography* unless they become available online at an affordable price.

It is useful to have an organized approach to weeding so that within a particular time period all materials have been reviewed. A weeding team is a good approach so that materials in question can be discussed and decisions made as to whether to discard, move to the circulating collection, or put in storage.

Writing a Reference Collection Development Policy

Reference collection development policies provide a way to document current practices in a reference department and to set directions for their future development. This is useful for guiding the present staff in their work, orienting new staff, and providing information to the users. It also provides consistency and continuity within the library as staff changes. Although the reference collection development policy need not repeat details about collection development that have already been documented in the library's overall collection development policy, it does help to document separately the collection development activities of the reference department, especially as it reflects some practices that differ from the rest of the library. The primary parts of this policy should include:

- Introduction that describes the library, its clientele and its areas of research or reference service
- Description of the scope and size of the collection
- Formats of materials collected, with a separate section on electronic resources
- Collecting levels by subject
- Types of reference materials collected
- Description of the responsibilities of staff and others for selection
- Criteria for selection, assessment, and weeding
- Sources of funding
- External relationships with other libraries, consortial arrangements, and resource sharing

In the *introduction* the policy should describe briefly the library, its goals, and its clientele. This introduction should also provide an overarching statement about the goals of the reference collection, which might be to provide accurate, up-to-date information or to support educational and informational needs. If others use the library who are not the primary clientele, this should be mentioned, as well as how the library serves them. For example, some university libraries are open to the general public as well as to the school's employees and students. With the increase in distance learning the policy might want to discuss how the library serves this part of its users.

In the *description of the scope and size* of the collection the library needs to describe the subject areas covered by the reference collection. This may be different from the circulating collection or may mirror it. In any case, it is important to describe what the collection does and does not include. For example, the library may not buy textbooks or may not purchase materials in certain subject areas. The size of the collection is equally important. Today the size must include both print and electronic resources so the description may begin to differ from previous policies.

The *formats of materials collected* should be outlined. Here the library should discuss how it decides whether to buy a reference work in print or in an electronic format and when it might buy both. It is also important to state whether microform collections continue to be maintained and whether CD-ROMs continue to be purchased. This area of electronic resources has become an important part of the collection. Guidelines must be set up to help staff and users understand how these decisions are being made. Some of the issues that need discussion are whether electronic resources will be offered for remote use, criteria for purchase of electronic resources, and consortial relationships. Future plans for electronic resources might be outlined here.

Subject collecting levels and the *types of reference* materials collected reflect the use of the reference collection. The subject levels might be explained using the Research Library Group system or another system that describes subject levels. The library might also want to list some specific types of reference materials it collects, such as government documents, maps, etc. The reference collection is developed and maintained based on user requests and interests. This can change over time as user needs move in new directions.

Staff usually have specific collection development responsibilities. Each staff member may be responsible for a certain area of the collection. In an academic library the faculty as well as the library staff may have some responsibility for collection development. Some libraries use committees to discuss proposed additions to the reference collection. This may be particularly true for electronic resources, since their cost is so much greater than that of a reference book.

The library should outline the *criteria used for selection and for weeding*. General guidelines are discussed elsewhere in this chapter.

It can be helpful to discuss in general terms *the funding of the library's collection*. Many people have no idea of how a library is funded and the limits of its budget.

Finally, the policy should *discuss relationships* that the library has with other libraries, such as the consortia agreements between academic institutions discussed throughout this chapter. The policy will document whatever agreement has been developed with other libraries, whether for print or electronic materials.

An example of a general statement about the reference collection is the following from Indiana University-Purdue University Fort Wayne:

> The reference collection supports the research needs of IPFW students, faculty and staff. It contains such materials as abstracts and indexes, encyclopedias, dictionaries, atlases, directories, bibliographies, statistical compilations, and handbooks. The reference collection primarily supports IPFW academic programs. Reference works that provide basic bibliographic access to or an overview of other academic disciplines are also selected. (www.lib.ipfw.edu/2909.0 html)

Promoting and Marketing Reference Materials to Library Users

Promoting and marketing reference materials have recently increased in importance because of the advent of electronic resources. These new resources often remain hidden from users unless they are making extensive use of the library's Web site. Most libraries believe that their electronic resources are underutilized by their users. In the hopes of rectifying this situation, many have begun to take more active steps to increase the visibility of these resources among library users.

Two important areas must be addressed in promoting these resources: The first is the staff. Many electronic resources are added to the collection in a short time such that the staff does not have much time to get acquainted with them. It is important to go back and refresh the staff's knowledge of these databases. Some libraries send out a writeup on a different database each week or month. Other libraries ask staff members to each study a particular database and then make a presentation. For the users, the library can feature a "database of the week" or month on the library's Web site. The librarians can feature databases in newsletters and on bookmarks, or they can encourage staff to tell users about the electronic databases.

Regardless of the approach taken, it is crucial that the contents of the collection be advertised to the library's users. Reference work is, after all, predicated on service, and unless the collection is put to use in real, practical scenarios it does little good.

Recommendations for Further Reading

Beals, Jennifer and Ron Gilmour. 2007. "Assessing Collections Using Brief Tests and WorldCat. Collection Analysis." *Collection Building* 26, no. 4: 104–107. A report on using the Brief Test approach to collection evaluation.

Bradford, Jane T. 2005. "What's Coming off the Shelves? A Reference Use Study Analyzing Print Reference Sources Used in a University Library." *The Journal of Academic Librarianship* 31, no. 6 (November): 546–558. A four-month study of print materials at the Stetson University Library concluded that the reference collection was too large and was not well used.

Clendenning, Lynda Fuller, J. Kay Martin, and Gail McKenzie. 2005. "Secrets for Managing Materials Budget Allocations: A Brief Guide for Collection Managers." *Collections, Acquisitions & Technical Services* 29, 1: 99–108. A step-by-step guide to managing individual funds within a library's materials budget.

Crosetto, Alice et al. 2007. "Assessment in a Tight Time Frame: Using Readily Available Data to Evaluate Your Collection." *Collection Management* 33, no. 1/2: 29–50. The William S. Carlson Library at the University of Toledo needed to move the reference and circulation collections to make room for an information commons. This proved to be an opportunity to evaluate the collection.

Doll, Carol A., and Pamela Petrick Barron. 2002. *Managing and Analyzing Your Collection: A Practical Guide for Small Libraries and School Media Centers.* Chicago, IL: American Library Association. An easy-to-use guide to collection analysis and weeding.

Johnson, Peggy. 2009. *Fundamentals of Collection Development and Management.* 2nd ed. Chicago, IL: American Library Association. An excellent recent addition to the literature on collection development.

Landesman, M. 2005. "Getting It Right—The Evolution of Reference Collections." *The Reference Librarian* no. 91/92: 5–22. Discussion of the changing nature of reference collections.

Samson, Sue, Sebastian Derry, and Holly Eggleston. 2004. "Networked Resources, Assessment and Collection Development." *Journal of Academic Librarianship* 30, no. 6 (November): 476–481. An evaluation of networked resources as they relate to the library's collection development policy.

Singer, Carol A. 2008. "Weeding Gone Wild: Planning and Implementing a Review of the Reference Collection." *Reference & User Services Quarterly* 47, no. 3: 256–264. A review of the reference collection at the Jerome Library at Bowling Green State University because of the proposed move of the science reference collection to the Jerome Library.

Tucker, James Cory, and Matt Torence. 2004. "Collection Development for New Librarians: Advice from the Trenches." *Library Collections, Acquisitions & Technical Services* 28, no. 4: 397–409. Practical advice on collection development for the new librarian.

Twait, Michelle. 2005. "Undergraduate Students. Source Selection Criteria: A Qualitative Study." *The Journal of Academic Librarianship* 31, no. 6 (November): 567–573. Twait studied a group of undergraduate students to determine what criteria they used in selecting sources to use.

Tyckson, David. 2005. "Reference Classics Ahead of Their Time." *Against the Grain* 17, no. 4 (September): 22–28. Based on an ALA program in 2005 that discussed what makes a reference classic.

Wilkinson, Frances C., and Linda K. Lewis. 2005. "Reference eBooks: Does an eBook on the Screen Beat One on the Shelf?; Discussion on Electronic Reference Books with Seven Academic Librarians." *Against the Grain* 17, no. 4 (September): 1, 18, 20, 22. This article explores the rapidly changing world of reference books—the ways that electronic reference books are being selected, purchased, and budgeted.

Wu, Michelle M. 2005. "Why Print and Electronic Resources Are Essential to the Academic Law Library." *Law Library Journal* 97, no. 2 (Spring): 233–256. The author argues that both print and electronic resources are needed.

Resources Discussed in This Chapter

Kieft, Bob, ed. *Guide to Reference.* Chicago, IL: ALA. Available: www.guidetorefer ences.org/HomePage.aspx.

New Walford's Guide to Reference Resources. 2005. 3 vols. London: Facet; distr. by Neal-Schuman.

O'Gorman, Jack, ed. 2008. *Reference Sources for Small and Medium-Sized Libraries*. 7th ed. Chicago, IL: ALA.

Recommended Reference Books for Small and Medium-Sized Libraries and Media Centers. 1981–. Englewood, CO: Libraries Unlimited. Annual.

Resources for College Libraries. 2006. 3rd ed. New Providence, NJ: ACRL/ CHOICE and R. R. Bowker.

Bibliography of Works in This Chapter

Bates, Marcia J. 1986. "What Is a Reference Book: A Theoretical and Empirical Analysis." *RQ* 28 (Fall): 40–43.

Doll, Carol A., and Pamela Petrick Barron. 2002. *Managing and Analyzing Your Collection: A Practical Guide for Small Libraries and School Media Centers*. Chicago, IL: ALA.

Gwinnett County Public Library. 1998. *Weeding Guidelines*. Chicago, IL: Public Library Association.

Nolan, Christopher W. 1998. *Managing the Reference Collection*. Occasional Paper #27. Chicago, IL: ALA.

Perez, Alice J. 2004. *Reference Collection Development: A Manual*. 2nd ed. Chicago, IL: RUSA.

18

Managing Reference Departments

Of Car Designs and Learning Styles

Much before the general economic recession that came to a head in 2008, General Motors, once the largest employer in the United States, had the thankless job of announcing the layoff of 30,000 workers, just prior to the Thanksgiving holiday of 2005. Many of those workers, according to a commentator, "... were its best and most productive. Their bosses simply couldn't give them a car to build that Americans really wanted to buy" (Bai, 2005:15). In other words, despite stellar staff and a conscientiously produced product, it was management that had failed in its primary duty of making effective business decisions. The fallibility of their decision making was further traced to an inability or unwillingness to "let consumers drive its designs."

Library management has traditionally looked to corporate management for guidance. For reference managers of the twenty-first century a clear cautionary tale can be salvaged from GM's managerial pileup. The consumers of reference services are information seekers, and information is mined according to their individual learning styles. Do information seekers of the twenty-first century have learning styles that are intrinsically different from the past? If we peer through the mists of time, we can see Socrates surrounded by a group of students who have presumably traveled from many directions to quite literally be at the feet of the master in their search for answers. If we flip forward two-and-a-half millennia to the Simon Fraser University in Canada or Harvard University in Boston, we see reference librarians toting laptop computers, primed to instantaneously assist students in their search for answers. So yes, the "design" has changed and there is such a thing as a twenty-first-century learning style.

It is a style that has developed a muscular expectation for rapid and on-demand information. Fueled by this expectation, the organization of reference delivery and access continues to change in many ways. The reference manager of the twenty-first century must not only be acutely sensitized to the evolving environment, but must be prepared to ably administer and manage dramatic new service models, information delivery systems, and innovative staff configurations. All this must be done while gracefully accepting the additional new roles thrust upon them by the continuing changes.

Organizing Reference Departments

Traditionally, the management of reference departments has cohered to a hierarchical principle that upholds a scalar chain of command. While elements of that chain continue, the hierarchy is perforce flattening out to accommodate the vibrant new roles and services necessitated by the new learning style (see Table 18-1).

Table 18-1. Changing Paradigms in Reference Management		
Traditional	**→**	**Emerging**
Hierarchical	*Organization*	Flattened
Stationary	*Service Delivery*	Spatial
Specialized	*Staffing*	Multidisciplinary
Isolated	*Work*	Integrated
Independent	*Structure*	Interdependent
Inductive	*Logic*	Deductive
Materials	*Mission Focus*	Users

Self-directed or team-based management has made some inroads into traditional hierarchies. Since 1998 the Ohio State University Health Sciences Library has instituted the Reference and Information Services Team (RIST), a "self-regulating management team" that has adopted a system of rotating coordinators rather than a head of reference to manage the team. All members of the team are given the opportunity to learn one another's jobs with the idea of making reference services more integrated (Bradigan and Powell, 2004). The Valley Library at Oregon State University has also subscribed to "team-based management" that employs workgroups and coordinating advisory councils to replace top-down decision making (McMillen and Rielly, 2003).

Various persuasive analyses have been offered attesting to the intrinsic value of self-managed teams. It has been argued that "members feel a moral sense to make the approach work so as not to let down other members" (Young, 2004: 185); there is flexibility in being able to respond quickly to problems without consulting a chain of authority (Poon-Richards, 1996); and the opportunity exists to provide professional development for a wider swathe of reference librarians (McMillen and Rielly, 2003).

However, these are all perceived advantages accruing to nonhierarchical administrative models in any scenario, not specifically the one facing the twenty-first-century reference manager. The reason these models are appearing in the current environment is *because* of the current environment. The explosion of changing technology requires a far more diverse body of talents and experience. As James Neal (2005) points out in his presentation at the ACRL (Association of College and Research Libraries) Twelfth National

Conference, a "new generation of feral professionals" is brought about by the "expanding number of positions in functional specialist, computer systems, and administrative services." In addition, the rapid change in service needs demands a higher degree of coordination and "synergistic problem-solving" (Kelly, 1998: 8). These have combined to limn the advantages of flexibility, dimensionality, and personal motivation inherent to self-directed management.

By logical extension, once the environment is not marked by such intense flux and changing expectations, the relevance of self-directed teams could dim. This in fact already holds true for smaller public libraries, where the change in user needs and the induction of technological innovations is more gradual. The emergence of self-directed teams is, not surprisingly, dominant in academic libraries, where both the expectation and delivery of changing technologies is most insistent. In a study covering changes in the role of academic librarians, it was found that the highest percentage of change in both job activities and reference tools was a spin-off of changes in technology. Electronic collection development, e-mail reference, online searching, and designing Web pages marked the largest change in job activity. Online databases, the World Wide Web, e-mail, and electronic dictionaries and indexes counted for the most dramatic change in reference tools used (Cardina and Wicks, 2004).

Organizing Staff

Given that staff costs account for 50 to 80 percent of a public library's operating budget (Goodrich, 2005), the onus of providing the wisest possible allocation of staff time lies heavily on the head of the reference manager. According to an earlier time-management analysis, "the allocation of staff time to the reference desk is one of the most important library personnel issues" (Dennison, 1999: 158).

The Reference Desk

In 1967, a minimum standard for staffing public libraries was published by the American Library Association such that x number of staff, y number of books, and z square footage of building per capita was deemed as necessary. The logic girding this prescriptive and quantitative model did not prove very effective. Currently, and in the foreseeable future, the staffing of reference derives from the type of deductive logic provided by confirmed user needs.

At the Winona State University Library, for example, data on actual usage of the reference desk was recorded for both the number of requests and the level of difficulty in answering the requests. Based on these data, suggestions for double staffing the desk at particular times of the day and designating on-call reference librarians were proposed (Dennison, 1999). "Staffing for Results," published as part of the PLA (Public Library Association) Planning for Results series, also subscribes to deductive principles of staffing so that the number and type of staff is a function of proven local needs and priorities rather than a formulaic allocation based on a priori assumptions (Mayo and Goodrich, 2002).

In many cases, the primacy of the reference desk as the nexus for all information needs is being consciously muted. As Karyle Butcher states, "The physical reference desk has become the place where librarians catch their breath between patrons. It is less and less the place where actual reference service takes place" (1999: 351).

In the academic libraries of York College, Pennsylvania, the Merced Library at the University of California, and Northwest Missouri State University, for example, the reference desk has been completely phased out and reference librarians are seen by appointment. Ready reference questions are handled at a general-purpose desk that covers circulation and the more basic technological problems faced by users. This model has taken on different variations in different institutions. The medical library at the Johns Hopkins University and the Arizona State University West libraries staff the all-purpose desk with paraprofessionals. Brandeis University libraries employ graduate students. The University of North Carolina at Charlotte uses both paraprofessionals and student assistants to staff a "first point of service," complemented by referrals to more in-depth research by professional reference librarians (Bailey and Tierney, 2002). At the University of Arizona, if ready reference available at the general-purpose desk is not what is required by the user, a subject specialist is either called or the user fills out an online form for the specialist who will then get back to the user (Bracke, Chinnaswamy, and Kline, 2008).

The model of an "information commons" aims to integrate all reference activities into a one-stop shop, so that students and faculty are provided with a "seamless continuum...from planning and research through presentation into final product" (Bailey and Tierney, 2002: 284). Further discussion on how such models feed into a viable picture of the future of reference is found in Chapter 21.

Management of Service Delivery

Service delivery has undergone perhaps the most dramatic transformations. With the growing pervasiveness of digitized information, electronic databases, the all-consuming Internet, IM (instant messaging), podcasting, blogging, RSS (Really Simple Syndication), and virtual and chat reference, teamed with the ubiquity of desktop, laptop, and notebook computers, wireless networking, and cell phones with IM capability, the delivery of reference services is at a whole new level.

Roving or Mobile Services

Traditionally, the term "roving reference" implied a model whereby reference librarians were encouraged to be less stationary in their traditional posts behind a reference desk and more proactive in approaching users. As Suzanne Tronier, the manager of the East Millcreek Library of the Salt Lake County Library System, succinctly explained in a Publib Listserv exchange,

Our librarians are expected to contact people in the library during the first part of their roving shift, helping as needed. After that they provide back up for the reference desk, put out new arrivals and straighten displays; they can weed or do other projects in the stacks and otherwise make themselves available for questions. In some areas of the library…just working in that area will invite questions. (12/22/2005)

Reference librarians at the Salem-South Lyon District Library in Michigan have found it effective to carry a tablet PC with them as they rove the stacks and help patrons as they browse (Hibner, 2007).

A more dramatic interpretation of roving librarians has them ranging far beyond the confines not only of the desk, but of the library building as well. At Harvard University, the roving librarian provides "reference on the road" by strategically roving the undergraduate student center with laptop in hand. Given the wealth of electronic databases and online resources available, these librarians are able to either answer or direct a large part of the research interests of the students milling around the center. Similarly, the "Ask Us Here!" initiative at the Bennett Library of the Simon Fraser University in Canada has two choice "service locations" with a "high volume of pedestrian traffic" (Wong and O'Shea, 2004: 91). Here the research needs of students are either referred appropriately or answered by reference librarians with wireless laptops. The librarians at the University of Montana subscribe to "outpost reference," which involves roving around student dormitories and the student union. It was found that the student union was the more effective venue because there was more consistency and reliability in location and schedule (Hines, 2007).

Virtual Services

The successful integration of remote access to reference information and services has created an important additional responsibility for reference managers. Hiring or training staff to provide this service, apportioning staff time, effectively evaluating the services provided, and staying on top of the quicksilver advances in remote access technology must all become part of the management environment.

24/7 Access

The most robust form of virtual reference has been live, 24/7 access, i.e., "chat" reference. Recent literature on the provision of this form of virtual reference suggests that its cost-effectiveness can vary dramatically from one institution to another. While individual libraries that provide virtual reference can pay up to $12,000 annually for merely retaining the infrastructure, consortial arrangements can whittle down the cost to $3,000 (Bailey-Hainer, 2005). A thought-provoking study by Steve Coffman and Linda Arret (2004) questioning the viability of chat reference has been answered by equally convincing proponents of its cost effectiveness (Tenopir, 2004). Reference managers following the debate may also want to track the developments of various national and statewide collaborations, some of which are listed in Table 18-2.

Table 18-2. Select Examples of Collaborative Virtual Reference Services

Service	URL	Area	Activated	Libraries
ASKaLibrarian	http://askalibrarian.org	Florida	2003	109
Q&A NJ	www.qandanj.org	New Jersey	2001	51
NCknows	www.ncknows.org	North Carolina	2004	121
L-net	www.oregonlibraries.net	Oregon	2003	38
KnowItNow	www.knowitnow.org	Ohio	2004	78
AskUsNow	www.askusnow.info	Maryland	2003	40
AskColorado	www.askcolorado.org	Colorado	2003	74
QuestionPoint: 24/7 Reference	www.questionpoint.org	Global	2001 (merger 2005)	Nearly 1500

The attraction of virtual reference collaborations can also be traced internationally. The People's Network Enquire is a U.K. initiative that has been put together by over eighty public libraries under the sponsorship of the Museums, Libraries and Archives Council. The ZLB (*Zentral-und Landesbibliothek*) of Berlin provides e-mail reference in German, English, French, and Turkish through active partnerships with other libraries in Europe (IFLA 2005). These collaborative ventures, then, appear to be the most viable models of 24/7 virtual reference access (Bailey-Hainer, 2005).

Reference managers wanting to organize virtual reference services for their institution can refer to ALA's guidelines at www.ala.org/ala/mgrps/divs/rusa/resources/guidelines/virtrefguidelines.cfm. Helpful survey planning documents marking the initiation of these services can also be found at the URLs given in Table 18.2. Project management software tools, such as MSP2000 (Microsoft Project), are handy organizers to both scope and monitor the introduction of such services. An example of the use of this tool is found in the study by Zhang and Bishop (2005).

"Ask A" Services

In addition to virtual reference offering both e-mail and live reference services through statewide collaboration, a dizzying variety of individual initiatives are available to the reference manager.

- Michigan State University, for example, installed a Trillian-based IM service with the idea that it enhanced virtual reference by providing "convenience" to the many users who already used IM (Behm, 2005). The Schreyer Business Library at Pennsylvania State University also embraced IM as a potentially high-use addition to its virtual services (Zabel, 2005).

- The Orange County Library Systems were the first public library system to adopt RSS (Really Simple Syndication) to enhance its content distribution and have been followed by thousands of other libraries. The Pepperdine University Libraries, MIT Libraries, and Baylor University Libraries, for example, offer RSS feeds for newly cataloged titles. The Hennepin County Library and the Seattle Public Library provide feeds for items checked out and titles on hold. The new generation of feeds also includes audio files (Podcasts) and video files (Vodcasts).
- Reference libraries are also including special enhancements to Web contact center software such as VoIP (voice-over Internet protocol), which allows for vocal interaction; "knowledgebases" that hold frequently asked questions and answers; and improved co-browsing even with proprietary databases (Coffman, 2001). The Salem-South Lyon District Library in Michigan has enhanced speedy and effective reference service through the induction of VoIP so that staff can communicate with one another when they have a question (Hibner, 2007). One of the earliest and most comprehensive "knowledgebases" is "Start," created by a member of MIT's InfoLab Group at the Artificial Intelligence Laboratory and accessible at http://start.csail .mit.edu/index.html.

Increasingly, all libraries, be they academic, public, corporate, special, or school libraries, are setting up Web sites with some form of "Ask a Librarian" service.

New Roles

In a study of the Executive Leadership Institute instituted by the Urban Libraries Council to develop strong future managers, the authors found that successful participants were, among other things, "intrigued by recreating libraries through new business models" and "comfortable with messy, complex partnerships" (Nicely and Dempsey, 2005: 3–4). As outlined above, new business models marked by a flattening of the hierarchy, multi-professional staffing, and innovative service delivery systems unrestricted by stationary physical locations are par for the course being followed by reference managers of the twenty-first century. In addition, though, is the recognized value of getting comfortable with "messy partnerships." Some recurring areas requiring reference managers to get "messy" are in the field of electronic resource management, Web management, and reference marketing.

Electronic Resource Management

"Buying electronic information is more expensive and more complicated than purchasing print information" (Butcher, 1999: 350). That truism must leap out to the reference manager who must plan, choose, negotiate, and finally budget for every database that is purchased. Guidelines for implementing collection development policies, such as whether a print resource needs to be replaced or complemented with an electronic counterpart, must be prepared. Given that academic libraries reportedly budget 61 percent of their resources on electronic material (Albanese, 2004), planning a reflective and judicious budget can be a demanding task, requiring a change in traditionally held collection policies.

Vendor negotiation and site licensing agreements have evolved into art forms demanding far greater sophistication on the part of the reference manager (Brevig, 2008). The variety and scope for negotiation tends to fracture into as many possibilities as vendors available to provide them. Given this, decisions on whether and how to join the simplifying construct of a consortium become relevant (Hiremath, 2001). Consortial initiatives such as the International Coalition of Library Consortia at www.library.yale.edu/consortia; the Washington Research Library Consortium at www.wrlc.org; or the Statewide California Electronic Library Consortium at http://scelc.org, to name just a few, have the potential to exponentially power both the breadth and depth of access to electronic databases for individual libraries. Legal issues of copyright compliance need to be mastered and conveyed to users in effective ways, even as these issues continue to get "more complex and more blurred" (Wamken, 2004).

Web Management

A library's Web site is both the introductory façade to the institution and the user's first step to dipping into the library's reference services and tools. It is no wonder then that the responsibility of Web site content invariably falls on the reference department. Managers of the twenty-first century must be geared to either take on—or at minimum, share—the task of developing and maintaining Web sites.

A 2001 survey of the 122 members of the American Research Libraries found that 98 percent of reference librarians worked at "developing, editing, revising, and updating" Web content (Ragsdale, 2001: 9). Depending on the size, structure, and motivations of the library, the management of Web projects can take on many permutations, from the employment of a single Webmaster to a Web committee, to a distributed system involving input and coordination with collection development staff, catalogers, and bibliographers. The reference manager must also prepare for messier strains of Web responsibilities. As pointed out by Butcher, with the digitization of information becoming a rising expectation, "faculty look to librarians to participate in campus partnerships concerning the storage and retrieval of information" (Butcher, 1999: 351).

The soaring popularity of Web2.0 social networking tools has further complicated the content management of library Web pages. Increasingly interactive online experiences have conditioned users to expect a site that is not only informative, but also personalized to their needs, capable of active bi-directional communication, and collaborative. Next generation Web management must necessarily incorporate the idea that what was once "a solitary experience has become a social one" (Del Pinto, 2009: 41) and both design and manage library Web sites accordingly.

Reference Marketing

Although nonprofits have been using marketing techniques in recent decades, libraries have been slow to realize the need to *market* reference resources and services. Relative to Google and Wikipedia, electronic resources are invisible to most users. This feeling of invisibility has caused librarians to ensure that their users are more aware of what they have available by creating "an E-Buzz" that uses new technologies to both market and promote resources in strategic and creative ways (Dubicki, 2008). "Marketing" is a broad term that includes public relations, advertising, contacts with community groups, and more. Marketing can involve a cost to the library or can be almost cost free.

Developing a plan for the reference marketing project is the first step. For a public library it will be necessary to define a target audience, which might include students, senior citizens, teachers, businesspeople, freelancers, government officials, professionals, etc., and faculty, students, and administrators for an academic library. The library's market could also be defined by demographics such as age, gender, income, education, occupation, ethnicity, etc. The next step is to list the reference resources and services that the library offers and wishes to promote to its users. This could include electronic databases, the library's virtual reference service, or the library's e-book collection.

Many strategies can be used to promote these resources and services. Consider both the low-cost and more costly possibilities. These range from brochures, newsletters, newspaper articles, newspaper ads, direct mail, radio and TV advertising, and promotion on the Internet. For potential users, the library could develop subject pathfinders in print or on the Web that will bring an awareness of relevant and available electronic databases. Information on any reference resource or service can be highlighted on the library's home page. The Web is an inexpensive and powerful way to provide information to the library's users, such as online newsletters that can be sent to them on a regular basis. A simple bookmark with information about reference resources and services can also serve as a reminder to library users. The library's public relations office may want to place news stories or articles about the library's reference resources and services. Staff can promote reference resources by making presentations to community groups, faculty or student groups, or to the employees of local institutions and organizations. With a budget for paid advertising, the library can promote its reference services and resources through newspaper ads and radio or TV spots. Define what results are being sought before beginning, so there is a way to measure success.

Although general marketing of services and resources is effective, libraries can also consider the techniques of niche marketing, which is aimed at a specific audience such as senior citizens, students, businesspeople, etc. By using niche marketing the message can be made more detailed and specific. To do this, the reference manager will need to focus on a particular resource or service (or a group of them) and consider who might benefit from these resources and services (Walters, 2004). For example, a message aimed at the business community could discuss the kinds of information available through electronic databases that identify new places to advertise, new audiences for their products, and new advertising techniques that are cost-effective.

Relationship marketing is another technique that reference managers should consider. This kind of marketing goes a step beyond traditional marketing by developing interactive programs with the customers. This is an excellent technique for reference libraries because it allows long-term partnerships based on listening closely to user needs and developing strategies that respond to those needs. In this kind of marketing, all staff play a role in carrying the library's message to the users. Relationship marketing involves a greater degree of flexibility and creativity in meeting the user's needs and interests (Walters, 2004), but is ideally suited to the marketing of reference resources and services.

Virtual Reference Service Evaluation

In addition to evaluating traditional reference services, one of the new duties demanded of the reference manager is to administer and evaluate the many permutations of virtual reference services. Whereas in-person reference transactions quite naturally focus on the reference interview and answer, virtual reference has a dual focus. Both human interaction and digital competency vie for attention. A successful virtual reference transaction is highly dependent on effective chat software, bandwidth speed, and a robust workstation.

The ability to co-browse so that the librarian can directly demonstrate a search to the user; page-pushing software that can transfer files and screen shots without cutting and pasting; file sharing from proprietary databases; the ability to archive pages; concurrent usage with more than one user at a time; customizable user and library information; queuing options such as call selection; scripted messages; transference of active sessions; provision of final transcripts with hyperlinks; in-built statistical assessment tools and surveys; and troubleshooting assistance are just some of the cogs that keep the wheels of virtual reference moving smoothly. These are also some of the criteria for initial selection of software technology.

In addition to the choosing, assessing, and constant upgrading of virtual technology, managers are responsible for relatively involved logistical factors. Collaborative virtual services, such as those listed earlier in this chapter, are increasingly becoming the norm. The parameters of individual contributions have to be decided, effective liaison procedures need to be instituted, and the scheduling of staff time, training, and evaluation slotted into place.

Further Considerations

In their study of the management of libraries and information centers, Stueart and Moran (2007: 15) present five "functions common to all managers":

1. Planning
2. Organizing
3. Staffing
4. Directing
5. Controlling

For reference managers, technological innovations of tsunami proportions have compulsively created changes in all five functions. *Planning* of both strategic and long-term reference services and tools must necessarily incorporate the expectations of a demanding new learning style typical of users of the twenty-first century. The learning style, in turn, has fed into new experiments with the *organization* of reference departments so that a variety of models leaning toward lateral coordination can facilitate quick information services, rather than pyramidical hierarchies that are typically less flexible. *Staffing* must necessarily be more multidisciplinary to cater to different varieties of reference service delivery ranging from traditional in-person desk reference to 24/7 remote access services. Reference managers, faced with rapid changes, must be motivated to take on new and unexpected roles that could involve "messy partnerships" with players as varied as Web developers, electronic database vendors, and statewide consortia. Finally, the *control* of reference services is best maintained through a canny mix of effective marketing and vigilant evaluation.

Recommendations for Further Reading

Arthur, Gwen, ed. 2000. *Get Them Talking: Managing Change Through Case Studies and Case Study Discussion*. Chicago, IL: American Library Association. Published as RUSA Occasional Paper # 25, this hands-on approach to management problems regularly faced by reference departments in both academic and public libraries is useful to help managers think through the recurring challenges brought about by change.

Boss, Stephen C., and Lawrence O. Schmidt. 2007. "Electronic Resources (ER) Management in the Academic Library: Process vs. Function." *Collection Management* 32, no.1/2: 117–140. The article studies best practices of private industries as they dealt with change-management and applies it to academic libraries faced with dramatic changes in structure, workflow, and reference format brought about by technological advances.

Brevig, Armand. 2008. "Getting Value from Vendor Relationships." *Searcher* 16, no. 9 (October): 28–34. According to a recent study (see "Managing Mass..."), managing e-content is the biggest worry for reference managers. This paper clearly lays out strategies for assessing collection goals and vendor relations in order to develop excellence in the art of negotiation. Real-life examples are helpfully provided by the author from his library at AstraZeneca, the Anglo-Swedish pharmaceutical company that has directly linked corporate strategy with an information acquisition vision for the library's e-resources. This is a stimulating paper for reference managers ready to face their first vendors.

Buff, Hirko, and Mary Bucher Ross. 2004. *Virtual Reference Training: The Complete Guide to Providing Anytime, Anywhere Answers*. Chicago, IL: American Library Association. With the increasing prominence of virtual reference, this book not only provides an in-depth review of Washington's Statewide Virtual Reference Project, but supplies the reference manager with an easy-to-follow program for training virtual staffers, developing policies, and assessing effectiveness.

Gandhi, Smita. 2004. "Knowledge Management and Reference Services." *The Journal of Academic Librarianship* 30, no. 5 (Summer): 368–381. This article provides a clear and compelling argument for reference managers to embrace the corporate reliance on knowledge management (KM), whereby cumulative staff knowledge is retrievable. KM initiatives such as Refquest and Common Knowledge Database that already exist in some academic libraries are also reviewed.

Kinkus, J. 2007. "Project Management Skills: A Literature Review and Content Analysis of Librarian Position Announcements." *College & Research Libraries* 68, no. 4 (July): 352–363. Given the increasing complexity of the library world, the author argues that expertise is needed from multiple departments. This, in turn, argues for a strong need to place project management as a core requirement in new library management skills, much as it is in professions such as construction, pharmaceuticals, finance, and the software industry. The author reviews the content of both 1,180 library job advertisements and library curricula to support the contention that project management is an increasing requirement for all successful library managers and must become an integral part of basic training as well.

Neal, James G. 2005. "Raised by Wolves: The New Generation of Feral Professionals In the Academic Library." Paper presented at the ACRL Twelfth National Conference, Minneapolis, MN, April 7–10. Available: www.ala .org/ala/acrl/acrlevents/neal2-05.pdf. In this article, the author poses interesting questions on the organization, training, and overall management of academic library staff with formal training in disciplines other than library science.

Resnick, Taryn, Ana Ugaz, Nancy Buford, and Esther Carrigan. 2008. "E-Resources: Transforming Access Services for the Digital Age." *Library Hi Tech* 26, no. 1 (Winter): 141–157. A thought-provoking case study of new styles in staffing management tried out at the University Libraries of Texas A&M found that the reference experience for users of electronic resources was greatly enhanced by the inclusion of reference librarians who were adept at managing and licensing electronic resources. The importance of technical service librarians who can keep up with the explosion of database resources was suggested by this study.

Sarkodie-Mensah, Kwasi, ed. 2003. *Managing the Twenty-First Century Reference Department: Challenges and Prospects*. Binghamton, NY: The Haworth Press, Inc. With a stellar collection of articles selected from the 2003 issue of *The Reference Librarian*, this resource brings focus to management as it pertains specifically to reference departments in libraries. From training a new head of reference, to core competencies required for a leader, to managing an academic reference department, and collaborative leadership, the collection is informative.

Bibliography of Works Cited in This Chapter

Albanese, Richard Andrew. 2004. "The Reference Evolution." *Library Journal* 129, no. 19 (November 15): 10–12, 14.

Bai, Matt. 2005. "New World Economy." *New York Times Magazine* (December 18): 15.

Bailey, Russell, and Barbara Tierney. 2002. "Information Commons Redux: Concept, Evolution, and Transcending the Tragedy of the Commons." *Journal of Academic Librarianship* 28, no. 5 (September): 277–286.

Bailey-Hainer, Brenda. 2005. "Virtual Reference: Alive & Well." *Library Journal* 130, no. 1 (January 15).

Behm, Leslie. 2005. "Adoption of Instant Messaging for Chat at a Research Library in Conjunction with the Formal Chat Software Used." Presented at the Virtual Reference Desk Conference, November 15. Available: http://librarianinblack.typepad.com/librarianinblack/2005/11/adoption_of_ins.html (accessed January 18, 2006).

Bracke, Marianne Stowell, Sainath Chinnaswamy, and Elizabeth Kline. 2008. "Evolution of Reference: A New Service Model for Science and Engineering Libraries." *Issues in Science and Technology Librarianship*, no. 53 (Winter-Spring). Available: www.istl.org/08-winter/index.html (accessed January 24, 2009).

Bradigan, Pamela S., and Carol A. Powell. 2004. "The Reference and Information Services Team." *Reference & User Services Quarterly* 44, no. 2 (Winter): 143–149.

Brevig, Armand. 2008. "Getting Value from Vendor Relationships." *Searcher* 16, no. 9 (October): 28–34.

Butcher, Karyle. 1999. "Reflections on Academic Librarianship." *Journal of Academic Librarianship* 25, no. 5 (September): 350–354.

Cardina, Christen, and Donald Wicks. 2004. "The Changing Roles of Academic Reference Librarians Over a Ten-Year Period." *Reference & User Services Quarterly* 44, no. 2 (Winter): 133–142.

Cassell, Kay Ann. 1999. *Developing Reference Collections and Services in an Electronic Age: A How-To-Do-It Manual for Librarians*. New York: Neal-Schuman.

Coffman, Steve. 2001. "Distance Education and Virtual Reference: Where Are We Headed?" *Computers in Libraries* 21, no. 4 (April): 20.

Coffman, Steve, and Linda Arret. 2004. "To Chat or Not to Chat." *Searcher* 12, no. 8 (September): 49–56.

Del Pinto, Frank. 2009. "Trends and Observations: Adapting to Needs of the New Consumer (EMC: Web Content Management)." *EContent* 32, no. 1 (January–February): 41.

Dennison, Russell F. 1999. "Usage-based Staffing of the Reference Desk: A Statistical Approach." *Reference & User Services Quarterly* 39, no. 2 (Winter): 158–165.

Dubicki, Eleanora I. (ed.) 2008. *Marketing and Promoting Electronic Resources: Creating the E-Buzz!* New York: Routledge.

Eggleston, Tim. 2008. "Managing Online Reference Enquiries." *Incite* 29, no. 12 (1/2): 12–13.

Goodrich, Jeanne. 2005. "Staffing Public Libraries: Are There Models or Best Practices?" *Public Libraries* 44, no. 5 (September-October): 277–281.

Grahame, Vicki, and Tim McAdam. 2004. *SPEC Kit 282: Managing Electronic Resources*. Washington, DC: Association of Research Libraries.

Hibner, Holly. 2007. "Reference on the Edge." *Public Libraries* 46, no. 1 (January-February): 21–22.

Hines, Samantha Schmehl. 2007. "Outpost Reference: Meeting Patrons on Their Own Ground." *PNLA Quarterly* 72, no. 1 (Fall): 12-13, 26.

Hiremath, Uma. 2001. "Electronic Consortia: Resource Sharing in the Digital Age." *Collection Building* 20, no. 2: 80–88.

IFLA (International Federation of Library Associations and Institutions). 2005. "Think Globally, Act Locally: Building National and International Cooperative Virtual Reference Networks." Meeting at the annual 71st IFLA General Conference and Council, Oslo, Norway (August 16).

Kelly, Graham. 1998. *Team Leadership: Five Interactive Management Adventures*. Hampshire, UK: Gower.

"Managing Mass of e-Content is Main Worry." 2008. *Library & Information Update* no. 12 (1/12): 9.

Mayo, Diane, and Jeanne Goodrich. 2009. *Staffing for Results: A Guide to Working Smarter*. Chicago: American Library Association.

McMillen, Paula, and Loretta Rielly. 2003. "It Takes a Village to Manage the 21st Century Reference Department." *Reference Librarian* 39, no. 81 (January): 71–87.

Neal, James G. 2005. "Raised by Wolves: The New Generation of Feral Professionals In the Academic Library." Paper presented at the ACRL Twelfth National Conference, Minneapolis, MN, April 7-10. Available: www.ala.org/ala/acrl/acrlevents/neal2-05.pdf.

Nicely, Donna, with Beth Dempsey. 2005. "Building a Culture of Leadership." *Public Libraries* 44, no. 5 (September-October): 297–300.

Poon-Richards, Craig. 1996. "Self-Managed Teams for Library Management: Increasing Employee Participation via Empowerment." *Journal of Library Administration* 22, no. 1 (April): 67–84.

Ragsdale, Kate. 2001. *SPEC Lit 266: Staffing the Library Website*. Washington, DC: ARL Publications.

Stueart, Robert D., and Barbara B. Moran. 2007. *Library and Information Center Management*. 7th ed. Englewood, CO: Libraries Unlimited.

Tenopir, Carol. 2004. "Chat's Positive Side." *Library Journal* 129, no. 28 (December): 42.

Walters, Suzanne. 2004. *Library Marketing That Works!* New York: Neal-Schuman.

Wamken, Paula. 2004. "New Technologies and Constant Change: Managing the Process." *Journal of Academic Librarianship* 30, no. 4 (July): 322–327.

Wong, Sandra, and Anne O'Shea. 2004. "Librarians Have Left the Building: Ask Us HERE at Simon Fraser University." *Feliciter* 3: 90–92. Also available through the Canadian Library Association Web site: www.cla.ca.

Young, William F. 2004. "Reference Team Self-Management at the University at Albany." *Library Administration & Management* 18, no. 4 (Fall): 185–191.

Zabel, Diane. 2005. "Trends in Reference and Public Services Librarianship and the Role of RUSA." *Reference & User Services Quarterly* 45, no. 1 (Fall): 7–10.

Zhang, Ying, and Corinne Bishop. 2005. "Project Management Tools for Libraries: A Planning and Implementation Model Using Microsoft Project 2000." *Information Technology and Libraries* 24, no. 3 (September): 147–152.

19

Assessing and Improving Reference Services

Why Assess

There is an unwritten assumption that libraries, like Mom and apple pie, will always be there. One of the more impressive buildings in an academic campus, for example, is invariably the library building. With an estimated 139,000 libraries in the country, even Anytown, USA, usually has a town hall, a post office, and yes, a library. In Canada, the 14,069 libraries in the country constitute three times the number of McDonald's restaurants. In the United Kingdom, public libraries have existed for more than 150 years and currently number 4,517 not counting the national, academic, specialized, and school libraries.

However, times are changing and the very existence of physical libraries is being questioned, even as funding for libraries is habitually finding a position at the bottom of the totem pole. At the end of 2008, despite an astonishing 1.5 billion visits to public libraries in the United States by adults, major library systems are seeing dramatic downgrades, ranging from reduced hours (Knox County Public Library System, TN), job elimination (Newark, NJ), and budget cuts (Los Angeles, CA) to proposed branch closures (Free Library of Philadelphia, PA, and Erie County Public Library, Erie, PA). With budget cuts is the unsettling parallel development of a quantum increase in funding resources required for erupting electronic information formats and resources essential to every modern library institution. Caught between spiraling costs and continued funding invisibility, library managers are fast jumping into the ethos of the business world. Words like "ROI" (return-on-investment), "performance indicators," "institutional accountability," and "outcome-based evaluations" are finding expression through increasingly sophisticated tools of survey and multivariate analysis.

Traditionally, library feedback has been strong in the realm of library material and usage. Circulation statistics and turnstile counts are an integral part of many libraries. Both provide direct indicators of the number of people entering a library and borrowing material from the library collection. Libraries have been content with these few areas of quantification. The value quotient of a library has drawn legitimacy from these numbers. This is no longer enough.

In 1993, the U.S. government passed the Government Performance and Results Act, which mandates federal agencies to "establish specific objective, quantifiable and measurable performance goals," thus setting the goal of accountability for all institutions. Academic libraries are increasingly accountable to regional accrediting agencies. Corporate libraries must demonstrate ROI on a recurring basis. Public libraries are also finding it beneficial to establish an ROI on every dollar spent; Florida published a study claiming a return of $6.54 for every $1.00, similar to a study by the British Library that pegged the return to 4.4 times the investment (Oder, 2005). Even school libraries are feeling the need to rely on more than historical precedent to justify their existence. Statistical truths and the institutional reliance on numbers are being used by all kinds of libraries across the nation both as validation and as a way to support changes, modifications, and additions to library services. Reference rooms do not have the backing of circulation statistics and are particularly vulnerable to marginalization if no clear mandate for their purpose and performance is readily available.

What to Assess

Every reference environment has three aspects that can and should be evaluated:

1. Reference collection
2. Reference staff
3. Reference services

Given the time and commitment levels required, the question naturally arises: is the assessment of a reference environment really necessary? Most town libraries, for example, tend to rely on multitasking librarians so that a day in the life of a reference librarian could involve computer troubleshooting, calming disturbed patrons, sorting personnel problems, mopping unfortunate spills, conducting diplomatic conversations with unexpected visitors from Town Hall, and sweating over an antique copier, tweezing out inky papers accordioned in the machine. In the midst of such busy days, is it any wonder that service assessment is more a theory than a practice?

Traditionally, reference staff has also relied heavily on the accuracy of a strong reference collection. The process of building up a good reference collection has been established in the field. Library literature is replete with monthly broadcasts of "best of" lists and "core collection" choices. But for who are these collections "best" and to what end? Do the small town public library and the large college library choose their selections because they are, after all, "the best of reference" or because their customers have a proven need for these specific materials? "A measure of library quality based solely on collections has become obsolete" (Hernon and Dugan, 2001: 119).

Furthermore, the formats in which collections are being accessed are multiplying at a dizzying rate. Do users prefer electronic to print resources? Is remote access to sources essential? A pressing challenge for each reference librarian today is to align quality of reference materials, formats, and service so that the fundamentals of what constitutes a "core" reference collection are constantly being questioned and molded in accordance with reference needs. To benefit from feedback, a reliable reference services assessment is essential.

Finally, the funds for setting up and supporting a reference room are increasingly propelled by an assessment of achievement levels in the provision of reference services. If an actuary can convert the value of missing eyes, limbs, and even thumbs to specific dollar amounts well within the purview of community understanding, surely the library can convert the value of reference services into calculable numbers—or so seems to be the thinking of the day.

How to Assess

The evaluation of reference services is of predominant importance simply because it gauges the satisfaction of the end user, with the collection and the staff as the critical means to attain satisfying end-user service. In that sense, an assessment of reference services encompasses the collection and the staff as well.

The evaluation of services is also abstract. Reference service requires multidimensional approaches for a reliable assessment. In many cases, there are little or no direct tracings of service activity so that evaluative indexes must be devised to accurately reflect user satisfaction. Given the need to establish convincing evaluative techniques, a number of strategies have evolved over the past few decades. It is incumbent on each reference manager to be familiar with all the following techniques so that the right combination of techniques can be selected, appropriate to the assessment at hand. The most prominently used methods are listed below along a continuum of simple to complex requirements.

Suggestion boxes > Observation > Surveys >
Focus Groups > Case studies

Suggestion Box

The most basic attempt at assessment is via feedback channels such as the humble suggestion box. Whether a generic container with a slot for slipping in suggestions; a book for writing in suggestions and comments; an online box for keyboarding in suggestions; or an e-mail address for sending in suggestions, the intent is the same. "Tell us what you think, or want, or hate, or love about anything and everything" is the simple appeal of the ubiquitous "box."

The advantages of this method are ease of access for the user and simplicity of design and implementation for cash-strapped reference managers. John Lubans, Jr., for example, introduced his wildly popular "Suggestion Answer Book" at both the University of Colorado and Duke University. In his experience, the thousands of suggestions entered in the book were used to leverage "improvements in facilities, services, policies, and staffing." Equally important, he notes, the "desire to help...was made manifest" to the users (Lubans, 2001: 240–245).

One of the strictures of the format is the lack of accountability inherent in answering random suggestions. The very randomness of the suggestions tends to feed more easily into tweaking improvements, rather than any systemic planning. Idiosyncratic feedback can spark insights, but is less amenable to detecting a pattern or trend in general reference user needs and assessments. While the importance of user needs and assessment is openly and consistently upheld with the provision of an ongoing feedback channel, a more formalized format would need to be instituted for a reference assessment requiring depth.

Surveys

One such format is the age-old survey method. A survey is simply a set of questions asked of a defined community in order to get a quantitative handle on community values, activities, qualities, or perceptions. Since the purpose of a survey is to tap into people's individual preferences, the method is most appropriate when personal information is required: "Were YOU satisfied with the help you received today?" or "Did YOU find the information you wanted?" or "Do YOU think the reference room should be open on Sundays?" Surveys are also helpful when information is required about community characteristics. Demographic information, the mainstay of collection developers, is, after all, derivative of the king of all surveys, the U.S. Census. Age, education, ethnicity, and affluence are critical survey results that undergird the shaping of library collections.

The rules of logic suggest that a response to survey questions provides a direct and effective way of assessing reference services, yet the reality and complexity of human behavior suggests otherwise. Users who answered they were "very satisfied" with the help they received at the reference desk may still not have found the answer to their question, but are responding instead to the strenuous efforts of a charming reference librarian. The seemingly innocuous structuring of survey questions so as to elicit the desired area of response is a tricky business. Users who want "more hours" available at reference may be users who never really utilize those extra hours. The chasm between stated perceptions and actual behavior is well documented. Surveys then are an intuitive, age-old method of collecting data on a community of users, but they gain in value when supported with collaborating data on observed behavior or when teamed with reasoned treatises.

Once conducted, surveys tend to develop a life of their own. They act as powerful, persuasive, and recurrent sources of justification for arguments, additions, or modifications made in the library world. The whole idea for roving reference librarians, for example, emerged when surveys showed that users were reluctant to walk up to a reference desk. Hernon and McClure's survey, which claimed that the average percentage of reference questions answered correctly in a library was 55 percent, has clung onto professional memory long after it was undermined on several counts and by several authorities (Richardson, 2002). Given the power of surveys, a number of formats have emerged through which a survey can be conducted. The primary choice of the twenty-first century appears to be the online survey; a brief list of formats in use by libraries is given below.

In-house Surveys

In-house surveys have been the most common method utilized by libraries. The advantage of such surveys is that they are relatively inexpensive and can be administered by staff as part of their daily routine. The staff of the Leavey Library at the University of Southern California, for example, describes an in-house survey that cost less than $250 (Eng and Gardner, 2005). According to the results of a College Library Information Packet Note venture that studied 214 colleges, "the most common instrument developed in college libraries is the self-administered user satisfaction survey" (Adams and Beck, 1995). Since they are administered on the spot, the rates of response are high. The assessments given out following an Internet instruction session, or after concluding a reference transaction, or using a new electronic database are all commonly used surveys. The Yuba County Library's Reference Department, for example, has conducted various in-house surveys to gauge patron satisfaction and collection usage. Below is an example of a survey conducted (Figure 19-1).

Figure 19-1. Reference Department Survey

Yuba County Library
Reference Department

Please take a few minutes to complete this survey so that we can enhance our services. All individual answers will be combined with others, thus remaining confidential.

1. Have you ever used any of the Reference Department's services?
    __ Yes   __ No*
   *If no, please stop here

2. Which of the services have you used in the past year?
   __ Reference Librarian   __ Brochures and fliers at the reference desk
   __ Small Business Resources   __ Reference collection
   __ Nolo press legal references __ Law Library computers
   __ *Buzz* newsletter   __ *Ping* newsletter
   __ ALP newsletter   __ Adult Literacy

3. If you have made use of the Reference Librarian's services, how was your "case" handled?
   __ In person   __ E-mail   __ Phone

4. Overall, what is your impression of the Reference Librarian and his/her service?
   __Poor   __ Adequate   __ Good   __ Excellent

5. If you used any of the brochures and fliers available at the reference desk, please list as many as you can remember on the back.

6. If you used the Small Business Resources collection, please give your evaluation by filling out the last page of this survey.

(Cont'd.)

Figure 19-1. Reference Department Survey *(Continued)*

7. If you used our Reference collection this past year, please give us your overall opinion of the quality and usefulness.

___ Poor   ___ Adequate   ___ Good   ___ Excellent

8. If you used our reference collection, what materials or subject areas do you feel need improvement?

9. Have you ever used our collection of Nolo press legal materials?

___ Yes   ___ No

If yes, which materials?

10. Have you ever used our Law Library computers?

___ Yes   ___ No

If yes, what is your general opinion of the computers, their programs, etc.?

11. Have you ever seen a copy of the *Buzz* newsletter? If you have, please fill out the last page of this survey.

___ Yes   ___ No

12. Have you ever seen a copy of the *Ping* newsletter?

___ Yes   ___ No

If yes, what is your impression of the newsletter? Please give us ways to improve.

13. Have you ever considered participating in our Adult Literacy program, either as a tutor or a learner? (For more information, please see the Reference Librarian.)

___ Yes   ___ No

Please return this survey to
The Reference desk

Thank you very much.

Source: Survey provided by Yuba County Reference Librarian Regina Zurakowski, Yuba County Library, Marysville, California. Used by permission.

Telephone

Ironically, the advantages of telephone surveys appear suspiciously close to their disadvantages. The telephone indisputably provides direct and instant entry into every household, qualities that appeal to every serious surveyor. However, that very aspect can lead to criticism from those being surveyed (for being too intrusive), and result in unwilling or less-than-sincere responses. The nature of the format also defines and limits the depth and breadth of questions. By definition, telephone surveys would be limited to relatively shorter questions and responses that require minimal or no relative rankings. While this increases the speed of responses, it limits the depth and variety of questions. Telephone surveys, while widely used in the past, enjoy less legitimacy in the aftermath of intrusive telemarketing and the subsequent law allowing households to block calls or monitor incoming calls through caller identification.

Mailed Questionnaires

Mailed questionnaires are the most nonintrusive way of conducting surveys. The time to fill out a survey and the inclination to complete one are left entirely up to the respondent. However, this could lead to low response rates as well as slow return rates. The cost required for postage is also relatively higher than other formats, especially since self-addressed, stamped envelopes are usually included in a survey package to encourage a return from the chosen respondent.

E-mail/Online

The online survey is undoubtedly becoming the primary tool of choice, especially for academic and corporate libraries. Given the ubiquity of chat and virtual reference sessions, instant surveys that pop up at the end of each session are par for the course and user receptivity is high to answering the required question on whether the session was useful. More elaborate online surveys are also conducted either by contracting with professionals or through easily available software applications such as Zoomerang and Survey Monkey.

When the library at the University of Louisiana-Lafayette needed to survey the attitudes of library staff, Perennial Survey, a professional survey firm, prepared a list of thirty-one questions specifically for online use. The survey was then posted on the university's Web site for eleven days with links provided to four popular listservs. Only one response per IP (Internet Protocol) address was permitted. Subsequent data were then analyzed using SAS System software (Goetting, 2004: 12–17). *Survey Monkey*, the "intelligent survey software for primates of all species," is a globally popular, flexible, and intuitive subscription-based online survey tool used by reference managers in a range of libraries such as the Marygrove College Library, Michigan, the Texas State Law Library, Texas, and the California State University libraries, California. Software to create personalized online surveys is also available, such as the Remark Web Survey, which allows for highly flexible formatting without the need for HTML expertise. Overall, the survey method is advantageous in that "information is gathered, summarized, analyzed, and put to use in a short amount of time" (Everhart, 1998).

Surveys that require data to be gathered from human subjects are mandated by federal regulations to undergo a review process both before and during the survey process. This is typically undertaken in academic institutions by "an appropriately constituted group" commonly referred to as the Institutional Review Board (IRB). Libraries that are less familiar with the review process can refer to the specific code (45CFR46.116) available at www.hhs.gov/ohrp/humansubjects/guidance/45cfr46.html.

Interviews

Surveys are often supplemented with another method of assessment, i.e., the individual interview. Interviews are used to either help in the making of survey questions, or to add depth and anecdotes to the quantitative parsimony of a survey. They are useful tools to collect personal experience and perception that can lead to meaningful assessment information. They can be conducted face to face or via telephone or e-mail. Much as in the survey method, the questions must be designed to take advantage of the insight and experience of individual users. A preguide that frames the interview assessment is recommended to ensure the integrity of the interview process, the unbiased selection of interviewees, and consistency in both questions and answer ratings.

Observations

An observation is the seemingly simple act of recording what took place. Did the reference librarian answer the question correctly? Did the reference user approach the desk for assistance? Are reference sources easily accessible to the user? A live transaction is recorded and evaluated in accordance with preset questions and expectations. The method is most applicable when actual behavior as opposed to values and perceptions is the required area of assessment. Whatever the area of assessment, there are three distinct types of observational methods: direct observation, hidden observation, and self-imposed observation.

Direct Observation

The most intuitive method is through *direct observation*. An activity or service is monitored and the observations are recorded. However, as Newton's humble apple can testify, the simple recording of an activity can lend itself to relevance only if it is placed within a context of well-developed suppositions and expectations. In the case of reference assessments, a set of clear questions needs to establish the grounds for observation. A sampling plan needs to set the periodicity of the observation. Finally, a plan for analyzing the data gathered through observation must be in place so that the criteria for observation are fully answered.

The Pennsylvania State University Libraries, for example, undertook direct observational analysis of the usability of a new online catalog introduced in 2001 and known as CAT (Novotny, 2004). A clear set of questions and rationale for analysis was prepared in advance. As can be seen in the box below, in order to add more dimension to the observations, users were not only observed, but were also asked to "think aloud" as they searched.

The method has much to offer. It is relatively simple and the results resonate with the sincerity of direct observation. On the negative side, the procedure can be intrusive; reference staff or reference users are aware they are being watched constantly. The observations can be potentially colored by the biases and idiosyncratic perceptions of the all-too-fallible human observer. The quality of the questions and the strictures of plan analysis methods can skew observational studies. Relying on a tried and tested question plan can dilute some of the methodology angst.

A PROTOCOL ANALYSIS STUDY

1. A friend recommends that you read a book called History by Hollywood. Does the Penn State Libraries have this book?

   Question Rationale: *To examine how users search for known items and whether they could locate a book when they knew the title. The title was chosen so that the broadest keyword search resulted in fewer than fifty matches.*

2. Please use the library catalog to ask for a copy of the book *History by Hollywood.*

   Question Rationale: *This task was designed to see if users could determine how to use the "I Want It" button in CAT to request materials. Analysis of e-mail queries revealed that many users were unable to determine how to request materials.*

3. The article you need is in the journal *Kansas Law Review*, volume 49, issue 5, June 2001. Is this issue of the journal in the Penn State libraries? If so, where is it?

   Question Rationale: *A unique title was chosen so that users retrieved only one match regardless of which search type was selected (keyword or browse). The research team was interested in determining how users interpreted a serials record.*

4. Another article you need is in a journal called *Civil Engineering*. Specifically, you need volume 70, December 2000. Is a copy for this year available on the University Park campus? If so, which library can it be found in?

   Question Rationale: *To see how users navigated a potentially complex search. The default keyword search options results in over 2,000 matches. The record display includes multiple holdings, with the UP copy at the bottom of a very long record.*

5. You have been assigned to write a paper on the topic "Efforts to combat teen smoking." For this paper, you need to find four books at the Penn State Libraries. Please note the call numbers and locations of four books on this topic.

   Question Rationale: *To see how users search for materials on a subject. The topic was constructed so as to make it likely that multiple strategies would be required. Teen smoking as a keyword only retrieves two of the necessary four matches. The LC subject heading is Teenagers-United States-Tobacco-Use-Prevention, but other keywords would also work: teens, adolescents, smokers, and so on.*

Source: Eric Novotny. 2004. "I Don't Think I Click: A Protocol Analysis Study of Use of a Library Online Catalog in the Internet Age." *College & Research Libraries* 65, no. 6 (November): 537.

Hidden Observation

A variation on direct observation is the method of the *hidden observer*. A frequently used method, the modus operandi is inculcated right from library school, when students are asked to observe and record reference interviews being conducted by librarians at their neighborhood library. In this method, the same set of predetermined questions and plan of analysis need to be in place, but the staff is unaware that they are under scrutiny. The rationale is that the results would mirror more typical behavior, much as naturalist portrait photography claims to a more profound presentation of the "true" person, than does a formal studio photograph.

For example, between 1998 and 1999 the University of Arizona libraries evaluated reference service as a function of both approachability and reliability; this was evaluated through a three-step approach involving a survey questionnaire, observation, and focus groups. According to the coordinator of this assessment, "most of the important information the team uncovered was from the unobtrusive observation" (Norlin, 2004: 553). The questions structuring the observation are given below as an example of how hidden observations can be planned (see Figure 19-2).

Although the claim of veracity might make this a more appealing form of observation, the use of this method must be tempered by questions of ethics and accuracy. Staff that is subsequently told they were under observation may feel embarrassed or upset. Proxy questions that required staff time in research may be considered a waste of time and energy and engender hostility. Studies that have circumvented this problem have typically involved large, multi-branch libraries where the identity of the observed librarians can be kept anonymous.

Figure 19-2. Unobtrusive Observation Worksheet

UNOBTRUSIVE OBSERVATION WORKSHEET (QUESTIONS)

1. Observe the reference desk for approximately two to five minutes (incognito). What are the reference staff members doing? (Write down everything.) Do they look approachable?

    Yes   No   1   2   3   4   5

2. How long is the average wait for service?

3. Which person are you going to approach? Why?

4. What is your research question? (Write down the general idea.)

5. What did the person say when you initially asked the question?

6. What was the person's attitude while you explained the problem?

7. Which resources did the person recommend?

8. Did you find the resources useful?

    Yes   No   1   2   3   4   5

9. Did the sources directly answer your question?

    Yes   No   1   2   3   4   5

10. Would you approach the same person again? Why?

11. Did the person follow up to see if you needed additional help?

Take this time out to list two strengths and two ideas for improvement about the reference/service.

Source: Elaina Norlin. 2000. "Reference Evaluation: A Three-Step Approach—Surveys, Unobtrusive Observations, and Focus Groups." *College & Research Libraries* 61, no. 6: 546–553.

Online reference transactions that apply hidden observation techniques are also relatively easier, given the invisibility of the assessor. In 2001, for example, a set of specific assessment questions were sent to 111 sites of the Association of Research Libraries that offered e-mail reference services. The unobtrusive study allowed comparisons across institutions and could lend itself to a wider and more comprehensive assessment of e-mail reference in general. Timeliness, scope of answer, and policy statements versus actual delivery were some of the aspects of e-mail service that were studied through this method (Stacy-Bates, 2003: 59–70). When a study of such scale is required, unobtrusive online observation can be the best method available.

Self-imposed Observation

Transaction diaries, journals, preset forms, and reference activity notebooks are all examples of *self-imposed observations* (see Figure 19-3). The most basic observation is the number and general type of reference question answered. Almost all libraries have or should have a recording of this. The use of hash marks to denote reference, directional, or technological queries was instrumental in providing the foundation for the innovative Brandeis Model of reference service whereby staff (Herman, 1994) were apportioned to graded levels of service.

Figure 19-3. Reference Transaction Diary

DAY	TELEPHONE	IN PERSON	COMPUTER
MONDAY			
TUESDAY			
WEDNESDAY			
THURSDAY			
FRIDAY			
SATURDAY			
SUNDAY			
COMMENTS:			

A more intensive format for self-imposed observation is a preset transactional form that not only records the number and type of questions but also provides information on how the question was answered or referred. Such observational data can be highly useful in a number of assessment scenarios. The reliance on one format over another, the efficacy or inefficacy of one source over another, and the success of one reference librarian's search strategy over another are all areas where preset transactional forms can throw evaluative light.

Many librarians also use unformatted reference activity notebooks. Given hectic schedules at a reference desk, a hurried scrawl on the text of a question is sometimes the only record that a librarian is physically able to manage. Analyzing such notebooks is far more challenging, but great utility is found in such books, because the reference manager has more than individual memory to back up a statement like "we get a lot of health questions during winter." Figure 19-4 shows the transcript of a page from the reference desk notebook of West Orange Public Library, New Jersey.

Diaries and journals are the hardest self-observation tools to institute, decipher, and present as a consolidated finding. However, they are rich sources of information that can supplement or fill in the blanks left by other more succinct modes of observation.

Focus Groups

A focus group involves the creation of a setting and agenda calculated to elicit a group response on any issue. Like the individual interview method, the focus group aims at probing community experience and perceptions. Unlike individual interviews, the responses are a function of individual thoughts

---

Figure 19-4. Reference Desk Notebook, Sample Page

Monday, 4/18/2005

• Bergen's 'Record'	• Writing a screenplay
• Ledger—March 27th—'Detailer' ad?	• Reviews of Guare—six degrees of sep
• T-bills- tax considerations	• e-mail reviews of Gilead to xxxxxxxx
• Out of print books—how to purchase?	• Lemony Snicket pseudonym
• Assertiveness training	• Japanese population in NJ
• Math review for aptitude test	• Montessori
• How to teach an adult to ride a bicycle	• Slavery in north vs. south
• Fashion during Harlem Renaissance	• Johnnie Cochran—bio
• Business plan for screen script	• Scholarly articles on HIV/AIDS
• Microsoft Publisher	• Historic real estate values
• Jane Watson—nursing?	• AIDS in Africa

Source: Transcript of page from the Reference Notebook of the West Orange Public Library, New Jersey.

tempered or catalyzed by group dynamics. Focus groups act like old-fashioned butter churns, stirring up the most resonant or democratically held values and perceptions curdling in a group.

When does a focus group become the most useful tool available? Typically, the format serves best in the following situations:

- Immediate follow-ups on responses would provide a richer study. (For example, when a preliminary survey conducted by the Microsoft Library found that users needed more in-depth technical data, a follow-through focus group was organized to "drill down" into the exact kinds of data required. The survey set up the area of priority and the focus group honed down the exact nature of the library's user needs.)
- Individual surveys are hard to carry out for logistical or other reasons.
- Statistically larger data are required in a limited time slot.
- Group consensus on issues is as valid as or more valid than individual preferences.
- Existing data are puzzling and require community interpretation.
- Areas of modification or change are unclear so that a preliminary sense of group priorities is required.
- Community investment is an issue that needs to be jumpstarted or fanned into greater intensity.

Overall, because group interpretation is the purpose of the format, it has been most beneficial when used as an exploratory tool or when an issue needed further clarification or interpretation. For example, after three SERVQUAL surveys were administered by the Texas A&M University Libraries, it was clear that a gap existed between user expectations and perceptions; but details remained unclear. A final series of focus groups was held, which the researchers found "useful for identifying areas of improvement" (Ho and Crowley, 2003: 86). The librarians at the New Jersey Institute of Technology (NJIT) at Newark conduct a focus group every year to explore different aspects of reference service. A draft of the questions asked is posted in Figure 19-5.

Though a pedestrian format that has been frequently used by many different types of libraries and institutions, focus groups are challenging to organize. As in the interview method, the elaboration of questions and their interpretation can be complex. For example, one of the questions at a focus group aimed at assessing "technostress" at the reference desk was "Your job today is to paint the reference desk and everything on it. What colors will you use?" (Rose, Gray, and Stoklosa, 1998: 311). How would stippled sage be interpreted? The imagination boggles.

There is also the additional complexity of training facilitators, as the success of a focus group depends largely on the expertise of the facilitator in both moderating the discussion and recording what transpires. The very creation of a focus group requires a high level of preplanning. Random sampling is not conducive to productive discussion, so by definition group members must be selected on the basis of their interest or experience in the issues under consideration. The "snowball technique" is frequently used to develop further focus

---

Figure 19-5. Focus Group Questions Draft

2005 NJIT Library Focus Group Questions-DRAFT
February 3, 2005

Unless otherwise noted, every question is to be posed to all focus groups (faculty, graduate students, undergraduate students, architecture students).

Web site

1. How frequently do you use the library Web site?

2. How effective are you at finding what you need on the library Web site?

3. What did you use the last time you were on the Web site?

4. What have you looked for on the library's homepage that you have had trouble finding?

5. What are your suggestions for improving the library Web site?

6. What's the best place you go to when looking for a journal article?

7. Where do you go to do your current awareness reading? Do you have trouble finding full text? (fac)

8. Where do you start when you have a research project?

9. What have your experiences been with the following: Renewing books online? Placing a hold on a book? Checking your library accounts? Discuss your successes/difficulties in finding a book in the catalog. Finding a journal?

10. Have you used the library Web site at Rutgers? What other library's Web sites do you use?

11. What have your experiences been using databases on site and remotely?

12. When you use the library Web site, do you feel certain that you've found what you're looking for or not? (excl arch)

13. *Have moderator go down the navigation bar and ask for each item:* "What do you use this for? What else?" (arch, grad and undergrad) (note for arch moderator: use arch Web site)

14. How often have you used the Image database? Did it suit your research needs? (arch)

Source: Richard Sweeney, University Librarian, New Jersey Institute of Technology, 2006. Used by permission.

---

groups based on the suggestions of initial participants who may know others in the community who are interested or experienced in the issue area.

Despite these challenges, the focus group format continues to be used by many different libraries because of the rich dividends it tends to yield. Academic libraries such as Texas A&M have used it to set priorities, and corporate libraries such as the Microsoft Library have used it to add depth to an existing study.

Given its popularity and usage, the ideal dimensions of a focus group have been increasingly identified as:

- Unbiased, unselfconscious, and trained facilitators
- Six to twelve participants in each group
- Forty-five-to-ninety-minute sessions

- Six to ten questions
- A minimum of three groups for a preliminary investigation, with the understanding that the larger the number of groups the greater the relevance of the method.

A stellar example of a successful focus group venture is the experience of the Clemson Libraries, which held focus group "summits" that were used as the "basis for...strategic and business plans" for the library. The University of Texas adopted the same summit method to develop its own strategic plans. Brown University Library hired a professional firm "for several thousand dollars" to conduct its focus groups and found that the data was well worth the investment; it "helped the Library build a case with university administrators to fund specific projects for improvement" (Shoaf, 2003: 124–132).

Case Studies

Case studies are much like magnifying glasses. They focus on one aspect of librarianship, which is then studied in expanded detail. The case study method has a venerable history that can trace its ancestry to the law schools of 1870 that first introduced case method as a system of learning. What was initially a system of learning has now extended into an accepted tool of assessment in a number of social sciences.

Unlike the other methods outlined so far, the instrumentation used in this method is nonspecific. Whereas surveys use questionnaires and focus groups use mediators, case studies use any or all of the other methods to reach a conclusion. The primary imperative in this method is to posit the case. Once the magnifying glass has settled on a case, it is studied from all angles with whatever means available or possible. The method serves as an excellent organizing tool for in-depth evaluation.

Does nonverbal communication affect patron perceptions of a reference interaction? How well does collaborative digital self-service work? Are student workers effective at reference desk service? Annotated cases can be found in *Evaluating Reference Services* (Whitlach, 2000). The methods employed in these cases included surveys, interviews, direct observation, and diaries. Why then are they case studies? If more than one tool is used to study the same issue, then it becomes a case study. The difference is one of detail and emphasis rather than the adoption of an entirely different evaluation tool. Since the case study poses the imperative of focus and in-depth evaluation, the method is distinguished by:

- Multiplicity of assessment instruments
- Greater depth of evaluative understanding
- Greater reliability
- Relatively limited replicability

The results following a case study are invariably less "catchy" than those following a quantitative survey. Unlike a pithy percentage or number, the case study relies on triangulating the results of different assessments to best approximate the workings of a reference service or initiative. The results, by definition, are less succinct and far denser.

Case studies are most effective when:

- A single survey method is unconvincing
- A novel service or new collection has been introduced
- Staff has the time and expertise to expend on multiple assessments and analyses
- Advance weighting is attributed to each method in case of discrepancies between two results

Acting on Assessments

At a first level, assessments allow a reference manager to follow the dictum of "knowing thyself." In that knowledge lies the potential ability to establish priorities, scrape away redundancies, allot proper funding, allow new initiatives, and provide defensible institutional justification. All of the assessment techniques covered previously are important as a means to the end of "knowing thyself." Given that a great deal of time, energy, finances, and effort go into the completion of an assessment, it is imperative that a reference manager, having gained the necessary knowledge, should act on it. Microsoft Library conducts an annual survey of user needs with the express guideline that "all questions must lead to potentially actionable results" (Plosker, 2004: 50).

The New Americans Program at the Queens Borough Public Library found direction in both funding and programming through the survey analysis conducted by its Information and Data Analysis Librarian, Wai Sze Chan. Ms. Chan mapped ethnic correlates extracted from the census to create neighborhood profiles that in turn fed into relevant collection development and program initiatives. It is unlikely that something as exotic as a "Toddler Learning Center in Bengali" for the children of recent immigrants from Bengal could have been planned and funded by an external grant without strong survey analysis and presentation.

After a three-step survey of reference services was conducted at the University of Arizona Libraries, a roving reference librarian was introduced to enhance services; signage was improved including name tags on staff; and referrals for technology were organized since that was an area that students had found weak. The coordinator found the results of the assessment study to be "very meaningful" (Norlin, 2000: 546–553).

Quantify

If major funding is at stake, a statistical analysis of collected data goes a long way toward exciting external support. However, statistical analyses will invariably involve ancient mathematical beasts such as factor analysis, Likert scales, data reduction tools, chi squares, and measures of association. Trivial to the average statistician or statistically inclined librarian, data analyses even through the simplifying construct of programs such as SAS and SPSS can be daunting to many a stouthearted reference manager. At this point, investing in a professional surveyor, or locating a statistically endowed colleague, or purchasing a preset service such as LibQUAL+® is money and time well spent. Information about the LibQUAL+® kit is available at www.libqual.org, including the 2011 ALA Midwinter Meeting presentation by Michael Maciel "12 Years of LibQUAL+® at the Texas A&M University." Older surveys of libraries that have used the kit can be found in the 2005 publication *Libraries Act on Their LibQUAL+ Findings* (Heath, Kyrillidou, and Askew, 2005).

Strategize

Absolute clarity in assessment needs also goes a long way toward choosing both the level and type of assessment technique. Some questions to ask are:

- *Do you want to launch a new reference initiative?* For example, do you want to start 24/7 virtual reference services or live online reference or tiered reference? Survey methods have worked well when broad information on subjective preferences is required.
- *Do you merely want to get a "pulse" on user needs and expectations?* For example, are patrons satisfied with the answers they have found to their reference questions? Are databases useful? Are reference hours satisfactory? Suggestion boxes and observation methods have succeeded in opinion-based studies such as these.
- *Do you want to reprioritize funding allocation?* For example, will information assistants suffice for basic reference questions? Should print resources be diverted to electronic purchases? Should a certain area such as local history or small business be given special financial focus? For analytical studies, individual opinions are rarely enough. A focus group that forces deeper interpretations would be far more effective.
- *Do you want to attract new funding?* For example, will bibliographic instruction in computer technology enhance the reference profile? Will adding lifelong learning commitments to traditional reference add value to overall services? For diagnostic studies that aim to improve services, opinion-based studies alone present relatively feeble input. Case studies that incorporate both subjective opinions and objective quantification are best suited.

Visualize

The following are scenarios that you may face as a reference manager:

- The vice president of your graduate college has made several unsubstantiated remarks about faculty having to look elsewhere for their higher research needs. How would you convince her that the reference department is indeed serving the needs of the staff?
- Professional literature claims that 24/7 virtual reference is the library of the future. How would you design a technique to assess whether such services are necessary to your particular library?

- You have just been appointed as the supervising reference librarian of a multibranch county system. Your "feeling" is that annual updates of online general encyclopedias are preferable to purchasing the more expensive print updates. What assessment or data would you use to test your instinct?
- You are the head of reference at a medium-sized public library. Your director claims that the following year's budget will be much lower and would like you to reduce reference standing orders by 10 percent. What would you discard and how would you justify your decision?

Ongoing Assessments: An Imperative

Time-consuming though they may be, ongoing assessments of the reference environment are an imperative. Especially given the current diversity and flux in reference services, formats, and information expectations, each reference library will of necessity need to establish as conclusively as possible what makes the current reference environment successful and what to project as long-range reference needs.

Referring to libraries as a whole, the authors of *Future Libraries* state, "The surest path to irrelevance is to allow yourself to be defined by someone else" (Crawford and Gorman, 1995: 182). Although the statement sounds suspiciously close to something heard on *Oprah*, it is a valid observation in a world of shifting reference environments. The level of digitized reference material required by a law library may not be anywhere near the level required by a rural public library. The definition of a roving reference librarian could mean anything from moving out from behind the desk to laptop-toting reference librarians positioned strategically within academic departments, as practiced at Brandeis and Harvard, to mobile outdoor "reference stations" assembled at university campus hot spots, as at the University of Florida (Hisle, 2005). The need and extent of reference services requiring virtual-chat software can also range widely among different types of libraries serving different communities.

The evaluation and assessment tools described in this chapter are just that: tools. They are a means to an end. The end to keep in mind at all times is that assessments are well-thought-out, and thereby convincing measures of performance. The very act of assessing one aspect of reference swivels focus on that aspect. The focus can then lead to a compelling argument for:

- evaluating practices, performance, procedures, and services of the existing reference environment;
- foreshadowing reference services, formats, and practices of the future; and
- marketing the value of reference services to others, such as the community at large, funding agencies, and even the reference staff itself.

The pivotal role played by assessments cannot be underestimated. Assessments affect a decision maker who must decide which of multiple alternatives is the best choice; a manager who must allocate resources to one reference activity over another; and a spokesperson for a reference room that needs to attract legitimacy and funding from external sources.

Recommendations for Further Reading

Cobus, Laura, Valeda Frances Dent, and Anita Ondrusek. 2005. "How Twenty-Eight Users Helped Redesign an Academic Library Web Site: A Usability Study." *Reference & User Services Quarterly* 44, no. 3 (Spring): 232–246. The authors provide compelling evidence that usability testing, with even a small sampling population, was not only instructive, but provided sufficient insight to effect concrete changes. A comprehensive list of similar studies, distinguished by their small sampling populations, can be found at www.jkup.net/terms-studies.html.

Diamond, Tom, and Mark Sanders, eds. 2006. *Reference Assessment and Evaluation*. Binghamton, NY: The Haworth Press. University and college libraries are the target audiences for this collection of ideas, methods, and case studies for evaluating digital reference, staff training, desk staffing and other reference activities.

Dudden, Rosalind Farnam. 2007. *Using Benchmarking, Needs Assessment, Performance Improvements, Outcome Measures, and Library Standards: A How-To-Do-It Manual for Librarians*. New York: Neal-Schuman. The examples provided in this book are presented with the clear aim of allowing replicability in both small and large libraries. Dudden's work is focused on those institutions that acknowledge the importance of constant evaluations and assessment of reference services in theory, but end up giving it low priority in terms of actual practice.

Fink, Arlene. 2009. *How to Conduct Surveys: A Step-by-Step Guide*. 4th ed. Thousand Oaks, CA: SAGE Publications, Inc. This is not a manual for reference libraries per se; however, it contains a pragmatic and comprehensive guide to all kinds of surveys with examples of real surveys that have been used in a variety of institutions that can be adapted to reference services as well.

Heath, Fred M., Martha Kyrillidou, and Consuella A. Askew, eds. 2005. *Libraries Act on Their LibQUAL+ Findings: From Data to Action*. Binghamton, NY: The Haworth Press. This title is invaluable for reference departments interested in using LibQUAL+ to conduct surveys. The experiences of more than two dozen college, university, health sciences, and consortial libraries are presented, so that the survey tool has an immediacy not found in the many structural descriptions of LibQUAL+.

Holt, Glen, and Donald Elliot. 2003. "Measuring Outcomes: Applying Cost-Benefit Analysis to Middle-sized and Smaller Public Libraries." *Library Trends* 51, no. 3 (Winter): 424–440. This article is unique in that it addresses a relatively neglected area of assessment study, namely, the smaller-sized public library. The authors describe their efforts to tailor an existing cost-benefit analysis methodology they had earlier devised for the assessment of five large public library systems.

Howley, Sue, and Andrew Stevens. 2003. *WILIP: Summary Report and Next Steps*. London: The Council for Museums, Archives and Libraries. The assessment of reference services can be tightly focused on a single initiative or across a broad spectrum of services. This primary document provides an absorbing account of assessment on a national scale. The Wider Information and Library Issues Project (WILIP), sponsored by a nondepartmental body of the U.K. government in 2002, essentially mapped all the different types of information resource centers in the nation, conducted in-depth interviews, and provided over 200 suggestions aimed at ensuring the maximum fit between information users and providers.

Hubbertz, Andrew. 2005. "The Design and Interpretation of Unobtrusive Evaluations." *Reference & User Services Quarterly* 44, no. 4 (Summer): 327–335. The author supports this assessment tool by presenting it as a standardized test method. Such a method, he argues, is potentially valuable for establishing relative rankings across libraries. The (mis)use of this tool to assess overall service quality is deemed improper.

Maness, Jack, and Sarah Naper. 2007. "Assessing Inappropriate Behavior: Learning from the AskColorado Experience." In *Virtual Reference Service: From Competencies to Assessment,* edited by David Lankes, Scott Nicholson, Marie L.Radford, Lynn Westbrook, Joanne Silverstein, and Philip Nast. New York: Neal-Schuman. The chapter specifically studies "trends in inappropriate behavior" during virtual reference transactions and traces these trends across markets. The somewhat novel goal of the chapter is to assess bad practices, rather than best practices, with an eye to improving the virtual reference experience for both users and staff.

Matthews, Joseph R. 2007. *The Evaluation and Measurement of Library Services.* Santa Barbara, CA: Libraries Unlimited. Matthews tailors the book around the single question of what differences libraries make in the lives of their patrons and whether these are quantifiable through various measuring techniques. The book is a general exposition on evaluating library services as a whole; however, a great part of the material is devoted specifically to reference services. He also argues that traditional measurements such as number of reference transactions are less effective unless teamed up with customer-centric metrics such as whether the reference patron was satisfied by the transaction.

Novotny, Eric. 2002. *Reference Service Statistics and Assessment.* Washington, DC: Association of Research Libraries. Published as part of the SPEC Kit series (#268), the survey of seventy-seven member libraries provides a highly useful compilation on the various methods used by research libraries of all sizes. An interesting general observation by Novotny states that the high level of activity in reference departments, juxtaposed against data that show a decrease in the number of transactions, appears to be fostering a growing opinion that data collection techniques should be revamped.

Novotny, Eric, ed. 2007. *Assessing Reference and User Services in a Digital Age.* Binghamton, NY: The Haworth Press. Both best practices and case studies are explored by various authorities, in this compilation of e-reference evaluation in academic and public libraries. Topics include the effective evaluation of chat reference, online instruction, electronic resources, budgets and consortial undertakings, and the VET or Virtual Evaluation Toolkit.

Ronan, Jana, and Carol Turner. 2002. *Chat Reference*. Washington, DC: Association of Research Libraries. This book has a worthwhile section on evaluating chat reference. Evaluation forms for virtual reference at the University of Guelph, surveys of Ask-A-Librarian at the University of Illinois at Urbana-Champaign, Live Assistance at the Louisiana State University, LibChat at Syracuse University, and online reference at York University (defunct when checked on 2/18/2006) are all covered in separate chapters of the section.

Bibliography of Works Cited in This Chapter

ACRL. 1997. "Sources of Information on Performance and Outcome Assessment." Available: www.ala.org/ala/mgrps/divs/acrl/publications/whitepapers/sourcesinformation.cfm (accessed May 3, 2009).

Adams, Mignon, and Jeffrey Beck, compilers. 1995. *User Surveys in College Libraries*. (CLIP Note #23). Chicago, IL: ACRL.

American Library Association. 2010. *Quotable Facts about America's Libraries*. Available: http://www.ala.org/ala/aboutala/offices/ola/quotable facts/quotablefacts.cfm (accessed February 3, 2011).

American Library Association. 2011. *Funding News at Your Library*. Available: www.ala.org/ala/issuesadvocacy/libfunding/public/index.cfm (accessed February 3, 2011).

Blog. Available: http://libraryassessment.info.

Crawford, Walt, and Michael Gorman. 1995. *Future Libraries: Dreams, Madness, and Reality*. Chicago, IL: American Library Association.

DIG_REF. Available: www.webjunction.org/listservs/articles/content/438707.

Eng, Susanna, and Susan Gardner. 2005. "Conducting Surveys on a Shoestring Budget." *American Libraries* 36, no. 2 (February): 38–39.

Everhart, Nancy. 1998. *Evaluating the School Library Media Center: Analysis Techniques and Research Practices*. Englewood, CO: Libraries Unlimited.

Goetting, Denise. 2004. "Attitudes and Job Satisfaction in Louisiana Library Workplaces." *Louisiana Libraries* 67, no. 1 (Summer): 12–17.

Government Performance Results Act of 1993. Available: www.whitehouse.gov/omb/mgmt-gpra/gplaw2m.html (accessed April 29, 2009).

Griffiths, José-Marie and Donald W. King. 2008. "Interconnections: The IMLS National Study on the Use of Libraries, Museums and the Internet." Available: http://interconnectionsreport.org/ (accessed April 28, 2009).

Heath, Fred M., Martha Kyrillidou, and Consuella A. Askew, eds. 2005. *Libraries Act on Their LibQUAL+ Findings: From Data to Action*. Binghamton, NY: The Haworth Press.

Herman, Douglas. 1994. "But Does It Work? Evaluating the Brandeis Reference Model." *RSR: Reference Services Review* 22, no. 4 (Winter): 17–28.

Hernon, Peter, and Robert E. Dugan. 2001. *An Action Plan for Outcomes Assessment in Your Library*. Chicago, IL: American Library Association.

Hernon, P., and C. R. McClure. 1986. "Unobtrusive Reference Testing: The 55 Percent Rule." *Library Journal* 111, no. 7 (April 15): 37–41.

Hisle, Lee W. 2005. "Reference Questions in the Library of the Future." *Chronicle of Higher Education* (September 30): B6–B8.

Ho, Jeannette, and Gwyneth H. Crowley. 2003. "User Perception of the 'Reliability' of Library Services at Texas A&M University: A Focus Group Study." *Journal of Academic Librarianship* 29, no. 2 (March): 82–87.

LIBREF_L. Available: www.library.kent.edu/page/10391.

Liu, Jia. 2007. *The Evaluation of Worldwide Digital Reference Services in Libraries*. Cambridge, UK: Chandos Publishing (Oxford) Ltd.

Lubans, John, Jr. 2001. "'Where Are the Snows of Yesteryear?' Reflections on a Suggestion 'Box' That Worked." *Library Administration and Management* 15, no. 4: 240–245.

Mosely, Pixey Anne. 2007. "Assessing User Interactions at the Desk Nearest the Front Door." *Reference & User Services Quarterly* 47, no. 2 (Winter): 159–167.

Norlin, Elaina. 2000. "Reference Evaluation: A Three-step Approach—Surveys, Unobtrusive Observations, and Focus Groups." *College & Research Libraries* 61, no. 6 (November): 546–553.

Novotny, Eric. 2004. "I Don't Think I Click: A Protocol Analysis Study of Use of a Library Online Catalog in the Internet Age." *College & Research Libraries* 65, no. 6 (November): 523–537.

Oder, Norman. 2008. " Budget Report 2008: Treading Carefully." *Library Journal* 133, no. 1 (January 1): 49–51.

Plosker, G. 2004. "Learning from Best Practices." *Online* 28, no. 3: 50–52.

PUBLIB. Available: http://lists.webjunction.org/publib/.

Read, Eleanor J. 2007. "Data Services in Academic Libraries Assessing Needs and Promoting Services." *Reference & User Services Quarterly* 46, no. 3 (Spring): 61–76.

Richardson, John V. 2002. "Reference Is Better Than We Thought." *Library Journal* 127, no. 7 (April 15): 41–42.

Rose, Pamela, Sharon A. Gray, and Kristin Stoklosa. 1998. "A Focus Group Approach to Assessing Techno-stress at the Reference Desk." *Reference & User Services Quarterly* 37, no. 4 (Summer): 311–317.

Shoaf, Eric C. 2003. "Using a Professional Moderator in Library Focus Group Research." *College & Research Libraries* 64, no. 2 (March): 124–132.

Stacy-Bates, Kristine. 2003. "E-mail Reference Responses from Academic ARL Libraries: An Unobtrusive Study." *Reference & User Services Quarterly* 43, no. 1: 59–70.

Staff. 2004. "Better Service Through Data Numbers—Wai Sze (Lacey) Chan." *Library Journal* 129, no. 5 (March 15): 34.

Survey Monkey. Available: www.surveymonkey.com. A detailed key on how to use the tool can be found at: www.library.kent.edu/files/Library_Live_II_Survey_Monkey.pdf.

Ward, David. 1999. *Getting the Most Out of Web-Based Surveys*. (LITA Guide #6). Chicago: American Library Association.

Whitlach, Jo Bell. 2000. *Evaluating Reference Services: A Practical Guide*. Chicago, IL, and London: American Library Association.

20

Reference 2.0

Changing Vocabulary Attests to Changing Times

More than two decades ago we entered a new world where a mouse no longer referred to Mickey; a floppy rarely described a hat; and Apple and BlackBerry became proper nouns. We are now entering a universe where "twittering" is no longer the preserve of birds; communication in addition to food is "del.icio.us"; and to have an avatar in a Second Life does not require the penance of an Asian mystic. We are, in short, entering the universe of Reference 2.0.

This universe has moved at such a fast clip that defining it and understanding its ramifications continue to skitter across many viewpoints. The goal of effective reference remains timeless, namely, the satisfaction of the user. However, the dramatic technological tools thrown up by Web 2.0 in which mass participation and Web socialization have become both the norm and the expectation have added a new dimension to business as usual.

In the world of reference, information is increasingly more than a one-way delivery of facts from those who know to those who seek to know. It is a multi-way, interactive dialogue, drawing from a vast anonymous social network that believes the sum to be greater than its parts. Users expect information to be individually developed so that the uniqueness of the user's needs are both acknowledged and satisfied. This information delivery system is expected to reach out and connect with users wherever they are rather than remain in the static splendor of a physical site. It is not a simple change where information is being provided in a new format brought about by new technology as has been the case ever since the clay tablets of Mesopotamia, the scrolls of Alexandria, the quipa of the Incas and even the advent of print. The informational model for all formats drew unchallenged from the central premise that information was to be collated in a central place or format that people could access.

In the brave new universe of 2.0, the focus is on social networking—leading to "designer information." This chapter touches upon some of the more vigorous tools being utilized by reference librarians across the globe. They have been selected to underlie what currently appear to be the four main sounding notes of the 2.0 universe: collaboration, social networking, customization, and seamlessness.

What Is the 2.0 Universe?

By the end of 2008, *Library Journal* was already covering the imminence of Reference 3.0 and the possible routes it might follow. Collaboration, spontaneity, customization, and multimedia formatting were all part of the future as defined by selected librarians and publishers. It was less clear in what ways Reference 3.0 was different from 2.0. More interesting still was the fact that no single definition of 2.0 has really stuck as being definitive. As passionately argued and elaborately substantiated by Walt Crawford (2006: 31), the term "Library 2.0" had sixty-two views and seven different definitions befuddling the concept, leading him to the generalization that 2.0 "encompasse(d) a range of new and not-so-new software methodologies." Lankes, Silverstein, and Nicholson (2006: 9) also characterized the whole notion of a Web 2.0 as "an aggregation of concepts." Reference 2.0 as well is really a congregation of concepts variously approached and rated by different practitioners.

With the fast-spreading "viral" quality of new technology associated with 2.0 developments, the necessary distance to catch one's breath and view the change has really not existed and will not exist for some time to come. Yet waiting for that distance before trying to come to a comprehensive definition does not make sense either, given the active use of flourishing tools such as wikis, RSS feeds, blogs, widgets, podcasts, streaming videos, mashups, and wildly popular sites such as Facebook, Flickr, LibraryThing, MySpace, and Second Life. Caught in the maelstrom of expanding Internet capabilities and user curiosity and maturity, it is possible to find patterns in what it is that makes 2.0 such an attractive tool to the traditional reference arsenal, even if a complete definition remains ambiguous. Copious examples of how these tools are currently being used are given as an experiential alternate to the holistic picture typically afforded by time and distance.

The following sections outline the four most prominent patterns found in the Reference 2.0 universe:

1. *Collaboration* refers to cooperative content creation. Tools used for this include wikis, blogs, microblogs, folksonomies, and podcasting. Sites like MediaWiki, Bloglines, Twitter, Delicious, LibraryThing, GoodReads, Bookcrossing, and Shelfari are all representative of this aspect of Reference 2.0.
2. *Social Networking* is associated with the outgrowth of online communities that are relevant for reference outreach, i.e., "where people are". Sites such as MySpace and Facebook are prime examples of social networking.
3. *Customization* is also a strong corollary to social networking; tools like widgets, RSS feeds, mashup initiatives like Google Maps, Facebook Plug-ins, and Meebo IM, and creation sites such as Ning and Wordpress are important components of Reference 2.0.
4. *Seamlessness*—global, transparent platforms that allow for seamlessness between mediums is evident in environments like Second Life; and multi-format reference through IM (instant messaging), SMS (short message service or text messaging), and mobile reference.

The tools themselves overlap over all four pattern categories so that providing Meebo IM reference, for example, testifies both to seamlessness in allowing for a creative combination of traditional reference data mashed up with the functionality provided by a 2.0 tool like Meebo; customization afforded by Meebo Me widgets can be embedded in sites where users can directly use IM. The University of Calgary Library (Canada), for example, started a successful Meebo IM reference service in late 2007 and added Meebo Me widgets to its library catalog so that students and faculty who were consulting the catalog could instantly chat with a reference librarian without having to toggle between sites. The Eastern Kentucky University (Kentucky) added a Meebome widget to its FindArticles site that has led to a doubling of its IM reference (Judd, 2007). Reference initiatives launched in Second Life can be perceived as collaborative (as evident in the sprawling *InfoIsland Archipelago*), customized, (as in the art-imitating-real-life library buildings populating the eerily familiar Second Life topography), and a product of the new seamlessness (as made startlingly clear by the talking, visually arresting 3-D librarian avatars of Second Life). The patterns, then, are not hitched exclusively to one tool, but stand as broader and calming descriptive harnesses to the welter of "shiny toys"(Crawford, 2009) inundating the 2.0 landscape.

Cooperative Content Creation

Reference Wikis

Imagine for a minute that you are sitting with a book, highlighting in yellow marker the sentences that you want to remember and jotting in the margins the thoughts and associative knowledge that the reading material has inspired in you. Imagine then that your jottings and highlighting are absorbed into the pages of the book so that they merge to create a new book, one that has incorporated your wisdom and knowledge into its pages. Whereas the print medium would have to view such a scenario as pure fantasy, the online medium has realized it in the form of a "wiki." Wikis are quite simply interactive sites that can be asynchronously amended, corrected, or expanded by the user. The further glory of the wiki dictates that no user needs to master Web technology to be an active wiki player. Wiki engines such as MediaWiki, Traction, TeamPage, and PmWiki provide the software; wiki providers such as seedwiki, Google Sites, and PBwiki can act as hosts so that the user is left to focus on the material and interaction with the material. Since its inception in 1994, wiki implementations have expanded exponentially so that they now come in all types and can be attached to just about any system.

How can the inherent structure of a wiki lend itself to enhancing reference services? Though "wikiwiki," started as a Hawaiian term for being super fast, the defining quality of a wiki is not so much speed as the ability to be cooperative and interactive. As usage around the nation and the globe attest, it is this interactivity that is being mined in various, creative ways by reference institutions.

Ready Reference

Given that instant updates are the hallmark of a wiki product, ready reference is one of the prime areas where the technology can flourish. The most popular and dramatic ready reference tool online is the much-debated *Wikipedia*. As elaborated in Chapter 5, *Wikipedia* draws its greatest strength and its most acute vulnerability from the same feature, namely its openness to content collaboration. A global community of almost 800 million monthly visitors and its consistent reign as one of the top ten most visited sites in the world (Alexa, 2011) attests to its success as a wiki resource of uncommon popularity. In the United Kingdom, *h2g2* aims to provide encyclopedic wiki content to "life, the universe, and everything." Small-scale ready reference by individual libraries is also played out with notable success by many institutions. *Andover Answers* is run by the Memorial Hall Library in Andover (Massachusetts) and hosts a public ready reference wiki on the town's history and social, cultural, and economic establishments at www.mhl.org/answers/. The Burbank Public Library in Burbank (California) hosts a local community wiki at http://burbank.wikidot.com/; however, the wiki is closed to instant editing and all changes must be submitted by e-mail.

Subject Guides

The Camden County Library (New Jersey) has more than fifty pathfinders and subject guides available on its Web site. The New York Public Library has almost 100 research guides on its site. Libraries have traditionally created these guides to aid their users. The onus of updating all these guides all the time is a constant requirement of good reference service. Wikis can assist in the process as seen in a number of examples. *Question Point*, the 24/7 reference service provided by the Library of Congress and OCLC, have set up a subject wiki for chat librarians "to provide quick, authoritative starting points for librarians" at http://wiki .questionpoint.org/readyref. Chad Boeninger, a Reference and Instruction Librarian at Ohio University Libraries, created *Biz Wiki* to transform the countless business resources traditionally listed in subject guides and pathfinders into a wiki format that the entire university community could update; it is available at www2.library.ohiou.edu/subjects/bizwiki/index.php/Main_Page. The Grand Rapids Public Library (Michigan) hosts a whole collection of subject guides that can only be updated by reference librarians within the library system at www.grpl.org/wiki/index.php/.

Discussions and Proceedings

Reference librarians have also been using wiki formats to keep an ongoing, interactive record of meetings, conference proceedings, and staff discussions. The ALA Annual Conferences, for example, host a wiki at http://presentations .ala.org that is open for posts from all attendees and exhibitors. The Oregon State Library (Oregon) uses Confluence to provide an ongoing source of internal information for its reference librarians. The issues of "reference desk managers," "subject research guides," and "digital access services" are all contained in "spaces" that the librarian can consult to get a sense of what has been discussed both longitudinally across time, latitudinally across committees, and annotated by staff through wiki access. A representative example from this wiki can be seen at http://wiki.library.oregonstate.edu/confluence/. The Albany County Public Library (Wyoming) staff aim to capture the elusive institutional wisdom of their system by documenting "how to do things" via a wiki at http://albystaff.pbwiki.com/.

Reference Instruction and Manuals

Wikis are potentially capable of reducing the constant reinvention of the wheel with regard to instruction manuals. Reference librarians looking to create how-to manuals for basic computer classes, or class syllabi for bibliographic instruction, or handouts dealing with information literacy are well served with wiki versions that can be updated and repackaged in keeping with the times and the institution using it. "Using a wiki to integrate the library instruction knowledge of many librarians enables a library instruction program to better meet our patrons' needs," states reference librarian Charles Allan (2007: 242). An example can be seen in the Library Technology Training Wiki that provides comprehensive tutorials on how to conduct an online survey and make a wiki at http://trainingwiki.pbworks.com. Online wiki-based tutorials on medical reference, reader's advisory, and information literacy can be found through the "Wiki Online Learning Opportunities" offered freely at http://statelibrary .ncdcr.gov.

Project Management

Wikis can be useful tools of knowledge management for specific projects. In trying to improve the computer services offered by the reference department at the Durham County Library (North Carolina), the staff became part of a larger Strategic Plan Wiki that aimed at both informing and encouraging active participation from the library board, trustees, the town government, and the community at large to effect a public transformation of the library system. The site, now retired, can still be seen as a historical snapshot at http://dclstrategic plan.pbworks.com and testifies to the successful use of wiki technology to further the goals of a reference project. The University of Minnesota Libraries set up a successful Libraries Staff Wiki to manage website content at https:// wiki.lib.umn.edu.

Reference Blogs, Microblogs, and Podcasts

In the early 1990s, the term "Weblogs" was used to loosely describe online postings or logs on a Web site. In less than a decade, the expansion of the tool led to a contraction of the word, and "Weblogs" was reduced to "blogs." The popularity of blogs and the rich variety of blog formats, in turn, gave birth to a host of corollary words such as bloggers (those who blog), blogging (a verb describing the act of posting a blog), microblogs (really short blogs), blogosphere (the universe of blogs), blogrolls (list of links to other blogs), blog search engines (engines that search blog postings and content), trackbacks (acknowledgment of communication between blogs), vlogs (video blogs), qlogs (question and answer blogs), MP3 blogs (music blogs), and podcasts (audio blogs). As of 2008, a reported 1 million posts were being added each day in eighty-one different languages across the globe (Technorati, June 2008). As of 2010, corporate bloggers were receiving an average of over 300,000 unique visitors per month.

Blogs are frequent posts made on a site, with the posts typically listed in reverse chronological order. There is nothing very new about this act. In the world of print reference, columns titled "What's New in Reference" or "Reference Updates" held the basic ingredients of a "blog." How then are blogs different? For one thing, blogs are not static columns, but actual Web sites navigable through hyperlinks. This allows blog sites to link with other blogs, accept online discussion and commentary, and archive past blogs so that the site is marked strongly with its own rugged personality. Topic, genre, content structure, motivation, media type, and composing device all play a role in marking the individualistic world of blogging. Hyperlinks, feedback, and open discussion forums accentuate the distinctiveness of the blog, even as they harness the 2.0 hallmarks of dynamic collaboration, networking, and cooperative content creation. A working paper conducted by the University of Essex (United Kingdom) on blogging refers to it as a means of "public knowledge-building on the web" that creates "self-organizing communities" (Brady, 2005). The world of reference blogs has been developing a great many such "self-organizing communities."

Reference Blogs as Campus Newsletters

The Lillian Goldman Library at Yale Law School has a "Reference Blog" that serves as a catchall for things that may be pertinent to the academic law community ranging from global and national news bulletins to in-house library acquisitions and bibliographic instruction (see Figure 20-1). A cloud of hyperlinked subject tags brackets the blog, serving as an index that the user can instantly click to retrieve blogs of personal interest.

Reference Blogs as Reader's Advisory

The Bensenville Community Public Library (Illinois) hosts a Web site that is rich in blogs directed at reader's advisory for all ages (see Figure 20-2). Library staff contribute to an ongoing blog on book reviews titled "52 Books, 52 Weeks Program" accessible at http://52books.org/. Author blogs are linked under a comprehensive listing so that users can access their favorite author through the library site. "Book trailers" are also collected so that a video preview of the book is available with the option to place a hold on the title.

Reference Blogs as In-house Communication

Internal blogs are handy tools to enhance communication within a busy or wide-ranging reference department. Not only is the original message or update open to all staff, but also changes over time, or other viewpoints can be

Figure 20-1. Screen Shot of Reference Blog at the Yale Law Library

Source: Screen shot reproduced with permission from Yale Law School.

Figure 20-2. Reader's Advisory Blog at the Bensenville (IL) Community Public Library

Source: Printed with permission from the Bensenville Community Public Library district.

incorporated or appended to the blog. "Blogs are a crucial element of the Web 2.0 landscape not just for the information they publish, but for the spider web of relationships they spawn," observes Funk (2009), and this holds very true to in-house reference blogs. The Barnard College Library blog (shown in Figure 20-3), the Libarians' Blog at Hennepin County Library, the Science Updates at Washington and Lee University Libraries, are all examples of blogs used in interesting ways to keep reference librarians on the same page. Issues as small as a consistent way to report problems with the local printer to long-term issues of digitizing the local history collection are examples of subjects; the efficacy and nature of an in-house blog is very much a function of institutional requirement and staff commitment.

Reference Blogs as News Bulletins

Mainstream newspapers, with their guiding principle of providing updates on news, are fertile ground for blogging. In fact, 95 percent of the top 100 newspapers currently have reporter blogs (The Bivings Report, 2007). Concurrently, large news blogs such as the wildly successful *Huffington Post* have taken on the persona of mainstream newspapers so that the boundary between the mainstream print sites and blog format is merging. Reference

---

Figure 20-3. Blog as In-house Communication at Barnard (NY) College Library

barnardrefdesk

THIS BLOG SERVES TO KEEP BARNARD LIBRARIANS POSTED ABOUT REFERENCE DESK GOINGS ON.

Tuesday, March 24, 2009
Student access to fax machines
Basically, there is no student access to a fax machine on campus. (I called office services; their fax machine requires an administrative code for use.)

However, there are tons of free fax services online, where you upload your file and they send it to the recipient's fax machine. Some have ads or require registration or other pesky things. If anyone has a recommendation about one service over another. Please post it in the comments.

Labels: fax machine

// posted by Jenna @ 1:06 PM 0 comments

Monday, March 16, 2009
REFERENCE SYMPOSIUM: FRIDAY MARCH 13, 2009

The 7th Annual Reference Symposium, "The Making of a Reference Librarian" was held on Friday March 13. Thanks to colleagues who helped the reference librarians by taking additional reference hours. Many of the papers and presentations are available on the symposium's website with more to come this week:

Source: Used by permission of Barnard College Library.

Figure 20-4. Blogs as News Bulletins at the University of Montana

GOVERNMENT NEWS FOR MONTANA

RECENTLY PUBLISHED GOVERNMENT INFORMATION
SPONSORED BY THE MANSFIELD LIBRARY AT THE UNIVERSITY OF MONTANA,
WITH SUPPORT FROM MONTANA GOVERNMENT INFORMATION PROFESSIONALS

WEDNESDAY, MARCH 25, 2009

Montana Bill on Stimulus Funds

From the *Missoulian*: "Capping more than a week of marathon committee sessions and one-on-one negotiations among its members, a key legislative panel Tuesday approved the bill outlining how to spend Montana's $870 million share of federal economic 'stimulus' money."

The House Appropriations Committee passed House Bill 645, Implement receipt of and appropriate federal stimulus and recovery funds, yesterday. You can find the latest text of the bill on the Montana Legislature website. The bill now heads to the floor of the Montana House.

Source: Dennison, M. (25 March 2009). "Legislature 2009: Key panel approves stimulus measure." *Missoulian*. A1.

Labels: budget, legislature, Montana, recession

POSTED BY J. BURROUGHS AT 12:59 PM   0 COMMENTS

Contact a Government Information Librarian for Assistance

Jennie Burroughs, University of Montana
jennie.burroughs@umontana.edu

Carol Jestrab, MSU-Northern
jestrab@msun.edu

James Kammerer, Montana State Library
jkammerer@mt.gov

LINKS

Montana State Website
USA.gov
GPO Access
THOMAS
About the FDLP

PREVIOUS POSTS

Montana Bill on Stimulus Funds
GAO Report on the Labor Department
NIOSH Vermiculite Study

Source: Government News for Montana, sponsored by the Maureen and Mike Mansfield Library of the University of Montana, http://mt-govinfo.blogspot.com.

librarians, especially those connected with special interest collections, have been quick to emulate the trend. News blogs, aimed at specific constituencies, can be seen in the field. The Government Documents and Reference librarian at the Mansfield Library, University of Montana-Missoula for example, has collaborated with staff to create a news update for "recently published government information" in blog form accessible at http://mt-govinfo.blogspot.com (see Figure 20-4).

Reference Blogs as Personal Statement

In 2006, *Time* magazine selected "You" as its "Person of the Year" based on the wildfire appeal of blogging and related user-created Web sites. Blog software is simple enough that publishing Web content, formerly the preserve of a technical department, is accessible to all. Personal blogs are the most common form of blogging to be found and also the most vulnerable to abandonment over time. A study in 2006 found more than 200 million dead blogs (Funk, 2009). Despite this high fatality rate, personal blogs have found favor with reference librarians both as personalized commentary and as institutional branding tools, most typically presented as library director blogs. Paul Courant, the University Librarian and Dean of Libraries at the University of Michigan, for example, has been writing "Au Courant," a personal blog on topics related primarily, though not exclusively, to the library universe at http://paulcourant.net/. The University Librarians' Blog, posted by Yale University Library, functions as a personalized branding tool for the library. Each post describes some special exhibit or feature of the library as seen in Figure 20-5.

Figure 20-5. Blogs as Personal Statement

Yale University Library

RESEARCH TOOLS   LIBRARIES & COLLECTIONS   ABOUT THE LIBRARY   LIBRARY SERVICES
Departments & Staff / Working at the Library / Giving to the Library / Access & Use / Computers in the Library / Ask! a Librarian

University Librarian's Blog

February 9, 2009

Celebrating the Power of Ideas

The first weeks of 2009 mark some extraordinary anniversaries, each one with a heightened resonance in the context of the seismic changes that are going on in the economic and political life of the nation. Martin Luther King, Jr. would have been eighty years old, Abraham Lincoln was born two hundred years ago, and we are also celebrating the bicentenary of Lincoln's exact contemporary Charles Darwin. The Library will celebrate Black History month, and so honor Dr. King, with a notable trio of lectures coming up. Abraham Lincoln's anniversary will be celebrated across the campus in many different forums, classes, and symposia. Charles Darwin, meanwhile, that reclusive and reflective scientist and man of letters, never visited North America, but the impact of his work on this country's political, philosophical and theological discourse, let alone our science, continues to animate controversy and passions that Darwin himself might never have imagined.

Though he did not visit, Darwin corresponded at length with scientists in North America, including Yale's James Dwight Dana, Silliman Professor of Natural History and Geology. Darwin's and Dana's association as explorers, scholars, and pioneering scientists fostered a rich and rewarding correspondence between 1849 and 1863 and the display of Darwin's letters to his friend and mentor (which are part of the collection of Manuscripts and Archives) in Sterling Memorial Library is one of a group of exhibits in different parts of the Library system, celebrating the Darwin bicentenary. Kline Science Library has mounted two displays, and there are others at the Medical, Music, and Divinity Libraries. They provide between them some fascinating insights, based on Yale collections, into Darwin's own life, times, and thought, and into the reception of his theory of evolution in the one hundred and fifty years since he published On the Origin of Species. They also give food for thought about the way ideas are transmitted, and the power of one man and his book to transform the world's view of itself.

Posted by Alice at 1:48 PM | Comments (0)

Alice Prochaska

FEBRUARY 2009
Sun Mon Tue Wed Thu Fri Sat
 1   2   3   4   5   6   7
 8   9 10 11 12 13 14
15 16 17 18 19 20 21
22 23 24 25 26 27 28

ARCHIVES

Source: Screen shot reproduced with permission from Yale Law School.

Microblogs

Microblogs are exactly what they sound like, blogs that inform, update, comment, or notify users in pithy form. The most popular version of a microblog is twitter, which currently claims more than 55 million daily users (Galante, 2009). Twitter's limit to a text-based post is a maximum of 140 characters. In a 2.0 world where fact is frequently stranger than fiction, it would have been hard to predict that the sending of 140 characters, or "tweets," could become a viable reference tool. Yet tweeting is increasingly recognized as an efficient way to provide quick updates, bulleted information, enhance publicity, or reinforce library messages. From the Library of Congress (see Figure 20-6) to academic, public, and small-town libraries, tweeting is currently being used for a variety of purposes. The Casa Grande Public Library (Arizona) uses it to provide program updates; the Perkins Library Reference Desk at Duke University tweets out answers to reference questions, bibliographic updates, and even the library room temperature; Maryland's cooperative 24/7 online service, *AskUsNow!*, offers tweets for quick question-and-answer sessions; the Nebraska Library Commission provides ready reference through its twitter account. Examples of reference questions answered through tweets at the Commission's site (http://twitter.com/NLC_Reference) shows how microblogging is capable of providing ready reference.

Q: *Where can I search to see who owns a particular corporation in Nebraska?*
A: *Tweet: http://tinyurl.com/384na4*

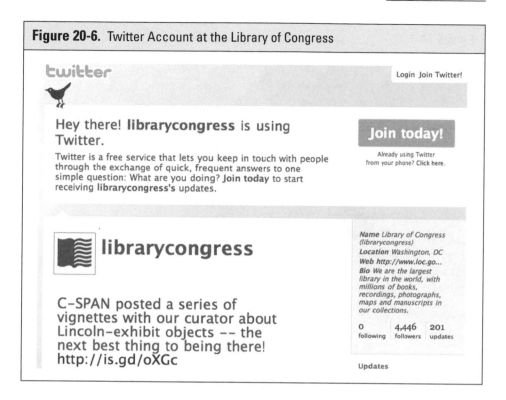

Figure 20-6. Twitter Account at the Library of Congress

Q: *Where are the state statutes online?*
A: *Tweet: http://tinyurl.com/b4px4w*

Podcasts

Much like blogs, podcasts also provide updates over the Internet, except they are audio files. The same structure of Web syndication and feeds allows for podcasts to be accessible effortlessly to vast numbers of users linked to a single site. Reference libraries have used podcasts to conduct tours of the collection, distribute reference programs to a wider audience that could not attend an in-house session, and deliver bibliographic instruction. The Claude Moore Health Sciences Library of the University of Virginia, for example, has open access to podcasts of its health lecture series. Those interested in subscribing to an automatic feed of these podcasts can subscribe to it, or opt to listen to any one of the podcasts offered at their Web site available at www.hsl.virginia.edu/historical/lectures.cfm. The Sheridan Libraries of the Johns Hopkins University uses podcasts to assist its constituency in effectively navigating the library's reference resources. Instructive podcasts on *JHsearch*, a metasearch platform for searching through multiple library databases, *Ask a Librarian* services offered by subject specialists, and mapping software available to analyze geospatial data and create customized maps, are part of the repertoire on bibliographic instruction offered by the library (see Figure 20-7).

Figure 20-7. Podcasts at the Sheridan Libraries, Johns Hopkins University

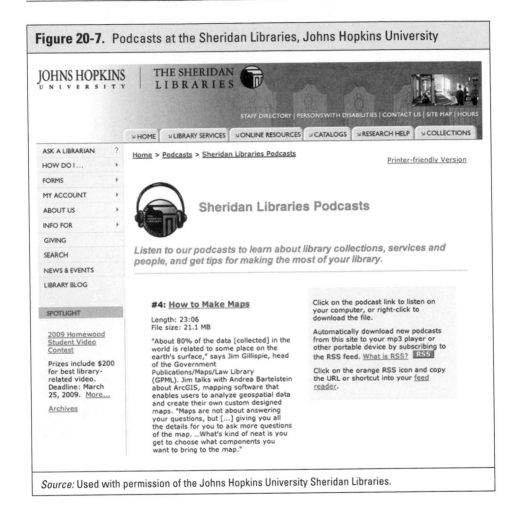

Source: Used with permission of the Johns Hopkins University Sheridan Libraries.

Reference Folksonomies

Another dramatic manifestation of cooperative content creation has been in the area of socially tagged informational sites. The classification of information, far from being slotted into traditional subject indexing, develops taxonomy based on keyword usage from multiple folks; hence the term, "folksonomy." The visual display of this form of keyword indexing is popularly projected through graphical words or tag clouds, where words used most often by the user community have larger fonts, and correspondingly, words with lesser usage are displayed in smaller fonts. All the variously sized words are typically hyperlinked so users can drill down into the subject in which they are interested. The familiar hierarchy or connecting relationship between terms, which constitutes the bedrock of subject classification, is simply nonexistent in folksonomies where keywords float in their own user-created space.

Flickr is one of the most popular online photo management and sharing application sites that is freely available to all users. Libraries interested in maintaining a visual profile have been quick to upload institutional photographs on Flickr. As with all public images that are used for library marketing, the convoluted laws of patron privacy need to be followed (Carson, 2008). In Figure 20-8, the photos associated with the University of British Columbia (Canada) have developed a folksonomy that is graphically depicted with a tag cloud. The majority of photographs appear to describe the "campus," the "library," and "ubc" (given that the fonts for these words are the largest in the cloud). Clicking on any one of these indexing words would lead the user to see the associated photographs.

Del.icio.us is a widely used social bookmarking service that allows all users to freely tag and save sites that they choose in order to share it with others at a future date. Unlike the old system of having to save such sites on individual computers as "Favorites," this service manages saved Web pages from a centralized source that can be accessed from anywhere. In Figure 20-9, the Witkin State Law Library (California) has pertinent sites bookmarked. The popularity of the subject matter is indexed in a folksonomy with a tag cloud in which "California" has the largest collection of bookmarked sites. Drilling down in the hyperlinked tag allows the user to encounter the sites seen in the next graphic: "How To File A Claim," "California Codes," "LA Law Library," etc. (see Figure 20-10).

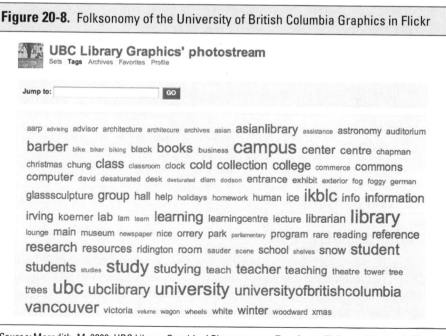

Figure 20-8. Folksonomy of the University of British Columbia Graphics in Flickr

UBC Library Graphics' photostream
Sets **Tags** Archives Favorites Profile

Jump to: [   ] GO

aarp advising advisor architecture architecure archives asian asianlibrary assistance astronomy auditorium barber bike biker biking black books business campus center centre chapman christmas chung class classroom clock cold collection college commerce commons computer david desaturated desk desturated diam dodson entrance exhibit exterior fog foggy german glasssculpture group hall help holidays homework human ice ikblc info information irving koerner lab lam learn learning learningcentre lecture librarian library lounge main museum newspaper nice orrery park parliamentary program rare reading reference research resources ridington room sauder scene school shelves snow student students studies study studying teach teacher teaching theatre tower tree trees ubc ubclibrary university universityofbritishcolumbia vancouver victoria volume wagon wheels white winter woodward xmas

Source: Meredith, M. 2009. UBC Library Graphics' Photostream—Tags (www.flickr.com/photosubclibrary/tags/).

Figure 20-9. Cloud Tag for the Witkin (CA) State Law Library

Figure 20-10. A Drill-down of Single Tag for the Witkin (CA) State Law Library

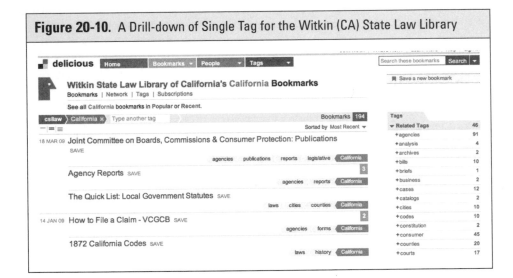

Social Networking

Facebook and MySpace

Much like Flickr, which is a media site, Facebook, MySpace, Bebo, Friendster, StudiVZ, Hi5, and Orkut are social sites that are structured to facilitate online user interaction and the open sharing of data. Given the emphasis on providing timely reference "where the users are," attention to these social networking sites has risen amongst reference librarians because of the rising popularity of these sites. By January 2011, for example, Facebook had posted over 600 million active users. Within these millions of users, interest groups voluntarily coalesce based on stated interests and invitations to be part of the group. Each group features a "profile" with information on the group or institution, and a "wall" with threaded discussion lists and scrolled messages allowing for data collation and interactive discussion.

For reference librarians, the sites provide yet another "space" in which to offer services. "Ask A Librarian" groups, book discussion groups attracting outlier populations that may not visit a physical library, and professional consultation groups that are able to discuss database vendor negotiation, conference proceedings, or library best practices are some of the iterations playing out in these still-early days of social networking site usage amongst reference librarians.

Public libraries like the Denver Public Library (http://myspace.com/denver_evolver); the Houston Public Library (www.facebook.com/houston library); and the Hennepin County Library (www.facebook.com/hclib) among many others, have set up a presence in these sites. Academic libraries like Mississippi State University Libraries (www.facebook.com/msulibrary); the Brooklyn College Library (www.myspace.com/brooklyncollegelibrary); and the Duke University Law Library (see Figure 20-11) have accounts. Larger professional groups such as *Librarians and Facebook*, *Library Applications in Facebook*, the *Libraries Without Walls* conference group, and the *University College and Research* group can all be located in Facebook.

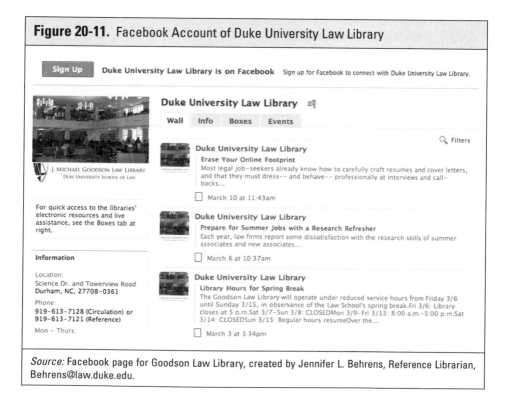

Figure 20-11. Facebook Account of Duke University Law Library

Sign Up   **Duke University Law Library is on Facebook**   Sign up for Facebook to connect with Duke University Law Library.

Duke University Law Library

Wall   Info   Boxes   Events

Q Filters

J. MICHAEL GOODSON LAW LIBRARY
Duke University School of Law

Duke University Law Library
Erase Your Online Footprint
Most legal job-seekers already know how to carefully craft resumes and cover letters, and that they must dress-- and behave-- professionally at interviews and call-backs...

☐ March 10 at 11:43am

For quick access to the libraries' electronic resources and live assistance, see the Boxes tab at right.

Duke University Law Library
Prepare for Summer Jobs with a Research Refresher
Each year, law firms report some dissatisfaction with the research skills of summer associates and new associates...

☐ March 6 at 10:37am

Information

Location:
Science Dr. and Towerview Road
Durham, NC, 27708-0361

Phone:
919-613-7128 (Circulation) or
919-613-7121 (Reference)

Mon - Thurs:

Duke University Law Library
Library Hours for Spring Break
The Goodson Law Library will operate under reduced service hours from Friday 3/6 until Sunday 3/15, in observance of the Law School's spring break.Fri 3/6: Library closes at 5 p.m.Sat 3/7-Sun 3/8: CLOSEDMon 3/9-Fri 3/13: 8:00 a.m.-5:00 p.m.Sat 3/14: CLOSEDSun 3/15: Regular hours resumeOver the...

☐ March 3 at 3:34pm

Source: Facebook page for Goodson Law Library, created by Jennifer L. Behrens, Reference Librarian, Behrens@law.duke.edu.

As may be seen in the Duke graphic, in addition to information about the Duke University Law Library's contact information and hours of service, the potential user can also directly launch into World Cat and catalog searches; chat with a reference librarian; access LexisNexis and other databases; and use the "Ask-a-Librarian" service, all without leaving the site. Herein lies the potential attraction of social networking sites like Facebook. Much like laptop-toting reference librarians who try to catch the physical user in high-traffic areas such as the student community area (as discussed in styles of roving reference [Chapter 18]), Reference 2.0 aims to catch tomorrow's user at online high-traffic areas.

Customization

Widgets Used for Reference

"Gadgets," "snippets," "modules," "add-ons," and "plugins" are some of the other terms used for widget technology. Widgets are miniscule programming codes that can be easily plucked and inserted into a larger Web page so that the page becomes more interactive and customized to user preferences. Reference libraries have used widgets, as well as offered widgets to their users for accessing library services in innovative ways.

A prominent use of widgets by reference librarians has been in the field of chat reference. Chat widgets such as MeeboMe, Qwidget, WIMZI, Plugoo, and Digsby have become prominent tools for chat reference. The University Libraries at the Pennsylvania State University attached chat widgets on various pages of its Web site so the user can access it at the point of need. The Ask-a-Librarian page, course guide pages, subject guide pages, and subject library homepages all have embedded chat widgets for speedy and anonymous reference interactions.

The University of Texas Libraries has a family of widgets that are helpfully divided into search widgets, information organizing widgets, and collaboration widgets (see Figure 20-12).

- *Search widgets* include a Toolbar Button that allows Google users to add a button for the library catalog on their Google page; a Web browser add-on that allows users to search the University of Texas Digital Repository; and a widget that opens up the possibility of using iPhones to search for material in the closest library through WorldCat searches.
- *Information organizing* widgets include a Facebook application that creates APA, Chicago Manual, MLA, Turabian and Harvard citation styles for material found in WorldCat; a Flickr Uploader that organizes photographs on the Web; and Zotero, a widget that helps users to collect, manage, and cite research sources.
- *Collaboration* widgets include a widget that helps "clip out" material from Web pages to then share with others through blogs, e-mails, and print-outs; and PBWiki, which allows users to set up their own free, hosted,

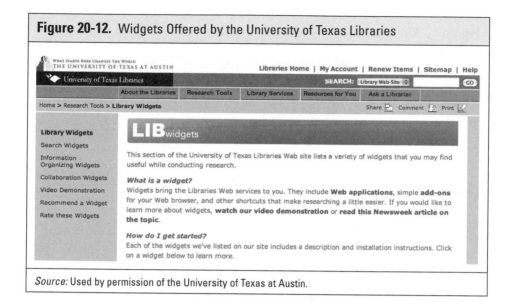

Figure 20-12. Widgets Offered by the University of Texas Libraries

Source: Used by permission of the University of Texas at Austin.

password-protected wiki in the time it takes to make a PB (peanut butter) sandwich.

RSS Feeds Used for Reference

In 2005, the powers that be at Firefox and Internet Explorer collaborated in an effort to standardize a little orange logo with white wavy lines rippling outward, denoting the "broadcasting of content." This was to become the ubiquitous RSS logo that stands for Really Simple Syndication. What is really simple about this customization tool is its ability to automatically view breaking new content from any number of Web sites in one single interface, without having to search each site independently. Since 1999, when RSS first originated, the software (feed reader or aggregator) used to read the feeds has expanded so that it can be Web based, desktop based, or available through hand-held devices. Whereas the current family of Internet browsers has built-in RSS readers, accessing feeds is limited to the computer in which it is saved. On the other hand, Web-based feed aggregators such as Google Reader, available at www.google.com/reader, and Bloglines at www.bloglines.com, are free, easy to use, and can be accessed from any computer with Internet access, key considerations in the popularity of 2.0 tools.

For reference librarians, RSS feeds can be used to alert patrons about new books, articles, library news and happenings, blogs, and even tables of contents from new journals (see Figure 20-13). The custom of updates, however, has far predated RSS technology and, in fact, continues through e-mail notification in a great many libraries. Why then is the popularity of RSS feeds gaining so rapidly in so many environments, including reference libraries? The answer may be contained in some of the functional differences between e-mail and RSS

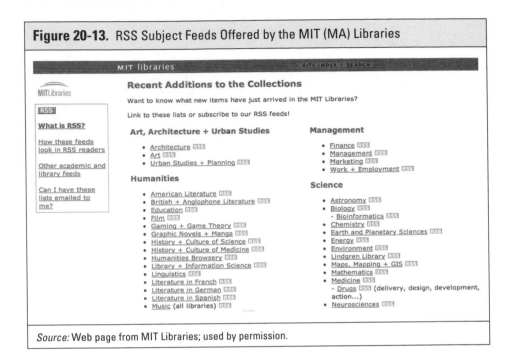

Figure 20-13. RSS Subject Feeds Offered by the MIT (MA) Libraries

Source: Web page from MIT Libraries; used by permission.

alerts. Unlike receiving updates via e-mail, RSS feeds allow for customizable formatting; the items are automatically deleted or marked as "read"; subscription to an RSS is typically anonymous; and updates are kept sacrosanct from the flotsam and jetsam populating the standard e-mail account. An in-built elegance to RSS updates for both the sender and the receiver promises its continued expansion in user base.

Mashups

Mashups are creative enterprises. They describe a single graphical interface for a distinctive service that is created when content and functionality from more than one Web application are brought together or "mashed up." Why would reference librarians want to mash things up?

First, mashups continue the traditions of good reference in allowing services to develop based on patron-driven wants. If the reference user is able to find peer-based and professional reviews of books on a single site such as Amazon.com, the likelihood of that site being used for evaluating the product is greater than if the user had to toggle through two or more sites to collect the same information. Hennepin County Library, for example, has mashed its ILS with its customer book review database so that its constituency now enjoys a compelling and popular new product, namely, a catalog that can also provide side-by-side comparative reviews of books by contemporaries. At the University of Huddersfield in the United Kingdom, the ILS is mashed with Amazon and other external data sites so that a search in the catalog not only brings up the usual locational and availability information, but a host of other user-focused tools. The user can rate and comment on the book as well as check out reviews by peers, see the cover of the book, instantly link to social bookmarking sites like Delicious, sign up for RSS feeds to be alerted of all new acquisitions in that call number category, and visually browse through a virtual bookshelf holding similar material (see Figure 20-14). An "Ask a Librarian" link completes the page for every single search made in the library catalog.

Second, mashups involve merging and can be used to foment cooperation between different entities. For example, at the University of Rochester, course management has benefited from a well-conceived mashup between reference library resources and the course system as a whole. When professors structure their courses, a feed is sent to the library, which then proceeds to match library resources with the course syllabus. As stated by Susan Gibbons, vice provost of the River Campus Libraries at the university, "mashups provide us an opportunity to better integrate the library with the rest of campus, so that our resources are not siloed but seen as part of an integrated whole of the University" (Storey, 2008: 9).

The Southeastern Libraries Cooperating (SELCO) in Minnesota, a library consortium, mashed up its Web site with both Google Maps and mapbuilder .net (see Figure 20-15). With the mashup, library users could immediately connect their library to the pertinent legislator of that legislative district. The legislator list was also linked to individual photographs and official sites of the legislative body. In addition to added value for the user, it turned out to be a great way of setting up linkages with the legislators themselves, some of whom had no idea of the number of libraries, in addition to the obvious public library, that they represented.

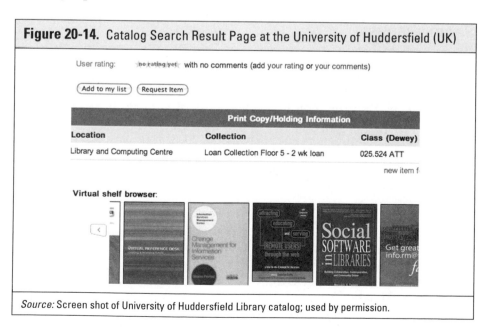

Figure 20-14. Catalog Search Result Page at the University of Huddersfield (UK)

Source: Screen shot of University of Huddersfield Library catalog; used by permission.

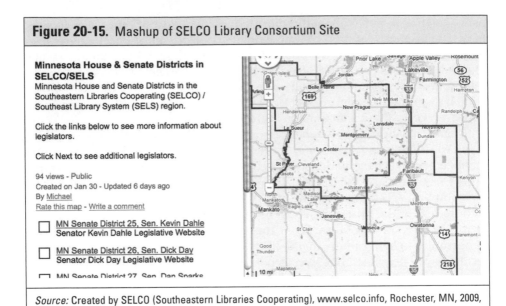

Figure 20-15. Mashup of SELCO Library Consortium Site

Minnesota House & Senate Districts in SELCO/SELS
Minnesota House and Senate Districts in the Southeastern Libraries Cooperating (SELCO) / Southeast Library System (SELS) region.

Click the links below to see more information about legislators.

Click Next to see additional legislators.

94 views - Public
Created on Jan 30 - Updated 6 days ago
By Michael
Rate this map - Write a comment

☐ MN Senate District 25, Sen. Kevin Dahle
Senator Kevin Dahle Legislative Website

☐ MN Senate District 26, Sen. Dick Day
Senator Dick Day Legislative Website

☐ MN Senate District 27, Sen. Dan Sparks

Source: Created by SELCO (Southeastern Libraries Cooperating), www.selco.info, Rochester, MN, 2009, using Google Maps; used by permission.

Finally, as with a great many 2.0 tools populating the library universe, some mashups require relatively basic technical knowledge and can be built by leveraging existing software and sites. In sum, mashups are technologically accessible engines of innovation and can quite simply create a more resonant product and a more unique user experience.

Seamlessness

A glowing orb acts as a liaison to a virtual reference librarian, flying cars provide tours of reference facilities, and books can be searched or questions can be answered in real time by texting through a mobile device: we have entered a certain level of technological seamlessness in the continually emerging world of Reference 2.0. The drive "to make quality information available anyplace, anytime, and for everyone" (Robinson, 2008: 4) undergirds the restless desire to keep experimenting with new forms of media formatting and interactivity, so that there is a palpable sense of increasing transparency between mediums.

Reference in Virtual Worlds

Drawing from realistic three-dimensional (3-D) modeling tools, and underwritten by the assumption that the one life lived physically is not quite enough for the imaginative genius of humans, a wildly popular online virtual world was created in 2003. Second Life (SL), as it was so aptly termed, used the compelling lure of 3-D to help its "residents" create an expanding digital world filled with people/"avatars," a thriving environment, and online experiences. Participants, both individuals and institutions, could buy land, build library buildings, set up reference desks, and hold discussions or answer questions in a somewhat sur-real, cartoon-like virtual world that, nonetheless, mirrors real-life environ-ments. Basic entry into this world and the setting up of an avatar to represent the user is free and easily accessible at www.secondlife.com.

Hundreds of university, college, and public libraries were established on SL, with one of the more spectacular initiatives being the *InfoIsland Archipelago*, where the user could "talk" in real-time, synchronous interaction with a visu-ally solid reference librarian. However, students at San Jose State University found out quite early that navigating through the SL world was clunky, required a steep learning curve, and left one with the perception that in this early stage, SL was more immersed in the "gee-whiz aspect . . . like building neat-o buildings and fountains" (Kelly Gordon in Gerardin, 2008: 324) and less successful at establishing a viable and vibrant reference presence. "Maybe 3-D online environments are just one of those technologies that sound cool but never fully materialize, like personal jetpacks," was Jeffrey Young's (2010) comment. Yet, the ongoing appeal of virtual worlds for the reference librarian is secured more by what may come about in the future than by what is cur-rently evolving. As pithily stated by Hurst-Wahl (2007: 53), "By being a part of SL now, librarians believe they are positioning themselves for the tools, ser-vices, and user environments that will come after it." And in fact, newer ven-tures such as Open Cobalt at Duke University, stand-alone versions of SL at Case Western Reserve University, and the creation of Open Simulator continue to testify to the attraction of reference in virtual worlds.

Mobile Reference

Although virtual reference has been discussed in other parts of the book, it is being highlighted in this chapter both to emphasize its vital role in the 2.0 landscape, as well as its continuing expansion from online, e-mail, chat, and IM reference to the world of handheld devices such as iPods, BlackBerrys, PDAs, MP3 players, notebooks, iPhones, and iPads. Personal digital devices may be on their way to becoming popcorn technology: easy to use, cheaper to buy, and accessible to more than a few. Equally important, the Millennials and NextGen generations appear to interact through e-mail, texting, chat, and Skype and regard handheld devices as an integral part of their persona. As Google CEO Eric Schmidt stated at the Web 2.0 Expo in San Francisco, "The biggest growth areas are clearly going to be in the mobile space. . . . And the reason is people treat their mobile phones as extensions of their person" (Claburn, 2007). There are an estimated 5 billion cell phone subscriptions around the globe, and the traditional use of the cell phone as a communication device has been rapidly redefined to include instant information as well. A 2007 survey of Harvard Medical School found that 52 percent of the students had PDAs that were used primarily (26 percent) for accessing reference information (Lippin-cott, 2008).

Libraries, especially academic institutions, are working toward mobile-ready reference services in different ways. The University of South Dakota offers reference books that are preloaded on PDAs. The University of Alberta in Edmonton, Canada, has a PDA Zone (see Figure 20-16) with technical support, reference bibliographies, and downloadable text from databases such as Access Medicine.

Libraries are creating Web sites and OPACs that are mobile friendly. Libraries at the University of Virginia, University of Richmond, Ball State University, the Grainger Engineering Library, Wayne State University Library, North Carolina State University Library, and the Boston University Medical Center have established "mobile libraries." Staff and students at the Boston University Medical Center, for example, can access the Medline database, check out e-books, and use a hyperlinked directory of library staff and services via the mobile library interface (see Figure 20-17).

Whereas SMS or text messaging has been adopted by libraries to deliver due notices and interlibrary loan request updates, many libraries such as those at University of California at Los Angeles, New York University, Yale Science Libraries, and the Worcester Public Library offer text-messaging reference. The Ohio University Libraries offer Skype reference via calls, video calls, or text messaging. Reference librarians from NYU studied more than 300 of their SMS reference sessions in 2008 and produced some interesting analyses. Questions that began as SMS queries could very easily develop into other venues more suitable to the depth of the question. Despite the nature of SMS, which is predicated on short questions and answers, actual usage involved single interactions marked with a furious volley of back-and-forth transactions. The University of California, Merced, which opened as recently as 2005, not only

---

Figure 20-16. PDA Zone at the University of Alberta, Edmonton, Canada

This site provides access to resources and library services that are available for users of handheld devices known as **Personal Digital Assistants (PDAs)**.

PDA Library Resources and Services

- Wireless PDA Support
- MDC Mobile - MDConsult's information service for PDAs
- PDA Bibliographies
- PEPID
- PICOmaker
- Access Medicine

PDA Guides

- Health Sciences Resources
- PDAs in Education
- Ressources en frani¿½ais
- E-Book / E-Text Sites for PDAs
- Downloading Library Resource Guides To Your PDA

Source: Reprinted with permission from the University of Alberta Libraries.

Figure 20-17. Mobile Library at the Boston University Medical Center

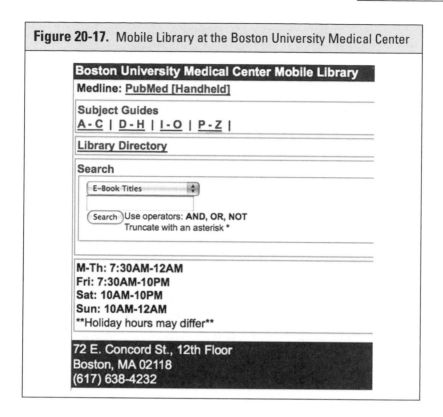

offers SMS reference, but maintains cell phones at the reference desk so that the librarians are not tied to the spot. Embedded chat reference through Mee-boMe (George Mason University Library and Darien Public Library), Plugoo (Brigham Young University Library and University of Wisconsin Law Library), libraryh3lp (Baylor University and Rochester Public Library), and Chatango (Oregon State University Libraries and University of Calgary) are also found in all kinds of reference libraries.

The Athabasca University Library (Canada), co-sponsor of the 2009 Second International m-Libraries Conference on handheld devices, has a mobile-friendly Digital Reading Room where the campus community can access course readings and mobile language Web sites such as ESL and accent reduction. The Roehampton University in London created a Green Room in 2008 for staff to experiment with mobile devices and exchange best practices in the active use of such technology. The Open University (UK), a distance learning institution with more than 200,000 students, has a similar initiative that they call the Digilab.

Concluding Remarks: The Tree of 2.0 Knowledge

A full-page advertisement in *The New York Times* (February 22, 2009: A26) displays a colorful iPhone3G, with twenty modern pictographs touting "apps" (widgets). These apps provide everything from Shazam ("Ever hear a song and wonder who sings it? Just hold your iPhone up to the music and, in seconds, you have the name, artist and album, plus a link") to RunKeeper ("GPS to track your run, hike, or walk. See your routes on a map, record time and distance and more"). The advertisement goes on to offer tens of thousands of such apps. And you thought a phone was a mere communication device.

President Barack Obama had more than 1.5 million friends on Facebook, more than 165,000 Twitter followers, a YouTube channel with more than 1,800 videos, a Flickr stream with more than 50,000 images, and an associated community-organizing Web site called mybarackobama.com (Steins, 2009). His unqualified success at attracting campaign funds from the "little person" and establishing a groundswell of popular opinion around the nation has been attributed in large part to successful strategizing and use of 2.0 tools.

In December 2008, Linda Braun of Librarians and Educators Online (LEO) presented a 2.0 workshop at the Boston Public Library (MA) titled "Meeting Customers on Their Own Turf" (with the unwritten but stated subtext that "The library Web page is dead"). Susan Gibbons of the University of Rochester echoed that approach with her observation that "The wider the gap between the passive experiences of library Web sites and the interactive ones, the more ripe libraries are for replacement by disruptive technologies and services that we may not even be able to yet imagine"(Storey, 2008: 11).

As a testament to the increasing use of 2.0, the Kingston Frontenac Public Library in Ontario, Canada, put out an advertisement for a full-time "Librarian 2.0 in preparation for the 2.0 World" (see Figure 20-18).

From the everyday use of telephones to the organization of a presidential campaign, Web 2.0 is a recognizable presence. Within the field of librarianship, simple professional workshops as well as institutionalized structures such as reference librarian job requirements are also marked by the 2.0 universe. The onrush of 2.0 technology in everyday life is both insistent and ubiquitous. Cartoonish words like Plugoo and Digsby; and words conjoined like centaurs such as Facebook and folksonomy; and a forest of acronyms such as MMOGs, SaaS, API, XML are all linguistic markers to the emergence and settling-in process of this bustling new technology.

It is quite possible that sections of the community are punch drunk with the availability of "shiny new toys." It is quite possible that large chunks of this new technology will glitter for a period and fall away into oblivion. It is even possible for reference departments to continue with business as usual, much as there are libraries that continue to use card catalogs.

What is not possible is to pretend that it is not happening. Having eaten from the tree of 2.0 technologies, there is no turning back. Getting intimate with the arsenal of tools available is good reference behavior. It allows the luxury of forgetting to innovate for the sake of innovation and continuing to focus on what is important, namely, the provision of stellar and resonant reference service to end users.

Figure 20-18. Screen Shot of Librarian 2.0 Position Announcement

Kingston Frontenac Public Library
Career Opportunities
http://www.kfpl.ca/

LIBRARIAN Permanent Full-Time

KFPL is a progressive, innovative, multi-branch library system with a mission to provide exceptional customer service within the context of a warm and welcoming environment. To this end, we are seeking a dynamic, creative individual to develop and promote the library as a continuous learning organization.

We are looking for a Librarian 2.0 in preparation for the 2.0 World

Are you an information specialist with a combined reference and technological orientation who will:
- Lead our virtual reference team, implementing transformative technology such as IM, podcasting, and streaming audio/video as well as participate in our traditional reference services
- Recommend and implement new and developing technologies such as wikis, blogs, etc.
- Contribute to the development of the library's website
- Contribute to our virtual services offerings, such as web 2.0, federated searching, open URL resolver, etc
- Provide training and support for other librarians in new technologies
- Manage our electronic resources and online databases, explore and recommend new online resources, and negotiate contracts with consortia and vendors
- Collaborate with other librarians to provide community development and outreach, particularly in regard to our virtual services.

Source: Used by permission.

Recommendations for Further Reading

Bradley. Phil. 2011. *How to Use Web 2.0 in Your Library Revised Edition.* London: Facet Publishing. A practical, how-to book on using Web 2.0 tools in libraries, the author also provides helpful illustrations and step-by-step instructions on setting up various initiatives. A companion Web site with author podcasts enhances the text version.

Farkas, Meredith (creator). 2005–ongoing. *Library Success: A Best Practices Wiki.* Available: www.libsuccess.org/. Launched in 2005, following the Chicago ALA meeting, the wiki was designed to provide a general and freely accessible repository for innovative ideas coming out of libraries. Farkas reports approximately 8,000 visitors a month, and deservedly so as the wiki provides a wide-ranging list of real-life examples that are illuminative. The sections on "Implementing Tech in the Library" and "Information Sharing and Education" are relevant for this topic.

Farkas, Meredith. 2007. *Social Software in Libraries: Building Collaboration, Communication, and Community Online.* Medford, NJ: Information Today. A comprehensive overview and explanation of 2.0 tools, heavily supplemented with examples of usage by different kinds of libraries. The book is strongly supported by a companion Web site accessible at: http://sociallibraries.com. The site includes Five Weeks to a Social Library, a dynamic initiative that was initially taught to forty students online; it provides freely accessible course content to learn about 2.0 tools and their use in libraries. The tools

TOP TEN REFERENCE 2.0 TOOLS AND SITES	
Tools	**Sites**
Wikis	MediaWiki
Blogs	Bloglines
Folksonomies	Twitter
Widgets/Gadgets/Apps	Del.icio.us
RSS Feeds	MySpace
Mashups/APIs (Application Programming Interface)	Facebook
Instant/Text Messaging	Ning
Podcasts	Flickr
Mobile/handheld devices	You Tube
Microblogs	Meebo

covered are blogs, RSS, wikis, Second Life, social networking, flickr, social bookmarking, and selling social software at your library to get past staff resistance to 2.0 changes.

Godwin, Peter, and Jo Parker, eds. 2008. *Information Literacy Meets Library 2.0*. London: Facet Publishing. Twelve experts discuss the use of 2.0 tools by library patrons and students and then go on to suggest ways in which libraries can integrate usage patterns with technology.

Kroski, Elyssa. 2008. *Web 2.0 for Librarians and Information Professionals*. New York: Neal-Schuman. A comprehensive survey of 2.0 technology is provided along with real-life examples of its use in various types of libraries.

Sanchez, Joe. 2009. "Implementing Second Life: Ideas, Challenges, and Innovations." *ALA Library Technology Reports* 45, no. 2. (February/March). The author, a doctoral candidate at the University of Texas at Austin, provides a broad context for Second Life by giving a detailed history of the evolution of text-based games to 3-D social virtual worlds. The pedagogical applications of digital storytelling, role-playing, community engagement, and working with teen populations are suggested. Guest author Jane Stimpson provides real-life examples of public libraries that have apparated into Second Life and discusses the large numbers that have dissipated into "ghost sims."

Steiner, Sarah K., and M. Leslie Madden, eds. 2008. *The Desk and Beyond: Next Generation Reference Service*. Chicago: ACRL/ALA. Thirteen chapters by different experts on various 2.0 technological tools and newly defined reference services, with a focus on moving "beyond the walls of the library."

Technorati. Accessible: www.technorati.com. *Time* magazine had the comment that if Google was the Web's reference library, Technorati was becoming its coffeehouse. It is the preeminent blog search engine and provides substantive information about the blogosphere.

Wood, M. Sandra, ed. 2007. *Medical Librarian 2.0: Use of Web 2.0 Technologies in Reference Services*. Binghamton, NY: The Haworth Press. Edited by a medical reference librarian of many years' experience and authored by both bloggers and well-known health science specialists, the book provides an interesting focus on the impact of 2.0 technology on medical librarianship.

Bibliography of Works Cited in This Chapter

Alexa. "Global Top Sites." Available: www.alexa.com (accessed January 27, 2011).

Allan, Charles. 2007. "Using a Wiki to Manage a Library Instruction Program: Sharing Knowledge to Better Serve Patrons." *College & Research Libraries News* 68, no. 4 (April).

Bebo. Available: www.bebo.com.

The Bivings Report. 2007. Available: www.bivingsreport.com/2007/american-newspapers-and-the-internet-threat-or-opportunity/ (accessed January 20, 2009).

Bloglines. Available: www.bloglines.com.

Bookcrossing. Available: www.bookcrossing.com.

Brady, Mark. 2005. "Blogging: Personal Participation in Public Knowledge Building on the Web." *Chimera Working Paper*. Available: www.essex .ac.uk/chimera/content/pubs/wps/CWP-2005-02-blogging-in-the-Knowl-edge-Society-MB.pdf (accessed February 15, 2009).

Braun, Linda. 2007. *Listen Up! Podcasting for Schools and Libraries*. Medford, NJ: Information Today.

Carson, Bryan. 2008. "How-To Laws for Using Photos You Take at Your Library." *MLS: Marketing Library Service* 22, no. 5 (September–October). Available: www.infotoday.com/mls/sep08/Carson.shtml (accessed May 5, 2009).

Chatango. Available: www.chatango.com.

Claburn, Thomas. 2007. "CEO Eric Schmidt Presents Google's Friendly Face at Web 2.0 Expo." *Information Week* (April 17). Available: http://tinyurl.com/ djmkkh (accessed May 4, 2009).

Crawford, Walt. 2006. "Library 2.0 and 'Library 2.0'." *Cites & Insights* 6, no. 2 (Midwinter): 1–32.

Crawford, Walt. 2009. "Shiny Toys or Useful Tools?" *Cites & Insights* 9, no. 3 (February).

Delicious. Available: http://delicious.com.

Digsby. Available: www.digsby.com.

Facebook. Available: http://www.facebook.com.

Farkas, Meredith. 2007. *Social Software in Libraries: Building Collaboration, Communication, and Community Online*. Medford, NJ: Information Today, Inc. Companion Web site: http://www.sociallibraries.com.

Friendster. Available: www.friendster.com.

Front Page. Available: http://c2.com/cgi/wiki.

Funk, Tom. 2009. *Web 2.0 and Beyond*. Westport, CT: Praeger Publishers.

Galante, Joseph, 2009. "Twitter Gets New Round of Venture Capital Funding." *Bloomberg* (February 13). Available: www.bloomberg.com.

Gerardin, Julie, Michelle Yamamoto, and Kelly Gordon. 2008. "Fresh Perspectives on Reference Work in Second Life." *Reference & User Services Quarterly* 47, no. 4 (Summer): 324–327.

Goodreads. Available: www.goodreads.com.

Google Sites (known as JotSpot prior to 2009). Available: www.jot.com.

Herman, Douglas. 1994."But Does It Work? Evaluating the Brandeis Reference Model." *RSR: Reference Services Review* 22, no. 4 (Winter): 17–28.

h2g2. Available: http://www.bbc.co.uk/h2g2/.

hi5. Available: www.hi5.com.

The Huffington Post. Available: www.huffingtonpost.com.

Hurst-Wahl, Jill. 2007. "Librarians and Second Life." *Information Outlook* 11, no. 6 (June): 50.

Judd, Cindy. Available (blog entry): http://library20.ning.com/forum/topics/515108:Topic:21235?page=3&commentId=515108%3AComment%3A30549&x=1#515108Comment30549 (accessed February 12, 2009).

Kille, Angela. 2005. "Wikis in the Workplace: How Wikis Can Help Manage Knowledge in Library Reference Services." Available: http://libres.curtin.edu.au/libres16n1/Kille_essayopinion.htm (accessed February 14, 2009).

Lankes, David R., Joanne Silverstein, and Scott Nicholson. 2006. "Participatory Networks: The Library as Conversation." Available: http://iis.syr.edu/projects/PNOpen/ParticiaptoryNetworks.pdf (accessed May 4, 2009).

Lippincott, Joan K. 2008. "Mobile Technologies, Mobile Users: Implications for Academic Libraries." *ARL* 261 (December): 1–4.

MediaWiki. Available: www.mediawiki.org.

Meebo. Available: www.meebo.com.

MySpace. Available: www.myspace.com.

Ning. Available: www.ning.com.

Orkut. Available: www.orkut.com.

PBwiki. Available: http://pbwiki.com.

Plosker, G. 2004. "Learning from Best Practices." *Online* 28, no. 3: 50–52.

Plugoo. Accessible: www.plugoo.com.

PmWiki. Available: www.pmwiki.org.

Qwidget. Available: www.qwidget.com.

Robinson, Kathryn. 2008. "Multimedia." Comment in "Future-Present: What's Possible Now and Coming Soon in Reference." *Library Journal* no. 19 (November 15): 4–5.

Secker, Jane. 2008. *Libraries and Facebook (Case Study 5).* London: University of London. Available: http://clt.lse.ac.uk/Projects/Case_Study_Five_report.pdf.

SecondLife. Available: http://secondlife.com.

seedwiki. Available: www.seedwiki.com.

Shapiro, Samantha. 2009. "Revolution, Facebook-Style." *The New York Times* (January 25): MM34, NY edition.

Shelfari. Available: www.shelfari.com.

Smith, Justin. 2009. *The Facebook Marketing Bible: 40+ Ways to Market Your Brand, Company, Product, or Service Inside Facebook.* 2nd ed. PDF version available: www.insidefacebook.com/category/opensocial/.

Steins, Chris. 2009. "Obama, Web 2.0 and Planning." *Planetizen* (1/19). Available: www.planetizen.com/node/37013 (accessed February 22, 2009).

Storey, Tom. 2008. "Mixing It Up: Libraries Mash Up Content, Services, and Ideas." *Next Space* no. 9 (June): 6–11.

StudiVZ. Available: www.studivz.net.

TeamPage. Available: www.tractionsoftware.com.

Technorati. 2008. *State of the Blogosphere.* Available: http://technorati.com/blogging/state-of-the-blogosphere/ (accessed February 15, 2009).

Twitter. Available: www.twitter.com.

YouTube. Available: www.youtube.com.

Young, Jeffrey. 2010. "After Frustrations in Second Life, Colleges Look to New Virtual Worlds." *The Chronicle of Higher Education* (January). Available: http://chronicle.com (accessed February 2, 2011).

WIMZI. Available: http://wimzi.aim.com.

Zotero. Available: www.zotero.org.

21
The Future of Information Service

Libraries in the twenty-first century are evolving at a rate that would have been unimaginable to Samuel Green when he first proposed the notion of a reference department well over a century ago. The rapid rate of change is reflected in many sectors of society from the economy to technology. Libraries are not an exception. As new technology makes its way into our lives, libraries are quick to use it. As our users adopt social software, so libraries want to use it to reach our users. Libraries are now on Facebook and MySpace; libraries have blogs and wikis and they have RSS feeds.

Change does not, however, entail an outright rejection of all that has come before. In Darwinian theory one finds the notion of evolutionarily conserved traits, elements of a species' genetic makeup that are so effective and powerful as to remain unchanged for millions of years, even as everything else about the organism and its environment are transformed. Although libraries in general and reference departments in particular have more than their share of conserved traits, change has come rapidly in the past decade. Reference services and sources are changing to meet new user interests and needs. In this chapter, we will attempt to map the winds of change while acknowledging that many principles of good reference service remain.

As one standard definition has it, reference is "the facilitation of the connection between researchers and the information they desire or need" (Summerhill, 1993: 74). Although this description remains accurate, reference services have changed dramatically. Advances in computing technology, the rise of the Internet, the advent of Wikipedia and the popularity of social networking have led to irrevocable paradigm shifts in the work of library and information science professionals. Crucially, such developments are not static, and the growth of the technological sphere is ongoing. A Pew Internet and American Life survey released in January 2009 indicated that since 2005 a fourfold increase occurred in the number of adults with a profile on an online social network, i.e., 8 percent in 2005 to 35 percent at the end of 2008 (Pew Internet and American Life Survey, 2009). Librarians must, by consequence, now focus on what technology their users have adopted and how they can use that same technology in the library to better support patron needs. The ease of using Google and question-answering systems such as "Cha Cha" (www.chacha.com) has made it hard for users to understand that all information is not the same and that search engines and question-answering systems do not always supply accurate or complete information. This is an ongoing challenge to librarians who have turned to a more active role in information literacy to try to help users understand how to evaluate and handle the information they find. Technology and easy access to information are part of the challenge facing librarians as they reassess their role in reference service. Librarians now realize that they must make their resources and services as easy to use as these simplified online portals.

Many experts have sought to provide us with a view of the future of reference. David Tyckoson identified features of libraries that will remain constant and those that will change. Tyckoson believed the constants were the service the libraries provide to their community—the four basic functions outlined by Samuel Green in 1876 (instruction, answering questions, reader's advisory service, and promotion)—and the personal service that librarians provide. The changes Tyckoson foresaw were newer and better tools as a result of technology, an increase in demand for instruction, a decrease in demand for ready reference, and a role for librarians in the creation of information as well as in its conservation (Tyckoson, 2003).

Joseph Janes suggested that librarians should continue to work in areas where their strengths lie. These, he suggested, are

> concerns about evaluation and quality of information sources, sophisticated tools and techniques for searching, understanding the nature of users, their communities, their needs and situations, compiling and organizing and packaging information resources for their use, helping them to understand how to help themselves and how to use and evaluate information.

Janes also envisioned a future that focuses

> less on the answers to specific questions and more on providing assistance and support to people with more detailed, more demanding, more comprehensive information needs of all kinds. (Janes, 2003: 24)

Last, Stephen Abram stated:

> In 2008 we are seeing the real action in our world of libraries move from the back office to the front desk. We are moving from a technology-centric strategy to one in which the real needs of our clients must predominate. Aligning technology with user behavior no longer suffices to ensure success. We need to understand, and understand deeply, the role of the library in our end-users' lives, work, research and play. (Abram, 2008: www.infotoday.com/searcher/sep08Abram.shtml)

New Ways of Doing Business—Reference 2.0

As the Internet has become part of our daily existence, libraries have chosen to compete by adding e-mail reference, chat reference, and, now, reference using IM (Instant Messaging) and SMS (text messaging). E-mail reference was a simple addition. Using basic e-mail software, libraries began to communicate with their users outside the confines of the library. Though it is harder to conduct the reference interview using e-mail, libraries have developed forms for users to fill out to assist in ascertaining the exact question. Though it can be an uneven service, as some e-mails are answered quickly and others take several days, it can be quite satisfactory; it gives the librarian a chance to think about the question and provide a more thorough answer.

Chat reference was patterned after some of the commercial enterprises already using this technology, such as L.L.Bean, who has a "Live Help" site where customers can chat with a customer representative. The software has improved and has been made more usable for libraries, although the best of it is expensive. The advantage of the chat reference is that it is done in real time, is interactive and immediate, and enables the librarian to do a better reference interview. Chat reference can be done through a consortium or regionally to spread the expense and allow the libraries involved to offer more hours of service. Some consortia offer chat reference 24/7. One of the early services was a pilot project set up by the Library of Congress called the Collaborative Digital Reference Service (CDRS). Its software, QuestionPoint, was then adopted by OCLC (Online Computer Library Center). Many libraries have chosen to use the QuestionPoint software while others use Meebo or other free software.

Instant messaging (IM) and text messaging (SMS) has been adopted especially by academic libraries because it appeals to their user population. It is immediate and interactive and can be done from any location. Libraries staff IM during regular hours or can add additional hours if needed. A successful IM project was reported at the Kansas State Libraries at the Reference Renaissance conference in 2008. This IM and text messaging reference project began using Meebo and later the library moved to the open source Libraryh31p, which allowed multiple operators and more flexibility (Theiss-White et al., 2008).

All of these new services continue to develop as librarians gain experience using them. There are definitely audiences for these new ways of communication, and the services continue to grow. Much of their success or failure may simply revolve around the marketing issue and whether the marketing is continuous. Nevertheless, it is an important effort to reach a mobile and diverse library user population. One way to continue to support this service is to make it a service of a consortium such as: CleveNet's KnowItNow in Cleveland, Ohio, Maryland's AskUsNow! or New Jersey's QandANJ.

Providing New Materials and Formats

Though print materials will always remain part of the reference picture, digital versions of print titles and new materials in digital format only have flooded the market. Slowly, reference titles available only in print are receding and digital titles are multiplying. Although this seems like a wonderful world for the library user, it is actually a complex world that is not easy to maneuver. In fact, the user often turns to Google or Yahoo, assuming equal quality rather than using the library's databases. Libraries have taken many approaches to encouraging the use of their online bibliographic and full-text databases from online tutorials and pathfinders to information literacy programs and marketing. They have added new software to aid users. The article linker software, for example, makes it possible for a user to find the full text of articles in another database owned by the library when there is only a bibliographic citation. The federated searching software makes it possible for users to search across several databases on a topic rather than having to identify which database should be used.

More access to online databases is available beyond the library. Thus the library's users can access the databases from home, in their office, or elsewhere. This improved access makes it easier for the user who finds it inconvenient to visit the library during its hours of service. The library's Web site provides access not only to the databases leased or owned by the library but to other information gathered by the library such as guides on how to research a term paper or a list of reliable Internet sites. A dynamic library Web site can engage library users in the use of many excellent sources of information.

Providing New Service Models

Face-to-face reference service has declined in the past few years as the Internet has become a more prominent part of users' lives. Coffman and Arret (2004) reported on recent ARL statistics that show a decrease of 40 percent in reference transactions in academic libraries between 1997 and 2003. Use of public libraries has remained more stable. Libraries have also noted the decline in the number of ready reference questions and an increase in more complicated questions. Users only consult the reference librarian after trying unsuccessfully to find the information on the Internet. New models of reference service have emerged as libraries have reached out to new user groups in an effort to compensate for this decline in face-to-face reference (see Table 21-1). Many libraries have opted not to have a reference desk but rather to have librarians available in their offices, by phone, by e-mail, chat and IM. Others have consolidated library services into one desk that provides reference service, photocopying services and assistance with computing.

Libraries have developed roving as a way to talk informally to users who do not approach the reference desk. Public libraries have always done outreach, but now we have new outreach models being developed by academic libraries. The State University of New York at Buffalo Library developed an outreach model that can be adapted by others. Its plan included getting office space in academic departments and arranging for Internet access (Wagner and Tysick, 2007). Librarians also have to provide access through the Web to the library and its resources in order to reach users wherever they are. This calls for continual user-friendly upgrades to the library's technological infrastructure and designing systems. Librarians must find easy-to-use ways to present quality information. It is important to tailor the information to users' needs.

Table 21-1. Models of Reference Service

Type	Description	Pros	Cons
Traditional reference desk	Librarian serves user at the reference desk	Easy to staff— one service point	Only serves users who come to the desk
Reference consultation model	Complex questions are referred to a consultation service	Uses librarians for complex questions	Limits the number of users that can be served
Tiered reference service	Three levels of service-information desk, general reference desk and consultation service	Users consult librarians for complex questions	Must train staff to do appropriate referrals & limits the number of users that can be served
Team staffing	Librarian and paraprofessional work together at reference desk	Librarian available to answer more difficult questions	Paraprofessional must make appropriate referrals to the librarian
Integrated service point concept	Integration of reference and circulation desks	Only one point of service for users	Requires ongoing training of staff
Roving	Librarians circulate throughout the reference area	Reach users who have not approached the reference desk	May require additional staffing
Virtual reference	Librarians answer questions by e-mail and chat	Users assisted who cannot visit the library	Technology still slow and harder to do reference interview
Outreach model	Librarians go out to departments, groups and organizations	Can reach new audiences	Requires additional staffing
No reference desk	Users can make an appointment with a librarian or contact them by telephone, email or chat	More flexibility for librarians and users	May be confusing for users who expect a reference desk

What Will Librarians Do? Competencies Needed

This newly defined reference service means that the role of the librarian must change. Among the competencies that twenty-first-century librarians will need are:

- Ability to provide information using Reference 2.0 technologies
- Knowledge of how to select electronic resources
- Online searching expertise

- Desire to share knowledge through teaching
- Reader's advisory skills
- Knowledge of how to develop an effective Web presence,
- Appreciation of the importance of marketing a program
- Familiarity with research on assessment and evaluation
- Interpersonal skills
- Ability to adapt to change
- Enthusiasm for career-long learning

Of course, librarians will continue to answer reference questions although they may encounter fewer ready reference requests and more complex questions. Many of these requests will be made online rather than in person (though users will continue to come to the library). Librarians may want to take on more of a consultation role to better help users with complicated questions that require more time and perhaps follow-up. Whitlatch suggests that "answering questions requires more focus on instruction in search strategies and other elements related to the basic information competencies of identifying the type of information needed, and finding, evaluating, and communicating the information successfully" (Whitlatch, 2003: 30).

Librarians need to understand how Reference 2.0 technology works and to keep abreast of changes and innovations. Librarians need to evaluate the potential of using Facebook, MySpace, blogs, wikis, tagging, RSS, podcasting, etc. These social networking technologies help libraries connect with users and potential users "where they are."

Librarians will continue to do collection development. With less print to order, librarians will concentrate their attention on the evaluation and selection of electronic resources. Each new resource added must then be fitted into the library's electronic collection. The new resources must also be introduced to the users for whom it is intended and marketed to an even broader audience. Along with the selection goes the ability to excel in online searching. As all librarians know, a well-planned search can yield much better results. Librarians owe it to their users to help them search effectively and efficiently.

Librarians will engage in more information literacy instruction—both one-to-one and in groups. Users need to learn to use electronic resources, the online catalog, and other databases that are available. The complexity of the library's resources, especially the online databases, has made it imperative that users receive assistance. The information literacy instruction may be one-to-one at the reference desk or in an e-mail or chat session; or it may be a class—either a one-shot class to get users started or part of a collaboration with a teacher or professor to help students get started on a particular assignment. E-learning is another important aspect of information literacy as librarians learn to insert learning packages into learning management systems such as Blackboard or hold an online discussion about research methods.

Librarians will develop their reader's advisory skills to provide more person-alized service to their users. Reader's advisory services now include nonfiction as well as fiction. Librarians will also spend time creating finding tools to guide their users in the ever-more-complex world of information resources. Finally, they will continue to develop Web pages to organize and present information to their users in a form that is easy to use and understand, such as pages on how to do research in general or guides to research on particular subject areas.

Librarians will learn more about marketing. "As part of their marketing competencies, library professionals must have the skill to systematically assess the information seeking needs and habits of their primary clientele" (Whitlatch, 2003: 29). These skills will be learned in library school or in a continuing education course.

Assessment and evaluation will be practiced on a much more regular basis by librarians. Decision making will be based on the results of surveys, questionnaires, and focus groups. Programs and projects will be based on both quantitative and qualitative information. Librarians have done a great deal of evaluation of their services. A recent article documents a multiple-methods study done at Villanova University and Falvey Memorial Library. The library used focus groups, benchmarking, surveys, transaction analysis, activity mapping, and secret shoppers to evaluate library service. The study resulted in the consolidation of the service points into one single large desk from which all services are available, the installation of a print center in the library in partnership with the university's graphic services, and the creation of a multipurpose instructional computer lab (Stein et al., 2008). Evaluation can take many forms, but the need for continual evaluation of reference services is a necessity.

Interpersonal skills will remain essential in this changing world. It has for many decades distinguished libraries and librarians and will continue to do so. The ability to change and the enthusiasm for lifelong learning will continue to mark the route of this profession. Libraries and librarians must continue to respond to the needs of their users and to be alert to changes in the world that will affect libraries. Reference librarians' role will change as reference continues to evolve. Their new role will be multifaceted and more proactive than in the past. They will work to design better systems that meet their users' more personalized needs.

Planning the Future

In a recent article Terence K. Huwe posed a series of diagnostic questions to help libraries stay on top of change. These questions can be a way to guide future planning.

- *Is the library following the interests of its community?* Huwe suggests keeping current on what technologies are being used in the community.
- *Is the new technology something that should be implemented immediately or should it be tested carefully first?* Huwe says that sometimes it's good to adopt a new technology immediately and other times to move more cautiously and look at the pros and cons of it.
- *How does a new technology impact on existing library services?* Huwe says, for example, that new technology can increase use of other library services.

- *How does a new technology link to other existing technologies?* Huwe says that often people move between various technologies so it is important to see how they link together. People may use, for example, wikis and e-mail interchangeably.
- *How do librarians keep themselves prepared and informed about new technologies?* Librarians must keep up with what is happening around them and try new technologies. (Huwe, 2009)

What Will the Future of Reference Look Like?

Reference in the future will be less attached to a particular location no matter what type of library, but its focus will be user centered. In a library building there will no doubt be one desk that serves a variety of functions such as assisting users to identify, use and evaluate electronic resources and helping them with various software packages. Users can reach librarians for assistance by making an appointment to meet with them or contacting them by phone, e-mail, chat, IM or SMS. This gives the librarians more flexibility to do other projects rather than staffing a desk and gives the user more choices. Most library reference work will be transacted virtually in the future.

Librarians will spend their time providing instruction in the use of resources. They will also develop tutorials and FAQs for the library's Web site. They will spend a great deal of time putting resources needed by their users on the Web and adding and subtracting information to keep the Web site timely and current. For example, librarians put up lists of resources on their Web sites after the September 11, 2001 terrorist attacks, and in March 2009, librarians developed a list of resources titled "Economic Crisis Reference Guide." Librarians will plan outreach services to reach prospective users—either in physical locations or virtually. Librarians will evaluate their efforts to judge what projects are most effective so they can use their funding wisely.

Does Reference Have a Future?

Questions about the ongoing relevance of all aspects of our profession have likely been ongoing concerns since the library of Alexandria burned to the ground. Although libraries are certainly subject to change, we need not fear their dissolution. Comparatively speaking, reference service is a new dimension of our institutions, but as we grow both more complex and more open it increasingly seems certain that this service is here to stay. Far more productive, then, may be to ask how that future should be approached. James Rettig has suggested that libraries must respond to their users' values, which are "immediacy, interactivity, personalization, and mobility" (Rettig, 2003: 19). As to immediacy, using chat reference and instant messaging is an attempt to meet this user need as well as provide reference 24/7. Interactivity has been responded to by chat and IM. Personalization has been implemented by personalizing the library's Web site to users' needs. The need for mobility has been responded to by making the library Web site and its resources available wherever the user is and at any hour. Rettig has also challenged librarians to become "expert anthropologists of our user communities" in order to serve them well (Rettig, 2003: 20).

Marketing is another important component of the library's future. As with any profit-making or nonprofit organization, libraries must make their present and potential users aware of their products and services. Marketing need not be terribly expensive, but it must be effective. Libraries offer a wide range of materials and services that are often not obvious to the users unless they are highlighted. Because so many of the resources and services are online and often remote, libraries must use a variety of media to market themselves—flyers and brochures, the library's homepage, newspapers, radio and television, Web sites and social networking sites such as Facebook.

The future of reference is best summed up as "high tech and high touch." Libraries will continue to upgrade their technology in an effort to better serve their users. They will also continue to develop personalized services for every user whether that user asks for service in person at the reference desk, by telephone, by e-mail, or by chat. The complexity of the available information services must be matched by support for the individual users (Ferguson, 2000: 303). Reference service will be integrated and seamless such that it will be provided to match the user's needs no matter where he or she enters the library's sphere. The personal aspect of library service will continue to distinguish itself from other institutions and will separate it from its competition and fill the needs of its users.

Recommendations for Further Reading

Auster, Ethel, and Donna C. Chan. 2004. "Reference Librarians and Keeping Up-to-Date; A Question of Priorities." *Reference & User Services Quarterly* 44, no. 1 (Fall): 59–68. A study of the competencies required for reference librarians in a changing environment and how librarians were using professional development to upgrade their skills.

Bradford, Jane T., Barbara Costello, and Robert Lenholt. 2005. "Reference Service in the Digital Age: An Analysis of Sources Used to Answer Reference Questions." *The Journal of Academic Librarianship* 31, no. 3 (May): 263–272. A study of whether librarians used print or online sources to answer questions. Print sources were only used 9.38 percent of the time.

Cardina, Christen, and Donald Wicks. 2004. "The Changing Roles of Academic Reference Librarians Over a Ten-Year Period." *Reference & User Services Quarterly* 44, no. 2 (Winter): 133–142. This survey documents the changes in the jobs of academic librarians over a ten-year period.

Radford, Marie L. 2008. "A Personal Choice, Reference Service Excellence." *Reference & User Services Quarterly* 48, no. 1: 108–135. Discusses the need for going the extra mile and providing excellent reference service.

Smith, Michael M., and Barbara A. Pietraszewski. 2004. "Enabling the Roving Reference Librarian: Wireless Access with Tablet PCs." *Reference Services Review* 32, no. 3: 249–255. Description of a roving reference strategy at

Texas A&M University Libraries where the librarians roved the student study areas using tablet PCs to access electronic resources.

Wolfe, Judith A., Ted Naylor, and Jeanette Drueke. 2010. "The Role of the Academic Reference Librarian in the Learning Commons." *Reference & User Services Quarterly* 50, no. 2 (Winter): 108–113. Reference librarians use their skills in a variety of reference service models which range from the traditional to the tiered to the information commons to the learning commons. Libraries might use one form of any model, a hybrid model, or a model in the process of transformation. Some libraries are adopting the learning commons model with good results.

Bibliography of Works Cited in This Chapter

Abram, Stephen. 2008. "Evolution to Revolution to Chaos? Reference in Transition." *Searcher* 16, no. 8: 42–48.

Coffman, Steve, and Linda Arret. 2004. "To Chat or Not to Chat—Taking Another Look at Virtual Reference, Part I." *Searcher* (July–August): 38–46.

Ferguson, Chris. 2000. "'Shaking the Conceptual Foundations,' Too, Integrating Research and Technology Support for the Next Generation of Information Service." *College and Research Libraries* (July): 300–311.

Flanagan, Pat, and Lisa R. Horowitz. 2000. "Exploring New Service Models: Can Consolidating Public Service Points Improve Response to Customer Needs?" *Journal of Academic Librarianship* 26, no. 5 (September): 329–338.

Frank, Donald G., Katharine L. Calhoun, W. Bruce Henson, M. Leslie Madden, and Gregory K. Raschke. 1999. "The Changing Nature of Reference and Information Service: Predictions and Realities." *Reference and User Services Quarterly* 39, no. 2 (Winter): 151–157.

Huwe, Terence K. 2009. "Reference Diagnostics for a Virtual World." *Computers in Libraries* 29, no.1: 27–29.

Jackson, Rebecca. 2002. "Revolution or Evolution: Reference Planning in ARL Libraries." *Reference Services Review* 30, no. 3: 212–228.

Janes, Joseph. 2003. "What Is Reference For?" *Reference Services Review* 31, no. 1: 22–25.

Pew Internet and American Life Survey. 2009. "Adults and Social Network Websites." Pew. (January 14).

Rettig, James. 2003. "Technology, Cluelessness, Anthropology and the Memex: The Future of Academic Reference Service." *Reference Service Review* 31, no. 1: 17–21.

Stein, Merrill, et al. 2008. "Using Continuous Quality Improvement Methods to Evaluate Library Service Points." *Reference & User Services Quarterly* 48, no. 1: 78–85.

Summerhill, K. S. 1993. "The High Cost of Reference: The Need to Reassess Services and Service Delivery." *Reference Librarian* no. 43: 71–85.

Tenopir, Carol, and Lisa A. Ennis. 2001. "Reference Services in the New Millennium." *Online* (July–August): 41–45.

Theiss-White, Danielle, Laura Bonella, Jason Coleman, and Erin Fitch. 2008 "'r u there? I need help:' Virtual Reference at Kansas State University." Presented at the Reference Renaissance Conference, August 4 and 5. Denver, Colorado.

Tyckoson, David A. 1999. "What's Right with Reference?" *American Libraries* (May), 57–63.

———. 2003. "On the Desirableness of Personal Relations between Librarians and Readers: The Past and Future of Reference Service." *Reference Services Review* 31, 1: 12–16.

Wagner, A. Ben, and Cynthia Tysick. 2007. "Onsite Reference and Instruction Services; Setting Up Shop Where Our Patrons Live." *Reference & User Services Quarterly* 46, no. 4: 60–65.

Whitlatch, Jo Bell. 2003. "Reference Futures: Outsourcing, the Web or Knowledge Counseling." *Reference Services Review* 31, no. 1: 26–30.

Wilson, Myoung C. 2000. "Evolution or Entropy? Changing Reference/User Culture and the Future of Reference." *Reference & User Services Quarterly* 28 (Summer): 387–390.

Appendix
RUSA Outstanding Reference Sources 2006–2011

The Reference and User Services Association (RUSA) of the American Library Association uses twenty-two criteria to select the best reference publications that can be recommended for small and medium-sized libraries. A committee made up of reference librarians from different kinds of libraries is responsible for final selections, a practice that has continued since 1958. Previous selections can be accessed through the RUSA site at www.ala.org.

The list provides a handy focus on the extraordinary variety of reference resources available to users—and the breadth of familiarity required of reference librarians. "Best of..." lists are expedient ways to keep abreast of titles that will be popularly requested.

2011

- *The Oxford Companion to the Book*. Michael F. Suarez, S.J. and H.R. Woudhuysen, eds. 2 vols. Oxford, 2010. (9780198606536).
- *Encyclopedia of Identity*. Ronald L. Jackson II, ed. 2 vols. Sage, 2010. (9781412951531).
- *Encyclopedia of Geography*. Barney Warf, ed. 6 vols. Sage, 2010. (9781412956970).
- *The Oxford Encyclopedia of Ancient Greece and Rome*. Michael Gagarin, ed. 7 vols. Oxford, 2010. (9780195170726).
- *The Encyclopedia of Religion in America*. Charles H. Lippy and Peter W. Williams, eds. 4 vols. CQ Press, 2010. (9780872895805).
- *Off Broadway Musicals, 1910–2007: Casts, Credits, Songs, Critical Reception and Performance Data of More Than 1,800 Shows*. Dan Dietz, ed. 1 vol. McFarland, 2010. (9780786433995).
- *Encyclopedia of World Dress and Fashion*. Joanne B. Eicher, ed. 10 vols. Oxford, 2010. (9780195377330).
- Berg Fashion Library. http://www.bergfashionlibrary.com/. Oxford, 2010.
- *Chronology of the Evolution-Creationism Controversy*. Randy Moore, ed., et al. 1 vol. Greenwood, 2009. (9780313362873).
- *The Oxford International Encyclopedia of Peace*. Nigel Young, ed. 4 vols. Oxford, 2010. (9780195334685).
- *21st Century Economics: A Reference Handbook*. Rhona C. Free, ed. 2 vols. Sage. 2010. (9781412961424).
- *Encyclopedia of Political Theory*. Mark Bevir, ed. 3 vols. Sage. 2010. (9781412958653).

- *Encyclopedia of Group Processes & Intergroup Relations.* John M. Levine and Michael A. Hogg, eds. 2 vols. Sage. 2010. (9781412942089).

2010

- *Archaeology in America: An Encyclopedia.* Francis P. McManamon, ed. 4 vols. Greenwood, 2009. (9780313331847).
- *Encyclopedia of African American History: 1896 to the Present.* Paul Finkelman, ed. 5 vols. Oxford, 2009. (9780195167791).
- *Encyclopedia of Modern China.* David Pong, ed. 4 vols. Charles Scribner's Sons, 2009. (9780684315661).
- *The Encyclopedia of the Spanish-American and Philippine-American Wars.* Spencer Tucker, ed. 3 vols. ABC-CLIO, 2009. (9781851099511).
- *Encyclopedia of Environmental Ethics and Philosophy.* J. Baird Callicott and Robert Frodeman, eds. 2 vols. Gale Cengage, 2009. (9780028661370).
- *Encyclopedia of Human Rights.* David Forsythe, ed. 5 vols. Oxford, 2009. (9780195334029).
- Social Explorer. http://www.socialexplorer.com/pub/home/home.aspx. Social Explorer, 2009.
- *Broadway Plays and Musicals: Descriptions and Essential Facts.* Thomas S. Hischak, ed. 1 vol. McFarland, 2009. (9780786434481).
- *American Countercultures.* Gina Misiroglu, ed. 3 vol. Sharp, 2009. (9780765680600).
- *Encyclopedia of Gender and Society.* Jodi O'Brien, ed. 2 vols. Sage, 2009. (9781412909167).
- *Encyclopedia of Marine Science.* C. Reid Nichols and Robert G. Williams, eds. 1 vol. Facts on File, 2009. (9780816050222).

2009

- *Books and Beyond: The Greenwood Encyclopedia of New American Reading.* Kenneth Womack, ed. 4 vols. Greenwood, 2008. (9780313337383).
- *Encyclopedia of Taoism.* Fabrizio Pregadio, ed. 2 vols. Routledge, 2008. (9780700712007).
- *Encyclopedia of the First Amendment.* John R. Vile, David L. Hudson Jr., and David Schultz, eds. 2 vols. CQ Press, 2009. (9780872893115).
- *Greenwood Encyclopedia of Folktales and Fairy Tales.* Donald Haase, ed. 3 vols. Greenwood, 2008. (9780313334412).
- *Encyclopedia of Education Law.* Charles J. Russo, ed. 2 vols. Sage, 2008. (9781412940795).
- *Climate Change: In Context.* Brenda Wilmoth Lerner and K. Lee Lerner, eds. 2 vols. Gale Cengage, 2008. (9781414436142).
- *Gale Encyclopedia of Diets: A Guide to Health and Nutrition.* Jacqueline L. Longe, ed. Gale Cengage, 2008. (9781414429915).
- *New Encyclopedia of Orchids: 1500 Species in Cultivation.* Isobyl la Croix. Timber Press, 2008. (9780881928761).

- *Encyclopedia of the Arab-Israeli Conflict: A Political, Social and Military History.* Spencer C. Tucker, ed. 4 vols. ABC-CLIO, 2008. (9781851098415).
- *African American National Biography.* Henry Louis Gates Jr. and Evelyn Brooks-Higginbotham, eds. 8 vols. Oxford University Press, 2008. (9780195160192).
- *Oxford Encyclopedia of Women in World History.* Bonnie G. Smith, ed. 4 vols. Oxford University Press, 2008. (9780195148909).

2008

- *APA Dictionary of Psychology.* Gary R. VandenBos, ed. American Psychological Association, 2007. (1591473802).
- *Encyclopaedia Judaica.* Staff, Macmillan Reference U.S.A., ed. 22 vols. Rev. ed. Gale, 2006. (0028659287).
- *Blackwell Encyclopedia of Sociology.* George Ritzer, ed. 11 vols. Blackwell, 2007. (1405124334).
- *Encyclopedia of Body Adornment.* Margo Demello. Greenwood, 2007. (313336954).
- *Encyclopedia of Race & Racism.* John Hartwell Moore, ed. 4 vols. Gale, 2008. (9780028660202).
- *The Oxford Encyclopedia of Maritime History.* John B. Hattendorf, ed. 4 vols. Oxford, 2007. (9780195130751).
- *Schirmer Encyclopedia of Film.* Barry Keith Grant, ed. 4 vols. Gale, 2006. (0028657912).
- *Encyclopedia of Asian Theatre.* Samuel L. Leiter, ed. 2 vols. Greenwood, 2007. (03133529x).
- *Brave New Words: The Oxford Dictionary of Science Fiction.* Jeff Prucher, ed. Oxford, 2007. (0195305671).
- *Postwar America: An Encyclopedia of Social, Political, Cultural and Economic History.* James Ciment. 4 vols. ME Sharpe, 2007. (079568067x).
- *Oxford Companion to World Exploration.* David Buisseret, ed. 2 vols.

2007

- *Colonial America: An Encyclopedia of Social, Political, Cultural, and Economic History.* James Ciment, ed. M. E. Sharpe, 2005. (0765680653).
- *Crusades: An Encyclopedia.* Alan V. Murray, ed. 4 vols. ABC-Clio, 2006. (1576078620).
- *Encyclopedia of Swearing: The Social History of Oaths, Profanity, Foul Language, and Ethnic Slurs in the English-Speaking World.* Geoffrey Hughes. M. E. Sharpe, 2006. (0765612311).
- *Encyclopedia of the American Revolutionary War: A Political, Social, and Military History.* Gregory Fremont-Barnes and Richard Ryerson, eds. ABC-Clio, 2006. (1851094083).
- *Encyclopedia of the Developing World.* Thomas M. Leonard, ed. 3 vols. Routledge, 2005. (1579583881).

- *Encyclopedia of US Labor and Working Class History.* Eric Arnesen, ed. 3 vols. Routledge, 2006. (0415968267).
- *Encyclopedia of Western Colonialism Since 1450.* Thomas Benjamin, ed. 3 vols. MacMillian, 2007. (0028658434).
- *Encyclopedia of Women and Religion in North America.* Rosemary Skinner Keller, ed. 3 vols. Indiana, 2006.
- *Historical Statistics of the United States: Earliest Times to the Present.* Susan B. Carter, Scott Sigmund Gartner, Michael R. Haines, et al., eds. 5 vols. Cambridge, 2006. (0521817919).
- *Insects: Their Natural History and Diversity.* Stephen A. Marshall. Firefly, 2006. (1552979008).
- *Oxford Encyclopedia of British Literature.* David Scott Kastan, ed. 5 vols. Oxford, 2006. (0195169212).
- *Oxford Encyclopedia of Children's Literature.* Jack Zipes, ed. 4 vols. Oxford, 2006. (01951146561).
- *Qu'ran: An Encyclopedia.* Oliver Leaman, ed. Routledge, 2005. (0415326397).
- *Right, Wrong, and Risky: A Dictionary of Today's American English Usage.* Norton, 2005. (0393061191).

2006

- *Americans at War: Society, Culture, and the Homefront.* John P. Resch, ed. 4 vols. Macmillan, 2005. (002865806x).
- *American Heritage Science Dictionary.* Houghton, 2005. (0618455043).
- *Black Women in America,* 2nd ed. Darlene Clark Hines, ed. Oxford University Press, 2005. (0195156773).
- *Encyclopedia of Cryptozoology: A Global Guide to Hidden Animals and Their Pursuers.* Michael Newton. McFarland, 2005. (0786420367).
- *Encyclopedia of the Documentary Film.* Routledge, 2005. (1579584454).
- *Encyclopedia of Multiethnic American Literature.* Emmanuel S. Nelson. Greenwood, 2005. (031333059X).
- *Encyclopedia of Psychoactive Plants: Ethnopharmacology and its Applications.* Christian Rätsch. Park Street Press, 2005. (0892819782).
- *Encyclopedia of Religion and Nature.* Bron Taylor, ed. 2 vols. Continuum International Publishing, 2005. (1843711389).
- *Encyclopedia of Twentieth Century Photography.* Routledge, 2005. (1579583938).
- *Encyclopedia of World War I: A Political, Social and Military History.* Spencer C. Tucker, ed. 5 vols. ABC Clio, 2005. (1851094202).
- *Immigration and Asylum from 1900 to Present.* Matthew J. Gibnery and Randall Hansen, eds. ABC Clio, 2005. (15706077969).
- *Oxford Encyclopedia of Latinos and Latinas in the United States.* Suzanne Oboler and Deena J. Gonzalez, eds. Oxford University Press, 2005. (0195156005).

Source: Outstanding Reference Sources is an award of the Reference and User Services Association (RUSA), a division of the American Library Association (ALA). This list is used with the permission of RUSA/ALA; www.ala.org/rusa.

Subject Index

Page numbers followed by the letter "f" indicate figures; those followed by "t" indicate tables.

Index of Reference Resources Described

About the Authors

Kay Ann Cassell received her BA from Carnegie Mellon University, her MLS from Rutgers University, and her PhD from the International University for Graduate Studies. She has worked in academic libraries and public libraries as a reference librarian and as a library director. Ms. Cassell is a past president of Reference & User Services Association of ALA and is active on ALA and RUSA committees. She is the editor of the journal, *Collection Building*, and is the author of numerous articles and books on collection development and reference service. She was formerly the Associate Director of Collections and Services for the Branch Libraries of the New York Public Library where she was in charge of collection development and age level services for the Branch Libraries. She is now a Lecturer and Director of the MLIS Program in the School of Communication, Information and Library Studies at Rutgers, the State University of New Jersey.

Uma Hiremath is Assistant Director at the Ames Free Library, Massachusetts. She was Assistant Director at the Thayer Public Library, Massachusetts; Head of Reference at the West Orange Public Library, New Jersey; and Supervising Librarian at the New York Public Library where she worked for five years. She received her MLS from Pratt Institute, New York, and her PhD in political science at the University of Pittsburgh.